Exegetical Commentary

ON

MATTHEW

SPIROS ZODHIATES

Advancing the Ministries of the Gospel

AMG *Publishers*

God's Word to you is our highest calling.

Exegetical Commentary on Matthew
By Spiros Zodhiates

Copyright © 2006 by AMG Publishers
Published by AMG Publishers
6815 Shallowford Rd.
Chattanooga, TN 37421

ISBN 0-89957-150-6

First printing—February 2006

Cover designed by Meyers Design, Houston, Texas
Interior design and typesetting by Reider Publishing, West Hollywood, California
Editing and proofreading by Dr. Dennis Wisdom, Fran Lowe, Gina Bucy,
    Dan Penwell, and Dr. Warren Baker

Printed in the United States of America

To my beloved wife, Joan Carol, to whose invaluable editorial skill I owe a great deal.

Contents

FOREWORD: LEGACY OF WHAT I BELIEVE	xi
INTRODUCTION	xv
CHAPTER 1	1
THE GENEALOGY OF JESUS (1:1–17)	1
THE VIRGIN CONCEPTION AND BIRTH (1:18–25)	2
CHAPTER 2	5
THE ARRIVAL OF THE WISE MEN TO WORSHIP THE KING (2:1–6)	5
HEROD'S FIRST ATTEMPT TO FIND THE MESSIANIC KING (2:7–12)	8
THE HOLY FAMILY'S FLIGHT TO EGYPT (2:13–15)	10
THE MASSACRE OF THE BABIES OF BETHLEHEM (2:16–18)	11
THE RETURN FROM EGYPT TO NAZARETH (2:19–23)	13
CHAPTER 3	16
THE APPEARANCE OF JOHN THE BAPTIST (3:1–10)	16
THE BAPTISM OF THE HOLY SPIRIT (3:11, 12)	21
JESUS BAPTIZED BY JOHN (3:13–17)	23
CHAPTER 4	25
JESUS TEMPTED BY SATAN (4:1–11)	25
THE GALILEAN MINISTRY BEGUN (4:12–17)	30
FOLLOWING CHRIST (4:18–22)	31
JESUS' RESPONSE TO THE MULTITUDE (4:23–25)	33
CHAPTER 5	36
THE BEATITUDES (5:1–12)	36
THE SALT AND LIGHT OF THE EARTH (5:13–20)	39
TEACHING ON ANGER (5:21–26)	42
ADULTERY AND DIVORCE (5:27–32)	44

ON TAKING OATHS (5:33–37)   46

LOVING AS GOD LOVES (5:38–48)   47

CHAPTER 6   **52**

ALMSGIVING, PRAYER, AND FASTING (6:1–18)   52

POSSESSIONS AND MASTERS (6:19–24)   58

THE CURE FOR ANXIETY (6:25–34)   62

CHAPTER 7   **67**

JUDGING FORBIDDEN (7:1–6)   67

BEHAVING AS GOD'S CHILDREN (7:7–12)   71

ENTERING THE KINGDOM OF HEAVEN (7:13–23)   74

TWO FOUNDATIONS (7:24–29)   81

CHAPTER 8   **85**

A LEPER CLEANSED (8:1–4)   85

THE CENTURION'S SERVANT HEALED (8:5–13)   87

PETER'S MOTHER-IN-LAW HEALED (8:14–17)   89

UNDERSTANDING DISCIPLESHIP (8:18–22)   91

THE WIND AND WAVES STILLED (8:23–27)   92

TWO DEMON-POSSESSED MEN HEALED (8:28–34)   95

CHAPTER 9   **97**

SINS FORGIVEN ONLY BY GOD (9:1–8)   97

THE CALL OF MATTHEW (9:9)   100

JESUS ANSWERED THE PHARISEES (9:10–13)   101

JESUS TEACHES HIS DISCIPLES (9:14–17)   103

JESUS HEALS A WOMAN WITH AN ISSUE OF BLOOD AND RAISES
    JAIRUS' DAUGHTER FROM THE DEAD (9:18–26)   105

JESUS HEALS TWO BLIND MEN (9:27–31)   109

JESUS HEALS A MUTE MAN (9:32–34)   111

JESUS' COMPASSION FOR THE MULTITUDES (9:35–38)   112

CHAPTER 10   **115**

JESUS CALLS AND COMMISSIONS THE TWELVE (10:1–15)   115

FUTURE PERSECUTIONS (10:16–25)   120

FEAR GOD, NOT PEOPLE (10:26–31)   125

PUBLIC CONFESSION AND DENIAL (10:32, 33)   128
CONFESSION AND PERSECUTION (10:34–39)   129
THE PRIVILEGE OF ACCEPTING BELIEVERS (10:40–42)   133

CHAPTER 11   **135**

JOHN THE BAPTIST (11:1–15)   135
PEOPLE ARE INNATELY REBELLIOUS AND CRITICAL (11:16–24)   140
GOD REVEALS HIMSELF TO BABES (11:25–27)   143
CHRIST'S INVITATION TO INNER REST (11:28–30)   144

CHAPTER 12   **147**

JESUS IS LORD OF THE SABBATH (12:1–14)   147
JESUS WOULD NOT BE INTIMIDATED (12:15–21)   150
A HOUSE DIVIDED AGAINST ITSELF CANNOT STAND (12:22–30)   153
THE BLASPHEMY AGAINST THE HOLY SPIRIT (12:31, 32)   155
THE JUDGMENT ON NATURE AND WORDS (12:33–37)   157
JESUS PREDICTS HIS DEATH AND RESURRECTION (12:38–42)   159
THE RETURN OF UNCLEAN SPIRITS (12:43–45)   161
THE FAMILY THAT DOES THE WILL OF GOD (12:46–50)   163

CHAPTER 13   **165**

THE PARABLE OF THE SOWER (13:1–9)   165
WHY PARABLES? (13:10–17)   166
THE EXPLANATION OF THE PARABLE OF THE SOWER (13:18–23)   171
THE PARABLE OF THE WHEAT AND THE TARES (13:24–30)   174
THE PARABLES OF THE MUSTARD SEED AND THE LEAVEN (13:31–33)   175
TEACHING BY PARABLES PROPHESIED (13:34, 35)   177
THE EXPLANATION OF THE PARABLE OF THE WHEAT AND   178
    TARES (13:36–43)
THE HIDDEN TREASURE, THE PEARL, AND THE DRAGNET (13:44–50)   180
THE RESPONSIBILITY OF UNDERSTANDING (13:51–53)   183
JESUS RETURNS TO NAZARETH (13:54–58)   184

CHAPTER 14   **187**

JOHN THE BAPTIST IS MURDERED (14:1–12)   187
JESUS FEEDS THE FIVE THOUSAND (14:13–21)   191

Jesus Walks on the Sea (14:22–33) — 194

Jesus' Fame Spreads Through Gennesaret (14:34–36) — 199

CHAPTER 15 — **201**

What Is Tradition? (15:1–9) — 201

What Defiles People? (15:10–20) — 204

Jesus Heals a Gentile Woman's Daughter (15:21–28) — 210

Jesus Heals the Multitudes (15:29–31) — 213

Jesus Feeds Four Thousand (15:32–39) — 215

CHAPTER 16 — **218**

Discerning the Signs of the Times (16:1–4) — 218

The Leaven of the Pharisees and Scribes (16:5–12) — 220

Peter's Confession of Jesus (16:13–20) — 223

Jesus Predicts His Death and Resurrection (16:21–23) — 228

Taking Up the Cross (16:24–27) — 230

Seeing the Son of Man Coming in His Kingdom (16:28) — 233

CHAPTER 17 — **235**

The Transfiguration (17:1–13) — 235

Jesus Heals a Boy Vexed with an Evil Spirit (17:14–21) — 244

Jesus Again Predicts His Death and Resurrection (17:22, 23) — 250

Jesus Pays Taxes to Caesar (17:24–27) — 252

CHAPTER 18 — **255**

The Greatest in the Kingdom of Heaven (18:1–5) — 255

Offending Young Believers (18:6–10) — 257

The Parable of the Lost Sheep (18:11–14) — 262

Restoration of a Brother (18:15–20) — 266

The Parable of the Unforgiving Servant (18:21–35) — 272

CHAPTER 19 — **282**

Marriage and Divorce (19:1–12) — 282

Jesus Blesses Little Children (13–15) — 291

The Rich Young Ruler (19:16–22) — 293

Possessions and the Kingdom of God (19:23–30) — 299

CHAPTER 20   302

   TWO CATEGORIES OF WORKERS (20:1–16)   302

   JESUS AGAIN PREDICTS HIS DEATH AND RESURRECTION (20:17–19)   307

   GREATNESS THROUGH SUFFERING AND SERVICE (20:20–28)   308

   JESUS HEALS TWO BLIND MEN (20:29–34)   313

CHAPTER 21   315

   JESUS ENTERS JERUSALEM TRIUMPHANTLY (21:1–11)   315

   JESUS PURIFIES THE TEMPLE (21:12–17)   321

   THE BARREN FIG TREE (21:18–22)   325

   JESUS' AUTHORITY QUESTIONED (21:23–27)   328

   THE PARABLE OF THE TWO SONS (21:28–32)   330

   THE PARABLE OF THE WICKED VINE-GROWERS (21:33–46)   335

CHAPTER 22   344

   THE PARABLE OF THE MARRIAGE SUPPER (22:1–14)   344

   RENDERING TO CAESAR AND TO GOD (22:15–22)   354

   JESUS ANSWERS THE SADDUCEES ABOUT LIFE AFTER   357
      DEATH (22:23–33)

   THE TWO GREAT COMMANDMENTS (22:34–40)   362

   DAVID'S SON AND LORD (22:41–46)   365

CHAPTER 23   369

   THE PRIDE OF PHARISAISM (23:1–12)   369

   THE EIGHT WOES (23:13–36)   375

   JESUS LAMENTS OVER JERUSALEM (23:37–39)   386

CHAPTER 24   389

   JESUS PREDICTS HIS RETURN IN GLORY (24:1–8)   389

   THE THREATS OF BETRAYAL AND MARTYRDOM (24:9–14)   394

   THE ABOMINATION OF DESOLATION (24:15–22)   397

   FALSE CHRISTS AND PROPHETS (24:23–26)   403

   THE RETURN OF THE SON OF MAN (24:27–41)   405

   WATCHING FOR CHRIST'S RETURN (24:42–44)   416

   THE FAITHFUL AND UNFAITHFUL SERVANTS (24:45–51)   420

CHAPTER 25   **427**

THE PARABLE OF THE TEN VIRGINS (25:1–13)   427

THE PARABLE OF THE TALENTS (25:14–30)   434

THE SON OF MAN RETURNS IN GLORY TO JUDGE THE   441
   NATIONS (25:31–46)

CHAPTER 26   **447**

THE PLOT TO KILL JESUS (26:1–5)   447

JESUS IS ANOINTED PRIOR TO HIS BURIAL (26:6–13)   448

JUDAS VOLUNTEERS TO BETRAY JESUS (26:14–16)   451

THE LAST SUPPER (26:17–30)   452

THE PROPHECY OF PETER'S DENIAL (26:31–35)   458

JESUS IN GETHSEMANE (26:36–56)   460

JESUS IS TRIED BEFORE THE SANHEDRIN (26:57–68)   469

PETER'S DENIALS (26:69–75)   474

CHAPTER 27   **477**

JESUS' CONDEMNATION AND JUDAS' SUICIDE (27:1–10)   477

JESUS BEFORE PILATE (27:11–26)   481

JESUS RIDICULED AND MISTREATED (27:27–31)   486

THE CRUCIFIXION AND FINAL MOCKERY OF JESUS (27:32–44)   487

JESUS' DEATH (27:45–54)   492

JESUS' BURIAL (27:55–66)   499

CHAPTER 28   **505**

JESUS' RESURRECTION (28:1–10)   505

THE CONSPIRACY (28:11–15)   512

THE GREAT COMMISSION (28:16–20)   513

Foreword:
Legacy of What I Believe

The Triune God

- God is one deity (*theótēs* [2320]) and is self-existent (John 8:58). Christianity is monotheistic.

- As the Lord Jesus Christ was fully God incarnate (Col. 2:9; Heb. 1:1–4), so each Person of the triune God (Matt. 28:19) is fully God: God the Father, God the Son (John 1:1c), and God the Holy Spirit (John 16:13, 14; Acts 5:3, 4; *ekeínos* [1565], that One).

- The Lord Jesus Christ is God's final and complete revelation (Col. 2:9; Heb. 1:1–4).

- God is forever Spirit (John 4:24) who became flesh (1:14) to reveal to humanity His nature (*phúsis* [5449]) as forever the same (*aídios* [126]; only in Rom. 1:20 referring to His divine power [*dúnamis* {1411}]).

Creation

- Heaven was and remains God's dwelling place. The Lord Jesus taught believers to pray, "Our Father who art in heaven" (Matt. 6:9; a.t.).

- God created (*epoíēsen* [4160], *éktisen* [2936]) the world, consisting of heaven and earth (Gen. 1:1; John 1:3).

- The benevolent God created all things good (*agathós* [18]; Gen. 1:25, 31) and not anything that was evil (*ponērós* [4190]).

- God's special creation is human beings, who are both spiritual (spirit/soul) and material (living bodies; 1 Thess. 5:23).

- God created life to enjoy Him, but, through Adam's sin, humanity lost its personal relationship with God and as a result became lost and dead in sin (Gen. 3:1–13; Rom. 5:12).

Satan and the Fall

- The devil and demons, Satan's servants, were not created by God as such but as angels who were to minister to people for good (Heb. 1:14).

- When Lucifer, an angel who sinned, broke his relationship with God, he became Satan, the devil. Those angels who followed him became demons. They fell from heaven to earth according to Luke 10:18, which states that Jesus saw (*etheṓroun*, the imperfect of *theōréō* [2334], to see and perceive with emphasis on perception) Satan fall (*pesónta*, the aorist active participle of *píptō* [4098], to fall; "having fallen") from heaven. This verse is in the context of the seventy disciples' evangelistic efforts and of the subjection of demons because the seventy called on the name of the Lord Jesus as God. The aorist participle *pesónta* indicates that Satan fell suddenly and permanently out of heaven to earth where he is now active with his demons. While on earth, the Lord and the above-mentioned seventy commanded demons to come out of people (Matt. 7:22; 9:33; 17:18, etc.), and they had to obey.

- Sin pervaded earth through Adam and Eve as a result of their disobedience. Genesis 3:1–13 and Romans 5:12 imply that one of their first thoughts was of disobedience. God had specifically forbidden Adam and Eve to eat the fruit of one tree, but they both believed the lie of the serpent and ate of it in spite of God's specific command. Through this rebellion, sin, suffering, and death entered the world.

Salvation

- Satan and demons are beyond salvation, but all humans are the target of God's salvation in Christ (John 3:16).

- The all-wise God (Rom. 16:27) offers His salvation to all people. The Savior of humankind is the Lord Jesus Christ who shed His blood as the incarnate God, a perfect sacrifice accepted by the Father (1 Tim. 2:6).

- The life of God for humanity is called eternal life. However, it is not imposed by God. It comes by faith (Rom. 3:25–28) that people exercise during their lifetimes (Col. 1:23).

- Although Jesus Christ had to offer His body as a blood sacrifice on the cross, people must appropriate this atonement individually

(John 1:12). Those who reject God's free gift of salvation exclude themselves from God's mercy, though it was the desire of Jesus Christ to include them in His plan of salvation (1 Tim. 4:10).

- Salvation is a spiritual resurrection. Second Corinthians 5:17 says, "Behold [this is a work of God], all things have become new [NKJV; from *kainós* {2537}, qualitatively new]." Jesus Christ, being God (John 1:1), became sinless man (Heb. 4:15) in order to reconcile sinful people to God. Reconciliation (*katallagé* [2643]; and the verb *katallásso* [2644]) is a one-sided restoration of sinful humanity to a never-changing God (James 1:17). Reconciliation to God begins when the Holy Spirit convicts people, and they are willing to turn from their sins to God.

- All saved believers constitute the body of Christ, and this of necessity means the spiritual body of Christ.

Hell

- God does not capriciously punish people. He rewards the good and punishes the evil according to their acceptance or rejection of His salvation and the good or evil they perpetrate during their lifetimes (John 5:29).

- God does not impulsively send anyone to hell, where rebellious unbelievers go because they refuse God's gracious gift of salvation. He prepared hell as an eternal abode for Satan and his followers (Matt. 25:41).

- To unbelievers, God will render retribution (*ekdíkesis* [1557], vindication, the bringing out of justice) first for unbelief (John 3:18) and then for a lifetime of disobedience (Rev. 20:12). *Ekdíkesis* (cf. the verb *ekdikéo* [1556]) is an execution of justice on those who persist in unbelief (Rom. 12:19). In contrast, God will reward (*antapódosis* [469]) believers (Col. 3:24) for their faith in His Son's blood sacrifice (Heb. 9:22) and then for their works, whether good or bad (2 Cor. 5:10).

- The Greek word "Hades" (*hádes* [86]) is translated as "hell" in Matthew 11:23; 16:18; Luke 10:15; 16:23; Acts 2:27, 31; and Revelation 1:18; 6:8; 20:13, 14. Until the resurrection of Christ, all souls went to Hades (*Sheol* in Hebrew) on their death. This was divided by a great gulf (Luke 16:26) that separated paradise (for believers) from the "place of torment" (Luke 16:28) for unbelievers.

In Luke 16:23, Jesus Christ presented Hades as a place to which both Abraham (the man of faith cited in Heb. 11:17–19 and James 2:21–23) and the rich, selfish man went after they died.

- Hades (*a* [1], the alpha privative, "without"; and *eídōn*, the aorist of *horáō* [1492], to see and perceive, with emphasis on perception) is one of the New Testament words translated by the English "hell." Other words include Gehenna (*géenna* [1067]) and Tartarus ([n.f.] from the verb *tartaróō* [5020], to incarcerate in eternal torment, cast down to hell; 2 Pet. 2:4).

- As there is reality and joy in being in Christ (Rom. 8:14–17), so there is corresponding torture (*odúnē* [3601]) in being out of Christ during an unbeliever's lifetime (1 Tim. 6:10) as well as after his physical life in this world has ended (Luke 16:23–25). Hebrews 9:27 unequivocally states that only in this life do we have the opportunity to believe and be saved. The sorrow and pain experienced by unbelievers in whatever form—physical, spiritual, or both—are diametrically opposite to what they thought their selfish enjoyment of life would bring.

- Lazarus received (*apélabe*, the implied aorist active indicative of *apolambánō* [618], to receive) "evil things" in life which God had allowed, just as the rich man received (*apélabe*) "[his] good things" in life (Luke 16:25). By faith Lazarus, like Job (Job 1:21, 22), received or accepted these experiences as from God. He did not rebel against His provider but rather endured his harsh poverty and infirmity patiently. Both Abraham, the father of the faith, and Lazarus received an endless reward, but the unbelieving, selfish, rich man received just the reverse—endless torment that could not be improved upon, for there was a "great gulf" (*chásma* [5490]) between the two places (Luke 16:26).

—Spiros Zodhiates

Introduction

The Synoptic Gospels

The Gospel of Matthew is the first of three Synoptic (from *súnopsis* [n.f.] from *sún* [4862], together; and *ópsis* [3799], sight, associated with the future of the verb *optánomai* [3700], to see; thus, an overview, summary, from which we derive our English "synopsis") Gospels, which include Mark and Luke. The preposition *sún* (*syn* in English) means several things that have been mixed together. With respect to the three Gospels, the mix has been identified with parallelism (chronology), style, and theology. The three Synoptics display a unique degree of interrelatedness, while the Gospel of John diverges sharply. Without doubt, we can conclude that God Himself inspired each author. Inspiration alone explains the complete agreement in meaning and purpose.

Authorship

Matthew was one of the Twelve Apostles, a former tax collector. While his authorship is not specifically stated anywhere in the body of the text—which has led some to believe it was originally anonymous—the Gospel of Matthew was received in the second century with the title *KATA MAΘΘAION*. According to Guthrie, "There is no positive evidence that the book ever circulated without this title" (Donald Guthrie, *New Testament Introduction*, 1970, 33).

Second-century writer Papias (A.D. 60–130), bishop of Hierapolis in Phrygia, Asia Minor, a disciple of the apostle John and friend of Polycarp the martyr, appears to have written a five-volume history of the Gospels entitled *Explanations of the Sayings of the Lord's* (from *kuriakón* [2960]) *Lógia* (from *logíon* [3051], a meaningful word). Unfortunately, the collection is no longer extant; only fragments survive in the writings of Irenaeus (ca. A.D. 130–200) and Eusebius (A.D. 263–339). Among these fragments, we find the earliest known reference to the authorship of Matthew.

Most New Testament scholars assume that the phrase *tá lógia* ("the collections") within this reference refers to Matthew's Gospel for several reasons:

- The context is canonical authorship.
- The term *tá lógia* is also used for Mark's Gospel.
- There were no other prominent Matthews.
- There is no evidence that Matthew wrote anything else.
- Irenaeus (see above) mentions the Gospel.

The Gospel heavily stresses Old Testament prophecy and theology (see two sections down), generally appearing to be designed to convince Jews that Jesus is the Messiah.

Date of Writing

The broad range of suggested dates of authorship (A.D. 40 to A.D. 110) reflects the scarcity of information. Though some liberal scholars place the writing in the last quarter of the first century (A.D. 75–100), the majority of conservative historians push the production back to well before A.D. 70.

Liberals generally do not accept a pre-A.D. 70 date because they reject supernatural prophecy. Jesus clearly predicted the destruction of Jerusalem in Matthew 22:7 and 24:15–22 and implicitly in Matthew 21:43. Liberals consider such forecasts as later insertions by unethical apologists. However, Matthew presents these as Jesus' verbatim predictions. To retrofit these monologues with allegedly verbatim prophecies is more than deception; it's conspiratorial lying—putting words in Jesus' mouth He never spoke. The liberals' antisupernatural bias is inconsistent with the supernatural power of the Son of God, and such a conspiracy is out of character with the Son of man who consistently upheld truth and condemned lying.

Since the most primitive reference to Matthew's authorship is Papias' statement, it's beneficial to ask when Papias lived. Eusebius, an early church historian, lists Papias as a contemporary of Ignatius (A.D. 107–117?) and Polycarp (A.D. 69–158?), early church fathers. He also calls him the "famous" bishop of Hierapolis "in the third year of Trajan's [A.D. 52–117] reign [*emperor* A.D. 98–117], [when] Clement I [A.D. 30–100] departed this life" (*History of the Church*, v. 3. 36, 34 respectively).

Irenaeus states that Papias "listened to John and was later a companion of Polycarp, and . . . lived at a very early date," but Eusebius notes that Papias said he was not the direct pupil of any of the apostles but rather of their students (Ibid., v. 3. 39) in the preface to one of his books.

If Papias wrote around A.D. 100, then Matthew is datable at least a generation earlier. The external evidence yields little more than this, and writers following Papias may have been influenced by him or others. For a thorough analysis of internal arguments for an early date, see Robert H. Gundry, *Matthew: A Commentary on His Literary and Theological Art*, 599–609; and Davies and Allison, *The International Critical Commentary: Matthew*, vol. 1, I-VII, 127–138.

Structure

Some scholars suggest that Matthew divided his Gospel into three sections based on the phrase from "then began Jesus" in 4:17 and 16:21. The first section marks Jesus' birth to preparation for ministry (1:1—4:16). The second section begins with the Lord's announcement of the introduction of the kingdom of God with the presence of the King (4:17). The third section marks a shift in emphasis to the death of the King (16:21) and the promise of a more remote, physical kingdom.

In addition to this general structure, Matthew includes five dialogues or discourses:

- Righteousness of the kingdom (5:1—7:27)
- Persecution within the kingdom (10:1–42)
- Sovereignty of the kingdom over good and evil (13:1–52)
- Humility, forgiveness, and punishment in the kingdom (18:1–35)
- Hypocrisy, apostasy, and exclusion from the kingdom (23:1—25:46)

Theology

The four Gospels are very different. Under the guidance of the Holy Spirit, each writer was inspired to select from among thousands of spoken words and innumerable events to emphasize certain points. Matthew's primary intent to prove the messiahship of Jesus to Jews can be inferred, for example, from his quoting more than twice the number of Old Testament prophecies the other writers quoted (a total of sixty). What each Gospel author emphasized by frequency, insertion, or even omission is significant. Each writer was a strategic apologist.

It would be impossible to list, much less discuss, every idiosyncratic piece of grammar, history, and theology from Matthew in this work. Accordingly, we have selected the more prominent dissimilarities from the other Synoptics and John.

Jesus Christ as Son of David, Messiah, and Lord

Second only to Luke in providing prebirth and birth narrative details, only Matthew's Gospel records Jesus' birth to "the" virgin (1:23) in fulfillment of prophecy. (The article "the" is clearly present in both the Hebrew prophecy in Isaiah 7:14 and its Greek quotation in Matthew 1:23.) Matthew includes meticulous details to keep his readers from misconstruing the term "virgin": "Before they came together, she was found with child of the Holy Spirit" (NKJV 1:18). Again in verse 25: "And [Joseph] knew [*egínōsken*, from *ginōskō* {1097}, to know, to have sexual intercourse with] her not [i.e., he kept her a virgin] until she gave birth to a son"(a.t.).

Matthew records the clearest trinitarian formula and, therefore, exhibits a high if not the highest Christology in the entire New Testament where he sums up Father, Son, and Holy Spirit as a single name that can only be the name of God (Matt. 28:19). Accompanying this exceptional wording is Matthew's unique testimony to the Father's passing to the Son "all authority [*exousía* {1849}, power, authority] . . . in heaven and on earth" (28:18 NKJV, NASB, NIV). Matthew also calls Jesus God's Son (2:15) and "Lord" (8:6, 21, 25, etc.) to whom divine worship is properly accorded (2:2, 11; 8:2; 9:18; 14:33; 15:25; 20:20; 28:9, 17). Although Luke and John respectively call attention to the belief of the shepherds (Luke 2:15) and Jews in general (John 7:42) that the Messiah would be born in Bethlehem, Matthew alone cites the fulfillment of Micah's prophecy that proclaimed the Messiah as "from everlasting" (Mic. 5:2; Matt. 2:5, 6).

Jesus' sovereignty extends over the angels, which He owns (13:41; 16:27; 24:31), within the universe (*pánta*, the neuter plural of *pás* [3956], all things) the Father has delivered to Him (Matt. 11:27). Matthew alone includes Jesus' teaching that He possesses the exclusive and sovereign right to reveal the Father (11:27; 19:11). Accordingly, Matthew alone cites Jesus' words to Peter, "Blessed are you, Simon Barjona, because flesh and blood did not reveal this to you, but My Father who is in heaven" (16:17 NASB).

Matthew alone includes the following passages: The Lord Jesus infallibly saves His elect: "He will save His people from their sins" (1:21 NASB). Thus, "the gates of Hades shall not overpower [*katischúō* {2729}]" the Lord's church (16:18; a.t.). The Father reveals truth to children in whom He has "prepared praise" for Himself (21:16) but hides revelation from the arrogant (11:25) because this is "well-pleasing in [His] sight" (11:26 NASB). "Every plant," Matthew *alone* quotes Jesus, "which My heavenly Father did not plant shall be uprooted" (Matt. 15:13 NASB). God's revelation is a sovereign blessing, not something brought about even by the powerful desires of the righteous:

> But blessed are your eyes, because they see; and your ears, because they hear. For truly I say to you that many prophets and righteous men desired [from *epithuméō* {1937}, to desire strongly] to see what you see, and did not see *it*, and to hear what you hear, and did not hear *it*. (13:16, 17 NASB)

Even if a person drinks the Lord's cup down to the last drop of obedience, following Him in sacrificial death, the reward is detached from choice, faith, and action: "My cup you shall indeed drink; but to sit on My right and on My left, this is not Mine to give, but it is for those for whom it has been prepared by My Father" (Matt. 20:23; a.t.). The universal response of the flesh to such independent (i.e., of merit) sovereignty is indignation (20:24, cf. 20:10–12; Mark 10:41), but God is still sovereign.

Jesus is sovereign as God incarnate, which means He is Lord as man. As the Son of man, He is the highest member of all creation. Even before His exalted resurrection and ascension to glory, we read that the Son of man has power on earth to forgive sins (9:6); the Son of man is Lord of the Sabbath (12:8); the Son of man is sovereign over angels (13:41); the Son of man will come in the glory of His Father with His angels (16:27); and the Son of man will sit on the throne of His glory (19:28; 25:31; 26:64) in His kingdom (13:41; 16:28).

Underscoring his evangelical aim to reach the Jews, as compared to Luke's more Gentile-directed christology (Luke 3:23–38), Matthew focuses on Jesus as the Son called out of Egypt (2:15), the Son of David (1:1; 9:27; 12:23), and Messiah (1:1, 16; 2:4; 11:3, etc.), the fulfiller and fulfillment of Old Testament types and prophecies (1:22, 23; 2:15, 17, 18, 23; 4:14–16; 8:17; 12:17–21; 13:14, 15, 35; 21:4, 5; 27:9, 10). Matthew alone introduces prophecy with the clause "that it might be fulfilled which was spoken by [the Lord, the prophet, the prophets]" (nine times: 1:22; 2:15, 23; 4:14; 8:17; 12:17; 13:35; 21:4; 27:35 NKJV). Only Matthew records the Magi's question, "Where is He that is born [i.e., destined to be] king of the Jews?" (2:2), a sharper focus than His Gentile counterpart's "tidings of great joy . . . to all people" (Luke 2:10). Yet Matthew does not view Gentiles as excluded, since this destiny was proclaimed to "wise men from the East" (2:1).

Jesus is David's heir of promise (Ps. 89:20–29), the Messiah, the anointed One, "the Christ [*christós* {5547} from *chríō* {5548}, to anoint], the Son of the living God" (16:16). He is "this rock" on which the church is built (16:18, Matthew only). Matthew alone quotes Jesus' claim that He is "greater than the temple" (12:6). While Mark (15:38) and Luke (23:45) mention the rending of the temple veil when Jesus died, Matthew's is the only Gospel to connect the "rent" with the resurrection of some saints, no doubt intended to be the firstfruits (cf. James 1:18) of Old Testament prophecies like Isaiah 26:19 and Daniel 12:2:

> The tombs were opened; and many bodies of the saints who had fallen asleep were raised; and coming out of the tombs after His resurrection they entered the holy city and appeared to many. (27:52, 53 NASB)

As the coming King of kings, this newborn Messiah was a threat to the devil, who quickly infused his fears into the mind of Herod, who in turn dispatched murderers to kill the Morning Star (2:16–18, Matthew alone; Rev. 22:16). Once he failed to kill the child immediately after birth, the devil tried unsuccessfully to tempt Jesus to jump from the pinnacle of the temple (4:5–7) and then later, he tried to frighten Him away from the cross in the Garden of Gethsemane (26:36–39). From at least two of these scenarios, we can infer that Satan did not want Jesus to reach Golgotha, but even stronger evidence is seen in his desperate plea through Peter to circumvent Jesus' death in Jerusalem (16:22, 23).

Kingdom Eschatology

Matthew alone uses the expression "the kingdom of heaven"—a profuse thirty-two times (3:2; 4:17; 5:3, 10, 19, 20; 7:21; 8:11; 10:7; 11:11, 12; 13:11, 24, 31, 33, 44, 45, 47, 52; 16:19; 18:1, 3, 4, 23; 19:12, 14, 23; 20:1; 22:2; 23:13; 25:1, 14). He speaks of the "Father [which is] in heaven" fifteen times (5:16, 45, 48; 6:1; 7:11, 21; 10:32, 33; 12:50; 16:17; 18:10, 14, 19; 23:9). He also uses "heaven" as a euphemism for God, a common feature of Jewish culture: "voice from heaven" (3:17); "swear by heaven" (5:34; 23:22); "treasures in heaven" (6:20); "exalted unto heaven" (11:23); "sign from heaven" (16:1). "The baptism of John, whence was it? from heaven, or of men?" (21:25 KJV). All of these have a distinctive Jewish ring.

Matthew selects twelve kingdom parables (ten of which are found only in Matthew) to depict God's universal sovereignty over good and evil. The wicked, particularly hypocrites, may grow within the kingdom, but they are destined to be rooted out, the vultures finally gathering over a corpse (Matt. 24:28 only)—not something with any life remaining in it. The parables include the tares (13:24–30, 36–43); the hidden treasure (13:44); the pearl of great price (13:45, 46);, the dragnet (13:47–50); the householder (13:52); the landowner (20:1–16); the two sons (21:28–32); the vineyard (21:33–43); the wedding feast (22:2–14); the ten virgins (25:1–13); and the talents (25:14–30). Two additional parables also are cited by Mark and Luke: the mustard seed (13:31, 32, cf. Mark 4:30–32) and the leaven (13:33–35, cf. Luke 13:20, 21).

Matthew uniquely depicts salvation within the kingdom as the sovereign God tying up the devil and pillaging his goods:

> Or else how can one enter into a strong man's house to seize [from *diarpázō* {1283}, to steal, capture, plunder] his goods, except he first bind the strong man? And then he will seize [*diarpásei*] his house. (Matt. 12:29; a.t.)

Matthew spends more time than the other Gospel writers advancing the theme that the kingdom of God will spread beyond the borders of Israel to the entire world. He alone includes a prophecy from Isaiah that calls attention to a messianic purpose other than military conquest:

> Behold my servant, whom I have chosen; my beloved, in whom my soul is well pleased: I will put my spirit upon him, and he shall shew judgment to the Gentiles. He shall not strive, nor cry; neither shall any man hear his voice in the streets. A bruised reed shall he not break, and smoking flax shall he not quench, till he send forth judgment unto victory. And in his name shall the Gentiles trust. (12:18–21, cf. Isa. 42:1–4)

Before the Messiah sends forth judgment to victory, there is a "till"—an interlude, an extended Spirit-empowered ministry of peace to the Gentiles, Israel's very enemies. This period of grace between peaceful and violent (see, e.g., Zech. 14:1–3; 12–15; Rev. 19:11–15) advents of the Messiah is alluded to in words from Christ that Matthew alone incorporates:

> Truly I say to you, Among them that are born of women there has not risen a greater than John the Baptist: notwithstanding he that is least in the kingdom of heaven is greater than he. And from the days of John the Baptist until now the kingdom of heaven suffers violence, and the violent take it by force. For all the prophets and the law prophesied until John. And if you will receive it, this is Elijah which is to come. He that has ears to hear, let him hear. (Matt. 11:11–15; a.t.)

Although Jesus, His disciples, and those who had "ears to hear" all accepted John the Baptist as Elijah to come (the forerunner of the Messiah; Mal. 4:5, 6), the religious authorities and the majority of common people rejected John and his message. Since John's message was about Christ, they rejected and killed their Messiah as well. Because Jesus was the Father's final Word (Heb. 1:1, 2), this completed not a cycle but a straight-line persecution of truth from the very inception of prophetic history with Abel. (For Abel's prophetic role, see Gen. 4:10; Heb. 11:4; 12:24). As Luke testifies to the Gentiles (Luke 11:50, 51), so Matthew witnesses to the guilt of the self-righteous of all history:

> Fill up then the measure of your fathers' guilt. . . . I send to you prophets, and wise men, and scribes: and some of them you will kill and crucify; and some of them you will scourge in your synagogues, and persecute from city to city that upon you may come all the righteous blood shed upon the earth from the blood of righteous Abel to the blood of Zechariah, the son of Barachiah, whom you slew between the temple and the altar. Verily I say to you, All these things shall come upon this generation. (Matt. 23:32–36; a.t.)

The analogous caution to God's people today is that they can expect the worst persecution against truth, not from unbelievers without (Gentiles) but from Pharisees, self-promoting hypocrites, within the church (the religious elite [Cain was a brother; Judas, one of the Twelve]; and thus Matt. 13:30; 22:11, 12; 26:50, cf. Gal. 4:29 [in context]; 2 Pet. 2:1): "For they that are such serve not our Lord Jesus Christ, but their own belly; and by good words and fair speeches they deceive the hearts of the innocent [from *ákakos* {172}]" (Rom. 16:18; a.t.).

As the Lord's ministry to the apostate nation unfolds, we find a progression of warnings in Matthew, first to rebellious individuals (3:7), then to whole cities (Chorazin, Bethsaida, Capernaum; 11:20–24, Matthew only), then finally to the entire generation (12:41–42). At the end of this progression, Jesus prophesied that Israel will be displaced by a nation comprised primarily of Gentiles: "Therefore say I unto you, The kingdom of God shall be taken from you, and given to a nation bringing forth the fruits thereof" (21:43; Matt. only). "Many shall come from the east and west, and shall sit down with Abraham, and Isaac, and Jacob, in the kingdom of heaven. But the children of the kingdom shall be cast out into outer darkness: there shall be weeping and gnashing of teeth" (8:11, 12; Matt. only). Similarly, only Matthew records the Jews' acceptance of whatever guilt was attached to the death of Christ. They said, "His blood be on us, and on our children" {27:25, cf. Rom. 11:25}].

Matthew alone records Jesus' parable of the two sons, which teaches that tax collectors (of whom Matthew is the spiritual firstborn) and harlots enter the kingdom of God before self-promoting scribes and Pharisees (21:31, 32)—a clear gradation of evil, hypocrisy, and arrogance. Similarly, the parable of the wedding feast (22:1–14) shows the transition of the kingdom of God from exclusive Jewish ownership to possession by all nations. Matthew alone records Jesus' strategic move from Nazareth to Capernaum to fulfill a prophecy of the inclusion of Gentiles in the kingdom:

> And leaving Nazareth, [Jesus] came and dwelt in Capernaum, which is upon the sea coast, in the borders of Zabulon and Nephthalim: This was to fulfill what was spoken through Isaiah the prophet, saying, The land of Zabulon and the land of Naphtali, by the way of the sea, beyond the Jordan, Galilee of the Gentiles—The people who were sitting in darkness saw a great light, and to those who were sitting in the land and shadow of death, upon them a light dawned. (4:13–16; a.t., cf. Isa. 9:1, 2)

Finally, two parables already noted view the advancement of the kingdom beyond the boundaries of Israel. The mustard seed starts out as the smallest of seeds, but it grows into a huge tree (13:31, 32). Though the tree is planted in

Israel, the coming of birds may represent the attraction of Gentiles to the Jewish salvation (see John 4:22). Similarly, the leavening of the whole container of meal (13:33) more naturally connects with the advancement of the gospel to the entire world than to the nation that has the kingdom taken from it (21:43).

Matthew's Gospel includes the only record of the Lord's promise to build an unassailable church on a "rock," which we take to be Peter's confession of Jesus as the Son of God (16:16–18; see our notes below). Also exclusively reported in Matthew is the giving of the keys to the kingdom—the power to acquit and punish (bind) sin—to the disciples (Matt. 18:18), represented in one instance by Peter (16:19, 20). The church's authority to bind and loose is an expression of the eternal will of God (16:19; 18:18–35).

Since the kingdom is destined to expand through all nations, evangelism is a key theme in Matthew. Early in the book, Matthew uniquely exposes his readers to Jesus' vision of a plentiful harvest, for which disciples should pray for workers (9:37, 38). The Great Commission (28:19, 20; cf. Mark 16:15) closes the book with the distinguishing commands to make disciples, baptize them in the name of the triune God, and teach new believers to observe all of Jesus' commands. Our current age does not end until this "gospel of the kingdom [is] preached in the whole world as a testimony to all the nations" (24:14 NASB).

Christ's return to this field of workers is imminent—as in the days of Noah (24:37–39; Luke 17:26, 27). The Lord will come as a thief (24:43; Luke 12:39). Matthew and Luke depict the separation of coworkers and even spouses in bed together (24:40, 41; Luke 17:34–36). Matthew stresses imminence in three additional unique parables: the evil slave (24:45–51), the ten virgins (25:1–13), and the talents (25:14–30).

The threat of this separation is mitigated by the promise to the Twelve: "You also shall sit upon twelve thrones, judging the twelve tribes of Israel" (19:28 NASB). Matthew's Gospel alone records Jesus' scenic picture of a final judgment that is based on how people treated His sheep (25:31–46).

The Old Covenant Citizen and Hypocrisy

The Old Testament citizen is collectively represented under the categories of Jew (28:15), scribe (23:13, although Jesus uses this term in a positive sense in 13:52), Pharisee (23:13), Jerusalem (23:37), generation (3:7; 11:16; 12:34, 39, 41, 42, 45; 16:4; 17:17; 23:33, 36), and nation (21:43).

The contexts of these terms show that they do not stand numerically for every individual within Israel but for those having the characteristics of self-centeredness (self-worship, self-righteousness, and self-promotion) and hypocrisy.

Matthew's Gospel alone records Jesus' eight woes on the formalism, legalism, and hypocrisy (inconsistencies) of scribes and Pharisees (23:13–36).

Hypocrisy is condemned throughout the Gospel. False prophets abound, counterfeiting true righteousness (7:21–23; 23:1–36). The show of righteousness falls short of true, inner righteousness in every way (5:19, 20; see next section). Matthew alone (23:3–5) suggests that hypocrites use the Law not only to leverage their own reputations but to enslave others to their didactic authority, thereby hindering (23:13) unsuccessfully (16:18) people's entrance into the kingdom. Matthew cites some of the hypocrites' more prominent malevolences, such as taking widows' houses (23:14), making prayers for pretense (23:14), and traveling over land and sea to produce converts who end up "twice the sons of hell" (23:15; a.t.).

The depravity of hypocrisy goes from bad to worse. In the context of Matthew 12, Jesus describes the progression of evil in the heart of the self-righteous person with a unique anecdote:

> Now when the unclean spirit goes out of a man, it passes through waterless places, seeking rest, and does not find it. Then it says, I will return to my house from which I came; and when it comes, it finds it unoccupied, swept, and put in order. Then it goes, and takes along with it seven other spirits more wicked than itself, and they go in and live there; and the last state of that man becomes worse than the first. That is the way it will also be with this evil generation. (12:43–45; a.t., Matt. only, cf. 23:15, "twice as much a son of hell as yourselves")

As evil goes from bad to worse, so does judgment. Matthew more frequently cites Jesus' teaching that God will be more lenient toward Sodom and Gomorrah on the day of judgment than toward those who reject His authority (10:15; 11:23, 24; 23:14; elsewhere only in Mark 6:11 and Luke 10:12, 14).

Historical depravity peaks in Matthew's sole account of the Jew's plan (see Schonfield's, *The Passover Plot*, 1965 and our note on 28:15) to spread the rumor that Jesus' disciples stole His body to promote the claim that He had risen from the dead, which the Jews call a "last deception . . . worse than the first" (Matt. 27:62–66 NASB, cf. 28:11–15).

New Covenant Believers and True Righteousness

Matthew twice quotes a verse from the Old Testament which anticipates the qualitative distinction between the old and new covenants: "I will have mercy, and not sacrifice" (9:13; Matt. only; 12:7, cf. Hos. 6:6; Heb. 10:5, 8). Inner righteousness is not ritual. Accordingly, the Sermon on the Mount (Matt. 5:1—7:27) is not so much an intensification as it is the true spirit of the Law.

The hypocrite may hammer his physical body into chastity, but the pure in heart deplores the thought of adultery.

This explains Matthew's frequent use of the noun "righteousness" (*dikaiosúnē* [1343]; six times clustered into four chapters [3:15; 5:6, 10, 20; 6:33; 21:32]), while Luke uses it but once (1:75), John twice (16:8, 10), and Mark not at all. Entire sections committed to the kingdom righteousness of God's people are found only in Matthew:

- Being salt and light in the earth (5:13–16)

- Complying with the least commandment (5:17–19)

- Exceeding the righteousness of scribes and Pharisees (5:20)

- Repelling thoughts of murder, adultery, divorce, anger without cause, humiliation of others (5:21–32)

- Refusing to use superficial vows (5:33–37)

- Exalting grace over justice (5:38–48)

- Abstaining from ostentatious alms giving and prayers (6:1–13)

- Adopting forgiving hearts (6:14, 15)

- Avoiding pretentious fasts (6:16–18)

- Repenting from anxiety over earthly treasures and the need for food and clothing (6:19–34)

- Conforming to correct protocol for treating sinning believers (18:15–25, Matthew *alone*)

- Rejecting titles like "rabbi" (23:8), "father" (23:9), "master" or "leader" (23:10)

- Humbly serving rather than despotically ruling over others (20:25, 26; 23:11).

Jesus "fulfill[s] all righteousness" (3:15, Matthew only), even paying taxes to avoid offense (17:24–27, Matthew only). Whereas Luke quotes Jesus as saying, "But rather seek ye the kingdom of God; and all these things shall be added unto you" (Luke 12:31), Matthew inserts "and his righteousness" as an object ritual-minded Jews might overlook (6:33). The Lord's disciples "thirst after righteousness" (5:6) but are persecuted for it (5:11). Believers must persevere (10:5, 6, 23, 40–42; 15:23, 24; 17:24–27; 25:31–46) in their confession of Christ before others (10:32, 33) in prayer (4:2; 6:16–18; 9:14, 15; 26:31–46, 69–75) and in good works (5:13–16). At the end of the age, the "righteous will shine forth . . . in the kingdom of their Father" (13:43 NASB).

True righteousness originates in the heart, not in the peripherals of actions (5:8, 28; 11:29; 13:15; 18:35); it is not ostentatious (6:1-18; 23:13–36) or meritorious (20:1–16); it rejects titles (23:8–10); it humbles itself (18:4; 23:12); it becomes like a child (18:3; 23:11), meek, trusting, and servile (5:5; 11:29; 20:20–28; 21:5); and it surpasses the ritualism of scribes and Pharisees (5:20; 9:10–12). All these characteristics reflect the contents of two commands that sum up the requirements of the Law: loving God and loving others as ourselves (22:36–40).

Forgiveness is not optional righteousness. Only in Matthew do we find the Lord warning disciples who fix limits on forgiveness: "Even so will my heavenly Father do to you if you do not from your heart forgive your brother his sins" (18:35; a.t.). The threat? "And his lord was angry and delivered him to the tormentors until he paid all that was owed him" (18:34; a.t.).

Matthew particularly emphasizes discipleship, which includes not only learning (13:13–15, 19, 23, 51, 52; 27:57; 28:19) but also obeying (21:6, 28–32; 28:20) and following Jesus' lead (4:22; 8:1, 22, 23; 10:38). Disciples teach Christ's law (13:52; 28:20); they heal and cast out demons (10:1); and they evangelize (10:23)—to the Jew first (10:6) as Jesus did (15:24).

These are some of the more outstanding theological features of Matthew's Gospel to which we now introduce you. We have included Strong's numbers to provide easy cross-referencing to Greek words found in AMG's Complete Word Study Series of reference books.

1

❦

The Genealogy of Jesus
(1:1–17; Luke 3:23–38)

The "**book**" (*bíblos* [976], a written record) Matthew left us is a trustworthy, historical record of the life of Christ, as we noted in our introduction. It is the first of three Synoptic Gospels, including those produced by Mark and Luke.

[1] Immediately, Matthew thrusts us into his purpose to convey to the Jews "**the generation** [from *génesis* {1078}, a feminine noun from the verb *gínomai* {1096}, to become] of Jesus Christ" from Abraham, convincing us that Jesus is the Son that God promised to Abraham long before Moses and the Mosaic Law. By contrast, Luke traces Jesus' lineage back to Adam (Luke 3:23–38).

Behind the human face of Jesus is the incarnation of the eternal Word (*Lógos* [3056], intelligence, rational expression), according to John 1:1. To reveal the Father to His people, the Word that was God entered a predetermined time and space and became flesh (John 1:14). He was not conceived the way others are. In Galatians 4:4, Paul writes, "But when the fulness of the time was come, God sent forth his Son, made [from *gínomai* {1096}, to become] of a woman, made under the law" (KJV). The same verb is used in John 1:14: "And the Word became flesh" (NASB). Thus, Matthew 1:1 speaks not simply of the birth of Jesus Christ but of the incarnation of the eternal Word.

While "Jesus" is a proper name, the title "Christ" (from *Christós* [5547], the anointed one), equivalent to the Hebrew "Messiah" (*māšiyaḥ* [4899, OT]) refers to the special anointing of the Holy Spirit on Jesus' humanity. When He entered history, He was both God and man, capable of suffering death yet equally capable of raising Himself out of death to prove His deity and redeem His people.

[2–16] From verses 2 to 16, the verb *egénnēsen*, the aorist active of *gennáō* (1080), to give birth or beget, is used when conception includes the physical father listed in the genealogy. However, in verse 16, a conspicuous shift to *egennḗthē* occurs (the aorist passive of *gennáō*). The birth (not the conception) is highlighted, since the Lord was conceived by a virgin.

For this reason, verse 16 says, "**out of** [*ex* {1537}, out of, from within] whom [i.e., Mary] was born Jesus, the One called Christ" (a.t.). Joseph became Mary's husband, but Jesus was conceived prior to any conjugal relations between the two (vv. 20–22).

[17] Matthew divides the genealogy of Jesus into three divisions (with various omissions, since Jewish genealogies generally listed only prominent individuals): from Abraham to Solomon (vv. 2–6), from Solomon to the Babylonian captivity (vv. 7–11), and from the return of the Babylonian captives to the appearance of Christ (vv. 12–16). The intervening fourteen generations in each period are loosely and purposefully calculated to reach the time when the eternal Word entered verifiable history. This may have been arranged for the purpose of easy memorization, since few books were available at that time.

This genealogy proves that Jesus, the Holy One of God who became man, is going to be exalted as King in spite of His redemptive humiliation. The Gospel of Matthew frequently refers to Jesus as the King of the Jews (2:2; 27:11, 29, 37, 42 [the King of Israel]). The time will come when He will descend to assume His reigning messiahship (25:31), assert His eternal rule, and be revealed as the "only Potentate, the King of kings and Lord of lords" (1 Tim. 6:15 NKJV).

It is interesting that Matthew refers to the Babylonian captivity as a *metoikesía* (3350), a change of domicile. God did not consider it a captivity for the Israelites so much as a change of residence (vv. 11, 12, 17). We, too, should interpret our removal from one place to another as coming from divine providence for our own good, since God has so ordained it (Rom. 8:28).

The Virgin Conception and Birth
(1:18–25; Luke 2:1–7; John 1:1, 2, 14)

[18] Matthew does not give details on how Mary conceived, simply that "**she was found with child.**" She had not had sexual relations with her fiancé, Joseph, but the Holy Spirit directly caused her impregnation. When God speaks, things happen (Gen. 1:3, 6, 9, 11, 14, 20, 24, 26; Jon. 2:10). He is not limited by or dependent on the processes of nature, which He established.

At the time, an engagement was called a "betrothal." Even though the marriage was not consummated for a full year, the virgin (*parthénos* [3933]) bride to be was considered a wife (*gunē̂* [1135]). During this time of abstinent waiting, the bride stayed at her parents' home. To be engaged was "to be remembered" (*mnēsteúō* [3423]). This verb was used in the NT only three times, always in the passive, referring to Mary's betrothal to Joseph (here and in Luke 1:27; 2:5). It was derived from *mnáomai* (3415), to remember. The betrothal was such a firm and binding promise that its dissolution was considered a divorce.

[19] God graciously sent an angel directly to Joseph to inform him of what had taken place so he would not dismiss Mary. Dismissal or divorce would have been permitted only if Mary had been unfaithful, in which case it would have been considered adultery (5:31, 32; see Zodhiates, *What About Divorce?*).

If Joseph had rejected Mary when she was pregnant by the Holy Spirit, he would have been acting unjustly. However, Matthew clearly states that Joseph was a "**just man**" (*díkaios* [1342]). He was holy in his character and did not want to hurt Mary's reputation.

To be a truly "just" person is also to be kind. Joseph did not intend to make Mary "**a public example**" (*paradeigmatízō* [3856], to expose to public shame) by putting her away publicly but was only "**minded**" (*boúlomai* [1014], to intend, to desire to do, to entertain an idea) to put her away "**privily**," that is, in secret (*láthra* [2977]). But even the thought "**to put [her] away**" (*apolúō* [630], to dismiss—the same verb used in 5:32) must have been a heavy burden on Joseph.

Joseph was a son of David (see Luke 3:23, 31) as was also Jesus Christ in Matthew 1:1. Joseph was in the same royal lineage and would not do anything to hinder the fulfilment of prophecy.

[20] The embryo in Mary's womb is called literally, "**that which is begotten** [aorist passive participle of *gennáō* {1080}, to give birth to] in her." This pushes life back to conception, not to some later stage of development.

According to Luke 1:26, 31, the angel Gabriel announced to Mary that she was going to have a son, a male child. This would fulfill Isaiah's prophecy some seven hundred years before (Isa. 7:14).

[21–24] The angel of the Lord explained that Jesus' purpose in coming was to "save his people from their sins" (v. 21). He would not be another mere human prophet but the very incarnation of God (v. 1). This is revealed in the selection of the additional name in verse 23, as given in Isaiah 7:14, "Emmanuel" (*immanûel* [6005, OT] in Heb., which means lit., "with us, God").

The Greek word for "**virgin**" (*parthénon* [3933]) in verse 23 is from the Hebrew word *almāh* (5959, OT), which means either a young woman or a virgin. The context, however, clearly identifies Mary as a virgin at the time of her conception by the Holy Spirit.

[25] Matthew comments on Joseph's obedience to the angel's command to take Mary as his wife (v. 24). Then he adds that Joseph "**knew** [*egínōsken*, the imperfect tense of *ginōskō* {1097}, to know] her not till she had brought forth her firstborn son." The imperfect tense highlights Joseph's abstention from physical relations with Mary for the entire course of her pregnancy.

An interesting textual variant occurs here, with the manuscript evidence about evenly distributed on both sides. Most modern versions follow half of the Alexandrian manuscripts and some of the Byzantine texts that say Joseph "knew her not until she had borne a son." But the King James Version and the Textus Receptus follow the other manuscripts that say that Joseph "knew her not till she had brought forth her firstborn son" (from *prōtótokos* [4416]). The word is derived from *prōtos* (4413), first or foremost, and *tókos* from *tíktō* (5088), to bear, bring forth. But whether Matthew actually used the word "firstborn" or not, we know that the word *prōtótokos* is appropriate here, because Luke also uses it in Luke 2:7, "And she brought forth her firstborn son, and . . . laid him in a manger." We cannot infer from the term that Mary had other children, since the only child in a Jewish family was called the firstborn, even if no siblings were forthcoming. However, Matthew 12:47–50 strongly implies that Mary did have additional children following the birth of Jesus. Jesus Christ was not only Mary's firstborn, but He was also the firstborn of every created thing (Col. 1:15), the firstborn of every new creation (Rom. 8:29; 2 Cor. 5:17; Gal. 6:15; Eph. 2:10; Heb. 2:10). John 3:16 tells us that Jesus is also "the only begotten Son of God" (from *monogenēs* [3439], lit., the only One of His kind, from *mónos* [3441], only, and *génos* [1085], family, species), specifying His deity (as also used in John 1:14, 18; 3:16, 18; Heb. 11:17; 1 John 4:9).

Joseph called the baby "Jesus" (from *Iēsoún* [2424]) as the angel instructed. The Hebrew equivalent, "Joshua" (*yᵉhōšua'* [3091, OT]), means "Jehovah His help," a name conceptually associated with the idea of Savior: "Thou shalt call his name JESUS: **for** [*gár* {1063}, because] he shall save his people from their sins" (v. 21).

Our Savior is designated by "Christ" alone in nearly three hundred passages; by "Jesus Christ" or "Christ Jesus" less than one hundred times, and by "the Lord Jesus Christ" less than fifty times. Following His resurrection, a more frequent use of "Christ Jesus" emphasizes His messianic title (Acts 19:4; Rom. 8:1, 2, 39; 1 Cor. 1:2, 30; Gal. 3:26, 28; Eph. 2:6, 7, 10, 13; Phil. 3:3, 8, 12, 14; Col. 1:4, 28; 1 Tim. 1:12, 14, 15; 2 Tim. 1:1, 2, 13; 1 Pet. 5:10, 14).

2

The Arrival of the Wise Men to Worship the King (2:1–6)

Bethlehem was not newly selected to be the town of Jesus' birth. It was prophesied hundreds of years before by Micah the prophet (Mic. 5:2).

[1] The historical setting was "**the days of Herod**" (47–4 BC), the notorious king seated by Julius Caesar who built the Jewish temple in Jerusalem. The Romans had appointed Herod king of the Jews. He was married to a beautiful woman named Mariamne, whom he later put to death.

Even the coming of the Magi was prophesied: "And the Gentiles shall come to thy light, and kings to the brightness of thy rising" (Isa. 60:3; see vv. 9, 10 for more details). "**Magi**," the plural of *mágos* (3097), was the name given to priests and wise men of the Medes, Persians, and Babylonians (see Dan. 2:12, 18, 24, 27; 5:7, 8). They specialized in the study of astrology. Inexplicable events were attributed to their natural skills or supernatural powers.

The magi did not understand where the star would lead them and why. The verb "**there came**" (from *paragínomai* [3854] from the preposition *pará* [3844], close proximity; and *gínomai* [1096], to become) means they entered the immediate vicinity of Jerusalem, and Bethlehem was now only six miles away.

[2] We can explain the statement, "We have seen his star in the east, and are come to worship him," only in terms of the Lord's supernatural leading. The reference to worship implies that the Magi were believing Gentiles, outside of the local redemption history of Israel but obviously not beyond the blessing of the Abrahamic Covenant (Gen. 12:3).

The star (from *astér* [792]) that led the Magi to Bethlehem pointed to the most significant event of history—God becoming man (1:1; John 1:1, 14).

We do not know exactly when the Magi first saw the star in Chaldea how long they had traveled, or how long Jesus had been born before their arrival.

Nor are we given any details about the Magi. We do know they were the first to call Jesus "the King of the Jews," knowledge they could obtain only by divine revelation. The Greek word translated "**worship**" (*proskuneō* [4352]) used here means that they fell prostrate before Jesus. They worshiped a little baby as a reigning king!

[3] Herod's jealousy disquieted him. He was "**troubled**" (from *tarássō* [5015], to disturb, agitate, stir up as water in a pool; cf. John 5:4) concerning what this new King might mean to his own sovereignty. Paradoxically, the birth and presence of the "Prince of Peace" (Isa. 9:6) was a source of anxiety for him.

Not only the king was troubled but also "all Jerusalem with him." The Jews eagerly expected a Messiah to deliver them from their bondage to Rome, but they also feared the conflict and suffering that would come if they tried to throw off the Roman yoke.

[4] Although Herod, an Idumean (Mark 3:8) from Edom and a descendant of Esau, was hostile to the Jews, he consulted the Sanhedrin, both chief priests and scribes—the students and expounders of the Old Testament Scriptures. The chief priests were the authorities, but the scribes were knowledgeable of the scrolls they reproduced.

Herod suspected that something important was taking place. Why would prominent men follow a star all the way from Persia? Because these were not ordinary people and this was not an ordinary experience, something unusual must be happening, Herod reasoned. The Jews were expecting the Messiah. Was this baby the One? Herod determined to find out. And so "**he demanded** [from *punthánomai* {4441}, to inquire, learn; not the harsh connotation of the English] of them where Christ should be born," hiding his intentions to destroy their Messiah King.

Prophecies of the birth of Christ seven hundred years earlier prove that the event was not an accident but part of God's plan. Isaiah 7:14 foretold Jesus' birth from a virgin; Micah 5:2, the place—Bethlehem, an obscure little town in Judea; Hosea 11:1, His call out of Egypt; and Jeremiah 31:15, the great sorrow that would accompany Herod's attempt to kill the infant.

The fulfillment of prophecy proves the Bible to be God's Word, His revelation of Jesus Christ, the eternal truth. What is written has stood the test of time. Many prophecies (Matt. 2:15, 18, 23) were spoken and written down.

[5, 6] "**Bethlehem**" was a small, ancient (first mentioned in Gen. 35:19) town in hilly country about six miles south of Jerusalem. The name means "house of bread." Out of this insignificant town came the most significant person in history, Jesus Christ, who would divide history into two time periods: BC (before Christ) and AD (anno Domini, the year of the Lord).

"Thou Bethlehem . . . art **not** [*oudamōs* {3760}, absolutely not by any means] the least among the **princes** [from *hēgemōn* {2232}, leaders or rulers] of Judah." The least town in all the land of Judah would birth the most significant ruler of the world—God in the flesh (John 1:1, 14).

The noun translated "**princes**" refers to leaders or those who go before. The prophet Micah (5:2) tells us that after the coming of Christ, the leader of Judah, Bethlehem will no longer be considered insignificant. The birth of Jesus Christ will cause her to be honored forever. This has clearly been fulfilled. Christians all over the world want to visit Bethlehem, the Lord's birthplace.

In the next clause, the corresponding noun translated "**Governor**" (*hēgoúmenos*, the present middle participle of *hēgéomai* [2233], to lead, **a ruler**) is described in terms of his future role: "**that shall rule** [*poimaneí*, the future tense of *poimaínō* {4165}, to tend as a shepherd] my people Israel." Here, the prophet Micah (quoted by Matthew) presents Christ as the Shepherd. Later, Jesus says of Himself, "I am the shepherd, the good one. The good shepherd giveth His life for the sheep" (John 10:11; a.t.). Shepherding includes provision, protection, and sacrifice. The sheep recognize the voice of their Shepherd and follow Him (John 10:4).

The term "governor," a participial noun of *hēgéomai* with its root idea of leading, is an appropriate term for One who is to shepherd His people, because the shepherd always leads his sheep. He goes before them (John 10:27). He does not drive them with a whip as one would a team of horses. His leadership is gentle and considerate. Consequently, "**my people**" must be understood as Christ's redeemed people for whom He lays down His life and whom He sovereignly protects in His hand (John 10:28). They are those who follow Him—His church. They consist of Jews and Gentiles (Rev. 7:4, 9–17), redeemed by the blood of the sacrificial Lamb (*amnós* [286]; John 1:29, 36) who will shepherd both His people (Rev. 7:17).

First Peter 2:9 sums up the honors of Christ's "people" (*laós* [2992]) whom Paul literally calls God's "peculiar treasure" (*perioúsios* [4041], treasured, beyond usual) in Titus 2:14. In Christ's work of redemption, God has created a people that are a valued possession, a special and unique treasure. This is not "Israel after the flesh" (1 Cor. 10:18), those who belong to the "stock of Israel" (Phil. 3:5), nor are they "the commonwealth" (*politeía* [4174], citizenship) of Israel" (Eph. 2:12). Rather, they are the "Israel of God" (Gal. 6:16) from which many, even Jews by birth, are "aliens" (Eph. 2:12). Christ's redeemed people are the spiritual Israel—all the faithful, the whole number of the elect who have been, are, and shall be gathered into one body under Christ. These are all the believers of all time constituting the church universal.

But while the true sheep willingly follow the shepherd's crook, John gives an interesting twist to Jesus' shepherding career in the book of Revelation. Now Jesus is lovingly shepherding (*poimaínō* [4165], to govern as a shepherd who tends his sheep) His own people who hear His voice and follow Him willingly. But in the millennial kingdom, the same verb is used (*poimaínō*) to describe His ruling all nations but with an additional qualification, "with a rod of iron" (Rev. 12:5; 19:15). The initial citizens of the millennial kingdom are all born-again believers with unglorified bodies. However, their children and descendants will be born with the same fallen natures that all humans have been born with since Adam's fall. They must make up their own minds. Many will accept Christ's sacrifice for their sins and receive the same redeemed natures that we present-day saints have, willingly submitting to their Ruler. But many others who refuse to be saved will be forced to submit outwardly because of Christ's rod of iron and will wait for the opportune time to rebel. This will only come when Satan, the dragon, is released from chains at the end of the millennial kingdom (Rev. 20:7–9).

Jesus' rule over the nations lies in the future—the final shepherding (*poimaínō*) with a rod of iron across the back of sin. Christ's shepherding or rule, then, has two distinct meanings. God will wipe away every tear from the eyes of the righteous, but He will rule over the rebellious with the iron rod of His wrath (Rev. 2:27; 19:15), the "wrath of the Lamb" (Rev. 6:16). The "called" (*klētoí* from *klētós* [2822]; Rev. 17:14 and the Epistles in general; or the "called out" [*eklektoí* from *eklektós* {1588}, called out, or chosen, found in the Gospels]) and "faithful" (*pistoí*, from *pistós* [4103]) will reign with the Lamb of God. The shepherding of Christ, therefore, extends from the incarnation to His coming again and beyond.

Herod's First Attempt to Find the Messianic King
(2:7–12)

[7] Herod assumed the veracity of the report about the star and acted malevolently on it, considering the birth of a messianic king as a threat to his local rule.

Accordingly, Herod inquired "**privily**" (*láthra* [2977], secretly—a Greek word rarely used in the NT; see Matt. 1:19; John 11:28; Acts 16:37) of the wise men. Planning the death of the baby Jesus, Herod questioned the wise men "**diligently**" (*ēkríbōsen*, the aorist tense of *akribóō* [198], to inquire accurately, exactly) about the precise time the star appeared in order to calculate the approximate age of the child.

[8] Herod then told the wise men (probably through officials, translators, rather than directly) to search "**diligently**" (*akribôs* [199], accurately, exactly) for the young child. He learned the approximate age of the child by ascertaining the time when the wise men saw the star (v. 7). He also learned the place of the child's birth because of Micah's prophecy (Mic. 5:2) as quoted by the chief priests and scribes (vv. 4, 5). Apparently, he believed the prophecy enough to attempt to thwart it.

But who can fight against God? In Acts 5:38, 39, Gamaliel, a prominent Pharisee, says, "If this counsel or this work be of men, it will come to nought: but if it be of God, ye cannot overthrow it; lest haply [perhaps] ye be found even to fight against God" (KJV). Herod planned to fight God. He sent the magi directly to Bethlehem where it had been prophesied that the Messiah would be born. He said to them,

> **Having gone** [*poreuthéntes*, the aorist passive deponent participle of *poreúo-mai* {4198}, to go; an implied imperative based on precedence of the main imperative verb that follows], **accurately** [*akribôs*] **search** [*exetásate*, the aorist imperative of *exetázō* {1833}, examine, inquire, verify] concerning the **young child** [*paidíon* {3813}, a little child, a baby]; and when you have found him, bring me word again, that I may come and worship him also. (a.t.)

Herod commanded the Magi to inform him of whatever facts they found consistent with their supposition. If this were the leader (*hēgemōn* [2232]) prophesied by Micah and confirmed by a supernatural star, He would be a threat to Herod's kingdom. If not, Herod had nothing to fear. But Herod was wickedly deceptive, and his pretentious sincerity deceived even "the wise."

[9, 10] After leaving Herod, the Magi continued to follow the star:

> When they had heard the king, they departed; and, lo, the star, which they saw in the east, **went before** [*proēgen*, the imperfect tense of *proágō* {4254}, to go before; lit., was going before] them, till it came and stood over where the **young child** [*paidíon* {3813}] was. When they saw the star, they rejoiced with **exceeding** [*sphódra* {4970}] great **joy** [from *chará* {5479}].

The Greek word *idoú* (see Matt. 3:16), elsewhere translated "behold," calls attention to the phenomenon of the miraculous star, the revelation of the One who originally created "lights in the firmament of the heaven to . . . be for signs" (Gen. 1:14). Accordingly, this was an intensely personal leading:

"And when he putteth forth his own sheep, he goeth before them" (John 10:4). "For as many as are led by the Spirit of God, they are the sons of God" (Rom. 8:14).

Since the Magi were led by the Spirit, they undoubtedly were Gentile believers, children of Abraham by faith, though not by flesh, and called by God in fulfilment of a specific prophecy:

> And the Gentiles shall come to thy light, and kings to the brightness of thy rising. . . . The abundance of the sea shall be converted unto thee, the forces of the Gentiles shall come unto thee. The multitude of camels shall cover thee, the dromedaries of Midian and Ephah; all they from Sheba shall come: they shall bring gold and incense; and they shall shew forth the praises of the LORD. (Isa. 60:3–6).

No wonder the Magi rejoiced with great joy when they found the child, God's salvation.

[11] The Magi entered the house Jesus was moved into following His birth and found the child with His mother, Mary. They had no doubts about the identity of the baby as they worshiped Him. They immediately opened their treasures and presented them to the child. The gifts consisted of gold (an acknowledgment of royalty), frankincense (of deity), and myrrh (prophetic of His death; see Ps. 72:10; Isa. 60:6).

[12] Had God not intervened, the Magi would have returned to Herod, telling him exactly where Jesus was. The verb "**warned**" (from *chrēmatizō* [5537], to have business dealings) is associated with God's prophetic warnings (Matt. 2:22; Heb. 11:7; 12:25). The Magi believed and obeyed God rather than the king. By recognizing God's voice, they discerned Herod's deception.

The Holy Family's Flight to Egypt
(2:13–15)

[13] Because the Magi obeyed God, Mary, Joseph, and the baby Jesus were spared from Herod's deceptive plan. Consistent with the principle of the headship of the husband no matter how important and unique the wife is (as Mary certainly was), the angel assigned Joseph the task of leading his family to Egypt (v. 13, cf. 1 Cor. 11:3).

The most important part of this family was "**the young child.**" The angel did not say "your child," because Jesus was not Joseph's child. Nor did the angel say, "Take the young child and **your wife**" but rather "**his mother.**" The verb "**flee**" (*pheúge*, the present imperative of *pheúgō* [5343], to depart, go) is singular, meaning that Joseph was expected to lead his family to safety.

The angel continued, ". . . and **be** [from *eimí* {1510}, to be] thou there until I bring thee word." The singular person again stresses Joseph's headship.

The Lord who sent His angel to say "Go!" would send the same angel to say "Return!" He did not reveal how long the refugees would be in this strange country but rather, "until I tell you" (2:13 NASB). Since the timing of the return was ultimately in God's hand, Joseph and Mary were not to be anxious.

The Lord knew Herod's wicked plan, the imminence of which is expressed in the verb *méllei*, the present active indicative of *méllō* (3195), to be about to do. His plan was to immediately "**seek**" (*zēteín*, the present infinitive of *zētéō* [2212]) the baby Jesus in order to kill Him. The verb used is not the ordinary verb *apokteínō* (615), to kill but *apolésai*, the aorist active infinitive of *apóllumi* (622), to utterly destroy. Herod did not realize this child was the Son of God (Matt. 1:1), who always had been (John 1:1, 2) but had become "flesh" (*sárx* [4561])—something He did not possess prior to His incarnation (John 1:14). Herod figured that by taking the physical life of Jesus, he could eliminate Him. He did not realize that the child born in Bethlehem was the preexistent *Lógos* (3056) who could never be destroyed.

[14] Joseph and his family traveled by night, probably to avoid needless exposure (v. 14). Egypt's border was about seventy-five miles from Bethlehem.

[15] Joseph and his family remained in Egypt "until the **death** [*teleutḗ* {5054} from *télos* {5056}, end, termination, goal; the only time the noun is used] of Herod." He "was finished," as the saying goes.

Herod's evil acts led to the fulfilment of the prophecy recorded in Hosea 11:1: "When Israel was a child, then I loved him, and called my son out of Egypt." All circumstances, even Herod's wicked actions, led to the fulfilment of prophecy. Nothing is a product of chance in the development of the life of Christ or the lives of Christians (Rom. 8:28). God uses even adverse circumstances for our benefit and His glory.

The Massacre of the Babies of Bethlehem
(2:16–18)

[16, 17] When the magi did not return to Herod, he was "**very** [*lían* (3029)] **furious** [from *thumóō* {2373}, used only here]" (a.t.), feeling that he had been **mocked** (from *empaízō* [1702]).

The unbelievably cruel revenge that followed was done in a fit of anger. Bethlehem was small enough that possibly no more than twenty or thirty children two years old and under were killed. However, Herod may have attacked contiguous towns as well on the assumption that parents could move any time following the birth of the child (see our comments on Rama in v. 18). His motive was purely selfish—to prevent the newborn baby from becoming king. But Herod did not know that this King was not meant to succeed or replace him (3:2; Mark 1:15) but to provide forgiveness of sins for those who believe (Matt. 1:21). Moreover, His reign would be eternal (John 3:15).

In these verses we have the third prophecy of the four recorded in this chapter (vv. 6, 15, 17, 18, 23), which all affirm the unity of God's revelation.

[18] Here Matthew quotes the weeping prophet Jeremiah (31:15), who predicted terrible mourning as a result of Herod's slaughter. Rama is the name of six towns in Palestine, but here it refers to a city of Benjamin near Jerusalem. During the reign of Nebuchadnezzar, captives were kept there under guard, among whom was the prophet Jeremiah (Jer. 39:8–12; 40:1). Thus, Herod's slaughter reached beyond Bethlehem.

Four words are used to qualify the sorrow. The **first** is "**voice**" (*phōnē* [5456]). The idea is that just as there was loud grieving in Jeremiah's time, so also there was agonizing wailing over the killing of the children in Bethlehem.

The **second** word is "**lamentation**" (*thrēnos* [2355]), a common grief expressed in poems as, for example, David's grief over Saul and Jonathan (2 Sam. 1:17). A few older manuscripts omit *thrēnos* here, and the UBS text and most modern versions also omit it, regarding it as an accommodation to the LXX rendering of Jeremiah 31:15 as quoted here. The vast majority of Greek manuscripts do have it, however, and it certainly fits here. The Old Testament book of Lamentations was possibly written by Jeremiah as poetic sorrow over the destruction of Jerusalem.

Third, we have "**weeping**" (*klauthmós* [2805] from the verb *klaíō* [2799], to weep; Luke 19:41), a verb distinct in meaning from *dakrúō* (1145), to shed a tear or tears (John 11:35). Tears are the expression of sorrow, but sometimes we weep quietly without wailing.

The **fourth** word, translated "**mourning**" in the King James Version, is *odurmós* (3602). The English word "mourning," however, more accurately translates *pénthos* (3997). *Odurmós*, by contrast, is not so much mourning as actual pain as when a woman delivers a child (*ōdín* [5604], birth pang). Under excruciating grief, persons might inflict pain (*odurmós*) on themselves by pounding their chests or beating their heads against walls.

Sorrow which is not vented can become unbearable. Some ease their grief by writing down their thoughts, like in the book of Lamentations. If we put words to our grief to form lamentations (*thrénos*), others may be blessed. However, sometimes the deep sorrow of our hearts is so great, it can be expressed only through tears.

But Rachel's pain (*odurmós*) was not accompanied by hopelessness. The babies Herod killed were not annihilated, for the Lord spoke of children when He said, "Of such is the kingdom of heaven" (Matt. 19:14). Moreover, the mothers of Bethlehem could find comfort in the inferred promise of resurrection that completes the prophecy God gave to Rachel in Jeremiah 31:16–17:

> Refrain thy voice from weeping, and thine eyes from tears: for thy work shall be rewarded, saith the LORD; and they shall come again from the land of the enemy. And there is hope in thine end, saith the LORD, that thy children shall come again to their own border.

Resurrection is necessarily implied in this promise. Although Rachel's children "were not" (Jer. 31:15), they "shall come again to their own border." The return from the spiritual realm is likened to a return from a foreign country, the "land of the enemy," namely the "last enemy" which is death (1 Cor. 15:26).

The Return From Egypt to Nazareth
(2:19–23; Luke 2:39, 40)

[19] The *teleuté* (5054) or "**finishing**" of Herod mentioned in verse 15 is repeated here to emphasize that God limited Herod's ability to perpetrate evil, just as He does to all people.

[20] Again an angel appeared to Joseph and told him to "**Take** [from *paralambáno* {3880}, to receive alongside] the young child and his mother, and go into the land of Israel."

It is noteworthy that the expressions "the child" and "his mother" are repeated, both certifying again Jesus' virgin birth. At no time is reference made to Joseph as the father of Jesus. This time the angel of the Lord does not say "flee" (*pheúge* [5343]) but "**go**" (from *poreúomai* [4198]). The singular tense of the imperative again implies Joseph's leadership (1 Cor. 11:3).

The Greek verb for "**are dead**" is *tethnékasin*, they have died, the perfect third-person plural of *thnésko* (2348), to die. Herod, who thought that he could frustrate God's plans, succumbed to the final event appointed to all people (Heb. 9:27).

[21] For the fourth time (vv. 13, 14, 20, 21), the phrase "**the** little child [a.t.; *to paidíon*] and **his** mother" confirm that Joseph was not the child's father.

[22] Archelaus (*Archélaos* [745]) became the governor of Idumea, Samaria, and Judea on the death of his father, Herod the Great (v. 22). His character was cruel and vindictive. Naturally, Joseph feared to bring back his family under Archelaus' government. Without doubt, Joseph sought God's guidance, and God gave it.

Again the verb "**having been warned**" (from *chrēmatízō* [5537]) is used as in verse 12, and again God communicates His revelation through a dream. Joseph "**departed**" (from *anachōréō* [402], to return, to withdraw) for Galilee, the northern province of Palestine, a region about fifty miles long and twenty to twenty-five miles wide. Herod had left this part of his kingdom to his son Herod Antipas and the region to the northeast and beyond Jordan to Philip. Archelaus was ruthless and did not remain king after killing three thousand of the most influential people in the country. No wonder God led Joseph to an area where this evil man did not rule.

Joseph "**was afraid**" (from *phobéomai* [5399], to be afraid). He did not panic, which is expressed by another verb—*throéomai* (2360), troubled. Jesus told us not to be "troubled" when we hear of "wars and rumors of war" (Matt. 24:6; Mark 13:7).

[23] While Joseph did not panic when he learned who was ruling, he readily obeyed God. He decided not to go to Palestine but to Galilee where Herod Antipas, another son of Herod, was reigning. God revealed the **region** where Joseph was to take his family, but Joseph chose the **city**. If we trust God and seek His guidance, we need not panic, even if God reveals only the broad sweep and not the fine details of His plans for us.

Joseph decided on the city of Nazareth where he first received the announcement that Mary was pregnant by the power of the Holy Spirit. Joseph and Mary were probably well acquainted with Nazareth from their previous stay there (Luke 1:26; 2:4, 39). Even our reason tells us not to ignore relatives and friends in our journeys through life.

In recording this decision, Matthew does not indicate any specific prophecy that pinpointed Nazareth as the town in Galilee where the family should settle, but neither did the prophecies contradict Joseph's decision. On the contrary, he saw that the meaning attached to Nazareth would identify Jesus as from that city. In fact, the prophets had predicted, "**He shall be called** [from *kaléō* (2564), to call] a **Nazarene** [*Nazōraíos* {3480}, an inhabitant of Nazareth]."

Jesus claimed to be a Nazarene (John 18:5, 7, 8; Acts 22:8). According to the Jewish elders and scribes, Stephen spoke of "Jesus of Nazareth" as the One who would destroy the temple and change the customs Moses had delivered to the Jews (Acts 6:14). The Lord's enemies recognized Him as "Jesus of Nazareth" (Matt. 26:71). Those who needed His help also called Him by this name (Mark 10:47; Luke 18:37; Acts 3:6). The disappointed disciples, on their way to Emmaeus, confessed that "Jesus of Nazareth . . . was a prophet mighty in deed and word" (Luke 24:19). When His enemies wanted to identify whom they had crucified, they placed the inscription, "Jesus of Nazareth, the King of the Jews," on the top of the cross (John 19:19). No one else in history was as well known as "Jesus of Nazareth."

The Hebrew word *neṣer* (5342, OT) from which "Nazarene" and "Nazareth" derive means a shoot or a branch. This is an allusion to such passages as Isaiah 11:1: "And there shall come forth a rod out of the stem of Jesse [the father of David; Matt. 1:6], and a Branch [*neṣer*] shall grow out of his roots" (see also Isa. 53:2; Zech. 3:8; 6:12). Nazareth, it seems, was held in contempt (John 1:46; 7:52) as were the early followers of Jesus who were referred to as "the sect of the Nazarenes" (Acts 24:5).

Indeed, who would have believed that Jesus, the Son of God, would emerge at age thirty from contemptible, ill-reputed Nazareth to accomplish miracles and teach as He did in the next three to three-and-a-half years of public ministry?

Note that while one prophet is mentioned in Matthew 1:22; 2:5, 15, 17, this verse says, "**by the prophets**," that is, all the prophets. Jesus in Matthew 5:17 said, "Think not that I am come to destroy the law, or the prophets: I am not come to destroy, but to fulfil." His residence in Nazareth as a result of Joseph's choice and God's command to dwell in Galilee was in fulfillment of "what was spoken through the prophets" (2:23 NASB).

3

⟳

The Appearance of John the Baptist
(3:1–10; Mark 1:1–6; Luke 3:2–15; John 1:19–28)

The silent years of Jesus' life in Nazareth were broken only by the events described in Luke 2:41–52 when Joseph and Mary took the twelve-year-old Jesus to visit the temple in Jerusalem at Passover.

[1] For the second time in Matthew, we have the verb *paragínomai* (3854), to come, to arrive (see Matt. 2:1), used. Here in verse 1, it indicates the coming of John the Baptist in the wilderness of Judea. The term "**wilderness** [from *érēmos* {2048}, desert, wilderness] **of Judaea** [from *Ioudaía* {2048}]" described the desolate area extending from the hill country near Jerusalem down to the Jordan Valley and the Dead Sea. It is a limestone country, rough and barren, with only patches of grass. It seems to have had many inhabitants but no large cities. We do not know whether John the Baptist baptized anybody from the Jerusalem side of the Jordan River or not, but we do know that by the time Jesus was baptized, John 1:28 tells us that John was baptizing at Bethabara (UBS: Bethany) beyond Jordan or on the eastern side of the Jordan River.

John was the son of Zacharias and Elizabeth (Luke 1:5–25, 39–45, 57–80), and "**the word** [*rhēma* {4487}, articulation, utterance] of God came unto John the son of Zacharias in the wilderness" (Luke 3:2). God specifically told him what to say.

[2] John's message was simple and direct: "**Repent**" (*metanoeíte*, the present imperative of *metanoéō* [3340], to repent). His use of the present imperative indicates that this was a call not only to initial repentance to salvation but also to the continuous repentance subsequent to salvation. He called people to repent and keep on repenting. It is interesting that Jesus preached the same message: "Repent [the same present imperative]: for the kingdom of heaven is at hand" (4:17).

On the other hand, when Peter preached his Pentecostal address (Acts 2:38), he did not use the verb "repent" (*metanoeíte*) in the present imperative but in the aorist imperative (*metanoésate*), thus urging his hearers to repent initially. This was to be externally evidenced by water baptism that was to occur only once subsequent to repentance and faith, as indicated by the verb *baptisthéto*, the aorist passive imperative of *baptízo* (907), to baptize. Baptism as a physical act performed by one person to another does not change an individual's mind-set. This is done by the Spirit of supplication (Zech. 12:10) that creates *metánoia* (3341), repentance, a gift from God (Acts 5:31; 11:18).

Both John and Jesus preached that sinful people not only begin the Christian life through repentance but continue to repent because they now have a new and tender consciousness of sin (see also James 4:17; 1 John 1:9).

Paul also believed and preached the same as John and Jesus as apparent from his message to the Athenians in Acts 17:30: "But now [God] commandeth all men every where to repent." This verb for "repent" (from *metanoeín*) is the present infinitive. It is not *metanoésai*, the aorist active infinitive, which would mean the initial repentance Peter urged his hearers to do at Pentecost (Acts 2:38).

The root idea of the Greek words *metanoéo*, to repent, and *metanoía*, repentance is "to change the mind." They both contain the word *noús* (3563), mind. From *noús* come words like *noéo* (3539), to perceive, understand; *nóema* (3540), thought; *katanoéo* (2657), to comprehend; *diánoia* (1271), penetrating mind; *ánoia* (454), lack of mind, folly; *énnoia* (1771), notion; *epínoia* (1963), a reasoned-out thought, conclusion; and *nouthetéo* (3560), to set the mind, to admonish.

To think like God does, our minds must be changed. Our minds, as God created them, provide mirrors that enable us to look at ourselves as God sees us and yardsticks to measure ourselves by God's standard. But when Adam fell, he rejected the proper image, and his mind became perverted, producing wrong conclusions. Adam determined in his mind, in his thought process, that he knew better than God. Thus, he disobeyed God's explicit command to not eat from a particular tree. He conceived sin in his mind before he stretched out his hand to take the forbidden fruit. Sin starts as a thought and ends as an act (James 1:14, 15). If we want to cleanse our lives from evil, we must stop thinking evil thoughts, for they lead to spiritual death.

Sin leads also to physical death, so the result of an evil-thought process is both spiritual and physical death. This occurred as God said it would, for people are now dead in their trespasses and sins (Rom. 3:23; Eph. 2:1) and need to change. But in order to change our actions, we need to first change our minds. This is our greatest need—repentance (*metánoia*).

When we change our minds, we no longer justify and accept our sinful natures. Instead, we accept God's pronouncement that we are all sinners and ask for His forgiveness. From that moment, we begin entrusting ourselves to God, believing not only that He tells us the truth but that He is the truth (John 14:6). At this point, our *noús* (minds) become *phrónēsis* (5428), (intellectual or morally insightful) and begin to be controlled by Christ. When we accept and believe in Him, He can transform our sinful minds to the mind of Christ (1 Cor. 2:16). The word *phrónēsis* derives from the obsolete term *phréō* or *phráttō* or *phrássō* (n.f.), meaning to curb or reign in. In Christ we acquire curbed or controlled minds, and the One who curbs them is Jesus Christ. John drew parallels between our need for repentance and the approach of the kingdom of heaven, because the initial experience of heaven on earth can come to people only through repentance and faith in the gospel (Mark 1:15). With Christ's incarnation, God arrived among us. And John the Baptist came to announce that arrival.

"**Kingdom**" is translated from *basileía* (932), reign. Jesus Christ, who always reigned in heaven, brought heaven to earth by His presence among us (John 1:18; see Zodhiates, *Was Christ God?*).

This is the invisible kingdom or the reign of God in the hearts of believers (Luke 17:20, 21). Those who have experienced this invisible reign within will also experience Christ's visible kingdom (Matt. 16:28; 25:34; Rev. 12:10).

The phrase "**is at hand**" is translated from *éggiken*, the perfect tense of *eggízō* (1448), to be near. The verb is used intransitively, meaning to come near, to approach, and the perfect tense indicates it has already arrived. Christ brought it here.

Heaven is God's throne (5:34, 45, 48) from where Christ descended (John 3:13, 31; 6:32, 33, 38). He being Spirit (John 4:24) became (from *gínomai* [1096], to become; John 1:14) flesh.

[3] The Jews expected Elijah the prophet to introduce the kingdom of God (Mal. 4:5), but God chose John the Baptist (Isa. 40:3). He is identified in Isaiah 40:3 as "the voice of one crying in the wilderness," calling attention to Jesus' coming as Emmanuel, "God with us" (Matt. 1:23).

When God spoke to him, John the Baptist was living in the desert. This is clearly stated in Luke 3:2: "The word [*rhéma* {4487}; in this case the exact verbalization of God's message] of God came unto John . . . in the wilderness." He had lived in the desert of Judea since childhood (Luke 1:80), and God called John to preach in that very desert. God further directed John to start his ministry just prior to Jesus' public ministry.

The verb "**crying out**" is *boōntos*, the present participle of *bodō* (994), to cry aloud. What was John crying out? Three imperatives make up the content of John's message: "**repent**" or "**be repenting**" (*metanoeíte*) of verse 2; "**prepare**" (*hetoimásate*, make ready, the aorist imperative of *hetoimázō* [2090], to prepare), and "**make**" or "**keep making**" (*poieíte*, the present imperative of *poieō* [4160], to make) straight. This message needed to be heard loudly and clearly. The call to "be repenting" here was a call to a permanent change of mind. Likewise, "keep making straight" was a call to a changed way of life, to continuously walk in the right ways of the Lord and not in crooked ways.

God's call can be heard even in a dry and barren desert. John obeyed immediately, and obedience brought blessing in the midst of desolation.

[4] John's dress and food were simple and adequate (v. 4). His life and message were so clear and convincing that people from Jerusalem, all Judea, and the region around Jordan came to see and hear him. Nothing showy or ostentatious attracted the crowds, only the simple preaching of the Word of God.

[5, 6] Many who came to hear John were "**being baptized** [*ebaptízonto*, the imperfect of *baptízō*, to baptize; from *báptō* {911}, to cover wholly] of him in Jordan, confessing their sins" (a.t.).

To "**confess**" (*exomologoúmenoi*, the present participle of *exomologéō* [1843] from *ek* [1537], out; and *homologéō* [3670], to express agreement) means to agree with the Holy Spirit (John 16:13, 14) as He convicts of sin (John 16:8). John did not baptize people unless they were convicted of their sins and confessed them.

[7] Among those who came to hear and John were Pharisees and Sadducees. These Jewish elite were not motivated, however, by a conviction of sin and a desire to turn from it or to escape God's judgment. To them, baptism was just another superstitious, self-righteous act. Since John saw no evidence of their conversion, he was fully justified in being disturbed.

He addressed them accordingly:

> O **generation** [from *génnēma* {1081}, offspring] **of vipers** [from *échidna* {2191}, poisonous snake], who **hath warned** [from *hupodeíknumi* {5263}, to warn, instruct, admonish] you **to flee** [from *pheúgō* {5343}] from the **wrath** [from *orgē* {3709}] **to come** [from *méllō* {3195}, to come in the future]?

John called the Pharisees and Sadducees poisonous snakes because they considered baptism equivalent to acceptance by God (cf. John 8:44). No human external act can result in salvation, for it is a spiritual transformation realized through faith in Christ and by God's grace (Eph. 2:8–10). The physical act of baptism cannot help anyone escape God's wrath. John taught that an outward baptism by water should be accompanied by an inward baptism of repentance for the remission of sins (Mark 1:4; Luke 3:3).

[8] John wanted to see that immediate change that repentance brings. This is evident from the aorist active imperative *poiēsate*, from *poiéō* (4160), to make or do.

In regard to fruit, this is the first time the adjective "**meet**" (from *áxios* [514], worthy) is used. It refers to the kind of fruit rather than to its maturity. For example, "the fruit [*karpós* {2590}] of the Spirit" in Galatians 5:22, 23 speaks of only one fruit, yet it has several qualities that characterize the regenerated sinner. These are love, joy, peace, longsuffering, kindness, goodness, faith, meekness, and temperance. In the believer, these qualities mature. To "**make**" or "**bring forth**" (from *poiéō*) emphasizes the production of the fruit, not the maturity. "Worthy" refers to a lifestyle that is distinctly different from that of a nonrepentant person. Repentance, therefore, produces true value.

[9] As Jews, the Pharisees and Sadducees claimed Abraham as their father, and they believed this was sufficient to merit salvation. Nevertheless, in John 8:44, Jesus told them, "Ye are of your father the devil." Although they were the physical descendants of Abraham, they were spiritual descendants of the devil. Apart from repentance, they would receive the same punishment reserved for Satan himself (Matt. 25:41). Escape from such punishment could only come through repentance and belief in the gospel (Mark 1:15).

John used the ample supply of stones in the desert to make an important point:

> For I say unto you, that God **is able** [from *dúnamai* {1410}, to be able to accomplish] of these stones [even Gentiles, as the Jews might interpret the reference] to raise up **children** [from *téknon* {5043}; see John 1:12] unto Abraham. (Matt. 3:9)

John stressed that the Jews would not inherit the kingdom of God (8:10–13) just because they were descendants of Abraham.

[10] John continued, "And **now**" (*éde* [2235], already), stressing the urgency of repentance and belief, "also the axe is laid unto the root of the trees." He threatened both Jews and Gentiles with ultimate punishment. The Jews depended on their ancestry and the keeping of the Law of Moses for salvation. John now declared that this religious system had come to an end because it had not produced worthwhile fruit. With the coming of Jesus Christ, this religious system "tree" was about to be cut down and destroyed.

The imminence of punishment on this fruitless tree is indicated by the present tense of the verb "**is laid**" (*keítai*, the present passive of *keímai* [2749], to be outstretched, applied). The passive voice leaves unanswered the question of who is the subject, but it is evident that God is the Judge. We expect "**every**" (from *pás* [3956]) tree to bear fruit. God has similar expectations for the trees He plants. He seeks "**good** [from *kalós* {2570}, inherently good] **fruit** [from *karpós* {2590}]," according to its kind (see Luke 13:6–9).

The verb "**bringeth**" in the phrase "bringeth not forth good fruit" is the present active participle of *poiéō* (4160), to bring forth (see Luke 13:9). Fruit should develop according to its season; otherwise, it "**is hewn down**" (from *ekkóptō* [1581], to cut off or out). Why should a tree occupy space if it does not accomplish its intended purpose? If this is logical in earthly matters, how much more so in spiritual? The fire figuratively represents the destruction of uselessness.

The Baptism of the Holy Spirit
(3:11, 12; Mark 1:8; Luke 3:16; John 1:33)

Here we have two individuals contrasted: John the Baptist, a man who came to announce the coming of Christ; and Jesus, who being God, became a man (John 1:1, 14) so He could die and save His people from their sins (Matt. 1:21). One was human and the other divine.

[11] John also contrasted the work each came to do. John's work was to baptize in water those who repented and confessed "their sins" (v. 6) whereas Christ would baptize believers with the Holy Spirit. John's was a physical act while Christ's work of forgiveness (*áphesis* [859], sending forth, remission) parted sinners from their sins so they would no longer be under the power of sin (Mark 2:5).

Paul, in 1 Corinthians 12:13, speaks of the once-and-for-all baptism in the Holy Spirit of all believers into the body of Christ as the work of Christ: "For by [in] one Spirit are we all baptized into one body . . . and have been all made to drink into one Spirit." This puts us who believe into the true church of Jesus Christ, which He promised to build (Matt. 16:18; Eph. 5:32).

Another significant contrast between John and Christ is that John was fallible and could easily attribute truth to a false confession, as Philip may have done in the case of Simon Magus. Simon had bewitched the people of Samaria with his magic, and when he himself professed faith in Christ, Philip administered baptism to him. However, his later actions strongly indicate that he may not have really been saved (Act 8:9–24).

John was wise to doubt the real motives of these Pharisees and Sadducees who came to him pretending repentance. However, Jesus Christ, the baptizer in the Holy Spirit, could not be so deceived. They could possibly have deceived John the Baptist but not Jesus Christ. To avoid the wrath of God, they needed to truly repent and believe for the forgiveness of their sins. Only then would they be baptized in the Holy Spirit.

Another important contrast between the baptisms of John and Jesus is the element in which they were baptizing believers. In the case of John, it was the water of the Jordan River; in the case of Christ, it was the Holy Spirit. The one was material and the other spiritual. Baptism in water was the physical act confirming a spiritual transformation by the Holy Spirit. Only if one's confession of faith was genuine would this act be meaningful.

The Holy Spirit is not like common water (*húdōr* [5204]) but is a Person, a member of the triune God whom Jesus revealed as Father, Son, and Holy Spirit (Matt. 28:19). Water symbolizes cleansing from physical filth. The Holy Spirit cleanses the soul through revealed truth (John 16:13; 17:17). What is the truth? That we are sinners; that God is righteous; and that, if we do not believe in Christ, we will be judged. Of the Holy Spirit, the Lord Jesus said, "He shall glorify [from *doxázō* {1392}, to honor] me: for he shall receive of mine, and shall show it unto you" (John 16:14).

The baptism in the Holy Spirit should be distinguished from the infilling of the Holy Spirit. The baptism in the Holy Spirit is the work of uniting believers to the body of Christ. The infilling (*plērōma* [4138] from *plēróō* [4137], to fill; see Eph. 3:19) of the Holy Spirit is a continuous work through which believers are empowered to do all that God desires of them (Eph. 5:18). The Holy Spirit also seals (*sphragís* [4973]) believers (Eph. 1:13; 4:30), guaranteeing that he will live (from *enoikéō* [1774]) in them (Rom. 8:11; 2 Tim. 1:14).

Scriptures that deal with the baptism in the Holy Spirit are the words of John the Baptist recorded here and also Mark 1:8, Luke 3:16, and John 1:33.

As water baptism is meant to be administered just once after true repentance and admission into the visible church of Christ, so the baptism in the Holy Spirit is accomplished just once for the incorporation of believers into the universal spiritual church of Christ. (See author's study on 1 Cor. 12:13 and Acts 1:5; 11:16.)

[12] As John compares humanity to a grain field, he portrays Jesus as separating the wheat from the husk (v. 12). Only Jesus Christ can winnow the wheat. No human can separate believers from unbelievers, not even John the Baptist, Christ's forerunner. We should not take the winnowing fork into our own hands and try to judge who is a real believer and who is not.

Christ Himself will judge the genuineness of each individual who claims to be born again. This will be done when the goats are separated from the sheep (Matt. 25:31–46). "*His* wheat" symbolizes the Lord's sheep whom He calls by name (John 10:3), and "*the* chaff" (note that it does not say *His* chaff) represents unbelievers who will suffer unquenchable fire (3:12).

The unquenchable fire is called "**everlasting**" (from *aiṓnios* [166], perpetual) in Matthew 25:41. God gives believers in Jesus Christ eternal life (John 3:16) characterized not only by unending duration but also by divine character. In the same way, eternal fire is both divine and perpetual; those who reject eternal life choose eternal punishment.

Jesus Baptized by John
(3:13–17; Mark 1:9–11; Luke 3:21, 22)

[13] At an unspecified time when Jesus was about thirty years old, He came from Galilee to the Jordan to be baptized by John (v. 13). This event marked Christ's approval of John's ministry.

[14, 15] John's baptism was a "baptism unto repentance." Since he knew that Jesus had no sin for which He should repent, for He was "without sin" (Heb. 4:15), John hesitated to baptize Him. Jesus also did not want people to think that His own baptism was related to personal repentance from sin. Rather, He desired to do His Father's will in every detail. Thus, Jesus told John that His baptism signified the fulfillment of all righteousness (v. 15).

John's baptism of Jesus, then, was a sign of the perfection of Christ's life and death. Jesus Himself was righteousness personified because He was the Son of God. (See *díkaios* [1342], righteous; *dikaiosúnē* [1343], righteousness; *dikaióō* [1344] and *díkē* [1349], judgment, in the author's *The Hebrew-Greek Key Study Bible.*) As such, He could be the propitiation for the sins of the world.

[16] Jesus was immersed, as the verb "**baptized**" (from *baptízō* [907]) indicates here. The word *baptízō* derives from *báptō* (911), to dip. In water baptism, the water touches every part of the external body. In the baptism in the Spirit, the Holy Spirit touches every part of the human personality, affecting the sanctification of the spirit, soul, and body. Believers are completely changed in every fiber of their beings, spiritually affecting their relationship with God, psychologically affecting their societal attitudes toward others, and physically affecting even the care they give their own bodies (1 Thess. 5:23).

Notice that as Jesus **went up** (from *anabaínō* [305], to go up) from the water, the Holy Spirit **descended** (from *katabaínō* [2597], to go down) from heaven on Him.

Matthew continued his report of the event: "And **lo** [*idoú* {2400}, the imperative of *eídon*, the aorist of *horáō* {3708}, to perceive]," which refers not only to the simple act of seeing but also to understanding. This word is different from the words *blépō* (991) and *óptomai* (3700), both meaning to see physically. When *idoú* (lo, behold) is used, it calls observers not to physical sight but to prepositional insight and frequently signifies that something significant or miraculous is taking place. Here it calls attention to God the Father's approval of Jesus.

In Jesus' baptism, "the **heavens** [from *ouranós* {3772}, the dwelling place of God, the sky] were opened," symbolizing the meeting of the spiritual and the physical in one body. The Word (*Lógos* [3056], intelligence), which is spiritual and therefore immaterial, became (*génesis* [1078] as in Matt. 1:1) flesh, and His birth was not the birth (*génnēsis* [1083]) of a mere child. The baptism of Jesus was the assertion of the incarnation of the Son of God in humanity.

As Jesus was baptized, He actually "**saw** [from *eídon* {1492}] the Spirit of God descending like a dove." This word "saw" means to know intuitively, to recognize and implies more than physical sight. Jesus innately knew that the Spirit of the Father was descending on Him because of His eternal relationship with His Father.

The present participle of the verb "**lighting upon**" (from *érchomai* [2064], coming) presents a dynamic "coming" of the Spirit on the human nature of Christ (cf. Col. 2:9). In other places, Jesus is called *ho erchómenos*, the coming One (Matt. 3:11; 11:3; 21:9; 23:39; 24:30; Mark 11:9; 13:26; Luke 7:19, 20; 13:35; 19:38; 21:27; John 1:15, 27; 3:31; 6:14, 33; 12:13; Heb. 10:37). Just as frequently, the New Testament writers say *érchetai*, "He is coming" (Matt. 24:42, 44; Mark 1:7; Luke 3:16; 12:40; John 1:30; 12:15; 1 Thess. 5:2; Rev. 1:7).

[17] Matthew repeated his "**and lo**" (see v. 16) to anticipate the importance of the statement to follow. This was the "**voice**" (*phōnḗ* [5456]) of God the Father from heaven. By saying "**my . . . Son**," the Father pointed to the uniqueness of His Son. Here the Father called Jesus "**the beloved** [One]" (*ho agapētós* [27], inherently dear), the definite article again adding the sense of uniqueness to the love the Father has for His only begotten Son (Matt. 12:18; 17:5; Mark 1:11; 9:7; Luke 3:22; 9:35; 2 Pet. 1:17). God the Father expressed His pleasure in His beloved Son by stating that He was "**well pleased**" (from *eudokéō* [2106]), which means to be very satisfied, to think well of.

4

Jesus Tempted by Satan
(4:1–11; Mark 1:12, 13; Luke 4:1–13)

The Holy Spirit lives within believers (Rom. 8:9), while Satan is limited to the outside (see 2 Cor. 12:7 where the verb "buffet" [*kolaphízō* {2852}, to strike the *outside*] describes how Satan abused Paul). Satan prowls "as a roaring lion" (1 Pet. 5:8) in search of prey. We should learn to spot him from far off as those "not ignorant of his thoughts [from *nóēma* {3540}]" (2 Cor. 2:11; a.t.).

Since the devil can think, he is a personal being, but he was created by the Word (*Lógos* [3056]) of God: "All things [from *pás* {3956}, all without exception] were made by him [the *Lógos*, the Word]: and without him was not any thing made that was made" (John 1:3). This is explicitly stated by Ezekiel: "Thou wast perfect in thy ways from the day that thou wast created, till iniquity was found in thee" (Ezek. 28:15). You will note, however, that the prophet supports the truth that everything God created originally was "very good" (Gen. 1:31)—"perfect . . . from the day that thou was created, till. . . . "

Another name in Scripture for Satan is "Lucifer" (meaning "Light- bearer"; see Isa. 14:12). Isaiah tells us that Lucifer's pride made him attempt to ascend to God's throne (Is. 14:12–16). Today people fall for the same reason, and the devil, appearing as the angel of light he once was, tempts us to act consistently with our fallen natures (James 1:13–15).

[1, 2] Jesus was "**led up** [or **away**, from *anágō* {321}]" into the desert by the Holy Spirit. There is an interesting contrast in the verb used here and the one in Mark to describe the Holy Spirit's activity. The verb "**led up**" (*anágō*) in Matthew pictures the Holy Spirit as going before Him, leading Him on, while the verb used in Mark 1:12 is "driveth" (from *ekbállō* [1544], lit., to cast out or throw out), picturing the Holy Spirit as pushing from behind. The forceful- ness of *ekbállō* in Mark has led some to conclude that Jesus was unwilling to go to the desert. The true sense is that the Spirit generated in Him a compulsion to be alone in communion with His Father. While He was seeking this communion, the devil attacked. We, too, can experience temptation when we seek to draw close to the Father.

The word usually translated "temptation" in the New Testament is *peirasmós* (3986), which is the noun form of the verb used here, *peirázō* (3985), to tempt, test, try. The devil tempts us to make us sin, but God's tests or tries us by giving us the choice to love and obey Him. Satan believed he could tempt Jesus to sin as he does other people, either ignoring or disbelieving God the Father's attestation from heaven that Jesus was His beloved Son (Matt. 3:17).

An illuminating statement is found in James 1:13: "Let no man say when he is tempted, I am tempted of God: for God cannot be tempted [*apeírastos* {551}] with evil, neither tempteth he any man." God "tests" or "tries" (*peirázō*) us to strengthen our integrity before Him, not to produce rebellion. The morality of a temptation, therefore, lies in the motive of the tester. The best example of a double motive in a single act is given in Genesis 50:20 where Joseph commented on his brothers' act of selling him to the Egyptians: "But as for you, ye thought evil against me; *but* God meant it unto good, to bring to pass, as it is this day, to save much people alive."

Satan, as always, was wrong to think he could overpower Jesus with temptation. He did not comprehend that, although Jesus subjected Himself to many human weaknesses, His sinless human nature was fully permeated and controlled by His own deity working in conjunction with the Holy Spirit. Christ's human nature, therefore, could not sin against His overpowering divine nature, "for in him dwelleth all the fullness of God *bodily*" (Col. 2:9; a.t., emphasis added). We must remember, however, that our Lord's divine nature did not overpower His pain. He felt fatigue and hunger in His body, and He felt physical pain on the cross as well.

[3] The "**if**" in Greek is *ei* (1487) and is used here with a present-tense verb in a first-class condition, assuming that the "if" clause is real. The devil, desiring to keep Jesus off guard, said, in effect, "If you are the Son of God, and I assume you are, you can change these stones into bread and satisfy your hunger." This first temptation was aimed at Jesus' human and divine natures simultaneously. The devil mercilessly tempted the Son of man to eat during a time of prolonged fasting, but he could not successfully lure Him to convert stones into bread.

[4] Three times (vv. 4, 7, 10) the Lord met Satan's "if" head-on:

> But he answered and said, **It has been written** [*gégraptai*, the perfect passive of *gráphō* {1125}, to write], man shall not live by bread alone, but by **every**

[from *pás* {3956}] **word** [from *rhéma* {4487}] that proceedeth out of the mouth of God. (cf. Deut. 8:3; a.t.)

The perfect tense of *grápho* indicates that what God inspired His prophets to write down over the 1,500+ years from the time of Moses, the author of the Torah, was still valid; literally, "It has been written, and it still stands as written." A person's life is not just physical, but a spiritual side requires God's truth in order to fully live. The expression, "**it is written**," is repeated three more times, in verses 6, 7, and 10.

[5, 6] Having lost the first round, the devil moved on to a second temptation:

Then the devil **took** [from *paralambáno* {3880}, to take alongside] Him up into the holy city, and set Him on a pinnacle of the temple, and said to Him, **If** [*ei*] You are the Son of God, cast Yourself down: for it is written, He shall give His angels charge over You: and in their hands, they will bear You up, lest at any time You dash Your foot against a stone. (a.t.)

This second temptation was designed to test our Lord's trust in the Father. If He refused to throw Himself down from the highest point of the temple, Satan mocked, it would prove that He really did not trust His Father. Once again, Satan used the *if* clause of the first-class condition, assuming that Jesus really was the Son of God. This was not the first time Satan challenged God:

For thou hast said in thine heart, I will ascend into heaven, I will exalt my throne above the stars of God: I will sit also upon the mount of the congregation, in the sides of the north: I will ascend above the heights of the clouds; I will be like the most High. (Isa. 14:13, 14)

[7] Satan essentially quoted Psalm 91:11, 12 correctly but reasoned fallaciously from it. The psalm is indeed a promise of angelic protection to the righteous, but it is not a command for the righteous to test that protection. The *ought* cannot be logically deduced from the *is*; specifically here, it was invalid to deduce the morality of testing a promise from the promise itself. Whether or not Jesus ought to jump, given the promise that angels would catch Him, must come from somewhere else.

Jesus quoted that somewhere else: "It is written again, Thou shalt not **tempt** [from *ekpeirázo* {1598}, to test] the Lord thy God" (cf. Deut. 6:16).

Here we have a dilemma. If God is untemptible (*apeírastos* from *a* [1], the alpha privative "without"; and *peirázo* [3985], temptation) of evil (James 1:13), then why is there a command to not tempt Him? To apply the dilemma to the this scenario, if Jesus had jumped and the angels had caught Him as promised by God, what effect would this have had on the One who cannot be tempted? How can an impossible event—tempting the Untemptible—be immoral?

To answer this, we can differentiate between an internal and an external temptation. God cannot be tempted internally because He is immutable: "I am the Lord, I change not" (Mal. 3:6, cf. Num. 23:19; Job 23:13; Heb. 6:17; James 1:17). If we define an internal temptation as a chance to change, to react or to re-think, then such a form of temptation has no valid place in One who does not change and who is, therefore, timelessly omniscient. Omniscience cannot change its mind. To change one's mind from something to something else logically requires partial knowledge. If God, for example, learned one day that two and two is actually five, then, when He earlier thought four, He was mistakenly ignorant. This presupposes fractional knowledge. God learning anything is contradictory to omniscience.

On the other hand, Satan and humans can **externally tempt** God, but this reduces to an empty attempt—a worthless try, like punching a brick wall or lying to Omniscience (Acts 5:4). Even Gamaliel recognized that while some fight against God, they "cannot overthrow" what He does (Acts 5:39). If God is internally untemptible because of His immutability, He cannot react by definition. He foreknows every single attempt of people and angels before they exist, and it is impossible for them to do anything in history contrary to what He has foreknown from eternity: "Whatever God does is forever; nothing can be added to it, and nothing can be taken from it, but God does it so that men might fear Him" (Eccl. 3:14; a.t.). Creatures are not unrelated to God's foreknowledge. Either they do precisely what He has foreknown, or His foreknowledge is fallible. Accordingly, neither sin nor righteousness causes the Immutable One to change:

> If you sin, what do you accomplish against Him? Or, if your transgressions are multiplied, what do you do to Him? If you are righteous, what do you give Him? Or what does He receive from your hand? (Job 35:6, 7 NKJV; Paul argues the same point in Rom. 11:35, 36.)

If God is immutable, then He cannot change Himself by strict logical necessity: "He **cannot** deny Himself [i.e., His immutability]" (2 Tim. 2:13). For the same reason, "God [i.e., Truth] . . . **cannot** lie" (Titus 1:2). If God could change Himself, then He would not be immutable.

In conclusion, Satan tried and failed to tempt God on two counts. Not only is God's internal nature unchangeable, but also the human Jesus would not have thrown Himself down from the pinnacle. He absolutely would not sin.

Mature believers know better than Satan. They do not tempt God for two reasons. They believe that the fruitless attempt, however impossible of success, is immoral because God has declared it so. They also put their faith in God's attributes of immutable truth, wisdom, and love, and His immutable plan of every detail of their lives, down to the numbering of the hairs on their heads.

[8, 9] Whereas we find an assumed reality and the same Greek word *eí* in verses 3 and 6, the "**if**" of verse 9 is different. It is a supposition of possibility.

Again, the devil took him up into an exceeding high mountain and showed Him all the kingdoms of the world and the glory of them; and said unto Him, All these things I will give you, **if** [*eán* {1437}] You, **having fallen down** [*pesón*, the aorist participle of *píptō* {4098}, to fall], **worship** [*proskunéses*, the aorist subjunctive of *proskunéō* {4352}] me. (a.t.)

Here Satan tempted Jesus to fall down and worship him at least once (reflected in the aorist tense of *proskunéō*). But on what basis? On the basis of "the easy way out." If, in a moment of weakness, the Lord could be tempted to self-servingly ascend to a quick and alternate redemption of the world from sin in exchange for a single instance of idolatry, this could be a great victory for the devil. It took only one sin from Adam to bring the human race under judgment in the first place (Rom. 5:18, 19). Perhaps, the devil would think, a single sin from the Lamb of God would nullify the atonement.

The offer was based on the lie that the world was Satan's to give. God had not given His "good" world (Gen. 1:31) to Satan—only the "sinful kingdom" (Amos 9:8), the "darkness of this world" (Eph. 6:12), the "present evil [from *ponērós* {4190}] age" (Gal. 1:4 NASB). Who in their right mind would want to rule over even a single era of sin, darkness, and malevolence?

The Lord chose the far more difficult path of suffering for our sakes, first to prepare for His priestly duties between advents: "For we have not an high priest which cannot be touched with the feeling of our infirmities; but was in all points tempted [from *peirázō* {3985}] like as we are, yet without sin" (Heb. 4:15). Second, He chose this path as a model for our perseverance: "For even hereunto were ye called: because Christ also suffered for us, leaving us an example [from *hupogrammós* {5261}, an underwriting, a diagram to be traced], that ye should follow his steps" (1 Pet. 2:21). The Lord's perseverance against sin was due to the total sovereignty of the triune God over His human nature. It is the same sovereignty of God that secures our conformity to Christ (Rom. 8:28) "that he might be the firstborn among many brethren" (Rom. 8:29, cf. Heb. 2:10–13).

The verb *paralambánei* (from *paralambánō* [3880]), translated "**taketh**" in verse 8 (cf. v. 6) includes the concept of nearness or proximity (*pará* [3844]). Like Judas, the "devil" (John 6:70), as Satan the opposer and the arch tare, followed close to Jesus, the arch wheat—growing together according to Matthew

13:30. This is operationally necessary for betrayal, which requires a great deal of deceit. You can't stab someone in the back unless you are within close range.

We must remember that while Satan and Judas spaced themselves inches from Christ as often as they could to accomplish their evil plan of betrayal, they were miles away from Christ morally. While we should be on guard against similar experiences, we must remember that our Lord subjected Himself to the betrayal and became obedient to death (Phil. 2:8) for the joy set before Him (Heb. 12:2). "When he was reviled, [he] reviled not again; when he suffered, he threatened not" (1 Pet. 2:23).

[10] Again, the Lord rebuked Satan from Scripture:

> Then saith Jesus unto him, Get thee hence, Satan: for it is written, **Thou shalt worship** [from *proskuneō* {4352}, to prostrate, from *prós* {4314}, toward; and *kuneō* {n.f.}, to kiss, to adore] the Lord thy God, and him only **shalt thou serve** [from *latreúō* {3000}].

The Lord probably had in mind both Exodus 34:14: "For thou shalt worship no other god: for the LORD, whose name is Jealous, is a jealous God," and Deuteronomy 6:13: "Thou shalt fear the LORD thy God, and serve him, and shalt swear by his name." *Proskuneō* is the physical posture of one who is completely submitted to the will of His Master. It is the outward manifestation of an inner attitude of humble dependence. *Latreúō*, on the other hand, is physical service that follows worship. We "serve" our God indirectly by ministering to His people (see our exegesis of Matt. 25:35–40).

[11] The devil "taketh" (v. 8) and the devil "**leaveth**" (from *aphíēmi* [863], to leave alone). Like us, the Lord had only intermittent relief from the devil. Even the devil exhausts himself by sinning; he cannot tirelessly persevere against the living God. Eventually, he abandoned his labors, but note Luke's comment that this was only "for a season" (Luke 4:13).

After this, we read, "**Behold** [*idoú* {2400}, look and understand; see Matt. 3:16], angels came and ministered unto him." Jesus needed ministry after this prolonged conflict.

The Galilean Ministry Begun
(4:12–17; Mark 1:14; Luke 4:14, 15)

Herod arrested and imprisoned John the Baptist in the Castle of Machaerus because he had rebuked the ruler for marrying his brother's wife (see Matt. 14:3–12).

[12, 13] Meanwhile, we read in these two verses that Jesus left Judea to enter Galilee, the northernmost part of Palestine, and chose Capernaum for His home. Galilee was fifty miles from north to south, twenty-five miles from east to west, and was densely populated and fertile. The name "Galilee" is derived from the Hebrew word *galil* (1550, OT) meaning "circle." Because many Gentiles lived there, it was known as "Galilee of the Gentiles" (v. 15).

Originally, Galilee was assigned to the tribes of Asher, Naphtali, and Zebulun after the Israelites came into the land (Josh. 19:10–16, 24–39). In the eighth century BC, the Assyrians engulfed Galilee completely and carried a great part of the population into exile. Gentiles came in at this time and mingled with the inhabitants who were left. On the Jews' return from the Babylonian exile under Nehemiah and Ezra, many the Galileans came to live in Jerusalem.

[14–17] Matthew interprets the coming of Jesus to Galilee as the fulfillment of Isaiah 9:1, 2, identifying the Galileans as the people sitting in darkness upon whom the light shines (vv. 14–16; see also John 8:12). Jesus' message was the same as that of His forerunner, John (v. 17; Matt. 3:2). The verb *metanoeíte* (from *metanoéō* [3340]), "**repent**," is in the present tense because sin is ever present with us in our flesh. Jesus Christ brought the kingdom of heaven into the world, first invisibly within the hearts of those who repent and believe, then He will do so visibly at the end of the age (Luke 17:20–22).

Following Christ
(4:18–22; Mark 1:16–20; Luke 5:1–11)

[18] While Matthew, a Jew, here calls Galilee a "**sea**" (*thálassa* [2281]), the well-traveled Gentile, Luke, chose the word "lake" (*límnē* [3041]; Luke 5:1, 2; 8:22, 23, 33).

The River Jordan, which begins at the foot of Mount Hermon to the north (the tallest mountain in the area—over 9,000 feet), runs into the Sea of Galilee and meanders south to the Dead Sea. The Sea of Galilee is 680 feet below sea level, thirteen miles long, and a little less than seven miles wide at its broadest part. During New Testament times, it had nine populous cities on its pear-shaped shore; today, only Tiberias remains.

This was not the first time Jesus saw two brothers, Simon Peter and Andrew (see John 1:35, 40, 41). At this point, they were probably already His disciples part-time.

The Lord did not call idle people but busy fishermen. These men were partners with Zebedee, the father of James and John. When Jesus saw them this time, they were "casting a **net** [*amphíblēstron* {293}] into the sea" (v. 18). The noun derives from *amphí* (n.f.), a prefix meaning "on both sides" (as in "amphitheater"). It occurs only in this section and in Mark 1:16. One person could throw this type of net over his shoulder, but it worked better when two people held it on both sides. "Fishing" for people also is more productive when believers cooperate.

Another type of fishing net was the *sagénē* (4522), a seine, a dragnet with weights on one edge and floats on the other. These nets were hung vertically in the ocean—floats up, weights down—then their ends were drawn together to entrap fish (Matt. 13:47). Our Lord used this type of net to illustrate the final eschatological ingathering of believers and unbelievers (13:47–50).

The word that describes all kinds of nets is *díktuon* ([1350]; used here in vv. 20, 21; also Mark 1:18, 19; Luke 5:2, 4–6; John 21:6, 8, 11 [twice]).

The Holy Spirit specifically selected each Greek word translated "net" to fit the purpose of the intended lesson.

Why did the Lord use the metaphor of fishing? He referred to Himself as a shepherd, not a fisherman. Abraham, Jeremiah, and Moses were all shepherds. Jesus commanded Peter, formerly a fisherman, to "feed my sheep" (John 21:16, 17), not "my fish." Even though Jesus' birth was announced to shepherds, He did not assign them the task of announcing His coming, and none of the Twelve were shepherds.

The metaphor highlights our first priority to fish the sea of fallen humanity with single hooks (*ágkistron;* Matt. 17:27), nets for casting (*amphíblēstron*), and dragnets (*sagénē*), thus reflecting individual and corporate evangelism.

[19] Challenging His disciples, Jesus said, "**Follow** [*deúte* {1205}] **behind** [*opísō* {3694}] **Me**, and I will make you fishers of men" (a.t.). He offered neither destination nor distance. The disciples must follow Him wherever He led, trusting Him step by step.

Jesus wanted to make the disciples new creatures. Until now they were fishermen. Fishermen need discipline, patience, perseverance, courage to face turbulent seas (Mark 4:37; Luke 8:23), and wisdom (e.g., different types of bait for different fish). Catching souls is difficult; some must be baited, while others must be snatched "out of the fire" (Jude 23) with nets.

[20] The reaction of the disciples to the Lord's call was swift: "And they **straightway** [*euthéōs* {2112}, immediately, right away] left [from *aphíēmi* {863}] their nets, and followed him."

Professional fishermen work for money. The catching of souls may not yield the temporary wealth of this world, but it yields eternal, spiritual treasures in heaven (Matt. 6:33; 2 Cor. 4:16–18).

[21, 22] The reaction of the next two whom Jesus called, James and John, was just as swift. "And they immediately [*euthéos* {2112}] left the ship and their father, and followed him." Just as Peter and Andrew had left their nets, James and John left their ship and their father Zebedee. But the verb "**left**" (from *aphíēmi* [863]) does not mean foolish and thoughtless abandonment. is God's call is a priority (see Matt. 8:21, 22; 10:34–39; Luke 9:61, 62).

Followers of Christ should not recklessly abandon their possessions or family to follow Him, but possessions and family must not detract them either. Our relationship to Jesus Christ is first, yet we must not neglect property or family (Matt. 10:37, 38; Luke 14:25–33).

Jesus' Response to the Multitudes
(4:23–25; Luke 6:17–19)

After calling James and John, the sons of Zebedee, who immediately left their fishing trade, Jesus launched His ministry in Galilee. Here "**multitudes**" (from *óchlos* [3793], unorganized crowds; v. 25) began to flock to Him. Although exposed to Jesus' teaching, preaching, and healing, most of these people did not become disciples in the fullest sense (see Luke 9:57–62). They were simply inquisitive.

[23] Jesus chose to go everywhere in Galilee, as implied in "**went about**" (from *periágō* [4013], to lead around). The four disciples whom He had invited to follow Him (vv. 19, 21) probably went with Him on these journeys.

Jesus first visited numerous synagogues where people gathered together to worship, pray, and read the Torah and the prophets. The president of the synagogue usually appointed a nonprofessional to preach. The pulpit was open, and on one occasion Jesus took the opportunity to read from the prophet Isaiah (Luke 4:16–30).

The Lord's method of instruction was didactic (instructive), signified here by the verb "**teaching**" (from *didáskō* [1321]). Rabbis were expected to perform such services, even if they had not yet become professional preachers. Both distinguished strangers (cf. Acts 13:15) and ordinary community members might be invited to address those in the synagogue. The duty of teaching children was originally assigned to the father of a family (Deut. 6:7), but later on, instruction became the duty of the synagogue.

Jesus thus became an itinerant teacher in the synagogues—the education centers of the day. His primary message to both Jews (Judea) and Gentiles (Galilee, Syria, Decapolis) was that God had anointed Him to preach the gospel to the poor (Luke 4:16–30).

All three verbs, teaching (*didáskōn* from *didáskō*), preaching (*kērússōn* from *kērússō* [2784]), and healing (*therapeúōn* from *therapeúō* [2323]), are present participles, indicating that these made up the normal workday for Christ.

The order of these verbs may indicate priority. "Teaching," the first priority, was directed toward the Jews. They needed to understand the new covenant prophesied for Israel and the general fulfillment of the Law and the prophets in the Person of the Messiah (Matt. 5:17). A new edifice was being built, and once it was built, the old would not be needed anymore, having served its prophetic and typical purposes.

The second task Jesus committed Himself to was preaching (from *kērússō*) the gospel (*euaggélion* [2098], good news). Teaching and preaching are different. Teaching is primarily addressed to the mind (*noús* [3563], from which comes the word *metanoéō* [3340], to repent or change one's mind). But the good news, which appeals to the heart as well, also needs proclamation so that others may hear and believe.

The third ministerial priority of Christ was healing (from *therapeúō*), the temporary physical restoration of those who were suffering. The order of these priorities is reflected in 1 Thessalonians 5:23 where we find the three elements of the human person. The spirit (*pneúma* [4151]) is first because it constitutes the contact point between God and a human. The soul (*psuchē* [5590]) is second, the animating principle of the body. The body (*sōma* [4983]) itself is the third element, the housing of the spirit/soul.

The human spirit and soul need to be saved, but so does the body, which has equally died "in Adam" (Rom 5:14; 1 Cor. 15:22). The full restoration of a body in *therapeía* (2322), healing, includes compassionate care as well as physical restoration. When people believed God had come among them, they looked to Him not only for physical relief but also spiritual care.

Notice the extent of the Lord's healing: "**all** [from *pás* {3956}] manner of **sickness** [from *nósos* {3554} from which the English word "nosology," the study of types of physical illness, is derived] and **all** [from *pás*] manner of **disease** [from *malakía* {3119}, infirmity, debility] among the people." On this special occasion, the Lord chose to heal everyone in the vicinity.

[24] Some, we read, were "**possessed with devils**" (from *daimonízomai* [1139], to be "demonized," i.e., possessed by one or more **demons** [from *daimónion* {1140}]). This condition is distinct from other illnesses, though there are physical symptoms.

Others were "**lunatic[s]**," translated from *selēniázomai* (4583), which means to be "moonstruck" (an archaic word). These people were probably afflicted with epilepsy, which, it was believed, was aggravated during lunar cycles. The word did not carry the stereotypical connotation of insanity that it does today. Still others were "**paralyzed** [NIV]" (from *paralutikós* [3885]) partially or totally.

These diseases were no obstacles to Christ. As Matthew continued in his report: "**He healed** [from *therapeúō*] them," ministering to whatever needs they had. Note again the deliberately redundant adjective "**all**" (from *pás*) here. All who were brought were cured. This had never been done by any doctor or prophet before.

[25] As usual, after dramatic healing events, multitudes of people began to follow Jesus:

> And there **followed** [from *akoloutheō* {190}, to follow; from the collective *a* {1} from *háma* {260}, together; and *kéleuthos* {n.f.}, a way; "accompany"] him great multitudes of people from Galilee, and from Decapolis, and from Jerusalem, and from Judea, and from beyond Jordan.

The verb *akoloutheō* is first encountered in this Gospel in Matthew 4:20: "And they straightway left their nets, and followed him." The original call to follow must have come with great power since the strange words from the Stranger, "Follow me, and I will make you fishers of men," would otherwise have evoked sardonic wit. After all, by definition we fish for fish, not for people. Why follow a profession from which no one could make a living?

The multitudes were comprised of people from the region of Galilee ([1056]; most likely Jews and Gentiles); Decapolis (literally, "ten cities," all of which except Scythia lay east of the Jordan River; cf. Mark 5:20; 7:31); Jerusalem (2419), the capital of Palestine where the temple was located; and Judea (2449), the third district west of the Jordan and south of Samaria.

5

❦

The Beatitudes
(5:1–12; Luke 6:20–23)

To highlight the importance of these lessons, Jesus taught them sitting down, *ex cathedra*, "from the chair." Rulers customarily sat on their thrones when they made authoritative pronouncements. Three distinct groups of people listened to Jesus: the committed disciples, the mere believers, and the outside circle of unbelievers. By addressing His teaching to the two inner circles, Jesus also impacted those outside the faith. (For a complete exegesis of this section, see the author's *The Beatitudes*.)

[1, 2] The adjective *makárioi* from *makários* (3107), "**blessed**," occurs eight times in verses 3 to 10. In Scripture, "blessed" means those indwelt by God in Christ and consequently, fully satisfied. In 1 Timothy 1:11, God is called *makários*. *Makários* is the state of believers in Christ who, in possessing God, possess everything, since God is the creator and provider of all things (Col. 1:16; James 1:17). Because believers are indwelt by the Holy Spirit (Rom. 8:9), they are fully satisfied no matter what their circumstances (Phil. 4:11). *Makários* or "blessed" differs from the word "happy" in that persons are happy if they have good luck. "Happy" comes from the root *hap*, which means a favorable circumstance or happening. By contrast, to be blessed is equivalent to having the Blessed One's kingdom within the heart (Matt. 5:3, 10). The Greek philosopher Aristotle contrasts *makários* with *endeés* (1729), the needy one. Accordingly, *makários* refers to those who have no longing for worldly things, because their sole satisfaction is in God, not favorable circumstances.

In Luke 1:28, 48, the virgin Mary is pronounced blessed (from *makarízō* [3106], to pronounce as blessed) or indwelt by God. Prophets and others who endure persecution for Christ's sake are also called blessed (from *makarízō*; see

James 5:11). Blessedness describes believers to whom God imputes righteousness (Rom. 4:6).

All the Beatitudes have the plural definite article "**the**" (*hoi* [3588]) before the adjectival noun: the poor, the mourning, the meek, the hungering and thirsting, the merciful, the pure in heart, the peacemakers, and the persecuted. Only those who are in such conditions for Christ's sake are blessed. This is brought out in verse 11 in the phrase, "**for** [*héneken* or *héneka* {1752}, for the sake of] **my sake**." Not all the poor, all the mourners, etc., are blessed.

[3] The Beatitudes are eight attitudes with promises attached. The first subject is the "**poor in spirit**" (from *ptōchós* [4434]) meaning helpless as contrasted to *pénēs* (3993), poor but able to help oneself through labor or toil. "In spirit" tells us where this helplessness is located. Only those who recognize their spiritual helplessness will accept the salvation Christ has provided (11:28).

[4] The second Beatitude, "**the mourning ones**" (a.t.; from *penthéō* [3996]), includes the believer's attitude toward those who have not yet believed and are spiritually dead.

We mourn at funerals. Likewise, believers who have the kingdom of God within them (Luke 17:21) are so joyful in the Lord that they shed tears for those who are spiritually dead and do not realize it. Those who weep over the state of unbelievers in this life "**shall be comforted**" (from *parakaléō* [3870]). Their heavenly comfort will be proportionate to their grieving over sin while on earth.

[5] In attempting to define the word "**meek**" (*praús* [4239]), Aristotle positions himself between two extremes: *orgilótēs* (3711), extreme anger, and *aorgēsía* (n.f.), indifference, not getting angry when one should. No person should be at either extreme.

In between the two concepts, we have the attitude of *praútēs* (4240) or *praótēs* (4236), meekness. One can be *praús* or *práos* and still be stirred to anger (*paroxúnō* [3947]; Acts 17:16) for the proper reasons. This is a tempered attitude toward what believers cannot control in others (1 Cor. 13:5). Remember that Moses was described as the meekest man in the world (Num. 12:3), and Jesus described Himself as meek (Matt. 11:29; see also 21:5).

[6] The phrase, "they which do **hunger** [from *peináō* {3983}] and **thirst** [from *dipsáō* {1372}] after righteousness" refers to a continuous attitude of yearning or desire. The promise is that "**they shall be satiated**" (a.t.; from *chortázō* [5526], to fill to satisfaction). Only in heaven where righteousness prevails will believers be totally satisfied.

[7] The "**merciful**" (from *eleḗmōn* [1655]) offer relief from sufferings. We must share with others the mercy we receive from God. In our future lives we shall receive in the same measure that we provided for others in this life (see also James 2:12, 13).

[8] The "**pure** [from *katharós* {2513}, cleansed] in heart" are those who possess the unadulterated holiness without which no person will see the Lord (Heb. 12:14).

[9] The "**peacemakers**" (from *eirēnopoiós* [1518]) are those who have received the peace of God in their hearts but do not keep it to themselves. They encourage God's peace and share it with others by helping them to know Christ. This does not guarantee that they will enjoy external peace here on earth, because Christ predicted that in the world we will have tribulation even as He had (John 16:33).

[10] The blessed ones will be persecuted "**for** [*héneken* {1752}, on account of] righteousness' sake." Peacemakers show the Prince of Peace to the world, but they are despised and rejected. In spite of persecution, they can rest assured that they possess the kingdom of heaven.

The first and last Beatitudes are the only ones that have the promise in the present tense: "for theirs **is** [from *estí* {2076}] the kingdom of heaven" (vv. 3, 10). All the other promises are in the future. Only the promise of the kingdom is in the present tense. If we do not have heaven in our hearts in this life, we will not have it in the future.

[11] Jesus now addresses the disciples directly:

> Blessed **are ye** [*esté* {2075}, the present indicative of *eimí*, to be], when [*hótan* {3752}; not *ei* {1487}, if, which might indicate doubt] men **shall revile** [from *oneidízō* {3679}, to defame, disparage, reproach, chide] you, and **persecute** [from *diṓkō* {1377}] you, and shall say **all manner** [from *pás* {3956}, every kind] of **evil** [from *ponērós* {4190}, malevolent evil] **against** [*katá* {2596}] you falsely, for my sake.

The world maligns committed Christians, not for any evil they do, but for the things they do for Christ's sake. We must be careful that the evil they accuse us of is false because of our commitment to the Lord (1 Pet. 3:16). Unbelievers resent Christians because their very presence and holy lives convict them of their sin.

[12] What attitude should the present maligning and persecution create in committed disciples of Christ?

Here we have it: "Rejoice and **leap for joy** [from *agalliáō* {21}, to be exuberant], for your **reward** [*misthós* {3408}, expected reward, pay for work performed] is great in heaven" (a.t.). Committed Christians willingly suffer abuse and persecution that compromise could possibly avert. They realize that their comfort on earth is limited and that they will not receive all their rewards here and now. Such rewards will be greatly multiplied in heaven. The concept of living in two worlds, the temporal earthly life and the eternal heavenly life, is entirely missing from unbelievers (Matt. 6:19–21). Jesus intended His comments to His disciples to motivate uncommitted disciples to desire similar rewards (what 2 John 8 calls the "full reward") and unbelievers to desire salvation.

Finally, Jesus appealed to the lives of the prophets, none of whom escaped persecution, and to the greatness of their rewards in heaven as further incentives to endure persecution.

The Salt and Light of the Earth
(5:13–20; Mark 9:50; Luke 14:34, 35)

Jesus continued His encouragement to committed disciples by using direct address instead of speaking generally about the blessedness of believers and what they can expect as rewards in this life and in the future. Both earthly and heavenly rewards are scaled to performance.

[13] Our Lord said to those closest to Him, the committed believers, "Ye are the salt of the earth." Here He speaks figuratively, explaining that what salt is to the earth, they are to the world.

What does salt do? Salt preserves food for future use. God uses committed Christians to preserve the human race, which Christ Jesus came into the world to save (John 3:16). Believers are a precious commodity, even as salt is vitally important.

God would have spared the cities of Sodom and Gomorrah had He found as few as ten righteous people living there (Gen. 18:32). The world has experienced the coming of the Word of God (John 1:1, 14), and although the majority in this wicked world reject Him, a minority of righteous believers are the salt of the earth. Only small quantities of salt help preserve food, and the minor presence of believers suppresses major evil. Before the Lord destroys the earth as He did Sodom and Gomorrah, He will take believers to Himself and destroy the wicked by fire (2 Pet. 3:4–13).

Salt flavors food when used in proper proportions. Food without salt lacks taste. When, however, one seasons food with too much salt, it becomes undesirable. Similarly, overbearing Christians can make the gospel unpalatable to unbelievers.

But Jesus added a warning. "**If**" (*eán* [1437], the suppositional conjunction of potential) the salt **loses its flavor** (from *mōraínō* [3471], to act foolishly, to make flat, tasteless), it has lost its value. How can salt lose its flavor? Primarily by being diluted. If Christians allow too much of the world to permeate their lives, they lose their effectiveness. Thus, they must allow truth to permeate the whole of their lives, displacing the pervading influences of the world. They must make the Christian life attractive and desirable to others and so fulfill its purpose, which is the glory of God.

[14] Whereas Jesus said, "**I** am the light of the world" (John 8:12; 9:5), here He says, "**Ye** are the light of the world."

The word used for "**light**" in all three instances is *phō̂s* (5457), inherent light whose function is to illuminate. Since Christ dwells in Christians and since He is the original Light, He shines through believers, making them light in the world.

The aggregate of shining Christians makes the city in which they live luminous (v. 14). Thus, the function of luminous Christians is to be seen and discerned as having Christ glowing within them (Rom. 8:10).

[15] Another related noun used in this verse is *lúchnos* (3088), a portable lamp or illuminator like our **candle.**

The verb used, however, is from *kaíō* (2545), to cause to burn, to kindle. In John 5:35, speaking of John the Baptist, Jesus said, "He was the lamp [*lúchnos*], the burning and shining one, and you were willing for a season to rejoice in his light" (a.t.). The role of Christians is not only to be light but also to be like lamps whose contents are consumed as they burn. While being consumed, they radiate light to guide those in darkness.

Let us accept our role as consumable lamps, not hiding our lights under "**bushel[s]**" (*módion* [3426], a Roman measuring basket)!

[16] Let us display our burning lamps on lampstands so they will "**shine**" (from *lámpō* [2989], to give light) to all around us. Collectively, believers are a light on a mountain top that can be seen from a distance, but they must also be individual lamps shining in their own dwellings.

This is supported by the literal translation of verse 16: "**In this way** [*hoútōs* {3779}, thus], **let shine** [from *lámpō*] your light before **the** men [i.e., those among whom you live and work]."

The result of such shining is inevitable. It is not a believers' calculated shining in order to impress others, because that would have been expressed with the conjunction of purpose *hína* (2443), in order that. It is rather expressed by *hópōs* (3704), so that. Not only are those living in the Christians' environment going to "**see** [the believers'] **good works,**" but many will also discern why they do them, and they will believe. Shining is not for self-aggrandizement but is an outcome of the indwelling Christ who is our light and glory. The result will glorify the Father who is in heaven. The verb "**glorify**" (from *doxázō* [1392]) derives from the verb *dokéō* (1380), to consider or recognize. Observers will correctly recognize that our heavenly Father is the cause of our radiance and goodness. Believers' faith is visible through their good works. The adjective "**good**" is from *kalós* (2570), good constitutionally. Thus, believers should live righteous lives that show forth the glory of God, not their own goodness (Rom. 12:1, 2; Eph. 5:10; Phil. 4:18; Col. 3:20; Heb. 13:21).

[17] God had given Jews the Law of Moses, which is also called the Law of the Lord (e.g., see Ps. 1:2; 19:7; Amos 2:4; Luke 2:23, 24, 39) to guide them.

To some, Christ's words and deeds appeared "**to destroy**" (from *katalúō* [2647], to dissolve, demolish, cancel) the Law. Yet He emphatically stated that He did not come to destroy what His Father had built (v. 17) but rather to build the superstructure of grace on it, the good news of the gospel. The Law required obedience, and disobedience required punishment. But Jesus provided the ransom for transgressors of the Law, that is, all of us (Rom. 3:23). Instead of punishing us for our sins, He paid the penalty of death, suffering in our places so that if we believe on Him, we will have eternal life (John 3:16).

Christ did not come to destroy either the Law or the prophets. Note the comparative particle "**or**" (*ḗ* [2228]) in verse 17. The prophets foretold the coming of the Messiah, and Christ did not negate their prophecies. Instead, He fulfilled those prophecies and the Law. Concerning Him, Paul wrote in Romans 10:4, "For Christ is the end [*télos* {5056}, completion] of the law for righteousness to every one that believeth." So the Law was the first teacher, but it was completed in the final Teacher, Jesus Christ.

When a lawyer asked Jesus what commandment of the Law was the greatest, He answered, "Thou shalt love the Lord thy God with all thy heart, and with all thy soul, and with all thy mind . . . and the second is like unto it, Thou shalt love thy neighbor as thyself" (Matt. 22:37–39). The Lord Jesus reduced Law and prophecy to love (*agápē* [26]) in contrast to the Jewish understanding of the Law and the prophets. In the New Testament sense, love is the fulfillment of the Law. Although it punishes sin, it does not punish the sinner but the sinless Savior who died in place of the sinner. That does not destroy the Law but fulfills it (Rom. 5:8).

[18] Jesus added that not a single letter or mark of the Law will be canceled. He used the ninth letter of the Greek alphabet, *iōta* (2503).

[19] This means the smallest details of the Law will be fulfilled. All God's commands are important, and we should heed them. But we must make sure that they are His commands (*entolḗ* [1785]) and not human rules (*éntalma* [1778]; see Matt. 15:9; Mark 7:7; Col. 2:22) that are passed on.

[20] The righteousness of the scribes (teachers) and Pharisees was external and superficial. This is why the Lord said His disciples' righteousness must exceed that of the scribes and Pharisees—not in quantity but in quality. It is not enough to wash the hands if the heart is filthy (Matt. 15:1–11). The inside of the cup must be cleaned as well as the outside (Matt. 23:25, 26).

Teaching on Anger
(5:21–26)

The principle Jesus addressed here is the cause of evil action. People consider others as offenders if they perpetrate crimes, not when they think evil thoughts. But Christ says that evil thoughts themselves are culpable.

[21] Murder begins with anger. Human justice may consider anger as temporary insanity, thus an excuse for killing another person. But Jesus taught that anger without a cause is not only inexcusable but also is an evil that needs to be remedied. There is, however, a righteous anger against sin (see Mark 3:5).

[22] A few older Greek manuscripts and some church fathers differ from the King James Version and the large majority of Greek manuscripts in omitting the adverb *eikḗ* (1500), which should be translated here, "without proper cause." Even if we assume that the omission is correct, the second half of the verse clearly explains what kind of anger Christ is talking about—a contemptuous anger that leads to verbal abuse.

Sometimes we should be angry. Jesus Himself was justifiably angry. In Mark 3:5 we read, "And when he [Jesus] had looked round about on them with anger, being grieved for the hardness of their hearts. . . ." Jesus was angry at those in the synagogue who did not want Him to heal a man with a withered hand because it was the Sabbath. They interpreted His benevolence as working on the Sabbath. Here Jesus used the present participle *orgizómenos* (from *orgízō* [3710], to be angry), **being angry,** to indicate that He condemned the state or habit of anger against someone. Christians should develop the attitude of longsuffering toward others, knowing that they themselves are sinners before God (1 John 1:8). Continuous anger against another has no just cause and, therefore, no place in the Christian's heart.

More sinful than being angry without reason is flippantly calling people words such as *raká* (4469), **worthless or empty one** or *mōré*, **fool**, from *mōrós* (3474), **dull, stupid, moron**. When people are verbally abusive, they deserve to be punished. The punishment, according to Jesus, is consignment to "**Gehenna**" (*Géenna* [1067], Purós; translated "hell fire" in the KJV). This place was symbolized by the Valley of Topheth in Jerusalem where garbage constantly burned. No persons can call others worthless and be worthy themselves. Today this is known as libel and is punishable by law.

[23] In bringing our offerings to God, we should have no pride (as, e.g., over our generosity) or anger in our hearts but rather humbly consider whether others have valid complaints against us. If we remember such complaints, we should attempt to rectify the problems and then bring our gifts to the Lord. God is more pleased with love and peace among brethren than with sacrifices.

[24] The verb "**be reconciled**" (*diallágēthi* [from *dialássō* {1259}, to reconcile]) is an imperative used only here where it implies a positive ethical change in both offended parties. This verb *dialássō* stands in contrast to *katallássō*. Concerning God reconciling the world to Himself, both the verb and noun involve a change only on our part since God is holy and immutable.

[25] The word translated "**adversary**" (v. 25) is from *antídikos* (476), one who is about to institute a court suit against another. The assumption is that he or she will proceed with the lawsuit if reconciliation is not made. In 1 Corinthians 6:1–8, Paul urged that lawsuits among believers be prevented even if injustices have been done. (See author's volume on 1 Corinthians 6, *How Far Does Christian Freedom Go?*)

As far as it depends on us, we should not allow disputes among believers to be settled by ungodly court judges. When Christians contend with one another publicly, they bring shame on the name and cause of Christ. Such disputes usually, as Paul stated in 1 Corinthians 6:3, 4, concern worldly things (from *biōtikós* [982], things pertaining to this life).

[26] This is further evidenced by the possibility of fines being imposed, which must be paid to the last "**penny** [NKJV]" (from *kodrántēs* [2835], the coin with the smallest value). Reconciliation pays, and it is to everyone's advantage to seek it.

Adultery and Divorce
(5:27–32; 19:9; Mark 10:11, 12; Luke 16:18)

[27] As murder is absolutely forbidden in verse 21, so is moral seduction (Ex. 20:14). Murder begins with anger, moral seduction with straying eyes. Marriage is sacred before God, and the destruction of the family God has ordained is the destruction of the moral fiber of society. Therefore, God said, "Thou shalt not commit adultery [from *moicheúō* {3431}]." He does not permit adultery now or in the future.

[28] As in the case of murder, Christ explained how to prevent adultery: "But I say unto you, that whoever **keeps looking** [from *blépō* {991}, to see, regard] at a woman in order to lust after her **already** [*édē* {2235}, even now] [*has*] **committed adultery** [from *moicheúō* {3431}] against her in his heart" (a.t.).

This is adultery of the heart. Jesus taught that what a person conceives in his or her "**heart**" (*kardía* [2588]) is culpable. The heart is the center of human thought, will, and emotions, and this is where adultery begins. The most common stimulator of this sin is the eyes, and from the gaze of the eyes comes the passion of the heart (Matt. 6:22, 23).

[29] For the first time, the verb *skandalízō* (4624), to cause one to **stumble,** to **entice** ("offend" in the KJV), is used in the New Testament.

What our eyes see stirs our hearts to desire. If the things we look at create evil desires, we should avoid looking. It is an easy thing to turn our eyes away, but oh, how our evil hearts resist! In verse 28, the verb *blépōn* (from *blépō* [991]), "**looketh on,**" is the present participle, meaning "[one] who keeps on looking." The one simple way to avoid adultery is to curb that constant stare that arouses impure thoughts.

Now the Lord argued the case for preferring partial or total destruction of the body (v. 29). If our eyes entrap us, it is preferable to get rid of them rather than have our entire body cast into the valley of burning garbage (*Géenna* [1067]; see v. 22). The Lord used this well-known place to symbolize **hell,** the place of final and enduring punishment.

[30] Most people are right-handed and begin their actions with that hand, even though they are not conscious they are using it.

Similarly, we should diligently guard against sin and stop at the first instance of temptation before lust has had the opportunity to conceive (James 1:15). The right eye is to be **plucked out** (from *exairéō* [1807], to pluck out) and the right hand **cut off** (from *ekkóptō* [1581]). These functions symbolize actions we should perform at the inception of temptation. The second we are conscious of it, we must cut off the temptation. When we lose the function of our hands or eyes, we are severely handicapped. So if that which causes us to sin is destroyed, sin loses its power over us.

The verb "**it is profitable**" is from *sumphérō* (4851), to bring together, make advantageous or profitable. Partial loss is better than total loss. Earthly loss is heavenly gain.

Of course, we must realize that Jesus is speaking rhetorically here. These are figures of speech, intended to emphasize the importantance of resisting temptation. Jesus never expected anyone to actually cut off his hand or pull out his eye. After all, he just told us that sin in the mind is just as serious as sin actually committed. Basically, sin is in the mind. It is the mind that tells the eye to continue looking, and it is the mind that tells the hand to pick up the dagger and kill the neighbor. The body is simply the instrument that the mind uses to carry out its sinful choices. Many a blind person has adulterous thoughts.

[31] Jesus taught that the marriage of one woman to one man is a sacred establishment by God (Matt. 19:5). And Paul taught that Christian marriage is binding for life (Rom. 7:3, 4).

God hates divorce (Mal. 2:16), and Moses permitted it only because of the hardness of people's hearts (Matt. 19:8; Mark 10:5, 12). And when this did take place, however, he commanded that the one divorcing should give the spouse a separation document called an *apostásion* (647), a **document of divorce**. This neuter noun is derived from the preposition *apó* (575), from; and *stásion* (n.f.), a noun from the verb *hístēmi* (2476), to stand. It is a certificate given to the dismissed spouse by the dismissing spouse to indicate that the separation was initiated by him or her.

If someone (Mark 10:12) dismisses a spouse, then he or she is obligated to give the former mate divorce papers. This is expressed by the verb *dótō*, "**let him give**," the aorist imperative of *dídōmi* (1325), to give. This is not a matter of choice but a requirement. The certificate must declare the reason for dismissal, whether legitimate or illegitimate.

[32] One improper cause of divorce is given in the context—adultery in the heart, as detailed in verses 27 and 28. Sensual desire leads to illicit action. But here we find that the only legitimate reason for divorce is *porneía* (4202), "**fornication**," a noun that includes any immoral sexual relationship, bearing in mind that sexual relationships are permitted only between a husband and wife. Jesus made this clear when He said, "**except** [*parektós* {3924}] for the **reason** [*lógou*, from *lógos* {3056}] of fornication" (a.t.).

The one who dismisses his wife for any other reason than fornication or immorality "**causes** [from *poiéō* {4160}, to make] her **to commit adultery** [from *moicháō* {3429}; i.e., if she should marry again]." It is contrary to God's command to dismiss a wife for any reason other than her sexual immorality. The bill of divorcement was permitted in Deuteronomy 24:1–4 for any "uncleanness" that a man might find in his wife (probably impure sexual behavior or suspicion of adultery). In Jesus' day, some suggested that "uncleanness" could be as slight as poor housekeeping or bad cooking (see Zodhiates' *What About Divorce?* and *May I Divorce and Remarry?* See also the comments on Matthew 19:7–9).

On Taking Oaths
(5:33–37)

[33] An oath is a binding promise to perform some action or speak the truth. "**Forswear thyself**" translates *epiorkḗseis*, the future indicative used as an imperative command of *epiorkéō* (1964), to swear falsely, to break an oath. At no time is perjury permitted, no matter how beneficial it may seem. Truth must permeate every aspect of our lives. Jesus Christ said, "I am . . . the truth" (John 14:6). Jesus also said that the truth will ultimately be revealed about all people and things. We should not compartmentalize our lives, sometimes telling the truth and at other times lying. Nor should we tell "white lies" either.

The verb "**but shalt perform**" is translated from the Greek verb *apodídōmi* (591), literally meaning to give back, to pay back. We must give an accounting to the Lord for our oaths. Every time we promise something, God will hold us accountable. It is far more serious if we invoke His name, as, for example in the all-too common expression, "I swear to God!" To take an **oath** is to place a moral restraint on oneself not to lie. When people invoke the name of the Lord, they are calling on God to be their witness.

[34–36] Here the Lord Jesus introduced a more exacting standard beyond invoking the name of God.

"But I say unto you, **swear** [from *omnúō* {3660}] not **at all** [*hólōs* {3654}, altogether, not by any means whatever]." Jesus told His disciples that their lives and reputations must be such that their word will be considered absolutely trustworthy apart from oaths (Gal. 1:20; Col. 3:9; 1 Tim. 2:7).

Nor are we to invoke anything on earth or in heaven to authenticate our words since everything is God's creation, even down to a single hair. Our lives must be so reliable and trustworthy that we never make oaths. We must tell the truth at all times in honor of God and His creation, no matter how insignificant the matter may be (see Ex. 20:7; Heb. 6:16; James 5:12 and the author's exegesis on James entitled *Faith, Love, and Hope*.)

[37] Jesus now summarized the logic of this teaching on oaths.

Our *yes* must be *yes*, and our *no* must be *no*. Anything "**more**" (*perissón* [4053]), such as an oath, is of *toú poneroú* (the article with the genitive singular of *ponērós* [4190], wicked, malicious), which can be translated either as the King James Version does: "**of evil**," or, as most modern versions do: "of the evil one" (see 6:13; 13:19, 38; Luke 11:4; John 17:15; Eph. 6:16; 1 John 2:13, 14; 3:12; 5:18, 19). Obviously, if we have given our word to anybody, we should make every effort to carry it out, as if it were a vow to God.

Loving as God Loves
(5:38–48; Luke 6:27–36)

Neither Christ nor the Law of Moses allowed personal retaliation. Paul, an expert in the Law of Moses, said that human government should carry out justice in Romans 13:1–7. The priests of the Old Testament performed every function of government—executive, legislative, and judicial. The judges at that time not only judged but governed as well. In Romans 13:4, Paul calls the one who governs a "minister [*diákonos* {1249}, servant, deacon] of God."

[38] One function of government, which exists by God's will (Rom. 13:1–5), is to settle differences that arise between people. In God's Law, He placed limitations on punishment: **eye for eye, tooth for tooth,** etc. (Ex. 21:24; Lev. 24:20; Deut. 19:21). Punishment should not be more severe than the crime. Correction, not retaliation (Matt. 5:39–42), should be the motive of punishment. Desired corrections come through love for the one who is punished. (For a description of these accomplishments of love, read 1 Corinthians 13 and the author's exegetical study of this chapter entitled, *To Love Is to Live*.)

[39] In the context of Christ's discussion of retaliation—"Resist not **evil** [from *ponērós*, malevolently wicked, as contrasted with *kakós* {2556}, bad; see v. 37]"—He did not give a universal command, but a **general** principle not "**to resist**" (from *anthístēmi* [436]). The inference is that resistance to the wicked person should be qualified. We should extend love to both friends or enemies (vv. 44–47). To destroy those attacking should not be the ultimate

goal of resistance but rather to win them to Christ (1 Cor. 9:19–22). Jesus did not absolutely forbid us to resist those who harm us, but if we do resist, we should do so redemptively as a matter of principle. If people brutalize or torture us, Christ did not require that we endure it.

"But whosoever **shall smite** [*rhapísei* from *rhapízō* {4474}, to slap] thee on thy right cheek, turn to him the other also." Carefully judge the situation. If there is a chance for redemption and letting someone strike each cheek will win that person to Christ, personal self-sacrifice is well worthwhile. Note that the verb "**shall strike**" (*rhapísei*) is the future active indicative, indicating a one-time act. It is not the present tense *rhapízei*, implying continuous striking. If our actions embolden and tempt evil ones to perpetrate more harm, we defeat our purpose. Love permits evildoers to realize the need of something they do not possess and that they can have through the grace of God.

[**40**] The **outer garment** (*himátion* [2440], cloak) of verse 40 was usually more valuable than the inner garment (*chitōn* [5509], coat). It was a heavy robe that kept its wearer warm and was used as a blanket at night.

[**41**] This illustration concerns service. The verb "**compel**" (from *aggareúō* [29], to compel or press into service) was used of a public courier who was commanded to carry something a distance. He had the authority to commandeer any person or thing he wished to accomplish his task. Needless to say, the privilege was flagrantly abused as he forced others to do his work. But Jesus taught us to go the extra mile. Again, believers should be willing to go beyond what they are obliged to do (see the parable of the unprofitable servants in Luke 12:45–48, 17:7–10.)

[**42**] If someone **asks** (from *aitéō* [154], to beg), we should **give** (from *dídōmi* [1325]); and if one seeks to "**borrow**" (from *daneízō* [1155]), we "**should not turn away**" (from *apostréphō* [654]). Both the verb "give" and the verb "turn away" are in the aorist tense, meaning that each time a grant or a loan is requested, it should be examined on its own merits and dealt with accordingly. The fact that personal discretion is involved is presumed in the use of singular verbs.

[**43**] For the sixth time, Jesus said, "**It hath been said**," and not, "It was written." The Law of Moses never said that we should hate our enemies (see Matt. 15:1–20). This invalid inference from "**love thy neighbor**" was a tradition taught by the scribes and Pharisees, not the Law of God.

Who was considered to be a "**neighbor**" (*plēsíon* [4139], close by, near) by the Jews? (See Lev. 19:18; Matt. 19:19; 22:39; Mark 12:31, 33; Luke 10:27; Rom. 13:9, 10; Gal. 5:14; Eph. 4:25; James 2:8.) This question prompted

Jesus' parable of the Good Samaritan (Luke 10:30–37). Only Jews were considered neighbors of Jews. Gentiles were considered little "dogs" (Matt. 15:21–28). Christ here rejected the Jewish tradition, since He commanded us to love our enemies as our own people. Personal enmity is forbidden. When Christ said, "Love your enemies," He did not mean national enemies but personal enemies on whom we might wish injury. Jesus designated any persons we come in contact with as neighbors, made so by God's providence. In Luke 10:30–37, at the end of the parable of the Good Samaritan, Jesus asked, "Which now of these three, do you think, has become [from *gínomai* {1096}, to become] neighbor unto him that fell among the thieves?" (a.t.). Thus, the answer to the question, "Who are our neighbors?" are ones who are far away as well as ones who are near, enemies as well as friends, abusers as well as victims.

[44] Christ commanded us to "**love**" (from *agapáō* [25]) our enemies. The verb here for loving is in the present tense, implying an ongoing process directed toward both friends and foes as a result of faith in Christ (1 John 5:1). We Christians have enemies because we have been chosen out of the world (John 15:19), and the cross of Christ is an offense to the world. Jesus loved His enemies enough to die in order to reconcile them to His Father. Christ commanded us to do three actions to prove love for our enemies, all in the present tense, indicating a continuous pattern of action.

First, we are to "**bless**" (from *eulogéō* [2127], to speak well of) those that curse us. "Well" or "good" means in accord with the true concept of good found in the Word of God, not in the world's definition(s) of good. To speak good **to** (i.e., to bless) evil persons is not to speak good **of** them. To speak well to those who curse us includes praying for God's intervention in their lives. God, in speaking well to His enemies, changes their hearts so they will no more curse those who love Him.

Second, we are told to "**do good** [*kalós* [2573, well]," another imperative, to those who "**hate**" (*misoúntas*, the present active participle of *miséo* [3404]) us.

Third, we are commanded to "**pray**" for those who despitefully use (from *epēreázō* [1908]) and persecute (from *diókō* [1377]) us.

The present tense of the verbs describing these evil behaviors toward believers argues that this is the norm, not the rare occasions that would be expressed by the aorist. By contrast, our Christian response should include speaking good, doing good, and praying to God for intervention.

Some older manuscripts do not have the two clauses concerning blessing those who curse us and doing good to those who hate us or the participle concerning those who despitefully use us. However, these phrases are clearly in

Luke's account of the sermon (Luke 6:27, 28), and therefore we know that they were part of the original message.

[45] In dealing with others, Jesus calls us to imitate the God we belong to and serve. The conjunction *hópōs* (3704), "**so that**," indicates the result of loving our enemies. We thus exhibit the Christ likeness that shows the nature of our heavenly Father.

These Christlike actions will not *make* us sons and daughters of our Father but rather reveal that we already *are* His children, possessing our Father's nature. We cannot demonstrate God's nature if we do not have it through the birth from above (John 3:3, 7) by which we become children (from *téknon* [5043]) of God through Jesus Christ (John 1:12; 1 Pet. 1:14). If Christ is in us (Rom. 8:10), He will manifest Himself through us.

Why does Christ say, "that you may be **sons** [from *huiós* {5207}, son] of your Father" (a.t.) and not simply children (from *téknon*) of God? A son is a mature grown-up, willing to conform to his father's desires and purposes, not immature and self-willed. A son of God cannot have a divergent way of life from his heavenly Father.

The heavenly Father not only created all humanity (Gen. 1:1), but He lovingly sustains the lives of all, including His enemies. He loves all people, as proven here by His indiscriminant provision of sun and rain. If He wanted to, He could deprive those who hate Him of these two necessary life factors. Like God, we, as mature sons and daughters of our heavenly Father, must show the same characteristics of love, toleration, and benevolence until He chooses to separate His sheep from the goats (Matt. 25:31–46) and the wheat from the tares (13:24–30, 36–43).

[46, 47] These two verses are each introduced with the "**if**" of potential (*eán* [1437]) as contrasted with the "**if**" of supposition *ei* (1487).

The first is, "For if you love those who love you, what reward do you have?" (a.t.). This question anticipates the answer, None! "Do not even the **publicans** [from *telónēs* {5057}, public tax collectors who were acknowledged as sinners] **do** [from *poiéō* {4160}, to make or do] the same thing?" (a.t.).

Similarly, Jesus asked the "**if**" of potential (*eán*): "If you **greet** [from *aspázomai* {782}] only your **brothers** [from *adelphós* {80}], are you any better than these **tax collectors** [from *telónēs* {5057}; many manuscripts use Gentiles {from *ethnikós* (1482)}]?" (a.t.).

Sinners' outwardly benevolent acts (e.g., loving others) are not evidences of good character. We must advance from the outer benevolence of peers to a deep inner love and concern for those who do not particularly like us, even our enemies!

[48] The verb translated "**Be ye**" (*ésesthe*, the future indicative of *eimí* [1510], to be) carries the imperative emphasis of what Christ wants His children to be through divine enablement (regeneration) and personal effort.

We are to be not only children (*tékna*) but also grown-up sons (*huioí*) in behavior (v. 45). When we behave like mature sons and daughters of our heavenly Father, others will discern that we are different from Pharisees and scribes (v. 20)—the hypocrites of our Lord's day. We grow into the likeness of what God already is. God was, is, and shall ever be the same, as is also Jesus Christ because He and the Father are one (John 10:30).

The word rendered by many translators as "**perfect**" (from *téleios* [5046]) comes from *télos* (5056)—a definite point or goal, a purpose. God, being our creator, places in us capacities He wants us to reach, and through Christ, those goals become evident. As we grow physically, so we must grow spiritually. We first must have divine life (2 Pet. 1:4), but that has to be exercised and cultivated (Phil. 2:12). The Corinthian believers lacked such growth (1 Cor. 3:1–4).

God our heavenly Father, however, is and has always been perfect, as the translation commonly attributed to *téleios* indicates. The verb is *estí* (2076), the present indicative of *eimí*, to be. The present tense expresses the immutability of God's essence and character (Heb. 13:8). Our perfection is God's goal. His corporate goal for the church is for us to be "perfect" or mature" (Eph. 4:13), even as the Father, Son, and Holy Spirit are perfect. We become one new entity in the same sense that the three Persons of the Trinity are one God.

6

cᵔᴼ

Almsgiving, Prayer, and Fasting
(6:1–18; Luke 11:2–4)

The first word of this chapter (v. 1), "**Take heed**" (*proséchete*, the present imperative of *proséchō* [4337], to pay attention, to apply one's mind to), used here for the first time in the New Testament, introduces three warnings against doing right things for the wrong reasons. Christ gave proper instruction on the right way to do almsgiving (vv. 1–4), prayer (vv. 5–15), and fasting (vv. 16–18).

Jesus did not command almsgiving, prayer, or fasting; rather, He assumed them with the clauses, "when thou doest thine alms" (v. 2), "when thou prayest" (v. 5), and "when ye fast" (v. 16). Some earlier Greek manuscripts have the accusative of *dikaiosúnē* (1343), that which is right, righteousness, for the accusative of *eleēmosúnē* (1654), the giving of **alms,** in the first verse. If this reading is adopted, then Jesus said, "Be careful not to do your 'acts of righteousness' before men" (NIV), and then gave an example of "acts of righteousness" when He mentioned almsgiving in verse 2. We could coin the word "theatricalize" to describe what Jesus warned against in our giving alms, because the word used for "**to be seen**" (*theathḗnai*, the aorist passive infinitive of *theáomai* [2300], to make a spectacle) of people, is the word from which comes our English word "theater." By using the aorist tense for "to be seen," Jesus commanded us not to parade our alms even once—"**before men**." Human admiration not only falls short of the glory of God; it is counterproductive.

[2] Hypocrites are rewarded when they receive praise from people, but human admiration is restricted to this life; there is no room for it in the world to come. The verb "**have**" (from *apéchō* [568], to receive payment in full), in the phrase "have their reward" is used here, then repeated in verse 5 with regard

to prayer, and in verse 16 with regard to fasting. It is also found in Luke 6:24 with respect to wealth.

Apéchō means **to have full payment**. The creator of all things has prepared dwellings, crowns, kingdoms and, most importantly, His personal presence for those who glorify Him in this life. To sacrifice the eternity of these things for a few seconds of vanity destined to disappear with the world (1 Cor. 7:31) is foolish.

[3, 4] Alms must be done "**in secret**" (from *kruptós* [2927], privately), so secretively, in fact, that one hand does not reveal to the other what it is doing. The word "**openly**" (from *phanerós* [5318], publicly) is not found in several manuscripts and versions, but the thought is certainly true of God's character. In 2 Corinthians 5:10, Paul told us that each one (*hékastos* [1538], each one individually) of us must "appear (from *phaneróō* [5319]) before the judgment seat of Christ." The Lord will grant public, heavenly rewards for every altruistic act performed in secret. The temptation we face now is self-promotion: "And whosoever shall exalt himself shall be abased; and he that shall humble himself shall be exalted" (Matt. 23:12).

[5] The fact that this discourse (vv. 5–7) concerns private prayer is indicated in the Greek texts by the singular: "when **thou prayest** [from *proseúchomai* {4336}]." By saying "**when**" (*hótan* [3752]), the Lord implied that prayer is the norm in the believer's life.

One of the shortest verses in the Bible is the admonition, "Pray **incessantly** [*adialeíptōs* {89}, without interruption" (1 Thess. 5:17; a.t.)]. Incessant prayer assumes uninterrupted dependence. This communion of dependence should be kept secretive. Hypocrites, we are told, feign dependence on the Lord to "be seen of men." Both Scribes and Pharisees prayed loud and long in synagogues and on town squares (*plateía* [4113], broad streets).

[6] But the Lord commended private prayer when we enter into our **closets** [*tameíon* {5009}, a place of privacy]," beyond the temptation to display and for the sake of intimate confession. He forbad ostentatious prayer. This does not preclude, however, prayer with other believers, as we are instructed in Matthew 18:19, 20 and as we see in Acts 4:24ff.

[7] Furthermore, Jesus told us not to "**babble**" (from *battologéō* [945] from *báttos* [n.f.], to stammer; and *lógos* [3056], word; "to repeat words" and therefore chatter meaninglessly). Rather, we should pray in a succinct, purposeful way. In their blind desire to impress others, the Pharisees recited long and meaningless prayers. The Lord's Prayer (vv. 9–13) is the perfect model for the form and content of prayer, but even this can be meaningless if we repeat it carelessly and without thought.

God does not answer babble: "For they **think** [from *dokéō* {1380}, suppose, conjecture] that in **many words** [from *pologóia* {4180}] they shall be heard" (a.t.). The Lord clearly implied that this supposition is incorrect, the product of self-deception.

Not all repetition is babble. While in spiritual agony in the Garden of Gethsemane, Jesus Himself "prayed the third time, saying the same words" (Matt. 26:44). (See author's *The Lord's Prayer*.)

[8] We have a good reason not to babble. The Father "**innately knows**" (from *oída*, the perfect tense—used as a present—of *horáō* [3708], to see and perceive with emphasis on perception) our needs "**before**" (*pró* [4253]) we ask, so while prayer is not dismissed as useless, meaningless repetitive prayer is.

"**Ask**" (from *aitéō* [154]) implies an element of humility—requesting from a superior. Though the verb frequently occurs in the imperative mood, prayer is never a demand. It is, rather, a petition to someone who has the superior power and authority to grant the request.

[9] "**Pray ye**" (from *proseúchesthe* [4336]) can be indicative—telling how we should pray or imperative—that we must pray. In this particular place, it refers to both in the content that follows. Note that there are no *battologíai*, "vain repetitions" (v. 7), in the Lord's prayer that follows.

"**Hallowed** [*hagiasthḗtō*, the aorist passive imperative of *hagiázō* {37}, to sanctify, set apart] be Thy name." This is not a request for God to make Himself holier than He is—an impossibility—but rather to manifest His holy name in the earth at every point in time (the aorist tense) so that all people will acknowledge His holiness. God's name is already holy, set apart from every other name, and His name includes all that He is and ever has been. It is our duty as children of God to become holy as He is holy and to repel any unholy behavior that would defile His name or shame His cause.

[10] God's "**kingdom**" (*basileía* [932]; see also Col. 1:13; Rev. 1:9) is coming whether or not some do not want it. Because the Lord continuously prevails in human history (Ps. 103:19), even the idea of intervention is anthropomorphic—an appearance as in the incarnation of Jesus Christ. Sensational events appear miraculous to us not because God has "re-entered" history, but because He performs such events infrequently. God ultimately does not "intervene" ("come **between** points of time or events," *Merriam-Webster's Collegiate Dictionary, Eleventh Edition*, 655) in history. He constantly controls and regulates everything down to a single sparrow that falls to the ground (Matt. 10:29) and the number of hairs on our heads (10:30).

The prayer, "Thy kingdom come. Thy will be done in earth, as it is in heaven," is a request for the full manifestation and visible glory of the Lord's invisible rule (Luke 17:20, 21, 24)

[11] The Lord's prayer now moves from worship to personal needs (vv. 11–13). The first need is "our **daily** [from *epioúsios* {1967}, necessary for existence] bread."

Epioúsios is derived from *epí* (1909), upon; and *ousía* (3776), being. The first request is for the food our bodies require for daily subsistence, the amount we need to continue living today, as Paul said: "Having food and raiment let us be therewith content" (1 Tim. 6:8).

[12] We owe God all that He commands. To the extent that we do not fulfill our obligations, we accumulate "**debts**" (from *opheílēma* [3783]), which are primarily defaults on righteous beliefs, choices, attitudes, and acts.

The parable of the unmerciful servant (see 18:21–35) teaches us that the debt humans owe God—once Adam lost his original righteousness in the Garden of Eden and was sold into the slaveries of the devil and his own demonic nature—is staggering (Matt. 18:24–26). But Paul told us that the Father sent His Son into the world to blot out (cancel) this debt:

> And you, being dead in your sins and the uncircumcision of your flesh, has He quickened together with Him, having forgiven you all trespasses; having blotted out the handwriting of ordinances that was against us, which was contrary to us, and took it out of the way, nailing it to His cross. (Col. 2:13, 14; a.t.)

The verb "**forgive**" is from *aphíēmi* (863), to lift up and take away. This prayer acknowledges that only God has the power to forgive sins (Matt. 9:6), and from Paul we learn that He chooses to do it through faith in Jesus Christ (Rom. 3:25; Eph. 1:7).

Hōs (5613), "**as**" or "**in the same way that**," does not mean "on the basis of." If that were the case, none of us would be saved; salvation would be by works, and the cross would be unnecessary. Even the statement, "If ye forgive not men their trespasses, neither will your Father forgive your trespasses" (see v. 15 following), does not mean that salvation is merited by forgiving others.

The phrase simply implies that when our hearts have been regenerated, forgiveness is the necessary product of our new natures. This is why we do not ask, "Forgive **because** we forgive," but "**Forgive in the same way that** our new natures forgive." The new nature may not be unforgiving: "A good tree cannot produce bad fruit" (Matt. 7:18 NASB).

[13] The prayer continues,

> And lead us not **into** [*eis* {1519}] **temptation** [from *peirasmós* {3986}, testing], but deliver us **from** [*apó* {575}] **the** [from *ho* {3588}] **evil** [from *ponērós*

{4190}, malevolent one]: For Yours is the kingdom, and the power, and the glory, forever. Amen. (a.t.)

When the Lord tests us, His purpose is to strengthen us in order to approve and entrust us with greater tasks (1 Pet. 4:12, 13). God is incapable of being tempted or tempting anyone to sin (James 1:13, 14). If the test is for the purpose of causing someone to be untrustworthy or to fail, the word would be best translated "tempt," and that is the work of Satan, the opposer. (See author's *The Lord's Prayer*.)

Peter warned us to be vigilant, because the devil prowls like a roaring lion, "seeking whom he may devour" (1 Pet. 5:8). The verb "**deliver**" (from *rhúo-mai* [4506]) means to rescue, and to rescue is to attract to God. When we are in Him, the devil does not dare touch us. God is the only Savior from the power of Satan. When we appeal to our heavenly Father for deliverance, He causes the devil to flee and sends angels to minister to us (Heb. 1:14).

Notice the preposition used to indicate the kind of deliverance from the evil one. It is a rescue "**from**" (*apó* [575])—not "out of" (*ek* [1537])—the evil one. We believers are never an integral part of Satan, for the kingdom of God is within us (Luke 17:21). The devil may encircle us as a wild beast encircles his prey, but we are never part of him (1 Pet. 5:8) or in him (1 John 4:4). While Satan tries to devour us, Christ's overpowering Spirit dwells within us (Rom. 8:10, 11). The last half of verse 13 is not found in some earlier manuscripts and is not included in the UBS text and many of the newer English versions, but it is found in most of the Greek manuscripts and certainly reflects biblical truth. The Lord never abdicates His kingdom to anyone—friend or foe. To Him alone belongs the authority to rule as King with the executive power (*dúnamis* [1411]) and the glory (*dóxa* [1391]), that is, the splendor acknowledged by His children.

[14, 15] We believers may fall short of God's expectations:

> For [*gár* {1063}, explaining the prior verse] if [*eán* {1437}, the "if" of potential, "whenever"] ye forgive men their **trespasses** [from *paráptōma* {3900} from the preposition *pará* {3844}, near; and *píptō* {4098}, to fall], your heavenly Father will also forgive you: but **if** ["whenever" as above] ye forgive not men their trespasses, neither will your Father forgive your trespasses.

"Falling aside" as from a path is probably the best sense we can give to the noun "**trespass**," while preserving the meaning of the preposition *pará*. God frequently viewed His people as deviating from the eternal, straight, narrow, and well-lit path for some temporary, dark byway, side street, or back alley:

> Because My people hath forgotten Me, they have burned incense to vanity, and they have caused them to stumble in their ways from the everlasting [Sept.:

from *aiṓnios* {166}] paths, to walk in paths, in a way not cast up. (Jer. 18:15; a.t.)

Jesus Himself made use of this imagery:

> Enter ye in at the strait gate: for wide is the gate, and broad is the way, that leadeth to destruction, and many there be which go in thereat: because strait is the gate, and narrow is the way, which leadeth unto life, and few there be that find it. (Matt. 7:13, 14)

We have a single path to follow toward God's ultimate destiny for us which is conformity to Christ (Rom. 8:29). But distractions may trip us, and we fall to the side of the straight and narrow way. The verb for "**trespasses**" is *parapíptō* (3895), to fall by the side, and it occurs only in Hebrews 6:6. (For a thorough exegesis of Heb. 6:4–6, see the author's commentary on James entitled *Faith, Love, and Hope*, 766–792; see also the verbs *aphíēmi* [863], to forgive, and *parapíptō*, to fall by the side, in the author's *The Complete Word Study Dictionary: New Testament*.) The noun *paráptōma* is found in the Gospels (accompanied by the verb *aphíēmi*) in Matthew 6:14, 15; 18:35; and Mark 11:25, 26.

Paráptōma (3900) is sin that can be committed by believers as well as unbelievers. Unbelievers fall aside in agreement with their natures to commit *hamartía* (266), sin, as a missing of the mark, or *parábasis* (3847), transgression, walking contrary to the Law of God. The prefix *pará* can also mean deliberately against; and *básis* (939) means stepping over, derived from the verb *baínō* (n.f.), to walk. Thus, sinners deliberately step over the line and walk contrary to God's Law, whereas we believers may slightly, inadvertently, and temporarily fall aside in our customary walk with Christ (1 John 3:9).

[16–18] The Greek adverb *hótan* (3752), "**when[ever]**," begins this section as it did the sections on almsgiving (vv. 2–4) and prayer (vv. 5–7).

The Lord commended self-effacing humility with every occasion of benefaction, petition, and privation—three essentials of the Christian life. None of these should be done ostensibly—to be seen by others—but for the glory of God. Note that the command here is not to **fast** but to be inconspicuous during fasting which, like the other two, is taken as a matter of course for true believers. The Lord Jesus provided salvation when we were unable to help ourselves, and in turn He wants us to anonymously sacrifice for the benefit of others and the advancement of His kingdom.

One sacrifice is food, as when one fasts (from *nēsteúō* [3522], to fast). While fasting is assumed, the action should not be dictated. Fasting, like giving alms and praying, is strictly a personal decision between believers and their Lord. Jesus told the John the Baptist's disciples that it was not proper for His own disciples to fast while He was still with them (Matt. 9:14, 15; Mark 2:18,

19; Luke 5:33–35). The important thing is not how much is done, but why it is done. Fasting is a personal choice when one desires to get closer to God, as Cornelius in Acts 10:30, or to seek direction from God, as in Acts 13:2, 3. If it is for self-aggrandizement, as with the Pharisee in the temple in Luke 18:12, then, according to Christ, recognition in this world will be the limit, an awful exchange for eternal recognition. For the third time, we have the thought, "They **have** [from *apéchō* {568}, to receive full payment] their **reward** [from *misthós* {3408}; see also vv. 2, 5]."

Note the interesting contrast between hypocrites who "**disfigure** [*aphanízousi*, the present tense of *aphanízō* {853}, to mar the appearance] their faces" (v. 16) and believers who **anoint** (*aleípsai*, the aorist middle imperative of *aleíphō* [218], to rub as, e.g., with oil) their heads and wash their faces (see v. 17). Notice also how the regularity—the **present** tense—of hypocrisy compares with the instance—the **aorist** tense—of humility, as we might expect.

The disfigurement is deliberate, as Jesus says, to "appear unto men to fast." By contrast, believers hide their personal sacrifices for the Lord's work.

Possessions and Masters
(6:19–24; Luke 12:33–34)

Christians live in two worlds. We know that earth is not a permanent home but a preparation for our eternal dwelling place in heaven. Planning for the future is part of the function of our God-given intelligence.

[19] "Do **not be** treasuring [*thēsaurízete*, the present imperative of *thēsaurízō* {2343}] **treasures** [from *thēsaurós* {2344}] for yourselves on the earth" (a.t.), Jesus said.

The problem is not the laying up of treasures (*thēsaurízō*), but for whom we lay them up (ourselves). In 2 Corinthians 12:14, Paul said that, although the children have no obligation to **lay up** (from the same verb, *thēsaurízō*) treasures for their parents, the parents do have an obligation to lay up treasures for their children. But if we lay up for our children or for the Lord's work, we are not treasuring treasures, that is, retaining them to satisfy our own greed. The emphasis here falls on psychology and ethical values, not strategic investment planning. In the parable of the talents, when the servant returned 100 percent on the principal given to him (Matt. 25:20, 22), his master did not say, "Where did this come from? You should have given it all away a long time ago!"

The reason assigned to not treasuring worldly treasures was the risk of loss. Jesus noted only the risks of corruption (depreciation of value) and robbery (annihilation of value)—two prominent threats to wealth. "**Thieves**" here translates *kléptai* (from *kléptēs* [2812]), those who steal under cover of darkness and secrecy—a noun that contrasts with *lēstēs* (3027), the robber or thug who steals openly. Thieves are described as "**breaking through**" (from *diorússō* [1358] from *diá* [1223], through; and *orússō* [3736], to dig) because the walls of houses in the Middle East at this time were built of clay, and holes could be dug through them.

In light of these warnings, David's general advice is sound: "If riches increase, set not your heart upon them" (Ps. 62:10).

[20, 21] The risks do not apply, however, to heavenly treasures, and here Jesus told us to "**be treasuring treasures for yourselves in heaven**," the literal translation of verse 20. Consider once again David's words:

> One thing have I desired of the LORD, that will I seek after; that I may dwell in the house of the LORD all the days of my life, to behold the beauty of the LORD, and to enquire in his temple. (Ps. 27:4)

Even if corruption and robbery never happen, earthly treasures ultimately are torn from their owners at death. Accordingly, God asked the rich farmer who was going to build greater barns for all his crops, "Thou fool, this night thy soul shall be required of thee: then whose shall those things be, which thou hast provided?" (Luke 12:20).

We can lay up heavenly treasures by utilizing our time, talents, and money for the Lord's work. In 2 Corinthians 4:16–18, Paul advised us to differentiate between visible things that are temporary (from *próskairos* [4340]) and invisible things that are eternal (from *aiōnios* [166]). If we treasure material things, our souls will die according to Paul: "The mind set on the flesh is death" (Rom. 8:6 NASB). But if we "set our minds on things above, not on things of the earth" (a.t.; Col. 3:2), we will build a storehouse of spiritual rewards, and our spirits will live to the fullest: "The mind set on the Spirit is life and peace" (Rom. 8:6 NASB).

Jesus summed all this up by adding that our hearts are located where our treasures lie. Our hearts think and choose the values (treasures) resident in our hearts.

[22] The "**light**" (*lúchnos* [3088]) Jesus referred to was a portable oil-burning lamp. The **eye** (Luke 11:34), like a lamp, brings light into the body.

"If therefore thine eye be **single** [*haploús* {573}], thy whole body shall be full of light." *Haploús* stands in contrast to *diploús* (1362), double or many.

Even though we have two eyes, they are designed to pick up a single object, preferably the Lord Himself, as David counseled (see discussion of v. 20). Jesus connected the purity of the body with the holy character of an eye that does not vacillate between treasures on earth and treasures in heaven. Similarly, in James 1:8 we read that the "double minded [*dípsuchos* {1374}] man is unstable [*akatástatos* {182} from *a* {1}, without, not; and *kathístēmi* {2525}, to settle] in all his ways" (cf. James 4:8). A circularity of "unsettling" effects exists between the soul and the physical eye. Just as double-minded ("two-souled") persons can direct their physical eyes between good and bad objects, so physical eyes can transmit good and bad signals into the soul. If we think about the blurred and conflicting (double vision) messages our brains attempt to process when we merely cross our eyes, we can understand how our physical eyes can destabilize our souls when they receive and transmit conflicting data.

The "eyes of [our] understanding" (Eph. 1:18)—our spiritual eyes— work in conjunction with our physical eyes to our good or to our detriment.

[23] The worst condition, of course, is the single-souled, single-eyed person who focuses on evil without wavering. This is not, indeed it cannot be, the true believer in Christ. At this ultra-low level of depravity, the whole body, Jesus said, becomes dark:

> But if thine eye be **evil** [*ponērós* {4190}, malevolent], thy whole body shall be full of **darkness** [from *skoteinós* {4652}, moral and spiritual darkness]. If therefore the light that is in thee be darkness, how great is that darkness!

How can light within one be darkness? Is this a contradiction? No, it is the same kind of light Paul speaks about: "Satan himself is transformed into an angel of light" (2 Cor. 11:14). The most hideous form of darkness wraps itself with a garment of light, like the wolf that puts on sheep's clothing for the purpose of deception and destruction. The devil apparently is so malevolent he cannot face anyone directly—possibly not even unbelievers who were made in the image of God (James 3:9). He must deceive—which is what hypocrisy is—if he plans to stab in the back. Why risk a fair fight? Thus, Jesus' very applicable warning: "Beware of false prophets, which come to you in sheep's clothing, but inwardly they are ravening wolves" (Matt. 7:15).

Here, however, Jesus was not warning against some external enemy: "If . . . the light that is **in** [*en* {1722}, within, inside] **thee** be darkness." This is about the strongest warning against self-deception imaginable. We must always check what we believe against the Holy Scriptures as our objective norm for revelation. We cannot trust any form of self-examination: "The heart is deceitful above all things, and desperately wicked: who can know it?" (Jer. 17:9). The way we "examine [ourselves] to see if we be of the faith" (a.t.; 2 Cor. 13:5) is by checking the content of our beliefs against God's Word.

This is why the Word of God is called "the Light, the true [from *alēthinós* {228}] one" (a.t., cf. John 1:9; 1 John 2:8). This is not redundant (as, e.g., true truth). A false light merely gives an appearance of light. At his very best, Satan can only appear as an angel of light.

[24] A logic, thank God, operates against the potential mix of light and darkness in the self-deceived soul, and it is this:

> No man can serve two masters: for either he will hate the one, and love the other; or else **he will hold to** [from *antéchomai* {472}, to grip firmly] the one, and **despise** [from *kataphronéō* {2706}, to think down on or against some subject, i.e., negatively] the other. Ye cannot serve God and mammon [from *mammōnás* {3126}, money, wealth].

At the end of this section, Jesus returned to the dichotomy between treasures on earth (mammon, money) and treasures in heaven (God). The contrasts are varied: serving and not serving, loving and hating, holding and despising, and, from prior verses, temporal and eternal (vv. 19, 20), and light and darkness (vv. 21–23). It's one or the other—God or money. Serving, loving, and holding are conjoined, as are not serving, hating, and despising. The absence of neutrality is conspicuous.

"**No man**" is *oudeís* (3762; literally: not even one). It goes without saying that multiple bosses never work. Two owners will fight over the priorities and work of a single employee. If both impose equal work, the employee either has to work two shifts or prioritize at the risk of angering one of his bosses. Contradictory orders from two owners are impossible to carry out. Opposing employers wear out their employees. In plain language, Jesus said, it cannot be done.

The phrase, "Not even one **can** [from *dúnamai* {1410}, to be able] serve" (a.t.) implies that prior to conversion, men and women are enslaved to treasures on earth. Accordingly, they are not neutral (free) toward God; they hate and despise Him, so they are unable to serve Him. In Romans 1:30 Paul called them "haters of God" (from *theostugés* [2319]). At conversion, they love, hold to, and serve God while now hating, despising, and not serving the world.

The verb "**will hold**" (from *antéchomai*) does not mean that we hold onto God autonomously. As Paul explained, in a reciprocal sense, God has a stronger hold on us, even as we hold on to Him: "I follow after, if that I may apprehend that for which also I am apprehended of Christ Jesus" (Phil. 3:12).

"**Serve**" (*douleúein* from *douleúō* [1398]) is a present infinitive, meaning on a regular basis. As usual, the Scripture allows for sins of ignorance in the life of the believer. But no one can consistently serve two masters: God and the devil, "treasures in heaven" and "treasures on earth."

The Cure for Anxiety
(6:25–34; Luke 12:22–31)

[25] "**On account of** [*diá* {1223}] **this** [*toúto* {5124}, a singular neuter pronoun, "this thing"], I say unto you" (a.t.). On account of what? "**This**" (*toúto*) is singular, but what is the antecedent?

The nearest conceptual antecedent is the impossibility of serving two masters, a fitting introduction to the subject of anxiety. Attempting to serve God and the devil, heaven and the world, will certainly create a great deal of anxiety. All attempts to live out contradictions produce anxiety.

The Lord continued,

> Do **not** [*mḗ* {3361}] **put anxiety** [*merimnáte*, the present imperative of *mer-imnáō* {3309}, to fret] into your **soul** [*psuchḗ* {5590}], what you will eat, and what you will drink, nor your body, what you shall put on. Is not the life more than food and the body than clothing? (a.t.)

The three verbs, "**eat**" (*phágēte* from *esthíō* [2068]), "**drink**" (*píete* from *pínō* [4095]), and "**put on**" (*endúsesthe* from *endúō* [1746]), are all in the aorist tense. Because the Greek aorist interprets actions as points, the emphasis is "at any point [of time]." Yet the verb "**do not be anxious**" (*merimnáte*) is in the present tense. Not only are we to stop regularly agitating our souls and bodies over the future, but we are to continually stop every single instance of agitation over every single thing.

This does not mean that we should sit and wait for God to provide our needs. It does mean that anxiety should not replace God's command, "Six days thou shalt do thy work" (Ex. 23:12), as the primary motivator of the spirit and body. Since God commands work, Paul contended against welfare for the fit and able: "If any would not work, neither should he eat" (2 Thess. 3:10).

[26] Jesus now appealed to nature:

> Behold the fowls of the air: for **they sow** [from *speírō* {4687}] not, **neither** [*oudé* {3761}] do **they reap** [from *therízō* {2325}], **nor** [*oudé*] **gather** [from *sunágō* {4863}] into barns; yet your heavenly Father feedeth them. Are ye not much better than they?

The fact that it is foolish for us to worry about our needs is seen in this example from nature. God has given us far greater intelligence, and therefore responsibility, than that of fowl. Birds do not have human intelligence to plan what is needed immediately against what must be stored for later use. Since birds manage to feed themselves under the providential hand of the Father, our anxiety is without excuse.

And all the more so because of God's valuation of people: "Do you not **differ** [from *diaphérō* {1308}, to differ in value] from them?" (a.t.; see Matt. 10:31). God values us and our faith higher than He values birds.

Too often we care about the wrong things. We should care for our eternal souls and the souls of others that survive the body. The verb "**to be concerned**" (from *merimnáō* [3309]; a.t.) is actually neutral, carrying a good or bad connotation depending on the object to which it is joined. Care is a vice when directed toward the devil and his world, but it is a commendable virtue when directed toward the wellbeing of others. In 1 Corinthians 12:12–26, for example, Paul taught that we should care (*merimnáō*) for other members of the body of Christ (v. 25).

[27] To demonstrate that selfish care is useless, Jesus asked, "Which of you by taking thought can add one cubit unto his stature?" This question has two possible connotations. The word translated "**stature**" (*hēlikía* [2244]) means basically "length of life" and usually refers to the stage in life one has reached (John 9:21, 23; Heb. 11:11). But it is definitely used figuratively of one's height in referring to Zacchaeus as being "little in **stature** [*hēlikía*]" in Luke 19:3. The word translated "**cubit**" (*péchus* [4083]), on the other hand, is a measure equal to the length of a person's arm from the elbow to the end of the middle finger—between eighteen and twenty-one inches, obviously differing depending on who is measured. The King James Version and New King James Version assume that *péchus* should be taken literally, and *hēlikía* should be taken figuratively of adding anything to one's height. But most modern versions take *péchus* figuratively and *hēlikía* literally to describe adding anything to one's life span. For example, the New International Version translates this verse, "Who of you by worrying can add a single hour to his life?"

Of course, the answer to this question (however we translate it) is, no one. Since anxiety cannot increase our heights or lengthen our lives, it is absurd to worry about God's provisions of food and clothing.

[28, 29] Here we have another imperative:

> And why take ye thought for raiment? **Consider** [from *katamanthánō* {2648} from *katá* {2596}, an intensive preposition; and *manthánō* {3129}, to learn] the **lilies** [*krína* {2918}] of the field, how **they grow** [*auxánei*, from *auxánō* {837}, to grow]; they **toil** [*kopiósin* {2872}, to wear oneself out to the point of fainting] not, neither do they spin.

Katamanthánō means to thoroughly learn from creative ability as a *mathētēs* (3101), a disciple or learner of Christ (5:1). This is the only place in the New Testament where this verb is used.

For something to "**grow**" (*auxánō*), an external power must act upon it to place the element of life within. The life God implanted in **lilies** is unique, and no one can duplicate it (Matt. 13:32; Mark 4:8; Luke 12:27; 1 Cor. 3:6, 7). Seeds cannot be manufactured; they are reproduced. The statement is absolute for they do not toil. The beautiful life in a lily simply emerges from its hiding place.

The verb "**spin**" (from *nēthō* [3514]) is a veiled reference to the production of beautiful robes for King Solomon. This verb occurs only in Matthew 6:28 and Luke 12:27, and in both instances refers to lilies. So lilies are unparalleled by anything made by human hands (v. 29). Since God creates such natural beauty, we should not be anxious to "toil and spin" for our outer (physical) bodies.

The lilies Jesus referred to were wild but beautifully multicolored. Their beauty, He said, surpasses even the elaborate, multicolored royal robes of King Solomon.

[30] This verse begins with the conjunction *ei* (1487), which is either a subjective hypothesis ("**if**") or a contingency to which there is no doubt, as in the English "since" (see Matt. 19:10; Acts 5:39; Rom. 8:25).

Thus, we could translate it as, "Since God so clothes. . . ." Jesus here moved from beautiful lilies to the equally transient "**grass** [from *chórtos* {5528}] of the field." Grass beautifies the ground, but after it has served that purpose, it is still useful as fuel in the "**oven**" (from *klíbanos* [2823], a clay furnace fueled with grass or wood and used to bake bread).

Our faith should be strengthened by the fact that God surpasses even all Solomon's glory when He clothes lilies and grass:

Since God **thus** [*hoútōs* {3779}, so, in this manner] **clothes** [from *amphién-numi* {294} derived from the prefix *amphí* {n.f.}, round about; and *énnumi* {n.f.}, to robe] the grass of the field, which today is and tomorrow is cast into the oven, shall he not much more clothe you, O you of **little faith** [from *oligópistos* {3640}]? (a.t.)

The verb implies that the covering God gives to lilies and grass is not merely external. Jesus also used this word in Matthew 11:8 with regard to John the Baptist's clothing: "But what went ye out for to see? A man clothed [from *amphiénnumi*] in soft raiment? behold, they that wear soft clothing are in kings' houses" (cf. Luke 7:25). John the Baptist's clothing was different. Every fiber of his being was committed to Jesus Christ, and his sacrifice of fine food and clothing was the manifestation of his robe of righteousness.

"**Little faith**" presupposes some faith; however, the Lord wants us to believe that He will provide our need for food and clothing. The Father values us higher than the birds He feeds and the lilies He clothes with glory greater than Solomon's.

[31] The teaching was complete, so Jesus now commanded:

> Therefore [i.e., on the basis that God will provide your needs], do not **agitate yourselves** [from *merimnáō* as in v. 25], saying, What shall we eat? or, What shall we drink? or, How will we be clothed? (a.t.)

The Lord knows that when we become His children, we still carry some worldly anxiety, even though we have acquired His nature (2 Pet. 1:3, 4). No amount of faith can fully exempt us from the consequences of Adamic sin.

[32] Two explanatory clauses are in this verse, each introduced by "**for**" (*gár* [1063]). The first one is treated as a parenthetical expression in the King James Version, giving the reason why we might be tempted to worry. Don't be anxious because the Gentiles [typifying unbelievers] "eagerly seek ["anxiously" is implied] all these things" (NASB). In other words, "Don't be anxious like unbelievers who act like there is no tomorrow!"

The second "**for**" clause summarizes the real basis for Christians' freedom from anxiety:

> For [*gár*] your heavenly Father **knoweth** [*oíde*, the perfect tense—used as a present—of *eídō* {1492}, the aorist of *horáō* {3708}, to perceive, to innately know] **that** [*hóti* {3754}] **ye have need** [*chrḗzete*, the present tense of *chrḗzō* {5535}, to have need] of all **these** [*toútōn* {5130}] things.

This means that God actively and innately knows all our needs. It is a good thing He does. Otherwise, we would have serious problems coping with His granting all our desires instead of our needs.

"**All . . . things**" is translated from the adjective *hápas* (537), which is derived from *a* (1), an abbreviated form of *háma* (260), at the same time; and *pás* (3956), all, therefore "all [these] things simultaneously."

We often are like little children when we pray to our heavenly Father. While we realize He can provide "all things," we want them all at the same time—now (*háma*)! The Lord, however, not only knows what we need; He knows when we need it. He gives us what we need first, second, third, and each time following because He is the God of order (*táxis* [5010]; 1 Cor. 14:40), not confusion (*akatastasía* [181]; 1 Cor. 14:33). His order brings peace and progress. A child must first have milk to grow, then gradually solid foods.

[33] This is the key to Jesus' advice:

> **But seek ye** [*zēteíte*, the present tense of *zēteó* {2212}] **first** [*próton* {4412}] the kingdom of God, and his righteousness; and all these things **shall be added** [*prostethésetai*, the future passive indicative of *prostíthēmi* {4369}, to add] unto you.

"First" means a quantitative (chronological) and qualitative priority. Jesus wants us to desire God first and make our spiritual lives our top priority. When God possesses our hearts, we know how to live righteously.

We do not know what worldly goods are best for us or when we should have them. Jesus said that if we pursue the kingdom of God and His righteousness first, everything else will be added to us in God's time. The passive voice of *prostíthēmi* means that God will do the adding according to His omniscient wisdom. We do not have to be concerned, for He promises to give what we need when we need it. Mature Christians desire only their needs and wait for God's timely, all-sufficient (*autárkeia* [841]) provision to bring them perfect peace and contentment (2 Cor. 9:8; 1 Tim. 6:6). This is the meaning of blessedness (*makários* [3107]; Matt. 5:6)—full satisfaction with God's provision.

[34] Now we have the summary of Christ's teaching regarding worry:

> Take therefore no thought for the **morrow** [*aúrion* {839}, tomorrow]: for the morrow shall take thought for the things of itself. **Sufficient** [*arketón* {713}] unto the day is the **evil** [*kakía* {2549}, evil, calamity, trouble, malevolence] thereof.

In other words, live one day at a time. Tomorrow belongs to the Lord. It is enough for us to contend with and overcome the evil of each day. We are reminded that we live daily in environments which are intrinsically bad (*ponēría* [4189], evil, harmful). However, even though "the whole world lies in the power of the evil one" (1 John 5:19 NASB), 1 John 5:18 assures us that "the evil one" [*ho ponērós* {4190}] cannot touch [from *háptōmai* {681}, to touch from the inside] us (a.t.) since Satan does not indwell believers. Nevertheless, as 2 Corinthians 12:7 states, he does buffet us. Thus, a little faith can dispel a lot of worry!

7

Judging Forbidden
(7:1–6; Luke 6:37–42)

Jesus began His next imperative (v. 1) with the words "**do not**" (NASB) to put a restriction on the moral judgments we make on other persons. Because we are not omniscient, we do not have the right to evaluate our fellow human beings, although, elsewhere, we are commanded to "judge righteous judgment" (John 7:24) and to "prove all things" (1 Thess. 5:21).

God's commands are absolute. The verb "**judge**" (vv. 1, 2), from the Greek verb *krínō* (2919), means generally to separate, to discriminate between good and evil.

We can better understand this root verb when we examine some compound verbs derived from it: *anakrínō* (350), to judicially investigate; *diakrínō* (1252), to separate thoroughly, to discriminate; *egkrínō* (1469), to approve; *epikrínō* (1948), to criticize; *katakrínō* (2632), to judge against, to condemn; and *hupokrínomai* (5271), to speak or act under false identity. A related adjective, *eilikrinés* (1506), means sincere.

The noun *diákrisis* (1253), from the respective verb above, also carries the idea of penetrating judgment, thorough discernment. The Spirit of God grants to some believers "discernment [*diakríseis*] of spirits" (a.t.; 1 Cor. 12:10). This is neither a psychic gift nor guessing of people's motives, plans, or attitudes. John reminds us that the judging of a spirit is necessarily tied to that spirit's verbal confession concerning the person and work of Jesus Christ.

> Beloved, believe not every spirit, but try the spirits whether they are of God: because many false prophets are gone out into the world. Hereby know ye the Spirit of God: Every spirit that confesseth that Jesus Christ is come in the flesh is of God: and every spirit that confesseth not that Jesus Christ is come in the flesh is not of God: and this is that spirit of antichrist, whereof ye have heard that it should come; and even now already is it in the world. (1 John 4:1–3)

The present imperative *má krínete* of verse 1 can be translated, "**Do not be judging**," forbidding a pattern of action. Our lives should not be characterized by negative judging of beams, motes, hypocrisy, etc. Condemning our brother for a "mote" in his eye is an example of a superficial (*kat' ópsin* from *katá* [2596], according to; and *ópsis* [3799], appearance) judgment (see John 7:24).

We can make significant mistakes when we judge superficially. Apart from what people reveal about themselves, we do not know the thoughts and motives of others. All this is below the surface. People can be self-deceived or consciously lying. If they do not tell us their motives, we have nothing concrete on which to judge. We can as easily guess their motives from the color of the clothes they are wearing.

When Israel was seeking a king to replace Saul, the Lord reminded Samuel, "The LORD seeth not as man seeth; for man looketh on the outward appearance, but the LORD looketh on the heart" (1 Sam. 16:7). Since we cannot see their hearts, we cannot penetrate the minds and wills of others as Christ does (John 2:25; 8:44), so we are in no position to measure integrity. Sinners hide their sin—which is guilt, and righteous persons hide their righteousness—which is humility. Each group seeks anonymity in their own worlds, the first to avoid being caught, the second to glorify the name of Christ alone.

The reason to avoid continual judging is now assigned: "**that** [*hína* {2443}, for the purpose of, in order that] ye be not **judged** [*krithête*, the aorist passive subjunctive of *krínō* {2919}, to judge]." The comparison between the present and aorist tenses of "judge" is dramatic: "Do not **continually judge** in order that you will not be **judged once for all**," a picture of the final judgment following death (Heb. 9:27; see also Matt. 10:15; 11:22, 24; 12:36; Mark 6:11; 2 Cor. 5:10; 2 Pet. 2:9; 3:7; 1 John 4:17). In general, believers will be sentenced in accordance with their sentencing of others during their earthly lives.

The present tense of "judge not" conveys the idea that we should not look for faults. We should rather keep looking until we find something praiseworthy in others. God will judge all of us individually (*hékastos* [1538], each one), as Paul stated in 2 Corinthians 5:10.

The second verb *krithête* is the aorist passive subjunctive of *krínō* (2919), to judge or to separate. The aorist refers to the ultimate, once-for-all judgment by God whose judgment will not be superficial but thorough, down to the very motives.

We must remember that God will judge according to holy perfection, not only external actions but also internal motives—simple and complex. Since this day is inevitable, we should avoid the superficiality of negative judgments and concentrate on living pure lives before God. Let us set our minds on the perfect judgment ahead and look for God's graces—not His judgments—in all people.

[2] Often we are able to see a legitimate "mote" in someone's eyes, and Jesus affirmed that the mote exists. The problem does not seem to be our discerning faculty so much as the penal judgment (*kríma* [2917]; the suffix *–ma* indicating the result of judgment) we apply as we judge. When we judge others negatively, we punish them by avoiding them, gossiping about them, getting even in some way, or correcting them (v. 4). But we do not consistently apply the same punishment or correction to ourselves.

The warning here is that the same measures will be applied to us:

> With what judgment ye judge, **ye shall be judged** [*krithésesthe*, the future passive of *krínō* {2919}]: and with what measure ye mete, it shall be measured [from *antimetréō* {488}] to you again.

On the day of judgment, God's standard will be the sinless perfection of the Son of man. So the first judgment we make in this life that has any bearing on our eternal destiny and rewards is our judgment of Jesus Christ. To judge Him short of perfection, to criticize Him, is certain death. The next class of judgments we make—on peers, fellow believers (v. 3), or other people (v. 12)—will be judged on the basis of inconsistent application (James 2:12, 13; cf. the author's commentary on James, entitled *Faith, Love & Hope*).

[3] Jesus now qualified the inconsistency—our bias to favor ourselves:

> And why **beholdest** [from *blépō* {991}, to see, but lacking the perceptive depth of the comparative verb *horáō* {3708}, to see and perceive] thou the mote that is in thy brother's eye, but **considerest** [from *katanoéō* {2657}, to thoroughly understand] not the beam that is in thine own eye?

The two present tenses correspond with the present tense of "**judgeth**" in verse 1. Jesus addressed those of us who by continually gazing at others' motes miss our own beams. Self-deception is rooted in proud, external judgments.

The illustration shows the blinding effect of mote gazing. The problem is not inconsistent metrics—the use of different scales—since we gazers are not even aware of beams to measure. "You are not considering," Jesus said. The distraction of our looking at (from *blépō*), if not looking for, others' sins blind us to even thinking (from *katanoéō*) about our own. Scrutinizing others overpowers self-reflection. It's not that we measure our beams with a different scale; we're altogether blind to their existence.

Though we may not even be conscious of something to measure, our sin is measurably worse—this by Christ's pronouncement. Our fellow believers have "**motes**" (*kárphos* [2595], little splinters) of dry wood, straw, or chaff in their eyes, while we ourselves have "**beams**" (from *dokós* [1385], logs used in buildings, rafters) in our own. The size difference between a splinter and a beam is tremendous, so the point is well taken. We who judge are blind to our own huge sins by the small offenses of others.

[4] "**Or**" (*é* [2228]) introduces a comparative thought, the transition from condemning and punishing others to correcting them: "Or [i.e., in contrast with condemning and punishing] how will you say to your brother, 'Let me pull out the mote that is in your eye'?" (a.t.).

Whether our intention is to punish or correct, the rationale for our actions is the same—self-justification. We believe we are holier than others. We preemptively seize the power to condemn or correct, blinded to the beams within our own eyes by our perpetual gaze at others' motes.

[5] While Jesus did not endorse condemning and punishing, He did offer instructions on how to correct people and avoid hypocrisy. By "**first casting out**" (from *ekbállō* [1544]) the logs in our own eyes, the Lord told us, we will be able to "**see clearly**" (from *diablépō* [1227], literally, to "see through") to take the splinters out of our fellow believers' eyes. God now grants access to their hearts, because this access is no longer blocked by our focus on their sins.

Obviously, we should first decide to take our critical gaze off our fellow believers. If we don't take this first step, we're hopeless. Our gazing blinds self-reflection. And if mote gazing blinds us to the truth of our own beams, think how blinding beam-gazing will be. (Certainly, our brothers have beams as well as motes.)

The order of events, "first cast out," includes confession. If we confess our sins, the Lord will honor our humility with self-effacing wisdom and good results, perhaps even predisposing our fellow-believers to receive us.

[6] Through confession and repentance, the Lord promised an open door to the hearts of those we judged. If they shut the door, they may not be believers after all.

This is how we clarify the seeming paradox between this verse and verse 1. How are we supposed to "**give not** that which is holy unto the dogs, neither cast . . . pearls before swine" if we are commanded to "judge not" (v. 1) whether people are dogs or swine? If we judge persons as dogs or swine, will we be measured by the same criterion?

Although this is necessarily a prejudgment—an expectation of future bad behavior, it does not mean there has been no prior experience of "dog" or "pig" behavior. We should never prejudge without prior experience.

But it is still a negative judgment, and this contributes to our favorably disposing of the seeming paradox. As here, the "judgment" in verses 2 and 3 is not mental differentiation; it is, rather, retaliatory action (cf. God's "judgments in the earth" in both Testaments). God commands us to not render evil for evil in this way (Rom. 12:17; 1 Thess. 5:15; 1 Pet. 3:9). Similarly here, while we are to differentiate believers from nonbelievers, we are not to judge unbelievers.

We may evangelize unbelievers at a distance, but we are forbidden to share holy things with them, especially if they "trample them under their feet." We believers are holy, set apart for God. Thus, the Lord's words once again serve as the basis for Paul's later theology:

> Be ye not unequally yoked together with unbelievers: for what fellowship hath righteousness with unrighteousness? and what communion hath light with darkness? And what concord hath Christ with Belial? or what part hath he that believeth with an infidel? And what agreement hath the temple of God with idols? for ye are the temple of the living God; as God hath said, I will dwell in them, and walk in them; and I will be their God, and they shall be my people. (2 Cor. 6:14–16)

Our salvation is holy and more precious than pearls! A beautiful, valuable pearl is formed from an inconspicuous, valueless grain of sand. When we know that this pearl is going to be despised and trodden underfoot, we should use spiritual discernment to prevent ridicule and contempt. This is the basis for all separation: "Wherefore come out from among them, and be ye separate, saith the Lord, and touch not the unclean thing; and I will receive you" (2 Cor. 6:17, cf. Isa. 52:11; Rev. 18:4).

This verse is applicable to our possessions as well, which, after all, are the Lord's. We believers are not required to underwrite the sinful lifestyles of wayward children, drunkards, drug addicts, or other irresponsible persons. In the end, it is not only detrimental to the rebels, it is bad stewardship, diverting God's provisions away from those who are truly helpless through no fault of their own. Because we must someday give an accounting of God's gifts to us, we should not cast them indiscriminately to dogs or pigs.

Behaving as God's Children
(7:7–12)

[7, 8] Jesus now told us to go to our heavenly Father with our requests:

> **Ask** [*aiteíte*, the present active imperative of *aitéō* {154}, to request from a superior], and it shall be given you; **seek** [*zēteíte*, the present active imperative of *zētéō* {2212}], and you will find; **knock** [*kroúete*, the present active imperative of *kroúō* {2925}], and it shall be opened unto you: for the one asking receives; and he that seeks finds; and to him that knocks it shall be opened. (a.t.)

This is the natural behavior of mature sons and daughters. Even though a father knows all the needs of his children, they do not hesitate to continually (given in the present imperatives) ask (mouth), seek (eyes), and knock (hands). This recognition and confession of comprehensive dependence—oral, visual, tactile—is pleasing to the father. And so it is with our heavenly Father, for through prayer we express our complete dependence on Him. He answers in kind with speaking, displaying, and touching—all revelation, which is given, found, and opened. The three verbs presuppose familiarity; we rarely ask, seek, or knock on the doors of strangers.

By definition, asking is not demanding, and the verb used here, *aiteō*, means to request from a superior. All requests to our Father should be accompanied with the deepest humility, knowing that He is both wise and omniscient. On the other hand, since Christ is our mediator (1 Tim. 2:5), we can approach God confidently and boldly (*parrēsía* [3954]; 2 Cor. 3:12; Eph. 3:12; Col. 2:15; 1 Tim. 3:13; Heb. 3:6; 4:16; 10:19; 1 John 2:28; 3:21; 4:17; 5:14).

The three articulated present participles in verse 8, "**the asking one**" (*ho aitōn*), "**the seeking one**" (*ho zētōn*), and "**the knocking one**" (*tō kroúonti*) imply a normal condition for believers who continually ask and seek humbly from the Father.

The respective promises are receiving, finding, and having doors opened. Note the verb "**receiveth**" (*lambánei*, the present tense of *lambánō* [2983], to receive). The present tense places the emphasis on God's giving in this present life, although the remote future (e.g., the world to come) is not excluded in principle from the promise. The verbs "**findeth**" (from *heurískō* [2147], to find) and "**shall be opened**" (from *anoígō* [455], to open) also imply the Giver, although He is not named with any of these three verbs. In general, we know that "a man can receive nothing, except it be given him from heaven" (John 3:27). The same applies to finding and walking through opened doors.

[9, 10] Jesus again appealed to the rational faculty of His hearers:

> Or what **man** [*ánthrōpos* {444}] is there **of** [*ex* from *ek* {1537}, out from within] you, whom if his **son** [*huiós* {5207}, a mature child, contrasting with a *téknon* {5043}, a growing child] **asks** [*aitḗsē*, the aorist active subjunctive of

aitéō, to request from a superior] bread, he will not **give** [from *epidídōmi* {1929}, deliver over to] him a stone. Or if he asks for a fish, he will not give him a **serpent** [*óphis* {3789}, snake]. (a.t.)

The obvious conclusion is that no good parents would give their children anything that would not satisfy them or would harm them.

[**11**] Jesus did not expect answers from these rhetorical questions. No one was going to come forward and say, "I would!" He launched immediately into His conclusion:

> **If** [*ei* {1487}, since, inasmuch as] ye then, **being** [*óntes*, the present active participle of *eimí* {1510}, to be] **evil** [from *ponērós* {4190}, harmful], **know** [*oídate*, the plural of *oída*, the perfect of *horáō* {3708}, to see and perceive with emphasis on perception, used as a present] how **to give** [from *dídōmi* {1325}, to give voluntarily] **good** [from *agathós* {18}] **gifts** [from *dóma* {1390}] unto your children, **how much** [from *pósos* {4214}] **more** [*mállon* {3123}] shall your Father which is in heaven give good things to them that ask him?

Notice that the gifts are "good," but the givers are described as "continually [reflected in the present participle *óntes*] evil," a terrible picture of the depravity of human nature (see Gen. 6:5). Since Jesus was addressing His disciples, He affirmed that even they are malevolent (*ponērós*) by nature, that is, "in the flesh" that remains unsanctified. Notwithstanding this low level of sin, even evil parents can differentiate good gifts from malevolent (harmful) gifts and give the right ones to their children.

God is truly the only one who is innately benevolent (*agathós* [18]). To call attention to the incomparable love of God, the Lord asked, "How much more?" Our heavenly Father is not malevolent (*ponērós* [4190]); He is good (*agathós*; see Matt. 19:17; Mark 10:18; Luke 18:19). If then malevolent parents can select good gifts for their children, how much more should our good Father be able to give good gifts?

> Every good gift and every perfect gift is from above, and cometh down from the Father of lights, with whom is no variableness, neither shadow of turning. (James 1:17)

The good that God gives cannot be compared with the "good gifts" parents give their children. Consider, for example, the gift described in John 3:16: "For thus [*hoútōs* {3779}, likewise, or of such quality] God so loved the world, that he gave" (a.t.). God's gift of His Son is incomparably unique.

The synoptic parallel in Luke 11:13 mentions another good gift: "How much more shall your heavenly Father give the Holy Spirit to them that ask him?" Luke interjects the Holy Spirit because He is the source of all spiritual gifts that by their very nature are good (*agathá*).

[12] Jesus concluded His teaching:

> Therefore, **all things** [*pánta* {3956}] **whatever** [*án* {302}] **you wish** [from *thélō* {2309}, to wish determinately] that people do to you, **do you** [*poieíte*, the present imperative of *poiéō* {4160}, "do continually"] even so to them, for this is the law and the prophets. (a.t.)

Verse 12 seems to relate more to verses 1–5 than to verses 6–11. Verses 7–11 concern prayer to the Father, not relationships between persons. If then verse 12 is indeed a summary of verses 1–5, we have further evidence that the primary meaning of this entire passage (vv. 1–12), beginning with "Judge not, that ye be not judged," refers to judgments between Christian believers in this life.

Entering the Kingdom of Heaven
(7:13–23; Luke 13:24)

At the beginning of the Sermon on the Mount (Matt. 5:1, 2), we saw that three groups surrounded Jesus: curious bystanders, interested inquirers, and committed disciples. Up to this point in the sermon, the Lord had instructed His disciples, while the rest listened. Now He extended an evangelistic invitation to the whole group.

[13] The aorist tense of the imperative verb "**enter**" (from *eisérchomai* [1525]) indicates an initial entrance into "life" (v. 14) and an exit out of destruction (here), implying a permanent state, that is, without exit and reentry.

Jesus came into the world to introduce the kingdom of heaven (or kingdom of God; Matt. 19:24). The proclamation of this coming kingdom is the gospel, the good news (4:23), and His invitation is, "Come unto me" (11:28). In this verse, "coming" is portrayed as an entry through a "**straight** [from *stenós* {4728}, narrow] **gate** [from *púlē* {4439}]." In the days of our Lord, entrances to cities or edifices often had wide gates ten or twenty feet high. Crowds could easily pass through them.

Multitudes today pass through gates into local churches, but here Jesus spoke of two distinct gates, one that "**leads** [from *apágō* {520}, to lead away] to **destruction** [from *apóleia* {684}, ruin of soul and body]" and another that leads to life (see next verse). The gate that leads to destruction is "**wide**" (from *platús* [4116] from which we get our English word "plateau"), and the path to it is "**broad**" (*eurúchōros* [2149], comfortably spacious, roomy). And, Jesus added, "**many**" (from *polús* [4183]) in His day were entering the wide gate and traveling down the path to destruction.

The frightening impression we get here is one of herd psychology, a mad rush of sin driving crowds through the gate with the same demonic momentum that once drove pigs over a precipice:

> And the unclean spirits went out, and entered into the swine: and the herd ran violently down a steep place into the sea, (they were about two thousand;) and were choked in the sea. (Mark 5:13)

Breadth and width are quantitative terms, encompassing the vast number of deceivers in the world—religious leaders, philosophers, in general every savior but the one who said, "There is no saviour beside me" (Hos. 13:4). That Jesus had the many liars of the world in mind becomes evident in verse 15 where He spoke about false prophets (cf. 2 John 7: "For many deceivers are entered into the world, who confess not that Jesus Christ is come in the flesh").

[14] The adjectives, "**strait**" or "**straight**" (*stenḗ* [4728], not wide, allowing people to pass one at a time) and "**narrow**" (from *thlíbō* [2346], to press, like pressing an orange; related to *thlípsis* [2347], tribulation), respectively highlight two truths: first, there is only one personal, direct way to the Father. Jesus said, "I am the way, the truth, and the life: no man cometh unto the Father, but by me" (John 14:6); second, the way is a path of tribulation: "We **must** [*deí* {1163}, it is necessary] through much **tribulation** [from *thlípsis*] enter into the kingdom of God" (Acts 14:22, cf. Rev. 1:9; 2:9, 10; 7:14).

Entry is only through personal faith in Jesus Christ who is God (John 1:1) but became man (John 1:14): "Whosoever [*pás* {3956}, everyone who] believeth in him should not perish, but have eternal life" (John 3:15). The path is full of afflictions, but it is the most joyous and blessed life one can live (Col. 1:11).

Yet "**few** [from *olígos* {3641}] **are finding** [from *heurískō* {2147}; the Lord used the present tense, meaning in His day] it" (a.t.). For the rebellious who "[had] no king but Caesar" (John 19:15), the narrow gate was esoteric and repugnant. For others who lived in "kings' houses" (Matt. 11:8), the crushing path was restrictive and uncomfortable. Both path and gate would lead to probable persecution.

After Jesus ascended to the right hand of the Father and poured out His Spirit of power (Acts 2:33), many more believers were added to the church. Within a generation of that event, the Lord revealed to the apostle John a much brighter vision concerning the number of people saved:

After this I beheld, and, lo, a great multitude, which no man could number, of all nations, and kindreds, and people, and tongues, stood before the throne, and before the Lamb, clothed with white robes, and palms in their hands; and cried with a loud voice, saying, Salvation to our God which sitteth upon the throne, and unto the Lamb. (Rev. 7:9, 10)

[15] The Lord Jesus now expanded His exhortation concerning the broad path that leads to the gates of Hades.

Beware [from *prosécho* {4337}] of **false prophets** [from *pseudoprophétes* {5578} from *pseudés* {5571}, false; and *prophétes* {4396}, a prophet, from *pró* {4253}, before; and *phemí* {5346}, to speak with certainty], which come to you in sheep's clothing, but inwardly they are ravening wolves.

The verb *prosécho* is frequently used as a nautical term, meaning to hold a ship on course or to sail towards a point. As we hold our course, we must avoid all distractions. This is the first mention of *pseudoprophétes*. Matthew 24:11 tells us that in the latter days many such prophets will arise to "**deceive** [from *planáo* {4105}, or to deviate, follow the wrong signal] **many** [from *polús* {4183}, much, many individuals]." In 24:24 Jesus said that among them will be "**false Christs**" (from *pseudóchristos* [5580] from *pseudés*; false; and *christós* [5547], anointed one), claiming to be Israel's messiah.

"Prophets," according to the Bible, both reveal future events and declare God's revelation of Himself. The inseparability of these two functions is witnessed in the Old Testament teaching that the Lord tests ("proves") His people's adherence to truth with false prophets:

If there arise among you a prophet, or a dreamer of dreams, and giveth thee a sign or a wonder, and the sign or the wonder come to pass, whereof he spake unto thee, saying, Let us go after other gods, which thou hast not known, and let us serve them; thou shalt not hearken unto the words of that prophet, or that dreamer of dreams: for the LORD your God proveth you, to know whether ye love the LORD your God with all your heart and with all your soul. . . . And that prophet, or that dreamer of dreams, shall be put to death; because he hath spoken to turn you away from the LORD your God, which brought you out of the land of Egypt, and redeemed you out of the house of bondage, to thrust thee out of the way which the LORD thy God commanded thee to walk in. So shalt thou put the evil away from the midst of thee. (Deut. 13:1–3, 5)

The purpose of the false prophet is to steer God's people toward other gods. The Lord's purpose in this, however, is different—not to destroy but to prove the integrity of His people. The warning to us in both Deuteronomy and in our

Lord's "**beware**" is that the words spoken by a prophet are far more significant to the legitimacy and authority of his ministry than any signs and wonders he might perform, since the Lord does test the spiritual character of His people.

Early Greek culture included a false prophet called a *mántis* (n.f.), a sooth-sayer (from *manteúomai* (3132), to divine or utter spells; see Acts 16:16). The place where he delivered his oracles was called a *manteíon* (n.f.). Delphi, near Corinth, was one of the main cities for this frenzied activity.

A false prophet can predict that it will both rain and not rain. Obviously, his prediction will be fulfilled eventually. The gullible who witness the fulfilled prophecy will be impressed enough to become followers. Some will demand further verification, e.g., that he predict the weather more than once. But we should "prove all things," and "hold fast that which is good" (1 Thess. 5:21). We should hold to what agrees with the Word of God and discard the rest.

False prophets are in the world now, but as the end of the age approaches, Jesus said their number will increase (Matt. 24:11). He cautioned that those who do not care about His sheep will not enter through the door into the sheepfold but will climb over the walls as thieves and robbers (see John 10:1). He warned here that these false prophets will wear sheep's clothing to give the appearance of docility and harmlessness but only to hide their tooth-and-claw "**ravening**" (from *hárpax* [727], rapacious) and their snatching away of prey. The wolf, like the thief in John 10:10, comes only to steal, kill, and destroy.

The wolf in sheep's clothing is stealthy, but such clothing is unsuccessful here, since our God is stealth-defeating: "All things are naked and opened unto the eyes of him with whom we have to do" (Heb. 4:13, cf. Matt. 10:26).

[16] Wolves in sheeps' clothing cannot stay hidden for long. The Lord cautioned,

> **Ye shall know** [from *epiginōskō* {1921}, to know, from *epí* {1909}, an intensive; and *ginōskō* {1097}, to fully or additionally know by experience] them **by** [*apó* {575}, as a result of, from] their **fruits** [from *karpós* {2590}]. Do men gather grapes of thorns, or figs of thistles?

A fig tree produces only figs and an orange tree, oranges. Each tree produces fruit according to its kind. If a tree has oranges on it, you know it is an orange tree. So the answer to the two-pronged question is: no, such is impossible. From this rhetorical question, the Lord intended His hearers to infer that logical consistency, particularly consistency with biblical revelation, is the test for truth: "For every tree is known by his own [from *idios* {2398}, private, pertaining to] fruit" (Luke 6:44). If you find an apple on an orange tree, somebody tied it on. It's a joke, an inconsistency.

[17] But truth is always logically consistent:

> **Even so** [*hoútōs* {3779}, thus, in this matter, concluding] **every** [from *pás* {3956}] **good** [from *agathós* {18}, beneficent; but here "healthy"] tree bringeth forth **good** [from *kalós* {2570}, good, proper] fruit; but a **corrupt** [from *saprós* {4550}, rotted] tree bringeth forth **evil** [from *ponērós* {4190}, malevolent, harmful, here "inedible"] fruit.

In spite of sheep's clothing, a wolf can only be a wolf: "Can the . . . leopard [change] his spots? then may ye also do good, that are accustomed to do evil" (Jer. 13:23). The wolf can neither change his wolfness nor be sheepish. His stealthy advance toward a prey is not the hoax of a comedian who attaches an apple to an orange tree. He doesn't "play sheep" to make people laugh at a party, and he doesn't laugh himself—he howls. Actually, all he really wants to do is kill so he can eat. The danger Jesus warned His disciples about is very real.

"Wherefore," Jesus aptly concluded, "by their fruits ye shall know them" (v. 20). Eventually, the false prophet will say, "Let's seek other gods." What better reason do we have to memorize the "word of truth" (Ps. 119:43; 2 Cor. 6:7; Eph. 1:13; 2 Tim. 2:15; James 1:18)?

[18] Jesus expanded His teaching with logical inference, specifically definition. Not only is it true that good trees do not produce bad fruit, but good trees cannot produce bad fruit. This is the nature of logical necessity by definition; a fruit tree includes fruit in its definition:

> A good tree is not **able** [from *dúnamai* {1410}] **to make** [from *poiéō* {4160}] evil fruit; neither is a corrupt tree able to make good fruit. (a.t.)

Jesus here taught the impossibility of cross production. People produce what they are and they cannot produce what they are not. Unless God changes persons from rotten to good trees, they cannot do anything good.

[19] God limits the production of bad trees that are eventually destroyed:

> Every tree **not producing** [from *poiéō*] **good** [from *kalós* {2570}, intrinsically good] fruit **is cut down** [from *ekkóptō* {1581}, to cut down; from *ek* {1537}, out of from within or among; and *kóptō* {2875}, to cut] and cast into the fire. (a.t.)

Who cuts down the worthless tree? The farmer who is worthy of the name "farmer." He cuts it down because he has the good sense to know the difference it will make in the yield of his crops.

[20] "Wherefore," Jesus concluded as He did in verse 16, "by their fruits **ye shall know** [from *epiginōskō* {1921}; v. 16] them."

Believers are known by the fruit of the Spirit of Christ, which can produce only good fruit, just as unbelievers are recognized by fruit that is consistent with their depraved natures and the work of the devil who leads them captive (2 Tim. 2:26). We can only judge individuals after a considerable amount of time. Consistent actions and attitudes, particularly during persecution, show one's true character (Matt. 13:20, 21). Hypocrisy always looks good in the short term.

[21] The hypocrite's words and actions do not agree:

> Not **every one** [*pás* {3956}, every individual] **that saith** [*légōn*, the present participle of *légō* {3004}, to intelligibly speak] unto me, Lord, Lord [from *kúrios* {2962}], shall enter into the kingdom of heaven; but **he that doeth** [*poiōn*, the present participle of *poiéō* {4160}, to make, to produce] the **will** [*thélēma* {2307}, the determinate will of God viewed as a product; thus, the —*ma* suffix] of my Father which is in heaven.

Verbal confession of Jesus Christ as Lord is not enough. Jesus said, "This people honoreth me with their lips, but their heart is far from me" (Mark 7:6; cf. Isa. 29:13; Matt. 15:8, 9; Mark 7:6). A sincerity of heart must accompany these words; thus, the apostle Paul wrote:

> If thou shalt confess with thy mouth the Lord Jesus, and shalt believe in thine heart that God hath raised him from the dead, thou shalt be saved. For with the heart man believeth unto righteousness; and with the mouth confession is made unto salvation. (Rom. 10:9, 10)

Only as we partake of Christ's "divine [*theía* {2304}] nature [*phúsis* {5449}]," as described in 2 Peter 1:4, are we able to grow and produce divine fruit unto sanctification (*hagiasmós* [38]; Rom. 6:22), which is a holy life. This is the only way we sinners by the power of God are changed and justified, that is, declared or constituted righteous and converted.

Such a person is the subject of the participle "**he that doeth**," meaning "continually does," the will of the Father. In an ultimate sense, only Jesus Christ our righteousness (Jer. 23:6; 1 Cor. 1:30), the final object of our faith, continually (i.e., without sin, qualitatively) did the will of the Father.

Thélēma here is equivalent to what Acts 2:23 describes as "the **determinate** [from *horízō* {3724}, to determine] **counsel** [from *boulḗ* {1012}] . . . of God" that delivered Christ to the cross, which was part of the broader plan of the Father who "works all things according to the **counsel** [from *boulḗ*] of His **will** [from *thélēma*]" (Eph. 1:11 NKJV).

The choice of *thélēma* here, then, means that the "will of God" is the determinative cause, and "doing" is the effect. "Continually doing," therefore, is a product of God's will. Jesua told His disciples to acquiesce to this determinative will of God when they prayed, "Thy will [*thélēma*] be done [from *gínomai* {1096}, to occur, to take place]" (Matt. 6:10).

[22] The path to destruction is broad:

> **Many** [*polloí*, the plural of *polús* {4183}] **will say** [*eroúsi*, the future tense of *eréō* {2046}, to say with exactness; distinct from *légō* {3004}, to intelligibly say; and *phēmí* {5346}, to say with assurance] to me in **that** [*ekeínē* {1565}] **day** [*hēméra* {2250}], Lord, Lord, have we not prophesied in thy name? and in thy name have cast out devils? and in thy name done many wonderful works?

This refers to the day of the final judgment following the return of Christ. The Father has delegated all judgment to His Son: "For the Father judgeth no man, but hath committed all judgment unto the Son" (John 5:22). Since "there is not even one righteous person [*díkaios* {1342}, righteous]" (Rom. 3:10; a.t.) except the sinless Jesus (Heb. 4:15), He alone qualifies to judge humankind. In this we can see the perfect justice of God the Father in that He Himself will not judge anyone but commits judgment to the one person of the Godhead who took our sins on Himself and suffered for humanity.

The repetitive "Lord, Lord" expresses the intense final pleas of "**many**" desperate unbelievers. The power of self-deception is seen in their tenacious claims of prophecies, exorcisms, and "wonderful works"—all in Christ's name. For the unsaved, self-deception is strong, and these people ask a question expecting a yes answer: "We did do all these wonderful works in your name, didn't we?" The unspoken follow-up question is, "How can you condemn us?"

Hypocrites cannot address Christ as "my Lord," which Thomas did (John [20:28]) in spite of his doubts, because the Lord has not possessed them personally at any time. At best, "Lord, Lord" concedes the undeniable—Christ's authority to judge.

[23] Christ's response is terrifying:

> And then **will I confess** [from *homologéō* {3670} from *homoú* {3674}, together; and *légō* {3004}, to intelligently say] unto them, I **never** [*oudépote* {3763} from *ou* {3756}, not; *dé* {1161}, even; and *poté* {4218}, ever; "not at any time"] **knew** [from *ginōskō* {1097}, to know personally] you. **Depart** [*apochōreíte*, the present imperative of *apochōréō* {672} from *apó* {575}, away from; and *chōréō* {5562}, to clear space, make room; from *chōros* {5565}, space; i.e., "space yourselves away from me"] from me, **you that are working** [*ergazómenoi*, the present participle of *ergázomai* {2038}, to work] the [*tēn* {3588}] **iniquity** [from *anomía* {458}, lawlessness]. (a.t.)

The present participle, "**you that are working**" (i.e., even to this present moment) the wicked reality, undercuts the religious profession. "I did not

know you at any point in time" (see below) is the most terrifying pronouncement in the entire Bible since it slashes through the arrogant self-assurance
of those who convince themselves daily that they are believers. On that day,
however, the hypocrites' deceived opinion that they are born again—lies they
told themselves and others—will not count. God's opinion alone, which is
objective truth, will prevail (Prov. 19:21). The Lord knows everyone, but this
knowledge reflects the higher level of intimacy found in Amos 3:2, "You only
have I known of all the families of the earth: therefore I will punish you for all
your iniquities."

In the final judgment (John 5:27–29), all humanity will stand before
Christ. Sincere faith will be revealed and hypocrisy exposed. According to the
Lord's words, some will face that judgment with the self-generated faith of evil
spirits (James 2:19) in lieu of "the faith of God's elect" (Titus 1:1), the fruit
of the Spirit (Gal. 5:22). In terror, hypocrites will appeal to all their works only
to hear at the end that the Lord did not ever know them. The claims, therefore, are not objective; they are sayings, not doings: "Every one that saith unto
me" (v. 21); "many will say to me" (v. 22); "and then will I [not 'say' but] profess [*homologēsō*] unto them" (v. 23). They "say" lies; Jesus "professes" truth.

Oudépote, **absolutely never,** covers every point in history. These people,
then, were never converted or regenerated, never personally related to Jesus
Christ in their professed miracle-working. Accordingly, the Lord does not grat-
ify them with so much as a single concession to their lives' volumes, all products of the flesh. He simply announced He never knew them, an implied, "No,
you did not at any time do these things for My glory; you did them for the
sake of your own legacy that ends right now."

"**Iniquity**" (lawlessness) is what they "**are working,**" not prophecies, exorcisms, or other miracles. The present participle extends their lies right up to
the face of the King. This is the Lord's opinion of what they did and are doing
as they face Him, which means their claims are lies, self-deceptions, even now
before the Judge. The definite article before "iniquity" possibly refers to mimicking "the" offense of the devil (see Matt. 13:41; 2 Thess. 2:3, 7).

Two Foundations
(7:24–29; Luke 6:47–49)

The Sermon on the Mount was intended to build character, and the first thing
any building needs is a good, solid foundation (1 Cor. 3:10–15). Everyone is
responsible for the base he or she selects.

[24, 25] In this parable, two bases are presented: "**rock**" (from *pétra* [4073]; v. 24) and "**sand**" (from *ámmos* [285]; v. 26). Two kinds of builders are also here: the "**wise**" (from *phrónimos* [5429], prudent) builder selects the rock; and the "**foolish**" (from *mōrós* [3474], silly, stupid, from which we obtain the English word "moron"; v. 26) builder selects sand, probably because it is much easier to build on than rock.

Notice that the adjective "**wise**" is *phrónimos*, not the better-known word for wise, *sophós* (4680), which is related to the most common word for wisdom, *sophía* (4678). The difference is significant here. Although *sophía* can be used to refer to "fleshly wisdom" (2 Cor. 1:12) or even wisdom given by demons (James 3:15), it usually refers to spiritual wisdom (James 3:17). In Romans 16:27, God is called "only [*mónos* {3441}] wise [*sophós*]." Furthermore, Jesus is called "the wisdom [*sophía*] of God" (1 Cor. 1:24; see also Matt. 13:54; Luke 11:49; Rom. 11:33; 1 Cor. 1:20, 30; 2:7).

Here, however, the adjective "wise" is *phrónimos*, which could also be translated "prudent." In modern as well as in Hellenistic Greek, the New Testament noun *phrēn* (5424) means "brake," something that curbs or restrains. In modern Greek, the term is used for the brakes of a car. Some prudence remains in humans by virtue of creation apart from redemption. In Luke 16:8, for example, we read that the Lord approved the commendable act of an "unjust" steward, because he was "more prudent [from *phrónimos*; translated 'wisely' in the KJV] than the sons [from *huiós* {5207}] of light" (a.t.). Although this man was not a son of light, an element of natural prudence apparently coexisted with his moral unjustness. (For a detailed study comparing natural prudence with divinely given wisdom, see Zodhiates, *How to Manage Money*, on Luke 16:1–13, and *The Complete Word Study Dictionary: New Testament*, particularly words #4678 *sophía*, wisdom; #4680 *sophós*, wise; #5428 *phrónēsis*, prudence; #5429 *phrónimos*, prudent; #5424 *phrēn*, moral brake.)

The wisdom of God in Christ, which complements natural prudence, is one benefit of salvation and is part of the regeneration of the mind. That this wisdom is enhanced prudence is evident from Paul's vivid use of two complex Greek terms: one in 2 Timothy 1:7: "**sound mind**" (from *sōphronismós* [4995] from *sóos* [n.f.], sound, and *phrēn* [5424], moral brake), and the other in Titus 2:8: "**healthy logic**" (from *hugiēs* [5199] from which we derive our English word "hygiene" and from *lógos* [3056], rational speech, logic)—both gifts to believers from the regenerating Spirit of God.

In this parable, "**hears**" (from *akoúō* [191]) is detached from "does" (from *poiéō* [4160]). Some people hear and do, and others hear and do not do. The reference is clearly associated with physical hearing, not the hearing of the Spirit, which involves obedience.

Concerning the one who hears and does, Christ said, "**I will liken** [from *homoióō* {3666}, to compare with] him unto a **wise** [*phrónimos*] **man** [from *anḗr* {435}, a man, a male], which built his house upon a rock (v.24)."

Prudent people plan for inclement weather. Whereas some prudent persons would never build their physical houses on sand, they build their spiritual houses on sandy foundations. Like the rich farmer in Luke 12, they fail to consider the imminence of death, ignoring the one who said, "This night thy soul shall be required of thee" (Luke 12:20).

The foundation is the most important part of a building. After the storm passed, the prudent man "**had founded** [*tethemelíōto*, the pluperfect tense of *themelióō* {2311}, to lay a solid foundation] the house upon a rock."

Paul told us that the only foundation we can build on successfully is Jesus Christ (1 Cor. 3:11, cf. Matt. 16:18). Accordingly, faith, in Hebrews 11:1, is defined by the author as the "substance [*hupóstasis* {5287}, that which stands below] of things hoped for." Because Christ is the foundation or the substance of faith, believers can have *parrēsía* (3954), bold confidence, especially in proclaiming their foundation to an unbelieving world (Acts 2:29; 28:31; 2 Cor. 7:4; Eph. 3:12; Phil. 1:20; Heb. 3:6; 10:35).

[26] The man described as "**foolish**" (*mōrós*, someone who acts thoughtlessly or contrary to reason), by contrast, takes an irrational risk.

Though in modern Greek the word *mōrós* is used for "baby," the New Testament consistently attaches the term to adults who willfully (i.e., consciously) and irresponsibly ignore God's commands. Christ's address to the scribes and Pharisees, for example, "Ye fools [*mōroí* from *mōrós*] and blind" (Matt. 23:17, 19), is a condemnation of their rebellion, not pity toward their immaturity. Adults know that what they are doing is wrong but do it anyway.

[27] Judgment comes on the fool and his possessions: "And the rain descended, and the floods came, and the winds blew, and beat upon that **house;** and it fell: and great was the fall of it."

The fool sins, and his house is judged—presumably with him in it. While the teaching is applicable to individuals, Jesus no doubt anticipated the fall of the "house of Jerusalem" under the headship of religious leaders who corporately rejected their Messiah (note that Jerusalem's house is the subject in the following verses):

O **Jerusalem, Jerusalem**, thou that killest the prophets, and stonest them which are sent unto thee, how often would I have gathered thy children together, even as a hen gathereth her chickens under her wings, and ye would not! Behold, **your house** is left unto you desolate. For I say unto you, Ye shall not see me henceforth, till ye shall say, Blessed is he that cometh in the name of the Lord. (Matt. 23:37–39)

In principle, this house "**is** [morally] **desolate** [*aphietai*, the present tense of *aphiēmi* {863}, to abandon]" the instant Christ speaks these words. Historically, however, it collapsed in A.D. 70.

[28, 29] When Jesus completed all these sayings, the crowd "**was being astonished**" (*exeplēssonto*, the imperfect passive of *ekplēssō* [1605], to strike with amazement).

Everyone was struck not only by His "**doctrine**" (from *didachē* [1322], teaching) but also by His "**authority**" (from *exousía* [1849], physical and moral power; v. 29), which contrasted with the manner in which the scribes taught. Now that we have the full Word of God and the Spirit of Christ indwelling us, we, too, can preach or teach the Word of God with authority. As Paul noted, this will make a remarkable difference:

Knowing, brethren beloved, your election of God. For our gospel came not unto you in word only, but also in power, and in the Holy Ghost, and in much assurance; as ye know what manner of men we were among you for your sake. (1 Thess. 1:4, 5)

CHAPTER

8

⚬∕∕⚬

A Leper Cleansed
(8:1–4; Mark 1:40–44; Luke 5:12–14)

[1] When Jesus descended from the mountain (v. 1), great "**multitudes**" (from *óchlos* [3793], unorganized crowds; see 4:25; 5:1) followed Him, amazed at His unique power and authority (7:28).

[2] Among the crowds was a leper. Lepers customarily were not allowed to associate with healthy people. Leprosy was a loathsome disease, and lepers were assigned to live "outside the camp" of Israel (Lev. 13:46 NASB). They were barred from Jerusalem and other walled cities. In synagogues, they were confined to small, isolated rooms, ten feet long and six feet wide. To promote easy identification, they were required to leave their hair disheveled, place coverings on their upper lips, and continually cry out, "Unclean, unclean!" (Lev. 13:45) to people who were around them.

   Those who touched lepers were considered ritually defiled, as they would be if they touched a dead body. People kept a distance of at least one cubit (eighteen to twenty-one inches; see comments on Matt. 6:27) from them. To prevent contact, some people, even rabbis at times, threw stones at them.

   No wonder this verse begins with the exclamatory remark, "And, **behold** [*idoú* {2400} from *eídō* {1492}, to perceive]," the imperative that calls attention to extraordinary events (see Matt. 3:16). It was extraordinary indeed for a leper to personally approach an individual, and yet Jesus not only welcomed his approach but touched him—two acts contrary to Mosaic Law and Jewish tradition.

   An interesting New Testament phenomenon is that the healing of leprosy is never qualified by the Greek nouns *therapeía* (2322), healing, or *íasis* (2392), curing; nor are the corresponding verbs *therapeúō* ([2323], cf. Matt. 4:23, 24) or *iáomai* ([2390], to heal) used. Rather, Jesus told His disciples to "heal [from *therapeúō*] the sick, [but] **cleanse** [from *katharízō* {2511}] the lepers" (Matt. 10:8). In one sense, leprosy represented the moral defilement of sin from which Jesus came to save His people. This salvation, accordingly, is not only a lifting up and taking away, a liberation (*áphesis* [859]; Luke 1:77; 3:3; 4:18) from the physical symptoms of sin, but a change of moral character. It is the taking away of sin, the defilement that separates people from God, and it involves a radical change in sinners. God makes "saved" persons spiritually healthy—saints enabled to do His will.

If the multitudes were shocked when they heard Jesus speak and act with divine authority, then this first encounter with a leper, symbol of the worst defilement, must have left them breathless.

The leper humbly addressed Jesus, "Lord, **if** [*eán* {1437}, if surely] thou wilt [implying Christ's divine ability], thou canst make me clean." The verb "**canst**" is from *dúnamai* (1410), to be able. The leper did not doubt Jesus' ability, so he appealed to His sovereign will.

[3] The verb "**touched**" (from *háptomai* [680], to handle an object) sums up Jesus' compassionate will in this case (cf. v. 15; 9:20, 21, 29; 14:36; 20:34). Note that, consistent with what we mentioned in verse 2, the verb "**cleanse**" (*katharízō*) is used. The cleansing was "**immediate**" (*euthéōs* [2112]), wholly apart from any sacrifices or even obedience other than faith (see next verse).

[4] After restoring him to health, Jesus commanded the man to have a priest certify his healing in the temple in Jerusalem.

Under the old covenant, a leper was physically examined by a Levitic priest who, on confirming the absence of the disease, offered two live birds, one of which was killed over running water. The living bird was dipped in the blood of the dead bird and allowed to go free. The man then washed himself and his clothes and shaved. In seven days, he submitted himself for reexamination by the priest. He then shaved his head, face, and eyebrows. This was followed by his sacrificing of two male lambs without blemish and one ewe lamb, in addition to a meal offering of fine flour mingled with oil. The priest then touched the leper on the tip of his right ear, his right thumb, and his right big toe with the blood and oil. After a final examination, the priest issued a certificate stating that the leper had been cleansed (Lev. 14). Here Christ healed the leper before he appeared before the priest.

The cleansing would present irrefutable evidence of Jesus' power as the Christ, the Messiah of Israel, although the Jewish priests probably would not accept the testimony of the leper.

The Centurion's Servant Healed
(8:5–13; Luke 7:1–10)

[5, 6] Capernaum was the Galilean city Jesus adopted as His hometown (Matt. 9:1). He may have lived at Peter's house. A Roman centurion had built a synagogue for the Jews there (Luke 7:5).

This Roman centurion (an officer over one hundred men) that now appears on the scene had been influenced by Jesus' miraculous works (Matt. 7:28, 29). When the officer's servant became sick with "**palsy**" (*paralutikós* [3885], paralytic) and in great torment (possibly polio), the centurion asked Jesus for help.

[7, 8] It is interesting that the Lord's confident response to the centurion's inquiry: not "I will **come** and try to heal him," but rather, "I **will come** and heal him."

The centurion's faith in the superiority of Christ's person and power were reflected in verse 8: "Lord, I am not worthy . . . . but speak the word only, and my servant shall be healed." His faith in the healing power of Jesus was complete.

[9] The centurion apparently had heard about and perhaps seen Jesus' extraordinary power. In an insightful analogy, he compared the Lord's power to his own authority to order soldiers under his command:

> For I am a man under **authority** [*exousía* {1849}, moral and physical right], having soldiers under me: and I say to this man, Go, and he goeth; and to another, Come, and he cometh; and to my servant, Do this, and he doeth it.

[10] When Jesus heard these words,

> **He marvelled** [from *thaumázō* {2296}, to admire a *thaúma* {2295}, a wonder, miracle, marvel] and said to them that followed, Verily I say unto you, I have not found so great faith, no, not in Israel.

What was different "in Israel" about this faith was that this Roman centurion believed Jesus could "**tenderly heal**" (from *theraeúō* [2323]) his paralyzed servant from a distance by commanding His healing angels to invade—"**Come, and he comes**"—or Satan's destructive demons to depart—"**Go, and he goes.**" This confidence was indeed a marvel, and no Jew had advanced to such a level of faith in Christ's sovereignty over the invisible realm.

[11, 12] The Lord now hinted prophetically at the oncoming expansion of His kingdom among Gentiles at the expense of the apostatizing nation of Israel:

And I say unto you, That many shall come from the east and west, and shall sit down with Abraham, and Isaac, and Jacob, in the kingdom of heaven. But the **children** [from *huiós* {5207}] of the kingdom **shall be cast out** [from *ekbállō* {1544}, to be cast out; from *ek* {1537}, out of from within or among; and *bállō* {906}, to throw; "to throw out"] into **outer darkness** [*skótos* {4655}]: there shall be **weeping** [*klauthmós* {2805}] and **gnashing** [*brugmós* {1030}, grinding] **of teeth.**

As we have shown, the word translated "**children**" in the King James Version is actually "sons," referring to those born of Hebrew ancestry. Although "sons of the kingdom," most Jews rejected their Messiah and were supplanted by Gentiles (see Rom. 11). Many Gentiles, like this centurion, become adopted children of God, and one day they will enter the kingdom of heaven, while the unconverted, physical children of Abraham, Isaac, and Jacob will be cast into outer darkness.

This centurion and other Gentiles from the ends of the earth, however, will participate in the great banquet at which only believers from among both Jews and Gentiles will be present (Matt. 22:1–14). Faith is the password to the heavenly kingdom.

What is the "**outer darkness**" where unbelievers "will be cast out"? The place where these unbelieving Jews will be thrown is called *skótos*, "**darkness**," a symbol of spiritual darkness (John 3:19; Rom. 2:19) and eternal misery (Matt. 4:16; Luke 1:79; Acts 26:18; 1 Thess. 5:4; 1 Pet. 2:9). The expression "outer darkness" is found only here and in Matthew 22:13; 25:30, although Luke 16:19–31 actually pictures the condition of a person who dies in his sins and exists in Hades. Though in darkness himself, the rich man can see Abraham and Lazarus far off.

The noun *klauthmós* is associated with the verb *klaíō* (2799), to weep, to cry. The first time this noun occurs is in Matthew 2:18 which reads, "In Rama was there a voice heard, lamentation, and weeping, and great mourning, Rachel weeping for her children, and would not be comforted, because they are not" (cf. Jer. 31:15). While the historical backdrop is the Babylonian Captivity, Jeremiah's prophecy predicted the slaughter of innocent children in Bethlehem, one mile from Ramah, after Jesus was born (Matt. 2:17, 18).

"**Gnashing of teeth**" depicts extreme frustration. Here Jesus predicted the transfer of the kingdom from the Jews to their Gentile enemies—represented by a centurion from Rome, the very nation that held Israel in bondage. Nothing could be more frustrating to Jewish leaders than this prophecy of the church age. As a nation, Israel has been in outer darkness from the time they rejected Christ to the present day. While individual Jews have been saved throughout history, the nation itself will remain in outer darkness until it repents (Rom. 11:25–27).

[13] The centurion's unique faith was amply rewarded:

> **And Jesus said** [from *eípon*, the aorist tense of *légō* {3004}, to say intelligibly] to the centurion, **Go** [from *hupágō* {5217}, to go; from *hupó* {5259}, under, therefore stealthily; and *ágō* {71}, to lead away], and as **you have believed** [from *pisteúō* {4100}, to believe], **be it done** [from *gínomai* {1096}, to become] to you. And his servant was healed in that very hour. (a.t.)

The belief in the specific healing presupposes faith in Christ's sovereignty (lordship) in general. In other words, the centurion had a saving faith in Christ when he believed that the Lord could heal his servant.

Peter's Mother-in-Law Healed
(8:14–17; Mark 1:29–34; Luke 4:38–41)

[14] Peter's mother-in-law was in Peter's house, having been "**laid down**" (from *bállō* [906], to place, in contrast to *rhíptō* [4496]; Matt. 9:36; 15:30; 27:5; Luke 4:35; 17:2; Acts 22:23; 27:19, 29, meaning to cast down). Although her precise sickness is not given, we read that she was "**fevered**" (a.t.; from *puréssō* [4445], burning with fever [*puretós* {4446} from *pur* {4442}, fire, heat]). No attribution of evil or sin is given for this fever that had come on her.

[15] The Lord "**touched**" (from *háptomai* [681], to touch in order to heal, affect beneficently) Peter's mother-in-law. Immediately, the fever "**left**" (from *aphíēmi* [863], to leave), and "**she arose**" (from *egeírō* [1453], to rise, to raise).

God is free to heal with or without medical procedures and drugs. Moreover, the Lord Jesus' healing touch produces far more than just physical restoration. Therefore, if we become ill, we are told to seek the Lord first, then the physicians (2 Chr. 16:12). But God's answer is not always yes. It may be no, later, or something better. The apostle Paul referred to God's will as a mystery (*mustērion* [3466]; Eph. 1:9). If we do not know God's will in any particular crisis, we should follow the Lord Jesus in full submission: "I seek not My own will [*thélēma* {2307} from *thélō* {2309}, to determine; and *-ma*, the final product] but the will of the Father who sent [from *pémpō* {3992}, to send] Me" (John 5:30; a.t.).

The verb "**ministered**" (from *diakonéō* [1247]) means that Peter's mother-in-law was able to return to the household tasks she was doing before.

[16] The evening brought an end to the Sabbath, and again the multitudes brought many sick people to Jesus. Some He "**healed**" (from *therapeúō* [2323], to heal with tenderness), and from others He "**cast out**" (from *ekbállō* [1544]) demons. The phrase translated "**all that were sick**" is literally "all [from *pás* {3956}] the ones **having** [from *échō* {2192}] [it] **badly** [*kakōs* {2560}, a broad term—the opposite of *kalós* {2570}, good—blanketing every sickness and disease] were healed." No sick persons returned home as they came—believers or unbelievers.

[17] Immediately after this, Matthew quotes the prophecy of Isaiah 53:4 that speaks of the suffering Messiah taking on Himself our infirmities and sicknesses:

> That **it might be fulfilled** [from *plēróō* {4137}] which was spoken **by** [*diá* {1223}, through, implying agency; i.e., Isaiah was not the origin of the Word of God] Esaias the prophet, saying, **Himself** [*autós* {846}, the emphatic pronoun] **took** [from *lambánō* {2983}, to receive] our **infirmities** [from *asthéneia* {769}, weakness, from *a* {1}, without; and *sthénos* {n.f.}, bodily strength], and **bare** [from *bastázō* {941}] our **sicknesses** [from *nósos* {3554}, disease].

The active voice of "**took**" and "**bare**" implies a voluntary action. The latter verb means to lift up and carry. Jesus bore the penalties of weakness and sickness for us, which God imposes because of sin. This does not mean that we believers are exempt from suffering in this life. Though saved by grace, we "groan within ourselves, waiting for the adoption, to wit, the redemption of our body" (Rom. 8:23)—which lies in the future. Paul assured us that "the sufferings of this present time are not worthy to be compared with the glory which shall be revealed in us" (Rom. 8:18).

Jesus has been "separated [from *chōrízō* {5563}] from sinners" (Heb. 7:26 NASB) and did not sin (2 Cor. 5:21; Heb. 4:15; see the author's *Sickness Why—Healing How?*), but He did take on Himself sin and its consequences, which include weakness, sickness (see above), and also death. He did not die of natural causes, but he voluntarily shed His blood (Heb. 9:22) for the sins of the world.

Peter cited Isaiah 53:5 in 1 Peter 2:24: "Who his own self bare our sins in his own body on the tree, that we, being dead to sins, should live unto righteousness: by whose stripes ye were healed [from *iáomai* {2390}]." But this does not mean that Jesus caught our colds or cancers any more than the sacrificial lamb did under the Levitical system of sacrifice. "To bear" the weight of a sickness does not mean "to get" the sickness, which is more like "collapsing under" than "bearing up under." Furthermore, to bear "**our**" sicknesses was not to bear His own. Ultimately, Christ bore the full consequence of our sins to redeem us from sin's penalty and power.

Although the verb *sṓzō* (4982) means to save spiritually and immediately from sin and its power, a delayed liberation of our bodies awaits the resurrection (see Rom. 8:23 above). Even though Christ is in us, Paul stated that "the body is dead because of sin" (Rom. 8:10). But he assured us that the Spirit of the Father "will also give life to [our] mortal bodies" (Rom. 8:11 NASB) to conform to our new spirits/souls (2 Cor. 5:17). In qualitatively new (from *kainós* [2537]; Rev. 21:5) bodies, we will be free from every weakness and disease forever.

Although it is true that physical healing is in the atonement in principal— "by whose stripes ye were healed [from *iáomai* {2390}, a verb consistently used in the NT for physical healing]" (1 Pet. 2:24)—God chooses when to apply this healing to our physical bodies. Physical death is the "last enemy" (1 Cor. 15:26) to be abrogated, and for believers this occurs at the rapture of the church (1 Thess. 4:16, 17).

Understanding Discipleship
(8:18–22; Luke 9:57–62)

[18, 19] Following so many healings, multitudes crowded around Jesus, so He decided to "depart unto the other side." Before He did, however, a scribe (*grammateús* [1122]), obviously overwhelmed with Jesus' healing power, offered a sincere but impulsive promise: "**Master** [from *didáskalos* {1320}, teacher, a title much lower than *kúrie* {2962}, Lord, see 8:2, 6, 8], I will follow you wherever you go" (a.t.).

According to verse 21 (cf. Luke 9:59), subsequent to this conversation Jesus addressed "**another** [from *héteros* {2087}] disciple," implying that this scribe was a disciple. While a disciple (*mathētḗs* [3101]) generally is a learner, we should remember that Judas was also called a disciple (John 12:4). Also, in response to Jesus' teaching about eating His flesh and drinking His blood, "many of his disciples went back, and walked no more with him" (John 6:66). Not all disciples were true believers in Christ, and, according to John, many apostasized. This "disciple" may have been an unbelieving disciple like Judas.

[20] However sincere the scribe was, the Lord's omniscient wisdom detected a hidden but heavy concern with worldly security, so He cautioned him:

The foxes have **holes** [from *phōleós* {5454}, a burrow, hole], and the birds of the air have **nests** [from *kataskēnōsis* {2682}, encampment, shelter]; but the Son of man hath not where to lay his head.

Worldly security has no proper place in the kingdom of God. The scribe sounded sincere, but he had not considered the full implications of his impulsive words. Jesus told him that following meant the risk of parting with many common comforts of life—like a roof and a bed. To follow Christ anywhere could mean to the cross. He offered no guarantee of worldly ease and comfort.

[21] Another man approached Jesus. "And **another** [*héteros* {2087}, another of a different type] of his disciples said unto him, Lord, **suffer** [*epítrepson*, the aorist imperative of *epitrépō* {2010}, to allow] me first to go and bury my father."

The Lord had just judged worldly security as an invalid excuse for not following. This prompted another kind of excuse.

[22] This, too, was judged unfavorably. "But Jesus said unto him, **Follow** [*akoloúthei*, the present imperative of *akolouthéō* {190}, to follow] me; and let the dead bury their dead." The present imperative means to continually follow uninterruptedly. (The aorist tense of *epitrépō* in the previous verse means that the disciple requested only a one-time interruption.)

The imperative that follows was harsh only if the man insisted that burying his father prevented him from preaching the gospel. Jesus was not telling him not to attend his father's wake or funeral. Remember the context: The man presented burial as an excuse for not following Jesus. Actually, he could do both by preaching the gospel to his unsaved relatives at the funeral. This is essentially what Jesus said in the parallel text of Luke 9:60: "Let the dead bury their dead: **but [you] go and preach** the kingdom of God" (a.t.). In other words, if you refuse to do both, if you insist on the either/or of burying or preaching, then let others bury your father to free you to preach the kingdom. But you can do both because "[you] can do all things through Christ who strengthens [you]" (Phil. 4:13). In either case, do not use the burial of your father as an excuse not to preach the gospel.

The Wind and Waves Stilled
(8:23–27; Mark 4:36–41; Luke 8:22–25)

[23] We don't know if the two who offered excuses were among the "disciples [who] followed him" (v. 23) onto the ship. In verse 18, we read that when Jesus

saw the multitudes gathered, He "gave commandment to depart unto the other side."

[24] The disciples who did enter the ship with Him soon found themselves in a precarious situation:

> And, behold, there arose a great **storm** [*seismós* {4578}, shaking] in the sea, so that the ship was covered with the waves: but He was **sleeping** [*ekátheuden*, the imperfect tense of *katheúdō* {2518}, to sleep; from *katá* {2596}, an intensive; and *heúdō* {n.f.}, to sleep, metaphorically to rest, be still; used of the mind or heart, to be at ease or content]. (a.t.)

We derive our English words "seismic" and "seismology," the study of earthquakes, from *seismós* a word used in the New Testament to describe upheavals on earth (Matt. 24:7; 27:54; 28:2; Acts 16:26; Rev. 6:12; 8:5; 11:13; 16:18) and in heaven (Heb. 12:26; Rev. 11:19). This is the first time the word *seismós* is used in the New Testament. In Matthew 24:7 Jesus predicted that earthquakes would increase randomly—"in divers [*katá*, according to] places [from *tópos* {5117}, place]"—prior to His return in glory. Earthquakes accompanied the giving of the Mosaic Law at Sinai (Ex. 19:18), the death (Matt. 27:54) and resurrection (Matt. 28:2) of our Lord, and the freeing of Paul and Silas from jail (Acts 16:26). They will accompany other judgments at the end of the age (Zech. 14:5; Rev. 16:18).

This shaking occurred either under the sea or in the sea, and huge waves pounded and overflowed the boat until it was in danger of sinking. It is interesting that the disciples were following Him when this happened. Obedience to Christ does not guarantee freedom from trouble or danger, but it does give us opportunities to trust Him in the storm.

Jesus' reaction to all this is amazing. He was enjoying a sound sleep, totally oblivious to the violent storm around him.

[25] Not so the disciples at this point, who were alert but panic-stricken:

> And his disciples **came to** [from *prosérchomai* {4334} from *prós* {4314}, towards; and *érchomai* {2064}, to come] him and **awoke** [from *egeírō* {1453}, to raise] him, saying, Lord, save us: we **perish** [from *apóllumi* {622}].

A violent storm often causes people to think God has abandoned them. The disciples' cry reflected that terror. The verb *apóllumi*, to **perish,** which is often juxtaposed with *sōzō* (4982), to save, defines both physical (Matt. 8:25; 14:30; 16:25; 27:40, 42, 49; etc.) and spiritual death (Matt. 1:21; Acts 2:40; Rom. 5:9, etc.). Although they were bewildered and terrified, the disciples—with the exception of Judas—were in danger only of losing their physical lives.

But they could be confident of their eternal destinies in the midst of this violent storm.

[26] Jesus' response to their fears was a powerful rebuke to their two enemies.

> And he saith unto them, Why are ye **fearful** [from *deilós* {1169}, either the adjective "cowardly" or the noun "coward"], O ye of **little faith** [from *oligópistos* {3640} from *olígos* {3641}, small; and *pistós* {4102}, belief, faith]? Then he arose, and **rebuked** [from *epitimáō* {2008}] the winds and the sea; and there was a **great** [from *mégas* {3173}] **calm** [*galénē* {1055}, tranquil, serene state].

These are not very flattering terms. "**Cowards**" (from *deilós*) will be the first group thrown into the lake of fire at the end of the millennial age (Rev. 21:8). Moreover, Jesus asked His disciples, "Why are you cowards, little-faith[ed]?" (a.t.). He implied that they had no legitimate excuse for cowardice and lack of faith when they were with the Master, in spite of the storm and His inactivity.

The adjective *deilós* occurs only in Matthew 8:26; Mark 4:40, and Revelation 21:8. In the latter reference, the "**fearful**" are cast into the lake of fire and brimstone along with the unbelieving, abominable, murderers, whoremongers, sorcerers, idolaters, and liars. These persons have such hard hearts that they are named by their dominant, habitual sins. They are not guilty of single instances of these offenses; rather, the offenses have consumed their souls.

"**Little faith**" does not mean no faith. Later, Jesus said that it takes only a grain of mustard seed of faith to move mountains (Matt. 17:20). However, faith is not something we can muster up on our own. It not only is a gift of God (Gal. 5:22; Eph. 2:8, 9; Phil. 1:29), but it is cultivated by the "husbandman" (*geōrgós* [1092], farmer; here, the Father; John 15:1) who prunes His choice vines. Since timidity is contrary to faith, we should repent of this with all the power God has given us. Paul told us, "God hath not given us the spirit of fear [from *deilía* {1167}]; but of power, and of love, and of a sound mind" (2 Tim. 1:7).

Although Jesus called the disciples fearful (from *deilós*) here, He graciously did something to create courage and faith in their hearts. He rebuked the winds and the sea, possibly addressing the angels that stirred them up (Rev. 7:1), much like He addressed Satan while looking at Peter. The Lord showed that He was God, the creator and sustainer of the universe (Col. 1:16. 17), the power over chaos and the restorer of peace.

[27] The disciples response? Amazement!

> But the men **marveled** [from *thaumázō* {2296}, to admire, to wonder at a *thaúma* {2295}, a marvel, wonder, miracle], saying, **What kind** [*potapós*

{4217}, what kind, what sort of; Mark 4:41 and Luke 8:25 both substitute the equivalent *tís* {5101}] is this that even the winds and sea **obey** [from *hupakoúō* {5219}] Him? (a.t.)

The Greek text shows that the question is much broader than the English versions indicate. None of the three Synoptic Gospels has the words "of man." The disciples were not asking the restricted question, "What manner **of man** is this?" but rather and more universally, "What kind of being is this? What are we dealing with here?" In their astonishment, they did not know whether they were in the presence of a Spirit-filled man, an angel, or a God. It did not make sense to them that a man could command the wind and sea. Surely, this was the domain of the sovereign God! What kind of being [cf. *monogeneâs* {3439} in John 3:16] is this?

Jesus Christ's sovereign command produced obedience, as it always does. This was the decree of God, a command of reality, not some ethical advisory that the sea and wind could potentially reject.

Two Demon-Possessed Men Healed
(8:28–34; Mark 5:1–21; Luke 8:26–40)

[28] The exact location where this healing occurred is a matter of conjecture. It was possibly near a town close to the lake called Gergesa (UBS: Gadara).

Two "**demoniacs**" (from *daimonízomai* [1139], literally, "ones being demonized") are mentioned in this verse, whereas Mark 5:2 and Luke 8:27 mention only one of them. They were so "**fierce**" (from *chalepós* [5467], violent, wild, as spoken of the "last days" in 2 Tim. 3:1) that no one "**could**" (from *ischúō* [2480], to have strength) pass by that road, that is, without an escort or weapons.

The Bible assumes the existence of demons. Satan or Beelzebub (954) is called "the prince of the devils [demons]" (Matt. 9:34). Satan tempted Adam and Eve in the Garden of Eden at the very beginning of human history according to the record in Genesis. First John 3:8 describes the devil (Satan) as sinning "from the beginning." His disposition to challenge the veracity of God was shown at the beginning of creation. God did not originally create Satan to be evil. Satan chose to become evil, and since God cannot tolerate evil, He cast Satan out of heaven. The devil is called that "**old** [from *archaíos* {744}, original, beginning] **serpent** [from *óphis* {3789}, a nonpoisonous snake, as compared with *échidna* {2191}, viper]" (Rev. 20:2), no doubt an allusion to the serpent in the Garden of Eden (Gen. 3:4).

Demons are immaterial, evil beings endowed with personalities that can possess both unbelievers (v. 28) and animals (v. 32), causing spiritual and physical disorders. However, people who have physical disorders are not usually possessed by demons (Mark 5:25–34). Demonic possession may be permanent or temporary (see Matt. 12:43, 44).

In Mark 1:23 and 5:2, we read the phrase, "a man with an unclean spirit [from *pneúma* {4151}]." Christ revealed that God is a Spirit (John 4:24). As Spirit, He knows all spirits. He sends good angels from heaven to minister to people on earth (Heb. 1:14), but the "angel of the bottomless pit" (Rev. 9:11) and demons harm humans and are properly called evil (*ponērá* [4190], harmful; Luke 7:21; 8:2) spirits. Unclean spirits also can vex unbelievers (Luke 6:18). But the greater power of the Spirit of God causes believers to overcome the spirit of antichrist:

> And every spirit that confesseth not that Jesus Christ is come in the flesh is not of God: and this is that spirit of antichrist, whereof ye have heard that it should come; and even now already is it in the world. Ye are of God, little children, and have overcome them: because greater is he that is in you, than he that is in the world. (1 John 4:3, 4)

While in the Gospels evil spirits seem to indwell mostly adult men, demons seem to be no respecter of age or gender. Jesus cast evil spirits from women (Luke 8:2; 13:11, 16), a young boy (Luke 9:39), and also the little daughter of the Syro-Phoenician woman (Mark 7:25).

[29] "And, **behold** [*idoú* {2400}]," the familiar imperative calling attention to something extraordinary (see Matt. 3:16), in this case, the recognition of Jesus Christ as the Son of God: "[The demons] cried out, saying, What have we to do with thee, Jesus, thou **Son** [from *huiós* {5207}] **of God?**"

[30–34] In Matthew 4:3, 6, the devil said to Jesus, "If [*ei* {1487}, the 'if' of supposition] thou be the Son of God," a suppositional "if." The **"if"** in verse 31 is also the suppositional *ei* ("suppose" or "inasmuch as"), presupposing a direct recognition of Jesus' Spirit-to-spirit opposition. These demons were forced to confess not only the Lord's knowledge of them but also the lack of any common ground between them. They knew that Jesus would oppose their evil work and inevitably cast them into the lake of fire (Rev. 20:10).

Already assuming that Christ would cast them out, they asked **permission** (from *epitrépō* [2010]) to enter a herd of swine.

The death of an entire herd of pigs must have been a serious financial loss to these people, so they "**besought**" (from *parakaléō* [3870]) Jesus to leave their area (v. 34). Evidently, they did not consider the healing of the demoniacs worth the financial loss of their pigs.

9

⚜

Sins Forgiven Only by God
(9:1–8; Mark 2:1–12; Luke 5:18–26)

[1] Jesus' "**own** [from *ídios* {2398}] city," His "home" according to Mark 2:1 NASB, refers to Capernaum (v. 1). Here friends brought to Jesus a paralyzed man, who was carrying a burden of sin on top of his wretched physical condition.

Mark comments that so many people were gathered together at the house that "there was no longer room, not even near the door" (Mark 2:2 NASB). Unable to approach Jesus, the man's friends literally "removed [from *apostegázō* {648}, to unroof] the roof [from *stégē* {4721}; a.t.]" and lowered him on a pallet in front of Jesus (Mark 2:2–4).

[2] Matthew begins his narrative with "**Behold**" (*idoú* [2400], the imperative of *eídon* [1492], the aorist of *horáō* [3708], to perceive), calling attention to the extraordinary (Matt. 3:16) miracle. The Word made flesh was about to perform in accord with His purpose for coming to earth: "Thou shalt call his name Jesus: for he shall save his people from their sins" (Matt. 1:21). The reader is alerted to this additional proof that Jesus Christ is the omnipotent Son of God. The greatest manifestation of the Son of man's authority on earth was His ability to forgive sins. To declare that a man's sins were forgiven was to claim to be God, a blasphemous contention to unbelieving Jews.

The Lord saw more than a paralyzed man lying on a bed. Both Matthew and Mark note Jesus' perception of the friends' persistence and creativity in bringing the paralytic before Him. The phrase "**seeing their faith**" translates the aorist participle *idōn* (from *eídon* [1492]) and could properly be translated as "having seen their faith" or "when He saw their faith . . . [cf. Mark 2:5, which uses the same phrase]." Faith, of course, is not seen physically; it is a spiritual reality, something beneath the empirical gaze of people and angels but not beyond the Son of God's knowledge. "Their faith" probably included the faith of the sick man himself as well as the ones who brought him to Jesus. The man was surrounded by faith in the Lord.

Jesus spoke immediately to the man's spiritual condition:

> **Son** [*téknon* {5043}, child], **be of good cheer** [from *tharséo* {2293}, to take courage]; thy sins **be forgiven** [from *aphíemi* {863}] thee.

This was planned. Jesus could have healed the man first, if that had been His intention. But by telling the man his sins were forgiven and knowing that the scribes would object that He was usurping God's authority, He laid the groundwork for the proof of this authority that followed—the physical healing itself.

[3] Amazingly, the scribes did not outwardly contend with Jesus, some of them saying only "within themselves, This man blasphemeth." Even though they believed that Jesus blasphemed by claiming to do something only God could do, they feared the people of faith (previous verse).

[4] Jesus attested His deity not only by His forgiving sins but also by His knowledge of the scribes' wicked thoughts.

And Jesus **knowing** [*idón*, the aorist participle of *eídon*, the aorist of *horáo* {3708}, to see and perceive] their **thoughts** [from *enthúmēsis* {1761} from *en* {1722}, in, within; and *thumós* {2372}, passionate thought as, e.g., evil reasoning and intent] said, "Wherefore **think ye** [from *enthuméomai* {1760}; Mark uses *dialogízomai* {1260}, to reason thoroughly] **evil** [from *ponērós* {4190}, malevolent things; here, motives] in your hearts?"

Even though healing could be accomplished through secondary causes, only God could forgive sins (Mark 2:7). Jesus healed many, but this was not His primary ministry on earth. He became incarnate to save us from our sins. Healing was a subordinate, authenticating ministry.

[5] The manner in which Jesus handled the scribes' objection is fascinating. He had already claimed He had authority to forgive sins by pronouncing forgiveness over the paralytic. But forgiveness—a new relationship with God—is invisible by nature. He knew the scribes would never accept what they could not see, but they would accept physical data as proof. Accordingly, He asked:

> For whether is **easier** [for *eukopóteros*, the comparative of *eúkopos* {n.f.}, easy; from *eu* {2095}, good; and *kópos* {2873}, labor}, to say, *Thy* sins be forgiven thee; or to say, Arise and walk?

This question demanded more from Jesus than the question, Which is easier for Me to pray for [as a man]? There is no mention of His praying or depending on God at all. Jesus actually claimed to have the full decretive power of the Almighty Himself! The scribes probably already dismissed the idea that Jesus' prayers would be answered, since "God heareth not sinners" (John 9:31), and Jesus had just blasphemed in their thinking. But now Jesus implied that He did not even need to pray; He only declared! Essentially, the question was this: Which is easier to decree (cause): forgiveness or healing? The man's sins were forgiven, but the scribes could not verify this. They could, however, verify a physical healing, especially of a paralyzed man. And they knew that only God could do this by commanding, "Arise!" If Jesus could not do this, He was exposing Himself to public ridicule.

[6] As usual, Jesus did not wait for His opponents to answer the unanswerable. No human can answer a question concerning the relative ease of two divine acts. Moreover, the notion "difficult for omnipotence" is contradictory. "Difficult" makes no sense to Omnipotence, since Omnipotence creates all forces out of nothing. Both healing and forgiveness are equally easy to a God who creates out of nothing.

> **But** [*dé* {1161}, i.e., "but regardless of how you may answer the question"] **that** [*hína* {2443}, in order that] you may **know** [from *eídon*, the aorist of *horáō* {3708}, to see and comprehend] that the Son of man has power on earth **to forgive** [*aphiénai*, the present active infinitive of *aphíēmi* {863}] **sins** [from *hamartía* {266}], (then said He to the palsied), **Having arisen** [*egertheís*, the aorist passive participle of *egeírō* {1453}, to rise up], **take up** [*áron*, the aorist active imperative of *aírō* {142}] your bed, and go to your house. (a.t.)

The present infinitive of *aphíēmi*, "forgive," encompasses the entire time of Jesus' ministry on earth, but here His authority to declare forgiveness (given in the active voice) was proven immediately by the paralytic's obedient response to the imperative "Arise!" The One who forgives by decree heals by decree; and no one but God can do such things. The scribes believed that God in heaven could forgive and heal but not the "Son of man . . . on earth." This was a new truth they could not accept.

Sin means to miss the mark, God's mark of perfection (Matt. 5:48). Matthew develops his theme of the Messiah who came to earth to "save His people from their sins" from the very beginning of his Gospel (Matt. 1:21; 3:6; 9:2, 6; 12:31; 26:28). With one exception ("all manner [from *pás* {3956}, all] of sin [*hamartía*]" in Matt. 12:31), he uses the plural noun, "sins," compared with John who prefers the singular "sin" (John 1:29; 8:34, 46; 9:41 [twice]; 15:22, 24; 16:9; 19:11), referring to the quality of sin. John uses the plural only in John 8:24 (twice); 9:34; and 20:23.

[7, 8] The proof was incontestable to the majority, though nothing specific is said of the scribes' reaction: "And [the paralytic] arose, and departed to

his house. But when the multitudes saw it, they marvelled, and glorified God, which had given such power unto men." Mark quotes the crowd as saying, "We never [*oudépote* {3763} from *ou* {3756}, not; *dé* {1161}, even; and *poté* {4218}, at any time] saw it thus [*hoútōs* {3779}, in this manner]" (a.t.; Mark 2:12).

While this was the general response of the crowd to the novelty (*oudépote hoútōs*) of this healing, we do not know whether the scribes joined them in glorifying God or just went away murmuring out of jealousy.

The Call of Matthew
(9:9; Mark 2:14; Luke 5:27–29)

[9] From this scene, Jesus moved on:

> And Jesus, **passing forth** [from *parágō* {3855} from *pará* {3844}, the closest proximity; and *ágō* {71}, to lead] from there, saw a man named Matthew, sitting at the **receipt of custom** [*telōnion* {5058}, an office where customs duties were received]: and He said to him, **Follow** [from *akolouthéō* {190} from *a* {1}, a particle of union; and *kéleuthos* {n.f.}, a road; "accompany"] Me. And he arose, and followed Him. (a.t.)

Matthew was a tax collector, a post granted by Roman authorities to a high bidder and often used to extort money above the requisite taxes for the personal benefit of the collector. The Jews considered this officially endorsed robbery and betrayal by one of their own people. In Matthew's case, Jesus saw a man burdened with the guilt of this sin against his own people. The Lord sees inner suffering in the worst of individuals, while people judge by external appearances (1 Sam. 16:7).

Jesus did not ask the advice of others concerning His invitation to Matthew nor did He make His call conditional. He neither added contingencies or promises but simply said, "Follow Me." Matthew's call was like Saul's (Acts 9:1–9). Saul even asked who it was when the Lord called him by name from heaven. In both instances, the Lord authoritatively commanded responses (Matt. 7:28, 29).

Note Matthew's immediate response to the sovereign grace of Christ: "And **having arisen** [*anastás*, the aorist participle of *anístēmi* {450}, to stand up], he followed Him" (a.t.). This is a response of action, not just words (cf. Luke 9:57–62).

Jesus Answered the Pharisees
(9:10–13; Mark 2:15–17; Luke 5:29–32)

[10] Matthew was impressed enough with this encounter to immediately host a party at his home in the Lord's honor. He invited many other tax collectors and sinners (Luke 5:29–32) to meet Jesus and the disciples. What an interesting mix—tax collectors, sinners, uneducated fishermen, and Jesus Christ, the Son of God!

> And it came to pass, **as** Jesus **sat at meat** [from *anákeimai* {345}, to sit at a table for a meal] in the house, **behold** [*idoú* {2400}, the imperative of *eídon* {1492}, the aorist of *horáō* {3708}, to perceive, calling attention to the extraordinary {see Matt. 3:16}], many publicans and sinners came and **sat down with** [from *sunanákeimai* {4873}, to sit together for the purpose of eating] him and his disciples.

"**Behold**" directs our attention to the surprise that publicans (tax collectors) and sinners would eat with Jesus and His disciples. The verb "**sat down with**" is also used in Matthew 14:9 for Herod's banquet with his friends. Frequently, when sinners dine together, they talk about sinful subjects or even conspire to sin further. Herod's banquet, for example, was the occasion of the beheading of John the Baptist (Mark 6:22–28). But Matthew opened his house to publicans and other burdened sinners who wanted to meet Jesus. What an encouraging example Matthew is of a person's witness to others of Christ.

Not all who dined in the Lord's presence were true believers "in Christ" (John 14:20), as Judas certainly proved.

> Then shall ye begin to say, We have eaten and drunk in thy presence, and thou hast taught in our streets. But he shall say, I tell you, I know you not whence ye are; depart from me, all *ye* workers of iniquity. (Luke 13:26, 27)

[11] The reaction of the Pharisees was traditional: "Holy" people do not mix with sinners. The word "Pharisees," in fact, means "separated ones." But Jesus was not a Pharisee. For Him, while holiness certainly does not mix with sin, the holy Son of God did mix with sinners in order to save them. To avoid direct confrontation with Christ, the Pharisees addressed the disciples: "Why eateth **your Master** [*didáskalos* {1320}, teacher] **with** [*metá* {3326}] publicans and sinners?"

While we list *metá* as a synonym of *sún* in *The Complete Word Study Dictionary: New Testament*, 1333, we also note that *sún* frequently connotes a nearer, closer connection (1331). In their self-righteousness, the Pharisees could not tolerate any proximity to publicans and sinners. Holiness to them meant distancing themselves from such vile people. Notice how they even distanced themselves from Jesus by saying "your Master."

[12] Jesus overheard their question and explained in His unique way why He had chosen to eat with these people:

> They that are **whole** [from *ischúō* {2480}, to have *ischús* {2479}, natural strength] have no **need** [from *chreía* {5532}] of a **physician** [from *iatrós* {2395}], but they that are sick. (a.t.)

This short response said a great deal. The analogy implied that these publicans and sinners were sick—with sin. They knew they were sick and He was the doctor. It implied that He was a doctor wholly independent of their beliefs. Finally, it implied that some others thought they were well and did not require a doctor. The next verse clarifies the Lord's meaning a bit further.

Jesus' use of *iatrós* showed further that people need more than a psychologist. The Old Testament picture of regeneration is nothing short of a heart transplant (Ezek. 36:26). Jesus proved that He had the credentials to restore all spheres of human existence permeated by sin: spirit, soul, and body (1 Thess. 5:23).

[13] Jesus quoted from Hosea 6:6, a prophecy in which God stated that He prefers that people show mercy rather than sacrifice bulls and goats—a frontal assault on the formalism of the Pharisees:

> But **having gone** [*poreuthéntes*, the aorist passive participle of *poreúomai* {4198}, not the imperative "go ye" but the fact prior to the imperative expressed in *máthete*], **learn** [*máthete*, the aorist imperative of *manthánō* {3129}, the verb associated with *mathētḗs* {3101}, disciple] what that means, I desire [*thélō* {2309}, to will, to wish to have] **mercy** [from *éleos* {1656}, compassionate and active pity] and not **sacrifice** [from *thusía* {2378}]: for I did not **come** [from *érchomai* {2064}] to call the righteous but sinners to repentance. (a.t.)

The terms in this statement paralleled those in the prior verse. The "righteous" corresponded to those who did not need a physician, and "sinners" corresponded to the sick. Jesus did not call the righteous, just as a doctor does not make house calls on those who are well. The purpose of His call was to invite those who were sick in sin to repent of their sins.

To soften the blow, Jesus stated the accused object twice in the third person—"they that" (v. 12) and "the righteous" (v. 13)—but the Pharisees knew these words were aimed directly at them.

Obviously, not all sacrifice is antithetical to acts of mercy. A woman might sacrifice her life to save a drowning child, for example. God commands a "sacrifice of praise" (Jer. 33:11; Heb. 13:15) that has nothing to do with showing mercy and does not fall under His condemnation of sacrifice. The injunction in Hosea is restricted to the external sacrifice of bulls and goats, that is, the legalism of the Pharisees, not to the internal sacrifices of praise to God and service to His people.

God desires His people to be merciful, as He is. Thus, He describes Himself with these words, "I will have mercy [from *eleéō* {1657}] on whom I will have mercy, and I will have compassion [from *oikteírō* {3627}, to have compassion, which includes emotion as well as action—a deep empathy for its objects] on whom I will have compassion" (Rom. 9:15). The Lord Jesus grieved over humanity's lost condition and sacrificed Himself, "the sacrificial Lamb [*amnós* {286}, a lamb destined to be sacrificed, cf. Acts 8:32; 1 Pet. 1:19] of God who takes away the sin of the world" (John 1:29; a.t.). As they appeared in the New Testament, the self-righteous Pharisees grieved over no one; they loaded up people with burdens too difficult to bear; and, as Jesus said, they did not extend so much as a finger to lighten the loads (Luke 11:46). But they did sacrifice bulls and goats.

God desired the mercy of self-sacrifice rather than the legalism of animal sacrifices.

Jesus Teaches His Disciples
(9:14–17; Mark 2:18–22; Luke 5:33–39)

[14] The disciples of John the Baptist and the Pharisees had one thing in common. They both fasted (from *nēsteúō* [3522], a total or partial abstinence from food).

In Israel, public fasts were common, such as the one appointed for the Day of Atonement that lasted through the month of October (Acts 27:9) and to which great merit was attached. The Pharisees fasted frequently, sometimes twice a week (Luke 18:12). The fasts mentioned in the New Testament were usually private (Matt. 6:16–18; 9:14; Mark 2:18, 19; Luke 5:33; 18:12; Acts 10:30; 13:2, 3) and were connected with sorrow and mourning (*penthéō* [3996], Matt. 9:15).

The question in this verse was probably occasioned by the different lifestyles of Jesus and John the Baptist. John's disciples asked why they and the Pharisees fasted "**frequently**" (from *polús* [4183], a.t.; lit.; "many things" meaning "many times," synonymous with *pollákis* [4178]), whereas the Messiah, to whom John the Baptist pointed, and His disciples did not.

Earlier in this Gospel, we noted that the Pharisees were motivated to fast by human praise, but Jesus cautioned His disciples against this hypocrisy:

Moreover when ye fast, be not, as the hypocrites, of a sad countenance: for they disfigure their faces, that they may appear unto men to fast. Verily I say unto you, They have their reward. (Matt. 6:16)

[15] Jesus' answer set the matter at rest. Using the analogy of marriage, He said that fasting was an expression of grief over the absence of the bridegroom. As long as the bridegroom was present, his friends did not need to fast.

And Jesus said unto them, The children of the bridechamber are not **able** [from *dúnamai* {1410}, to be able] to mourn, as long as the **bridegroom** [*numphíos* {3566}] is with them, are they? But the days will come when the bridegroom **shall be taken** [*aparthḗ*, the aorist passive subjunctive of *apaírō* {522}, to take away] from them, and then they will fast. (a.t.)

The "groom" had come in the incarnation of the Word (John 1:1, 14), and this was a time of rejoicing (Matt. 25:1). However, the time would come when this bridegroom would be "taken away," the aorist tense more likely specifying the event of Christ's ascension (Acts 1:9–11) rather than His physical death. It's true that the disciples grieved for Jesus after His death, but the resurrection three days later was a time of great, overcompensating joy. The separation of the Lord from His people following His ascension into heaven, however, has been much longer, and we find several references to the early church fasting and mourning for His presence (see Acts 14:23; 1 Cor. 7:5). How we, too, long for the return of the Lord—"Come, Lord Jesus" (Rev. 22:20)! The Lord's presence in the Spirit converts unbelievers (Acts 4:29–37). To not see this happen for a time is grievous.

Yet even though the bridegroom would ascend to His Father in heaven, He promised His disciples (His bride) that He would not leave them as orphans (from *orphanós* [3737], bereaved, parentless, comfortless; John 14:18), but He would be with them until the consummation of the age in the Person of the Holy Spirit (Matt. 28:20; John 14:16–18: note the change in subject from the third person Holy Spirit, "Him," to the first person, "I will come to you"). When the present age is consummated, the bridegroom will return to wed His bride (Rev. 19:7; 21:2).

[16, 17] Jesus resumed His attack on the legalism of the Pharisees:

No man [*oudeís* {3762}, no one] puts a **piece** [*epíblēma* {1915}, patch] of **new** [from *ágnaphos* {46}, unshrunk] **cloth** [from *rhákos* {4470}] on an **old** [from *palaiós* {3820}] garment, because that which is put in to fill it up takes from the garment, and the **rent** [*schísma* {4978}, tear, divide] is **made worse.** **Neither** [*oudé* {3761} from *ou* {3756}, "not"; and *dé* {1161}, even; "not even," "nor"] do men put new wine into old bottles: else the bottles **break** [from *rhḗgnumi* {4486}, to break in pieces], and the wine **runs out** [from *ekchéō* {1632}, to pour out], and the bottles perish: but they put **new** [from *néos*

{3501}, younger] wine into **new** [from *kainós* {2537}, qualitatively new] bottles, and both **are preserved** [from *suntēréō* {4933}, to conserve]. (a.t.)

Jesus used illustrations from the natural world to display the irrationality of hypocrisy. These hypocrites layered legalistic, external conformity to the Law over their wicked hearts and, from the analogy, their hearts were "**made worse.**" The irony was that they did not do such foolish things to cloth nor wine because they knew better. Apparently, they were more concerned with preserving worldly things than their own souls.

In general, cottons and wools used to shrink considerably with the first washing. (First century people did not have the preshrunken synthetics we have today.) Applying the metaphor, trying to patch up an old, sinful life by adding something new is useless. It only makes matters worse. What is needed is a qualitatively new garment (note the contrast above between the "chronologically new" [from *néos*] wine and the "qualitatively new" [from *kainós*] bottles, as well as "the robe of righteousness" and "the garments of salvation"; Isa. 61:10). "If any man is in Christ," Paul told us, "he is a new [from *kainós*] creation [*ktísis* {2937}]" (2 Cor. 5:17; a.t.).

Similarly, wineskins dry out and harden with age and use. As new wine ferments and expands, new skins expand with it but not old, inflexible ones. They split, the wine is lost, and the flask is "**destroyed**" (from *apóllumi* [622], to perish, a word that speaks figuratively of eternal perdition, the judgment on persevering unbelief; John 3:36).

Jesus did not come to add new commands to the old Jewish religion. He came to pour out His Spirit to create faith, a fruit of the Spirit (Gal. 5:22), in the hearts of His people whom He came to save (Matt. 1:21). The Jews could not accept this. Their religion was "old wineskins" that could neither expand nor accept new wine. Salvation is not a patch on something old, like bad behavior; it involves a new nature. Consequently, Jesus became a "rock of offense" to the Jews (Rom. 9:33; 1 Pet. 2:8).

Jesus Heals a Woman with an Issue of Blood and Raises Jairus' Daughter from the Dead
(9:18–26; Mark 5:22–43; Luke 8:41–56)

[18] An elder in the synagogue of Capernaum named Jairus (see Mark 5:22) came to Jesus on behalf of his daughter who had died. Like Nicodemus (John 3:1), he was a distinguished "**ruler**" (*árchōn* [758]) devoted to Judaism and prominent in the synagogue.

Before the crowds and the critical Pharisees surrounding Jesus, Jairus boldly worshiped Christ. "**Worshipped**" is from the word *prosekúnei*, the imperfect tense of *proskunéō* (4352), to fall prostate, from *prós* (4314), to; and *kunéō* (n.f.), to kiss, to adore. The imperfect tense means the ruler continued to worship Jesus.

Jairus means "Jehovah enlightens," a name that took on some prophetic color as Jairus apparently had been enlightened by Jesus' teaching in the synagogues of Galilee (Matt. 4:23, 24). Although not everything Jesus taught was recorded, this sudden introduction shows that Jesus' words had produced faith in Jairus' heart that He could raise the dead. He loved his daughter and was grief-stricken over her loss.

The verb *eteleútēsen*, translated "**dead**"—more accurately, "**she died**"— is closer in meaning to "**she's finished**," derived from the root noun "end" (*télos* [5056]), a reference to the girl's life in the flesh, not her existence in spirit. "**Even now**" (*árti* [737]) implies that she had already died. In spite of this, the ruler had no doubt the Lord could raise her from the dead: "But come and lay thy hand upon her, and **she shall live** [from *záō* {2198}, to live]." If this ruler were a Pharisee, he believed his daughter was alive in spirit, but he wanted the Lord to restore her composite existence of spirit and flesh. This is what he meant by "she shall live" (again).

[19, 20] Jesus could have raised Jairus' daughter from a distance with a single word (Matt. 8:8, 16), but He decided to go to Jairus' house. As the Son of God, He was aware that along the way He would encounter "a woman who had been **hemorrhaging** [a.t.; from *haimorroéō* {131} from *haíma* {129}, blood; and *rhéō* {4482}, to flow] for twelve years" (a.t.).

The Old Testament taught that bodily issues were generally unclean. If clean persons touched unclean persons or things, they became unclean also. What torture this woman must have endured for twelve years! No wonder she came behind Jesus and only "**touched** [from *háptomai* {680}] the hem of His **outer garment** [from *himátion* {2440}; that is, His robe]" (a.t.). No one but the Lord Himself could detect such faith in her heart, and absolutely nothing could make Him unclean, since He was innately pure. To the contrary, anything unclean that contacted Him was overwhelmingly cleansed: "Wash me, and I shall be whiter than snow" (Ps. 51:7).

[21] Evidently, the woman knew who Jesus was: "**If** [*eán* {1437}, the 'if' of potential] only **I may touch** [from *háptomai* {680}, to touch] His garment, **I shall be made whole** [from *sōzō* {4982}, to be saved]." (a.t.)

The woman's faith was genuine and extensive; she believed she could be healed physically by merely touching Jesus' outer garment.

[22] Jesus understood her fear and comforted her. He did not attribute her healing to touching the hem of His garment but to the gift of faith He saw in her heart (Eph. 2:8). The aorist verb *esōthē* (from *sōzō*, to save physically, spiritually, or both) in the expression, "the woman **was saved**" (a.t.), refers to the immediate healing, while the perfect tense of the same verb, *sésōken*, "your faith **has saved** you," stretches back to the woman's faith prior to the physical healing. *Sōzō* is used frequently to refer to physical healing (Mark 5:23, 28, 34; Luke 7:50; 8:36, 48; John 11:12; Acts 4:9; James 5:15) as well as to the bestowal of eternal life (Matt. 18:11; Rom. 11:14; 1 Cor. 1:21; 1 Tim. 4:16; Heb. 7:25; James 1:21). The meaning of the verb can be determined from the contexts.

This explains why Jesus called this woman "**daughter**" (from *thugátēr* [2364], female child). She had a personal relationship with Christ prior to the physical healing and was a child of God by faith, as evidenced by her words, "If I can only touch the hem of His garment, I will be made whole" (a.t.).

In another place, Jesus referred to a woman of faith as a "daughter of Abraham": "And ought not this woman, being a daughter of Abraham, whom Satan hath bound, lo, these eighteen years, be loosed from this bond on the sabbath day? (Luke 13:16, cf. Rom. 4:16)

[23] By the time Jesus arrived at Jairus' house, "**minstrels**" (from *aulētḗs* [834], flute players) were playing inside in readiness for the funeral procession.

Reading this verse in conjunction with 2 Chronicles 35:25 and Jeremiah 9:17, 18; 48:36–38, we learn that from the earliest days mourning was accompanied by the music of pipes or flutes. The sorrow of death was commercialized early in Israel's history. Flute players and professional mourners were hired by the well-to-do, like Jairus. Yet even the poorest in Israel provided two flutes and a waiter during mourning. The waiter was usually a woman who attended to the visitors.

The crowd was "**noisy**" (from *thorubéō* [2350], to disturb). The verb, used here for the first time in the New Testament, formally means to make noise—in the context, wailing or lamentation. The crowd was loud because the people were emotionally distraught over the death of one so young. But Jairus' daughter was probably a believer, having been brought up by a faithful father.

According to Luke 8:51, Jesus permitted only Peter, James, John, and the girl's parents to remain with him. From Luke 8:52 and the continuing narrative in Matthew, it seems that many people were in the house already.

[24] Planning to resurrect the girl but hindered by the crowd of unbelievers, Jesus dismissed them with a statement that generated ridicule:

Give place [*anachōreíte*, the present active imperative of *anachōréō* {402} from *aná* {303}, again; and *chōréō* {5562}, to space out, depart, withdraw; from *chōra* {5561}, region, space; "make room"], **for** [*gár* {1063}, because] the **little girl** [*korásion* {2877}] did not [*ou* {3756}] **die** [from *apothnḗskō* {599}] but **sleeps** [from *katheúdō* {2518}, to sleep]. And they laughed Him to scorn [*kategélōn* {2606}]. (a.t.)

When Jesus said that the girl was asleep, the crowd immediately "**was ridiculing**" (*kategélōn*, the *imperfect* tense of *katageláō* [2606], to publicly mock, ridicule, scorn) Him. (This compound verb is used only in connection with this incident; see also Mark 5:40; Luke 8:53.) The crowd considered Christ's equating death with sleep to be ridiculous.

Jesus did not mean that the girl had not died physically, for she had, but the crowd misunderstood him. By using a verb with a double meaning and knowing in advance the crowd's mental attitude, the Lord set the stage for a change from derision to praise. Only one meaning of the verb "died" makes sense in this context—the little girl did not die spiritually (eternal loss) but only slept (temporal rest) in death.

Before they entered the room where the body of the girl lay (Mark 5:39), Jesus attempted to comfort the girl's parents by saying that their daughter was asleep. Two verbs in Greek mean "to sleep": *katheúdō* and *koimáomai* (2837). Both highlight the impermanence of the dissolution of body and soul prior to the day of judgment, as Acts 24:15 says, "There shall be a resurrection of the dead, both of the just and unjust" (cf. John 5:28, 29). The verb used here, *katheúdō*, is also used in the Septuagint version of Daniel 12:2 to describe the preresurrection, temporary slumber of the physical bodies of both believers and unbelievers:

> And many of them that sleep [from *katheúdō*] in the dust of the earth shall awake, some to everlasting life, and some to shame and everlasting contempt. (Sept.; Dan. 12:2)

Katheúdō emphasizes laying down in sleep, being derived from *katá* (2596), an intensive, or *kátō* (2736), down; and *heúdō* (n.f.), to sleep. It is used for the first time in Matthew 8:24 when Jesus fell sound asleep in the midst of a storm while crossing the Sea of Galilee. The second use of *katheúdō* is found here in verse 24. The second verb for "sleep" (*koimáomai*) is used more frequently to refer to the death of believers (Matt. 27:52; John 11:11; Acts 7:60; 13:36; 1 Cor. 7:39; 11:30; 15:6, 18, 20, 51; 1 Thess. 4:13–15; 2 Pet. 3:4), which is why in modern Greek a cemetery is known as *koimētérion* (n.f.), the place of sleep. Both *katheúdō* and *koimáomai* probably encompass both the natural sleep of the body and the supernatural rest of a believer's spirit following physical death.

[25] So the crowd was "**put forth**" (from *ekbállō* [1544], to eject, forcibly cast out; from *ek* [1537], out of; and *bállō* [906], to cast, throw, drive out). Their unbelief and ridicule made them spiritually unworthy to witness a resurrection. For the same reason, Jesus did not display His resurrected body to unbelievers.

Jesus, however, permitted the parents and His disciples (see v. 19) to witness the girl's resurrection (Mark 5:40). The miracle occurred at the touch of His hand. Luke the physician describes the event: "And her spirit [*pneúma* {4151}, the inner person that departs at death and continues on apart from the body; see 1 Thess. 5:23 and the author's book, *Life After Death*] came again, and she arose [from *anístēmi* {450}, to rise; Matthew uses *ēgérthē*, the aorist tense of *egeírō* {1453}, to rise up] straightway; and he commanded to give her meat" (Luke 8:55).

The little girl was restored to her former state and arose. This was an earthly resurrection. The resurrection God promises us is not a restoration to the physical life as we now know it, but a qualitatively new state of being where spirit predominates in human personality, as described by Paul in 1 Corinthians 15. (See the author's exegetical study of 1 Cor. 15 entitled, *Conquering the Fear of Death*.)

[26] The "**fame**" (*phḗmē* [5345], fame, report, news) of Jesus spread throughout all that land. This is the only fame worth spreading.

Jesus Heals Two Blind Men
(9:27–31)

[27] By now everybody in Galilee and the surrounding area must have heard that Jesus had raised Jairus' daughter from the dead. Among them were two blind men.

As Jesus "**departed**" (from *parágō* [3855], to pass on further; see also v. 9) from this region, the two followed Jesus (cf. 20:29, 30), crying out, "Son of David." The Syro-Phoenician woman (15:22), the blind men of Jericho (20:30), and the multitude witnessing His triumphal entry into Jerusalem (21:9)also used this messianic title.

Although these men desperately wanted and needed their eyesight, they did not ask for it directly. Instead, they simply said, "**Have mercy** [from *eleéō*

{1653}] on us." Mercy is the relief God brings to the consequences of sin. God gives us both grace and mercy (1 Tim. 1:2; 2 Tim. 1:2; 2 John 3). Although grace saves us (Eph. 2:8), we still will die as a result of Adam's original sin (1 Cor. 15:22). In all our sufferings, however, we experience God's mercy; and as His children, He asks us to show mercy to others (Matt. 5:7).

Although blind, these men could "see" that they were suffering the consequences of sin. Their request was for relief and mercy with respect to their blindness, but they left it in the Lord's hands to determine the means of relief. That is the best prayer we can offer to the Lord in the midst of suffering. We should seek relief but not try to dictate to God what kind to give us.

[28] Jesus then entered the house (we are not told whose), and the blind men approached Him.

The Lord's next question implied that their request for mercy was an indirect request for sight: "Believe ye that I am able to do this?" Just as faith was present in several others Jesus had healed (the man sick with palsy, vv. 1, 2; Jairus' daughter, vv. 18–25; the woman with an issue of blood, vv. 20–22), so it was with these two blind men.

They quickly responded, "Yea, Lord!" They now addressed the "Son of David" as "Lord." This is the "yea, Lord" of implicit faith, as we find the "yea, Lord" of deep humility in the Syro-Phoenician woman (Mark 7:28) and the "yea, Lord" of absolute love in Peter (John 21:15).

[29] Here also, as in Matthew 8:15; 9:20, 21, the verb *háptomai* (680), to touch, to affect, or influence, is used. The result was immediate.

[30] "**Straitly charged**" is translated from *embrimáomai* (1690), which means to admonish strongly or charge strictly, to warn against disobedience, implying that Jesus expected obedience and had a reason for His command. The same prohibition was given to the cleansed leper in Matthew 8:4.

The general reason the Lord did not want most of His miracles publicized (8:4; 12:16; 16:20; 17:9) is that He did not want people to acclaim Him as the Messiah prematurely. He knew He must first suffer and die before being enthroned as King (John 6:14, 15). Nor did He want to arouse premature hostility from the Romans out of fear that a competing king had arisen. There was a perfect time for everything, however, Jesus made one exception to this general rule. After the demon-possessed man had been healed, he wanted to accompany Jesus. But Jesus told him to go home and tell his friends what God had done for him (Mark 5:19). Apparently, in that region there was no danger of a Jewish uprising that could precipitate a Roman backlash.

When public acclaim was likely to arise, Jesus avoided it. In this, too, we see His humility compared with the human tendency to prefer popularity. Jesus was God on earth, Emmanuel, but He chose the predominantly Gentile Galilee (Matt. 4:15) for much of His activity and even the desert where few ventured to live (Matt. 14:13). Then, too, less populated places had more room for large numbers to congregate. Those truly interested would make an effort to go, hear, and follow. In every case, Jesus carefully subordinated His fame (Matt. 12:16–21; note the emphasis on Gentiles in vv. 18, 21).

[31] The formerly blind men were so grateful and happy for their sight that they disobeyed the Lord and proclaimed the miracle throughout the land. The verb "**spread abroad**" is from *diaphēmízō* (1310), to advertise, from *diá* (1223), throughout; and *phēmízō* (n.f.), to speak, declare, which occurs in only two other places (Matt. 28:15; Mark 1:45). We can certainly understand their euphoria.

Jesus Heals a Mute Man
(9:32–34)

[32] Another "**behold**" (*idoú* [2400], the imperative of *eídon* [1492], the aorist of *horáō* [3708], to perceive, calling attention to the extraordinary; see vv. 2, 3, 10, 18, 20, also Matt. 3:16) draws our attention to a unique miracle that caused multitudes to stand in awe and the Pharisees to drum up fresh criticisms.

Someone brought a dumb man "possessed with a devil" (from *daimonízomai* [1139]) to Jesus. In the Greek, the word translated "**dumb**" is *kōphós* (2974), which indicates that the man was both deaf and dumb; he could not hear or speak. In Matthew 12:22 we find a demoniac who was both blind and dumb. These are two of the four instances (see also Mark 9:17–27; Luke 11:14) in Israel's long scriptural history where we read of dumbness being attributed to demon possession. We do find in Mark 7:32–37 a deaf man who spoke with difficulty (from *mogilálos* [3424]), but we are not told that the cause was demons.

[33] The uniqueness of this situation did not daunt Jesus. His presence alone was powerful enough to expel demons, and Matthew skips over the exorcist monologue found in the other synoptics:

And the **demon** [*daimónion* {1140}, the diminutive "little demon," implying that there may be "big" demons; certainly, there are "worse" according to

Matt. 12:45], **having been cast out** [from *ekbállō* {1544}, to cast out], the deaf person **spoke** [from *laléō* {2980}, to speak, emphasizing the breaking of silence more than the content of speech]. (a.t. See the author's exegetical works on 1 Cor. 12–14.)

In this verse, we have the reaction of the "**multitude**" (from *óchlos* [3793], a crowd). Based on what they saw, "**they were saying**" (from *légō* [3004], to speak logically) that such a thing had never occurred in the entirety of Israel's history.

[34] Secondly, we have the reaction of the Pharisees who opposed Jesus. They, too, saw what had happened. Being educated Jews, they also knew their history. But while they were intelligent, they were also hypocrites (Matt. 23:13–15, 23, 25, 27, 29) who needed an alternative explanation for Jesus' extraordinary authority. They could not deny the uniqueness of what He had done, but to accept Jesus as God incarnate (Emmanuel) was out of the question. So, since they believed that demons existed and that Jesus was an impostor, they assumed that He derived His authority from another source, namely the "**prince** [*árchōn* {758}, chief, originator, ruler] of the devils [demons]."

But the Pharisees did not see the trap they had set for themselves. Why would the chief of demons cast demons out of anyone? In the other Gospels, Jesus pointed out this incongruence, the self-defeating nature of such a practice, by arguing that such a kingdom would be an anti-kingdom (see Mark 3:24–30; Luke 11:18–22).

Jesus' Compassion for the Multitudes
(9:35–38)

[35] Jesus' itinerary is described here as it was in Matthew 4:23–25. He traveled to all the "**cities** [from *pólis* {4172}] and **villages** [from *kṓmē* {2968}]." Generally, He first taught in synagogues, because He knew that the people assembled there had come to learn more about God. Here He proclaimed the "**gospel** [*euaggélion* {2098}, good news] of the **kingdom** [from *basileía* {932}]." While this Gentile-dominated area had many evils, He focused on the good news (*kainós* [2537], qualitatively good as in Acts 17:19) that the King had come to live among them, bringing the kingdom of God (Matt. 3:2; 4:17; Luke 17:20, 21).

Preaching (from *kērússō* [2784]) did not exhaust Jesus' compassion for the whole person (1 Thess. 5:23). Closely following preaching was His **healing**

(from *therapeúō* [2323], to heal with tenderness). The text says that His authority to heal extended to "**every** [from *pás* {3956}] **disease** [from *nósos* {3554} from which the English word "nosology" derives, the classification of known diseases] and **weakness** [*malakía* {3119}, softness, bodily weakness] among the **people** [from *laós* {2992}]" (a.t.).

[36] As Jesus looked (from *eídō* [1492], to perceive) on the people, He understood their problems. This was an unorganized multitude (from *óchlos* [3793]) in contrast to organized groups like the Pharisees, Sadducees, and scribes. All kinds of people were gathered, but they had no leader. Jesus was moved with compassion for them, seeing them as "**sheep** [from *próbaton* {4263}] having no shepherd."

Jesus' unique authority was obvious. At the same time, His compassion reached far beyond that of any person. This is expressed in the verb "**was moved with compassion**," which translates from *splagchnízomai* (4697), bowel, intestine. This is the strongest verb for compassion in the Greek language and was used only of Jesus, as a rule (see also Matt. 14:14; 15:32; 20:34; Mark 1:41; Luke 7:13, except Matt. 18:27; Luke 10:33; 15:20). The word reflects the sick feeling we get in our stomachs when we are exposed to extreme or prolonged suffering.

All Jesus did flowed out of His compassion. His preaching was a compassionate concern for the dreadful judgment on unrepentance and unbelief, which is destruction. Preaching without compassion is ineffective. He also healed out of compassion.

An interesting textual variant occurs here concerning how our Lord saw the multitudes. The King James Version and New King James Version follow the Textus Receptus in characterizing these sheep as "**fainted**" or "weary" (from *eklúō* [1590], to be loose, exhausted, faint). But the New International Version, the New American Standard Bible, and other versions characterize them as "harassed" or "distressed" (from *skúllō* [4660], to skin, flay, lacerate). This is how Christ generally saw the masses, as sheep without a shepherd, wounded and abandoned.

Furthermore, Jesus saw the people "**scattered abroad**" (from *rhíptō* [4496], to throw, hurl, dispense). Jesus the Good Shepherd (John 10:11, 14) longed to lead them, feed them, and give them rest. Because the people were weary and oppressed, He challenged His disciples to the same tasks (vv. 37, 38). He probably gave this challenge to more than the Twelve.

[37] Jesus used the term "**harvest**" (*therismós* [2326]), one of His favorite similes, earlier at Jacob's well (John 4:35 ff.) and again when He sent out

the seventy (Luke 10:2). Here He contrasted the abundance of the harvest with the scarcity of workers. Food must be harvested at a precise time or the opportunity is lost. "**On the one hand** [*mén* {3303}], the harvest is abundant, **but on the other hand** [*dé* {1161}] the **workers** [from *ergátēs* {2040}] are few" (a.t.). Christ pleaded for His disciples to become workers to reap the fields.

The explicit promise is that when we do what Jesus did—proclaim that the kingdom of God has come, teach the Word of God, and show the same loving concern for people's needs—we will reap an abundant harvest. It is tragic not to have enough reapers. Implied is the idea that God will ripen the grain with His Holy Spirit.

The word "laborers" or "workers" are people the Lord of the harvest uses to reap souls and heal bodies as He continues His work. Consider how hard our Lord worked. Sometimes, it seems, He never rested! Paul admonished us also to work, not to merit salvation (Eph. 2:8) but to demonstrate our love for Christ and our faith in Him (v. 9). Workers use their hands to care for the sick as well as to benefit others (Eph. 4:28; 1 Thess. 4:11; 2 Thess. 3:10 ff.). We must not only teach, preach, and heal, but also care for the sick.

[38] The word for "**pray**" is *deéthēte*, the aorist imperative of *déomai* (1189), to pray for a specific work of God. Here the particular request is that the Lord will "**thrust out** [from *ekbállō* {1544}, cast out] workers into his harvest" (a.t.). Believers ought not to be lazy and easygoing but energetic and fast-paced, because the Lord told us the harvest is great—"a great multitude, which no man could number" (Rev. 7:9).

Yet we must take seriously the implication here that apart from prayer we will not be motivated, and souls will not be saved.

10

Jesus Calls and Commissions the Twelve
(10:1–15; Mark 3:13–19; 6:7–13; Luke 9:1–6)

Although Jesus commissions all believers to be workers (*ergátai* [2040]) in His vineyard in general, He did call to Himself a special group of twelve men whom He empowered in unique ways.

[1] This chapter begins with the reflexive middle voiced verb *proskalesámenos*, the aorist middle participle of *proskaléomai* (4341), "**having called to Himself**" (a.t.), from *prós* (4314), unto; and *kaléo* (2564), to call, used here for the first time in Matthew.

Jesus established a special spiritual relationship between this group and His unique sinless humanity and deity. He gave the Twelve some of the universal authority He received from His Father:

> Unto Me was given [*edóthē*, the aorist passive of *dídomi* {1325}] all [*pása* {3956}] authority [*exousía* {1849}, a noun related to the verb *éxestin* {1832} which means "that which stands outside or above"; Matt. 12:2, 4, et. al.] in heaven and on earth. (Matt. 28:18; a.t.)

The "**power**" (*exousía*) was intended to give the Twelve success in world-wide evangelism. This noun combines the ideas of moral authority and physical power, specifically the ability to reward and punish. Moral power requires physical strength (cf. Matt. 9:8; 28:18). If a ruler does not have the power (*dúnamis* [1411]) to reward and punish, his moral or constitutional rights are useless. Needless to say, God's rights are not derived from any law above Him.

Jesus gave the Twelve two powers: the abilities "**to cast out**" (*ekbállein*, the present infinitive of *ekbállo* [1544]) unclean spirits and to "**tenderly heal**" (*therapeúein*, the present infinitive of *therapeúō* [2323], to heal compassionately) the sick.

The first power addressed one of the consequences of sin, namely, the presence of "**unclean** [*akátharta* {169}, unclean; i.e., *ponērá* {4190}, malevolent, as in Luke 7:21] **spirits** [*pneúmata* {4151}]," that is, incorporeal, evil beings, demons]. Because these unclean spirits are continually harmful (*ponērá*), casting them out alleviates the torment they inflict (Matt. 17:14–18). A demon enters (*eisérchetai* [1525]) unbelievers at will, but it exits (*exérchetai* [1831]) only under God's compelling command (Luke 11:24, 26). When it is forced out, God confines it to waterless regions (Luke 11:24) like the abyss (Luke 8:31; Rev. 9:1–11; 11:7; 20:3). The Lord will totally destroy demons at the end of the age (Matt. 25:41; Rev. 20:10).

The second ability given to the Twelve Apostles was to heal the sick of every "**disease**" (*nósos* [3554]) and "**weakness**" (*malakía* [3119], softness; see notes on Matt. 4:23; 9:25).

In spite of this empowerment, demons, sickness, and subsequent weakness are still with us. They will last until the destruction of Satan and the annihilation of sin itself. The Lord Jesus will restore the world to its pristine condition at the time of His return in glory (Matt. 25:31; Acts 3:20, 21). These will be "the times of restitution [*apokatástasis* {605}] of all things" (Acts 3:21). Jesus did not give the apostles this scope of universal authority and power. Only Christ Himself will restore all things at the appointed time.

[2–4] In Mark 3:14, we read that Jesus "ordained [*epoíēsen*, the aorist tense of *poiéō* {4160}, to appoint] twelve," and in Luke 6:13, that "he named [*ōnómasen*, the aorist tense of *onomázō* {3687}] apostles." The list is always headed by Peter (Luke 6:13–16) and concluded by Judas. Representative characterizations are given of Matthew, the publican (Matt. 9:9–13), Judas, the betrayer (Matt. 10:4), and James and John, the sons of thunder (Mark 3:17).

[5] "These twelve Jesus **sent on a specific mission** [*apésteilen*, the aorist tense of *apostéllō* {649}, to send out from]" (a.t.). From verse 1 we learned that Jesus first invited the Twelve to Himself (*proskalesámenos* [4341]), then He sent them out from Himself. Only a disciple who had been with Jesus as a learner (*mathētḗs* [3101], disciple) could serve as an apostle (*apóstolos* [652], a sent one). As long as the disciples were with the Lord, He could instruct them, but when they were going to be separated, He gave them special instructions in verses 5 through 15.

Jesus told the apostles where to start and to confine their ministry to Israel. This restriction was limited to the Twelve; it was not imposed on the much larger group of disciples the Lord later sent forth to all nations (Matt. 28:19, 20). Whereas Jesus appointed only twelve to serve Israel, He gave the Great Commission to the church (Matt. 28:19).

Jesus told the Twelve not to take the road leading to the Gentiles and not to cross into Samaria, the district that lay between Galilee and Judea. Later, from within Samaria, Jesus said, "Lift up your eyes, and look on the fields; for they are white already to harvest" (John 4:35).

[6] Why did Jesus command them, "Go rather to the lost sheep of the house of Israel"? His mission (Matt. 15:24) now became their commission (Luke 24:47; Acts 13:46; Rom. 1:16).

This was a temporary focus (Matt. 8:11; 10:18; 21:43; 22:9; 24:14). As the Gospel to the Jews, the book of Matthew cites this brief limitation, whereas Luke exalts Christ as the Light of the Gentiles (Luke 10:1ff.; 24:47). Neither all Jews nor all Gentiles would be saved. The apostles were to go first to the lost sheep among the Jews (see also Rom. 1:16). However, the apostles' message—and later, the message of the seventy (Luke 10:9)—was to be the same to all (Matt. 3:2; 4:17).

The Twelve were to be on the move, as expressed by the verb "**go**" (*poreúesthe*, the present imperative of *poreúomai* [4198], "keep going"). They were to go not just once but as many times as they had opportunities.

[7] Here we find the use of the present participle *poreuómenoi*, "**as you keep going**" (a.t.). In their constant going, they were to

> **preach** [*kērússete*, the present active imperative of *kērússō* {2784}, be preaching], **saying** [*légontes*, the present active participle of *légō* {3004}, not just speaking randomly but giving the rationale], The kingdom of heaven **is at hand** [*éggiken*, the perfect active indicative of *eggízō* {1448}, to approach, to come near].

This was equivalent to telling the Jews that the God of the Old Testament, the King, was present. Heaven had come to earth; the *Lógos* (3056), the logical Word of God, had become flesh (John 1:1, 14).

[8] True believers cannot be indifferent to the sick and suffering people they encounter, thus, the added admonition: "**Keep tenderly healing** [*therapeúete*, the present imperative of *therapeúō* {2323}, 'keep healing with compassion']" (a.t.).

The apostles were also commissioned to "**keep cleansing**" (*katharízete*, the present imperative of *katharízō* [2511], to cleanse, the only verb used in the NT for the healing of lepers [a.t.]). The Old Testament required certifications of healing so that former lepers would be accepted back into their communities.

In the Textus Receptus, following "cleanse the lepers," we find "**raise** [*egeírete*, the present imperative of *egeírō* {1453}, to raise] the dead [*nekroús*, the accusative plural of the adjective *nekrós* {3498}, dead]." No definite articles are before any of the subjects, signifying that the Lord did not give the disciples unlimited authority to heal every sickness or raise every dead person. In John 16:33, Jesus promised victory over sickness and death: "In the world ye shall have tribulation [*thlípsin* {2347}]: but be of good cheer; I have overcome [*neníkēka*, the perfect tense of *nikáō* {3528}] the world."

We find in 1 Corinthians 15:26 that "the last [*éschatos* {2078}, the farthest chronologically] enemy that shall be destroyed is death [physical death]." This clearly teaches that we believers are neither exempt from nor granted full authority over corruption, sickness, and death in this age; however, we can have victory in this life and at the resurrection when all sickness and death will be eliminated. Our bodies will be "raised in incorruption" (1 Cor. 15:42; see vv. 53, 54).

Jesus' commands did not come with the guarantee of universal salvation or healing. Of the original Twelve Apostles, only Peter raised a dead person— Dorcas of Lydda, a believer distinguished for benevolence. Peter came to the house where Dorcas (Tabitha) had died and commanded her to rise (Acts 9:36–43). God gave the apostles the privilege to do many wonders and signs but not universally so. The Holy Spirit clearly led them to particular ministries.

The Lord also raised a dead person through the ministry of the apostle Paul. While Paul was preaching in Troas, a man named Eutychus fell asleep and dropped from the third floor of a building. He died, but Paul (1 Cor. 9:1, 2) raised him back to life (Acts 20:7–12).

The phrase "raise [the] dead" is not universally accepted as part of Matthew 10:8, and it is not included in the Majority Text; however, it is included in the Textus Receptus—thus, its presence in the King James Version. Since we have a record of Peter and Paul (Acts 9:40; 20:7–12) raising Dorcas and Eutychus, there is no theological objection to its inclusion here (it does not appear in any of the other three Gospels). Possibly this power was given only to Peter and Paul, since we have no record that the other apostles raised the dead. In any case, the power associated with these three commands may be restricted to the "signs of an apostle" (2 Cor. 12:12) and, if so, may not be applicable to the entire church age.

The same may be said for cleansing lepers. We have no record that the apostles or other believers cleansed lepers as Jesus did in Matthew 8:3 and Luke 17:11–19. Even so, the ministry of healing and caring for the sick in the life of Jesus, the Twelve Apostles, and believers in general was particular, not universal, in scope, as we have noted. Not all lepers were cleansed, and not all dead people were raised, either by Jesus or others. Sick people remain with us, as they did in Christ's day. In accordance with His command, we can care for and heal some but not all.

"**Cast out** [*ekbállete*, the present imperative of *ekbállō* {1544}] devils" means to keep casting out, since the verb is a present imperative. The Twelve were thus to liberate people who were possessed and imprisoned by evil spirits.

Jesus then instructed the apostles not to charge for these services. "**Freely** [*dōreán* {1432}, gratis] ye have received, **freely give** [*dóte*, the active imperative of *dídōmi* {1325}, to give]." A God-given gift must not be sold. "What hast thou that thou didst not receive?" (1 Cor. 4:7). The servant of God is not to accumulate money or goods by charging for preaching or healing.

[9] The aorist tense of the verb in the expression, "**You may not** [*mḗ* {3361}, the relative 'not'] **provide** [*ktēsēsthe*, the aorist middle subjunctive—used as an imperative—of *ktáomai* {2932}, to acquire or buy for oneself]" (a.t.), implies a once-for-all procurement.

Jesus warned His servants to beware of greed. The King's children are not entitled to live royally on earth. This is the reward of heaven. The negatives in verses 9 and 10 are relative (*mḗ* [3361]), not absolute (*ou* [3756]). This means the commands must be considered in conjunction with other Scriptures (see Luke 22:35–37). Jesus did not forbid owning extra clothing, bags, or other reserves but rather profiteering from His free gift, the gospel. Merchandising (*kapēleúō* [2585], to hawk, translated "corrupt" in 2 Cor. 2:17) the Word of God is forbidden.

[10] While Christian workers are forbidden to charge, the church is commanded to support them: "If we have sown unto you spiritual things, is it a great thing if we shall reap your carnal things?" (1 Cor. 9:11).

Thus, the reason for not carrying money and two sets of clothes is that the worker is "**worthy** [*áxios* {514}, deserving] of [receiving] his **meat** [*trophḗ* {5160}]," that is, from others. In Luke 10:7, Jesus said, "The laborer is worthy of his hire [*misthós* {3408}, reward]." The workers' rewards, however, are not fully received on earth; most are reserved in heaven (Matt. 5:12). For now, Christians should care for God's servants, but warnings against greed and profiting from the gospel ministry are very clear.

[11–14] Jesus also told us that we will experience various receptions. We should therefore apply wise insight to different situations, what Paul calls "discerning [*diakríseis*, the plural of *diákrisis* {1253}] of spirits" (1 Cor. 12:10). Apostles and disciples bring the same message to all, and some welcome it as a message of peace. If others are not worthy (*áxioi*) and have no cultivated ground (Matt. 13:8, 23) for the reception of the seed, the blessing returns to us. Nothing we do for Christ wastes His time or our efforts. Having done our duty, we can rest assured it will be fruitful in our lives and in the lives of others.

[15] Jesus taught that the testimony (*marturía* [3141]) of His saving grace will either justify people in this life or condemn them on the day of judgment (v. 18; 24:14; Mark 13:9; Luke 9:5; 21:13, etc.). God punished the sinful cities of Sodom and Gomorrah, but He will punish those individuals and cities that reject the gospel with worse judgments.

Future Persecutions
(10:16–25; Mark 13:9–13; Luke 21:12–17)

In commissioning the Twelve, the Lord revealed both the near and the distant future for believers and disciples. Most of the Twelve Apostles were martyred, but in this section, Jesus reached beyond to disciples for generations to come.

[16] This portion starts with "**behold**" (*idoú* [2400], the imperative of *eidō* [1492], be aware, look) as Jesus called His disciples' attention to an extraordinary threat to evangelism. He cautioned them about wolves, the chief enemies of the Shepherd who guards His flock. Indeed, it is a great mystery that the One given all authority in heaven and earth (Matt. 28:18) does not subjugate these voracious carnivores now but allows them to prey on His sheep.

In light of this, Jesus gave two ways to be on guard. The first is "**be ye** [*gínesthe*, the present imperative of *gínomai* {1096}, 'keep becoming'] wise as **serpents** [*ópheis* {3789}]." This implies that wisdom is not static but dynamic. Believers keep growing in wisdom (*phrónimos* [5429], prudence, sagacity, discretion; from *phrḗn* [5424], moral restraint) so they can protect themselves from wolves. In what way are serpents (*ópheis*) sagacious? We read in Genesis 3:1 that "the serpent was more subtil than any beast of the field." The word means shrewdness in a neutral sense. A snake knows how to escape swiftly and silently and hide itself in times of danger.

The second way we can guard against wolves is to become "**harmless**" (*akéraioi* [185] from the privative *a* [1], without; and *keránnumi* [2767], to mix) as doves. Nearly synonymous with holiness, we are to be free of deceit and other malevolent attitudes (Rom. 16:19; Phil. 2:15). Like wise serpents, we should understand Satan's subtlety. But no evil is to be mixed with this wisdom. We must have purity and simplicity of heart like harmless, gentle doves. The dove, the emblem of perfect innocence, was used (Matt. 3:16) as a symbol of the Holy Spirit's descent on Jesus in recognition of His holiness (v. 17) and official consecration to His messianic ministry.

[17] While we are commanded to ceaselessly pursue prudence and innocence, we are also told to "**beware** [*proséchete*, the present imperative of *proséchō* {4337}, to give heed to, apply the mind] of men." We cannot live apart from others, but Jesus told us nevertheless to be on our guard because tares among the wheat will "**betray**" (*paradōsousin*, the future tense of *paradídōmi* [3860], to be delivered over, betrayed) us. As the world hated the Lord, so it will hate us (John 15:18; 17:14), not for evil but for the good we do (Matt. 23:34; Mark 13:9; Acts 22:19; 26:11).

[18] The persecution against us, Jesus said, will be "for [His] sake." However, believers will stand before governors and kings as a "**testimony**" (*martúrion* [3142], witness, prosecution) against them—a noun which contrasts with *marturía* (3141), a defense. The testimony will be reserved for prosecution on the day of judgment.

In Jesus' day, the Jews of the synagogues had a council of twenty-three judges (Acts 22:19; 26:11; 2 Cor. 11:24).

[19, 20] The Lord advised His disciples what to say when they would be brought before governors and kings:

> But when they deliver you up, you may take **no** [*mḗ* {3361}, the relative "not"] **thought** [*merimnḗsēte*, the aorist subjunctive of *merimnáō* {3309}, to worry] **how** [*pōs* {4459}, in what manner] or **what** [*ti* {5101}, the content] you shall speak: for it shall be given you in that same hour what you shall speak. For it is not you that speak, but the Spirit of your Father which speaks in you. (a.t.)

This dynamic presence of the Father was fully in the Son. Jesus said, "The words that I speak unto you I speak not of myself: but the Father that dwelleth in me, he doeth the works" (John 14:10). Now Jesus encouraged His disciples that when they testified of Him, the Spirit of His Father would speak through them. Clearly, He did not mean that every word out of their mouths would be inspired. Only those words that testify of Him (i.e., the gospel) are inspired by the Father, consistent with the His testimony at Jesus' baptism: "This is my beloved Son, in whom I am well pleased" (Matt. 3:17).

A significant testimony, therefore, includes both the manner (*pōs*) and the content (*ti*), that is, the Word (*lógos* [3056]) of the cross, which is the power of God (1 Cor. 1:18). The Word is another name for Jesus Christ (John 1:1, 2, 14, 18). This is a good message for preachers to hear. The Word of God is self-authenticating (John 12:48) and alive (Heb. 4:12). It accomplishes whatever God sends it to do (Isa. 55:11) and requires nothing more than simple proclamation. Pompous charisma can add nothing to it.

[21] The persecution Jesus warned of is unimaginably evil: "And the brother shall deliver up the brother to death, and the father the child: and the children shall rise up against their parents, and cause them to be put to death."

Atrocious breakdowns of family units are increasing, as, for example, when members of a family turn against nonconforming children or parents. This is common in non-Christian and atheistic countries. But nothing is worse than the defective theological justification for such brutality that Jesus predicted: "The time cometh, that whosoever killeth you will think that he doeth God service" (John 16:2).

Malachi prophesied this awful breakdown of families as the Day of the Lord approaches:

> Behold, I will send you Elijah the prophet before the coming of the great and dreadful day of the LORD: And he shall turn the heart of the fathers to the children, and the heart of the children to their fathers, lest I come and smite the earth with a curse. (Mal. 4:5, 6)

[22] Persecution will be universal:

> And ye shall be hated of all men for my name's sake: but he that **endureth** [*hupomeínas*, the aorist participle of *hupoménō* {5278}, to endure under, to have patience] **to** [*eis* {1519}, toward, unto, until] the **end** [*télos* {5056}, goal, termination] **shall be saved** [*sōthésetai*, the future passive of *sōzō* {4982}, to rescue, deliver].

Believers will need endurance during general persecution, especially when betrayed by their families. What could be worse than family members delivering other members to death based on the false promise that they are serving God?

Enduring "to the end" cannot mean physical survival until the Lord returns. That would force us to conclude that those who died during persecution will not be saved. But the Bible maintains that those who die as martyrs for their faith will be saved both spiritually and physically: "Be faithful until death [i.e., 'the end'], and I will give you the crown of life" (Rev. 2:10; a.t.). "[He] became obedient unto death" (Phil. 2:8). The "end," therefore, is physical death, not the end of the age.

The Tribulation will be a time of intense martyrdom (v. 21; 24:9; Mark 13:12; Luke 21:16; John 16:2; Rev. 6:9). At first glance, Luke's parallel account appears to have an inconsistency: "Some of you shall they cause to be put to death. . . . But not one hair of your head shall perish. In your patience, possess your souls" (a.t.; Luke 21:16, 18, 19). Whatever "not one hair . . . shall perish" means, it has to reconcile with being put to death—at least for "some of you," as Luke quotes Jesus.

Congruously, Luke does not say, "In your patience possess your bodies" but rather "your souls." If we assume that not possessing a soul means losing a soul, then it seems that Luke has spiritual salvation in mind as well. If so, we can take his reference to not one hair perishing in the context of physical death, not as a statement of immortality but of the resurrection when the Son of man returns. After all, "the very hairs of [our] head[s] are numbered" (v. 30; a.t.) for some reason (cf. the vividly detailed account of resurrection in Ezek. 37).

If this interpretation is correct, then "the end" cannot refer to the end of the age or the return of Christ but must refer to the end of physical life. Thus, "Be thou faithful unto death, and I will give thee a crown of life" (Rev. 2:10). Although many will be martyred during this time, they certainly will be saved spiritually and physically in the resurrection.

Such a salvation no doubt refers to the "better resurrection" (Heb. 11:35), "the resurrection out [*exanástasin* {1815}] from among the dead" (Phil. 3:11; a.t.). This "first resurrection" occurs at the rapture of the church. The hope of resurrection is the rock on which we believers stand and from which we cannot be moved.

Jesus did not advise recklessness but the sagacity of a serpent to preserve life and ministry. Neither seeking martyrdom nor forsaking evangelism is morally correct. We must avoid both extremes. We not only have the hope of the resurrection but the assurance of it. (See the verb *exegereí* [1825], will raise, in 1 Cor. 6:14 and the author's book on 1 Cor. 6 entitled, *How Far Does Christian Freedom Go?*)

"And ye shall be hated of all men **for** [*diá* {1223} with the accusative, because of, on account of] my name's sake" (v. 22). We Christians will not make enemies because we lack good character traits, but because we do have them (which convicts the ungodly) and because we stand for the exclusive lordship of Jesus Christ.

[23] We are not to quit under the pressure of intense persecution, but neither are we to stand still. We will prove our endurance by moving on, ahead, ever upward to the city of God:

> But when they persecute you in this city, flee ye into another: for verily I say unto you, Ye shall not have gone over the cities of Israel, **till** [*héōs* {2193}, until] the Son of man **be come** [*élthē*, the aorist subjunctive of *érchomai* {2064}, to come].

The coming of the Lord is certain. In Greek, the expression "till the Son of man be come" contains the untranslated particle "**if**" (*án* [302] the "if" of certainty, "if surely", following "till")—the suppositional particle of reality and experience. The aorist tense of *érchomai*—*élthē*—is a crisis event, but the timing of the event is not revealed (Matt. 24:36; Mark 13:32). The Lord is going to come whether we are faithful to His commission or not.

At His trial before the Sanhedrin, Jesus told Caiaphas, the high priest, "Hereafter shall ye see the Son of man sitting on the right hand of power, and coming in the clouds of heaven" (Matt. 26:64), probably dating the "hereafter" from the time of His ascension. Shortly after His ascension, the events of Pentecost were the beginning of the Son of man's process of coming: "Therefore, having been exalted by the right hand of God and having received of the Father the promise of the Holy Ghost, He has shed forth this, which you now see and hear" (Acts 2:33; a.t.).

[24, 25] Disciples cannot expect their opponents to treat them less brutally than they treated their Master:

> The disciple is not above his master, nor the servant above his lord. It is enough for the disciple that he be as his master, and the servant as his lord. If they have called the master of the house Beelzebub, **how much** [*póso* {4214}, how much, how many] **more** [*mállon* {3123}] shall they call them of his **household** [*oikiakoús* {3615}]?

The words "if they have called" read more like past history than prophecy, so, assuming Matthew's narrative is chronologically arranged, it is certain that the accusation recorded two chapters ahead was not made for the first time: "This fellow doth not cast out devils, but by Beelzebub the prince of the devils" (Matt. 12:24). Also, the accusation there is not as strong; to cast out "by Beelzebub" is the role of a subordinate. Here, however, Jesus said they had actually "called [Him]" Beelzebub—the chief of devils (see Luke 11:15).

If Beelzebub is the chief of demons, then how can those of Christ's household be called "much more"? We're not forced to translate *póso mállon* as "how much worse [in degree]," especially if there is no "worse" than "the chief." We can as easily read the Greek phrase as "how much more often?" (i.e., will His disciples be called this?) or "how many more?" (i.e., disciples will also be called by this name). The Spirit of Christ in the church ministers far longer than the three-and-a-half years the Son of man ministered.

The name "Beelzebub" has an interesting history. "Baal-zebub" means "lord of the fly," and this was the god of the Philistine city of Ekron, according to 2 Kings 1:2, 3, 6, 16. "Baal" was a generic god, a catch-all for numerous subspecies with just as many names. Ironically, this god was so named because he was considered both the creator of and savior from flies. By Jesus' time, the Jews used the name Beelzebub for the chief of evil spirits (Matt. 12:27; Luke 11:18, 19), the "ruler of the demons" (Matt. 12:24; Mark 3:22; Luke 11:15).

Fear God, Not People
(10:26–31; Luke 12:2–7)

[26] Jesus gave His disciples a powerful incentive against fear when He promised that, on the day of judgment, God will expose the sins their persecutors covered up before others:

> **Fear** [*phobēthēte*, the aorist passive deponent subjunctive of *phobéomai* {5399}, to fear] them **not** [*mē* {3361}, the relative "not"; also in vv. 28, 31] therefore: for there is **nothing** [*oudén* {3762}, not a single thing] **that has been covered** [*kekalumménon*, the perfect passive participle of *kalúptō* {2572}, to cover up, to hide], that **shall** not **be revealed** [*apokaluphthḗsetai*, the future passive of *apokalúptō* {601}, uncovered], and **hid** [*kruptón* {2927}, secret, concealed] that shall not be known. (a.t.)

The two verbs, *kalúptō*, to cover up, and *krúptō*, to conceal, essentially mean the same thing. The first means to put a cover or lid over something you do not want seen, and the second is to hide something for the same reason. The noun *kálupsis* (from *kalúptō*), something covered (hidden), is antithetical to *apokálupsis* (602), a revelation, an unveiling. From the verb *krúptō*, to hide, we have the adjectival noun *kruptón*, hidden or secret, and *apókruphon* (614), hid, which in the plural is the name given to noncanonical (extrabiblical) books from Hebrew-Christian tradition. In due time, God will reveal secret or hidden (*kruptón*) things to us.

Jesus told His people that someday He will publicly expose the evil motives Satan's emissaries have hidden. Such motives are not hidden from God, since "all things are naked and opened unto the eyes of him" (Heb. 4:13) but from people. On that day, we shall experientially know (*gnōsthḗsetai* [1097]) what was inaccessible in this life. God will unveil not only the stealthy, malevolent motives of the princes of darkness but also the good motives of the children of light that are shrouded in humility:

> Therefore judge nothing before the time, until the Lord come, who both will bring to light the hidden things of darkness, and will make manifest the counsels of the hearts: and then shall every man have praise of God (1 Cor. 4:5).

[27] Jesus continued this thought: "What I tell you in **darkness** [TR, MT, *skótos* {4655}, darkness; UBS, Nestle's, *skotía* {4653}], that speak ye in light: and what ye hear in the ear, that preach ye upon the house tops."

Here *skótos* or *skotía* must denote physical darkness (as in Matt. 27:45 and Luke 12:3 respectively), obscurity from public view, since darkness and light are equated to hearing in the ear (i.e., in darkness; note that Luke 12:3 says, "in closets")—which is neither a sin nor a consequence of sin—and preaching from the housetops (i.e., in public).

Furthermore, *skótos* and *skotía* elsewhere refer to sin as, for example, "he . . . who hates his brother . . . is in darkness" (1 John 2:9 NKJV). Obviously, in our verse under study, Jesus was not saying, "What I speak in sin" [*skótos*]—since Jesus did not sin. Nor was He saying, "What I speak in the consequence of sin" [*skotía*, i.e., God's judgments]—since Jesus did not experience God's judgments on personal sin. Neither did He cite an extraneous subject as if He were avoiding the threat of someone else's (moral) darkness. Even if this were the case, it would be a strange way of speaking of an imminent threat: What I tell you in the environment of someone trying to kill us. Jesus was not worried, and He was not avoiding an external threat. He was simply speaking of His own "telling" that He qualified as "in darkness," that is, privately. The plain meaning, therefore, is that what He told His disciples obscurely, privately, out of public view and hearing, He wanted them to preach publicly.

Throughout Scripture, we are told that God will universally expose the evil motives of unbelievers, particularly hypocrites and those who attack believers: "For God shall bring every work into judgment, with every secret thing, whether it be good, or whether it be evil" (Eccl. 12:14). Paul said that this will be done "in the day [of judgment] when God shall judge the secrets of men by Jesus Christ according to my gospel" (Rom. 2:16).

While many things are mysteriously dark to us now, Jesus commanded us to boldly proclaim the gospel from the "house tops," audibly and visibly. If we are persecuted, we can rest in this promise that God will expose and judge people's wicked secrets.

[28] Jesus commanded His disciples not to fear martyrdom.

> And **fear** [*phobéthéte* {TR}, the aorist passive subjunctive of *phobéō* {5399}] **not** [*mé* {3361}, the relative "not"] **them which kill** [*apokteinónton*, the present participle of *apokteinō* {615}, to kill; "those who are killing"; to separate soul from body] the body, but are **not** [*mé*] **able** [*dunaménon*, the present participle of *dúnamai* {1410}, to be able] **to kill** [*apokteínai*, the aorist infinitive of *apokteínō*] the soul: but rather **fear** [*phobéthéte* {TR}, the aorist passive imperative of *phobéō*] him **which is able** [*dunámenon*, the present passive deponent

participle of *dúnamai*] to **destroy** [*apolésai*, the aorist infinitive of *apóllumi* {622}, to cause to perish] both soul and body in **hell** [*Geénnē* {1067}, Gehenna, the Valley of Hinnom {Hebrew}].

Coupled with the negative *mḗ*, the aorist tense of *phobéō* means not to fear at any time, any single instance. But we are to fear Him who is capable of destroying both our souls and bodies in hell. This is God, of course, for He is the only One with such power: "There is one lawgiver, who is able to save and to destroy" (James 4:12).

The United Bible Society and Nestle's texts have the first imperative in the present tense, *mḗ phobeísthe*, meaning that we should not constantly be fearing (i.e., a process) people who can kill—no doubt to correspond with the present participle *apokteinónton*. The aorist, on the other hand, points to the time of death when God can destroy both soul and body. Jesus' point was the following: At that time of crisis when the blade is at our throats, our fear of the One able to destroy our eternal souls in hell should overpower our fear of ones able to kill our bodies. Then we will not apostatize under the threat of death. The fear of hell should motivate us to defy the fear of physical death in those moments. Christ's command to fear hell is for us as believers, not unbelievers.

Although not explicitly stated, the implication is that those who secure their physical lives by rejecting Christ lose their eternal souls. Martyrdom, then, is a form of obedience: "He . . . became obedient unto death" (Phil. 2:8); "Ye have not yet resisted unto blood, striving against sin" (Heb. 12:4); "Be thou faithful unto death, and I will give thee a crown of life" (Rev. 2:10).

The verb *phobéomai*, to fear, and the noun *phóbos* (5401), fear, admit of degrees. By nature, we have one fear of the physical harm people can do to us. By supernatural endowment—"I will put my fear in their hearts, that they shall not depart from me" (Jeremiah 32:40)—we have another fear of God (Luke 18:2, 4; 23:40; Col. 3:22; 1 Pet. 2:17). Only God determines the destinies of souls. Saved souls depart to Christ, a "gain" over this life (Phil. 1:21, 23).

People are able to break up the constituent parts (*apokteínō*) of others, that is, separate bodies from their spirits/souls, but they cannot determine the subsequent location of souls.

Our fear of God should far exceed our fear of people for two reasons. First, God commands us, "Thou shalt fear the LORD thy God" (Deut. 10:20). In many other Old Testament verses, God commands us not to fear other gods, people, or death itself. Secondly, our fear of God will cause us to persevere under the threat of martyrdom: "I will put my fear in their hearts, that they shall not depart from me" (Jer. 32:40). So our fear of God who can destroy bodies and souls in hell is a higher grade of terror than what we would have for someone threatening to kill us. ("Awe and respect" are totally out of place here.) Such fear is intended for our good so we can endure under terrible circumstances. We would do well to pray the prayer our Lord taught us, "Deliver [*rhúsai*, the aorist middle deponent imperative of *rhúomai* {4506}] us from evil" (Matt. 6:13) by drawing us closer to God.

[29–31] Even sparrows are killed, but believers are "of more value than many sparrows," which means God values sparrows. The perfect will, wisdom, and timing of our Father determine when a single bird falls to the ground. Note the reference to "your [not the bird's] Father." Only believers have God as Father (Matt. 6:9), and He has full control of their souls, whether they are united with or separated from their bodies.

The text does not say that God passively knows the number of hairs on our heads. Rather, they "**have been numbered**" (*ērithmēménai*, the perfect passive participle of *arithméō* [705], from which we get our word "arithmetic"] by Him; that is, He determines the number. Just as He determines the death of a valued sparrow by wisdom, so He numbers the hairs on our heads by wisdom. The point is, we can trust His wisdom to determine the most insignificant details of our lives.

We prefer the aorist imperative in verse 31 from the Textus Receptus and the Majority Text. The command not to be afraid is a conclusion (*oún* [3767], therefore) based on God's providential care of sparrows and hairs (cf. "Not a hair out of your head will perish" [Luke 21:18; a.t.]). No matter how much danger we face, we must be brave. We should not live in a constant spirit of cowardice (*pneúma deilías* [1167]; 2 Tim. 1:7), but in complete trust and dependence on a heavenly Father who cares for sparrows and hairs.

We do not easily learn such things because we commonly judge hairs and sparrows, like the details of our lives, to be insignificant. We think God's knowledge of such things is passive, which He acquires by observation rather than knowing innately. Since the "Spirit is truth" (1 John 5:6), God's concern for sparrows and hairs is true. And since this Spirit of truth lives in us (Rom. 8:9), we can be fearless against Satan's worst attacks. When we worry, we need only think about God's care for the tiniest bits of creation.

Public Confession and Denial
(10:32, 33; Luke 12:8, 9)

[32] When we meet other people, we should boldly tell them the gospel (1 Cor. 15:3) and be prepared to answer objections (1 Pet. 3:15).

To identify publicly with Christ is "to confess" (*homologéō* [3670], to assent, admit; from *homoú* [3674], together with; and *légō* [3004], to speak intelligently) His name and work, particularly His work within us: "Go home to your friends and tell them what great things the Lord has done for you and what compassion He had for you" (Mark 5:19; a.t.). The primary subject of confession is God's new creation (2 Cor. 5:17) within us.

In the Greek text, implied subjects are in Jesus' statement, "Whosoever therefore shall confess **[that he is] in** [*en* {1722}] me before men, him will I confess **[that I am] in** [*en*] him also before my Father which is in heaven" (a.t.). The phrases in brackets help us to better understand the verse. The reason for our courage is our unity with God (John 17:21–23). Others cannot comprehend what happened to us because they cannot understand what happened in us. It is the "within" that explains the changes apparent in our behavior; new creatures are no longer idolaters, immoral, greedy, thieves, drunkards, revilers, or extortioners (1 Cor. 6:9–11). God is in us, and we are in Him because Jesus Christ has changed us and made us fit to be saints (2 Cor. 5:17).

[33] Some, however, are overcome by fear and deny Christ before others. "[To] **deny**" (*arnéomai* [720]), the opposite of "to confess," is not just to keep silent but to declare we do not know Him (see Peter's denial in the next paragraph). A time will come when God and Jesus Christ will either confess or deny us. And there will be a place for this as well in heaven, where only angels (Luke 12:8) and believers in Christ live (Luke 15:10).

The first use of the verb "deny" here is *arnḗsētai*, the aorist middle deponent subjunctive, coupled with *án*, the supposition of reality. Peter openly denied Christ when he was threatened, but Jesus assured Peter that he would return in faith because He prayed for him: "I have prayed for you that [*hína* {2443}, in order that] your faith not fail: and when you are converted [*epistrépsas*, the aorist participle of *epistréphō* {1994}, to turn back], strengthen your brothers" (Luke 22:32; a.t.). The aorist participle *epistrépsas* assumes God caused Peter's faith to return in response to His Son's prayer and in spite of Peter's denial (apostasy). If Jesus did not pray for the perseverance of our faith, none of us would return to Him after denial. Let us thank God that "He ever lives to make intercession for [us]" (a.t.; Heb. 7:25, cf. Rom. 8:34).

Confession and Persecution
(10:34–39; Luke 12:51–53; 14:26, 27)

[34–36] Jesus preempted any thoughts that He came to bring peace and failed.

Think [*nomísēte*, the aorist subjunctive of *nomízō* {3543}, to think] **not** [*mē* {3361}, the relative "not"] that **I came** [*élthon*, the aorist tense of *érchomai* {2064}, to come] **to bring** [*baleín*, the aorist active infinitive of *bállō* {906}, to cast] peace on the earth. I came **not** [*ou* {3756}, the absolute "not"] **to bring** [*baleín*] peace, but a **sword** [*máchaira* {3162}]. **For** [*gár* {1063}, introduces an explanation of the prior verse] I came **to divide** [*dichásai*, the aorist active infinitive of *dicházō* {1369}, to divide] a man against his father, and the daughter against her mother, and the daughter-in-law against her mother-in-law. And a man's **foes** [*echthroí* {2190}, enemies] shall be those of his own household. (a.t.)

According to Luke 2:13, 14, the advent of the Messiah was accompanied by a heavenly heraldry of peace from, ironically, a "multitude **of soldiers** [*stratiás* {4756}]", saying: "Glory to God in the highest, and on earth peace among [*en* {1722}, in or among] men of good pleasure [*eudokías*, the genitive of *eudokía* {2107}, good pleasure, good will, approval]" (a.t.). Given this announcement, what were the disciples to think of conflicts that arose as the result of their witness?

They were to realize that the division within families (*dichostasía* [1370]) would be accidental to any intentions on their part; in fact, it would be the product of the peace of Christ in their hearts. Family members confronted with these radical, unfamiliar changes, especially peace, succumb naturally to alarm or jealousy. What anxious heart can endure the presence of a peaceful one? Accordingly, among other reasons, the chief priests delivered up Christ "for envy" (Mark 15:10).

Jesus carefully differentiated inner peace from conflict that exists in the external world:

> These things I have spoken unto you, that in me ye might have peace [*eirḗnen* {1515}]. In the world ye shall have tribulation: but be of good cheer; I have overcome the world. (John 16:33)

From the fall of Adam, history has been filled with local, national (civil), and world conflicts. Yet the peace of Jesus Christ has ruled (Col. 3:15) in the hearts of many believers surrounded by strife. Note the precise wording in the above verse: The peace heralded by the angels in the second chapter of Luke is qualified by Jesus as in Him, not in the world. The Lord's promise of peace is particular, not universal, although He is infinitely larger than the world. In our composite world of good and evil, light and darkness, He said, "I did not come to bring peace, but a sword" (Matt. 10:34 NASB). On the island of Patmos, John saw a vision of the last days: "It was given to him that sat [on the red horse] to . . . take peace from the earth in order that they might kill one another" (Rev. 6:4; a.t.).

The inner peace of the believer is the result of personal justification: "Being justified by faith, we have peace with God through our Lord Jesus Christ" (Rom. 5:1). Thus, our first peace is "with God," not people. Prior to reconciliation, the Lord wars against unbelief and hypocrisy.

> Repent, therefore, for if not, I [Jesus] come to **you** [the entire church of Pergamos] suddenly, and I will wage war [*polemésō*, the future active tense of *poleméō* {4170}, to wage war, to fight] with [not *katá* {2596}, "against" {KJV}, implying that the Lord is fighting indirectly; but rather *met'* from *metá* {3326}, with, meaning both parties are battling] **them** [unbelievers within the church] with the sword [*romphaía* {4501}] of My mouth. (Rev. 2:16; a.t., cf. 17:14: "These [ten kings and the beast] shall make war with the Lamb, and the Lamb shall overcome them.")

When people are justified through faith, the Lord no longer battles to initiate repentance, even though the Spirit of God continues to strive against the flesh (Gal. 5:17). God and new believers in Christ lay down their swords and peace ensues. This is called reconciliation (*katallagḗ* [2643]; Rom. 5:11; 11:15; 2 Cor. 5:18, 19).

Since the Lord Himself "wages war" against our enemies, even family members, to pressure them to repent, this should raise our confident expectations. Thus, while "division" causes immediate, short-term conflicts, it may ultimately produce repentance. Consider two teachings from the apostles Paul and Peter: "In nothing terrified by your adversaries: which is to them an evidence [both] of their destruction and your salvation, and that from God" (Phil. 1:28; a.t.); "If any obey not the Word, they also may be won without word[s] by . . . conduct [*anastrophḗ* {391}, lifestyle, manner] . . . as they behold your pure [*hagnós* {53}] conduct in fear" (1 Pet. 3:1, 2; a.t.).

Without "division"—differentiation or schism (*schísma* [4978], tear), an equivalent Greek concept—there would be no "evidence of destruction" or "pure conduct" for unbelievers to notice. God creates this division by removing unbelievers' hearts of stone and replacing them with hearts of flesh (Ezek. 11:19; 36:26), making them new creatures in Christ (2 Cor. 5:17; Gal. 6:15).

Jesus acknowledged the family as a divine institution by becoming (*génesis* [1078]; see Matt. 1:1) a man and participating in a human family. Though dissension may be in a family unit because sin has affected its members, the Lord does not intend to destroy the sacredness of the family. The Greeks have a special word for family love, *storgē* (n.f.). In Scripture, the adjective is found only in the negative, *ástorgoi* (794), **without** family love, something that characterizes the end times (2 Tim. 3:3) just as it did in the earliest days of humankind (Rom. 1:31). When Jesus was dying on the cross, He committed His mother to the care of John (John 19:26, 27), one of His disciples. So Jesus encouraged family love and practiced it Himself, even during His agonizing moments on the cross.

Two other kinds of love advance beyond familial affection. They are *agápaō* ([25]; John 3:16), to love sacrificially the way God loves, and *philéō* ([5368]; v. 37), to befriend, from which we have the noun *philía* (5373), friendly love. When God's love (*agápē*) is appropriated by one family member but rejected by others, opposition is created. Division (*dichásai* as in v. 35, from *dicházō* [1369], to divide in half) occurs. The peace of Christ in the heart and life of the one stimulates the anxiety of the others: "A man's foes shall be they of his own household."

[37] But we are to stand firm against such opposition:

He [*ho* {3588}, the definite article] **who loves** [*philōn*, the present participle of *philéō* {5368}, to befriend] father or mother **more than** [*hupér* {5228}, above] Me, is **not** [*ouk* {3756}, the absolute "not"] **worthy** [*áxios* {514}] of me. (a.t.)

When family members persecute us, we should defer to our higher love for Christ. If we value relatives, even fathers or mothers, above Christ, we have not truly recognized His unique status as the incarnate God who gives new birth. We must rest in the fact that accountability for family divisions falls on those who reject the Spirit of Christ within us.

We must rank our love for the Lord first (*prótos* [4413], cf. *proteúōn* in Col. 1:18), thus Christ's warning to the church of Ephesus: "I have this against you, that you left your first [*prótēn*] love [*agápēn* {26}]" (Rev. 2:4; a.t.). John explains that "we love [*agapōmen*, the present tense of *agapáō* {25}, to love] him, because he first [*prótos*] loved [*ēgápēsen*, the aorist tense of *agapáō*] us" (1 John 4:19). This reciprocating love is the product of the Holy Spirit in us: "The love [*agápē*] of God is shed abroad in our hearts by the Holy Ghost which is given unto us" (Rom. 5:5).

Here in verse 37, however, the verb *philéō* means to befriend, and the present participle calls our attention to the habit of befriending. James tells us that Abraham was called the "friend [*philos* {5384} of God" as the result of his willingness to sacrifice his son Isaac (James 2:23; see author's *Faith, Love & Hope: An Exposition of the Epistle of James*). This event mirrored God's sacrificial love for the world: "Herein is love, not that we loved God, but that he loved us, and sent his Son to be the propitiation for our sins" (1 John 4:10).

[38] This leads to another positive principle for the us as believers. Whereas we must endeavor to maintain family love (*storgē*), we must also realize that the acceptance of God's unique love (*agápē*) will weaken human relationships (*philía*). Such diminishing is a "**cross**" (*staurós* [4716], striking the bar across) to bear. Ironically, the bearing of this cross of death is the path to life, to being "worthy of me [Christ]."

[39] The phrase "**he that findeth**" translates *ho heurōn*, the definite article (3588) and the aorist active participle of *heurískō* (2147), to find. The aorist marks entry into the kingdom, the initiation "of the faith of Abraham; who is the father of us all" (Rom. 4:16). Abraham trusted in God's righteous provision for a sacrifice in place of his son Isaac.

The word translated "**life**" is *psuchē* (5590), soul. Thus, we believers lose or destroy our souls in order to find them in Christ (see our exegesis of the parables in Luke 15). The word "**lose**" is *apolései*, the future active tense of *apóllumi* (622), meaning "to destroy." The souls of our old natures are crucified or destroyed in salvation, and our newly created spirits give life to our bodies (Rom. 8:10, 11). Those whose spirits have been re-created in Christ (Eph. 2:10) are willing to risk them for our Lord, since people can kill our bodies but not our souls. We know that our regenerated spirits liberated from our bodies will live on forever in Christ's presence (2 Cor. 5:1–8; Phil. 1:21).

The Privilege of Accepting Believers
(10:40–42; Mark 9:41)

[40] Jesus revealed the exalted value of believers whom God has "made [to] sit together in heavenly places in Christ Jesus" (Eph. 2:6). Because we are indwelt by both the Father and the Son, an inevitable linkage impacts everyone we meet: "He that **receiveth** [*dechómenos*, the present middle deponent participle of *déchomai* {1209}, to receive, welcome] you receiveth me, and he that receiveth me receiveth him that sent me."

Even if unbelieving relatives reject us, we must remember that the living, triune God Himself lives within us (John 14:23; Rom. 8:9–11; 1 Cor. 6:19; 2 Cor. 6:16; Col. 3:16). Those who repent and receive us, receive the Father, Son, and Holy Spirit.

The negative aspects of rejection have already been stressed (vv. 16–39). Now Jesus encourages us by saying that we will not experience total rejection for those whom God the Father draws to His Son will welcome us (John 6:44, 65).

[41, 42] We are prophets—preachers of God's grace—and righteous, because we are clothed in His righteousness (Eph. 6:14), the basis of our assurance of God's reward. The Greek word for "**reward**" (*misthós* [3408]) means a payment proportionate to character and work.

> He that receiveth a prophet in the name of a prophet shall receive a prophet's reward; and he that receiveth a righteous man in the name of a righteous man shall receive a righteous man's reward. And whosoever shall give to drink unto one of these little ones a cup of cold water only in the name of a disciple, verily I say unto you, he shall in no wise lose his reward.

True believers are able to discern those who belong to Christ, from prophets to "little ones." Christians do not have to be great, famous, or do outstanding work to be blessed by God. The Lord rewards us for the little things we do, even something as simple as giving a cup of cold water to a person in need "in the name of a disciple."

We should recall the Lord's encouraging words concerning our actions toward other believers: "Inasmuch as ye have done it unto one of the least of these my brethren, ye have done it unto me" (Matt. 25:40). Assuming the Lord is ranking the importance of believers in descending order—i.e., "prophet . . . righteous man . . . only [*mónon* {3440}] . . . a disciple"—His point is that from the greatest to the least, all of us are indwelled by the living God. Our relative, operative values, therefore, are not intrinsic but derivative, owing to the elements we commonly share (*koinōnéō* [2841], to partake):

> There is one body, and one Spirit, even as ye are called in one hope of your calling; one Lord, one faith, one baptism, one God and Father of all, who is above all, and through all, and in you all. (Eph. 4:4–6)

God alone can make a society out of people. He gives us laws and the power to conform to them by infusing His holy nature (2 Pet. 1:4) through salvation—the legal forgiveness (*áphesis* [859]) of sin and the release (*athétēsis* [115]) from its power.

CHAPTER

11

cↄ

John the Baptist
(11:1–15; Luke 7:18–35)

[1] At this point, Jesus **ended** [*etélesen*, the aorist tense of *teléō* {5055}, to finish] His **commanding** [*diatássōn*, the present active participle of *diatássō* {1299} from *diá* {1223}, through; and *tássō* {5021}, to appoint, arrange, order] of the twelve disciples . . ." (a.t.)

Although Jesus had given the Twelve authority to cast out unclean spirits and tenderly heal the sick from every kind of disease and weakness, we find no evidence that they all exercised this authority. But Peter and John restored the legs of a lame man they met in the temple (Acts 3:6–12). We are not told which apostles were used in various miracles performed at Solomon's porch. Peter, however, was so outstanding that people thought even his shadow could heal (Acts 5:15). He healed a man named Aeneas who had been sick with palsy for eight years (Acts 9:33, 34). This healing was incidental to Peter's visit to the town of Lydda. A third miracle performed by Peter was the resurrection of a girl named Tabitha (Acts 9:36–42).

The authority the Twelve received did not protect them from persecution and imprisonment (Acts 5:17–20), and King Herod was not restrained by Christ's authority conveyed to the Apostles (Matt. 10:1). He imprisoned Peter and even killed James, the brother of John (Acts 12:1–4).

On the other hand, persecution did not stop the Apostles from teaching in the temple. They chose deacons to take on ministerial services so they could devote themselves to teaching, fasting, and praying. This was the beginning of the *diatássōn*, the giving of special duties and orders in the church.

[2] John the Baptist, the forerunner of Jesus Christ, was imprisoned with the prospect of death overshadowing him. The enigma of God's sovereignty is why

He allows evil to coexist with and sometimes temporarily triumph over good in the world (Job 1:11, 12; 2:5, 6; Dan. 7:7, 12; 8:10–14; Rev. 13:5–7).

The authorities were evil men who had attained civil power. During a visit to Rome, Herod Antipas of Galilee had seduced his brother's wife and married her. When John the Baptist condemned this illicit affair, Herod put him in the prison (*desmōtērion* [1201]) of Machaerus near the Dead Sea. John never showed any sign of fear that would lead him to compromise his ethical stance against Herod. He was a brave man, willing to face even death by condemning this common case of adultery.

[3] While in prison, John heard of Jesus' works, but Satan tempted him to doubt that Jesus was Israel's Messiah. Consequently, he dispatched some of his disciples to ask Jesus,

> Are You the **Coming One** [*erchómenos*, the present middle deponent participle of *érchomai* {2064}, I am coming], **or** [*ḗ* {2228}, i.e., if You are not] **do we wait for** [*prosdokōmen*, the present subjunctive of *prosdokáō* {4328}, to wait for] **another** [*héteron*, the masculine accusative of *héteros* {2087}, another Messiah, another Person {masculine gender} of a different kind]? (a.t.)

John used this participial noun to announce the Messiah's coming in Matthew 3:11. He thought there might be a series of messianic appearances— one Messiah to redeem people from sin, another to rescue the redeemed out of this sinful world, and a third to create a new world where righteousness would reign unhindered. Jesus' disciples and John himself, hampered with persecution, looked primarily ahead to the victorious reign of Israel's Messiah.

[4] John had asked if he and his disciples should wait for another "Coming One." To substantiate His messianic claim, Jesus told these disciples to tell John about His miraculous words and deeds:

> **Go** [*poreuthéntes*, the aorist passive deponent participle of *poreúomai* {4198}, having gone] and **report to** [*apaggeílate*, the aorist imperative of *apaggéllō* {518} from *apó* {575}, from; and *aggéllō* {n.f.}, to announce] John again those things that you do hear and see. (a.t.)

John's messengers were commanded to report directly **to** John **from** (*apó*) the things they had personally heard and seen. Jesus' words and miracles would give John assurance in the face of death that he had genuinely been the forerunner of Israel's Messiah.

[5] Jesus listed the proof that He was truly the Anointed One of God so John and his disciples no longer had to "wait for another one":

The blind receive their sight, and the lame walk, the lepers are cleansed, and the deaf hear, the dead are raised up, and the **poor** [*ptōchoí*, the plural of *ptōchós* {4434}, helpless] have the gospel preached to them.

In Matthew 5:3, the "**poor in spirit**" (*ptōchoí tō pneúmati*) are the spiritually helpless. Because He knew their burdens, Jesus targeted these especially with the preaching of the gospel (*euaggelízontai* from *euaggelízō* [2097]). Since this list of miraculous events mimics the prophecies concerning the Messiah in Isaiah 61:1–3, John would be encouraged to hear of Jesus' authenticity.

Suffering believers are tempted to think that God has either lost His power or changed His character. God is always the same, but He does sovereignly deliver each of us with perfect wisdom and timing. He especially blesses those who can accept suffering without complaining.

[6] Perhaps to preempt John's perseverance to the end, Jesus added,

And **blessed** [*makários* {3107}] is he, whosoever **shall** not **be offended** [*skandalisthē̄*, the third person singular aorist passive subjunctive of *skandalízō* {4624}, to cause to sin] **in** [*en* {1722}, in, with, or by] me.

John was indeed blessed because he accepted martyrdom in lieu of compromising His Lord's ethics. He was not "offended" in Him, for he remained imprisoned because he defended God's law against adultery.

Makários is used in the plural throughout the Beatitudes in Matthew 5:3–11, but here it is singular and predicative, describing the full satisfaction of being indwelt by "the Blessed One" (*ho makários*; 1 Tim. 1:11; 6:15; see the author's *The Beatitudes—The Pursuit of Happiness* and word #3107 in *The Complete Word Study Dictionary: New Testament*). In the context of persecution, God's indwelling presence is particularly relevant because those fully satisfied in Him are not offended by circumstances controlled by Him. Had He chosen, Jesus could have as easily rescued John as personally come down from the cross. But John neither needed nor wanted rescuing because he was fully satisfied (blessed) with God's presence. When Jesus is our all (Col. 3:11), we have, as Paul says, "all things" (1 Cor. 3:21).

[7, 8] While John's disciples were returning to him, Jesus began to tell the "**multitudes**" (*óchloi*, the plural of *óchlos* [3793], crowd) around Him about John the Baptist.

Here we find the verb *theásasthai*, the aorist middle deponent infinitive of *theáomai* (2300), "**to see** [with wonderment or amazement]." As we noticed earlier, this is the word from which "theater" is derived. Jesus asked the multitudes if they had come out into the desert to marvel at (*theásasthai*) or to be entertained by a reed shaken by the wind. In other words, was John the Baptist a spineless victim shaken by circumstances? If they had known him before going out to see him, they would not have thought he delighted in a soft life. John ate what he could find in the wilderness and wore clothing made of camel's hair (Mark 1:6), which was spun into a coarse cloth used to make tents. Poor peasants used it also for outer garments, and some prophets of Israel may have as well (2 Kgs. 1:8; Zech. 13:4).

Jesus told His listeners that His prophets suffered discomforts and did not live soft, easy lives. He emphasized this with the word "**behold**" in verse 8 (*idoú* [2400] from *eídō* [1492], meaning to see and perceive or comprehend). He called attention to the full meaning of what a prophet was and that John met all the qualifications. John was self-effacing; he adopted the wilderness as his home, and he understood that Jesus was God who became man to save people from their sins. He preached Jesus' message that humanity's greatest need was repentance.

In Zacharias' song of blessing (Luke 1:67–79) for his son John, he cited the ancient prophets (Luke 1:70) and called his child "a prophet of the Most High" (Luke 1:76 NIV). John the Baptist was the transitional prophet between the Old and New Testaments, closing one era of history and introducing a new era with the coming of the Messiah.

[9, 10] Jesus confirmed this with the words, "Yea, **I say** [*légō* {3004}] unto you," meaning, "I know what I am saying to you." He then added that John was "more than a prophet," quoting Malachi's prophecy of a "messenger" who would herald His coming: "**Behold** [*idoú* as in v. 8], I send my **messenger** [*ággelon* {32}, angel] before thy face" (see Mal. 3:1). A definite article before "messenger" means there was only one unique fulfillment.

Jesus urged the people to note that something extraordinary was happening. They were observing a miracle. The prophet who had been predicted hundreds of years before the coming of the Messiah as His forerunner was now alive. God Himself had said,

> **I send** [*apostéllō* {649}, to send on a mission, akin to *apóstolos* {652}, apostle, one who is sent] my messenger, [meaning that this personally known prophet will carry the very words of God. John's specific mission is predicted:] . . . who **shall prepare** [*kataskeuásei*, the future tense of *kataskeuázō* {2680}, construct, prepare fully and make ready] your **way** [*hodón* {3598}] before You. (a.t.)

[11] Jesus hailed John as the greatest of those "**born** [*gennētoís* {1084}; note that the word has two *n*'s and comes from the verb *gennáō* {1080}, to give birth to, not *gínomai* {1096}, to become as in *génesis* {1078}; see note on Matt. 1:1] of women," a veiled pointer to the incarnation—easy to miss if we are not careful. Besides Christ, no one had been born without the involvement of a man (*anếr* [435]; see John 1:13 and the author's book entitled, *Was Christ God?*). Of those born to women, Jesus said, none was "**greater**" (*meízōn* [3187], greater in character) than John the Baptist. Yet, He continued, the least person born into the kingdom of God is greater than John.

John the Baptist announced the coming of the kingdom or reign of heaven in Jesus Christ (Matt. 3:3). That era would see the establishment of a new order of things, and the common people misunderstood this. They thought that John's water baptism would spare them from the wrath of God. This superficial view of salvation precipitated a rush to be baptized. This is why John's message was, "Bring forth therefore fruits meet for repentance" (Matt. 3:8).

[12] The people's haste to justify themselves through a physical action was nothing new. Jesus said it was prevalent "from the days of John the Baptist **until** [*héōs* {2193}] **now** [*árti* {737}, the present]."

Baptism by John was becoming a ritual, an easy way for people to assuage their guilt and fear of God's wrath. Since it was popular and did not cost anything, they clamored for it. The *entolế* (1785), commandment of God (Matt. 15:3), was being replaced by another *éntalma* (1778), a religious precept (Matt. 15:9). This "**now**" of which Christ spoke extends to the present time, for humans have not changed.

"**Violence**" translates *biázetai*, the present middle tense of *biázō* (971), to force, to violate, akin to *bía* (970), violent force. Those who do not repent "take [the kingdom of heaven] by force" through self-righteousness, not submitting to the righteousness of God (Rom. 10:3). They are like false shepherds who enter the sheepfold by climbing over the wall to steal or destroy the Great Shepherd's sheep (John 10:1, 7–18). These "**violent people**" (*biastaí* [973]; found only here) force their way into the fold, though they are not sheep. They "**take it by force**" (*harpázousin* [726], sudden seizure as by a robber, appropriation) in their own way and time. But they are ultimately unsuccessful, fighting, as they are, the King of kings!

[13] Because Christ fulfilled the old covenant's Law and prophecies (Matt. 5:17), that covenant ended with the coming of the new Elijah, John the Baptist, according to Jesus: "For all the prophets and the law prophesied until John."

[14] Here the word translated "**if**" is *ei* (1487), the "if" of hypothesis. "**To receive**" (*déxasthai*, the aorist infinitive of *déchomai* [1209], to accept) the truth that John the Baptist was "Elijah **about** [*méllōn*, the present participle of *méllō* {3195}] to come" was a matter of choice. To interpret this verse, we should keep in mind Gabriel's prophecy to Zacharias:

And he shall go before him in the spirit and power of Elijah, to turn the hearts of the fathers to the children and the disobedient to the wisdom of the just, to make ready a people prepared for the Lord. (Luke 1:17; a.t.; cf. Mal. 4:5, 6)

[15] Not all would receive this truth, so Jesus reinforced it with the words: "He who has ears, let him hear" (NIV). This verb *akoúō* (191) carries the double meaning of both hearing and understanding. That Jesus intended the latter follows from the inference that some had ears and heard (i.e., understood), while others did not. Although they had physical ears to hear the sounds, they did not perceive for they closed their spiritual ears to the Lord's conviction of sin.

People Are Innately Rebellious and Critical
(11:16–24; Luke 10:13–15)

[16] Jesus now told the people that "**this** [*taútēn*, the feminine accusative of *hoútos* {5026}] **generation** [*geneá* {1074}]" was like "**children**" (*paidía* [3813], little children) who could hear but were unable to understand. They were petulant and irritable because of their immaturity.

He compared His listeners to children who sat in the "**markets**" (*agoraís* [58]) where people gather and "**called**" (*prosphōnéō* [4377]) to their "**fellows**" (*hetérois* [2087], other in a different sense [MT, Nestle's, UBS]; or *hetaírois* [TR], those of the same company, companions; see word #2083 in the author's, *Complete Word Study Dictionary: New Testament*). Whom would children call to listen to them? Clearly to other children, companions (*hetaireía* [n.f.] akin to *hetaíros* [2083]). Accordingly, the Textus Receptus makes more exegetical sense.

[17] The word "**piped**" (*ēulḗsamen* [832]) means to play a wind instrument. It is associated with the noun *aulós* (836), a pipe or flute usually played at weddings. "**Dance**" translates *ōrchḗsasthe*, the aorist middle deponent indicative of *orchéomai* (3738), to dance, from which our English verb "orchestrate" comes.

These children expected others to dance to their tune, as Herodias' daughter did (Matt. 14:6; Mark 6:22), and to "**mourn**" (*ethrēnḗsamen*, the aorist tense of *thrēnéō* [2354], to lament in an audible manner, to wail loudly, as was done at funerals; see Matt. 9:23) the way they did. They could not tolerate consistency. The word for "**lamented**" is interesting. It is translated from *ekópsasthe*, the aorist middle indicative of *kóptō* (2875), to cut, strike, or beat one's body, particularly the chest. Displaying grief was common in those days.

Mourners not only beat and cut their bodies, but they also tore out their hair and ripped their garments. No matter what tune was played, these contrary individuals did not respond accordingly. The children, in turn, were dissatisfied, and this illustration served as a lead-in to "**this generation's**" immature censure of two of God's prophets.

[18] Something was wrong with this first prophet. They said, "He hath a devil." The Greek word translated "**devil**" is *daimónion* (1140), a demonic spirit. The dance music was addressed to John. Austerity was not the proper response. John not only did not dance, but he did not indulge in any form of entertainment. He was austere, sober, zealous—and, in their eyes, wrong!

[19] People directed the opposite criticism to Jesus, the second Prophet. He did not beat Himself; He simply ate and drank normally. They accused Him of being a "**glutton**" (*phágos* [5314], a man who overeats) and a "**winebibber**" (*oinopótēs* [3630], one who drinks too much wine).

John's critics considered him demon-possessed because he deprived himself of ordinary food, drink, and clothing. Yet the same critics accused Jesus of overindulgence when He conformed to normal consumption. The lesson here is simple: Whether we deprive ourselves or conform, critics will criticize. The best we can do is ignore unjust criticisms and study God's will for our lives as given in Scripture. Jesus endured this hostility, and because we are not above Him, we will experience similar criticisms (Matt. 10:24, 25).

The insults hurled at Jesus included His associations: He was "a friend of publicans and sinners." Indeed, in His earthly life, Jesus was not like the Pharisees whom He repeatedly called "hypocrites" (Matt. 23:13–15, 23, 25, 27, 29). Pharisees were separatists in name and practice. Jesus, on the other hand, reached out to publicans and sinners by living among them. But people could not accuse Him of discriminating in favor of the poor since, on three occasions, He accepted dinner invitations to the homes of Pharisees (Luke 7:36–39; 11:37–41; 14:1–6). In no case did Jesus compromise His ethics. He just met the needs of those who needed Him—rich or poor, famous or anonymous.

Jesus did not care what the Pharisees thought: "Who when he was reviled, reviled not again; when he suffered, he threatened not; but committed himself to him that judgeth righteously" (1 Pet. 2:23). Proof of Peter's testimony follows here:

But **the** [*hē* {3588}] **wisdom** [*sophía* {4678}, i.e., "the wisdom of God," not generic wisdom or man's wisdom in general] **was justified** [*edikaiōthē*, the aorist passive of *dikaióō* {1344}, to prove right] **by** [*apó* {575}, from—either directly or indirectly] **her** [*autēs*, the genitive feminine singular of *autós* {846};

the feminine gender of this pronoun corresponds to the feminine gender of the noun, *sophía*] **children** [*téknōn* {TR, MT}, the genitive plural of *téknon* {5043}, those who are born of God]. (a.t.)

All the Greek texts of Luke 7:35 add "all" to "her children." Furthermore, instead of the phrase "by her children," the more ancient and complete Greek texts of Matthew 11:19 have "by her works [*érgōn* {2041}]," meaning the works of Christ, the indwelling Logos who is the "power . . . and wisdom [*sophía*] of God" (1 Cor. 1:24; note: Luke 7:35 has "by her children").

Both statements are true, and the simplest synthesis is, "Wisdom was justified by her works of [i.e., within] her children." This avoids the theological difficulty of God depending on humans, even believers, to "justify" His wisdom.

The argument, then, is this: The same wisdom (*Lógos*) of God worked both deprivation in John the Baptist and normal consumption in the Son of man. The Pharisees criticized both works of God's wisdom. But God—always the subject of *dikaióō*, since "it is God [*theós* {2316}] that [*ho* {3588}] justifieth [*dikaíōn*, the present participle of *dikaióō* {1344}]" (Rom. 8:33)—justified His wisdom in both cases; that is, He decreed that both deprivation and normal consumption were right. But no matter what God did, the Pharisees declared His wisdom to be wrong.

[20–23] Jesus now tied together opportunity and responsibility. The greater the opportunity, He taught, the greater the responsibility.

In three neighboring cities in Galilee—Chorazin, Bethsaida, and Capernaum (v. 23)—Jesus had performed many powerful manifestations of His deity. He called these miracles "**mighty works**" (*dunámeis*, the plural of *dúnamis* [1411], power, accomplishment; vv. 20, 21, 23; see also Matt. 13:54, 58; Mark 6:2; Luke 10:13).

Jesus argued that if the miracles performed in Chorazin and Bethsaida had been done in Tyre, Sidon, and Sodom, the people would have repented, implying that miracles were generally sufficient to lead to repentance. Nevertheless, the people of Chorazin and Bethsaida, "**repented not** [*ou* {3756}, the absolute 'not']" (v. 20). Jesus performed miracles, but they rejected them. The word "**if**" (*ei* [1487]) in this verse is the "if" of hypothesis: "**If**" the Gentile cities of Tyre and Sidon had had the same opportunities, they would have repented "as if" (the objective *án* [302], if, i.e., "as if they were") in sackcloth and ashes, that is, in great humility. (The Greek particle *án* is not translated in the KJV.)

Then Jesus said that if the same demonstration of power performed in Capernaum had been shown in Sodom, one of the most sinful cities of antiquity (Gen. 13:10–13; 18:20; 19:1–29), the people would have repented, and the city would not have been destroyed. In general, Romans 1:20 tells us that

God's eternal power and divinity (*theiótēs* [2305]) revealed to all humanity in creation leaves people without excuse (*anapológētos* [379], without apology). On the day of judgment, those who have rejected God's general revelation will stand condemned before Him to be judged and punished.

[24] The judgments on ancient cities that witnessed no miracles will be "**more tolerable**" (*anektóteron* [414], the comparative of *anektós*, tolerable [a.t.]; from *anéchō* [430], to hold up) than on those cities that saw Jesus' miracles. The comparative adjective proves there will be degrees of punishment according to available light, just as there will be degrees of rewards for believers (2 Cor. 5:10).

God Reveals Himself to Babes
(11:25–27; Luke 10:21, 22)

[25, 26] This portion of Scripture is a "**response**" (*apokritheís* from *apokrínomai* [611], to answer) to the query John the Baptist's disciples made when they came to Jesus, asking whether He was the "Coming One" or whether they were to expect someone different (v. 3). In His prayer, Jesus spoke audibly to the Father so His disciples and others could hear Him.

> At that time Jesus answered and said, **I thank** [*exomologoúmai*, the present middle indicative of *exomologéō* {1843}, to acknowledge, confess, agree fully] thee, O Father, Lord of heaven and earth, because **thou hast hid** [*apékrupsas* {TR, MT} from *apokrúptō* {613}, to hide; see Matt. 10:26; Nestle's and UBS have *ékrupsas*] these things from the wise and **prudent** [*sunetós* {4908} from the verb *suníēmi* {4920} from *sún* {4862}, together; and *híēmi* {n.f.}, to send or put; to comprehend], and hast revealed them unto babes. Even so, Father: for so it seemed good in thy sight.

Although God has endowed humans with superior knowledge, their comprehension of the things of God is extremely limited. There are two kinds of wisdom—the world's wisdom and God's wisdom (1 Cor. 1:20, 21). The people whose faith is in the world's wisdom cannot know God' wisdom except through the gift of faith. They can receive such wisdom only by asking with the simplicity and trust of a child (James 1:5).

The word translated "prudent" is the mind. According to Scripture, neither the world's wisdom nor human prudence could discover what God hid (1 Cor. 1:21). Consequently, God "**revealed**" (*apekálupsas* [602], to uncover) what people could not discover (*anakalúptō* [343], uncover; see Luke 24:25, 45; Rom. 16:25).

[27] Then the Lord Jesus added,

> **All things** [*pánta*, the plural of *pás* {3956}, all and everything in particu-
> lar] **are delivered** [*paredóthē* {3860}, to deliver, implying intimacy of nature;
> from the preposition *pará* {3844}, indicating close proximity; and *dídōmi*
> {1325}, to give abundantly as a gift] unto Me of [*hupó* {5259}] My Father. And
> **no one** [*oudeís* {3762} from the absolute negative *ou* {3756}; the particle *dé*
> {1161}, even; and *heís* {1520}, one; "not even one"] **knows** [*epiginōskei* {1921},
> to know completely] the Son but the Father, neither does anyone know the
> Father but [save; KJV] the Son, and he to whomsoever the Son chooses to reveal
> Him. (a.t.)

Here Jesus spoke as the unique (*monogenēs*; see John 1:14, 18; 3:16, 18;
1 John 4:9) Son of God. The English "by" in "by my Father" is not *apó* (575)
that allows for mediation through another party but rather, *hupó* (5259), indicating direct, unmediated relationship to the Father. God the Father is not the
same Father to us that He is to His Son (*huiós* [5207]). The Father and Son,
together with the Spirit, are one God.

The word translated "but" is *ei mḗ* (1508). This expression is made up of
the subjective *ei* (1487), if or suppose, and the relative negative *mḗ* (3361).
Taken separately, the expression *ei mḗ* means "suppose not" or "if not." The
exception clause introduced by these two words clearly indicates that the only
One who exhaustively knows the Son is the Father and vice versa. The co-
omniscience between Father and Son is uniquely stated. Only thus does the
Son have the absolute authority to reveal the Father to an individual—"he to
whomsoever the Son will reveal him." This expresses the absolute unity of the
will of the Son and the Father. As one God, they have a single will concerning what and to whom they reveal spiritual truth.

Christ's Invitation to Inner Rest
(11:28–30)

[28] Jesus now called those who realized their need to come to Him. He first
used this word "**Come**" (*deúte* [1205]) in Matthew 4:19–21 where He called
four of His disciples to become fishers of men. However, this time Jesus did
not call His disciples but those who carried two special burdens. The term,
"**the** [*hoi* {3588}] **laborers** [*kopióntes*, the present participle of *kopiáō* {2872}
from *kópos* {2873}, to work until fatigued]," refers to people who are worn out
and weary from hard work, especially those in the Lord's vineyard.

The next description is "**heavy laden**" (*pephortisménoi* [5412] from *phortízō* [5412], load; see v. 30). We all must carry our own "loads" (*phortíon* [5413]; Gal. 6:5). Life is hard for all of us, both physically and spiritually. Even wealth is a burden, since the material things of this world do not satisfy. So Jesus calls all who are wearied from earthly burdens. The word *phortíon* (load) compares with *báros* (922), the burdens our friends bear that we choose to share (see 2 Cor. 4:17; Gal. 6:2; 1 Thess. 2:6). Whereas *phortíon* is a consequence of Adamic sin, *báros* is a burden each individual must responsibly carry, even when shared with others.

Jesus promises inner "**rest**" (*anapaúsō*, the future tense of *anapaúō* [373], to give inner rest, peace), which can be ours in spite of the fatigue and responsibility of carrying our own personal loads.

[29] Jesus used the corresponding noun *anápausis* (372) here as His promise to those who come to Him as little children.

While it is difficult to understand how we can have inner rest in an evil world, such rest is the result of repenting and trusting. Jesus does not cancel the consequences of sin, but creates an inner tranquility in our spirits that gives us victory.

Cessation of work is *katápausis* (2663), the act of resting (from the verb *katapaúō* [2664], to settle down, to cease). Christ does not cause this to happen in this life, although "there remaineth a Sabbath rest [*sabbatismós* {4520}] to the people of God" (Heb. 4:9; a.t., cf. Heb. 4:10, 11) in the age to come. For now, we believers must continue to work hard, enabled by Christ to shoulder our personal loads. Because of *anápausis* (inner rest from above), we are willing and able to bear (*bastázō* [941]) the burdens (*báros*) of others (Gal. 6:2).

Christ bids us to approach Him not only **for** inner rest but **with** a willingness to take a "**yoke**" (*zugós* [2218]) on ourselves. A yoke is a piece of wood enabling two to share a load. Jesus not only gives inner rest, but He shares in the pulling of our personal loads (*phortíon*). We soon discover that after we yoke together with Christ, He shoulders the heavier part of our burdens. The command is to personally take the yoke on ourselves. If we are not willing to do so, He cannot share our burdens.

Jesus also commanded that we "**learn**" (*máthete*, the imperative of *manthánō* [3129], to learn as a disciple, a *mathētḗs*) about Him, specifically that He is both "**meek** [*práos* {4235}] and **lowly** [*tapeinós* {5011}, humble] in **heart** [*kardía* {2588}]." What a condescension that the Son of God should humble Himself to the point of dying for our sins.

The word "**meek**" (*práos*) implies "balanced." Our Lord carries neither more than necessary to strengthen us, nor less to overburden us. Jesus wants us to grow in Him and to learn responsibility. He cannot share our burdens if we do not put on His yoke. (See the author's study of meekness [Matt. 5:5] in his work, *The Beatitudes.*)

Now we learn of Jesus' humility, for He was not proud. The Son of man did not dominate His disciples, because He was eager for them to learn about His character of humility. The yoke is level (*tapeinós*, not uneven) so that each individual pulls according to his or her strength. Jesus never forces us beyond our abilities nor intimidates us by showing how much He can do and how little we can do.

No matter how great our load in life, Christ promises that we "**shall find**" (*heurésete* [2147], to get, obtain, receive) rest. That is part of the learning process. When we learn to pull our share by properly positioning the yoke, we always will experience inner rest.

[30] Jesus assured us that His yoke is "**easy**" (*chrēstós* [5543], profitable; from the verb *chráomai* [5530], to furnish what is needed). Because Christ freely gives us grace, His yoke is easy and His burden "**light**" (*elaphrós* [1645]). What a wonderful yoke grace is compared to the pharisaical yoke of the Law that only "loads men with loads too hard to be borne" (Luke 11:46; a.t.). Christ does not merely "touch the load with one of [His] fingers" (ibid.), but He shoulders it completely.

CHAPTER

12

Jesus Is Lord of the Sabbath
(12:1–14; Mark 2:23–28; 3:1–6; Luke 6:1–11)

The fourth commandment set apart the Sabbath (v. 1), the last (seventh) day of the week, to be holy and free of all labor (Ex. 20:8, 9). As we noted in the last chapter, Christ promised *anápausis* (372), inner rest, in this age, not *katápausis* (2663), structural rest, the Sabbath rest of the age to come, which "remaineth . . . to the people of God" (Heb. 4:9–11). *Anápausis* is rest and peace of soul in the midst of hard labors, while *katápausis* is a periodic cessation from labor.

[1] The Pharisees observed the disciples picking grain on the Sabbath. Their criticism was not that the disciples were stealing, since it was permissible for hungry persons to eat grain or corn in a field so long as they did not harvest it in quantity (Deut. 23:25).

[2] Instead, the Pharisees faulted the disciples for working on the "**Sabbath**" (4521), which was not permissible or "**lawful**" (*éxestin* [1832] or *exón*). They called Jesus' attention to this with the imperative, "**Behold**" (*idoú* [2400], look; see our notes on *idoú* in Matt. 1:20).

[3, 4] Jesus reminded the Pharisees that David and his men once ate showbread in the tabernacle that was forbidden to all but priests (1 Sam. 21:1–6). As in the present situation of the disciples, this was a case of the priority of hunger over ritual. Acts of mercy do not fall within the class of the ordinary work forbidden on the Sabbath.

[5] Again, Jesus argued, because the priests prepared (i.e., did work) offerings in the tabernacle or temple on the Sabbath (Num. 28:9, 10; see also Lev. 24:8 for the changing of showbread on the Sabbath), it therefore was permissible to feed hungry people. And what was permissible in the temple was certainly permissible outside the temple (see vv. 11, 12).

[6] Assuming from this clear example that the Pharisees would have to acknowledge that the temple sanctified certain types of work on the Sabbath, Jesus etched His authority above that of the temple:

> But [*dé* {1161}] **I say** [*légō* {3004}, to speak logically] unto you, That **in this place** [*hóde* {5602}, here] is one **greater** [*meízon* {3185}, the neuter singular of *mégas* {3173}; "greater thing," the neuter no doubt pointing to the "one thing" {*hén* {1520}; John 10:30; i.e., one Spirit} that the Father and Son are] than the **temple** [*hierón* {2411}, the total structure of the temple, including the *naós* {3485}, the inner sanctuary].

Jesus had referred to His body as a temple (*naón*) in John 2:19, so in this sense—the incarnation of God—He was the true inner sanctuary (*naós*), "**greater**" than the physical temple (*hierós*) before them. When He was sacrificed on the cross, therefore, the lamb, the inner sanctuary, and the altar were all rendered permanently ineffective (*lúsate*, the aorist imperative of *lúō* [3089], to loose, to release; John 2:19). This ended the old covenant's sacrificial system (Heb. 9:25–28). Correlatively, when Christ was raised from the dead and ascended to the right hand of the Father, the *naós*—His body—ascended with Him. This is why the apostle John saw both the inner sanctuary (*naós*) and the ark (*kibōtós* [2787]) of the covenant in heaven in his vision (Rev. 11:19). Since Christ's *naós* was sacrificed outside Jerusalem (Heb. 13:11–13), the true temple moved without the gates of the city, leaving Jerusalem and its physical temple "desolate" (Luke 13:35) but opening the only way to all peoples and nations.

By elevating His authority to a level higher than the temple that sanctified the work of priestly preparations on the Sabbath, Jesus readied the Pharisees for a conclusion they would not want to hear (see v. 8).

[7] For the second time (cf. Matt. 9:13), Jesus quoted Hosea 6:6 to prove that God was more pleased with "**mercy**" (*éleos* [1656]) than with animal sacrifices. They could never replace God's mercy offered to us in the sacrifice of His Son for our sins (Heb. 9:22–28).

> But if ye had known what this meaneth, I will have mercy, and not sacrifice, **ye would** not **have condemned** [*katedikásate*, the aorist of *katadikázō* {2613} from *katá* {2596}, against; and *dikázō* {n.f.}, to judge, pronounce sentence] the **guiltless** [*anaítios* {338} from *a* {1}, without; and *aitía* {156}, cause, warrant for arrest, reason to appear in court].

By using the same adjective to describe both the disciples and the priests who profaned the Sabbath (*anaítioi*; v. 5), Jesus established the innocence of both parties. Both were guiltless because God "**wills**" (*thélō* [2309]) mercy over sacrifices. The entire old sacrificial system was subordinate to this superior attribute that God looked for in humankind.

Accordingly, Jesus indicted the Pharisees under two counts. First, because the Law allowed priests to prepare meals on the Sabbath, there was no more legal basis for condemning the hungry disciples than David and his men. Secondly, "sacrifice," a term obviously intended to comprehend the entire ritualistic system of the old covenant, was never an end in itself. Sacrifice must serve mercy, because the latter is God's preference, His choice (*thélō*).

[8] Jesus completed the argument: "For the Son of man is Lord even of the sabbath day." (While He did not explicitly say so, He inferred that He was Lord of the temple as well, according to the words of v. 6.) Note here that Christ's humanity as well as His deity constituted His lordship. The Son of man, not just the Son of God, is Lord over the Sabbath.

Just as sacrifice was subordinate to mercy, so the Sabbath was not intended to rule over people in an oppressive way, especially when they were hungry: "The sabbath was made for man, and not man for the sabbath" (Mark 2:27).

[9] To show that acts of mercy were not forbidden but were commended, Jesus traveled on the Sabbath (another "forbidden work" in tradition) to a synagogue in Galilee. He knew a man would be there with a withered hand toward whom worshippers were mercilessly indifferent (Mark 3:1–3; Luke 6:8).

[10] Observe the "**behold**" (*idoú*; see our exegesis of this word in Matt. 1:20, 23; 2:1, 9; Rev. 21:3, 5; 22:7, 12) as Jesus called attention to inexcusable indifference in the face of need:

> And behold, a man had a withered hand, and **they asked** [*epērōtēsan*, the aorist tense of *eperōtáō* {1905}, specifically inquired] him, saying, **If** [*ei* {1487}, the subjective "if"] it is lawful **to heal** [*therapeúein*, the present infinitive of *therapeúō* {2323}] on Sabbath days? that **they might accuse** [*katēgorēsōsin*, the aorist subjunctive of *katēgoréō* {2723}, to charge, condemn, critically judge, from which we get out English word "categorize"] him. (a.t.)

The critical texts have *therapeúsai*, the *aorist* infinitive, which indicates they asked if it was lawful to heal at that time. Matthew states the purpose for the query, but the Pharisees did not mention it.

[11, 12] Jesus asked a question that forced them to expose their inconsistency, for they would rescue one of their own sheep that had fallen into a pit on the Sabbath:

> And he said unto them, What man shall there be among you, that shall have one sheep, and if it fall into a pit on the sabbath day, will he not lay hold on it, and lift it out? How much then is a man better than a sheep? Wherefore it is lawful to do well on the sabbath days.

Of course, healthy sheep are as much assets as the sick and needy are liabilities (Matt. 15:30), but can the well-being of a person be compared to that of an animal? To Jesus, the sick who "have need of a physician" (Matt. 9:12 NKJV) were of such great value that He laid down His life so that "whosoever believeth" (*pás ho pisteúōn*) might have everlasting life (John 3:16).

[13] Since this victim was so precious to Jesus, He commanded the man to stretch forth his hand, and then He healed him.

[14] The incredulous response to this healing was that the Pharisees planned how "**they might destroy** [*apolésōsin*, the aorist subjunctive of *apóllumi* {622}]" Jesus, presumably to fulfill the Law. This shows how far astray legalism can lead people. They actually thought that preserving the law of the Sabbath and even killing someone for breaking it was more important than showing mercy to a suffering person. In contrast, Jesus did not come to destroy the Law but to fulfill it (Matt. 5:17).

The lesson of this story is that it is lawful "**to do** [*poieín*, the present infinitive of *poiéō* {4160}] **well** [*kalōs* {2573}] on the sabbath" (v. 12). The present active infinitive means not just once but every time, that is, repeatedly. On another note, we also learn that "the hour comes when everyone who kills [us] thinks he is offering a sacred service to God" (a.t.; John 16:2). Such was the self-deception of the Pharisees.

Jesus Would Not Be Intimidated
(12:15–21; Mark 3:7–12)

[15] Jesus discreetly moved to another region as He had directed His disciples to do (Matt. 10:23). Great multitudes followed Him as He departed from the synagogue where He had performed this healing miracle. For the fourth time (Matt. 4:23–25; 8:16–17; 9:35–37), we find Him attracting and healing crowds.

[16] It was not yet "His hour" for crucifixion; so in order to offset the Pharisaic mind-set to destroy Him (v. 14), He:

> **charged** [*epetímēsen*, the aorist tense of *epitimáō* {2008}, to admonish strongly, to warn; cf. Mark 8:30] them that they should **not** [*mē* {3361}, the relative negative] make him **known** [*phanerón* {5318}, publicly known, manifest].

Jesus gave similar instructions to a leper whom He had cleansed (Matt. 8:4).

[17] Matthew's Gospel includes this note that Jesus' desire not to make His work public (see also Matt. 1:22; 4:14) was in accord with the prophecy that

He would not strive, cry, or proclaim His message loudly in the streets (see v. 19). This prophecy from Isaiah 42:1–4 also shows that the Messiah would preface His victorious conquest of Israel's enemies with a sacrificial redemption for all people. Matthew is the only author of a Gospel who quotes this prophecy.

[18] The quote begins with the imperative "**Behold**" (*idoú* [2400]; cf. Matt. 1:20), stressing that this first coming of the Messiah would be a surprise to Jews who were expecting a military victory (cf. Matt. 1:20, 23; 2:1, 9, 13, 19; 3:16, 17; 4:11; 7:4; 8:2, 24, 29, 32, 34; 9:2, 3, 10, 18, 20, 32; 10:16; 11:8, 10, 19; 12:2, 10).

In the prophecy, the Lord Jesus is called "my servant." The word "**servant**" (*pais* [3816]) means a young boy, meaning that Jesus would be a servant to His Father even in His youth. "**I chose**" (a.t.; *hērétisa*, the aorist tense of *hairetízō* [140], to choose or to take) implies suitability for the task. This is the only occurrence of this verb in the New Testament. The Lord Jesus took on Himself a special body and spirit/soul peculiar to the ministry He would accomplish as the incarnate God for humanity (Acts 2:27; Heb. 10:5). Jesus Christ was the chosen child-servant for the particular task of redemption.

The Father also refers to His Servant as "**my** [*mou* {3450}] **beloved** [*agapētós* {27}, an adjective in the Gospels applied exclusively to the Son of God; Matt. 3:17; 12:18; 17:5; Mark 1:11; 9:7; 12:6; Luke 3:22; 9:35; 2 Pet. 1:17]," or "the One who is inherently loved by Me." "**In**" translates the Greek preposition *eis* (1519), unto or into, which indicates purpose. *Eudókēsen*, "**is well pleased**," is the aorist tense of *eudokéō* (2106). It indicates the eternal pleasure the Father has in His Son including, of course, the Son's sinless spirit and body and His overall ministry of redemption, culminating at the cross.

This human nature would also have the Holy Spirit "**upon him**" (*ep' autón*). All three Persons of the triune God were present in and through Jesus' human nature.

The Word of God became flesh to "**show** [*apaggeleí*, the future tense of *apaggéllō* {518}, to announce] **judgment** [*krísin* {2920}, separation, judgment, the divine law proclaimed in the Gospels] to the nations" (a.t.). This gospel would be preached not only to the Jews but also to every other people. "Judgment" has the dual meaning of separating good from evil and calling into account various responses to the gospel.

[19] The prophecy explains how this gospel would be proclaimed. It speaks of Christ's meekness in ministry and suffering for humankind. The word "**strive**" (*erísei* [2051] to complain out loud, protest; used only here in the

NT) means to contend or dispute. The Lord Jesus did not strive in His first coming. Although He reasoned with the Pharisees on numerous occasions, He did not enter into heated arguments (see also Isa. 53:7, 8; Acts 8:32, 33).

Christ came in meekness. The Son of man proclaimed the kingdom of God through the "still small [invitational] voice" (1 Kgs. 19:12). "**Cry**" is the future tense of *kraugázō* (2905), meaning to shout or cry out. As you read the Scriptures, notice how frequently the silence of the Lord Jesus is mentioned in His ministry and suffering. Today the message of Jesus Christ can be heard only deep within the silence of the heart, because He came in the meekness and quietness of a lamb [*arníon* [721]), not in the ferocity of a lion, which will characterize His Second Coming (Rev. 5:5, 6). *Arníon* is used almost exclusively in the book of Revelation (5:6, 8, 12, 13; 6:1, 16; 7:9, 10, 14, 17; 12:11; 13:8; 14:1, 4, 10; 15:3; 17:14; 19:7, 9; 21:9, 14, 22, 23, 27; 22:1, 3) while the Gospels use primarily *amnós* ([286]; John 1:29, 36).

[20] The prophecy continues with Christ's loving concern for and patience with humankind. The "**bruised** [*suntetrimménon* {4937}] **reed** [*kálamos* {2563}]" could refer to a reed bent by the wind or stepped on, or, more likely, to the reed used as a writing instrument during Isaiah's time. A plant's stem was sharpened to a point, then dipped in ink. In time, the point either became saturated with ink and softened beyond use, or the reed bent from pressure at the point where it was held. Frequently, a writer would snap it in two and throw it away.

A second illustration is the "**smoking** [*tuphómenon*, the present participle of *túphō* {5188}, to make smoke] **flax** [*línon* {3043}, a fiber used to make linen]." It referred to the linen wick of an oil lamp smoldering and nearly extinguished. To stop the smoke, one would crush the wick between his or her fingers.

Although we may be bruised by the cares of the world or broken by sin, Jesus cares. He will not abandon us or cast us aside. If the fire of our faith ebbs until nothing is left but smoke, Jesus will care for us. He wants to restore the flame of faith and infuse life into dying embers. The two negatives in this verse and the two in verse 19 are all the absolute "**not**" (*ou* or *ouk* [3756])—four guarantees of the Lord's protection.

His mercy will continue "till **he send forth** [*ekbálē*, the aorist subjunctive of *ekbállō* {1544}, to cast out] **judgment** [*krísis*] unto victory." Here the word "**judgment**" is used for the second time (cf. v. 18) with the double meaning of separation and judgment. Those who line themselves on the side of the chosen and beloved Servant (v. 18) will win the "**victory**" (*níkos* [3534]).

[21] "His **name** [*onómati*, the dative singular of *ónoma* {3686}, name]" refers to all that Christ's name stands for; and the "**Gentiles** [*éthnē* {1484}, nations

other than Israel] **shall trust** [*elpioúsin*, the future tense of *elpízō* {1679}, to hope] in Him" (a.t.). Believers dispersed among the nations are the flickering wicks that will prevail until God pronounces judgment.

A House Divided Against Itself Cannot Stand
(12:22–30; Mark 3:20–27; Luke 11:14–23)

[22] While Jesus was en route to Capernaum from Nazareth (see also Mark 1:21), friends brought a desperately needy man to Him. The man was not only demon-possessed, but blind and dumb as well.

The victim's handicaps were attributed to being "**possessed by a devil**" (*daimonizómenos*, the present passive deponent participle of *daimonízomai* [1139], to be demon-possessed, "demonized"). The result of his contact with Jesus was instantaneous: ". . . and he [Jesus] **healed** [*etherápeusen*, the aorist tense of *therapeúō* {2323}, to heal with compassion] him." The man could speak immediately when healed and did not have to learn how to form and pronounce words.

[23] The people were "**amazed**" (*exístanto*, the imperfect middle of *exístēmi* [1839], to be ecstatic), a Greek word from which we get the English word "ecstasy."

Jesus' repeated healing of the sick continued to amaze (reflected in the imperfect tense) the common people. This gave rise to the question, "Is not this the son of David?" meaning the Messiah (see 9:27). The word translated "**Is not?**" (*mḗti* [3385]) literally means "not perhaps?" from *mḗ* (3361), the relative "not", and *ti* (5101), anything. The question can be more accurately rendered, "Isn't this?" (see John 4:29). The people no doubt were confused concerning Jesus' use of power to heal and cast out demons but not to conquer their Gentile overlords.

[24] The Pharisees strongly objected to the crowd's accolades. The strength of their protest we deduce from the absolute negative "**not**" (*ou* [3756]) used here.

Categorically rejecting Jesus' messianic credentials, the Pharisees attributed His power to cast out demons to Beelzebub, the "**prince** [*árchonti* from *árchōn* {758}, chief, ruler] of the devils." The Pharisees concluded that since Jesus could effectively command demons, He must be their leader. But their logic was only as good as their starting point. They did not consider the other option: that Jesus was indeed the *Lógos* (3056) of God, the Logic personified, the Intelligence who became flesh (John 1:1, 14).

[25] It only makes sense that the Logic of God could read their minds:

And Jesus **knew** [*eidōs* from *eidō* {1492}, to know innately, to perceive] their **thoughts** [*enthumēseis*, the plural of *enthúmēsis* {1761}, device, contrivance; see Matt. 9:4; Acts 17:29; Heb. 4:12], and said unto them, Every **kingdom** [*basileía* {932}] divided against itself is brought to desolation.

The word "**desolation**" comes from the Greek *erēmoútai* (2049), which means to be deserted or self-destroyed. Here Jesus attempted to reason with the Pharisees. If He were using satanic power to expel demons, it follows logically that Satan's power was divided against itself. Such a contrary use of power would be divisive, self-defeating, and counterproductive to the demonic kingdom.

[26] Jesus began His hypotheses with the subjective "**if**" (*ei* [1487], suppose) from which He drew the conclusion that if Satan were to fight against himself, his kingdom could not possibly continue.

[27] Jesus extended His logic by using still another subjective "**if**" (*ei*, suppose). If the Pharisees' assumption that He cast out demons by Beelzebub, the prince of the devils, were correct, then by whom did their sons do the same?

They had three options: The first was not evident. Possibly the Pharisees' sons did not cast out devils at all, but this was not something an arrogant religious leader would admit. The second and third options were Beelzebub and the Spirit of God. The ideal answer would be: You (Jesus) cast them out by Beelzebub while our sons cast them out by the Spirit of God.

That may have sounded good, but the Pharisees were trapped. They knew if they admitted that both Beelzebub and the Spirit of God cast out demons, they would have no objective way of determining which was operating in either case. That was why the sons become judges. If their sons also cast out demons by Beelzebub, then there was no gain in charging Jesus with this (equal) crime. On the other hand, if their sons cast out demons by the Spirit of God, then Jesus possibly did as well. They were now adrift in a sea of skepticism. By admitting two powers, they were forced to concede that either Beelzebub or the Spirit of God was operating in any given instance. Consequently, any choice they made was self-defeating. Once again, the *Lógos* (Logic) of God trapped them in a quandary!

[28] Again, deepening the quandary, Jesus claimed that if (*ei*, suppose) He did cast out demons by the Spirit of God, a new conclusion followed: "**Then** [*ára* {686}, therefore, the logical consequence is that] the kingdom of God **is come** [*éphthasen*, the aorist tense of *phthánō* {5348}, to arrive] unto you."

The kingdom of God arrived when the Word (*Lógos*) became flesh (John 1:1, 14; see also the note on Matt. 1:1 on *génesis* [1078]). The word "**unto**" (*eph'* from *epí* [1909], upon) is better translated as "upon," meaning that the kingdom of God was imposed on the Pharisees whether they acknowledged it or not. The "**kingdom**" (*basileía* [932]) refers to the mediatorial reign of the Father through the incarnate God.

The obvious reference to the Trinity put the Pharisees in a precarious position. If Jesus cast out demons by the Spirit of God, then the Pharisees were rejecting the work of the Holy Spirit. Moreover, since the Spirit is the Spirit of the Father, then the Pharisees also implicated the Father in the charge. With one sweep of logic, Wisdom personified silenced the Pharisees' accusation.

[29] Jesus then taught the Pharisees something new. Casting out demons is not Satan toying with his subordinates, but rather the Son of God violently overpowering the archdemon and stealing his possessions:

> Or else how [*pôs* {4459}] can [*dúnatai*, from *dúnamai* {1410}, to be able, to be possible] one enter [*eiseltheín*, the aorist infinitive of *eisérchomai* {1525}, to enter] into a strong one's [*ischuroú* {2478}] house and spoil [*diarpásai*, the aorist infinitive of *diarpázō* {1283}, to thoroughly ransack, to snatch away] his goods [*skeúe*, the neuter plural of *skeúos* {4632}, object, vessel], unless he first binds [*désē*, the aorist subjunctive of *déō* {1210}, to bind] the strong one? And then he will spoil his house. (a.t.)

Satan is strong (*ischurós*), even stronger (*ischuróteros*) than we are, but he is no match for the power of Jesus Christ. Scripture calls the miracles of Christ *dunámeis* or "powers" (Matt. 7:22; 11:20, 21, 23; 13:54, 58; 14:2; Mark 6:2). Jesus' virtually overpowers the forces of sin, Satan, sickness, and death. He freely enters Satan's realms, ties him up, and takes his possessions.

[30] Jesus concluded with the warning that the one who is not for Him is necessarily against Him, and, correlatively, the one who does not "gather together with Him, scatters" (a.t.). Jesus warned the Pharisees that they could have no neutral position with respect to His person and work. This general statement introduced the subject of blaspheming against the Holy Spirit.

The Blasphemy Against the Holy Spirit
(12:31, 32; Mark 3:28–30; Luke 12:10)

To know what Jesus meant by blasphemy against the Holy Spirit, we need to understand the background of the occasion.

The Pharisees expressed their hatred and animosity toward Jesus by accusing Him of being in league with the devil. Jesus healed the blind and deaf demoniac in an instant, but the Pharisees attributed this miracle to Beelzebub, the prince of demons. Their hatred was so intense that they considered Jesus an accomplice of not just demons but of the prince of darkness himself. Had they been rational, they would have concluded that someone greater than Satan casts out demons. Since Satan's rule (*árchōn* [758], the active ruler) is restricted to the kingdom of darkness, they accused Christ of depending on the devil to stop evil in the world. But in so doing, they were forced to concede that Satan would be doing the work of the Holy Spirit, self-defeatingly casting out his own soldiers.

They refused to acknowledge Jesus' deity. They saw only the Son of man, not the Son of God who has no beginning or ending, who is self-existent, not a creature, but the Creator of all things (John 1:3–4). In revealing His relationship with the Holy Spirit, Jesus said in John 16:11–15 that the ruler of this world, the devil, "has [already] been judged [*kékritai*, the perfect passive of *krínō* {2919}, to judge]" (16:11; a.t.). At a certain time, "the Spirit of truth" (v. 13) would "come" (*élthē*, the aorist active subjunctive of *érchomai* [2064], to come) as that Person (*ekeínos* [1565], "that One" in the masculine, not neuter, gender that ordinarily designates the Holy Spirit [*tó Pneúma* {4151}]). ("He" that One [Person]; (v. 13; *ekeínos* again ascribing masculine personality to the Holy Spirit who might otherwise be conceptualized as an abstract power) "will glorify" (*doxásei*, the future active indicative of *doxázō* [1392], to recognize, honor, invest with dignity; v. 14) or reveal who Jesus Christ was and is. We can know the Son of God only through the Holy Spirit who has revealed Christ throughout all ages.

[31, 32] Jesus Christ frequently spoke of Himself as the "Son of man." These two verses emphasize the dual nature of Christ. Spiteful words aimed at His humanity—the Son of man—are forgivable. Those directed at the Spirit of God working in or through Him are not forgivable. This is the only unforgivable sin mentioned in the Bible. Since the Father gave Jesus the Holy Spirit "without measure" (John 3:34), it was indistinguishable from His divine nature as the Son of God. Thus, the Spirit of God is called the Spirit of Christ (see, e.g., Rom. 8:9; 1 Pet. 1:11). A rejection of the Spirit of God is, therefore, a rejection of Christ's deity.

The Pharisees' "**sin**" (*hamartía* [266]) against the Holy Spirit was "**blasphemy**" (*blasphēmía* [988], verbal abuse; derived from *bláx* [n.f.], meaning stupid; and *phēmí* [5346], to speak; therefore to predicate stupidity, to speak stupid things against). In their jealous rage, they concluded that Jesus leveraged Satan's power to cast out demons (v. 27). Such an argument was stupidity (*blakía*), an irrational rejection of the Spirit of Christ, Jesus' very Person, and, therefore, a flagrant denial of His deity and, by implication, of the triune God.

According to verse 31, any sin or blasphemy against the Son of man can be forgiven. Even on the cross, Jesus asked His Father to forgive those crucifying Him. But blasphemy against the One who reveals the truth about Christ cannot be forgiven. Jesus said that when the Holy Spirit would come, "He will reprove the world of sin, and of righteousness, and of judgment" (John 16:8). The one who irrevocably rejects this conviction has no recourse: It "shall **absolutely not** [*ouk* {3756}; the absolute negative used in both vv. 31, 32] be forgiven him" (a.t.).

Those who blaspheme the Holy Spirit will never be forgiven, "neither in this **age** [*aiōn* {165}, age, including the prevailing philosophy] nor in the **coming one** [*méllonti* {3195}, the one impending, coming soon]" (a.t.). What people embrace as truth in this life will follow them into eternity. "As it is appointed unto men once to die, but after this the judgment" (Heb. 9:27).

The Judgment on Nature and Words
(12:33–37; Luke 6:43–45)

The Pharisees were the legalists of their day. They attempted to keep the letter of the Law but despised anyone who fell short, and their words were correspondingly evil. So Jesus repeated the promise recorded in Matthew 7:15–20.

[33] Matthew alone incorporates Jesus' teaching that the accusation of the Pharisees—that Jesus cast out demons by the prince of demons—was the product (fruit) of their evil hearts. The fruit, He said, was "**rotten**" (*saprós* [4550], putrid; see Matt. 7:17, 18; 13:48; Luke 6:43), like spoiled fruit or decayed fish.

Since the Pharisees were hypocrites, Jesus told them to be consistent: "Either **make** [*poiēsate*, the aorist active imperative of *poiéō* {4160}] the tree good, and its fruit good; **or else make** [*poiēsate*] the tree corrupt, and its fruit corrupt" (a.t.). He thus expressed His desire for a final (the aorist) consistency between tree and fruit. Similarly, James objected to bitter and sweet water coming from the same fountain (i.e., mouth; James 3:10, 11). This agrees with the Lord's words to the church of Laodicea:

> I wish you were hot or cold [i.e., consistent, not pretending to be good when in fact you are evil]. So then, because you are lukewarm [inconsistent,

fraudulent] and neither cold nor hot [as above], I will spue you out of My mouth. (Rev. 3:15, 16; a.t.)

[34] Jesus then referred to the Pharisees as a "generation of vipers." The word "**generation**" (*gennḗmata*, the plural of *génnēma* [1081], offspring, product) derives from *gennáō* (1080), to give birth, and not from *gínomai* (1096), to become. The products of sin and hypocrisy are equivalent to the poisons of venomous snakes that prey on the unsuspecting.

Jesus did not expect anything but blasphemy to pour out of the mouths of such poisonous natures:

> How can you, **being** [*óntes*, the present participle of *eimí* {1510}, to be] **evil** [*ponēroí* {4190}, malevolent], speak **good things** [*agathá* {18}]? For out of the **abundance** [*perisseúmatos*, the genitive of *perísseuma* {4051}, surplus] of the heart, the mouth speaks. (Matt. 12:34 NKJV)

[35] And, Jesus added, this is the only possibility because, "A good man out of the good treasure of the heart bringeth forth good things: and an evil man out of the evil treasure bringeth forth evil things."

Those who are good have good hearts filled with good treasure and consequently produce good things. Evil people, on the other hand, have evil hearts filled with evil treasure. Jesus used the word "**treasure**" (*thēsaurós* [2344]) because people value good or evil. We find it difficult to believe that by nature we actually "treasure" evil, but we do until the Lord supernaturally changes our value systems by changing our natures. Apart from regeneration, evil persons cannot produce any good. They do not even want the freedom to do good; instead, they want freedom from God's righteousness: "For when ye were the servants of sin, ye were free from righteousness" (Rom. 6:20). Their treasured evil choice, the necessary product of evil natures—"you being evil" (Matt. 12:34)—is to be free from Christ. This was the Pharisees' choice. Legalism has no place for grace.

Here, *agathós* (18), benevolent, is contrasted with *ponērós* (4190), malevolent, just as *kalós* (2570), good, is the exact opposite of *kakós* (2556), bad. The first set of terms is attitudinal; the second is more frequently attached to actions. God alone is innately *agathós*, according to Mark 10:18, while Satan is frequently called *ho ponērós* (Matt. 13:19, 38; Eph. 6:16; 1 John 2:13, 14; 3:12; 5:18).

[36, 37] Jesus warned the Pharisees that while natures and values (treasures) produce good and evil "things," this will all terminate in judgment:

> But I say unto you, That every **idle** [*argós* {692} from *a* {1}, without; and *érgon* {2041}, work; "workless," without work, profitless] **word** [*rhēma* {4487}, exact saying] that men shall speak, they shall give account [*lógon* {3056}, accounting, reckoning, reason, justification] thereof in the day of judgment. For by thy words

thou shalt be justified [*dikaiōthésē*, the future passive tense of *dikaióō* {1344},
to justify, declare righteous], and by thy words **thou shalt be condemned**
[*katadikasthésē*, the future passive tense of *katadikázō* {2613}, to condemn].

Most people think that God is not interested in details, particularly idle
chatter, which, they assume, He overlooks. Yet here we learn not only that
such useless words exist but they also are being recorded for review on the day
of judgment. The Lord wants us to measure our words before we speak. He
wants us to speak valuable words that justify His presence in our lives and
advance His kingdom.

Argós sometimes connotes indolence, slothfulness, or laziness (1 Tim. 5:13;
Titus 1:12; 2 Pet. 1:8), but this should not be confused with the concept of
"slow" since we are commanded to be "slow [*bradús* {1021}] to speak" (James
1:19). There is a slowness in laziness and presumption, but there is also a slowness in strategy. In the realm of words, unbelievers care little about what they
speak. They speak foolishness, for they do not believe their words will be
judged: "A fool uttereth all his mind: but a wise man keepeth it in till afterwards" (Prov. 29:11). We believers, on the other hand, while fully capable of
thinking nonsense, should restrain ourselves from displaying it. We should
measure our words before we broadcast them to the public. To think before
we speak takes time; thus, the command to be "slow to speak."

Both believers and unbelievers need to envision the final judgment.
Judgment will not be equal for all. Unbelievers will be judged for their unbelief, which has been decreed already (note particularly the contrast of the tenses
of "believeth" and "condemned" in the following verse):

He that does not **believe** [*pisteúōn*, the present participle of *pisteúō* {4100}]
has been condemned [*kékritai*, the perfect passive of *krínō* {2919}, to judge]
already [*édē* {2235}], because he has not believed in the name of the only
begotten Son of God. (John 3:18; a.t.)

There will also be a scaled judgment of works (Matt. 11:20–24). For believers, heaven is our reward for justification in Christ by faith, but we will also
receive gradational rewards for service and faithfulness (2 Cor. 5:10).

Jesus Predicts His Death and Resurrection
(12:38–42; Mark 8:11, 12; Luke 11:29–32)

[38] Responding to Jesus' evident authority, some scribes and Pharisees
demanded a "**sign**" (*sēmeíon* [4592]) from Him. Although they had already
seen innumerable signs, they did not believe.

[39] Jesus responded with the general teaching that "an **evil** [*ponērá* {4190}, malevolent] and **adulterous** [*moichalís* {3428}] generation" seeks signs.

In verse 34, Jesus had called them an "offspring of vipers." Now He stated that the "evil and adulterous generation" continually "**seeks**" (*epizēteí* [1934] from *epí* [an intensive]; and *zētéō* [2212], to seek, inquire after, require, demand, strive after) authentication. Jesus had performed many miracles, but the more He showed the Pharisees, the more hardened they became. He refused to endlessly multiply miracles and noted that "no sign will be given to it [the evil, adulterous generation] except the sign of the prophet Jonah" (v. 39 NKJV).

God sent a recalcitrant Jonah to preach repentance to sinful Nineveh. While fleeing by boat in the opposite direction, Jonah was thrown overboard during a storm. God arranged for a large fish to swallow him, but after three days, the fish spit him out on dry land. God then repeated His call to Jonah to preach against Nineveh.

[40] From this history, Jesus drew an analogy: "As Jonah was in the belly of the **fish** [*kḗtos* {2785}, a huge fish; only here in the NT] for three days and three nights, thus shall the Son of man be in the heart of the earth three days and three nights" (a.t.).

The Greek uses a single word, "**night/day**" (*nuchthēmerón* [3574]), to define a twenty-four-hour period or any part of a full day. Jesus was in the grave part of Friday and Friday night, all day and night Saturday to early Sunday morning when He rose from the dead. (See the author's volume on 1 Cor. 15 entitled *Conquering the Fear of Death.*)

[41, 42] Nineveh will judge Israel because the city repented and turned from sin at the preaching of the prophet Jonah. In contrast, the Israelites had rejected not only the written Word of God for generations but now the incarnate Word, living, preaching, and working miracles in their midst. Because they rejected the Word over this long period of grace, God will judge (*krísis* [2920]) them. The day of judgment will include both justifying testimony (*marturía* [3141]; see John 1:7) and condemning testimony (*martúrion* [3142]; see Matt. 10:18).

This is made clear by the verb "**condemn**" (*katakrinoúsi*) in verse 41 and by the related *katakrineí* (2632) in verse 42. Jesus established the principle that those who repent are "condemning witnesses" against those who do not repent—proof that God will give ample opportunity for all.

Jesus used "**behold**" (*idoú* [2400]; see Matt. 1:20, 23), in both verses 41 and 42 to call attention to the superiority of His witness to those of Jonah and

Solomon respectively. This greater testimony was now in the very presence of the scribes and Pharisees. And yet they would not believe; they demanded more proof. In each age, God provides adequate light for judgment (John 1:9, 11, 12).

The greatest light is the true Light, Jesus Christ. Christ's preaching imposed the highest level of accountability (John 15:22–24).

The Return of Unclean Spirits
(12:43–45; Luke 11:24–26)

Although this paragraph is related to verses 22–30 concerning the healing of the demon-possessed, blind, and deaf man, Jesus no doubt intended an application to the decaying state of Israel for rejecting its Messiah for legalism (cf. the prior context of judgment and v. 45). One point of difference is that this demon seemed to leave voluntarily, whereas Jesus cast out (*ekbállō* [1544]; Matt. 8:16, 31; 9:33, 34) the demon in verses 22–30.

The Scriptures present the triune God as God Almighty (*pantokrátōr* [3841]). This word comes from *pánta* (all, the plural of *pás* [3956], all things) and *krátōr* (n.f.), the One who has dominion (*krátos* [2904]) over the whole creation (see 2 Cor. 6:18; Rev. 1:8; 4:8; 11:17; 15:3; 16:7, 14; 19:6, 15; 21:22).

By contrast, Scripture calls the devil and his hosts "world rulers" (*kosmokrátoras* [2888]), but their sovereignty is limited to "the darkness of this world" (Eph. 6:12). This compound noun combines the words *kósmos* (2889), world—particularly the earthly world, which is the abode of humanity, the present order of things—with *krátōr* (as above). This evil world stands in opposition to Christ's kingdom. The devil maintains the system of darkness (*skótos*, figuratively meaning sin) in this age until God brings the present order to an end.

[43] Unclean spirits can indwell humans or other creatures such as pigs (Matt. 8:31, 32), or they apparently can travel from place to place independently.

Demons that leave humans seem to be restricted to "**waterless** [*anúdrōn* {504}] **places** [*tópōn* {5117}]," that is, deserted places (*érēmos* [2048]; cf. Matt. 4:1; Luke 8:29; 11:24. Note in Rev. 9:14 and 16:12 that four angels are bound at the Euphrates River until the appointed time comes to dry up the river). Unclean spirits seek "**rest**" (*anápausin* [372], inner rest), which Christ offers only to those "who labour and are heavy laden" (Matt. 11:28, 29). But He

does not extend this rest to demons, so they "**absolutely** do **not** [*ouch* {3756},
the absolute negative] find it" (a.t.).

[**44**] Since a demon cannot find rest, he reenters his previous dwelling that he
calls his "**house**" (*oíkon* [3624], dwelling place, referring to the human spirit
and body). "**Having come** [*elthón*, the aorist participle of *érchomai* {2064}, to
come], he finds [the house] **empty** [*scholázonta* {4980}, unoccupied, uninhab-
ited]" (a.t.).

How different when Jesus cast out unclean spirits! He did not leave the
house empty but immediately filled it with His Spirit. This concurred with
His decree forbidding re-entry to an evil spirit (Mark 9:25; see below also).
Salvation from demonic oppression includes not just casting out demons but
replacing them with the Spirit of God (Rom. 8:9) who "abide[s] with [us] forever" (John 14:16). Once the Spirit of God fills persons, unclean spirits do
not find empty places to re-enter. We believers are "indwelt with the Spirit of
Christ," which is greater in power than "he that is in the world" (1 John 4:4).
In Christ "we are more than conquerors" (Rom. 8:37). Evil spirits attempt to
return to their former houses, but the Spirit of God has inscribed "no vacancy"
on believers' hearts and demons are forced to turn away. Unbelievers, on the
other hand, inscribe their own message: "Welcome back!"

A false prophet may claim to cast out evil spirits (Matt. 7:22), but the claim
is as false as the claim of righteousness in the context. At best the alleged
"power" (*dúnamis* [1411]) to cast out demons is temporary, no substitute for
the occupation of a human heart by God's Spirit. This takes the power of
Christ, the grace of God. Christ never casts out an unclean spirit and leaves
the human heart vacant, wretched, and miserable.

Two participles describe unbelievers who experience temporary release from
the oppression of demons. One is "**swept**" (*sesaroménon*, the perfect middle
participle of *saróō* [4563], to sweep with a broom). The departure of evil spirits causes no permanent change in persons' hearts. They are not cleansed by
the blood of Christ (1 John 1:7, 9). The persons are still sinners using brooms
to sweep out their houses by themselves to "clean up their act."

The second participle, translated "**garnished**" (KJV), is *kekosmēménon*, the
perfect middle participle of *kosméō* (2885), to adorn or decorate. It is akin to
kósmos, world, beauty, from which our English word "cosmetics" comes; thus,
the participle means "made beautiful." This is self-help without repentance
and the intervention of the Holy Spirit, what the Lord calls "patching up"
(*epíblēma* [1915]) in Matthew 9:16. The individual has made an improvement
to be sure, but because it is self-made, it cannot last. The effect is like drain-
ing an infected wound. Unless it is cleansed and sterilized, the putrefaction

remains and reinfects the wound. But the new birth from above (*ánōthen* [509]; John 3:3, 7), involving the blood of the Lord Jesus Christ, both cleanses and heals (1 John 1:7).

In Mark 9:25, when healing a demon-possessed boy, Jesus commanded the demon, "Thou dumb and deaf spirit, I charge thee, come out of him, and enter no more [*mēkéti* {3371} from the relative negative *mē* {3361}; and *éti* {2089}, yet] into him." When Jesus Himself orders (*epitássō* [2004]) an evil spirit to come out of a person, it is a complete and permanent cleansing. The Lord makes a qualitatively new (*kainós* [2537]) creature (2 Cor. 5:17), fit for the presence of the King of kings! In Luke 8:2, we are told that Jesus cast seven evil spirits out of Mary Magdalene, who subsequently joined the company of elect women who served Jesus.

Without the indwelling Spirit of God, the person described in these verses had no rest. He was tormented with an emptiness created by the vacated evil spirit.

[45] Meanwhile, the unclean spirit decided to "**go**" (*poreúetai*, the present tense of *poreúomai* [4198]), that is, return, with seven "**other**" (*hétera* [2087], other of a different kind) spirits.

The "different" spirits are "**more wicked**" (*ponērótera* [4191] from the comparative adjective *ponērós* {4190}, harmful, malicious). Throughout Scripture, seven indicates completeness (Gen. 2:2; Dan. 9:20–27; Matt. 22:25; Rev. 1:4). The last state of this person was presented as the worst of all (cf. Gen. 7:4, 10; 8:10, 12; 29:27; Heb. 4:1–11). Similarly, the seventieth week of Daniel's seventy-weeks prophecy will include the worst tribulation of all (Matt. 24:21), no doubt a time of extreme demonic activity.

Finally, Jesus applied the whole episode to "this wicked generation." Apart from grace, what is malevolent (*ponērá*) only gets "**worse**" (*cheírōn* [5560]).

The Family That Does the Will of God
(12:46–50; Mark 3:31–35; Luke 8:19–21)

[46–49] Jesus was in Capernaum, a city about nineteen miles from Nazareth. Having come from Nazareth, His family must have heard that multitudes were pressing around Him and His disciples (Mark 3:20), and they were concerned. His mother and brothers (Mark 3:32) stood outside the house, asking to speak with Him. Someone noted,

Behold [*idoú* {2400}, the imperative of *eídon/eídō* {1492}, understand, comprehend], thy mother and thy brethren **stand** [*estēkasi*, the perfect tense of *hístēmi* {2476}, to stand] without, desiring to speak with thee. But he answered and said unto him that told him, Who is my mother? and who are my brethren? . . . **Behold** [*idoú*] my mother and my brethren!

Jesus' answer confirmed that the highest relationship with Him was a spiritual one. The family of God is not based on physical relations but on faith in God's Son.

[50] Then Jesus explained: "For whosoever **shall do** [*poiēsē* {4160}, to do] the will of my Father who is in heaven, the same is my brother, and sister, and mother" (a.t.). He said in effect, God is My Father, and those related to Him by faith in Me are part of My family.

13

⌖

The Parable of the Sower
(13:1–9; Mark 4:1–9; Luke 8:4–8)

[1–2] Because of their importance, Jesus taught these parables sitting down (vv. 1, 2), as He did the Sermon on the Mount (Matt. 5:1–2). It was customary in those days to deliver important pronouncements or speeches from a seated positon. A judge sat on his judgment seat or a king on his throne when making such dictums.

[3] The parable began with "**behold**" (*idoú*, the imperative of *eídon/eídō* [1492] from *horáō* [3708], to see and perceive). Jesus wanted the multitudes to pay attention because what He was about to say had important spiritual significance.

The "**sower**" in this verse was *ho sporeús* (n.f.), a man whose vocation was sowing seed. The use of the nominative present participle, *ho speírōn* (4687), "**the sower**" or "the sowing one," implied that this was not a single sowing but an ongoing sowing of seed.

In this parable, we do not find the focused planting that characterizes the verb *phuteúō* (5452), which means to select proper soil and plant seed (Matt. 15:13; 21:33; Mark 12:1; 1 Cor. 3:6). Rather, this sowing (*speírō*) implied a broad scattering (*skorpízō* [4650]; Matt. 12:30) of seed, such as Jesus Himself sowed among the multitudes (v. 2).

[4] Likewise, we must widely sow or scatter the Word, allowing it to fall wherever God wills. Naturally, some seed sown will be snatched away. However, we should not stop spreading it, for some will fall on good soil and produce fruit.

Scattering seed may take many forms, such as distributing tracts, preaching in open air meetings and on television and radio, and advertising in magazines and newspapers. In contrast, planting includes personal witnessing and teaching the Word of God to our own children and in Sunday school classes.

It is more focused and personal, whereas scattering is broad but less personal. Jesus used both methods. Even though scattering may seem less effective than planting, it can bring great results. This is brought out in the parable of the mustard seed in verses 31 and 32. Even the parable immediately following this one speaks of dough that grows and multiplies from "hidden" leaven or yeast.

[5–7] The same scattered seed (*álla*, the neuter plural of *állos* [243], the same kind; "some") both fails (vv. 5, 7) and produces (v. 8). Consequently, success or failure is not attributed to different kinds of seeds but to different kinds of soils, which symbolize different hearts on which the seed falls.

[8] The seed produces different quantities of fruit, a hundredfold, sixtyfold, and thirtyfold. It is neither the one who plants (*phuteúōn*) nor the one who waters (*potízōn* [4222]), but God who gives the increase (*auxánō* [837]; 1 Cor. 3:6).

[9] Jesus closed this parable, as He did the one in Matthew 11:15, by saying, "He that hath ears **to hear** [*akoúein*, the present infinitive of *akoúō* {191}], **let him hear** [*akouétō*, the present imperative of *akoúō*]" (a.t.). The word "**hear**" includes the sense of "**heed**," that is, understand and obey.

Why Parables?
(13:10–17; Mark 4:10–12; Luke 8:9, 10)

[10] The Greek word *parabolḗ* (3850), "**parable**," comes from the compound verb *parabállō* (3846), which means to closely compare (from *pará* [3844], a preposition indicating close proximity; and *bállō* [906], to put).

Jesus put things close together to illustrate spiritual truth, to make abstract things clear. Parables help us understand conceptual truths through ordinary experiences. However, they cannot exactly represent reality because not every material reality has a spiritual analogue.

[11] Jesus answered His disciples' questions by telling them He had given them something special. The word "**given**" translates the Greek verb *dédotai*, the perfect passive indicative of *dídōmi* (1325), to give freely. The perfect tense implies that it had already been given so they might now experientially "**know** [*gnōnai*, from *ginōskō* {1097}, to experientially know] the mysteries of the kingdom of heaven."

Biblical **mysteries** (*mustéria* [3466]) are propositions we cannot fully understand but which we should accept and believe as truths. For example,

God becoming flesh is one of the great mysteries of the new covenant (1 Tim. 3:16, cf. Matt. 1:1; John 1:1, 14). Christ came to tell us about the kingdom of heaven that rules over the kingdoms of earth (Matt. 4:17). Formerly, these things were hidden from us (Matt. 11:25), but God reveals them to us when we receive Christ, like children, by faith.

God gives us believers knowledge to understand the mysteries of the kingdom, but He does not give such knowledge to unbelievers. Here, the word "**not**" here is the absolute negative *ou* (3756), implying complete exclusion. The Lord offers to all the opportunity to believe, but many do not (John 1:9, 11).

[**12**] God enhances the gifts He gives to believers:

> For whoever has, to him **shall be given** [*dothḗsetai*, the future passive indicative of *dídōmi* {1325}, to give], and **he shall have more abundance** [*perisseuthḗsetai*, the future passive indicative of *perisseúō* {4052}, to have left over, abound]: but whoever has **not** [*ouk* {3756}, the absolute "not"), **from** [*apó* {575}] him **shall be taken away** [*arthḗsetai*, the future passive of *aírō* {142}] even what he has. (a.t.)

Persons must have new hearts to receive God's gifts (Ezek. 18:31; 36:26). He will not force them on unregenerate hearts. God promises to add more knowledge, little by little, to new believers, the babes in Christ, so they will mature.

God also gives believers more than sufficient resources so they have enough left over to share with others. This is shown in the phrase, "more abundance." God adds the same overflowing measure to His special gifts that He does to general gifts, such as the excess food He created to feed the multitudes (Matt. 14:13–21; 15:32–39).

Apó compares with *ek* (1537), which means "out of from within." This solves the apparent paradox: "The one who does not have [i.e., within, e.g., faith], even what he has [i.e., without, e.g., worldly knowledge, power, possessions] shall be taken away" (a.t.).

[**13**] Jesus explained that He used parables to demonstrate that unbelievers have faculties they will not use:

> They seeing **see** [*blépousin*, the present tense of *blépō* {991}] **not** [*ou*, the absolute "not"]; and hearing they hear **not** [*ouk*], neither **do they understand** [*suzioúsi*, the present tense of *suníēmi* {4920}, to put together].

In the mystery of lawlessness, seeing and hearing produce neither the will nor the reason to accept revelation. If people refuse revelation long enough, God will take it away, along with the will and mind to receive it.

[14] Jesus then recounted a similar condition in the days of the prophet Isaiah who lived hundreds of years before. And He informed His disciples of a new **fulfillment** (*anaplēroútai*, the present passive of *anaplēróō* [378], to fulfill again) of Isaiah 6:9, 10: "**By hearing** [*akoḗ* {189}] **you shall hear** [*akoúsete*, the future tense of *akoúō* {191}], but you shall **not** [*ou*, the absolute negative] understand" (a.t.). In Greek, the absolute negative particle *ou* is followed by the relative negative particle *mḗ* (3361), a double negative (e.g., no never!) to emphasize the refusal to understand. Their minds are closed. The word translated "**perceive**" (*sunḗte*, the aorist subjunctive of *suníemi*) is the same word translated "understand" in verse 13. This ingressive aorist highlights a point action with continuing results. Each instance of hearing is accompanied with a corresponding rejection point of truth and a progressively hardening heart. The same principle applies to the eyes, though the verb *eídō* (1492), to perceive, is given as a synonym of *suníemi*, to understand.

In summary, God has given humankind a physical world that reveals enough of the spiritual world to leave them without excuse (Rom. 1:20). But Jesus Christ became man (*génesis* [1078]; Matt. 1:1) to give us revelation beyond the senses of seeing and hearing that we may know the kingdom of heaven (Matt. 4:17). If we reject this revelation, we are lost.

[15] Isaiah's prophecy continues with an explanation of why people endowed with God-given senses fail to understand (*suníemi* and *eídō*). Their hearts, we are told, "**were made fat**" (*epachúnthē*, the aorist passive indicative of *pachúnō* [3975], to make fat). Most commentators take the passive tense to mean that this is a judgment of God, a hardening of sinful (nonresponsive) hearts as in the case of Pharaoh (Rom. 9:18). However, the verb in the subsequent expression, "Their eyes they have closed," is in the active tense. It is interesting that the word "**heart**" (*kardía* [2588]) here is singular, implying that, as in the days of Isaiah, the people of Israel had degenerated to a common depravity. This depravity, like accumulated fat in the arteries, was now hardened against the very "bread of life" (John 6:35). From both medical science and revelation respectively, we know that accumulations of fat lead to death.

As a result of misuse, hearing deteriorates: "Their ears **heard** [*ḗkousan*, the aorist tense of *akoúō* {191}] with difficulty" (a.t.). The word "**difficulty**" is translated from *baréōs* (917), heavy or weighed down. *Báros* (922), from which *baréōs* comes, is a burden voluntarily carried.

A mental disorder illustrates this difficulty. Some people hear sounds but cannot understand words. The injuries are not in the ears but in the brain, making them incapable of comprehending the meaning of sounds. So it is with those who are spiritually deaf. They can hear the words of the gospel, but they cannot comprehend because their minds and hearts are spiritually dead.

A further result of misuse is deteriorated vision: "Their eyes **they have closed** [*ekámmusan*, the aorist active indicative of *kammúō* {2576}, to shut]" refers, again, to a voluntary shutting of the eyes to revelation that would otherwise lead them to the perception of spiritual realities like the kingdom of heaven. Romans 1:19–22 elaborates on this closed mind and heart attitude with verse 21 speaking of "their foolish [*asúnetos* {801}, unintelligent; the same word used in our present context for 'intelligence' but without the alpha privative prefix *a* {1}, without] heart."

The conjunction "**lest at any time**" (*mḗpote* [3379] from *mḗ* [3361], the relative not; and *poté* [4218], any time) leads to the explanation of what happens when eyes and ears are closed. "**They should see**" (*ídōsin* [from 1492] from *horáō* [3708]) means "they should perceive," that is, realize. The verb *akoúsōsin*, the aorist active subjunctive of *akoúō*, "**to hear**," must be taken as synonymous with *eídō*, perceive, therefore "**heed**" (see Matt. 11:15; 13:9).

The explanation is this: If people's physical seeing and hearing are not accompanied by receptive understanding, truth cannot enter their hearts. Those who have worked with children know that unless they are willing to listen and understand, it is almost impossible for them to learn.

The only remedy for heavy ears and closed eyes is a cleansed heart. When our hearts are cleansed, we can comprehend and receive the things of God. Remember that the "heart," according to the Bible, includes our human volitional and intellectual functions (Mark 6:52; Luke 24:25; John 12:40; Rom. 1:21; 2 Pet. 1:19).

When God regenerates our hearts, we act as we should. The verb "**be converted**" sounds passive, but it is actually the aorist active subjunctive of *epistréphō* (1994), to return. We willingly turned from God; upon regeneration, we willingly return to our Creator who gave us life and breath.

The response to God's call is repentance (*metánoia* [3341]) and belief (*pístis* [4102]) from the heart. In the Old Testament, God's Word promises that the new covenant will include the regeneration of the heart and the implant of a new spirit: "A new heart also will I give you, and a new spirit will I put within you: and I will take away the stony heart out of your flesh, and I will give you an heart of flesh" (Ezek. 36:26; see also Ezek. 11:19). When the heart is regenerated, the believer is a qualitatively "**new** [*kainḗ* {2537}] creature" who can look forward to full transformation and conformity to Christ.

"And **I shall heal** [*iásomai* {LXX, MT, UBS, and Nestle's}] them" is the future middle deponent indicative of *iáomai* (2390). The future tense implies not only the certainty but also an indefinite time of the healing, while the middle voice points to some reflexive action—perhaps that God is doing this for His own glory as well as for the benefit of His people. Contrasting with this, the Textus Receptus parses the verb *iásōmai* as an aorist middle deponent subjunctive. If correct, the aorist here points to the instant of God's healing, but the contingency reflected in the subjunctive voice reflects the sovereignty of God's choice (John 12:40 [TR, MT]; Acts 28:27).

In the active voice, *iáomai* is found in Luke 5:17; 6:19; 9:2, 11, 42; 14:4; 22:51; John 4:47, and Acts 10:38; 28:8. In the passive voice, it is found in Matthew 8:8, 13; 15:28; Luke 7:7; 8:47; 17:15; John 5:13, and Acts 3:11; 9:34. Frequently, it is employed with respect to moral diseases, in which case it is almost synonymous with saving from sin (here and in Luke 4:18 [cf. Isa. 61:1]; John 12:40; Acts 28:27 [quoted from Isa. 6:10]; Heb. 12:13; James 5:16; 1 Pet. 2:24). *Iáomai* is equivalent to "save" (*sōzō* [4982]; see also Matt. 9:21, 22; Mark 5:23, 28, 34; Luke 7:50; 8:36; John 11:12; Acts 4:9; James 5:15).

We adopt the verb tense and mood in the Textus Receptus as indicative of the Lord Jesus' return to transform believers (1 Thess. 4:16). This refers to our glorified, incorruptible (*aphtharsía* [861]) bodies that can die no more (1 Cor. 15:50–57). This is ultimate and permanent healing, compared with the healings we receive from the Lord now, which are only temporary.

[16] Jesus then told His disciples how specially "**blessed**" (*makárioi* [3107]) they were already because of their belief, since they possessed eyes that could see and ears that could hear.

[17] "For" (*gár* [1063], because, for the reason that) assigned not so much a cause as an exemplification of the blessing of the disciples' eyes and ears. They were blessed "for" they had seen and heard truths that were not revealed in former ages:

> For verily I say unto you, That many prophets and righteous men have **desired** [*epethúmēsan*, the aorist tense of *epithuméō* {1937} from *epí* {1909}, upon; and *thuméō* {n.f.}, to emote, from *thumós* {2372}, passion, emotion; to set one's heart upon, to desire or long for] **to see** [*ideín*; see v. 3] those things which ye see, and have **not** [*ouk* {3756}, the absolute "not"] seen them; and to hear those things which ye hear, and have not heard them.

The disciples could not only see naturally (*blépousin*), but they could also perceive (*ideín*). They heard physically and understood and heeded (*akoúō*) Christ's message. The prophets and righteous people of Old Testament days did not have the privilege we have today of Jesus Christ's teachings. However, according to Peter, they did zealously examine the Scriptures to determine the significance of the prophecies concerning Christ's sufferings and glory:

Of which salvation the prophets have enquired and searched diligently, who prophesied of the grace that should come unto you: searching what, or what manner of time the Spirit of Christ which was in them did signify, when it testified beforehand the sufferings of Christ, and the glory that should follow. (1 Pet. 1:10, 11)

But the average Jew who sought God through the self-righteousness of the Law encountered the "stumbling block" (Isa. 8:14; Luke 2:34; Rom. 9:32, 33; 1 Pet. 2:8) of "the righteousness of God without the law" (Rom. 3:21), which Paul refers to as a "veil":

But their minds were blinded: for until this day remaineth the same veil untaken away in the reading of the old testament; which veil is done away in Christ. But even unto this day, when Moses is read, the veil is upon their heart. Nevertheless when it shall turn to the Lord, the veil shall be taken away. (2 Cor. 3:14–16)

The Explanation of the Parable of the Sower
(13:18–23; Mark 4:13–20; Luke 8:11–15)

[18] Jesus began to explain the parable of the sower. Remember, this was not a parable of planting seed in prepared soil like the growth parable of Mark 4:26–29 but rather one of scattering (*speírontos* [4687]) seed.

[19] God's Word (*Lógos* [3056]) must not only be heard but "**ongoingly understood**" (*suniéntos*, the present participle of *suníēmi* [4920], to put together, understand) for adequate rooting to take place.

Apart from effective germination,

Then **comes** [*érchetai*, the present middle {i.e., for himself} indicative of *érchomai* {2064}, to come] the **wicked one** [*ponērós* {4190}, malevolent, hurtful] and **catches away** [*harpázei* {726}, to seize with violence and surprise] that which **was sown** [*esparménon*, the perfect passive participle of *speírō* {4687}, to sow, scatter] in his heart. (a.t.)

The devil is the arch-antagonist of Christ in the world. Since the heart is the field in which the sower scatters seed, this is prime territory for Satan where he apparently has access "at his will" (2 Tim. 2:26) prior to regeneration and the indwelling of the Holy Spirit.

We must not only place (*bállō* [906], to put; Mark 4:26) or plant (*phuteúō* [5452]; Matt. 21:33; Luke 13:6; 20:9) good seed in proper ground, but we must also scatter (*speírō*) good seed randomly on all kinds of soil. The ground in this parable is representative of the human heart, and the condition of the heart determines its receptiveness.

Three places where seeds are scattered represent this receptiveness: First, the seed that falls "**alongside** [*pará* {3844}] the **road** [*hodón* {3598}, way or path]" (v. 4; a.t.) represents people who ignore the message because they are engrossed with the things of the world.

[20] Secondly, the seed that falls on stones covered by a thin layer of soil are those who have initial enthusiasm but lack comprehension or genuine interest (vv. 5, 6). They accept the benefits of salvation but reject the tough obedience and perseverance required under the stress of persecution or trouble (John 16:33).

[21] Since this subject ". . . hath **not** [*ouk* {3756}, the absolute 'not'] **root** [*rhíza* {4491}] **in** [*en* {1722}, within] **himself** [*heautō* {1438}]," he only endures for a "**while**" (*próskairos* [4340], for a season, temporarily; Mark 4:17; 2 Cor. 4:18; Heb. 11:25).

The gospel, however, is not just an antidote for troublesome times, but it is life itself, eternal (*aiōnios* [166]) life (*zōē* [2222]; John 17:3). This is a quality far beyond physical life (*bíos* [979].

Note that it is not if persecution or tribulation arises but "**having arisen**" (*genoménēs*, the aorist middle deponent participle of *gínomai* [1096], to become). Here Christ predicted such tribulation "**on account of** [*diá* {1223}, due to] the Word" (a.t.), and because of His name (Matt. 24:9).

The King James Version's "anon" in verse 20 and "**by and by**" used here is the same Greek word *euthús* (2117), meaning quickly or immediately, that is, immediate acceptance (v. 20) and here, immediate offense. This person is "**scandalized**" (*skandalízetai*, the present passive indicative of *skandalízō* [4624], offend) by the Word of God and by Christ Himself. The gospel wonderfully impresses these people for a while, but they do not realize the long-term consequences. They grasp it quickly but drop it just as quickly when they learn they have to bear a cross.

[22] Thirdly, the seed scattered "**among** [*eis* {1519}, into] **thorns** [*akánthas* {173}]" (v. 7) are those who become overwhelmed with the anxiety of this age and the deceitfulness of wealth.

Thorns abound in Palestine. Long and sharp, they symbolize God's painful judgments on sin (Gen. 3:18; Num. 33:55; Prov. 22:5) that are intended to drive us to Him. Our Lord's crown of thorns was probably made from these.

One type of thorn is the "**care**" (*mérimna* [3308], anxiety) of the world. This refers to the kind of anxiety that distracts a person from thinking about anything else. It is a fixation or myopia over the physical life (*bíos*; Luke 8:14; 21:34) of this "**world**" (*aiônos* [165], an age and its prevailing philosophy). Such anxiety consumes those who do not know God as their Father (Matt. 6:30–34).

Another thorn is the "**deceitfulness** [*apátē* {539}, delusion] of **riches** [*ploútou* {4149}, wealth]." Overattachment to possessions never provides proper soil for the growth of the Word of God.

In general, as long as one's primary concern is physical life (*bíos*) instead of Christ's abundant life (*zōḗ*; John 10:10), the seed can never take root and bear fruit. Worldly desires (Gen. 3:1–6) cannot be satisfied by material abundance; as the Scripture says, "When goods increase, they are increased that eat them" (Eccl. 5:11). God Himself takes away the power to eat (Eccl. 6:2) by adding leanness (another thorn) to the souls of those who presumptuously ask and receive such things (Ps. 106:15). The more we have, the more we want, and the less it satisfies. True satisfaction and peace of mind come only from Christ. So if it is true that the more we have, the more we want, and the less it satisfies, then let us rather ask for more of Him! How can the Lord deny the request of a heart that pants for Him (Ps. 42:1)?

Worldly cares "**choke** [*sumpnígei* {4846} from *sún* {4862}, together {an intensive}; and *pnígō* {4155}, to choke, suffocate] the word." The preposition *sún*, together, is important because it indicates that anxiety and the deceitfulness of wealth work together against the Word of God. When Christ is all in all to individuals, they sublimate anxiety and riches to the things of God. Care does not go away; it just rests on its proper object, the Lord, not self (1 Cor. 12:25). We should not seek money for self-gratification but to advance the kingdom by helping others with far greater needs (Matt. 19:21). What we put first in our lives soon masters us (Rom. 6:16). The person engulfed by thorns has not experienced the birth from above (John 3:3, 7). We must exalt Christ above (*hupér* [5228]; see Matt. 10:37) everyone and everything, and then everything else falls into its proper place.

This third response is not descriptive of someone who experienced God's grace and subsequently lost it, but of one who chose worldly things instead of Christ.

[23] Fourthly, the "good ground" represents the one "**hearing**" (*akoúōn*) **and** "**understanding**" (*suniōn*)—both present participles—the Word of God (a.t.; see v. 8). The present participles show that this is the ordinary way of life for

the true believer. It poignantly contrasts with "hearing without understanding," which cannot override the negative responses seen in the first three scatterings. Such negative responses are normal for the unbeliever. Understanding, then, makes the difference and produces fruit. To that fruit, Christ adds a peace "defying description" (*anekdiēgēton* [411]; Phil. 4:7), more precious than any worldly treasure.

The good ground depicts those who not only receive God's grace but mature to various levels and produce a variety of volume and quality of fruit (accomplishments) for Christ. Consecration and sacrifice enable some to produce a hundredfold, others sixtyfold, and others thirtyfold. Those who appreciate what Christ has done for them do not count the cost to serve in the glorious kingdom of God.

The Parable of the Wheat and the Tares
(13:24–30)

[24] Jesus gave this parable to teach us that we, "the children of the kingdom" (v. 38), cannot regulate all that is sown in the world. Our duty now is to scatter the good seed, but the Lord will separate the good from the evil in His own time.

[25–29] Nevertheless, while we sow the good seed, "**enemies**" (*echthroí* [2190]) will sow "**tares**" (*zizánia* [2215], darnel) in our work. These plants, looking like corn or wheat with similar stalks and color, do not produce fruit. We may not discern the difference between the wheat and tares now, but the angels can tell the difference during the harvest at the end of the age, since the tares have not produced fruit.

[30] Instead, the householder wisely commands: "Permit both **to grow together** [*sunauxánesthai*, the present passive infinitive of *sunauxánō* {4885}; derived from *sún* {4862}, together; and the basic verb *auxánō* {837}, to increase; see also 1 Cor. 3:6] until the harvest" (a.t.).

The passive-voiced "permit" does not detract from the householder's sovereignty because the context defines it as the active decree (command), "Do not root up!" Additionally, the harvest is at an "**appointed time**" (a.t.; *kairō̃*, the dative of *kairós* [2540], season) that will disclose the tares' barrenness and their illusory similarity to wheat. This will be evident to reaper angels commissioned by the Lord Jesus (v. 41).

On the day of judgment, the Lord will tell these angels to gather the tares first and "bind them in bundles to burn them." It is the only time this expression occurs in the New Testament, concerning judgment on the enemies of the gospel. They will be bound together in "**bundles**" (*désmas* [1197]), so classified according to the degree of harm they have done, that they may receive their appropriate punishment (Matt. 11:20–24). "Bundles" (plural) tell us that unbelievers will not be punished equally but according to their hindrances to spiritual awakening and their attempts to corrupt and destroy the church of Jesus Christ. The punishment is designated by the infinitive "**to burn**" (*katakaúsai*, the aorist active infinitive of *katakaíō* [2618], to burn up, consume with fire; see also Matt. 3:12; 13:40; Luke 3:17; Acts 19:19; 1 Cor. 3:15; Heb. 13:11; 2 Pet. 3:10; Rev. 8:7; 17:16; 18:8). Since tares are material, the fire must be material. In Matthew 3:12 and Luke 3:17, the fire is characterized as unquenchable (*asbéstō* [762] derived from the privative *a* [1] and the verb *sbénnumi* [4570], to quench, put out, extinguish; the combination, therefore, meaning inextinguishable, from which we derive the English word "asbestos").

The verb translated "gather" in the phrase, "**Gather** ye together first the tares . . . but **gather** the wheat into my barn," are two different compound Greek verbs. The first is *sulléxate*, the aorist imperative of *sullégō* (4816) from *sún*, together; and *légō* (3004), to gather. This means to gather similar things together. The second verb is *sunágō* (4863) from *sún*, together; and *ágō* (71), to lead by going before. The first action (*sullégō*) pertains to gathering evil people by binding them in bundles to be burned by fire. It implies that these people are grouped by degrees of depravity. The second event (*sunágō*) pertains to believers who follow God. The angels lead them together (*sunágō*) to the place where the Lord is, that is, heaven (John 14:1–5).

Unbelievers are cast into the fire "**to burn**" (*katakaúsai* [2618] from *katá* [2596], an intensive, here meaning up, down, or away; and *kaíō* [2545], to burn). In contrast, believers are placed "**into** [*eis* {1519}] my [the Lord's] **barn** [*apothékē* {596}, a repository, granary]," a place of preservation for further consideration and reward (see Matt. 3:12; 6:26; Luke 3:17; 12:18, 24).

The Parables of the Mustard Seed and the Leaven
(13:31–33; Mark 4:30–32; Luke 13:18–21)

Jesus now used two examples from the common horticulture surrounding His hearers.

[31] The first, a "**grain** [*kókkos* {2848}, a kernel, a single seed] of mustard seed," is a good example of the fallacy of attaching insignificance to small things. Indeed, at the time, the proverbial phrase, "as small as a grain of mustard seed," was in frequent use. Yet the undistinguished beginning of this seed serves as a powerful lesson for faith.

[32] In spite of its diminutive size, the seed yields a **mustard plant** (*sínapi* [4615], a plant often growing to a considerable size; v. 31; Matt. 17:20; Luke 17:6) which eventually becomes (the size of) a "**tree**" (*déndron* [1186]).

Similarly, the kingdom (*basileía* [932], reign) of God starts in a person's heart as a small seed and is "**made to grow**" (*auxēthḗ*, the aorist passive subjunctive of *auxánō* [837], to increase) by God's power (1 Cor. 3:6). This growth presupposes the germ of life (*zōḗ* [2222]) put there by God. A dried splinter will not grow into a tree like a seed. The verb *auxánō* presupposes the God-given potential possessed by a seed or sperm. For all their scientific ingenuity, people cannot create the tiniest seeds because they cannot infuse life (*zōḗ*). In one sense, God has restricted humans to lifeless inventions.

The birds find shelter in the branches of this tree. Without God (John 1:4), life is inexplicable and depressing chaos. With God, the most feeble soul grows and produces meaningful fruit for a kingdom destined to glorify the earth with the Lord's presence as it already does in heaven. The faith of Christ automatically blossoms forth in good works and becomes a tree in which "**to lodge**" (a.t.; *kataskēnoún*, the present infinitive of *kataskēnóō* [2681], to find shelter as under a tent; derived from *kátō* [2736], down; and *skēnóō* [4637], tent) from the burning heat of the day to the larger storms of life.

[33] "**Leaven**" or yeast (*zúmē* [2219]) is a symbol used in the Bible for both good and evil. In this verse, it causes "three **measures** [*sáta* {4568}] of **meal** [*áleuron* {224}, flour]" to ferment and raise the "**whole**" (*hólon* [3650]; here, implicitly, the "whole dough [*phúrama* {5445}]"; 1 Cor. 5:6).

This is a continuation of the previous parable, illustrating not just growth but the full permeation of the Word of God through the "whole" dough. What does the dough represent? Several ideas are consistent with biblical eschatology: first, the whole person will be "preserved blameless" until the coming of Christ (Col. 1:28; 1 Thess. 5:23); second, the entire church will attain the whole measure of the fulness of Christ (Eph. 4:13); and third, in the final subjugation, God will be "all in all" (1 Cor. 15:28).

Leaven or yeast is also used as a symbol of evil, which is why the week beginning with the Passover was called "the feast of unleavened bread" (Matt. 26:17; Mark 14:1, 12; Luke 22:1, 7; see also Ex. 23:15; Lev. 23:6; Deut. 16:3,

4–8). Because evil spreads so quickly and easily, the Lord warned against "the leaven of the Pharisees and of the Sadducees," that is, their contagious and corrupt teaching (Matt. 16:6, 11; Mark 8:15), something Luke equates with hypocrisy (Luke 12:1). In line with this use, Mark refers to "the leaven of Herod" demonstrated, among other places, at his party (Mark 8:15).

As the mustard seed of faith in the human heart can grow into a life-sustaining tree, so the mustard seed of evil can burgeon into a life-destroying tree of its own.

Teaching by Parables Prophesied
(13:34, 35; Mark 4:33)

Several verbs used in these two verses deserve our understanding.

[34] First,

"All these things **spoke** [*elálesen*, the aorist tense of *laléo* {2980}] Jesus unto the multitude." This verb is associated with the idea of breaking silence. The same verb is used in the phrase, "and without a parable **He was not speaking** [*elálei*, the imperfect of *laléo*] unto them." (a.t.)

[35] Then following, we see a different Greek word for "speak":

That it might be fulfilled which **was spoken** [*rhethén*, the neuter aorist passive participle of *eípon*, the aorist of *légo* {3004}, to relate systematically, i.e., in the form of a discourse; or, less probably, from *eréo* {2046}, to speak exactly] by the prophet, **saying** [*légontos*, the present participle of *légo*], **I will open my mouth in parables; I will utter** [*ereúxomai*, the future middle deponent indicative of *ereúgomai* {2044}, to blurt out, speak out] things **which have been kept secret** [*kekrumména*, the perfect passive participle of *krúpto* {2928}, to hide, keep secret] from the foundation of the world.

The verb *ereúgomai* has an interesting background. In classical Greek, it was used for discharging, emptying, or casting forth, as when the sea casts foam when waves break on a shore. Here it is useful to describe the Son of God's intrusion on human history (Matt. 1:1; John 1:1, 14) to reveal mysteries from the foundation of the world.

In Psalm 78:2, David prophesies that the Messiah "will open [His] mouth in a parable. [He] will utter [Sept.; *ereúxomai*] dark sayings of old." Had God chosen to stay silent, humanity would remain lost. It is because He graciously reveals truth that people can be saved. God kept these mysteries of the kingdom secret for centuries, but Christ both spoke and unveiled them. In Romans 16:25, Paul calls God's revelation "the mystery, which has been kept secret [*sesigēménou*, the perfect passive participle of *sigáō* {4601}, to keep silent] in eternal [*aiōníois*, the dative plural of *aiōnios* {166}] ages [*chrónois*, the dative plural of *chrónos* {5550}]" (a.t.). Jesus revealed (*apekálupsas*, the aorist active indicative of *apokalúptō* [601], to take the cover off) the truths that underlie His parables to His disciples (Matt. 11:25).

The Explanation of the Parable of the Wheat and Tares (13:36–43)

Why does God permit the simultaneous existence and growth of tares with wheat? And why are they so similar if they represent true and false believers?

If the disciples ever thought the Lord would permit sowers to reap, the answer they received was an unequivocal no! This response would immediately quell their speculation. The reapers will be angels who will descend from heaven to divide the two groups at the "**consummation**" (*suntéleia* [4930], completion; from *sún* [4862], together; and *télos* [5056], end or goal) of the age (v. 39). As long as people have breath, there is hope for their repentance and belief. Peers cannot prejudge and draw down the curtain of eternal destiny.

[36] The disciples knew that they were privy to the explanation of this parable, so they waited until He entered the house before requesting, "**Declare** [*phráson*, the aorist imperative of *phrázō* {5419}, to expound, explain; see also Matt. 15:15] unto us the parable of the tares of the field." The verb is synonymous with "explain" (*exēgéomai* [1834], to exegete, make plain). This is the same word used regarding Jesus Christ who, while eternally in the bosom of the Father (John 1:18), declared or "exegeted" God to us.

[37–39] Jesus first declared that the One sowing the good seed is the Son of man, that is, Himself; then He explained:

> The field is the world; the good **seed** [*spérma* {4690}, the God-given potential to germinate] are the **children** [*huioí* {5207}, mature children—those who identify with their father's purposes; not *tékna* {5043}, immature children] of the kingdom; but the tares are the children of the wicked one.

The tares are defined as the "**sons**" (*huioí*) of the "**evil one**" (*ponērós* [4190], the harmful, malevolent one), that is, the devil or Satan (John 8:44). During our earthly lives, Satan, the instigator of all evil, is the enemy who sows the tares.

[39] In describing Satan's work, Jesus spoke of the devil as "the enemy that **sowed** [*speíras*, the aorist active participle of *speírō* {4687}, to sow]" to teach us that evil angels are behind the iniquitous events and persons we war against. He also reminded us that the object of our faith is not the prince of this world but the God who permits such growth: "Let both [the wheat and tares] grow together [*sunauxánesthai* {4885}; see v. 30] until the harvest." For Scripture references to evil angels, see 1 Sam. 16:15, 16, 23; 1 Kgs. 22:22, 23; 2 Chr. 18:21, 22; Job 4:18; Dan. 10:12, 13, 20; Matt. 25:41; 2 Pet. 2:4; Jude 1:6; Rev. 9:11 ("angel of the abyss"); 9:14 (where the reference, "have been bound" [*dedeménos*, the perfect passive participle of *déō* {1210}, to restrain, constrain], can hardly refer to good angels); 12:7; Sept. Ps. 78:49, God sends "*aggélōn ponērón* (malevolent)"; Sept. Prov. 17:11, an evil man who seeks rebellion is promised an "*ággelon aneleémona* (unmerciful)."

Jesus encouraged His disciples by pointing out that the final disposition of the evil one along with his children will take place at a definite time appointed by God. This is designated as the "**end**" or consummation (*suntéleia* [4930], completion; from *sún* [4862], together; and *télos* [5056], end, goal) of this present age (cf. Matt. 24:3; 28:20; Heb. 9:26). Only God determines and knows the time, and no angel or human can change it.

[40] Jesus completed the analogy:

As therefore the tares are **gathered** [*sullégetai* {4816}, to gather together into bundles according to kind; see v. 30) and **burned** [*katakaíetai* from *katakaíō* {2618}, to burn down; see v. 30] in the fire; so [*hoútōs* {3779}] **shall it be** [*éstai*, the future tense of *eimí* {1510}, to be] in the consummation [*suntéleia;* see v. 39] of **this** [*toútou* {5127}, the genitive singular masculine demonstrative pronoun] age. (a.t.)

There is no supposition in this phrase, only certainty, but we can thank God that in the present age of grace, people still have the opportunity to believe before they die (Heb. 9:27).

[41] The consummation of this age will complete (*suntéleia*) the opportunities to believe or destroy. When this point is reached, God will cast all "**offending** [or offensive] **things**" (*skándala*, the plural of *skándalon* [4625]) into the "furnace of fire" (v. 42).

Satan and his demonic and human emissaries use these deceptions and crafty methods to dissuade people from believing (v. 22; see Eph. 6:11). The offenses (neuter) are attached to the tares. They are the evil motives, decisions, and actions of "**them which do** [*poioúntas*, the present active participle of *poiéō* {4160}, to do] **iniquity** [*anomía* {458}, lawlessness]."

[42] The angels "**will cast**" (*baloúsin*, the future tense of *bállō* [906], to throw) these subjects into the furnace of fire. The phrase "**furnace** [*kámimos* {2575}] of **fire** [*púr* {4442}]; cf. v. 50; Rev. 9:2]" provides terrible visual imagery for both the place and type of punishment for the wicked. Other qualifiers include **everlasting** (*aiōnios* [166]; Matt. 18:8; 25:41), **unquenchable** (*ásbestos* [762]; Matt. 3:12; Mark 9:43, 45; Luke 3:17; also *sbénnutai* [4570]; Mark 9:48), and **Gehenna** (*Géenna* [1067], the Valley of Hinnom) of fire, translated as the "hell of fire" or "hell fire" (Matt. 5:22; 18:9; Mark 9:43, 45, 47).

According to the Old Testament, Gehenna, the Valley of Hinnom, was originally the place where parents made their children pass through fire to appease the Ammonite god Molech (2 Chr. 28:3; 33:6). Subsequently, King Josiah stopped this practice and turned the valley into a dumping ground for Jerusalem's garbage, a place of continual burning (2 Kgs. 23:10, 13, 14). By the time of Christ, Gehenna had been appropriated in Jewish thought as the place of final punishment for the wicked. In order to convey His teaching on final punishment, Jesus adopted this common symbol.

"**Wailing** [*klauthmós* {2805} from the verb *klaíō* {2799}, to wail, weep, lament] and **gnashing** [*brugmós* {1030}, grating] of teeth" are typical responses to physical pain and guilt. The thought of never receiving comfort or relief will make the tares greatly regret their choices that led to destruction (cf. 2 Pet. 3:7, 16).

[43] Jesus then revealed the glorious end of the righteous: "Then the righteous **will shine forth** [*eklámpsousin* {only here in the NT}, the future tense of *eklámpō* {1584}, to shine out, be resplendent] as the sun in the kingdom of their Father" (NKJV). What a difference! The destiny of those who do not repent and believe is a place of eternal torment, a furnace of fire, whereas those who have truly repented and believed shine forth like the sun in the kingdom of their Father.

The Hidden Treasure, the Pearl, and the Dragnet (13:44–50)

Jesus called His first four teachings "parables" (vv. 3, 10, 13, 18, 24, 31, 33), while the remaining are included in this category in a summary statement in verse 53. A parable is a simile, a comparative using the word "like" or "as" (*homoía* [3664], similar, like). In His parables, Jesus made good use of ordinary physical objects to explain unseen or intangible spiritual realities.

[44] The kingdom of heaven, He said here, is comparable to a "**treasure** [*thēsaurós* {2344}, something precious] **hid** [*kekrumménō*, the perfect passive participle of *krúptō* {2928}, to hide; 'which has been hidden'] in a field." This is the same basic verb used in Matthew 11:25 and 13:35. In Luke 17:20, 21, Jesus said that His present kingdom rules invisibly in the hearts of believers and is therefore hidden from physical eyes, though its impact in the world is apparent.

The person who found the treasure of the kingdom of heaven realizes its inestimable value and that material things are worthless by comparison. Although this treasure is hidden in a field, it can be found by all who seek it.

Finding the treasure creates a "**joy**" (*chará* [5479]) so great that a person is willing to exchange everything for it. While this parable does not teach that the kingdom of heaven can be bought, it does teach that salvation is worth more than all we possess, that our salvation should not be taken lightly, and that it is worth parting with worldly things we hold dear to fully enjoy our new wealth. A person who does not joyfully give of his material possessions to enable others to find the treasure of the kingdom of heaven is not a true possessor of that treasure. He does not freely possess his possessions; they, rather, possess and enslave him. A reluctant, sorrowful giver is a hypocrite.

[45] The parable of the pearl is similar, except that the man seeking good pearls is a "**merchant**" (*émporos* [1713], a tradesman who travels from place to place looking for bargains and opportunities to buy and sell). This infrequently used New Testament word is found only here and in Revelation 18:3, 11, 15, 23.

[46] In all his searchings and dealings, the merchant, we are told, finds only "one pearl of **great price** [*polútimon* {4186} from *polús* {4183}, very great; and *timé* {5092}, honor, special attributed value—as opposed to *axía* {n.f.}, objective value]." Like the treasure hidden in the field, the pearl, representing our salvation, is so precious that the prospective owner sells all he has to own it. There are no half commitments or cheap transactions here. When the pearl is owned, everything else drops in value.

The concurrent action of the aorist active participles *heurṓn*, "**having found**" (from *heurískō* [2147]), and *apelthṓn*, "**having gone away**" (from *apérchomai* [565]), shows that the merchant, immediately on finding the pearl, sold his possessions to buy it. The lack of an extended period of consideration reveals the depth of spiritual hunger and the full recognition of incomparable value in this soul.

The merchant, now, "**has sold**" (*pépraken*, the perfect tense of *pipráskō* [4097], to sell) everything he had to buy the pearl. The root of this verb *peráo* (n.f.), which means to transport to a distant land, implies that he apparently went as far and wide as necessary to accomplish this task.

There are two interesting points of comparison between the "man" who finds the treasure and the "merchant" who finds the pearl. First, the verb "**sell**" (*pōleí* [4453]; v. 44) in the first parable tells us that the man engages in local, as opposed to distant, selling. Secondly, the same man finds his treasure—it appears, accidentally, while the merchant is actively "seeking fine pearls." From these points, we learn that two types of people respond to the Word: those with no prior spiritual interest who have new desires created in their hearts on first hearing the gospel, and those like the merchant who have been "seeking pearls" perhaps all their lives.

[**47**] Now we come to our last parable. In this verse we have the only occurrence of the noun "**net**" (*sagénē* [4522], a dragnet, seine) in the entire New Testament. This was a long sweep net, the ends of which were spread out by boats to cover a large portion of open sea, then drawn together and taken to shore with the netted fish. To ensure a good catch required several people doing various tasks; no one person could handle the entire netting operation by himself.

This parable should be taken in conjunction with the parable of the wheat and the tares (Matt. 13:24–30, 36–43). As the tares and wheat grow together, so two kinds of fish are netted. The servants cannot collect tares without rooting up wheat, and fishermen cannot net only good fish. This may be compared with the mixed responses in an evangelistic meeting. The same invitation is issued to all. Some genuinely repent and believe; others pretend. Possibly the ratio of shallow, temporary decisions to deep-rooted, permanent ones is the same 75 percent (three out of four) deduced from the parable of the sower (see Matt. 13:1–9, 18); but we should never be discouraged by such numbers. In the short run, the Lord has "much people" (Acts 18:10) in this or that city; in the long run, a "multitude, which no man could number" are saved (Rev. 7:9).

[**48**] When the fishermen draw the net to shore, they have "**gathered** [*sunélexan*, the aorist tense of *sullégō* {4816}] of every kind."

An evident difference exists between the "**good**" (*kalá* [2570]) and the "**bad**" (*saprá* [4550], worthless) fish. The fishermen collect the good fish in "**vessels**" (*aggeía* [30], receptacles, containers), and "**cast** [*ébalon*, the aorist tense of *bállo* {906}, to cast] **out** [*éxō* {1854}, outside]" the bad ones, either outdoors or back into the sea.

[**49, 50**] This judgment is probably the same as the one given in the parable of the wheat and tares. Both occur at the "**end** [*sunteleía* {4930}, completion] of the **age** [a.t.; *aiōnos* {165}; see vv. 39, 40 respectively]," and both are accomplished by angels (vv. 39, 41). Angels can as well be fishermen (a term not used but implied in vv. 47, 48) as reapers (*theristaí* from *theristḗs* [2327], harvesters). Finally, the term "**thus**" (a.t.; *hoútōs* [3779], so) beginning verse 49, shows this as an amplification of the foregoing text. "Angels" in verse 49 are the natural succedents to "they" in verse 48.

The Responsibility of Understanding (13:51–53)

[51] Now Jesus asked, "**Have ye understood** [*sunḗkate*, the aorist active indicative of *suníēmi* {4920}] all these things?" What things did the Lord hope His disciples had learned? Let's summarize:

- The Son of man scatters the Word of God (v. 37);
- The good seed are the children of God (v. 38);
- Not all seeds fall on fertile ground (vv. 21, 22);
- The devil scatters tares among the wheat (v. 25);
- Believers must not attempt to uproot what appear to be tares (v. 29);
- God permits tares (unbelievers) to grow together with wheat (believers) until the time of the harvest (v. 30);
- The destiny of the wicked is conscious suffering in the furnace of fire (vv. 42, 50);
- Believers will shine like the sun in the kingdom of their heavenly Father (v. 43). Suffering unbelievers will witness this shining with hopeless remorse over not repenting and believing while they had the opportunity (vv. 42, 43);
- The kingdom of heaven is like a great treasure (v. 44);
- The kingdom of heaven is like a pearl of inestimable value (v. 45);
- The kingdom of heaven is worth parting with all we possess to gain this treasure or precious pearl (v. 46);
- These truths are to be perceived and heeded from the illustrations given in parables and similes (v. 53).

[52] When the disciples answer, "**Yes** [*naí* {3483}], Lord" (TR, MT; v. 51), Jesus concluded,

Therefore every **scribe** [*grammateús* {1122}, a professional student, a teacher of the law of the kingdom of heaven] which is **instructed** [*mathēteutheís*, the aorist passive participle of *mathēteúō* {3100}, to disciple] unto the kingdom of heaven is like unto a man that is an **householder** [*oikodespótē*, the dative of *oikodespótēs* {3617} from *oíkos* {3624}, house; and *despótēs* {1203}, a despot, absolute ruler, one who masters his house], which **bringeth forth** [*ekbállei*, the present tense of *ekbállō* {1544}, to eject; from *ek* {1537}, out of; and *bállō* {906}, to put] out of his [personal] treasure **things new** [*kainá* {2537}, qualitatively new, meaning things that he has gained in his new life in Christ] and **old** [*palaiá* {3820}, previously secured and held possessions].

The householder knows the value of the kingdom of heaven (v. 44) and the benefit of sharing this treasure with others. Accordingly, he knows what possessions to retain for his own needs and for those of the household (*oíkos*) for which he is responsible as master (*oikodespótē*) and what to share or dispense (*ekbállō*) so others may find the treasure of the kingdom of heaven.

A Greek verb that denotes such prudence is *apotássomai* (657), variously translated as "forsake" or "send away" (Mark 6:46; Luke 9:61; 14:33; Acts 18:18, 21; 2 Cor. 2:13). Luke 14:33 is pertinent here: "So likewise, whosoever he be of you that forsaketh [*apotássetai*] not all that he hath, he cannot [the absolute negative *ou* {3756}] be my disciple [*mathētḗs* {3101} to which the verb *mathēteúomai* {Matt. 13:52} is akin]." Sharing should not be reckless but orderly (*táxis* [5010], the noun akin to *tássō* [5021], to set or put in order, which is the basic verb in the compound *apotássomai*; from *apó* [575] and *tássō*, thus meaning to arrange away from oneself). In summary, prudent children of the kingdom dispense what is above and beyond their needs, not recklessly but orderly and promptly.

[53] When Jesus "**finished** [*etélesen*, the aorist tense of *teléō* {5055}, to complete] these parables, **he departed** [*metéren*, the aorist tense of *metaírō* {3332} from *metá* {3326}, after; and *aírō* {142}, to take up; used only twice in the NT] thence."

Jesus had accomplished His purposes in Galilee and now headed for Judea. Galilee was a ministry of compassionate healing and teaching; Judea was to become a ministry of self-sacrifice for His people.

Jesus Returns to Nazareth
(13:54–58; Mark 6:1–6; Luke 4:16–30)

Jesus' residence was in Capernaum, but He returned to His hometown of Nazareth, which was also in Galilee.

[54–56] Note that the synagogue where Jesus "**was teaching**" (*edídasken*, the imperfect tense of *didáskō* [1321], to teach) was called "**their**" (*autôn*, the genitive plural masculine personal pronoun of *autós* [846]), not "His" synagogue (cf. Matt. 4:23; 9:35; 10:17; 12:9). Likely, this had been the synagogue His family attended before He began His public ministry.

Jesus' teachings during this period were a constant cause of discussion. People were "**astonished**" (*ekplēttesthai*, the present passive infinitive of *ekplēttomai* [TR, MT]; or *ekplēssesthai*, the present passive infinitive of *ekplēssomai* [UBS {1605}]; both words mean to be amazed or astonished). They could not understand the origin of His wisdom that superseded all earthly wisdom. Nor would they admit that His wisdom (*sophía* [4678], divine wisdom as revealed and manifested in Christ; cf. Matt. 11:19; Luke 11:49) or mighty works (*dunámeis* [1411], miracles) were of God (cf. Matt. 7:22; 11:20, 21, 23 and the NT use of the word *sēmeía* [4592], signs).

These miracles pointed to the divine sonship of Jesus Christ. The Nazarenes were acquainted with the child and young carpenter until He was thirty years old, but now Jesus' teachings and works were revealing another nature behind His humanity that caught them by surprise. The unfamiliar overshadowed what was familiar to them as, for example, His mother and brothers (*adelphoí* [80]) and sisters whom they knew by name.

[57] Because Jesus' compatriots had no natural explanation, "**they were being offended**" (a.t.; *eskandalízonto*, the imperfect passive indicative of *skandalízō* [4624], to trip up). They failed to see His incarnation (*génesis* [1078]; see note on Matt. 1:1), though they could not help but notice He was different.

The explanation Jesus gave of Himself was extremely modest. He called Himself a prophet "**without honor**" (*átimos* [820] from the alpha privative *a* [1], without; and *timē̄* [5092], honor, attributed value) in His "**own country**" (*patrídi*, the dative of *patrís* [3968], native country). While not honoring Him, neither was anyone bringing accusations against Him. Even those in His own house who had lived with Him day in and day out had found no basis for maligning Him. Yet John 7:5 tells us that His own brothers did not believe in Him. It was only after they had seen Him die and rise from the dead that they believed. His mother and brothers subsequently assembled with the disciples in the upper room at Pentecost (Acts 1:14).

Jesus did not perform many authenticating miracles (*dunámeis*) in Nazareth. His miracles actually were never intended to create universal faith but to selectively corroborate His messiahship. When He even hinted at such sovereign impositions from past history (see Luke 4:25–28), the common reaction was explosive.

[58] Since this verse is often misinterpreted in favor of faith healing, it is important to point out that the text does not say Jesus "**could** [*edúnato*] **not** [*ouk*] **do** [*poieín*]" miracles there because of unbelief, but simply He "**did** [*epoíesen*] **not** [*ouk*]" do them, showing that He exercised His choice.

This is vastly different, and it is corroborated by the fact that Jesus **did** miracles in Chorazin, Bethsaida, and Capernaum **in spite of** unbelief (Matt. 11:20–24). Accordingly, this verse offers no theological justification for condemning specific illnesses (particularly terminal illnesses) as judgments on a lack of faith. The inference itself is false, and the use of such an inference is legalistic, oppressive, and evil, although such judgment may occur because of an immoral or profligate lifestyle.

Jesus was and is always free to do or not do miracles. He is not a puppet tethered to human belief or lack of belief. Always gracious, He may choose to shower us with gifts when we are weak in faith or take us to heaven at a time when our faith could move mountains. But He will always do what is right and best.

14

❧

John the Baptist Is Murdered
(14:1–12; Mark 6:14–29; Luke 9:7–9)

[1] "Herod" (v. 1) was actually the name given to a family of rulers in Palestine who reigned just prior to Jesus' birth until shortly after His ascension.

The Herods were descended from Antipater, an Idumean, a tribe that had descended from Esau (the Edomites). *Idoumaía* (2401), derived from the Hebrew *Edōm* (OT 123), extended from the Dead Sea southward to the Gulf of Aqaba and from the Valley of Arabah eastward to the desert of Arabia— about 125 miles long and 30 miles wide. The descendants of Esau lived in this area, ordinarily harboring hostility toward the Jews. David fought against them (2 Sam. 8:14), but they were not entirely subdued until John Hyrcanus, a priest and Maccabean king, conquered them around 125 BC. During the Babylonian captivity, they took possession of the southern parts of Palestine as far as Hebron so that the later name of Idumea came to include this region also (see Ezek. 36:5).

At the age of fifteen, Herod, surnamed "The Great" (Matt. 2:1, 3, 7, 13, 15, 16, 19, 22; Luke 1:5), was honored by Julius Caesar with an appointment to manage the province of Galilee. About 41 BC, he was given the title "tetrarch" with administrative responsibilities over a fourth part of the region.

Opposition forces caused Herod to flee to Rome where he was declared king of Judea. After gathering an army together, he recovered Jerusalem and extirpated the Maccabean family in 37 BC. Following the battle of Actium, he joined the party of Octavius who confirmed his appointment. He then rebuilt the temple of Jerusalem, constructed and enlarged many cities (especially Caesarea), and erected theaters and gymnasiums. He was notoriously jealous and cruel, at one time putting to death his wife Mariamne and her two sons, Alexander and Aristobulus. He died in AD 2 at seventy years of age, after a reign of about forty years.

Toward the close of his life, Herod commanded the massacre of infants in Bethlehem (Matt. 2:16) in a vicious attempt to kill the Jewish Messiah. At his death, the Roman emperor Caesar Augustus passed half of the kingdom (Idumea, Judea, and Samaria) to Herod's son Archelaus along with the title of ethnarch. The remaining half was split between two other sons, Herod Antipas and Philip. Antipas ruled Galilee and Perea, and Philip ruled Batanea, Trachonitis, and Auranitis (Luke 3:1), later called Caesarea Philippi, north of Galilee. Herod Antipas, we read here, "heard of the fame of Jesus."

[2] But he mistakenly thought that John the Baptist, whom he had killed, had been raised from the dead. The text implies that Antipas preferred the Pharisaic affirmation of the resurrection to the Sadducean denial of a resurrection and he believed John the Baptist to be worthy of such an honor. But before we credit Herod with any of this, we should remember that he probably sided with the majority party (the Pharisees) and John the Baptist strictly for political reasons. Luke comments that he was actually "perplexed" (*diēpórei*, the imperfect of *diaporéō* [1280], to severely doubt, hesitate; Luke 9:7) over the differing theories of Jesus' identity, some saying He was a resurrected John, others, a revived Elijah or a prophet (Luke 9:7, 8).

[3] According to Josephus (*Antiquities*, xviii:112), Herod Antipas imprisoned John at the request of Herodias and beheaded him in a fortress established in Machaerus (east of the Dead Sea), a town not mentioned in either Testament. Archaeological excavations in Israel show that Essenes occupied this area.

Matthew says Herod,

> . . . **having captured** [*kratēsas*, the aorist participle of *kratéō* {2902}, to arrest] John, **bound** [*édēsen*, the aorist indicative of *déō* {1210}, to bind] him and **placed** [*étheto*, the aorist middle indicative of *títhēmi* {5087}, to place] him in prison **for** [*diá* {1223}, for the reason, because of] Herodias' sake, his brother Philip's wife. (a.t.)

When followed by a noun in the accusative case, *diá* refers to the active reason something is done. Herod imprisoned John for Herodias' sake. In fact, elsewhere we read that apart from the perspective of the mob, "Herod feared John, knowing that he was a just and holy man, and observed him; and when he heard him, he did many things, and heard him gladly" (Mark 6:20; a.t.).

[4] Nevertheless, John repeatedly accused Herod Antipas and Herodias of adultery, a fact given by the imperfect tense of *légō* (3004), to speak meaningfully. *Élege* is best translated, "**He was saying**" to Herod, meaning, "He was accusing."

And John accused Herod Antipas in no uncertain terms: "It is [**absolutely**] **not** [*ouk* {3756}] **lawful** [*éxestin* {1832} from *ek* {1537}, out of from within; and *eimí* {1510}, to be; i.e., 'morally right'] for thee to have her." John did not mince words or hold back on "all the counsel of God" (Acts 20:27), in spite of the danger to his life.

[5] Only John's popularity with the people who considered him a prophet saved him at that time. Matthew informs us that Herod was

> . . . **willing** [*thélōn*, the present participle of *thélō* {2309}, desiring] **to put** [him] **to death** [*apokteínai*, the aorist infinitive of *apokteínō* {615}, to kill; the aorist infinitive stressing the idea of once for all], [but] he feared the multitude because they considered him as a prophet. (a.t.)

[6] The adversative "**but**" (*dé* [1161]) here implies that a ripe time for Herod to act had arrived. He had wanted to strike at John for a long time, but he needed an occasion and some special circumstances to offset the multitude's bias. The day and circumstances came together. On his birthday, Herodias' daughter danced and "**pleased** [*éresen*, the aorist tense of *aréskō* {700}, to fit, please, incline the heart of] Herod."

[7] Did Herod anticipate or even plan this whole scenario? By binding himself publicly to a carte blanche ("blank check"), he could shift the blame for John's death to the girl. Certainly, the multitude would be sympathetic toward a king who kept his word. From her request, we know that Herodias wanted John dead, but Herod, also, wanted John dead (v. 5).

[8] And so, prompted by her unscrupulous mother Herodias, the daughter requested, "Give me **here** [*hóde* {5602}] John the Baptist's head on a **platter** [*pínaki*, the dative of *pínax* {4094}, plate, platter]" (a.t.).

The "here" implies "now" or "at this time," and could be taken as intending to head off any further consideration of the matter. Any king, otherwise, would be demeaned by the presumption of "here and now," but Herod was trapped by his own words and perhaps considered the whole affair as a "now or never" opportunity.

Another shocking referent is the "platter," something that food and drink are ordinarily served on, yet an apt lead-in to a specific judgment of God: "For they have shed the blood of saints and prophets, and thou hast given them blood to drink; for they are worthy" (Rev. 16:6). That God would give such murderers the blood of the slain to satisfy their thirst is not a very pleasant picture but one that fits the crime. If they wanted the blood of the innocent so desperately, let them drink it!

What happened to childlike innocence and ethical parenting? Is the head of a man on a dinner platter a common request from a young girl? Whose idea was this? Mark says she asked her mother, Herodias, "What shall I ask [for]?" (Mark 6:24). Then we read here, "**being before instructed** [*probibastheísa*, the aorist passive participle of *probibázō* {4264}, to persuade or confirm in advance] of her mother." What kind of depraved advice to a child is this? And what generation of vipers accepts it? As Jesus said elsewhere, it would be better for such people to be collared with a millstone and cast into the sea before they cause some little one to sin (Matt. 18:6).

[9] "And the king **was sorry** [*elupéthē*, the aorist passive of the intransitive verb *lupéō* or *lupéomai* {3076}, to be grieved]." Matthew reports this as fact— not pretense. But how can this be predicated to the same person who was "would have put [John] to death" (v. 5)?

Certainly, Herod's mind and will were divided over the matter. Intermittently, he believed John to be a "just man and an holy," and he "heard him gladly" (Mark 6:20). But he more consistently succumbed to the will of his illicit lover. Defiling even her own daughter (v. 8), Herodias was evidently a master of persuasion. Herod's grief, therefore, is not inconsistent with his desire to put John to death. It just shows that while co-existing with some grain of righteousness and truth, sin (lust), apart from the grace of God and stimulated by an evil agent (Herodias), overcomes a person (Luke 11:22; 2 Pet. 2:19, 20). The apostle Paul says that there are two kinds of grief (*lúpē*), one "of the world" that works death and the other "of God" that works repentance (2 Cor. 7:10). But Herod did not repent; evil overcame him, inside and out.

Perhaps, like Judas, when Herod saw the ultimate fruit of his sin, he was sorry, as many people are when they finally see how far astray their sin has led them. But this is not a sorrow that produces salvation.

The adversative *dé* (1161), but, translated "**nevertheless**" in the King James Version, introduces Herod's higher will, so to speak. His ultimate decision was to conform to the minimal integrity expected of a king—keeping a solemn promise. *Diá* (1223), "**on account of** [the oath]," views the promise as a cause and conformity as an effect.

In addition to the oath, a second constraint on Herod's freedom to act existed: "And **them which sat with** [*sunanakeiménous*, the present participle of *sunanákeimai* {4873} from *sún* {4862}, together; and *anákeimai* {345}, to recline, sit down at the table; thus, to sit together with] him." The oath was public; the request was public; there was no way Herod could privately deny the request. The presence of even a single subject, not to mention a house full of guests, constricted his ability to renegotiate terms.

So "**he commanded** [*ekéleusen* {2753}] it **to be given** [*dothḗnai*, the aorist passive infinitive of *dídōmi* {1325}, to give] her." The oath and the presence of guests combined to motivate Herod to command this deplorable act.

[10] "And he [Herod] sent, and **beheaded** [*apekephálisen*, the aorist tense of *apokephalízō* {607}, to sever the head off the body] John in the prison," possibly the firstfruit of those "beheaded for the witness of Jesus" (Rev. 20:4).

[11] Per the original request, John's head was first given to the young girl, who in turn gave it to her mother. Some birthday gift this was!

[12] John's disciples took his body and buried it, possibly including his head, assuming Herodias' depravity had not sunk to the level of putting it on display.

Jesus Feeds the Five Thousand
(14:13–21; Mark 6:30–44; Luke 9:10–17; John 6:1–14)

[13] When Jesus heard these things, He went to a "**desert** [*érēmon* {2048}] **place** [*tópon* {5117}] **for** [*kat'* from *katá* {2596}, according to] **Himself** [*idían* {2398}]" (a.t.), but a crowd of people followed Him from several cities.

We can surmise that Jesus wanted a private place to pray and recover from grief over this personal loss. Mark explains that He was accompanied by His disciples, telling them to "rest a while" in the context of "many coming and going" (Mark 6:31). On other occasions, Jesus separated Himself from the hustle and bustle of crowds (Matt. 14:23; 17:1; 20:17; Mark 4:34; 7:33; 9:2).

[14] But as Jesus observed many coming and going,

> [He] **was moved with compassion** [*esplagchnísthē*, the aorist passive of *splagchnízomai* {4697}, to show compassion] toward them, and **he healed** [*etherápeusen*, the aorist tense of *therapeúō* {2323}, to heal with compassion] their sick.

Derived from *splágchnon* (4698), intestine, the verb *splagchnízomai* is frequently associated with action; that is, it is not a passive emotion that "feels but does nothing." Because we can feel the pain of others as if it were deep within our own bodies (our intestines) and since we always do what we can about our own pain, the verb includes the complex idea of sympathetic action. The frenzy of people—here their "coming and going"—often moved Jesus as He thought of them as "faint[ed], . . . scattered abroad, as sheep having no shepherd" (Matt. 9:36).

The word "**sick**," used here for the first time, is *arróstous*, the accusative plural of *árrōstos* (732) from the privative *a* (1), without; and *rhṓnnumi* (4517), to strengthen. The adjectival noun *árrōstos* means without natural strength, having some form of chronic illness. The sick here suffered from various chronic sicknesses that disabled them one way or another. The Lord was moved by both the sicknesses and the handicaps they produced.

A *therápōn's* work moves beyond the work of a *iatrós* (2395), a physician, in his attempt to restore the soul as well as the body. By analogy today, a physical therapist (*therápōn*) seeks to restore a person to wholeness through a customized regimen of physical and motivational exercises, following the skilled procedures of a physician (*iatrós*). The therapist combines coaching with encouragement using both commands and incentives.

In his account of this scene, to emphasize the miraculous physics of healing, "Luke, the beloved physician [*iatrós*]" (Col. 4:14) replaces Matthew's *therapeúō* with *iátō* (healed from sickness; Luke 9:11). John adds that the multitude grew in numbers as "they saw [*heórōn*, the imperfect tense of *horáō* {3708}, to see and perceive] his [Jesus'] miracles which he did on them that were diseased [*asthenoúntōn*, the present participle of *asthenéō* {770}, to be feeble, sick]" (John 6:2).

[15] The disciples, as usual, were long on advice and short on faith. Their suggestion here, however, was not unrealistic. Since no stores or markets were in the immediate vicinity, they suggested that Jesus send the people to nearby villages in order to buy "**victuals**" (*brōmata*, the plural of the noun *brōma* [1033], food).

[16] Jesus immediately responded by saying,

> They have **no** [*ou* {3756}, the absolute "not"] **need** [*chreían* {5532}] to depart; **give** [*dóte*, the aorist imperative of *dídōmi* {1325}, to voluntarily give] to them, you, **to eat** [*phageín*, the aorist infinitive of *esthíō* {2068}]. (a.t.)

Jesus wanted to teach His disciples two lessons. First, He can provide anything anywhere; and second, when He provides, He does so through His people. This applies to both physical and spiritual needs, immediate and remote, temporary and eternal. When we are tempted to think that we have to go somewhere else at some other time to find the Lord's will, these words remind us to "Stand still, and see the salvation of the LORD, which he will show to you today" (Ex. 14:13).

[17] The first English word, "**And**," is actually a translation of the Greek adversative *dé* (1161), "but." We always use "but" when our scope of God's sovereignty is too narrow. The verse summarizes the recurring alibi of the Lord's disciples throughout the church age: "We don't have enough!"

So it seemed to me, when the Lord challenged me at sixteen years of age to advertise the gospel message in secular Greek magazines like *Romance* and in Muslim, Hindu, Buddhist, and Communist magazines and newspapers throughout the world. Today, we at AMG International can point to former notorious enemies of the gospel who are now witnessing to a persecuting majority in their native countries.

John tells us that the five barley loaves and two fish mentioned here belonged to a "small child" (*paidárion* [3808]) and were most probably his lunch (John 6:8, 9). We know that bread made from barley was cheaper than that of wheat, so the child was carrying little of any value. John adds that Andrew asked, "But [*allá* {235}, an adversative like *dé*] what are they among so many?" As I point out in *The Complete Word Study Dictionary: New Testament*, 124, II, *allá* is sometimes used as a continuative having one of the following meanings: but now, but further, moreover, but indeed. In this verse, *allá* probably means the latter: "But indeed, how could so many be fed from so little?"

Jesus Christ can take the naturally insufficient and make it supernaturally sufficient-plus. If all the insufficient resources of a local congregation were put on the altar of God, how much more would God grant sufficiency plus to physically and spiritually feed numbers far beyond five thousand (John 14:12–14)? Let us have faith in His ability "to do exceeding abundantly above all that we ask or think" (Eph. 3:20).

In the phrase, "but five loaves, and two fishes," the "**but**" (*ei* [1487], the "if" of supposition; and *mḗ* [3361], the relative "not") highlights the inadequacy of the food to match the overwhelming need.

[18] The present tense of "**bring**" (*phérete*, the present imperative of *phérō* [5342], to carry) means to keep bringing, that is, continue bringing to Me what you think is insufficient. What a blessed invitation this is!

The "**here**" (*hṓde* [5602]), coupled with the unqualified, present imperative, implies "now." It is important for us to put what we have in the hands of the Lord Jesus immediately. To delay is disobedience.

[19] Jesus immediately blessed what was brought to Him:

> **Having looked up** [*anablépsas*, the aorist participle of *anablépō* {308}] to heaven, **He blessed** [*eulógēse*, the aorist indicative of *eulogéō* {2127}, to speak well to] and **having broken** [*klásas*, the aorist participle of *kláō* {2806}], **He gave** [*édoken*, the aorist indicative of *dídōmi* {1325}]the loaves to His disciples. (a.t.)

The blessing must be taken as a divine command. Jesus did not "speak well of" bread and fish. Rather, He "spoke well **to**" the bread and fish; that is, He determined the multiplication of the bread and fish. Contrary to those who think Jesus fed the crowd with miniscule portions of food, the disciples later gathered twelve baskets of fragments. That many baskets could not be filled with scraps from a small original volume that would not occupy such space.

As the record stands, the Lord did many miracles that no human could do (see Matt. 15:32–38; Luke 5:1–9; John 2:1–11).

[20] The multitude, we read,

> . . . ate and **were filled to satiety** [*echortásthēsan*, the aorist tense of *chortázō* {5526}, to satisfy], and they took up of the fragments **that remained** [*perisseúon*, the present participle of *perisseúō* {4052}] twelve **baskets full** [*kophínous*, the accusative of *kóphinos* {2894}, a small wicker basket used by women for shopping]. (a.t.)

Note the present participle *perisseúon*, "**the abounding remains**," which characterizes God's grace. God always provides a surplus, and He tells us to gather up the remainder, since He does not want us to waste His gifts.

[21] The word "**about**" translates *hōseí* (5616), "approximately" five thousand men in addition to women and children.

Jesus Walks on the Sea
(14:22–33; Mark 6:45–52; John 6:15–21)

Before we move on to the miraculous event of walking on water, we need to interject a comment found in John 6:15:

> Jesus, therefore, **having known** [*gnoús*, the aorist participle of *ginōskō* {1097}, to know by experience] that they would come and **take Him by force** [*harpázein*, the present infinitive of *harpázō* {726}, to suddenly and forcefully take away] to make Him a king, departed again into a mountain by Himself. (a.t.)

This event followed the feeding of the five thousand, but it did not hinder Jesus from continuing to perform miracles, confident as He was that "His hour" was "not yet" (John 7:30; 8:20). This would occur only at the *parousía* (3952), His return and subsequent personal presence in glory.

Nevertheless, the crowds in Bethsaida were feverish enough now to "**snatch away**" (see *harpázein* above) Jesus in order to make Him king. The aorist tense of *poiéō* (4160), to make, underscores their determination to do this once for all. The verb is used in 1 Thessalonians 4:17 to describe the unrestrained catching away of the church at Jesus' Second Coming.

[22] The text does not tell us how Jesus "**constrained** [*ēnágkasen*, the aorist tense of *anagkázō* {315}, to compel] his disciples to get into a ship," but it apparently was a countermeasure against the crowd's attempt to snatch Him away.

In our world, people constrain other people to act by physical force or by persuasion. Since the definition of the word presupposes resistance, constraint must be superior in order to be effective; otherwise it fails. God exerts neither physical force nor argument; He merely speaks, and it is done. But a good example of the Lord's determination to physically force a good result is the overwhelming power of three angels against a resistant Lot. They made him leave the city of Sodom prior to its destruction. This force, which Lot unsuccessfully resisted, is equated to the mercy of the Lord:

> And while he lingered, the men [i.e., angels] laid hold upon his hand, and upon the hand of his wife, and upon the hand of his two daughters; the LORD being merciful unto him: and they brought him forth, and set him without the city. (Gen. 19:16)

All we can infer by the use of "constrained" in our verse under study is that the disciples in some way resisted the Lord and He prevailed: "The king's heart is in the hand of the LORD, as the rivers of water: he turneth it whithersoever he will" (Prov. 21:1). It makes sense that the disciples, of all people, would be sympathetic with the crowd's (see prior verse) attempt to force Christ's kingdom prematurely.

Both Matthew's and Mark's narratives say "a" ship, but the Greek text has the definite article (*tó*), the, for no apparent reason. Nothing had been said about a particular boat. To take all the disciples, however, it must have been fairly large. Jesus planned to have all of them witness His suspension of one of His laws—gravity. In the meantime, His purpose in sending the disciples ahead "unto the other side" seemed to be His need to be alone with the Father.

[23] Jesus' intention "**to pray** [*proseúxasthai*, the aorist middle deponent infinitive of *proseúchomai* {4336} from *prós* {4314}, toward; and *eúchomai* {2172}, to express a wish] **in** [His] **own private place** [*kat'* from *katá* {2596}, according to; *idían* {2398}, own]" (a.t.) was realized after He ascended the mountain. He was now "**alone**" (*mónos* [3441]), and evening "**was come**" (*genoménēs*, the aorist middle deponent participle of *gínomai* [1096], to become). The imperfect verb *ēn* from *eimí* (1510), to be, implies He had been there for a while.

Regretfully, we do not know the content of this prayer, but we do know that Jesus frequently thanked His Father (Matt. 11:25; Luke 10:21; John 11:41) and requested certain things from Him.

[24] By the time Jesus had descended the mountain from His private place, we read,

> The ship **was** [én, the imperfect tense of eimí {1510}, to be] **now** [édé {2235} also translated "already"] in the midst of the sea, **tossed** [basanizómenon, the present participle of basanízō {928}, to buffet, toss, torment] with waves: for the wind was **contrary** [enantíos {1727} from en {1722}, in; and antíos {n.f.}, set against].

What follows is a classic test of faith for the disciples. Already having commanded them to the other side, Jesus would surely secure their safe arrival. Yet the disciples' faith collapsed under the weight of wind and tide.

[25] Jesus appeared to the disciples during the fourth "**watch**" (phulakḗ [5438], guard, implying the normal dangers on the waters). The first watch was 6 p.m.–9 p.m.; the second, 9 p.m.–12 midnight; the third, midnight–3 a.m.; and the fourth, 3 a.m.–6 a.m., dawn. In addition to surging seas and violent winds, the disciples had to contend with darkness.

While the text does not say, Jesus probably had been praying from late afternoon through the night up to this appearance of "**walking** [peripatōn, the present participle of peripatéō {4043}, to walk, to come] on the sea."

[26] This was an unprecedented sight; no prophet in the history of Israel had ever walked on water. When the disciples saw this,

> **they were troubled** [etaráchthēsan, the aorist passive tense of tarássō {5015}, to disturb, agitate, trouble], saying, It is **a spirit** [phántasma {5326} from phantázō {5324}, to make appear; an apparition, spector, phantom]; and they cried out for fear.

This was their best guess; surely, no man could walk on water. Mark adds (6:49) that they "supposed" (édoxan, the aorist of dokéō [1380], to assume, conjecture) they were looking at a spiritual essence as opposed to a weighty object.

[27] But Jesus gave them a good reason to be brave—His presence:

> But **straightway** [euthús {2112}, immediately] Jesus spake unto them, saying, **Be of good cheer** [tharseíte, the present active imperative of tharséō {2293}, to take courage, embolden]; it is I; **be not afraid** [phobeísthe, the present middle/passive imperative of phobéomai {5399}, to fear].

In sovereign grace, the Lord cuts off false thinking "immediately." When we are driven by storms into the abyss of fear, He quickly speaks to our hearts, "Be not afraid."

[28] Peter certainly became emboldened rather quickly.

> Lord, **if** [*ei* {1487}, the "if" of supposition] it is You, command me to come
> **toward** [*prós* {4314}] You on the water. (a.t.)

We cannot infer from this statement the content of Peter's doubt. If we stop with the clause, "if it is You," then clearly he doubted the presence of the Lord. On the other hand, if we assign the entire supposition/conclusion—"if . . . then"—to conjecture, Peter may be doubting the morality of his demand. After all, even if it were the Lord, why should He honor such a request?

[29] Yet the gracious Jesus, under no necessity as God or man, immediately responds, "**Come[!]**" (*elthé*, the aorist imperative of *érchomai* [2064], to come).

The aorist tense foretells the impending crisis. The Lord decreed an event that would fail in contrast with His own "walking on the sea" (the present participle) in verse 25. Accordingly, for a moment Peter "**walked** [*peripátēsen* {4043}] **on** [*epí* {1909}, on the surface of] the water and **came** [*élthen* {2064}] **toward** [*prós* {4314}] Jesus" (NASB).

[30] The moment was short-lived. Though to his credit Peter got within an arm's length of Jesus (see v. 31), the "**strength**" (*ischurón* [2478]) of the wind distracted him from the One known as "the Strength" (*Ho Ischurós*; LXX Neh. 1:5; 9:32).

Peter initially obeyed the Lord's decree to "be not afraid," but when he was caught up in the midst of danger, he

> . . . **became afraid** [*ephobéthē*, the aorist middle/passive of *phobéomai* {5399}] and, beginning **to sink** [*katapontízesthai*, the present passive infinitive of *katapontízomai* {2670} from *katá* {2596}, down; and *pontízomai* {n.f.}, to sink, no doubt related to *póntos* {4195}, the sea], he cried, **Lord** [*kúrie* {2962}, master, sovereign], **save** [*sóson*, the aorist imperative of *sózō* {4982}, to save] me. (a.t.)

This is what happens when we move our spiritual eyes from the Lord to the storm, from the Creator to the creation. In Asia Minor, Pontus (see *póntos* above) was a northeastern province on the Euxine Sea, sometimes called Cappadocia on the Sea. Although the English word "pontoon" comes immediately from the Latin *ponton*, the Latin term may have been influenced by the Greek or both may have come from a common source.

Despite his lapse of faith, Peter still believed enough in the power of the Lord to call upon Him. The verb *sózō* here is contextually restricted to physical rescue. Jesus physically helped him back into the boat.

The Lord is free to respond or not respond to an imperative, such as the one Peter blurted out when he was afraid. We should never presumptuously assume that the Lord is mechanically moved by meritorious faith or prayer, a notion consistently denied by Scripture: "Then shall they cry unto the LORD, but he will not hear them: he will even hide his face from them at that time, as they have behaved themselves ill in their doings" (Mic. 3:4; see Prov. 1:28, 29; Isa. 59:2). If the Lord chooses to save the desperate, He does so out of a pure grace that spites self-centeredness.

[31] We do not know how far Jesus was from the boat, but we can deduce that Peter "walked" to within His reach because the Lord,

> . . . **having stretched out** [*ekteínas*, the aorist participle of *ekteínō* {1614}, to extend] His hand, **caught** [*epelábeto*, the aorist middle deponent indicative of *epilambánō* {1949}, to take hold of] him, and said to him, O you of **little faith** [*oligópiste*, the vocative of the adjective *oligópistos* {3640} from *olígos* {3641}, little; and *pístis* {4102}, trust; "little faith"], why did you doubt? (a.t.)

Jesus is not speaking of saving faith in His atonement here but rather faith in His power to rescue from a specific threat, namely drowning. The Lord did not dismiss Peter as wholly *ápistos* (571), without faith.

Then Jesus asked, "**Wherefore** [*eis* {1519}, unto; *tí* {5101}, what; therefore, 'unto what end,' 'for what purpose,' 'why'] **didst thou doubt** [*edístasas*, the aorist tense of *distázō* {1365}, to hesitate]?"

As Peter was walking toward Jesus, fear overcame him, and he hesitated to continue on. Since he had no real need to walk on water, his request was unnecessary and foolish. We, too, should carefully consider our requests of God. As the only wise God (Rom. 16:27), the Lord knows what is best. When we ask God to do foolish things, we test Him (James 1:13) and become offensive (Matt. 4:6).

Jesus knew why Peter hesitated; but occasionally, He asked His followers questions, not to get information of which He was ignorant but to make them understand the consequences of unbelief.

From Peter's experience, we learn that it is not enough to trust God's sovereignty in general. We must trust the Lord's sovereignty over the details of life, always reminding ourselves that He has numbered our hairs and not a single sparrow falls to the ground without His sovereign will (Matt. 10:29, 30).

[32] "When they were come into the ship, the wind **ceased** [*ekópasen*, the aorist tense of *kopázō* {2869}, to end or exhaust from labor or fatigue or from having accomplished a purpose; used only here and in Mark 4:39; 6:51; LXX Gen. 8:1]."

This event is also found in the synoptic Gospel of Mark (6:45–52). Yet in an earlier event (Matt. 8:23–27; Mark 4:35–41), the Lord rebuked the wind and the waves, prompting the viewers to ask, "What manner of man is this, that even the wind and the sea obey him?" (Mark 4:41). Here in Matthew 14:32, however, the Lord didn't even bother with a verbal rebuke; we read, "When they were come into the ship, the wind ceased." This time, the disciples' response was not a quizzical, "What manner of man is this?" but a confessional: "Thou art the Son of God."

[33] The response to this miracle was worship:

> Then they that were in the ship came and **worshipped** [*prosekúnēsan*, the aorist tense of *proskunéō* {4352}, to bow and kiss towards] him, saying, **Of a truth** [*alēthôs* {230}, the adverb of the adjective *alēthḗs* {227}, truthful; from *alḗtheia* {225}, truth] thou art the Son of God.

At least eleven of the twelve disciples were true believers in Jesus Christ. We don't know how many were present at the feeding of the five thousand or at Christ's miraculous walk on water, but there is no reason to assume that Judas was absent from either. Since confession, bowing, and kissing (*proskunéō*) are external actions, none demands a corresponding heart of faith. How anyone could sustain unbelief before such displays of the Lord of creation is a mystery. It must have been pure rebellion, since the Son of God had adequately proven His lordship over the elements—gravity, wind, and waves. Not only did He make these things, He "sustains" (*sunístēmi* [4921], to stand together; from *sún* [4862], together; and *hístēmi* [2476], to stand; Col. 1:17) them all.

Jesus' Fame Spreads Through Gennesaret
(14:34–36)

This section gives us an idea of what common people thought of Jesus after He fed the five thousand and walked on water.

[34] How the disciples and others came across the lake is discussed in John 6:22–25. Once in the land of "**Gennesaret**" and possibly in the synagogue in Capernaum, Jesus preached His sermon on the Bread of Life (John 6:32–59). The Lake of Tiberias is also called the Lake of Gennesaret, and the small crescent-shaped strip of country on the northwest side of the Sea of Galilee is called the land or region of Gennesaret (Matt. 14:34; Mark 6:53). It extends along the lake for three or four miles and inland a mile or more where it is shut in by the hills. The plain was formerly rich and fruitful, possibly the scene portrayed in the parable of the sower (Matt. 13:1–8). Three important cities in

this region are Capernaum, Bethsaida, and Chorazin. The feeding of the five thousand occurred in Bethsaida.

[35, 36] When the men of this region

> . . . **learned** [*epignóntes*, the aorist active participle of *epiginōskō* {1921}, to experientially know] about Jesus, they brought to Him **all** [*pántas*, the plural of *pás* {3756}, all] **having** [*échontes*, the present participle of *échō* {2192}, to have] it **badly** [*kakōs* {2560}, bad; the full range of spiritual and bodily weaknesses and diseases]. (a.t.)

Interestingly, their faith in the Person of Jesus Christ was so complete that it extended to touching His clothing. Our Lord honored this faith. The pure holiness of the Son of God sanctified even "the hem of His garment," for

> as many as **touched** [*hápsontai*, the aorist middle subjunctive of *háptomai* {680}, to touch] **were made perfectly whole** [*diesōthēsan*, the aorist passive of *diasōzō* {1295} from *diá* {1223}, through, thoroughly; and *sōzō* {4982}, to save; to save completely].

In a similar incident, Mark records that when a woman merely touched Jesus' clothes and was healed, the Lord "knew in Himself that power [*dúnamin* {1411}] had gone out of Him" (Mark 5:30; a.t.).

The Greek word translated "**as many**" (*hósoi*, the masculine pronoun of *hósos* [3745]) restricts the number who touched Him but not the number healed. Everyone who touched was healed, but the text does not say that everyone touched Him. Those who touched had faith in His power to save, and "**they were saved through and through**" (*diesōthēsan*). The verb occurs here and in Luke 7:3; Acts 23:24; 27:43, 44; 28:1, 4; and 1 Peter 3:20.

CHAPTER

15

What Is Tradition?
(15:1–9; Mark 7:1–13)

In this section, Jesus first addressed the scribes and Pharisees (vv. 1–9), then the people in general (vv. 10–14), and finally, His disciples (vv. 15–20).

[1, 2] The Greek word *parádosis* (3862), translated "**tradition**," appears in this passage in verses 2, 3, and 6, all in the singular number, that is, tradition, not tradition**s**. In the parallel passage in Mark 7, it occurs in verses 3, 5, 8, 9, and 13.

The noun derives from the verb *paradídōmi* (3860), to voluntarily deliver; from *pará* (3844), a preposition that denotes proximity; and *dídōmi* (1325), to give, a verb ending in *–mi* which emphasizes completion, like a finished product. Tradition, therefore, was the completed product of the elders (*presbúteroi* [4245], older leaders; Matt. 21:23; 26:3, 47, 57; 27:1, 3, 12, 20, 41; 28:12). That tradition was the product of the elders across several generations is shown in verse 2 and also in Mark 7:3. In Mark 7:7–9, the "tradition of men" is contrasted with "the commandment [*entolḗ* {1785}] of God."

Here, a group of scribes and Pharisees from Jerusalem complain that Christ's disciples "**transgress** [*parabaínousi*, the present indicative of *parabaínō* {3845}, to transgress; from *pará*, against, contrary to; *baínō* {n.f.}, to go] the tradition of the elders." By using this verb, the elders elevated their tradition to the level of God's commandment. According to them, neither should be transgressed or violated.

The particular complaint was directed at the disciples eating bread without washing their hands. Washing hands before eating makes good hygienic sense, but the scribes and Pharisees were not concerned with hygiene. To them, this was a moral issue: "Why do your disciples contradict the tradition of the elders?"

[3] Jesus answered with a counter question: "**Why** [*diá* {1223} with the accusative that follows, on account of; *tí* {5101}, what; 'for what reason'] do ye also transgress the commandment of God **by** [*diá* {same as above}] your tradition?" The last phrase prepared the way for Jesus to demonstrate that they were being inconsistent.

[4] He then explained,

> For God **commanded** [*eneteílato*, the aorist tense of *entéllomai* {1781}, to command, in the KJV, TR, and MT; *eípen*, the aorist tense of *légō* {3004}, to speak logically, in the UBS and Nestle's Text; *eneteílato* is preferable because it qualifies "said" as an imperative—God "says" many things that are not imperatives], saying, Honour thy father and mother: and, He that curseth father or mother, let him die the death.

The scribes and Pharisees would agree that God had commanded these things, for they had no contention over Mosaic Law. Moreover, the first command pertaining to the family, which Jesus quoted here, was one of the Ten Commandments, the very foundation of the Israelite community and society in general (Ex. 20:12). The second command He quoted was from the same revelation to Moses on Mount Sinai (Ex. 21:17).

The Greek word for "**honor**" is *tíma*, the present imperative of *timáō* (5091), to honor. Contrasting with the aorist, the present imperative extends through life itself, that is, for as long as parents are alive. The corresponding noun *timḗ* (5092) presupposes value. Although *timḗ* is somewhat synonymous with *axía* (n.f.), price, worth, commercial value, it incorporates the idea of sentiment, therefore sentimental value—something we would not attach to money, for example.

In contrast to this value children should naturally place on their parents, Jesus spoke of a great evil recognized in the Law: "And **he that curseth** [*kakologṓn* {2551}, the present participle of *kakologéō* {2551} from *kakós* {2556}, evil; *légō*, to speak] his father, or his mother, shall surely be put to death" (Sept.; Ex. 21:17). The malignment here is not an occasional outburst but a lifestyle of intentional harm, thus, the use of the present—as opposed to the aorist—participle. We may also note that evil speech is not restricted to "speaking to"; it equally includes speaking "of" or "about", that is, gossip or complaints. The command blankets over direct and indirect discourse.

The punishment is harsh. While allowance was made in the Old Testament for stoning rebellious children (Deut. 21:18–21), the purpose clause associated with obedience to this specific command, "that thy days may be long upon the land which the LORD thy God giveth thee" (Ex. 20:12), implies that God Himself would shorten the life of a child given to a lifestyle of maligning his or her parents.

[5, 6] Another significant comparison follows: "For God commanded [v. 4]. . . . But ye say. . . ." Not only are God and humans compared but also the verbs "command" (*eneteílato*) and "say" (*légete*).

Jesus gave a specific violation that dishonors parents:

> Whoever shall say to his father or his mother, It is a **gift** [*dốron* {1435}, gift; Mark 7:11 adds the transliterated {from Hebrew} "corban"] [to God] which you would otherwise profit from and honors not his father or his mother, he shall be free. (a.t.)

What a shameful practice for spiritual leaders to display to their followers! In effect, a Pharisee said to his parents, I'd like to give you this money, which admittedly you need, but I have dedicated it to God. Jesus implied that there is no exception to honoring parents, so this tradition of withholding something needed by parents on the pretense that it was dedicated to God did not constitute a valid exception but clearly transgressed the Law (v. 3).

Moreover, the scribes and Pharisees had "**cancelled** [*ēkurốsate*, the aorist tense of *akuróō* {208}, to cancel; from the alpha negative *a* {1}, against; and *kuróō* {2964}, to confirm; translated 'made . . . of none effect' in the KJV] the commandment of God with [their] tradition" (a.t.).

This was a serious accusation. Of course, the Mosaic Law holds, so this was only a vain attempt to cancel God's original command for their personal profit, not a real cancellation that God will concede to on the day of judgment.

[7] Jesus characterized this subversion of the Law by calling the scribes and Pharisees "**hypocrites**" (*hupokritaí* [5273]), as He frequently called them (Matt. 22:18; 23:13–15; Mark 7:6, etc.).

[8] Then He quoted from Isaiah:

> This **people** [*laós* {2992}] **draweth nigh** [*eggízei*, the present tense of *eggízō* {1448}, to approach] unto me with their mouth, and honoureth me with their lips; but their heart is **far** [*pórrō* {4206}, an adverb meaning far away, distant] from me. (see Isa. 29:13)

"**Their heart**" [*hē kardía* {2588} *autōn*] is actually singular in number, signifying that while the hearts of the people are many, their attitude and unbelief is one. The Greek verb is *apéchei* (566) and means "**is held off**," the present tense of *apéchō* (568), to be far away, and it is also singular. When used impersonally (as here in the third person), *apéchei* means to restrain or hold off (cf. Mark 14:41; *apéchousin*, they have in full, in Matt. 6:2, 5, 16; and *apéchete*, you have in full, in Luke 6:24).

The Old Testament picture here, then, was that of Israel full of idols, holding God off, restraining His approach at an absurdly assumed "safe" distance. Since their common heart was locked in to idols, the most they could offer God was their mouth and lips—external appendages like "clean" hands. The illustration was quite appropriate, considering their complaint against the disciples.

[9] Isaiah's picture continued:

> But **in vain** [*máten* {3155} from *mátaios* {3152}, vain, uselessly] **they do worship** [*sébontai*, the present tense of *sébomai* {4576}, to revere, adore, worship] Me, **teaching** [*didáskontes*, the present participle of *didáskō* {1321}, to teach] for **doctrines** [or teachings, from *didaskalíais*, the plural of *didaskalía* {1319}, teaching] **commandments** [*entálmata*, the plural of *éntalma* {1778}, command, precept; from the verb *entéllomai* {1781}, to command, enjoin] of men. (a.t.)

The word "**for**," which has caused some to read in the idea of substitution, is not in the Greek text—the commandments of men in place of (for) doctrine. The most literal reading is "**teachings**" [an accusative case], commandments of men," thus identifying the "teachings" with the "commandments of men." This accords with the variety of human expression over and against the unity of God's thought.

What Defiles People?
(15:10–20; Mark 7:14–23)

[10] Jesus now addressesd the multitudes on the real cause of defilement: "**Hear** [*akoúete*, the present imperative of *akoúō* {191}, to hear, listen] and **understand** [*suníete*, the present imperative of *suníemi* {4920}, to comprehend; from *sún* {4862}, together; and *híemi* {n.f.}, to send, put]."

[11] The key is that the heart is self-defiling. It requires nothing from the outside—neither physical (like food) nor moral temptation. It is from these teachings of Christ that James concluded, "Every man is tempted, when he is drawn away of his own lust" (James 1:14). That lust is within the heart.

> **Absolutely not** [*ou* {3756}, the absolute "not"] **that which enters** [*eiserchómenon*, the present middle deponent participle of *eisérchomai* {1525} from *eis* {1519}, into from without; and *érchomai* {2064}, to come] into the mouth

defiles [*koinoí*, the present tense of *koinóō* {2840}, to make common, pollute, defile] the person but **that which comes out** [*ekporeuómenon*, the present middle deponent participle of *ekporeúomai* {1607}, to eject, to put out] of the mouth, this defileth a person. (a.t.)

The verb "defile" is associated with the adjective *koinós* (2839), common, defiled, unclean. Thus, *koinóō* etymologically means "to make common or unclean." The strict theological point here is that people are not defiled by something external. The root of sin is the human heart, and this condition is common among humankind, especially the unregenerate. However, this low estate is not the ideal and not the way God originally created people.

[12] Amazingly oblivious to Jesus' supernatural knowledge and ethics, the disciples asked, "**Knowest thou** [*oídas*, the perfect tense of *horáō* {3708}, to perceive] that the Pharisees **were offended** [*eskandalísthēsan* {4624}, to cause to stumble or fall, to scandalize], after they heard this saying?"

Think about this two-edged sword a moment! First, the disciples asked Jesus if He had perceived the Pharisees' reaction. Secondly, as if this were not enough, they questioned Jesus' sensitivity and ethical propriety. They came very close to siding with the Pharisees. After all, if the disciples were convinced that the Lord's teaching was right, why would they care whether He was sensitive to the Pharisees' false teachings?

[13] Jesus' answer reveals His detachment from any sensitivity to false teaching. He implied that the disciples should not concern themselves with Satan's tares (Matt. 13:25–38), since tares are destined for uprooting:

> **Every** [*pása*, the feminine of *pás* {3956}, each within the total] **plant** [*phuteía* {5451}] that My heavenly Father **did not** [*ouk*, the absolute "not"] **plant** [*ephúteusen*, the aorist tense of *phuteúō* {5452}, to plant] **shall be rooted up** [*ekrizōthésetai*, the future passive tense of *ekrizóō* {1610} from *ek* {1537}, out of from within; and *rhizóō* {4492}, to root, from which we get our English "rhizome"]. (a.t.)

Phuteúō, to plant, carries a stronger connotation of careful planning and managing than the arbitrary scattering reflected in the verb *speírō* (4687), to sow (seed). We say this because the parable of the sower presents a farmer randomly throwing seed without a great deal of care since some falls within range of scavengers, some on rocky ground, some on soil with no depth, some before a blazing, destructive sun (Matt. 13). It is clearly accidental that any seed falls on good earth at all, within deep, fertile soil and near water. The accidental growth arising from scattering (*speírō*) is contrasted here with the careful planting (*phuteúō*) of a loving heavenly Father who selects the good soil, nutrients, and water to secure growth (see Mark 4:26–29).

The corresponding nouns compare like the verbs. *Phuteía*, used only here, is actually a plant (seeds are not uprooted), whereas *spérma* (4690), that which is sowed, is ungerminated seed (cf. *dé karpophoreí;* Matt. 13:23). In the parable of the sower, the seed falling on good ground bears fruit, *phuteía*. Neither thorns, birds, bad ground, nor lack of water have been able to stop the increase (*aúxēsis* [838]) of the life of the seed.

From verse 13, we can deduce that God has not planted some plants. He does not "plant" tares; the devil does (Matt. 13:25–40). These tares will be rooted up, bound in bundles, and cast into the fire to be burned.

[14] This verse concluded what Jesus had just said. Since the Pharisees were not planted by the Father, Jesus said, "**Leave** [*áphete*, the aorist imperative of *aphíēmi* {863}, to leave; from *apó* {575}, from; and *híēmi* {n.f.}, to send forth] them" (a.t.).

The aorist tense leaves open the possibility that they might be evangelized later—"leave them [for now]." As long as they were in this crisis stage of resistance, leave them be. Let them remain in their current condition of being offended by what Jesus had just said. In other words, don't do anything to offset the offense. Since truth offended them, let them stay offended.

In their current condition, Jesus continued, "They are blind leaders of the blind" (a.t.). The scribes and Pharisees were indeed self-made leaders of the Jewish people. They could not see or hear spiritual truth. They saw Jesus Christ standing before them, but they could not understand who He was.

The principle that followed is applicable to everyone who gives or receives false teaching:

> And if the blind **lead** [*hodēgé* is the present subjunctive of *hodēgéo* {3594}, to lead] the blind, both **shall fall** [*pesoúntai*, the future middle deponent indicative of *píptō* {4098}, to fall] into the **ditch** [*bóthunon* {999}, a pit, a symbol of destruction].

The middle voice of *píptō* indicates a responsible but reflexive action. The blind should not be leading; they should be seeking eyes from the Lord.

[15] Although the teaching seems quite simple, Peter wanted further elucidation:

> **Declare** [*phráson*, the aorist tense of *phrázō* {5419}, to expound, explain; from which the English word "phrase" is derived] unto us this **parable** [*parabolén*, the accusative of *parabolé* {3850} from *pará* {3844}, near; and *bállō* {906}, to cast or put].

[16] Since Peter asked Jesus to clarify the parable to them, the Lord asked the disciples:

Are you [plural] also **yet** [*akmḗn* {188}, at this point in time] **without understanding** [*asúnetoi* {801} from *a* {1}, without; and *súnesis* {4907} from *sún* {4862}, together; and *hĭēmi* {n.f.}, to put]? (a.t.)

The "**also**" (*kaí* [2532]) grouped the disciples with the scribes and the Pharisees, and the predicate stated that they, too, were unable to "put together" what Christ said.

[17] Jesus repeated the teaching, appealing to a generally understood truth:

Do you not yet understand that **all** [*pán*, the neuter of *pás*, everything] that enters the mouth **goes into** [*choreí*, the present tense of *choréō* {5562}, to give space to, find room in] the belly and **is cast out** [*ekbálletai* {1544}] into the **draught** [*aphedrṓna* {856} from *apó* {575}, from; and *hédra* {n.f.}, a seat, toilet]? (a.t.)

Food does not defile because it does not reach human hearts or spirits. If people do not wash their hands, residual bacteria passes through their bodies into the sewer, leaving their hearts untouched. Jesus' point was that clean hands do not produce moral purity; conversely, unwashed hands do not defile the soul.

[18] Now Jesus touched the heart of the matter (literally):

But those **things which proceed out** [*ekporeuómena*, the present middle neuter **plural** participle of *ekporeúomai* {1607}] of the mouth **come forth** [*exérchetai*, the present middle **singular** of *exérchomai* {1831}] from the heart; and they **defile** [*koinoí*, the present active indicative **singular** of *koinóō* {2840}] the man.

Jesus said that the things (the participle is plural, the referent obviously the words) that leave the mouth are viewed as a collection (the verb is singular, the referent probably is the thought) that comes from the heart and defiles. So the heart itself is self-defiling.

Jesus made it clear that this is human nature apart from the grace of God. People's hearts are already hard. What evil thoughts erupt and pass into the world in the form of evil words only reinforce (defile) the evil already present within. Defiling, therefore, is not the creation of evil *ex nihilo*, that is, out of nothing, or turning good hearts into bad ones. It begins with the evil that comes forth from hearts in the first place. Any subsequent defiling, therefore, is merely reinforcement. So human hearts are not only self-defiling but self-destructive.

Although the middle voice is used with reference to "things which proceed out of the mouth," it is evident that words are passive, and the mouth is the cause. Words do not move themselves (reflexive) out of the mouth. Likewise, the heart causes the thoughts that form words. Neither words nor thoughts act; they are produced, respectively, by the mouth and heart.

[19] Here, Jesus clearly defined human hearts as thinking, choosing, and, self-defiling faculties.

The heart's productions include:

> **Evil** [*ponēroí*, the plural of *ponērós* {4190}, malevolent, harmful] **thoughts** [*dialogismoí*, the plural of *dialogismós* {1261}, the noun associated with the verb *dialogízomai* {1260}, to reason through, to comprehend, to mentally penetrate].

God is not responsible for the iniquity that circulates in the hidden recesses of humankind. The Bible teaches that we have malevolent natures that correspond to that of the devil (*ponērós*, Matt. 13:19, 38; Eph. 6:16; 1 John 2:13, 14; 3:12; 5:18). We, therefore, "being [*óntes*, the present participle of *eimí*, to be] evil [*ponēroí*]" (Matt. 7:11), without the overpowering work of the Holy Spirit, can manufacture only evil thoughts. Salvation, specifically, enlightenment based on the Word of God, infuses new thoughts into us. This is called the renewal of the mind (Rom. 12:2; Eph. 4:23; Col. 3:10).

- "**Murders**" (*phónoi*, the plural of *phónos* [5408], murder). *Phónos* is not the killing (*apokteínō* [615], to kill) endorsed by God in capital punishment and just wars. *Phoneúō* (5407) is killing the innocent, those not worthy of death, for some malevolent purpose. The two verbs, *phoneúō* and *apokteínō*, however, are not rigidly distinct since John, in his first epistle, says "No murderer [*anthrōpoktónos* {443}, mankiller, from *ánthrōpos* {444}, man; and *kteínō* {n.f.}, to kill] hath eternal life abiding in him" (1 John 3:15). However, in this verse John is restricting "murder" to someone who "hates his [innocent] brother." In any case, murder has no place in the heart of the believer, and a murderous heart is another one of those hideous states from which we are delivered.

- "**Adulteries**" and "**fornications**." At the beginning of human history, God ordained the bond of marriage between one woman and one man for reasons other than reproduction since He also commanded plants and animals to reproduce according to their "kind" (*génos* [1085]). Human rebellion extended to this institution, substituting for marriage "adulteries" (*moicheíai* [3430], physical unions beyond that with spouses) and "fornications" (*porneía* {4202}, physical unions between unmarried persons). Jesus said these specific rebellions begin in the heart, the thinking/choosing—and therefore planning—faculty before they reach physical expression. Our first guard, therefore, should be on what we think. If we regulate our thought lives, we can restrain our bodies.

- "**Thefts**" (*klopaí* [2829] from the verb *kléptō* [2813], to steal). The *kléptēs* (2812) is more of a stealthy thief as opposed to the *lēstēs* (3027), one who robs out in the open, the common mugger. The kleptomaniac is a clandestine operator who ingeniously hides articles on the way out of a building. Again the Lord's emphasis is on the mental and volitional planning stages of sin.

- "**False Witnesses.**" This is actually one compound plural Greek word (*pseudomarturíai*, the plural of *pseudomarturía* [5577] from *pseudḗs* [5571], false; and *marturía* [3141], a witness]. Lying was strictly forbidden in the Old Testament (Lev. 6:2, 3).

- "**Blasphemies.**" The English word "blasphemies" derives from the Greek noun *bláx* (n.f.; sluggish, stupid; in Modern Greek, idiot or fool) or the verb *bláptō* (984), to harm; and *phēmí* (5346), to speak. To include the ideas resident in the noun and verb, then, "blasphemy" is foolish and harmful content that pours out of the mouth. Once again, a lock on the mind and will stops the mouth. Believers should carefully plan their words.

[20] Jesus concluded His argument:

> These are the [*tá*, the plural neuter definite article] **defiling things** [*koinoúnta*, the present neuter plural participle of *koinóō* {2840}] to people, but eating with unwashen hands does not defile them. (a.t.).

To summarize, these "things" defile people, but the list is a set of silent, hidden, internal thoughts and choices before they become actions. This natural state of unregenerate persons is seen in the use of the present participle which underscores the uninterrupted process of evil.

Whatever impact unwashed hands has on bodily hygiene, there is no connection with moral purity. This was a false Jewish tradition. No external, bodily actions can clean up evil hearts. They may eliminate some filth, but they can neither sanitize or sanctify the individuals before God. However, such "washings," the writer of Hebrews tells us, prophetically typify the internal cleansing of the conscience "until [i.e., they were temporary] the time of reformation" (Heb. 9:10). God will then fulfill His promises to regenerate hearts, put a new Spirit within (Jer. 32:39, 40; Ezek. 11:19, 20; 36:26, 29), and cleanse the wicked from all iniquity (Jer. 33:8). The Jews took the typology as an end in itself.

The only hope for unregenerate people is to experience the cleansing blood of Jesus Christ shed on Calvary's cross. This alone is the power that victoriously overcomes the power of sin (1 John 1:7).

Jesus Heals a Gentile Woman's Daughter
(15:21–28; Mark 7:24–30)

[21] Jesus then crossed into the regions of Tyre and Sidon in Phoenicia. These two mostly heathen cities were only twenty-one miles apart. It was the Tyrenians who furnished the timber for Solomon's Temple and other great buildings of Jerusalem. The cedars of Lebanon were floated some eighty-five miles from Tyre to Joppa and from there taken to Jerusalem. During Jesus' ministry, He visited this populous and thriving city, and people came from there to hear Him (Matt. 11:21, 22; Mark 3:8; 7:24; 31; Luke 6:17; 10:13, 14). Paul also spent seven days at Tyre (Acts 21:3, 4) on one occasion.

[22] A Canaanite woman then approached Jesus:

> And, **behold** [*idoú* {2400}, the imperative middle of *eídō* from *eídon*, the aorist of *horáō* {3708}, to see and perceive with emphasis on perception], a woman **of Canaan** [*Chananaía* {5478}, the name "Canaan" having been given to the plains of the Jordan and the seacoast in contrast to the highlands; Num. 13:29; Deut. 7:1; Josh. 11:3] came out of the same coasts and cried to Him, saying, **Have mercy** [*eléēsón*, the aorist imperative of *eleéō* {1653}, to be merciful] on me, O **Lord** [*kúrie*, the vocative singular of *kúrios* {2962}, master], You son of David; my daughter **is being demonized** [*daimonízetai*, the present passive of *daimonízomai* {1139}] **badly** [*kakôs* {2560}]. (a.t.)

Mark calls this woman a Syrophoenician (Mark 7:26) and records that Jesus had entered a house near the border away from the suspicious, watchful eyes of the public, though this was impossible (Mark 7:24).

The aorist imperative indicates that the woman's request was for immediate help. Her daughter was "being demonized," the passive voice highlighting a demon's active oppression from which only the Lord could rescue. The woman's attitude was entirely different from that of the Jews (Matt. 15:1–20). She had a need, and she believed Jesus had the power to cast out the demon, something He had done on other occasions (Matt. 4:24; 8:16, 28–33; 9:32; 12:22).

Note the faith of this "[stranger] from the covenants of promise" (Eph. 2:12). First, her request implied that she believed Jesus was merciful (*eleémōn* [1655], compassionate), even beyond Jewish borders. Second, when she addressed Him as "Lord," she implied His lordship over demonic realms. She certainly believed He was the anointed Son of God. The aorist tense of "have mercy" shows she believed Jesus could immediately do something to meet her daughter's crisis. She also called Him "son of David," acknowledging not just His deity but His fulfillment of prophecy that the Messiah would come from the seed of David.

[23] "But he answered her **not** [*ouk*, the absolute 'not'] a word."

Jesus' silence was intentional, but we are not given the reason. However, we can deduce that the Lord has His perfect time, "His hour" to save. We cannot rush Him, no matter how frantic (like the woman) we are.

The disciples took this silence as a cue that He did not want the woman around. "**Send** her **away** [*apóluson*, the aorist imperative of *apolúō* {630}, to dismiss, release] **because** [*hóti* {3754}] she cries behind us" (a.t.). They assumed that the woman was becoming a nuisance to the Lord.

[24] "But he answered"—not the disciples but the woman, for two reasons. First, the disciples already knew that Jesus had come only for the "lost sheep of the house of Israel" because He had commanded such: "These twelve Jesus sent forth, and commanded them, saying, Go not into the way of the Gentiles, and into any city of the Samaritans enter ye not" (Matt. 10:5). They knew she was a Gentile, and this was only consistent with what He had already commanded them. Second, the woman responded to Jesus' answer, not the disciples, implying that Jesus was looking at her when He spoke.

This restriction to "the lost sheep of the house of Israel" was obviously not absolute, and Jesus wanted to teach His disciples this lesson. True, He came initially to the house of Israel. But not everyone in Israel is a "lost sheep" as is evident from those verses that state that the Lord saves every one of His sheep. Of the hundred sheep that "He has," the ninety and nine are safely in the fold, and He goes after the one remaining (Matt. 18:12; Luke 15:4; John 10:26–31). Thus, they are not all "lost sheep," only those "who believe not, because [*hóti*] ye [i.e., 'they'] are not of my sheep" (John 10:26).

And since "lost sheep" is a broader class than "the house of [physical] Israel," it may extend to the Gentiles of His people as well:

And other sheep I have, which are not of this fold: them also I **must** [*deí* {1163}, not moral—as if God "obeys"—but preordained necessity] bring, and they shall hear my voice; and there shall be one fold, and one shepherd. (John 10:16)

Paul goes to great theological lengths in the book of Romans to prove that God intended to extend His kingdom to the Gentiles (Rom. 9—11) during a period of what he calls "a partial hardening" (Rom. 11:25 NASB) of Israel: "They are not all Israel, which are of Israel" (Rom. 9:6). Logically, this statement can be interpreted two ways. Either an elect, spiritual Israel is totally within natural Israel (i.e., Israel according to the flesh), or the two classes intersect like rings. The latter case fits Paul's subsequent argument for the incorporation of Gentiles among which he describes Israel as: "He is not a Jew, which is one outwardly" (Rom. 2:28). If the house of spiritual Israel extends beyond natural Israel, even Jesus' original words do not exclude Gentiles.

[25] Ignorant of Jesus' plan to offer salvation to the entire world but cognizant of an accepting, even inviting, tone in His voice, the woman repeated her plea: "Lord, help me!"

> Then came she and **worshipped** [*prosekúnēsen*, MT, the aorist tense of *proskunéō* {4352} from *prós* {4314}, toward; and *kunéō* {n.f.}, to kiss, the aorist signifying a **momentary** act; or *proskúnei*, TR, UBS, Nestle's Text, the imperfect of the same verb, implying a **continuing** act] him.

In either case, the woman apparently fell on her face and kissed Jesus' feet. Notice the personal pronoun *moi*, me. This should not be understood as a self-centered request at the expense of her daugher. She clearly identified with her daughter; her daughter's torment was her own. (Note the close connection: "Help me. . . . My daughter is demonized" [v. 22; a.t.].)

[26] Still, Jesus tested the woman's faith:

> It is **not** [*ouk*, the absolute "not"] **good** [*kalón*, the accusative of *kalós* {2570}] **to take** [*labeín*, the aorist infinitive of *lambánō* {2983}; the aorist means "at this time," not generally] the bread of the **children** [*téknon* {5043}] and **to cast** [*baleín*, the aorist infinitive of *bállō* {906}] it to the **little dogs** [*kunaríois* {2952}]. (a.t.)

The root Greek noun *kúōn* (n.f.) is a house or domestic dog, but the diminutive *kunárion*, used here in the plural, is a small dog or puppy that kisses its master's hand—thus the connection with the verb *kunéō*. The verb *proskunéō*, therefore, has come to mean "to worship," to be thankful in the way a dog expresses its humble gratitude the only way it knows how. Three New Testament synonyms for *proskunéō* include *sébomai*, to revere (with its associative noun *sébas* [n.f.], respect, and verb *sebázomai* [4573]); *eusebéō* (2151), to show piety, worship; and *latreúō* (3000), to serve.

The Greek term translated "dogs" here, therefore, does not include the negative connotation it does in today's society of pit bulls, Weimaraners, Doberman pinschers, or just plain rabid curs. Moreover, the fact that the "children's bread" is not appropriate for "loving puppies" does not mean the puppies do not have their own proper food, either. We have to be careful that we do not put a harsh tone in Jesus' mouth from the word "dogs" itself.

[27] The woman persisted: "**Truth** [*naí* {3483}, yes], Lord: **yet** [actually two words: *kaí*, also; and *gár*, for] the dogs eat of the crumbs which fall from their masters' table."

In Greek there are two words which mean "yes." *Málista* (3122), the superlative adverb of *mála* (n.f.), means very, mostly, especially (Acts 20:38; 25:26; 26:3; Gal. 6:10; Phil. 4:22; 1 Tim. 4:10; 5:8, 17; 2 Tim. 4:13; Titus 1:10; Phile. 1:16; 2 Pet. 2:10). The other word, used here, is *naí*. What is the difference? *Málista* is an adverb of comparison that admits of degrees like good, better, and best, or possible, probable, and certain. *Naí*, on the other hand, is an adverb of affirmation that excludes degrees by definition. This is why the Lord said, "Let your yes [*naí*] be yes and your no [*ou*] no; for whatever is more than this is evil" (Matt. 5:37; a.t.).

The woman's *naí*, therefore, was an absolute assent to the Lord's teaching; she had no doubt that what He had said was true. From here, she could only risk inquiring whether this teaching, while nothing but the truth, was the whole truth. Note that she used neither the Greek adversative *dé* or *allá*, "but," to contradict the Lord, but rather *kaí gár*, meaning "for also" (i.e., in addition). She now suggested a derivative truth, not a denial of the original. In addition to the fact that bread was not cast to dogs, the dogs still benefit from crumbs that "**keep falling** [*piptónton*, the present participle of *píptō* {4098}, to fall] from their master's table" (a.t.).

[28] At this response, Jesus commended the woman:

O **woman** [*gúnai*, the vocative case of *gunē*], great is thy **faith** [*pístis* {4102}]: **be it** [*genēthētō*, the aorist passive imperative of *gínomai* {1096}, to become] unto thee even as thou wilt [*théleis*, the present tense of *thélō* {2309}, to desire].

Jesus' "**be it**" was not the wishful thinking of a pastoral benediction but a decree, as in, "Let there be [*genēthētō*] light, and there became [*egéneto*] light" (Gen. 1:3 LXX). The devil himself could not retain the demon inside this young girl once Jesus had spoken.

And so we read, "And her daughter was made whole from that very hour."

Jesus Heals the Multitudes
(15:29–31; Mark 7:31–37)

[29] Jesus now left the region of Tyre and Sidon in Phoenicia and "came **near** [*pará*, proximate to] unto the Sea of Galilee."

He was acquainted with a certain mountain there, perhaps the one where He had encountered the devil at the beginning of His ministry (Matt. 4:8). This too may have been the one on which He had taught the Beatitudes (Matt. 5:1; 8:1).

[30, 31] Here great multitudes, we are told, "**cast down**" (*érripsan*, the aorist tense of *rhíptō* [4496], to throw or let down) their sick before Jesus: the lame, blind, dumb (unable to hear or speak), maimed, and others.

The verb *rhíptō* is more often associated with throwing away or scattering refuse rather than with letting down. Consequently, the scenario is not very pleasant, and it vividly contrasts with Jesus' compassionate healing of the victims. These were not necessarily sick relatives but outcasts, rejects, beggars, those that society, represented by the multitude, had disowned. Throwing someone down on the ground is a sampling of the worst type of humiliation.

But as Paul concluded, maybe partly from this very scene, "Who will reject what God elects?" (Rom. 8:33; a.t.). The Lord Jesus restored these castaways completely and permanently as seen in the use of several present participles:

". . . the dumb **speaking** [*laloúntas*, the present participle of *laléō* {2980}, to speak, break the silence], the crippled **healthy** [*hugieís*, the accusative plural of *hugiés* {5199}, healthy ones], the lame **walking** [*peripatoúntas*, the present participle of *peripatéō* {4043}, to walk], and the blind **seeing** [*blépontas*, the present participle of *blépō* {991}, to see]. (a.t.)

The multitude did not stop with marveling, which alone stops short of salvation. The text says,

They marveled [*thaumásai*, the aorist infinitive of *thaumázō* {2296}, to marvel] . . . **and** [*kaí*, and, also] **they glorified** [*edóxasan*, the aorist tense of *doxázō* {1392}, to ascribe glory; from *dokéō* {1380}, to think, to predicate] the God of Israel. (a.t.)

Hopefully, the crowd also rethought its responsibilities to the helpless. Certainly, those who were believers did so.

To glorify is to subjectively predicate all the attributes of God to God, that is, to recognize God as God, as He is objectively. This mental cognition causes the emotions to burst forth in marvel and awe. One cannot be emotionally detached while praising God. Because of the trinitarian relationships, the Father and Son glorify One another: "If God [the Father] be glorified in him [the Son], God shall also glorify him [the Son] in himself [probably the Son], and shall straightway glorify him [the Son]" (John 13:32). At this point, the multitudes most likely gloried in God the Father through the Son who performed the works.

Jesus Feeds Four Thousand
(15:32–39; Mark 8:1–9)

[32] Jesus became concerned about the needs of the multitudes:

> Then Jesus called His disciples to Him and said, **I have compassion** [*splagchnízomai* {4697} from *splágchnon* {4698}, bowel, intestine; to feel pity at the deepest level] on the multitude, because they continue with Me now three days and have nothing to eat. I do not [*ou*, the absolute "not"] **desire** [*thélō*] to send them away hungry, lest they **faint** [*ekluthṓsin*, the aorist tense of *eklúomai* {1590} from *ek*, out of; *lúō* {3089}, break up, dissolve] on the way. (a.t.)

The Lord is concerned with our physical well-beings. In His human nature (*splagchnízomai* does not apply to His deity) at the deepest level, He groans under the burden of our suffering. Here the threat of people collapsing from hunger stirred Him to provide for their immediate needs. Sometimes the Lord does not want us to fast—not if it produces a collapse so we cannot effectively serve Him.

[33] Five thousand had been fed a short time before (see Matt. 14:15–21). Yet the disciples, walking by sight and not by faith, asked, "Whence should we have so much bread in the wilderness, as **to fill** [*chortásai*, the aorist infinitive of *chortázō* {5526}, to satisfy] so great a multitude?"

The disciples knew the crowd could not be satisfied with just a little food. Yet their incredulity as to where Jesus could find bread in the wilderness to again feed literally thousands when He had done so previously (note "**desert** [*érēmos* {2048}] **place** [*tópos* {5117}]" in 14:15) is utterly amazing.

[34] Jesus, ever patient, did not rebuke them but asked, "How many loaves have ye?" He already knew the count, and He could have created bread *ex nihilo* (out of nothing). But in this instance He revealed His providence over things already in existence, no doubt to remind us that He will increase whatever we place on His altar for His service.

This was necessary, for the number of loaves and fishes was insufficient to feed the great crowd. Moreover, it was not just a small number of fish, but they were "**little fishes**" (*ichthúdia* [2485], a small fish).

Mary's Magnificat celebrates the redemption history of Israel as one in which the Lord repeatedly "filled [*enéplēsen*, the aorist tense of *empíplēmi* {1705}, to fill] the hungry [*peinṓntas*, the present participle of *peináō* {3983}, to hunger] with good things [*agathṓn*, the genitive plural of *agathós* {18}, goods]; and the rich [*ploutoúntas*, the present participle of *ploutéo* {4147}, to be rich] He hath sent away [*exapésteilen*, the aorist tense of *exapostéllō* {1821}, to send away] empty [*kenoús*, the plural of *kenós* {2756}, empty, vain]" (Luke 1:53; a.t.).

[35] Now Jesus "**commanded** [*ekéleuse*, the aorist tense of *keleúō* {2753}, to bid] [them] **to sit down** [*anapeseín*, the aorist infinitive of *anapíptō* {377}, to lean back] on the ground" (a.t.). They had been standing and were fatigued to the point of passing out.

[36] Following this, Jesus blessed the available food.

> And He took the seven loaves and the fish and **having thanked** [*eucharis-tésas*, the aorist participle of *eucharistéō* {2168}, to thank] [His Father, implic-itly], He broke them and gave to His disciples, and the disciples to the multitude. (a.t.)

A large-scale eucharist and the proper order for the church: first, the giv-ing of thanks, then the breaking, then distribution to the elders, and from the elders to the people of God. Each loaf represents the body of Christ, broken on our behalf. Paul speaks of the one body of the Lord from which we sym-bolically partake and eat in remembrance of Him (1 Cor. 11:24).

In John 6, the Lord Jesus spoke of Himself as the bread (always singular, never "breads") of life coming down from heaven (vv. 32–35, 41, 48, 50, 51, 58). The physical bread represents His sinless body that was sacrificed for sin (Heb. 10:12).

Note that while the verb *éklase* (2806), broke, is an *aorist* tense, the verb *edídou* (UBS, Nestle's Text), giving, is imperfect, meaning "He kept giving."

[37] The result was,

> They **all** [*pántes*, the nominative plural of *pás*] ate and **were filled** [*echortás-thēsan*, the aorist passive of *chortázō* {5526}, to fill to satiety]: and they took up of the abundance of the pieces that were left seven **baskets** [*spurídas* {4711}] full. (a.t.)

Jesus had produced a "**surplus** [*perisseúon*, the present participle of *peris-seúō* {4052}, an amount beyond what is necessary] **of fragments** [*klasmátōn*, the neuter plural of *klásma* {2801}]" (a.t.).

A Greek synonym for *perisseúō* is *pleonázō* (4121), to have more than enough. But *perisseúō* has a sense of good and duty that is missing from *pleonázō*. The latter term is sometimes associated with greed (*pleonexía* [4124]), which is a sin (Mark 7:22; Luke 12:15; Rom. 1:29; 2 Cor. 9:5; Eph. 5:3; Col. 3:5; 1 Thess. 2:5; 2 Pet. 2:3, 14).

The word translated "**baskets**" here is *spurídas*, a small shopping basket, while in Matthew 14:20; 16:9; Mark 6:43; 8:19; Luke 9:17, and John 6:13, "baskets" translates *kophínous*, the accusative of *kóphinos* (2894), a wicker basket, a larger basket made of ropes or entwined twigs. In both instances, the surplus was not wasted. It was probably put to good use, perhaps to feed the needy. The Lord's grace never runs short and never goes to waste.

[38] Here and in Matthew 14, the numbers of thousands fed **excluded** (*chōrís* [5565], apart from, besides) women and children, a common custom of counting in those days. This means the total number fed was actually much greater.

[39] After this great miracle, Jesus, "**having dismissed** (*apolúsas*, the aorist participle of *apolúō*, to loose from, dismiss, release] the multitudes, went into a boat and came to the borders of Magdala" (a.t.).

Interesting but without explanation is the fact that the reaction of the crowd following this miracle was tame compared with the stirring created at the feeding of the five thousand when the crowd was prepared to declare Jesus king (John 6:15). Then He compelled His disciples to depart before He dismissed the crowds. This time, the crowd appeared to be less zealous.

16

Discerning the Signs of the Times
(16:1–4; Mark 8:10–12)

Jesus did not hesitate to call the Pharisees and Sadducees "hypocrites" (v. 3). The reason is clear enough; He had given them ample evidence that He was able to do what no person had ever done. Who had ever multiplied a few fish and loaves of bread to feed thousands of persons on two occasions? Who had healed the sick and raised the dead? Instead of acknowledging Jesus as the Son of God—the natural response to such miracles—they came "**tempting**" (*peirázontes*, the present participle of *peirázō* [3985], to tempt or test) Him.

[1] The word *"peirázō"* in the Bible can have two meanings: either a temptation to sin or a test of righteousness, and it depends on the motive. God tests His people to strengthen their faith. Unbelievers and particularly hypocrites, on the other hand, tempt people to sin.

James 1:13 tells us that God is not the responsible cause of sin:

> Let no person [*mēdeís* {3367}, not even one; from *mē* {3361}, the relative not; *dé* {1161}, even; and *heís* {1520}, one], when he is tempted [*peirazómenos*, the present passive participle of *peirázō* {3985}, tempt], say, I am tempted of [*apó* {575}, from] God [*theoú*, the genitive case of the noun *theós* {2316} without the definite article *toú*, meaning "from deity" as opposed to any created person, angelic or human]: for [*gár* {1063}, because] God [*ho theós*, here the definite article pointing to any of the Persons of the Trinity, probably the Father] is [*éstin* {551}] untemptable [*apeírastos* {551} from the privative *a* {1}, without; and *peirázō*, to tempt] by evil [*kakón*, the genitive plural of *kakós* {2556}, evil, meaning evil things either in character or effects], neither does He tempt anyone. (a.t.)

James 1:14 amplifies this thought by teaching that the responsible cause of sin is not an external agent at all but rather the internal state of lust:

But [*dé* {1161}, but; i.e., "but rather than God being the cause"] every man [*hékastos* {1538}, each, every one] is tempted [*peirázetai*, the present passive indicative of *peirázō*, to tempt], when he is drawn away [*exelkómenos*, the present passive participle of *exélkō* {1828}, to draw away; from *ex* {1537}, out of; and *hélkō* {1670}, to draw] of [*hupó* {5259}, by] his own [*idías*, the genitive feminine of *ídios* {2398}, own, the emphasis being on personal or private, one's possession] lust [*epithumías* {1939}], and enticed [*deleazómenos*, the present middle/passive participle of *deleázō* {1185}, to entrap; from the noun *délear* {n.f.}, bait]."

The Pharisees were not inclined toward good; rather, they wanted to thoroughly discredit Jesus' words and miracles by baiting Him to

. . . show [*epideíxai*, the aorist active infinitive of *epideíknumi* {1925}, occurring for the first time here and then in 22:19; 24:1; Luke 17:14; Acts 9:39; 18:28; Heb. 6:17, and meaning to show off, to exhibit] them a sign [*sēmeíon* {4592}, a signpost] from [*ek* {1537}, out of from within, heaven being the local origin of the sign] the [*toú* {3588}] heaven [*ouranoú*, the genitive of *ouranós* {3772}; "the heaven" is the place where God's special presence dwells]. (a.t.)

[2, 3] In response, Jesus chided the Pharisees and Sadducees for their inability to discern "the signs **of the times** [*kairṓn*, the plural of *kairós* {2540}, seasons]," though they could frequently predict weather based on current weather conditions:

When it is evening, ye say, It will be **fair weather** [*eudía* {2105}]: for the sky **is red** [*purrázei* {4449}]. And in the morning, It will be **foul weather** [*cheimṓn* {5494}, winter] today: for the sky is red and **lowring** [*stugnázōn* {4768}, gloomy, overcast].

They had been given prophecies concerning the first appearance of their Messiah, even the birthplace (Mic. 5:2) and time (Dan. 9:24–26) of His birth. Yet they ignored God's revelation because of their hypocrisy (*hupokritaí* [5273] from *hupó* {5259}, under, implying secrecy; and *krísis* [2920], judgment), wickedness, and adultery (v. 4).

[4] Earnestly seeking (*epizēteí*, the present tense of *epizētéo* [1934]) signs is not a neutral endeavor. Non-Christians believe they are unbiased before the Spirit of God removes their hearts of stone and replaces them with hearts of flesh, one promise of the new covenant (Ezek. 11:19; 36:26). Jesus called a generation that looked for signs both "**wicked**" (*ponērá* [4190], malevolent) and "**adulterous**" (*moichalís* [3428]).

Jesus' response to this desire for proof was emphatic: "There shall **no** [*ou* {3756}, the absolute 'not'] sign be given unto it, but the sign of the prophet Jonas." This did not mean that the other signs Jesus did in His lifetime were insufficient. In John 20:30 some signs are referred to as *álla* (243), other of the same quality, in contrast with *hétera* (2087), other of a different kind. Jesus' primary sign to Israel at that time would be His resurrection after three days in the grave, corresponding to Jonah's release from the belly of the large fish, following three days of confinement. That sign would be sufficient to bring Israel to the level of accountability to determine the fate of the nation. Indeed, Israel rejected this sign, and God destroyed Jerusalem and its temple in A.D. 70, according to Jesus' prophecies in Matthew 21:40–43; 22:7.

This section closes with the phrase "And **he left** [*katalipṓn*, the aorist participle of *kataleípō* {2641}, to leave behind, forsake] them, and departed." Jesus had had enough of their unrepentant wickedness and adultery.

The Leaven of the Pharisees and Scribes
(16:5–12; Mark 8:13–21)

[5] Now the scene changed. In Mark 8:13 we are informed that Jesus left the disciples on the east coast of the Sea of Galilee with the plan to meet them on the other side where He had fed thousands of people:

> And **having left** [*apheís*, the aorist participle of *aphíēmi* {863}, to leave] them, and **having entered** [*embás*, the aorist participle of *embaínō* {1684}, to enter in] into the ship **again** [*pálin* {3825}], **He departed** [*apélthen*, the aorist indicative of *apérchomai* {565}] to the other side. (Mark 8:13; a.t.)

He sailed; they walked. The disciples **forgot** (*epeláthonto*, the aorist middle indicative of *epilanthánomai* [1950], to forget) not only to carry bread with them but also to stock the ship Jesus traveled on with more than one loaf (Mark 8:14). But He used even what they had forgotten to make an important point concerning false teaching.

[6] It is important for us to understand what Jesus meant by His words, "Take heed and beware of the leaven of the Pharisees and of the Sadducees."

The first verb, translated "**Take heed**," is *horáte*, the present imperative of *horáō* (3708), to see and perceive. The present tense is gnomic; that is, it teaches a general principle (see A. T. Robertson, *A Grammar of the Greek New Testament in the Light of Historical Research*, 866). The disciples needed to see the difference between the false teaching of the Pharisees and Sadducees and the truth of the gospel, especially if the former had a leavening (penetrating) impact on people. The word "gnomic" comes from the Greek *gnṓmē* (1106), opinion, a determined mindset. Jesus wanted to make His disciples aware of the fundamental difference between law and grace, so they could clearly teach it later.

The second verb is "**beware**" (*proséchete*, the present tense of *proséchō* [4337], to take heed, to guard against; from *prós* [4314], toward, but in this case more likely "near"; and *échō* [2192], to have). Coupled with the first verb, it gave the sense that the disciples should be wary of false teaching when they were "near" the Pharisees and Sadducees. Jesus wanted the disciples to understand that the Pharisees and Sadducees were hypocrites. The only reason they came to Him was to tempt Him by asking for more signs to provide credentials for what He had already proven.

[7] The disciples did not immediately understand Jesus' words.

> **They were reasoning** [*dielogízonto*, the imperfect of *dialogízomai* {1260}, to dialogue, reason; from *diá* {1223}, through—an intensive preposition expressive of thoroughness; and *logízomai* {3049}, to reckon, figure out] among themselves, saying, "It is because we have taken no bread." (a.t.)

What a lack of bread had to do with being cautious around the Pharisees and Sadducees showed just how little they understood Jesus' metaphor.

They were also removed from recent miracles. Jesus had just miraculously fed more than four thousand. Why would He now be concerned that the disciples had brought no bread?

[8] Jesus called them, literally, "**little-faiths**" (*oligópistoi* [3640]), a term not equivalent to "unbeliever" (*ápistos* [571]). Jesus never called His disciples "faithless" (*ápistoi* [571]). Faith, *pístis*, in the New Testament has several objects and therefore can be qualified as great or little depending on the number of biblical propositions to which a believer assents.

From what follows in verse 9, we see that the disciples did not seem to understand the full sovereignty of the Lord Jesus. That was why He asked them to remember the feeding of both the five thousand (v. 9) and the four thousand (v. 10). Besides missing the whole point of the "leaven of the Pharisees and of the Sadducees," the disciples forgot that lack of bread would never be an obstacle for Jesus.

[9, 10] Accordingly, Jesus asked,

> Do you **not yet** [*hoúpō* {3768}, from *ou* {3756}, the absolute not; and *–pō* {4458}, how] **understand** [*noeíte*, the present tense of *noéō* {3539}, to think, comprehend; synonymous with *dialogízomai*, to reason] **neither** [*oudé* {3761},

not even; from *ou*, the absolute negative; and *dé* {1161}, but] **remember** [*mnēmoneúete*, the present tense of *mnēmoneúō* {3421}, to recall] the five loaves of the five thousand, and how many baskets [*kophínous* {2894}] you took up, neither the seven loaves of bread of the four thousand and how many baskets you took up? (a.t.)

[11] Jesus continued,

How [*pôs* {4459}] is it that you **understood** [*noeíte*, see v. 9] not that **I spoke** [*eípon*, the aorist tense of *légō* {3004}, to intelligently speak] to you not concerning bread, that you should **beware** [*proséchein*; see v. 6] of the leaven of the Pharisees and Sadducees? (a.t.)

The Lord Jesus wanted the disciples to know that the false teachings of the Pharisees and scribes were a powerful leavening agent they should guard against. Today, as then, the leaven of legalism works its way through the church, distracting people from the gospel of grace.

In biblical days, leaven (*zúmē* [2219]) was a catalytic agent like yeast that caused fermentation in dough, making it rise. Frequently, Jesus used this permeation process to describe the spread of sin. However, on one occasion, He also analogously described the penetration of the kingdom of God in the world: "The kingdom of heaven is like unto leaven, which a woman took, and hid in three measures of meal, till the whole was leavened" (Matt. 13:33).

Properly understood, the two leavens, the kingdom of God and the legalistic teaching of the Pharisees and Sadducees, penetrate daily life, spreading and advancing (*prokóptō* [4298]) automatically, not necessarily with conscious effort. This process compares with that expressed in the Greek verb *auxánō* (837), to grow, which presupposes the organism of life.

Concerning false teaching spreading throughout the world, Paul wrote: "Evil men and seducers shall wax worse and worse, deceiving, and being deceived" (2 Tim. 3:13) and "Their word will spread like gangrene [*gággraina* {1044}]" (2 Tim. 2:17; a.t.). Peter added, "There shall be false teachers among [*en* {1722}, within, among] you" (2 Pet. 2:1). Because the tares grow alongside the wheat until the time of the harvest, we can anticipate that legalism will be with us until Christ returns. In the interim, we are called to overturn legalism with grace.

[12] Now Jesus clearly identified leaven with "**doctrine**" (*didachês* {1322}), the singular Greek noun emphasizing the unity of Pharisaism. At the bottom of Pharisaism—its laws, rituals, external conformities—lay their simple doctrine of justification by works. The Pharisees and Sadducees were arrogant and hypocritical because their theology was false. False teaching is the root of bad

motives and behaviors. People think, choose, plan, and behave what they believe.

Didachḗ is the content that persons learn on their own or from others. Like the "doctrine" of the Pharisees and Sadducees, the teaching of Christ has an underlying unity, so it is frequently called by the singular *didaskalía* (1319), teaching. Jesus never taught the Law from one side of His mouth and grace from the other, justification by works on one day and justification by faith on the next, nor did He ever waver. He always taught the same, consistent gospel of grace everywhere He went. Teachings (*didaskalíai*, the plural of *didaskalía*), by contrast, are human productions.

Finally, "**they understood**" (*sunḗkan*, the aorist tense of *suníēmi* [4920], to understand, literally, "to put it all together"; from *sún* [4862], together; and *híēmi* [n.f.], to send, put together mentally, comprehend).

Peter's Confession of Jesus (16:13–20; Mark 8:27–30; Luke 9:18–20; John 6:68, 69)

[13] Caesarea Philippi was a city set on the southwestern slope of Mount Hermon and the furthest distance north Jesus travelled in His earthly ministry. Considerably north of Galilee, the city was located near the sources of the Jordan River. Mount Hermon was sometimes called Paneas, from the Greek word *pán*, the neuter of *pás* (3956), all, perhaps derived from the heathen Greek god, Pan, during the Hellenistic era. This would correspond with its reputation for being a center of idol worship.

Somewhere along the border of this city, Jesus asked His disciples regarding rumors concerning His Person and work.

Whom [*tína*, the accusative interrogative pronoun of *tís* {5150}, who] do **the** [*hoi*] **men** [*ánthrōpoi*, with the definite article, meaning "the men who have anything to say at all"] **say** [*légousin*, the present tense of *légō* {3004}, to select words to convey thought, the present tense highlighting regularity] that I the Son of **the** [*toú*, possibly a reference to Adam] man **am** [*eínai* {1511}, the present infinitive of *eimí* {1510}, to be]? (a.t.)

That the verb *légō* basically means "to select" is evidenced by its association with *logía* (3048), collection, or, in the organizational sense, of a gathering of likeminded persons (1 Cor. 16:1, 2). So we can paraphrase Jesus' question as follows: "What is the general opinion concerning the Son of man among those who speak of Him?"

[14] Two opinions, differentiated here by the Greek particles *men* (3303) and *dé* (1161), can be translated, "on the one hand, but on the other hand."

The set of terms, *hoi* ([3588], translated by the first "**some**") and *álloi* ([243], translated the second "**some**" and meaning others of the same kind), groups those who believed Jesus was John the Baptist with those who believed He was Elijah. This may have been because Jesus identified John as "Elijah who was to come" (Matt. 11:14 NIV), and Luke speaks of John as going before Him [Jesus] "in the spirit and power of Elijah" (Luke 1:17 NIV).

Then the disciples used another Greek word for "**others**," not *álloi* but *héteroi* (2087), meaning others of a different kind (in this case, persuasion). These people classed Jesus as one of the Old Testament prophets, like Jeremiah.

[15] Jesus was not concerned with the opinions among people who were not His disciples. He wanted to know what His followers thought: "**But** [*dé*] you, whom do you say that I am?" (a.t.).

Since they obviously knew His name and since Jesus knew what they thought, He apparently was seeking a public confession from them of what He was by predication and title.

[16] Simon Peter's answer was inspired, but we can assume that Peter answered for the other disciples since Jesus' question was to all: "Whom do you [plural] say. . . ?" (a.t.). Peter responded,

> **Thou** [*sú* {4771}, You, emphatic] **art** [*ei* {1488}, the present tense of *eimí* {1510}, You are] **the** [{3588}, the definite article meaning there is only one, unique] **Christ** [*christós* {5547} from the verb *chríō* {5548}, to anoint], the Son of the **living** [*zōntos*, the present participle of *záō* {2198}, to live] God.

The definite article "the" is extremely important; it is never used carelessly. Here it means that the Lord Jesus is not one of many sons; He is "the" only Son in His class. Moreover, He is not the son of a dead god but the Son of "the [i.e., only] living [the present participle indicating perpetuity] God [i.e., the Father]."

[17] This was the right answer, and because of it, Jesus called Peter "**blessed**" (*makários* [3107], a state of internal bliss, contentment, satisfaction). The adjectival noun is used to characterize God's general nature in 1 Timothy 1:11. Jesus blessed Peter because the Father had directly revealed to him the truth about His Son. Peter did not conclude this from any opinion circulating among non-disciples.

Thus, Jesus said,

> **For** [*hóti* {3754}, because; the reason why Peter is blessed follows] flesh and blood hath **not** [*ouk* {3756}, the absolute "not"] **revealed** [*apekálupsen*, the

aorist tense of *apokalúptō* {601}, to uncover, take the lid off] it unto thee, but my Father which is in heaven.

Because the sense was generic, this included the flesh and blood of Jesus Himself. The revelation of our Lord's deity was the product of the Trinity, the Father, Son, and Holy Spirit. No human mediation whatsoever caused this revelation. Regeneration is the operation of the Spirit of God directly on our spirits; as Jesus said, "That which is born of the Spirit [i.e., the Spirit of God] is spirit [a qualitatively new human spirit]" (John 3:6).

The apocalyptic character of this revelation implies mystery, but Jesus said as much when He preached the analogy between those born of the Spirit and the unpredictable wind (John 3:8). The aorist tense of "revealed" no doubt points to the crisis of the new birth.

While "flesh and blood" speaks of two material things, the verb "**revealed**" is singular in number. Of course, neither flesh nor blood per se could reveal such things, but here the composite expression refers to a living person. In general, flesh means human nature (Matt. 19:5; Mark 10:8; 1 Cor. 6:16; Eph. 5:31; Jude 7), so when Jesus said to Peter in effect, "Flesh absolutely did not reveal My deity to you," He meant that this was not a human revelation but a divine one.

[18] Jesus continued with His own blessing on Peter:

> And **I say** [*légō* {3004}, to speak intelligently] also unto thee, That thou art **Peter** [*Pétros*, a proper name meaning "stone," the masculine gender of the feminine noun *pétra* {4073}, a massive rock or cliff], and upon this **rock** [*pétra*] **I will build** [*oikodomḗsō*, the future tense of *oikodoméō* {3618}, to build] my church.

The noun translated "**church**" is *ekklēsía* (1577), mentioned here for the first time in the New Testament. It derives from the prefix *ek* (1537), out of; and *kaléō* (2564), to call. It means the set of individuals called out of the unbelieving world to become and remain believers. The enclitic pronoun *mou* (3450), "my," is the genitive of *egṓ* (1473), I. The Lord Jesus is not only going to build His church; He's going to possess it in the fullest sense. It is His church, and no one else's.

And He alone builds. As the apostle Paul says later, "I planted, Apollos watered, but God increased [*eúxanen* {837}, grew]" (1 Cor. 3:6; a.t.). The Lord is sovereign over the growth of His church. The church is presented as a structure with an immovable foundation (*themélion* [2310]): "And [ye] are built upon the foundation [*themelíō*] of the apostles and prophets, Jesus Christ himself being the chief corner stone" (Eph. 2:20). From this, we can see clearly that Jesus Christ Himself is the Rock (the chief cornerstone) on which the church is built. We are saved by confessing that Rock, the truth that "Thou art the Christ, the Son of the living God."

To offset any conjecture that He will fail to build His church, the Lord added:

> And the **gates** [*púlai*, the plural of *púlē* {4439}, a large gate as opposed to a *thúra* {2374}, door] of **hell** [*hádou*, the genitive singular of *hádēs* {86} from the alpha privative *a* {1}, not; and *eídō* {1492}, to perceive; therefore the "unseen" or "imperceptible" place] shall **not** [*ou* {3756}, the absolute "not"] **prevail** [*katischúsousin*, the future tense of *katischúō* {2729} from *katá* {2596} against; and *ischúō* {2480}, to prevail over] against it.

Hades occurs eleven times in the New Testament (Matt. 11:23; 16:18; Luke 10:15; 16:23; Acts 2:27, 31; 1 Cor. 15:55 [where it is translated "death"]; Rev. 1:18; 6:8; 20:13, 14). The Septuagint uses the Hebrew word *sheól*, which occurs sixty-three times. In Luke 16, the rich man who mercilessly disregards a poverty-stricken man named Lazarus is consigned to Hades following his death: "In Hades, he lifted his eyes, being [*hupárchōn*, the present participle of *hupárchō* {5225}, to subsist] in torments" (v. 23; a.t.). Hades is "unseen" by living men, yet the rich man is spoken of as having eyes that he lifts in order to see Lazarus "afar off" (*makróthen* [3113], from a distance; Luke 16:23).

The term also appears in Matthew 11:21, 23 where Jesus pronounced judgments on the unrepentant cities of Chorazin, Bethsaida, and Capernaum. The city of Capernaum, for one, had an overwhelming opportunity to receive Christ, since He did most of His miracles in that region. Jesus prophesied that Capernaum, which was exalted (*hupsōtheísa* [5312]) to heaven (*ouranoú* [3772]), will descend (*katabibasthḗsē* [2601]) into *hádēs*. No doubt, *hádēs* is spoken of in this section of Matthew as a place of punishment.

Since the gates are on Hades—not heaven—and since Christ has the keys to them (Rev. 1:18), the most natural meaning is that the Lord will beat down Hades' gates through His church. People will be saved; there is no satanic stoppage of the overpowering kingdom of Christ. In poetically strong, clear language, Jesus declared that all opposing forces of the enemies of the gospel shall fail.

[19] Jesus continued His blessing to Peter:

> And **I shall give** [*dōsō*, the future tense of *dídōmi* {1325}, to give] unto **you** [*soi*, the 2nd person **singular** {see the last paragraph of this section} dative pronoun of *sú* {4771}] the keys of the kingdom of the heavens: and **that which** [*hó*, the accusative singular neuter relative pronoun of *hós* {3739}] **if** [*eán*

{1437}, the "if" of reality] **you shall bind** [*désēs*, the aorist active subjunctive of *déō* {1210}, bind] on the earth, **shall be** [*éstai*, the future indicative of *eimí* {1510}, to be] [that which], **having been bound** [*dedeménon*, the perfect passive neuter participle of *déō*, to bind] in the heavens, and that which **you loosed** [*lúsēs*, the aorist active subjunctive of *lúō* {3089}, to loose] on earth, shall be [that which], **having been loosed** [*leluménon*, the perfect passive neuter participle of *lúō*, to loose] in the heavens. (a.t.)

The verbs appear to contradict, but they do not. There is no other way to express an event historically future to Peter but determinately past to God: "Whatever you shall bind on earth and whatever you shall loose on earth has already been bound or loosed in heaven" (a.t.). Heaven's decision to bind or loose is prior to the actual binding or loosing on earth. The two have to agree; the historical must match what heaven has already decided on.

Binding and loosing both relate to sin: "To Him who loved us and loosed [*lúsanti*] us from our sins by His blood" (Rev. 1:5; a.t., *lúsanti* [TR, UBS, Nestles Text]). Although salvation is depicted as the Lord breaking into Satan's house, binding him and stealing his treasured possessions, namely, unbelievers (Matt. 12:29), Jesus did not give Peter His power to save and destroy (James 4:12). The binding and loosing here most likely refer to corporate judgments the church makes on sin: "Whose soever sins ye [plural; see last paragraph below] remit, they are remitted unto them; and whose soever sins ye [plural] retain, they are retained" (John 20:23). An instance of this seems to have occurred in the church of Corinth:

> In the name of our Lord Jesus Christ, when ye are gathered together, and my spirit, with the power of our Lord Jesus Christ, to deliver such an one unto Satan for the destruction of the flesh, that [*hína* {2443}] the spirit may be saved in the day of the Lord Jesus. (1 Cor. 5:4, 5)

Here the whole church determined to bind an unrepentant believer in sin—specifically to pray not for his salvation but the "destruction of the flesh" that led him into sin. Yet the delivery of this person to Satan serves a good, final purpose—the salvation of his spirit on the Day of the Lord. Unwittingly, Satan's short-term goal of destruction self-defeatingly produced salvation (see also 1 Tim. 1:20).

Since the Roman Catholic Church and the Eastern Orthodox Church have based their theory of the primacy of Peter on the singular "you" (meaning to Peter alone) in Matthew 16:19, it is important to note that the same promise regarding binding and loosing is addressed to all disciples (the plural "you") in John 20:23. The singular "you" may reflect no more than the fact that Peter was the first to confess Jesus as the Messiah, the Son of God. In other words, the promise belongs to all those who "confess with their mouths that Jesus is Lord" (Rom. 10:9; a.t.). Peter was merely the firstborn of this confession, so Jesus addressed him personally.

[20] Yet this was not the time to publicly confess—at least not to the world of unbelief. Following this special promise to His church, Jesus

> . . . **charged** [*diesteílato*, the aorist middle indicative of *diastéllō* {1291}, to command; from *diá* {1223}, denoting transition; and *stéllō* {4724}, to send, to shrink back] he his disciples that they should tell no man that he was Jesus the Christ.

This is a good example of the use of the aorist tense to prevent contradiction. *Diesteílato* restricts the command and its obedience to the crisis of the moment. The Father had determined a proper season (*kairós* [2540]) to reveal the deity of His Son. Thus, while Jesus was always the Son of God, Paul explains to the Romans that the declaration of this fact was reserved for the time "out of [*ek*] the resurrection of the dead" (Rom. 1:4; a.t.). The resurrection, in fact, served as proof based on Jesus' prophecy that He would raise Himself.

Jesus Predicts His Death and Resurrection
(16:21–23; Mark 8:31–33; Luke 9:21, 22)

[21] After Peter's confession, Jesus "began **to show** [*deiknúein*, the present infinitive of *deíknumi* {1166}] unto his disciples."

What He taught from the beginning shows what He considered most important. And this was the fact that "he **must** [*deí* {1163}] go unto Jerusalem, and suffer many things of the elders and chief priests and scribes, and be killed, and be raised again the third day."

The necessity (*deí*) of the atonement was not moral; that is, God was not commanded to reconcile man by some higher god. The triune God had foreordained the atonement. The reconciliation, therefore, was not something He ought to have done any more than He ought to have created. Even though men secondarily caused the humiliation, suffering, and death of the Lord Jesus, the Bible teaches that they all acted under His divine permission and foreknowledge:

> The kings of the earth stood up, and the rulers were gathered together against the Lord, and against his Christ. For of a truth against thy holy child

Jesus, whom thou hast anointed, both Herod, and Pontius Pilate, with the Gentiles, and the people of Israel, were gathered together, for to do whatsoever thy hand and thy counsel determined before to be done. (Acts 4:26–28)

The triune God permitted this suffering and death for the humanly divine Jesus (Matt. 20:19; 23:34; 26:2; 27:22, 23, 26, 31, 35; 28:1; Acts 2:23) because "without shedding of blood [there] is no remission [of sins]" (Heb. 9:22; see also Heb. 9:25, 26).

Yet death would not end Christ's purpose in coming to earth—indeed, it was only a beginning. Here He predicted not only that He would rise (*egerthḗnai*, the aorist passive infinitive of *egeírō* [1453], to raise, the passive specifying the raising of the divinely human nature of Christ by the triune God—Father, Son, and Holy Spirit), but that He would do so on the third day.

[22] This was too much for Peter. Apparently, he could not "hear" resurrection, his thinking totally eclipsed by the irreversibility of death. We read,

> Peter **took** [*proslabómenos*, the aorist middle participle of *proslambánō* {4355}, to receive unto oneself] him, and began **to rebuke** [*epitimán*, the present infinitive of *epitimáō* {2008}] him, saying, Be it **far** [*híleōs* {2436}, the masculine adjective derived from the Attic *hílaos* {n.f.}, to be appeased, merciful, propitious, favorable] from thee, Lord: this shall not be unto thee.

From all we know of the disciples' subsequent evolution of faith, being "slow of heart to believe" even after the resurrection (Luke 24:25), these words reinforced the contention that they could not even conceive of a resurrection. After all, the referent of "be it far from thee" was not the resurrection but the death. Jesus had just said He would be raised on the third day; apparently, Peter and the other disciples either did not hear Him because of shock or they could not conceive of such a miracle, even though He had raised others from the dead. Perhaps they thought that He could not raise Himself, or that He would never allow Himself to be killed.

The verb *hiláskomai* (2433), to be propitious, to show mercy, includes the idea of relieving the suffering attendant upon sin. It is so used, for example, in Luke 18:13 when the publican looked up to heaven and smote his chest, saying, "God be merciful [*hilásthēti*, the aorist passive imperative of *hiláskomai*, to be propitious] to me a sinner," that is, relieve me from the judgments you have placed on my sin. In Hebrews 8:12, *híleōs* capsulizes what God will be to His people: "For I will be merciful [*híleōs*] to their unrighteousness, and their sins and their iniquities will I remember no more." Here, *híleōs* encompasses the grace (*cháris* [5485]) that changes a person's heart.

[23] Jesus' response was abrupt and sharp: "But he turned, and said unto Peter, Get thee behind me, Satan: thou art an offense unto me."

He "said unto Peter," but addressed Satan who apparently was close enough to be spoken to and motivated Peter to discourage the atonement. Peter, wanting to protect Jesus from physical death, used words inspired by the devil to tempt Christ with self-preservation. The Greek word translated "offense" is *skándalon* (4625), a trigger, a moral trap as a cause of sin.

Jesus did not impute the offense to Peter, the vehicle, but to Satan, the driver: "Thou [i.e., Satan] art an offence unto me: for thou **savourest** [*phroneîs*, the present tense of *phronéō* {5426}, to mind] **not** [*ou* {3756}, the absolute 'not'] the things that be of God, but those that be of men."

It is human ("of men") to shirk death, but this was to be no ordinary death. Perhaps even Satan realized "that through death [Jesus] might destroy him that had the power of death, that is, the devil" (Heb. 2:14).

Taking Up the Cross
(16:24–27; Mark 8:34–38; Luke 9:23–26)

[24] From this confrontation with Satan, Jesus taught an invaluable lesson concerning self-sacrifice.

If [*ei* {1487}, the suppositional "if"; assuming, on the condition that] **anyone** [*tis* {5100}, anyone without distinction; "man" {KJV} is not present] **wills** [*thélei*, the present indicative of *thélō* {2309}, to desire, choose, determine] **to come** [*eltheîn*, the aorist active infinitive of *érchomai* {2064}] after Me, **let him deny** [*aparnēsásthō*, the aorist middle deponent imperative of *aparnéomai* {533}, to deny; from *apó* {575}, from; *arnéomai* {720}, to disclaim, disavow, disown] **himself** [*heautón* {1438}, the reflexive pronoun, "himself"], and take up his cross, and **follow** [*akoloutheítō*, the present active imperative of *akolouthéō* {190}, to follow] Me. (a.t.)

Self-preservation, to which Satan appealed, is one of the most basic "things . . . of men" (*tá tôn anthrṓpōn*; v. 23; a.t.), but sacrifice is one of the supernatural "things . . . of God" (*tá toú theoú*; v. 23; a.t.). Jesus taught this lesson in word and especially in deed, as He gave Himself up to death for the sins of the world. While the imperative *aparnēsásthō* is in the aorist tense, meaning to deny once-for-all, an initial decision binding for life, the imperative *akoloutheítō* is in the present tense, signifying a lifelong action. Denial is the first decision; following is the ongoing, subsequent process. Every believer is called to follow the Lord's example: His choice, His self-denial, His crossbearing, His following after the Father.

[25] Jesus now explained further just what self-denial and crossbearing meant, particularly with reference to Satan's malevolent temptations of self-preservation and self-glorification.

> For whosoever if [*án* {302}, the conjunction of determination] he **wills** [*thélē*, the present subjunctive of *thélō* {2309}, to will, choose, determine] **to save** [*sōsai*, the aorist infinitive of *sōzō* {4982}, to save] his **soul** [*psuchēn* {5590}] **shall lose** [*apolései*, the future indicative of *apóllumi* {622}, "to destroy" but here "to lose," as contrasted with *heurései*, "to find"] it: and whosoever if [*án*; see above] he will lose his life for My sake **shall find** [*heurései*, the future indicative of *heurískō* {2147}, to find] it. (a.t.)

In the context, Satan had just tempted Christ to save Himself from the cross. It did not work. It is interesting, however, how Jesus consequently wove together physical and spiritual lives. Shirking the cross means more than just sparing a physical body; it means defying the very plan of the triune God. It means the loss of salvation—destruction. The Lord wants His disciples to know that the person who goes through life saving himself will ultimately lose his very soul, not just his physical life. A lifestyle of self-centeredness does not represent true Christian faith or experience (see Luke 16:19–31).

By extension, losing one's soul for Christ's sake does not mean killing one's body (suicide) or sacrificing the body for someone else or for God (martyrdom). Losing one's soul means the day-by-day sacrifice of self-centeredness, of self-salvation, for the glory of Christ. Consider Paul's words:

> I say the truth in Christ, I lie not, my conscience also bearing me witness in the Holy Ghost, that I have great heaviness and continual sorrow in my heart. For I could wish that myself were accursed from Christ for my brethren, my kinsmen according to the flesh. (Rom. 9:1–3)

In essence, Paul followed the example Christ set, who was "made a curse for us" (Gal. 3:13). The words from the cross, "Why has thou forsaken me?" represent a real substitutionary atonement. Jesus' human nature endured a temporary separation from the triune God so that we might not have to experience this. By faith, we escape the forsaking He endured on our behalf! Now, would we, like Him and the apostle Paul, do the same for our "kinsmen according to the flesh"? As Jesus said, "Greater love hath no man than this, that a man lay down his soul [*psuchēn* {5590}] for his friends" (John 15:13; a.t.).

Yet we should not lay down our souls primarily for our friends. The Lord Jesus qualified the loss as "for my **sake** [*héneken* {1752}]," that is, for His glory.

He is the referent or object of the denial. This means that as we stand for Him, for His cause, our opponents are ultimately opposing Him.

This is not equivalent to saying that in order to find eternal life we must first lose it. Such a possibility would deny the meaning of "eternal." The same One who said, "Why has thou forsaken me?" said shortly after, "It is finished (only in John 19:30)," even before He physically died. So the call to the destruction of our self-centeredness, to the death of our souls, extends only through this life. It is as temporary as the Father's forsaking the divinely human Jesus on the cross. The Father did not "leave [His] soul in hell [Hades]" (Acts 2:27).

[26] Always ready to appeal to the higher faculty of reason, Jesus asked,

> For what does it **profit** [*ōpheleítai*, the present tense of *ōpheléō* {5623}, to be useful] a man if **he shall gain** [*kerdésē*, the aorist active subjunctive of *kerdaínō* {2770}] the whole world and **lose** [*zēmiōthḗ*, the aorist passive subjunctive of *zēmióō* {2210}] his own soul? Or what shall a man give in **exchange** [*antállagma* {465} from *antí* {473}, against or instead of; and *allássō* {236}, to change] for his soul? (a.t.)

The only valid exchange for our souls is the divinely human soul of Christ: "when thou shalt make his soul an offering for sin" (Isa. 53:10). No other payment is satisfactory. Even if we could gain the wealth of the entire world, it would not be a sufficient payment to secure our eternal souls. The main point, however, is a reinforcement of the prior verse. Those who persevere in self-affirmation, in gaining the whole world for themselves will achieve eternal death. Only through self-denial and taking the cross do we "find" our souls. Before that, we're detaching from it.

And in the second rhetorical question, the verb *allássō*, to give in exchange, presupposes the existence of something of equal value (*állēs*, the feminine of *állos* [243], another of equal value). What the Lord Jesus asked is this: What thing of equal value could we offer as an equivalent exchange for our eternal souls? The answer is nothing! No worldly equivalent can compare with the price Jesus paid for our eternal souls. No persons can earn what only God can give. His gift is of grace (*cháris* [5485]) and therefore gratuitous or free (*dōreán* [1432]).

[27] The "for" (*gár* [1063]) here gives the reason why we should deny ourselves. It is simply because a day of justice, a day of reckoning is coming. God will reward self-denial and punish self-affirmation. He promises this in His Word.

"For the Son of man **is about** [*méllei*, the present tense of *méllō* {3195}, to be imminent] **to come** [*érchesthai*, the present infinitive of *érchomai* {2064}] in the glory of His Father with his angels" (a.t.).

Imminence characterizes "the Coming One" (see John 1:9, 15, 27, 29; 3:31), and the present infinitive used here implies the beginning of a series of events.

And **then** [*tóte* {5119}, then, involving not necessarily an instant but a period of time] **he shall reward** [*apodósei*, the future tense of *apodídomi* {591}, to render, repay, recompense] every man **according to** [*katá* {2596}, in agreement with—not based on or because of] his **works** [*práxin* {4234}, habitual practices].

The first determination is status in the Book of Life—an either/or status as a child of God; the second is works. Note the distinction in Revelation 20:12: "The books [plural, i.e., of works] were opened: and another book [singular] was opened, which is the book of life." Everything we do in our lifetimes is recorded in books by God. He will issue rewards in proportion to benevolent works done by His grace and punishments in proportion to self-centered works.

Katá, according to, does not mean "based on" but "correlative with (or to)"; that is, for example, reward and good works correlate. Good works do not cause rewards, but they scale with rewards, and that is all *katá*, best translated as "in agreement with," means. The ultimate cause of both good works and rewards is God's grace.

Among the culpable entities are "secrets" (Eccl. 12:14; Rom. 2:16) and "words" (Matt. 12:36, 37). In general, Jesus said, "There is nothing covered, that shall not be revealed; and hid, that shall not be known" (Matt. 10:26; cf. Mark 4:22; Luke 12:2). That means secret motives, plans, and actions will all be divulged.

Seeing the Son of Man Coming in His Kingdom
(16:28; Mark 9:1; Luke 9:27)

This verse is one of the more perplexing sayings of Jesus Christ during His earthly ministry. It is important that we study it carefully.

[28] Liberals banter that our Lord was evidently wrong concerning the imminence of His return. However, Jesus stressed the veracity of what He was about to say: "**Verily** [*amén* {281}, truly] I say unto you."

This phrase or a close equivalent is recorded thirty times in Matthew alone (5:18, 26; 6:2, 5, 16; 8:10; 10:15, 23, 42; 11:11; 13:17; 16:28; 17:20; 18:3, 13, 18; 19:23, 28; 21:21, 31; 23:36; 24:2, 34, 47; 25:12, 40, 45; 26:13, 21, 34);

thirteen times in Mark (3:28; 8:12; 9:1, 41; 10:15, 29; 11:23; 12:43; 13:30; 14:9, 18, 25, 30); seven times in Luke (4:24; 9:27; 12:37; 18:17, 29; 21:32; 23:43); and twenty-five times in John (1:51; 3:3, 5, 11; 5:19, 24, 25; 6:26, 32, 47, 53; 8:34, 51, 58; 10:1, 7; 12:24; 13:16, 20, 21, 38; 14:12; 16:20, 23; 21:18).

There be **some** [*tinés* {5100}, certain ones] **standing** [*hestēkótōn*, the perfect active participle of *hístēmi* {2476}, to stand] **here** [*hóde* {5602}, in this place], which shall **not** [*ou* {3756}, the absolute "not"] **taste** [*geúsontai*, the aorist middle subjunctive of *geúomai* {1089}, to taste] of death, **till** [*héōs* {2193}, until] **they see** [*ídōsi*, the aorist active subjunctive of *eídon/eídō*, the aorist of *horáō* {3708}, to perceive] the Son of man **coming** [*erchómenon*, the present middle participle of *érchomai* {2064}, to come] in his kingdom.

Evidentially, Jesus was speaking about physical death. The present tense of "coming" points to the whole process of the arrival of His kingdom more so than to any particular event in it. The transfiguration that immediately follows was part of the fulfillment of this prophecy. It accords with "some [not all] . . . shall not taste of death," specifically, Peter, James, and John. The transfiguration itself was a temporary reversal of the *kénōsis* (*ekénōsen* [2758], "He emptied [Himself]"; Phil. 2:6, 7; a.t.), an exaltation of the Son of man in which His radiant deity, veiled by his humanity, was unveiled. Similarly, Moses and Elijah appeared "in glory" (Luke 9:31) for this magnificent, unparalleled event. Later, at His trial, Jesus told the high priest that he too would "see the Son of man sitting on the right hand of power, and coming in the clouds of heaven" (Mark 14:62), a prophecy perhaps of the destruction of Jerusalem in A.D. 70.

In John 14:16, Jesus said the Father would give His disciples another comforter. Yet in verse 18 He immediately qualified this event with, "I will not leave you comfortless: I will come to you." He intended no doubt to have them understand Pentecost as one element of His coming in the Person of the Holy Spirit to be "with [them] alway, even unto the end of the world" (Matt. 28:20).

When Stephen was being stoned, Luke records that he saw "the heavens opened, and the Son of man standing on the right hand of God" (Acts 7:56), willing and ready to "receive [his] spirit" (v. 59). The entire book of Revelation is a sequence of comings as well. For example, the ascended Lord warned the church at Pergamos, "Repent; or else I will come unto thee quickly, and will fight against them with the sword of my mouth" (Rev. 2:16).

All these events are part of that ongoing intervention of "the Coming One" in our history. None of these events precludes a rapture or a Second Coming in final judgment. But the kingdom of God and of Christ is an eternal coming in mercy and judgment (Rev. 1:4; 15:4; 17:14; 19:16).

17

The Transfiguration
(17:1–13; Mark 9:2–13; Luke 9:28–36)

Scholars are not certain which mountain Jesus and His three disciples ascended for this great event. Luke just calls it "a mountain" (Luke 9:28). We do know that Jesus was in northern Galilee, since immediately following the transfiguration, He went to Capernaum. Both Mount Tabor and Mount Hermon (the taller of the two) have been suggested as the site.

[1] Peter, James, and John were selected to witness "**apart**" (*kat' idían*; privately; from *katá* [2596], according to; and *ídios* [2398], one's own) from others the high point of Jesus' visible glory as well as the low point of His humiliating agony in the Garden of Gethsemane (Matt. 26:37; Mark 14:33). These were rare privileges for these three, who also stood nearby when Jairus' daughter was raised from the dead (Mark 5:37; Luke 8:51).

[2] In Philippians 2:6, 7, we learn that Jesus Christ subsisted in the "form [*morphḗ* {3444}] of God" but emptied Himself, taking the "form [*morphḗn*] of a servant [*doúlou* {1401}]." Since sovereignty and service are antithetical concepts, the precise contrast in "form" seems to be between rule and obedience. The "form of God" is not service, and the "form of service" is not sovereignty. So Jesus added service to His sovereignty by becoming the God-Man, veiling His rule and accenting His service to the point of washing feet and dying on the cross. Theologians call this "kenosis," from the Greek word *ekénōsen* (2758), "He emptied Himself" ("made himself of no reputation" in the KJV), in Philippians 2:7. He emptied Himself by adding human—not subtracting divine—predicates, by adding service, not subtracting sovereignty.

The transfiguration is a momentary reversal of this humiliation, a temporary repositioning of the two permanent forms—one to the foreground, and one to the background. A complex verb derived from *morphḗ* is used here: "And [He] was **transfigured** [*metemorphṓthē*, the aorist passive of *metamorphóō* {3339} from *metá* {3326}, succession, change; and *morphóō* {3445}, to form, to structure] before them." Since the Lord Jesus is always God and man, the change is the relative positioning of forms, not the absolute replacement of one by the other.

The passive voice is used for the triune God's action on Christ's humanity. God the Father, Son, and Holy Spirit all repositioned the human form of Jesus Christ, unveiling and forwarding His deity while veiling his humanity, placing it in the background. The Son of man, then, was passive from the standpoint that God the Father did this and yet active from the perspective that whatever the Father does, the Son of God does likewise (John 5:19).

According to Luke 9:29, "The **fashion** [*eídos* {1491}, appearance, sight; from *eídō/eídon* {1492}, the aorist of *horáō* {3708}, to see and perceive with emphasis on perception] of his countenance was altered."

In His new form, Jesus' face "**did shine** [*élampsen*, the aorist tense of *lámpō* {2989}, to shine] like the sun," and His clothes became as white as light. Although Matthew uses the historic aorist to sum up the event, Mark chooses the present participle, *stílbonta* (from *stílbō* [4744], to radiate, glitter), "radiating," to emphasize the durative glory of His white radiance, unmatched by any snow on earth (Mark 9:3). Luke the historian adds that the transfiguration occurred "as [Jesus] prayed [*proseúxesthai*, the aorist middle deponent infinitive of *proseúchomai* {4336} from *euchḗ* {2171}, a wish; and *prós* {4314}, toward {the Father}]," His clothing becoming "white and glistering [*exastráptōn*, the present participle of *exastráptō* {1823}, to glisten, to shine forth]" (Luke 9:29).

In Romans 12:2, Paul defines the metamorphosis of believers as a renewal (*anakainṓsei* [342] from *aná* [303], again; and *kainós* [2537], qualitatively new) of their minds, an internal change of form from flesh to spirit. In 2 Corinthians 3:18, he elaborates:

> But we all, with open face beholding as in a glass the glory of the Lord, are changed into the same image from glory to glory, even as by the Spirit of the Lord.

This spiritual transformation is as radically white as the face and clothing of the transfigured Lord Jesus. Believers, in whose hearts the grace of God reigns, never stop manifesting the mind of Christ (1 Cor. 2:16). By using the word "all" (*pántes*, the plural adjective of *pás* [3956], all), Paul includes every believer. All Christians, then, behold the glory of the Lord and are changed into His glorious image—"predestin[ed] to be conformed to the image of his

Son" (Rom. 8:29). Looking at Christ, recognizing His glory, is the occasion of our being conformed to His image (2 Cor. 4:4). And it is "from glory to glory" as it is "from faith to faith" (Rom. 1:17).

[3] As Jesus' kenosis (self-emptying or humiliation) brought heaven to earth, so the transfiguration brought earth to heaven. We read that Moses and Elijah appeared, Luke adding "in glory" (Luke 9:31).

The verb "**appeared**" (*óphthēsan*, the aorist passive of *horáō*, to see and perceive, or of *optánomai* [3700], to see physically) includes the ideas of physical sight and possibly also of understanding. Since there are no reported formal introductions or revelations, we wonder how the disciples knew it was Moses and Elijah. Matthew simply reports the fact, but Peter seems to cognize (we can't say "recognize," since the two were "in glory") Moses and Elijah according to the next verse. As in other revelations, such as John's visions in Revelation, he was "in the Spirit" without local transport (Rev. 1:10). The point is that heaven transcends earth in ways not reducible to physical dimensions. The local appearance of Moses and Elijah proves as much.

The verb translated "**talking with**" (Jesus) is *sullaloúntes*, the present participle of *sullaléō* (4814) from *sún* (4862), together, and *laléō* (2980), to speak, to interrupt silence. Moses and Elijah had obviously been silent for some time, at least on earth.

Concerning the destinies of these prophets following their earthly ministries, we have meager information from the biblical records:

> So Moses the servant of the LORD died there in the land of Moab, according to the word of the LORD. And he [God?] buried him in a valley in the land of Moab, over against Beth-peor: but no man knoweth of his sepulchre unto this day. (Deut. 34:5, 6)
>
> Yet Michael the archangel, when contending with the devil he disputed about the body of Moses, durst not bring against him a railing accusation, but said, The Lord rebuke thee. (Jude 9)
>
> And it came to pass, as they [Elijah and Elisha] still went on, and talked, that, behold, there appeared a chariot of fire, and horses of fire, and parted them both asunder; and Elijah went up by a whirlwind into heaven. (2 Kgs. 2:11)

From these verses, we glean that: (1) Moses died and was buried, inferentially by the Lord Himself. (2) Satan and Michael the archangel argued over Moses' body, possibly a tussle over resurrection and ascension "to glory" (Luke 9:31). Or perhaps Satan wanted to display the corpse for idolatrous worship in Canaan, which could explain why the Lord buried him covertly in the first place. And (3) Elijah ascended to heaven in his natural body.

Even though both appear "in glory" according to Luke 9:31, there is no evidence that either was raised in a glorified body. In fact, this would seem to be eschatologically out of order with Paul's prophecies in 1 Corinthians 15:42–55 and 1 Thessalonians 4:14–17. On the other hand, the absence of a resurrection does not explain how Moses as a "spirit [that] hath not flesh and bones" (Luke 24:39) would appear to the physical senses of the disciples. But then, Samuel somehow appeared to Saul (1 Sam. 28:11–19); the rich man in torment apparently had some sort of spiritual eyes (Luke 16:23) and tongue (v. 24) and was seen by Abraham and (probably) Lazarus; and the martyrs under the altar were given robes (Rev. 6:9–11). The problem is interesting, thorny, and beyond the prescribed limits of a commentary. Theologians have suggested speculations like "intermediate [i.e., pre-resurrection] bodies."

We know Moses and Elijah appeared, because the text says so. One evidence for this is the fact that the two, according to Mark, "were talking with Jesus" (Mark 9:4). Luke, always given to historical detail, adds that they "spake of his [Jesus'] decease which he should accomplish at Jerusalem" (Luke 9:31). Moses and Elijah had to exist contemporaneously with Jesus in order to discuss a concurrent future.

[4] Peter, as usual, was the first to speak. Only six days prior (v. 1), Jesus had rebuked him sternly for suggesting that He spare Himself the dangers in Jerusalem. Again he spoke with little significant forethought: "Lord, it is good for us to be here: if thou wilt, let us make here three tabernacles; one for thee, and one for Moses, and one for Elias."

Peter did not understand that neither Moses nor Elijah "in glory" required "**tents**" (*skēnás*, the accusative plural of *skēnē* [4633]) like the Word (*Lógos*) who, prior to being "received up into glory" (1 Tim. 3:16), [tented] [*eskēnōsen* {4637}] among us" (John 1:14). Peter did not realize that this was a vision of another world—heaven itself. Perhaps based on Malachi's prophecy that Elijah would return to earth before the Day of the Lord (Mal. 4:5, 6), Peter assumed that this appearance was the beginning of the fulfillment of that event. Actually, the appearance does carry some eschatological symbolic weight: Moses typified the dead and Elijah the living at the return of Christ for His people (1 Thess. 4:16).

Peter was right about one thing: "It is **good** [*kalón* {2570}, intrinsically good] for us to be here." Yes, it was good; but the construction of tents—like churches—would not serve as a good reminder that "here have we no continuing city" (Heb. 13:14). The transfiguration was a momentary revelation of glories to come, not the beginning of Elijah's ministry on earth before the Day of the Lord (see the "two witnesses" in Rev. 11:3–12). But Peter was not altogether without humility, for he said, "Lord, . . . if **thou wilt** [*théleis*, the present tense of *thélō* {2309}, to determine]." At least, he submitted his proposal to the sovereignty of His Master.

[5] The present participle, "**speaking**" (*laloúntos* from *laléō* [2980], to break silence), coupled with the adverb "**yet**" (*éti* [2089], yet, still), shows that Peter's eloquent speech was cut off short of its finale. "While he yet spake," the Father interrupted. Assuming all the words in verse 4 were aired, Peter evidently had more to say.

Before the Father spoke, a bright cloud appeared:

> **Behold** [*idoú* {2400} from *eídon*, the aorist of *horáō*, to perceive sensibly and mentally], a **bright** [*phōteiné* {5460} from *phôs* {5457}, light] **cloud** [*nephélē* {3507}, a cloud formation] overshadowed them.

Such clouds of glory received Christ at His ascension (Acts 1:9) and will accompany His return (Matt. 24:30; 26:64; Mark 13:26; 14:62; Rev. 1:7). Living believers will be "caught up together with [the believing dead] in the clouds" (1 Thess. 4:17). The transfiguration prefigured this return.

The exclamatory "behold" occurs twice in this verse, once before the verb "**overshadowed**" (*epeskíasen*, the aorist tense of *episkiázō* [1982] from *epí* [1909], upon; and *skiázō* [n.f.] from *skiá* [4639], shadow, shade) which implies that the bright cloud produced shade.

The second "behold" calls our attention to "a **voice** [*phōné* {5456}, the emphasis on the sound] out of the cloud." Since the Son of God was not "declaring" (exegeting) the Father (John 1:18) who was now speaking on His own, how does this "voice" harmonize with Jesus' words, "Ye have [neither] heard his [i.e., the Father's] voice [*phōnén*] at any time" (John 5:37)? Possibly, the voice of the Father at this instant was mediated through angels—a theme common to both Testaments (Gen. 16:10; 48:16; Ex. 3:2, 6; 32:34; Isa. 63:9; Matt. 1:20; Gal. 3:19)—just as the vision of the Father was mediated by the bright cloud. This is the second time Matthew records a voice speaking from heaven (Matt. 3:17; 17:5).

> **This** [*hoútos* {3778}, this] is **my** [*mou* {1473}] **beloved** [*ho* {3588}, the definite article; *agapētós* {27}, beloved one; "The beloved One" is a title used only of God the Father or of the Lord Jesus Christ; see Matt. 3:17; 12:18; 17:5; Mark 1:11; 9:7; 12:6; Luke 3:22; 9:35; 20:13; Eph. 1:6; 2 Pet. 1:17] Son.

The two pronouns strengthen Christ's status as the only begotten Son. *Hoútos* is singular, literally "this **One**," meaning no others are in the class. Also, *hoútos* as opposed to *ekeínos* (1565), "that One," highlights the unique proximity of the trinitarian Persons, as do *prós*, "towards," in John 1:1; *kólpos* (2859), "bosom," in John 1:18, and *pará* (3844), "with," in John 17:5. Furthermore, *mou*, my, implies a unique possession differentiated from the Father's (and Son's, for that matter) ownership of all things (John 16:15). And finally, the definite article in the title, "the beloved One," also sets the Son apart as the particular object of the Father's love, wholly distinct from His general love for creatures.

The Father added, "In whom **I am well pleased** [*eudókēsa*, the aorist active tense of *eudokéō* {2106}]." The problem with this reading is that the verb is taken as present and passive, when it is actually aorist and active. An alternative reading would be, "**by** [*en* {1722} is frequently the instrumental 'by'; see Zodhiates, *The Complete Word Study Dictionary: New Testament*, D, 582] whom **I thought well**," meaning "by Him [i.e., His atonement and intercession] I thought well" toward fallen humankind. (For a similar construction, see *eudokías* in Luke 2:14.) The Father's good thoughts toward humanity were captured in His plan to send the Son to seek and to save the lost (Luke 19:10).

Based on His evaluation of the Son, the Father added, "**Hear ye** [*akoúete*, the present imperative of *akoúō* {191}, to listen] him." This means more than just hearing the sound of Christ's voice. It means obedient listening to His will.

[6] The bright cloud and the voice frightened the three disciples: "And when the disciples heard it, they fell on their face, and were **sore afraid** [*ephobēthēsan*, the aorist passive tense of *phobéō* {5399}, to fear]." The passive tense reflects the cause of their fear; they were made fearful or frightened by the bright cloud that appeared instantaneously and the booming sound (*phōnē* [5456]) of the Father's voice that interrupted Peter's speech. Fear is not an action we initiate, like taking a walk. Nor is it something we choose, as if any of us would want it. God imposes fear on both unbelievers (Ex. 23:27; Isa. 2:19; Rev. 6:16) and believers (Ps. 85:9; Jer. 32:40; Acts 5:5, 11).

[7] We dare not approach the Father without the holy righteousness of the Son. But through the Son's merit and propitiation, God's throne of wrath (Rev. 6:16) becomes His throne of grace that we can approach boldly (Heb. 4:16).

Accordingly, it was not the Father but Jesus, the human mediator (1 Tim. 2:5) who "**touched** [*hēpsato*, the aorist middle of *háptomai* {680}] them, and said, Arise, and **be not afraid** [*phobeísthe*, the present passive imperative of *phobéomai*, to be frightened]." The present tense means "continue not to be afraid."

Jesus did not expect them to turn their fears off permanently, as if this were something in their control apart from His gentle touch and calming words. Had He not touched them and said, "Do not be afraid," they would have had no rational basis for knowing they were not endangered by the bright cloud and the Father's immediate, holy presence. By contrast, the wicked, over the course of their lives, build up a "fearful [*phoberá* {5398}] expectation [*ekdoch̄e* {1561}]" of God's wrath (Heb. 10:27). But when the Lord tells us, "Do not be afraid," we can trust Him. The imperative "Do not be afraid," presupposes the propositional truth, "There is no reason to be afraid." His "touch" confirms His words.

[8] Jesus then rather suddenly terminated the vision:

> And when they had lifted up their eyes, they saw **absolutely no one** [*oudéna*, the accusative of *oudeís* {3762} from *ou* {3756}, the absolute "not"; *dé* {1161}, the adversative "but"; *héna*, the accusative of *heís* {1520}, one]. (a.t.)

According to Mark's record of this event, when the disciples looked around, Moses and Elijah, the shining garments, and the bright cloud had all "suddenly" (*exápina* {1819}, unexpectedly) vanished (Mark 9:8).

[9] As they descended, Jesus gave them a command:

> And **as they came down** [*katabainónton*, the present participle of *katabaínō* {2597}, to descend] from the mountain, Jesus **charged** [*eneteílato*, the aorist middle of *entéllomai* {1781}, to command] them, saying, Tell the vision to no man, until the Son of man be risen again from the dead.

The vision of Elijah and Moses was bound to stir up incredulity even among the nine disciples who did not see it. So Jesus told the three to keep the transfiguration event to themselves until after His resurrection, the arch confirmation of all that was given in the Law and the Prophets.

[10, 11] The transfiguration prompted the disciples to ask, "Why **then** [*oún* {3767}, therefore] say the scribes that Elias must first come?"

Why the "then"? Jesus had just said, "Tell the vision to no man, until the Son of man be risen." The "then" implies that the disciples thought Jesus was inverting the sequence of Elijah's appearance and the resurrection as given by the prophet Malachi (Mal. 4:5, 6).

At this stage of revelation, they, like the Pharisees, probably assumed that any particular resurrection—in this case, the Son of man's—would occur at the general resurrection on the Day of the Lord, the end of the age. If so, telling no one about the vision until the resurrection would make little sense, since Malachi prophesied that Elijah would appear before the Day of the Lord (the resurrection) with the purpose of changing the hearts of parents and children prior to judgment. If the transfiguration had anything to do with Malachi's sequencing of events, it did not make sense to conceal it.

When we say "this stage of revelation," we mean that the disciples had not yet heard the Olivet Discourse (Matt. 24), let alone Paul's advanced, prophetic schema in 1 Corinthians 15 and John's book of Revelation.

> And Jesus answered and said unto them, Elijah truly **comes** [*érchetai*, the present—not future—tense of *érchomai* {2064}, to come] first and **shall restore** [*apokatastése*, the future tense of *apokathístēmi* {600}] all things. (a.t.)

Before we undertake the adversative phrase in the next verse, we should understand that we cannot logically deduce from these words that Malachi's prophecy is **only** ahead of us. Jesus quoted Malachi's prophecy that was future to Malachi at the time he gave it. Jesus neither issued a new prophecy of the future nor confirmed the futurity of the old one; in fact, to the contrary, He was not even quoting the event but the principle of the prophecy. This was proven by the use of the present tense *érchetai* (see above), that is, "**Elijah comes**" (a principle) not "Elijah will come" (an event).

[12] The second, third, and fourth evidences of past fulfillment are the following three words: "But [*dé*, the more mild adversative] . . . Elias came [*élthen*, the aorist tense of *érchomai*, to come; answering to *érchetai* in the prior verse] already [*ēdē* {2235}]" (a.t.).

These words cannot refer to Elijah's pre-ascension life or to his appearance at the transfiguration. The first understanding is ruled out by the fact that Malachi's prophecy (400 B.C.?) was hundreds of years after Elijah's ascension (868 B.C.?). The second possibility is eliminated by the subsequent phrase, "and [i.e., when he came] they knew him not, but did to him whatever they wanted" (a.t.), which has no meaning at the event of the transfiguration. Unbelieving Jews did nothing to Elijah at the transfiguration; they weren't even there.

Still, there is little doubt that the transfiguration was a prophetic vision of the Second Coming of Christ in glory to judge the living and the dead and to set up a kingdom that has no end. The transfiguration prefigured His personal presence (*parousía* [3952], appearance) in this kingdom.

Until we read the next verse, there is some mystery in these words concerning Elijah:

> And **they knew** [*epégnōsan*, the aorist tense of *epiginōskō* {1921} from *epí*, upon; and *ginōskō* {1097}, to experientially know] him **not** [*ouk* {3756}, the absolute "not"], but **did** [*epoíēsan*, the aorist tense of *poiéō* {4160}, to make or do] to him whatever **they wanted** [*ethélēsan*, the aorist tense of *thélō*, to desire or want]. Likewise shall also the Son of man suffer of them. (a.t.)

From the last sentence, we can deduce that the Jews punished Elijah "likewise" as they punished Christ. But this finds no fulfillment in the Old Testament.

The Jews knew Elijah, and Jezebel persecuted him—Nor was it fulfilled in the New Testament (hardly at the transfiguration). So Jesus must have had someone else in mind when He plainly said, "Elijah came."

[13] Now we read, "Then the disciples **understood** [*sunēkan*, the aorist tense of *suntēmi* {4920}, to put elements together to make sense] that He spake unto them of John the Baptist."

Matthew does not say the disciples "mistakenly concluded." If John was not "Elijah," the conclusion is inexplicable since Jesus mentioned only Elijah by name—not John. More broadly, nothing verbatim in the prior conversation explained why the disciples would conclude "John" when Jesus had said only "Elijah." This, then, was a theological conclusion on their part. John fit the theological and historical criteria.

Historically, John "came already"—this much is obvious. Second, of historical note, both the Jews and the Gentiles "did to" John what "they wanted" to do. For the most part, the scribes, Pharisees, and Sadducees rejected John's prophecy of the coming Messiah. And the Gentile king Herod, at Herodias' request, imprisoned and killed him.

According to Luke, John fulfilled Malachi's prophecy:

> And he [John] shall go before him in the spirit and power of Elias, to turn the hearts of the fathers to the children, and the disobedient to the wisdom of the just; to make ready a people prepared for the Lord. (Luke 1:17)

Apparently, the "spirit and power" of Elijah rested on John as it did on Elisha (2 Kgs. 2:9–12). This was more than just the Spirit of God; the Spirit of God re-created the spirit of Elijah—the pattern of Elijah's ministry. This template enclothed John like a garment, fitting him like a glove. Consequently, he turned the hearts of fathers to their children, just as Malachi said Elijah would do (Mal. 4:6). John, then, bore the title and template—not the historic person—of "Elijah," whose name means "My God [is] Yah(weh)." And Jesus confirmed as much to the multitudes:

> For this is he, of whom it is written, Behold, I send my messenger before thy face, which shall prepare thy way before thee. Verily I say unto you, Among them that are born of women there hath not risen a greater than John the Baptist: notwithstanding he that is least in the kingdom of heaven is greater than he. And from the days of John the Baptist until now the kingdom of heaven suffereth violence, and the violent take it by force. For all the prophets and the law prophesied until John. And if ye will receive it, this is Elias, which was for to come (Matt. 11:10–14).

Because prophecy is a set of templates impressed on human history, subject to multiple fulfillment, none of this precludes a return of Elijah to earth to preach before the return of Christ (see Rev. 11:3–12). It is not unreasonable to assume that Elijah's bodily ascension and preservation in heaven was for this purpose. Also, at least one, if not both, of the "two witnesses" in the tribulation period repeat the miracles of Elijah (Rev. 11:5, 6).

As "the spirit of Elijah" in John the Baptist announced Christ's coming to establish His spiritual kingdom, so "the body of Elijah" will return to proclaim the inauguration of the physical kingdom at the Second Coming.

Peter recounted the transfiguration in his second epistle at a time when skeptics questioned the physical reality of miracles. In 2 Peter 1:16–18, he compares "wisdom-infused [*sesophisménois*, the perfect passive participle of *sophízō* {4679}, to make wise] myths [*múthois* from *múthos* {3454}, fiction, fables, tales, myths]" with the "majesty [*megaleiótētos* {3168}]" of that One [*ekeínou*, i.e., of Jesus Christ]" of which he, James, and John were "eyewitnesses" (*epóptai* [2030], observer, inspector; the masculine plural noun of *epopteúō* [2029], to inspect). He characterizes this event as the "power [*dúnamin* {1411}] and presence [*parousían*]" of the Lord Jesus (a.t.).

The transfiguration, then, was intended as a prophetic glimpse into the future power, presence, and glory of Jesus Christ, and it was accompanied by

. . . a voice borne [*enechtheísēs*, the aorist passive participle of *phérō* {5342}, to carry, bear] to Him, such [*toiásde*, the feminine {referring back to voice} of the pronoun *toiósde* {5107} from *toíos* {n.f.}, such; "of so great {a voice} as that"] by [*hupó* {5259}, by means of {the Agent is about to be named}] the Majestic [*megaloprepoús*, the genitive singular of *megaloprepés* {3169}, to be suitable, fit, right for the occasion] Glory [i.e., the Father]" (2 Pet. 1:17; a.t.).

The Father is called *ho megaloprepés toú stereōmatos*, the Majestic steadfast [hard or persevering] One in LXX, Deut. 33:26.

Jesus Heals a Boy Vexed with an Evil Spirit
(17:14–21; Mark 9:14–29; Luke 9:37–43)

[14] Luke says that Jesus and the three disciples descended from the mountain "on the next day," so they may have been there for a full day (Luke 9:37). A crowd (*óchlos* [3793], unrelated individuals) had gathered together at the foot of the mountain (see also Mark 9:14).

As Jesus approached, He noticed that the crowd had surrounded His disciples. Scribes were asking them why they could not cast a dumb spirit out of a child (Mark 9:14, 18).

From the mount of God to the valley of devils, from the height of praise to the depths of unbelief, the descent was as dark as it was deep. We must be prepared to descend with our Lord from the pinnacles of glory to the valleys of service and humiliation, even among Satan and his hosts.

[15] A desperate man spoke first to Jesus:

> **Lord** [*kúrie* {2962}, Master] **have mercy** [*eléeson*, the aorist imperative of *eleéo* {1653}, to be merciful toward] on my son: for **he is lunatic** [*seleniázetai*, the present passive of *seleniázomai* {4583}, to be moonstruck], and sore vexed: for oftimes he falleth into the fire, and oft into the water.

Luke adds a motive to this request for mercy: "because [*hóti* {3754}, for the reason that] he is my only-begotten [*monogenḗs* {3439}, the only genus, only {one of his} kind]" (Luke 9:38; a.t.).

Mercy is universally related to punishment. Historically, a criminal who pleaded for mercy before his judge or king requested the removal or mitigation of a merited punishment. Because the lawbreaker deserved the punishment, mercy was issued solely at the discretion of the king. Here, the father's request was a tacit acknowledgment that his son's suffering was due to sin. The aorist tense of *eleéo* shows that he wanted his son to have an immediate cure from the disease and relief from injuries sustained by fire and water.

The passive tense of *seleniázetai* reflected the ancient idea that the moon or lunar cycles caused seizures. (*Selḗne* means moon, as does the Latin root luna- [lunar] in "lunatic.") During these episodic attacks, the boy frequently fell into fire or water. Even if we identify his condition as epilepsy, the demon was the cause. This is substantiated by the fact that epilepsy produces random motions, not sadistic targets like fire and water.

[16] The father continued his depressing story: "I brought him to thy disciples, and they could not cure him."

Since the three—Peter, James, and John—were with Jesus on the mountain and the four of them descended to the commotion at the base, the man brought his son originally to the nine remaining disciples. They were now surrounded by the multitude, and the scribes questioned them, most likely concerning their inability to heal (Mark 9:14).

[17] Jesus responded with,

> O **faithless** [*ápistos* {571} from *a* {1}, without; and *pístin* {4102}, belief; wholly without faith] and **perverse** [*diestramménē*, the perfect middle participle of *diastréphō* {1294}, to pervert, make crooked, twist] **generation** [*geneá* {1074}, the living at the time of Christ], how long shall I be with you? how long shall I suffer you? bring him hither to me.

Jesus' answer was politely impersonal and generic, yet the accusation was universal. The disciples would be first in line to receive it, since Jesus did not expect unbelievers to cast out demons. On the other hand, since He did not do miracles on certain occasions "because of . . . unbelief" (Matt. 13:58), the crowd was equally culpable for discouraging the disciples with their skepticism.

How long shall I be **with** [*meth'* from *metá*, with, as in "God **with us** {*meth' hēmōn*}"; Matt. 1:23] you? how long shall **I suffer** [*anéxomai*, the future middle deponent indicative of *anéchomai* {430}, to endure; from *aná*, up, again, or *ánō* {507}, above; and *échō* {2192}, to have, hold; therefore "to bear up under" some crushing weight, as in 2 Cor. 11:1, "to bear with" or "tolerate"] you?

The incarnate Son of God's stay in the presence of this perverse generation was to be temporary: "He "tabernacled [*eskḗnōsen*, the aorist tense of *skēnóō*] among us" (John 1:14; a.t.).

In Mark 9:22, after summarizing the oppressive regularity of the demon's violence from the time the boy was a child, the father understandably addressed Jesus with a bit of doubt, not "if You will," but rather,

If [*ei* {1487}, the "if" of supposition] You **can** [*dúnasai* {1410}, to be able, to have power] do anything, **having been compassionate** [*splagchnistheís*, the aorist passive deponent participle of *splagchnízomai* {4697}, to have deep-felt compassion] to us, **help** [*boḗthēson*, the aorist imperative of *boēthéō* {997}] us. (a.t.)

This was not a rebellious spirit but a despairing cry. The father himself had borne this crushing weight for a long time.

Jesus answered contingency with contingency: "If [*ei*] thou canst believe, all things are possible to him that believeth" (Mark 9:23). All things are possible, not certain, which means that once faith overrules the impossibility, the Lord's will is still determinative. But first the impossibility must be removed through belief in His omnipotence.

The father responded, "Lord, I believe, help [*boḗthei* {997}, the present imperative of *boēthéō*] me [in, or] with respect to the [*tē̂*] unbelief [*apistía* {570}]" (Mark 9:24; a.t.). The father clearly had faith in the Lord Jesus; otherwise, he would not have brought his son to the disciples in the first place. Yet he had lingering doubts, weighed down by the severity of his son's case and reinforced by the disciples' impotence. Now he asked Jesus to remove his doubts.

From this we learn that our faith is not holy, reflecting the singleminded perfection the Lord commands. Christ alone increases faith. Therefore, we can ask Him to help us when we honestly doubt. We cannot hide from Him what He already knows.

[18] Jesus then commanded the demon to leave:

> And Jesus **rebuked** [*epetímēsen*, the aorist tense of *epitimáō* {2008} from *epí* [1909], upon; and *timáō* {5091}, to evaluate] the devil; and **he departed** [*exélthen*, the aorist tense of *exérchomai* {1831}, to come out] out of him: and the child **was cured** [*etherapeúthē*, the aorist passive of *therapeúō* {2323}, to compassionately heal] from that very hour.

As when Jesus rebuked the wind and the waves (Matt. 8:26; Mark 4:39; Luke 8:24), the effect was immediate. Jesus' verbal rebuke caused the demon to flee. Today, liberal thinkers dismiss most of these narratives as mythological overlays on history. We need, they say, to "demythologize" these fables, stripping them down to "real" history. Yet the New Testament is clear that the Lord Jesus not only acknowledged the existence of demons, but He addressed them, He linked many illnesses to their destructive behavior, and He cast them out with His omnipotent word.

The three aorists are simultaneous and logically so: Since an "effect" is "that which is caused" then causes and effects are never sequential. The instant Jesus spoke, the demon departed, and the child was cured. There were no delays between cause and effect, as if the demon was "thinking over" God's will: "For with authority commandeth he even the unclean spirits, and they do obey him" (Mark 1:27). He commanded; they obeyed—instantaneously!

[19] "Then came the disciples to Jesus **apart** [*kat'* from *katá*, according to; *idían*, private, particular], and said, Why could not we cast him out?" The disciples were embarrassed, frustrated by their failed attempt before the crowd, and humiliated by the scribes (see vv. 14, 16).

[20] "And Jesus said unto them, **Because** [*diá* {1223}, for the reason] of your **unbelief** [TR: *apistían* from *a*, without; and *pístis*, belief; UBS: *oligopistían* from *olígos* {3641}, little; and *pístis*]."

The UBS reading has better manuscript support. Also, it makes sense to set apart the disciples' "little faith" from the crowds' "faithlessness." (Remember, too, that "faithless" is joined to "perverse" in verse 17.) This does not weaken Jesus' argument. The disciples could be fairly ineffective against a powerful demon, with faith smaller than a single grain of mustard seed.

The "**for**" (*gár* [1063]) introduced a strong conclusion:

> For **verily** [*amēn* {281}, truly] **I say** [*légō* {3004}, to intelligently say] unto you, **If** [*eán* {1437}, the "if" of reality, as opposed to *ei*, the "if" of supposition] **ye have** [*échēte*, the present subjunctive of *échō*, to have] faith as a grain of mustard seed, **ye shall say** [*ereíte*, the plural tense of *eréō* {2046}, to say] unto this mountain, **Remove** [*metábēthi*, the aorist imperative of *metabaínō* {3327}, depart]

hence [*enteúthen* {1782}, from this place] to **yonder place** [*ekeí* {1563}, there, that place]; and it shall remove; and **nothing** [*oudén*, contracted from *ou*, the absolute "not"; *dé*, even; and *hén* from *heís*, one] **shall be impossible** [*adunatḗsei*, the future tense of *adunatéō* {101}, to be impossible] unto you.

By "this mountain," Jesus certainly referred to the Mount of Transfiguration in their immediate presence. Although we might be tempted to dampen if not negate the force of this teaching, Jesus Himself said this is the way it "shall be" with the faith of a mustard seed—a faith that no doubt includes its own wisdom and righteousness. Since Jesus gave this imperative, He implied that such a command even to a literal mountain would be rational. He Himself commanded the wind and sea that "obeyed" Him (Mark 4:41). He reinforced His point by adding that "not even a single thing" is impossible to the person of faith.

Nothing was impossible for the perfect Man of perfect faith far beyond that represented by a mustard seed. His point seemed to be that our less-than-mustard-seed size faith will never match His faith, by whose righteousness of faith alone we are justified (Rom. 5:18, 19; Gal. 2:16). If a seed of faith saves us from demons and our own demonic natures, then it is Him, to whom all glory belongs both now and in the ages to come (1 Pet. 4:11).

We should remind ourselves, first, that "possibility" is not "actuality" (i.e., the promise is that all things are "possible," not "certain"). Second, the Son of man Himself did not command any mountains to displace themselves in His short time on earth. Even if we did command a specific mountain, it will move eventually because they are all going to move in the future: "And the heaven departed as a scroll when it is rolled together; and every mountain and island were moved out of their places" (Rev. 6:14; see also Isa. 40:4; Rev. 16:20). We believers, destined to judge angels (1 Cor. 6:3), will probably take part in the renewal of the earth.

But this follows later. We should seek which mountains the Lord would have us move now. Babylon, the evil city of unbelief surrounded by the gates of Hades, is the mountain the church should bring down with the Word of God in our present evil age:

> Behold, I am against thee, O destroying mountain [identified as Babylon in the prior verse], saith the LORD, which destroyest all the earth: and I will stretch out mine hand upon thee, and roll thee down from the rocks, and will make thee a burnt mountain. (Jer. 51:25)

We will indeed move the mountains the Lord wills that we move in our lifetimes: "Greater works than these shall he do; because I go unto my Father. . . . If ye shall ask any thing in my name, I will do it" (John 14:12, 14).

[21] Jesus then advised His disciples that different types of evil spirits exist:

> **Howbeit** [*dé* {1161}, but] this **kind** [*génos* {1085}, genus, type] does not **go out** [*ekporeúetai*, the present tense of *ekporeúomai* {1607}, to go out of; from *ek* {1537}, out of from within; and *poreúomai* {4198}, to depart] except by **prayer** [*proseuché* {4335} from *prós*, to, or toward; and *euché*, a wish] and **fasting** [*nesteía* {3521}]. (see also Mark 9:29; a.t.)

Whether or not copyists inserted this verse in Matthew from a Markan source is irrelevant to the present discussion. The phrase is original in Mark and only serves to amplify, not contradict, what Matthew says. Since Jesus evidently said it, we will deal with it here.

With perhaps the one exception of Daniel's refrain from "pleasant bread . . . flesh [and] wine" (Dan. 10:3), the biblical fast is total abstinence from food and drink for a period of time (Esth. 4:16). The Mosaic Law indirectly legislated fasting for one day only by inclusion in the general prohibition of work (cooking) and the "affliction of souls" on the Day of Atonement (Lev. 16:29, 31; 23:27–32; Num. 29:7). This became known as the "day of fasting" (Jer. 36:6) or "the fast" (Acts 27:9). After the exile, fasting was included in additional feasts and private expressions of grief and penitence.

According to the New Testament, some strict Pharisees fasted every Monday and Thursday (Luke 18:12), and devout laypersons, like Anna, fasted often (Luke 2:37). The only record of Jesus fasting is during the time of His temptations at the outset of His ministry. When asked why His disciples did not fast like those of John the Baptist and the Pharisees, Jesus responded that it was not appropriate until He left their presence (Matt. 6:16–18; 9:14–15).

Since Jesus did not rebuke a disease or the symptoms, the antecedent to "this kind" can only be the demon itself. We know there are individual demons and sets of demons with names like "Legion" (Mark 5:9, 15; 9:17; Luke 8:30).

What does fasting add to prayer? Apart from the Mosaic command to "afflict your souls" (see above) on the Day of Atonement, no Scriptures teach us exactly what fasting does. By itself, fasting does not prove that believers are sincere. A case in point is God saying He did not honor fasting (Isa. 58:3, 4), and that true fasting is ministry to the poor (vv. 5–7). Yet fasting is evidence of a willingness to exchange material goods for spiritual goods, the temporal things of this world for eternal things, such as salvation from sin and demonic oppression. If we are willing to give up food so someone else might be saved, then our prayers are in agreement with God's will.

Had Jesus fasted before casting out the demon? Perhaps so, although there is no correspondence between the way Jesus casts out demons and the way we do. If His deity alone cast out the demon, then the appeal to fasting is incongruous, since God can't fast. Furthermore, the teaching falls on deaf ears, since none of the disciples is God. We must remember that the Son of man "cast(s) out devils by the Spirit [Luke 11:20 says 'finger'] of God" (Matt. 12:28), which is the way we will do it if we do it at all. The implied promise here is we can do it if we fast and pray.

Jesus Again Predicts His Death and Resurrection
(17:22–23; Mark 9:30–32; Luke 9:43–45)

[22] For the second time—the first was in Caesarea Philippi in northern Galilee (Matt. 16:21)—the Lord Jesus revealed to His disciples in Galilee God's plan:

> The Son of man **is about** [*méllei*, the present tense of *méllō* {3195}, to be about to do, to be at the point of, to be impending] **to deliver Himself** [*paradídosthai*, the present middle/passive infinitive of *paradídōmi* {3860}] into the hands of men. (a.t.)

Here Jesus declared that this event that "must be" (*deí* {1163}; Matt. 16:21), is imminent, near at hand. The voice of *paradídōmi* is middle, the action both directed by the Son of God and at the Son of man. The ultimate deliverer is not human, not even Judas, "the one [*ho*] who delivered [*paradoús*] Him [*autón*]" (Matt. 10:4; a.t.), but the triune God—Father, Son, and Holy Spirit:

> For of a truth against thy holy child Jesus, whom thou hast anointed, both Herod, and Pontius Pilate, with the Gentiles, and the people of Israel, were gathered together, for to do whatsoever thy hand and thy counsel determined before to be done (Acts 4:27, 28).

> No man taketh it from me, but I lay it down of myself. I have power to lay it down, and I have power to take it again. This commandment have I received of my Father (John 10:18).

> How much more shall the blood of Christ, who through the eternal Spirit offered himself without spot to God, purge your conscience from dead works to serve the living God? (Heb. 9:14)

The death of Christ is here unambiguously attributed to the prior, determinative counsel of the Trinity. Herod, Pontius Pilate, and the Gentiles did what God had determined beforehand to be done to His Son (Acts 4:27, 28). Furthermore, the death is accomplished actively by the Son: not "I permit man to take it from Me," but "no one [*oudeís*, 'not even one' created thing, man or demon] takes it from Me [i.e., it is not decreed to be taken], but I lay it down [actively] of Myself [i.e., not of anyone else]" (a.t.). And Jesus did this "through the eternal Spirit," that is, through the Holy Spirit, who, with the Father and Word, are one Spirit. The predetermined death of Christ included redemption, for in His death the way to eternal life was opened. Even Judas acted within the plan of God. Though he joined the Twelve for ulterior motives, he, without realizing it, fulfilled Old Testament prophecies (Ps. 41:9; Luke 22:21, 22).

[23] Unable to comprehend Jesus' bodily resurrection, the disciples "**grieved** [*elupḗthēsan*, the aorist passive of *lupéō* {3076}, to grieve] **very much** [*sphódra* {4970}, exceedingly]" (a.t.). If they had a preconception of a spiritual resurrection that left the physical body in the grave, they would naturally grieve for the loss of Jesus' bodily presence. Yet Jesus told them He would raise His physical body (John 2:19–21), not just ascend in spirit to the Father.

When we read the Synoptic passages, we learn more: "But they were ignoring [*ēgnóoun*, the imperfect active of *agnoéō* {50}, to ignore; Acts 17:23; 1 Cor. 14:38] this saying" (a.t.; Mark 9:32; cf. Luke 9:43–45). The translation, "they understood not" (KJV), is too passive sounding, so we have substituted the more precise translation "ignored" that captures the active, volitional sense. This does not mean, however, that they were fully conscious of their motives. We tend to ignore things that make us confused, angry, or frightened.

Mark 9:32, in fact, continues, "And they were fearing [*ephoboúnto*, the imperfect middle of *phobéō*, to be afraid] to ask Him" (a.t.). The middle voice implies that cause and effect are both internal; that is, they were causing themselves to fear. How so? They subjectively reacted (effect) to the subjective possibility (cause) that Jesus' hope of resurrection was wishful thinking on His part. But this was not objective. Objectively, it was impossible that He not be raised from the dead: "It was not possible [*ouk dunatón*] for Him to be held [*krateísthai*] by [Death]" (Acts 2:24; a.t.). Accordingly, the subjective fear that He was wrong and they would never see Him again prevented their talking about His death.

Luke looks beyond the facts and fears to the Lord's plan:

> . . . and it has been hidden [*parakekalumménon*, the perfect passive participle of *parakalúptō* {3871}, to cover; from *pará*, besides, alongside of, near; and *kalúptō* {2572}, to cover] from them in order that [*hína* {2443}, a purpose clause] they might not perceive [*aísthōntai*, the aorist middle subjunctive of *aisthánomai* {143}] it. (Luke 9:45; a.t.; cf. Sept.; Job 23:5; Prov. 24:14).

We should be careful to limit our understanding to the precise truth in the Greek verbs. For example, the perfect tense of "hidden" only brings the disciples up to the present; no strictures are put on future revelation. This is corroborated by the aorist tense of "perceive," meaning for an instant; that is, there is no sense of duration. Finally, the prior verse (Luke 9:44) tells us that the truth that was partially hidden was the Son of man "being delivered" into the hands of men.

Jesus had not disclosed any details of "the delivery" at this point. For one thing, although He said "is about" (v. 22), He did not reveal when the event would occur in terms of hours and days, so the imminence itself may have frightened the disciples. Also, Jesus veiled the fact that Judas would be the betrayer until he performed the act itself. But the veil was partial. Just before this, Jesus told them to literally "put [what was revealed] . . . into [their] ears" (Luke 9:44).

God sometimes covers up (*kalúptō*) elements that are "alongside" or "near" (*pará*) the disclosed elements of predictive prophecy. He waits until we are properly equipped "in His hour" to understand and absorb. We cannot rush God. His plan includes its own timetable. *Parakalúptō*, therefore, means neither full disclosure nor full nondisclosure. (Here study carefully 2 Cor. 3:12–18, which explains how the hope [*elpís* {1680}] of grace displaces the veil of the Law.)

Jesus Pays Taxes to Caesar
(17:24–27; Mark 12:13–17)

[24] After the scenario at the base of the Mount of Transfiguration, Jesus went to Peter's "house" (v. 25), where He stayed frequently. Upon His arrival in Capernaum, some tax collectors approached Peter concerning Jesus' accountability to Caesar. Only Matthew deals with this incident, possibly because it was his former occupation (Matt. 9:9–13).

Taxes were increased at the time of Nehemiah (Neh. 10:32) and again, later, to one-half shekel (two drachmas in Greek money) per person for temple services. Exacted in New Testament times (Matt. 17:24), a large part of the collections was sent yearly to Rome.

The tax collectors asked, "Does **not** [*ou* {3756}, the absolute 'not'] your Master **pay taxes** [*teleí*, the present tense of *teléō* {5055}, to pay taxes; from which *telónēs* {5057}, tax collector, is derived]?" (a.t.).

[25] Peter, standing outside, responded simply, "**Yes**" (*naí* [3483], truly), not "Yes, He does not," but "Yes, He does." Though the answer is syntactically ambiguous, as in most cultures, the negative aspect of the question is ignored. The collectors knew what Peter meant, since they understood their own question. Peter would not imply that Jesus would do anything immoral, and he knew that paying taxes was moral.

Then Peter entered his house. Jesus

> . . . **preempted** [*proéphthasen*, the aorist tense of *prophtháno* {4399}, to anticipate, used only here in the New Testament] him saying, What do you **think** [*dokeí*, the present active indicative of *dokéo* {1380}, to think], Simon? Of whom do the kings of the earth take custom or **tribute** [*kénson* {2778}, census, poll]? Of their own **children** [*huión* {5207}, sons] or of **strangers** [*allotríon* {245}, others]? (a.t.)

Jesus apparently knew what the tax collectors had asked outside the house. His lead question forced Peter to think beyond the mundane ethics of tax accountability to higher biblical truth. The King of kings will exact the righteous requirements of the Law from unbelievers while paying off the debt for His children, thereby setting them free. Later, Paul constructs a complete allegory on this theme in Galatians 4:22–31.

[26] The answer was self-evident. Peter knew that kings impose taxes on strangers, not their children.

Jesus concluded, "**Then** [*ára* {686}; *ge* {1065}, therefore doubtless] the children **are** [*eisin*, the present tense of *eimí* {1510}, to be] **free** [*eleútheroi* {1658}, free]" (a.t.). He did not say "will be" but "are" free, meaning as children. The relationship itself included freedom from this law of taxes that was imposed only on strangers. Similarly, we believers are freed from this imposition of the Law: "God sent forth His Son . . . to redeem them that were under the law, that we might receive the adoption of sons. Wherefore thou art no more a servant, but a son" (Gal. 4:4–7).

[27] God Himself, with equal discrimination, frees His own sons from the Law by fulfilling in Christ both its requirements and its penalty. Jesus was not implying that earthly kings were immoral by imposing taxes only on strangers. Nor was He implying that strangers should rebel for the status accorded to sons. The truth is, that's exactly what it would take—a revolution, for no king would adopt all his subjects to grant them equal status with his natural sons.

Because the Lord has ordained government to defend against external aggression and prevent internal anarchy, it is proper to finance it (Rom. 13:1–7). Taxes simply underwrite international peace and domestic civil order. So it is morally right to "render to Caesar the things that are Caesar's" (Mark 12:17).

Accordingly, Jesus said, "**But** [*dé* {1161}] **in order that** [*hína* {2443}, a purpose clause] **we** not **offend** [*skandalísōmen*, the aorist subjunctive of *skandalízō* {4624}, to offend, scandalize]," let's give Caesar what he rightfully demands. The aorist tense carries the idea of not offending even one time. We should never avoid or cheat on our taxes.

Not having the money, Jesus used the occasion to perform another miracle. As prophesied, the first fish Peter landed contained the exact amount of money required to pay the taxes for both Jesus and himself—a *statéra* ([4715]; "**a piece of money**" [KJV]), an Attic silver coin equal to four drachmae, equivalent to the Jewish shekel. Since one-half shekel was required per person, this was sufficient for the tax.

18

The Greatest in the Kingdom of Heaven
(18:1–5; Mark 9:33–37; Luke 9:46–48)

This narrative in Matthew actually begins a bit sooner, and Mark fills in a significant detail. It seems that before the disciples reached Peter's house, they were engaged in a dispute.

[1] This prompted Jesus to ask, "What was it that ye disputed [*dielogízesthe*, the imperfect middle deponent indicative of *dialogízomai* {1260}, to reason thoroughly] among yourselves by the way?" (Mark 9:33). The imperfect tense means that this had been going on for some time. In 1 Corinthians 3:20, Paul tells us that "the Lord knoweth the thoughts [from *dialogismós* {1261}, thorough reasoning] of the wise, that they are vain [from *mátaios* {3152}, empty, fruitless, aimless, pointless]." Unless the Lord gives insight, reasoning can go in circles forever.

The disciples were confused over the appearance of the kingdom of God. Assuming the visible kingdom was around the corner, they expected princely promotions and discussed who among them would be greatest. When Jesus inquired about the subject they were discussing, they became embarrassed. Guilt-ridden from the question, "they held their peace" (Mark 9:34). Matthew now tells us that they later built up the nerve to ask the question uppermost on their minds as to who would be the greatest in the kingdom of heaven.

[2] Jesus' response was unique. Instead of telling the disciples another parable, He gave them an object lesson on service and humility.

And Jesus, **having called to Himself** [from *proskaléomai* {4341}, to call toward oneself] **a young child** [*paidíon* {3813}, the diminutive form of *país* {3816}], **stood** [from *hístēmi* {2476}, to stand, cause to stand] him in the midst of them. (a.t.; Luke 9:47 says, "by [*pará* {3844}, proximate to, alongside] Himself [from *heautoú* {1438}].")

Proskaléomai derives from *prós* (4314), toward; and *kaléomai* (n.f.), to invite, to call to oneself, the middle of *kaléō* (2564), to invite, to call. The significance of the "call" depends on the caller. Here the Lord Jesus Christ, the Son of God (John 1:1, 14), gave the personal invitation. To enter the conversation concerning the greatest in the kingdom, He invited a child to Himself and stood him among the disciples who desperately needed to learn humility. Only Jesus could have innately known what was in the heart of the child, and He knew this child was a believer.

In Luke 18:15–17, we have a scenario of believing parents bringing "infants" (from *bréphos* [1025]) to Jesus hoping that His teaching would produce faith in their children. On this occasion, Jesus said, "Suffer little children [from *paidíon* {3813}] to come unto me, and forbid them not: for of such is the kingdom of God."

[3] Once the child was standing in their midst, Jesus said,

> Verily [*amén* {281}, truly], I say [*légō* {3004}, to speak as the incarnate God] to you, if **you are not converted** [from *stréphomai* {4762}, to turn oneself] and **become** [from *gínomai* {1096}, to be] **as** [*hōs* {5613}, like] **little children** [from *paidíon* {3813}], you shall **not** [*ou* {3756} and *mé* {3361}, an intensive meaning "not ever or at any time," "in no way"] **enter** [from *eisérchomai* {1525}] into the kingdom of heaven. (a.t.)

Straphéte is passive and therefore properly translated "**be converted**." The turning is initiated by the power of God's Spirit in our hearts. In ourselves, we do not have the power to turn to God. We need God's power from above to effect our conversion. Jesus' words reflect a similar teaching to that of the prophet Jeremiah: "Turn thou [from *epistréphō* {1994} from *epí* {1909}, upon; and *stréphō* {4762}] me, and I shall turn [from *epistréphō*], because thou art the Lord my God" (Sept.; Jer. 31:18; cf. Ps. 80:19; 85:4; 119:37; Lam. 5:21). The aorist tense in this verse describes the initial decision of turning, that point defined in the New Testament by the verbs *metanoéō* (3340), to repent, and *pisteúō* (4100), to believe (Mark 1:15).

Jesus emphasized here that we sinners can be saved only when we recognize we are as helpless as little children. This is why the Lord Himself "turns" us, accomplishing the work we cannot do ourselves. Only God can convert water into wine, only He can change hearts of stone into flesh, and only He can turn adults into children. It's not the physical size of an adult that needs shrinking; it's the oversized ego that requires no less than a deathblow. We adults are independent, self-made, and rebellious; children are dependent and trusting. So this is a supernatural change.

Salvation occurs in two phases: first, the Holy Spirit convicts us of sin; then the Spirit regenerates us with power from above. The work is the Lord's from start to finish, according to Paul in Philippians 1:6. By nature, we do not have the power to re-create ourselves. However, 2 Corinthians 5:17 teaches us that God can make us "new creatures" (literally: **new** [from *kainós* {2537}] **creation** [*ktísis* {2937}]), infusing us with His holy nature (2 Pet. 1:4). Conversion includes conviction of sin, repentance, and belief.

Although God is the cause of salvation, He is not responsible for making us sinful and distinctly different from His original, sinless creation. That is our doing.

[4] After Jesus had called the child to Himself as an example, He said, "Whosoever therefore **shall humble** [from *tapeinóō* {5013}] himself as this little child, the same is greatest in the kingdom of heaven."

True humility is submitting to God's righteousness (Rom. 3:21, 22; 10:3), which is fulfilled in the Person of Christ (1 Cor. 1:30). When God humbles "the poor in spirit" (Matt. 5:3), they repent, believing in Christ's satisfaction of the Father's righteous requirements and thereby entering through the door, which is His Son (John 10:9).

[5] Jesus now shifted the focus from personally becoming humble like a child to the treatment of children who, in the kingdom analogy, represent believers. Because of their innocent natures, God's children must be treated in a special manner before God.

Continuing, Jesus said, "And whoso shall receive one such little child in my name receiveth me." Since such a child as the one in verse 4 represents the humble believer indwelt by the Spirit of Christ (Rom. 8:9, 10), to receive that child is to receive the Lord Himself. The final judgment itself is based on this dynamic presence of the ascended Christ in His people; thus, the wording, "Inasmuch as you did it [not] to one of the least of these my brothers, you did it [not] to me" (Matt. 25:40, 45 respectively; a.t.).

"In my name" properly belongs with the verb "receive," and it means "for My sake," that is, for the purpose of glorifying Christ. Yet the identity between the Shepherd and His sheep is so strong that the Lord can even say:

> And whosoever shall give to drink unto one of these little ones a cup of cold water only in the name of a disciple, verily I say unto you, he shall in no wise lose his reward. (Matt. 10:42)

Offending Young Believers
(18:6–10; Mark 9:42–48; Luke 17:1, 2)

[6] No gray areas exist with respect to the treatment of young believers. One either "receives" or "offends"; there is no middle road. Children here are likened to believers:

> But whoso **shall offend** [*skandalíse*, the aorist subjunctive of *skandalízō*
> {4624}, to trip up] one of these **little** [from *mikrós* {3398}] ones **who believe**
> [*pisteuónton*, the present participle of *pisteúō* {4100}] in Me, **it would be bet-
> ter** [from *sumphérō* {4851}, to be of mutual advantage; from *sún* {4862},
> together; and *phérō* {5342}, to bring] for him that a **millstone** [*múlos* {3458},
> a mill; and *onikós* {3684}, the upper very large millstone turned by a donkey]
> were hanged about his neck, and he were drowned in the depth of the sea. (a.t.)

Alluring young, unsuspecting believers to any sin is extremely evil.
Children can easily be deceived, and habitual sins start by succumbing to
momentary gratifications or, more innocently, by simply imitating older people. Those who dare to tempt children are inviting God's wrath into their lives.
The punishment for such offenses is so terrible that the offenders would be
better off drowned before they commit the transgressions. The aorist subjunctive *skandalíse* is best translated "whoever might even once scandalize"—not
"whoever shall." The aorist highlights the instant of the event when the finger
is on the trigger (the Greek noun *skándalon* is actually used for the trigger
mechanism of a baited trap) and the mind decides to pull the trigger. According
to Christ, a single action of offending is one too many. Potential offenders will
do well to not even think about baiting the innocent for ill-gotten gain. Little
children do not have the mental or moral reserves to understand the consequences of sin. Things we do and say can have calamitous, long-ranging
impacts on them. Note how the aorist subjunctive of *skandalízō* here compares
with the present indicative of the same verb in verse 8 where the hand or foot
is "constantly offending" (*skandalízei*).

[7] Jesus solemnly warned:

> **Woe** [*ouaí* {3759}, alas; an interjection of grief or indignation; the oppo-
> site of *makárioi* {3107}, blessed; see the author's *The Beatitudes*] unto the **world**
> [from *kósmos* {2889}] **because of** [*apó* {575}, from, in consequence of] the
> **offenses** [from *skándalon* {4625}, cause of sin], for **it is a necessity** [*anágkē*
> {318}] that offenses come; but woe to that person **through** [*diá* {1223}, imply-
> ing agency] whom the **offence** [*skándalon*] comes! (a.t.)

Here we have the reason why our world is getting worse and worse: People
are perpetrating many crimes on children and new believers. The apostle Paul
prophesies about the progressive moral deterioration of our world:

> This know also, that in the last days perilous times shall come. For men
> shall be lovers of their own selves, covetous, boasters, proud, blasphemers,
> disobedient to parents, unthankful, unholy, without natural affection, truce-
> breakers, false accusers, incontinent, fierce, despisers of those that are good,

traitors, heady, highminded, lovers of pleasures more than lovers of God. (2 Tim. 3:1–4)

Woe is always associated with God's impending judgment, and the woe in the context here is "everlasting fire" (v. 8). Sinners are free to choose, but they are not free to choose the consequences of their sin—for instance, avoiding hell. God taught this fundamental lesson in Genesis 3:1–13, the very beginning of the Bible and creation. God, therefore, sets the consequences, and we would do well to take heed.

Apó (575), "because of" or "in consequence of" (see author's *The Complete Word Study Dictionary: New Testament*), here in verse 7, carries the sense of source, that is, the cause of woes resulting from offenses instigated by both unbelievers and believers. Jesus was speaking to His disciples (v. 1), and believers should practice what they preach.

When Jesus said it is a necessity (*anágkē* [318]) that offenses come, He did not mean it is a moral necessity, as if God has decreed it, and therefore it must happen. Rather, it is an inevitable consequence of our sinful world. Fallen human nature being what it is (as long as God allows sinful people to live on this earth) will tempt or otherwise cause others to sin. It is a component of freedom, for if people had to live in absolute obedience, they would have no freedom of choice.

God, on the other hand, has graciously reconciled people through the death of His only Son, but He calls them to voluntarily believe in this atonement. Though He gives humans the choice, He desires that all believe, for He is "the Saviour of all men, specially of those that believe" (1 Tim. 4:10).

When people choose not to believe, sin produces more sin in them. The ultimate sin was committed against the innocent man, Jesus, on the cross. And yet God, in His sovereign grace, has overruled sinful people to bring about the greatest possible benefit to humanity, redemption through Jesus Christ. Even though Judas betrayed the Lord Jesus, the final product of his wicked act ended in redemption for all who believe.

Throughout history, God has constantly overpowered evil with good. Sovereign benefits accrued directly or indirectly from good and, on many occasions, even evil, but praise God, the benefits are eternal (Rom. 8:28). God perpetually thwarts Satan's purposes for evil, and the nominal results he gets are incomparable to the eternal benefits God brings out of victory over evil.

As long as sin is present on earth, scandals or offenses will occur, but Jesus rightly sounded the danger alarm with "woe," which implies personal responsibility. In the last phrase of this verse, Christ conspicuously changed the subject from the general woe pronounced on general "**scandals**" (from *skándalon* [4625]) of the world to the particular woe coming on the particular "offense" (*skándalon*), which is the betrayal of Jesus Christ by "that man"—Judas. The woe meant Judas was responsible for his premeditated, voluntary (i.e., unforced) action. Such general scandals and Judas' betrayal are not acceptable excuses for personal shortcomings. They are sins in themselves; they reproduce like yeast (*zúmē* [2219]; see Matt. 16:6, 11, 12; 1 Cor. 5:6–8; Gal. 5:9); and they are destined for everlasting fire. Those who are an "offense to [Jesus]" are those who, like Satan, "do not think with the mind [from *phronéō* {5426}] the things of God" (Matt. 16:23; a.t.).

The Lord Jesus is called a "stone of stumbling, and a rock of offense [from *skándalon*]" in 1 Peter 2:8. Similarly, in Matthew 26:31 we read, "All ye shall be scandalized [from *skandalízō* {4624}] because of Me this night: for it is written, I [i.e., the Father] will smite the Shepherd [Christ], and [then, as a consequence] the sheep of the flock shall be scattered abroad" (a.t.). The disciples fled like cowards when officer arrested Jesus: "But all this was done, that the scriptures of the prophets might be fulfilled. Then all the disciples forsook [*aphéntes* {863}, they temporarily left Him] him, and fled [*éphugon* {5343}]" (Matt. 26:56). They left Him physically, but He continued to be in them spiritually" (see Rom. 8:11).

Jesus equated Judas' sin against the innocent Lamb of God with child abuse. As the next two verses stress, he would have been better off plucking out an eye or cutting off his hand rather than betraying the Son of man; in fact, "It would have been good for that man if he had not been born" (Matt. 26:24; NASB).

[8] Verses 8 and 9 present us with some of Jesus' most difficult sayings.

If a single offence (the aorist tense of *skandalízō* in v. 6) carries a threat, then how much more a habitual sin? In this verse and the next, Jesus changed from the aorist to the present tense of *skandalízō*.

> But if thy hand or thy foot **offend** [*skandalízei*, the present tense of *skandalízō* {4624}] thee, cut them off, and **cast** [from *bállō* {906}, to cast, to throw] them from thee: it is **better** [from *kalós* {2570}, good] for thee **to enter** [from *eisérchomai* {1525}] into **life** [from *zōé* {2222}] **halt** [from *chōlós* {5560}, lame, crippled] or **maimed** [cf. Matt. 15:30 from *kullós*, maimed; synonymous with *chōlós*; since the consonantal sounds are nearly identical, both words may derive from a common root], rather than having two hands or two feet to be cast into **everlasting** [*aiónion* {166}] **fire** [*púr* {4442}].

Jesus was realistic. He knew that no rational people sever their hands, feet, or eyes because those members led them to sin. Prudent persons know that sin begins in the heart, and if the heart is pure, the whole body is pure. (See also our discussion on Matthew 5:29, 30). In Romans 2:5, the apostle Paul spoke about **unrepentant** (from *ametanóetos* [279]) **hearts** (from *kardía*

[2588]) that cause eyes, hands, and feet to sin, forming sinful habits and finally reaping death (Rom. 7:5). Death for such people will be total punishment (see Matt. 25:46), torment for the entire person—body, soul, and spirit.

Kalós (good) is used here to describe the preference of temporal amputation to a perpetual hell. We cannot begin to imagine how horrible hell will be. But what did Jesus mean when He said, "It is better for thee to enter into life with one eye"? Obviously, He did not mean the literal extraction of an eye, a hand, or a foot, but that we must stop any activity leading to the spiritual entrapment of young believers.

The word *zōḗ* stands in contrast to the "Gehenna of fire" (see next verse) that people may enter having their eyesight intact. However, a believer may enter "the life" with one eye, one foot, and one hand, the other having been laid on the altar as a sacrifice made in standing for a principle.

[9] Jesus continued: "And if thine eye offend thee, **pluck** it **out**."

His threat against rebellion was the same here as in the previous verse, but He added the phrase, "the **Gehenna** [from *géenna* {1067}] of fire" (a.t.), a Greek transliteration of the Hebrew *gā-Hinnom*, which means the "Valley of Hinnom" (Josh. 15:8; Neh. 11:30). Originally, Gehenna was a garbage dump southwest of Jerusalem, originally the boundary of Judah and Benjamin (Josh. 15:8; 18:16) and the northernmost limit of Judah's territory. (See also Matt. 10:28 dealing with this subject.)

In this valley, refuse burned day and night. At times in the history of apostate Israel, wicked kings like Ahaz and Manasseh made their children "pass through the fire" in this valley (2 Kgs. 16:3; 21:6) as a sacrifice to Molech, the god to whom the Ammonites sacrificed their children (Lev. 18:21). Josiah put an end to this vicious practice (2 Kgs. 23:10–14).

The Greek word "Gehenna" is found twelve times in the New Testament: eleven in the synoptic gospels (Matt. 5:22, 29, 30; 10:28; 18:9; 23:15, 33; Mark 9:43, 45, 47; Luke 12:5) but none in John. It also occurs in James 3:6, which speaks of the savage nature of the human tongue inflamed by Gehenna. Broadly speaking, Gehenna is a state of open fire, but it is also a place of retributive justice made for Satan and his demons to which the bodies and souls of those who reject Christ's sacrifice on their behalf will go as a result of their own choices (Matt. 10:28). In 2 Thessalonians 1:8, Paul says Jesus will be revealed "in flaming fire taking vengeance [from *ekdíkēsis* {1557} from *ek* {1537}, out of; and *díkē* {1349}, justice, righteousness; commonly translated 'revenge' or 'vengeance']." In Romans 12:19, Paul quotes Deuteronomy 32:35: "Vengeance [*ekdíkēsis*] is Mine; I shall pay back [from *antapodídōmi* {467} from *antí* {473}, in place of; and *dídōmi* {1325}, to give voluntarily]" (a.t.).

Hell is the alternative to eternal life for those who refuse God's grace, and heaven is the eternal dwelling place of God, His angels, and believers.

[10] Jesus now came back to the subject of offending little children who believe in Him. He also shifted attention away from the physical violence of a hand or the lust of an eye to the mental attack of scorn:

> **Take heed** [from *horáo* {3708}, to see and perceive] that **ye despise** [*kataphronésete*, the aorist subjunctive of *kataphronéo* {2706} from *katá* {2596}, against, or *káto* {2736}, down; and *phronéo* {5426}, to think; thus "to think down upon or against," "look down upon mentally"] not one of these little ones.

The aorist tense stresses the avoidance of a single instance of "looking down" on little ones by despising or thinking evil of them, which can lead to physical abuse. It can also refer to misleading a child spiritually. Jesus was possibly holding a baby brought by a mother for His blessing (Mark 9:36; 10:16).

Then Jesus gave a new reason for treating children with respect—something is happening in heaven:

> For I say unto you, That in heaven their **angels** [from *ággelos* {32}, messenger] do **always** [*diá* {1223}, through; and *pantós* {3956}, all; "through all time"] **behold** [from *blépo* {991}, to see; equivalent to *optánomai* {3700}, to see with the eyes and understand] the **face** [*prósopon* {4383}] of my Father which is in heaven.

Hebrews 1:14 broadly defines angels as

> . . . ministering [from the verb *leitourgéo* {3008}, to publicly function like a priest, assisting in worship, charitable relief, or service; Acts 13:2; Rom. 15:27; Heb. 10:11] spirits, sent forth to minister for [*diá* {1223} with an accusative means "on the account of"] them who shall be heirs of salvation.

These angels, who always see the face of (the) Father in heaven, are presented as "ministering spirits" to believing children. *Blépo* means to see and perceive (Matt. 7:3), to pay attention (Matt. 11:4; 14:30; 24:2; Mark 8:24; Luke 11:33; John 1:29; 21:9). Their sight is directed toward God the Father as if they were on earth, and they seek God's help for helpless children, those who are "poor in spirit" (Matt. 5:3), utterly dependent on God's mercy.

The Parable of the Lost Sheep
(18:11–14; Luke 15:3–7)

[11] Jesus now interjected the parable of the lost sheep:

For [*gár* {1063}] the Son of man is come **to save** [*sósai*, the aorist active infinitive of *sózo* {4982}, to save] the **one who has become lost** [*apólolós*, the perfect active neuter singular participle of *apóllumi* {622}, to destroy, to lose]. (a.t.)

Jesus essentially elaborated on Matthew 1:21 that teaches that the Word of God became incarnate to "save his people from their sins." The infinitive *sósai* denotes the Son of man's purpose. While Matthew 1:21 limits this purpose broadly to "his people," here the object is an individual sheep (The participle *apólolós* [lost] is neuter, referring to the neuter noun "sheep" [*próbaton* {4263}], which will be introduced in the next verse.) that is lost, implying that if even one sheep were lost and needed salvation, Jesus would come to earth and die for him or her.

God innately knows "his people." The apostle Paul in 1 Timothy 4:10 tells us that Jesus "is the Savior of all people, especially of believers" (a.t.). In 1 John 2:2 we are told that when Jesus Christ shed His blood on the cross, it was a sufficient "propitiation" (*hilasmós* [2434], expiation) not only "for" (*perí* [4012], concerning) our sins but also for the sins of the "whole **world** [from *kósmos* {2889}]." Titus 2:11 says, "For the grace of God that bringeth salvation hath appeared to all men." First Timothy 2:4 says that God "will have all men to be saved, and to come unto the knowledge of the truth."

Since verse 11 is not found in some older manuscripts, certain commentators suggest it was added by later copyists from Luke 19:10 to provide a transition into the next three verses. But since it is found in most manuscripts, we suggest it is authentically from Matthew himself and Jesus used the same thought twice, once when He introduced the parable of the ninety-nine sheep here, and later when He spoke to Zacchaeus as recorded in Luke 19.

Although the verb *apóllumi* can have the transitive idea of either to destroy or to lose, it can also have the intransitive idea of being lost or perishing. In this case, the sheep was lost because of its own carelessness or its own choice. It chose to wander away from the shepherd and became lost.

God had given so much to Adam and Eve in the Garden of Eden—an abundance that required no work. But they thought He had deprived them by denying them one thing. And we know the sorrowful results that have followed ever since as a result of their greed.

People became like wandering sheep preyed on by wolves due to their own arrogance and stupidity and not due to God's intentional abandonment. He never loses, purposely or out of weakness, any sheep He saves and brings into His fold. People are not lost because of God, the Good Shepherd (John 10:14) but because of their own determination to wander.

[12] Jesus challenged His disciples to think these things through:

> **What** [*tí*, the neuter singular of *tís* {5101}] **do you think** [from *dokéō* {1380}, to think, use logic]? If a certain man had a hundred sheep and one **out of** [from *ek* {1537}, out of from within the group] them **went astray** [from *planáō* {4105}, to wander, roam, go astray], **does [or will] he** not **leave** [*apheís* from *aphíemi* {863}] the ninety-nine on the mountains and, **having gone** [from *poreúomai* {4198}], he **seeks** [from *zētéō* {2212}] that which **is going astray** [from *planáō*]? (a.t.).

The lesson was intended to encourage the disciples. He asked them what they would do if they were personally faced with this situation. Suppose you had a hundred sheep and one of them lost its way. "What would you do?" asked Jesus. "Would you not do as I did?" The assumption is that the disciples would do what their Master did. They would temporarily secure their flock to seek the one that was lost.

The verb *planáō*, to lead astray, to deceive, is never used with God as the subject. However, Jesus warned that false christs will attempt to deceive us (Mark 13:6; see also 2 Tim. 3:13; 1 John 2:26; 3:7). And 1 John 1:8 warns us that it is possible to deceive ourselves. But whether we are led astray by others or we choose to go astray, James tells us in James 1:13 that we should never blame God:

> Let no one when he is tempted say [from *légō* {3004}], I am tempted from [*apó* {575}, "from" in the sense of source] God, for God is untemptable [*apeírastos* {551} from the alpha privative *a* {1}, without; and *peirázō* {3985}, to tempt, i.e., to have the experience of evil] by evil things, and He Himself tempts [from *peirázō*] no one. (a.t. The inference is that anyone who would say such things is not speaking intelligently [*légō*].)

One sheep went astray (*planáō*), meaning to roam, wander, get lost. (The English word "planet" is derived from this verb, because the planets seem to wander off their orbits.)

Notice the shepherd left the ninety-nine sheep who did not wander on the mountain, and "having gone he seeks **that which is going astray** [*tó planómenon*, the present passive participle of *planóō*]." The lost sheep was still wandering when the shepherd began seeking it. At the same time, Luke 15:4 describes the wandering sheep as **that which has become lost** (*tó apolōlós*, the perfect active participle of *apóllumi* [622], to perish, be lost). The sheep had already become hopelessly lost and probably did not even realize it was lost.

What did the Good Shepherd do? He searched for the lost as any caring owner of a flock would do. He left heaven and became man to seek His straying sheep. The ninety-nine were assumed to be safe and secure; the Shepherd's leaving was not a threat to their well-beings. Moreover, the parable did not imply that the lost sheep was insecure either. The Shepherd "continually seeks" the one who is "continually straying"—two present tenses. What more can be said of the Son of man's love for a rebel? He continually seeks the one who continually sins (strays) against Him. As Paul quotes a "very bold" Isaiah, "I was found by those who did not seek Me" (Rom. 10:20 NKJV, cf. Isa. 65:1; Rom. 3:11).

As a confirmation of Matthew 18:14, we have the assurance in 2 Peter 3:9 that God is "longsuffering toward us, not willing [from *boúlomai* {1014}, to desire as one's own plan] that any **should perish** [from *apóllumi* {622}, to perish]" (a.t.). God does not want to send anyone to hell, but people choose to go there because they are not willing to repent, believe, and be saved.

[13] The shepherd eventually finds his one stray sheep:

And **if** [*eán* {1437}, better translated "when" since the finding is presupposed by what follows] it be that he **find** [*heureín*, the aorist active infinitive of *heurískō* {2147}, to find] it, **verily** [*amén* {281}, truly], **I say** [*légō* {3004}, to speak intelligently] to you, that **he rejoices** [*chaírei*, the present tense of *chaírō* {5463}] **more** [*mállon* {3123}] over it than over all the ninety-nine which **had not gone astray** [from *planáō*]. (a.t.)

The scenario is a lost (*apolōlós*) sheep that "was led astray" (*eplanéthē*) and "continues to be lost" (*planōmenon*). But Jesus compared the lost sheep to the ninety and nine who did not choose to go off course then. Of course, they may have wandered sometime in the past or might in the future, in which case the shepherd will seek them also. And what led this sheep astray? Probably greener grass that looked better than what he had. What a perfect example of us sin-prone human beings; we're never satisfied with and thankful for what we have.

The aorist tense of "find" corresponds to the event of conversion, but the contrasting present tense of "rejoice" emphasizes Jesus' ongoing joy over the event. While Luke 15:10 tells us that "there is joy in the presence of the angels of God over one sinner that repenteth," now we are informed that the Son of man (v. 13) Himself rejoices. In the parable of the prodigal son (Luke 15:32), such rejoicing was "necessary" (from *deí* [1163], must be).

[14] Jesus concluded this parable:

Even so [*hoútōs* {3779}, thus], it is not the **will** [*thélēma* {2307}, "will" meaning determination, in contrast with *boulé* {1012} or *boúlema* {1013}, the noun of the verb *boúlomai* {1014}, to wish] **before** [*émprosthen* {1715} in front of, in the presence of] your Father who is in heaven that one of these little ones **should perish** [from *apóllumi* {622}, to be lost, to perish]. (a.t.)

The "little one" here, we should recall, was earlier considered to be "converted" (v. 3), "humble" (v. 4), and a believer (v. 6). Jesus did not call or place in the midst of the disciples all the little ones in the area, only one (v. 2).

God as Father gave physical life to us all but spiritual life only to those who believe. Spiritual life is the possession of only some, because it depends not only on the giver, God Himself, but also on each person as an individual receiver. God wills to save every soul, but far too often, people will to resist, for each individual is created with the freedom of choice.

We can never separate God's wisdom from His omnipotence. His omnipotent wisdom is seen in the grace He provided humankind in the sacrifice of His Son for the sins of the world. The greatest miracle that occurs is the regeneration of the human spirit, soul, and body (1 Thess. 5:23). Then the accomplished will of God, His *thélēma* (Matt. 6:10; Gal. 1:4) is achieved, the realization of His desire (*boulē*; Eph. 1:11; Heb. 6:17). This is coincidental with the demonstration of His power and the transformation of any person who repents and believes.

Other aspects of God's will (*thélēma*) as Father are minor compared with the miracle of salvation. Matthew 1:21 presents this salvation as basic. According to this verse (18:14), it stands as ever "**in front**" (*émprosthen* {1715}) of God, an expression that shows God's attitude as Father.

Although the Father is described as being in heaven, 1 Kings 8:27 tells us that He is not confined to it or bound by it: "But will God indeed dwell on the earth? behold, the heaven and heaven of heavens cannot contain thee; how much less this house that I have builded?"

Restoration of a Brother
(18:15–20; Luke 17:3, 4)

[15] Jesus now changed from offenses against "little ones who believe in [Him]" and the illustration of the lost sheep to offenses between brothers:

> If your brother **trespass** [*hamartēsē*, the aorist subjunctive of *hamartánō* {264}, to sin] against you, **go** [from *hupágō* {5217}, to go stealthily, quietly] and **admonish** [*élegxon*, the aorist active imperative of *elégchō* {1651}, reprove] him between you and him alone: if **he hears** [*akoúsē*, the aorist tense of *akoúō* {191}] you, **you gained** [*ekérdēsas*, the aorist tense of *kerdaínō* {2770}] thy brother. (a.t.)

The aorist tense of "trespass" and "admonish" underscores our responsibility to address the sins of our brother as soon as they are committed. Literally, if our brother "sins once" (*hamartḗsē*) against us, we are commanded to do something about it. Jesus did not say to wait for a pattern or habit to emerge. By then, we are usually enraged anyway. The command says in effect, Don't wait for bitterness to overtake you. Address your brother at the first offense. And you go to him; don't wait for him to come to you!

The verb "admonish" (*elégchō*) occurs here for the first time in the New Testament. The noun that corresponds to this verb, *élegchos* (1650), occurs only twice in the New Testament, translated "evidence" in Hebrews 11:1 and "reproof" in 2 Timothy 3:16 (MT, TR). In modern Greek, *élegchos* is used for a report card, a summary of a child's performance in school. This word suggests that we should deal with facts, not speculations. In a sense, Jesus was saying, "Check your brother's report card. Is this the norm for him or a one-time stepping out of line?"

The verb *elégchō* is also used with respect to the Holy Spirit convicting, convincing, and reproving the world of sin (John 16:8). God does not assign us the task of convicting the world of sin, only of reproving fellow believers who sin against us personally.

Privacy is critical, "between thee and him alone," Jesus counseled. Precautions should be taken against publicity, which is why the verb *hupágō*, to go stealthily or secretly, is selected as opposed to *poreúomai* (4198), to march boldly. Covering and exposing sins are, respectively, love and hatred: "He that covereth a transgression seeketh love; but he that repeateth a matter separateth very friends" (Prov. 17:9). How different the body of Christ should be from the world! The world is filled with gossip and bad news and loves to spread it—read any newspaper. However, Jesus told us not to expose our Christian brothers' shortcomings before others.

Just as a single sin starts the process, a single conviction should follow, thus the aorist tense of *elégchō*. The specific sin should be targeted. This is no time to bring up other offenses or sin in general, which would be overwhelming. The scope is restricted to "a [i.e., one] sin against us." Hopefully, a single "hearing" will produce a single "gaining" (both verbs are aorist) of our brother. If it does, the issue will end, and peace will ensue. If not, this is not a work we dare abandon. Reconciliation is precious work and should be done in the spirit of Christ diligently and perseveringly. Consider how God promises to reward such victory in Revelation 3:12: "He that overcomes I shall make a pillar in the temple of My God" (a.t.), and in verse 21, "To him who overcomes will I grant to sit with Me in My throne" (a.t.). What wonderful privileges!

[16] However, because the exposure of an offense apart from the Holy Spirit's renewal only causes anger, the brother may reject our advance. If that happens, Jesus gave a specific, ethical path to follow.

> But if he will not **hear** [from *akoúō* {191}, to hear but contextually to accept and repent] thee, then **take** [from *paralambánō* {3880}, take alongside; from *pará* {3844}, alongside, near, close proximity; and *lambánō* {2983}, to take] with thee one or two more, **that** [*hína* {2443}, in order that] in the mouth of two or three witnesses every **word** [*rhḗma* {4487}, exact saying] **may be estab-lished** [from *hístēmi* {2476}, to stand on its own merit].

How different this containment process is from the revenge of the world that seeks the broadest exposure in the most sensational headlines! Even before appealing to the church, the offended brother has an opportunity to limit the exposure of his sin to the most intimate and trustworthy of associates.

Since gossip is strictly forbidden in Scripture because of its destructiveness (see Prov. 11:13; 18:8; 20:19; 26:20, 22), the assumption is that the one or two persons that are "taken" have witnessed the offense firsthand. This is evidenced here also by the use of the *hína* clause (see above) that connects "witnesses" to the "one or two." The appeal to "two or three" was well grounded in the Law of Moses (Num. 35:30; Deut. 17:6, 7; 19:15).

"Every word" includes the prior offense and the words associated with it as well as words spoken at the confrontation itself—all in preparation for a possible reporting to the church. Thus, the establishment of fact is "in the mouth" (not just the mind) of the witnesses; that is, they are to prepare to give testimony if necessary.

[17] However, the offending party may not even listen to the witnesses:

> And if **he refuses to hear** [*parakoúsē*, the aorist subjunctive of *parakoúō* {3878} from *pará* {3844}, nearby, proximate; and *akoúō* {191}, to hear; thus "to hear closely," that is, precisely, accurately, truthfully] them, **tell** [*eipé*, the aorist imperative singular of *épō* {2036} or *légō* {3004}] it to the **church** [*ekklēsía* {1577} from *ek* {1537}, out of from within; and *kaléō* {2564}, to call]: but if he **refuses to hear** [also from *parakoúō*] **also** [*kaí* {2532}] the church, let him be unto you as [*hṓsper* {5618}, as for sure] a **heathen man** [*ethnikós* {1482}, Gentile] and a **publican** [*telṓnēs* {5057}, tax collector]. (a.t.)

In Old Testament times, the testimony of two or three witnesses was sufficient to send a murderer to his death (see Num. 35:30). But even the two or three witnesses could not ambush and stone the accused themselves; they had to report to the priests. Likewise, Jesus added the step of reporting to "the church" for a final hearing.

When Jesus said to "tell it to the church," He did not prescribe any particular procedure. But presumably it would be the same that Paul and Barnabas used when they went to the church in Jerusalem to discuss the issue of forcing circumcision on the Gentiles (Acts 15:1–31). Galatians 2:2 tells us that Paul first discussed the gospel which he preached among the Gentiles "privately to them which were of reputation" (that is, the leaders of the church, probably the apostles and elders; see Acts 15:4, 6). Sharing a localized scandal in a public worship service with an entire congregation is far removed from the orderly procedure Jesus commanded here. It also is not in agreement with keeping the resolution of the matter as private as possible. Accordingly, if a sinning believer has refused to hear both the offended person and one or two witnesses, the proper procedure would be to take it to the church leadership. They would investigate and bring it before the entire church if excommunication were appropriate.

The aorist tenses of "refuse to hear" and "tell" do not extend much time to the offending party. It appears that as soon as he rejects the witnesses, the church is brought in, and as soon as he rejects the church, he is disciplined.

Note the interesting connection: "If [eán] he refuse to hear them, you [singular] tell the church." The offended party alone should make the presentation to the church.

Note also the use of kaí, "**also**," in the phrase, "also the church." This is placed for emphasis. Judgment intensifies as the person continues in his obstinacy against witness after witness. The last stop is the local church, which has the power to "bind" sins (Matt. 16:19; 18:18). Jesus gave us no evidence of an authority over many churches—church superauthorities. No ecclesiastical body should be superior to the local church, and God does not grant authority to the government or state over church matters like discipline.

How should such a "brother" be treated once he has defied the local church? The reference to "Gentile" and "tax collector" is very Jewish. Gentiles were considered heathen beyond the covenant God had made with Abraham and his seed: "You only have I known of all the families of the earth" (Amos 3:2). Despite the fact that Abraham himself was a Gentile and God extended His salvation to Gentile individuals like Melchizedek and Job, strict Jews believed Gentiles had no chance, let alone the certainty, of salvation.

If Gentiles represented the heathen without, tax collectors represented the hypocrites within—betrayers. Tax collecting obviously was a profitable job; otherwise, it would not have attracted anyone. But Jews considered working for Rome a betrayal. Hebrew traitors collaborated with the enemy to extract wealth from God's people. "Tax collectors [a special type] and [other types of] sinners" were regularly associated together (Matt. 9:10, 11; 11:19; 21:31, 32; Mark 2:15,

16; Luke 5:30; 7:34; 15:1; 18:10, 11, 13). If "Matthew the publican" (Matt. 10:3) had an objection, this certainly would have been the time to voice it.

Jesus' judgment was strong. A person who refused to repent before the church was to be treated as an outsider to the covenant of God as the Jews considered Gentiles, or as an inside traitor as the Jews considered a tax collector. We must remember that Jesus dealt with Jewish mentality here. Even the little preposition "**as**" (*hósper* [5618], exactly like; from *hós* [5613], in the manner of; and *–per* [4007], a particle of emphasis meaning "certainly") reinforces this identity.

[18] When the church as a whole disciplines, it manifests the eternal command of God. His commands are timeless, based on His immutable nature. To emphasize the fact, biblical authors speak anthropomorphically of these decisions as prior to the events themselves, sometimes as far back as "before the foundation of the world" (see Ps. 135:6; Is. 14:24, 27; 46:9–11; Acts 2:23; 4:28; 15:18; Rom. 8:29, 30; Eph. 1:5, 11; 1 Pet. 1:2, 20; Rev. 13:8).

Here Jesus taught that the historical binding and loosing of the church has been foreknown:

> Verily I say unto you, Whatever you bind [*désēte*, the aorist subjunctive of *déō* {1210}] on earth has been bound [*dedeména*, the perfect passive participle of *déō*] in heaven: and whatever you loose [*lúsēte*, the aorist subjunctive of *lúō* {3089}] on earth has been loosed [*leluména*, the perfect passive participle of *lúō*] in heaven. (a.t.)

Because the Lord does not admit any exceptions, we conclude that He was speaking to true believers, not hypocrites. Hypocrites cannot bind or loose anything, and their decisions are universally invalid. They have no authority whatsoever. It does not follow from this, however, that any particular local body or even denomination is infallible. Unfortunately, hypocrites are sown among the righteous: the tares and the wheat "both grow together until the harvest" (Matt. 13:30). Nevertheless, God promises that He will support the local body decisions of His elect. The proof is in the results.

In the immediate context, the binding, consistent with the aorist tense of *déō* and *lúō* above, is identified with the specific one-time church penalty of treating the unrepentant person as a Gentile and tax collector. The church collectively disassociates from the responsibility of this brother's behavior, yet with the hope that the punishment will lead him to repentance. The only two known occurrences of this in early church history say as much and are recorded by the apostle Paul:

> It is reported commonly that there *is* fornication among you, and such fornication as is not so much as named among the Gentiles, that one should have his father's wife. And ye are puffed up, and have not rather mourned, that he

that hath done this deed might be taken away from among you. For I verily, as absent in body, but present in spirit, have judged already, as though I were present, concerning him that hath so done this deed, in the name of our Lord Jesus Christ, when ye are gathered together, and my spirit, with the power of our Lord Jesus Christ, to deliver such an one unto Satan for the destruction of the flesh, that the spirit may be saved in the day of the Lord Jesus. (1 Cor. 5:1–5)

Holding faith, and a good conscience; which some having put away concerning faith have made shipwreck: of whom is Hymenaeus and Alexander; whom I have delivered unto Satan, that they may learn not to blaspheme. (1 Tim. 1:19, 20)

Paul makes the interesting contrast between pride and the mourning that puts away the unrepentant believer.

Too often the church allows the rebellious brother to remain intact, priding itself on its broadmindedness rather than mourning its loss of purity. But the church should mourn, especially since the purpose of delivery to Satan is the salvation of the spirit after Satan, apparently self-defeatingly, destroys the flesh. On the same positive note, most commentators take 2 Corinthians 2:5–11 as indicating that this particular fornicator did repent. The "destruction of the flesh" does not necessarily mean physical death. It could also mean the destruction of the principle of the self life or the "flesh" in the person.

Parenthetically, Paul's individual binding, "I delivered unto Satan" (Hymenaeus and Alexander), reflecting his apostolic authority, is not the norm. Jesus' teaching is normative for His body. The church collectively excommunicates only on nonrepentance before two or three witnesses.

This is binding. Loosing (an aorist tense) is the one-time forgiveness that attends confession and repentance, the "gaining your brother" mentioned in the immediate context (v. 15).

[19] Binding and loosing are not done without corporate prayer and that by at least two believers, as we see from this verse.

Again [*pálin* {3825}], verily [*amén* {281}, truly; Nestle's text, MT] I say unto you, That if two of you **shall agree** [from *sumphōnéō* {4856}, to agree, from which we derive the word "symphony"] on earth as touching any **thing** [*prágmatos*, the neuter singular of *prágma* {4229}] that **they shall ask** [*aitēsōntai*, the aorist middle subjunctive of *aitéō* {154}, to petition a superior], it **shall be done** [*genēsetai*, the future middle deponent indicative of *gínomai* {1096}, to cause to be, to become] **for them of** [*pará* {3844} with the genitive "by," meaning the source of] my Father who is in the heavens. (a.t.)

"Again" means Jesus repeated what He just said, although now He qualified the ministries of binding and loosing with prayer. He did not abandon the subject of agreement between two or three witnesses concerning binding specifically (v. 16) or the subject of binding and loosing generally (vv. 17–19).

Nor did Christ imply that two believers can receive anything they want. The "**any** [*pantós*] **thing** [*prágmatos*, the neuter 'something']" of this verse corresponds to the "what **thing** [*hósa* {3739}; which is also neuter] you bind" and "what **thing** [*hósa*] you loose" in the former verse (the linkage is established by the neuter gender of the nouns as well). Those who ignore the adverb "again" in order to isolate this verse to mean that two believers can agree in prayer and then expect to receive a check for a million dollars are losing the meaning of the text. Connectors and contexts all have a purpose.

The middle voice of *aiteō* is reflexive, meaning "**to ask for yourselves**," that is for your own benefit, the benefit of the church. The literal translation of the deponent verb *genēsetai* would be the active idea, "It shall occur." However, most English translations render the verb as passive: "It shall be done," because the "it" that is done is God's response to prayer. God causes the answer, so "it shall be done [i.e., by God]" is the most rational translation.

The preposition *pará* indicates that the Father will confirm the binding and loosing done by the church in agreement with His eternal decree. The order of events, then, is as follows: first, the binding or loosing has been decreed in heaven (v. 18). Then believers agree and pray regarding the matter (v. 19). Finally, "it shall be done" by the Father (v. 19).

[20] "**For** [*gár* {1063}] where two or three are gathered together in my name, there am I in the midst of them."

The connector "for," like "again," links this verse to the one just before it. The "two or three" stretches back to the "two or three" of verse 16 where the subject is "binding."

It is significant that Christians assemble in Christ's name, meaning in Christ's mind and will and for His glory. This is another limitation, but once the condition is met, the presence of the One who said, "I am," will unleash an irresistible power to bind and loose.

The Parable of the Unforgiving Servant
(18:21–35)

[21] Binding and loosing sounded like a nice power to have, but Peter was shrewd enough to know that the real world has a loophole—the "brother" who never continues the process to the bitter end of excommunication. Before this stage is reached, he repents . . . again and again from one sin or several.

So Peter asked an important follow-up questions in effect, "How many times do I let him gain over me? Am I forced to release him on his verbal re-confession into perpetuity?" In other words, how do I deal with a persistent hypocrite?

> Lord, **how often** [*posákis* {4212}, how many times] **shall** my brother **sin** [*hamartései*, the future tense of *hamartánō* {264}, to sin] against me, and I forgive him? **Till** [*héōs* {2193}, an adverb of time, until] **seven** [*heptákis* {2034}]? (a.t.)

Sin is both a state (*hamartía* [266]) and an act (*hamártēma* [265]), but Peter had in mind the act of sinning rather than the sin nature inherited from Adam (Rom. 5:12). In Ephesians 2:3 Paul calls us "children [from *téknon* {5043}] by nature [from *phúsis* {5449}] of wrath" (a.t.), because we have sinful natures. However, when we are saved by God's grace, we are "sharers [from *koinōnós* {2844}] of His divine [from *theíos* {2304}] nature [from *phúsis*]" (2 Pet. 1:4; a.t.).

At this point, Peter did not understand the full extent of the forgiving grace of God. First John 1:9 says that when believers confess their sins, they receive forgiveness through the blood of Christ. Such acts of sin do not cancel out salvation, and neither should they cancel our fellowship. Jesus gave an orderly method for dealing with them, but at no time are we to stop forgiving—not if we understand God's forgiveness.

At the time Peter was speaking, he had not received the Spirit of truth promised for Pentecost (Acts 1:4). Consequently, he did not yet know the fullness of truth about grace. Jesus was about to enlighten him. One of these truths is God's implanting new natures (*phúsis*) in us. Since we have partaken of God's nature (2 Pet. 1:4), He empowers us to forgive the way He has forgiven us. However, our ability to forgive is never has the same quality as Christ's forgiveness because of what He did on the cross.

In this parable, Jesus commanded unlimited forgiveness between believers. The number seven implies completeness in imitation of what God did and commanded. For instance, God created the world in six days and rested on the seventh. He gave humans a pattern to work for six days and to rest on the seventh, the Sabbath (Ex. 20:10). He instituted a Sabbath year (Lev. 25:2–6) and a Year of Jubilee following seven times sevens years (Lev. 25:8, 9). The Feasts of Unleavened Bread and Tabernacles both lasted seven days (Ex. 12:15, 19; Num. 29:12). Seven occurs frequently in connection with Old Testament ritual: the sprinkling of a bullock's blood seven times (Lev. 4:6), the burnt offering of seven lambs (Num. 28:11), the seven sprinklings of a cleansed leper (Lev. 14:7), the seven branches of the candlestick in the tabernacle (Ex. 25:37), and Naaman's seven washings in the Jordan river (2 Kgs. 5:10).

The Israelites circled Jericho seven times (Josh. 6:4). Elijah's servant looked for rain seven times (1 Kgs. 18:43). The psalmist praised God seven times a day (Ps. 119:164). Genesis 29:18; 41:29, 54 and Daniel 4:23 all mention seven. The early church had seven deacons (Acts 6:3), and John addresses seven churches in the book of Revelation and mentions seven golden lampstands (1:12) and seven stars (1:16). At the miraculous feeding of four thousand from seven loaves and a few fish (Mark 8:1–9), the seven baskets collected afterwards indicated that Jesus provides beyond daily satisfaction. Seven demons possessed Mary Magdalene (Luke 8:2), while the dragon of Revelation 12:3 and the beast of Revelation 13:1 and 17:7 each will have seven heads.

[22] Jesus showed His longsuffering in His answer to Peter:

"I say not unto thee, **Until** [*héōs* {2193}] seven times: **but** [*allá* {235}, contrariwise], **until** [*héōs*] seventy times seven."

Jesus used this occasion to differentiate between human forgiveness and God's forgiveness. When He forgives us, He saves us and makes us a "new [*kainós* {2537}, qualitatively new] creations [*ktísis* {2937}, KJV: *creature*)" according to 2 Corinthians 5:17 and Galatians 6:15. Peter describes this change in 2 Peter 1:4 as making us partakers (from *koinōnós* [2844]), or sharers of the "divine [from *theíos* {2304}] nature [from *phúsis* {5449}]." Therefore, we should forgive as God forgives. We need God's unrestricted, undeserved, nonexclusive forgiveness and also the same unqualified forgiveness from other believers without numbers attached. But what we hope to receive, we ought to give. According to John 1:16, God gives fresh grace for every grace expended, and since He never runs out of grace, we shouldn't either. We should ask for it continually.

Thus, Jesus used Peter's arithmetic to teach us the eternal principle that His forgiveness and our forgiveness of others should have no limits in quality or quantity. Jesus did not say "seventy times seven" (490) to present a new limit but rather to show that any selected number would be multiplied. As we receive grace, we should dispense it in the same measure. We must not keep count of how many times we forgive but apply God's inexhaustible stream of grace to others.

[23] Jesus now illustrated with a parable that used money as an analogy of spiritual things. He compared two coins, the talent (from *tálanton* [5007], a weighted currency of varying high value) and the denarius (*dēnária* [1220], a common currency used to pay salaries, usually for a twelve-hour day; see the parable of the vineyard in Matt. 20:1–16).

Therefore [*diá* {1223}, on account of; *toúto* {5124}, this; "for this reason"] the kingdom of the heavens **is likened** [from *homoióō* {3666}] to a **certain**

man, a king [from *basileús* {935}], **who determined** [from *thélō* {2309}, to desire, to determine] **to settle** [from *sunaírō* {4868}, to take account; from *sún* {4862}, together; and *aírō* {142}, to take] **account[s]** [from *lógos* {3056}] with his servants. (a.t.)

Certain words and expressions in this parable require our close attention. The first is the "**kingdom of the heavens**." We should recognize God as the Ruler of our lives. The kingdom of the heavens is the same as the kingdom of God (Matt. 19:23, 24) that now has invisible spiritual rule over our lives (Luke 17:20, 21). God has a timetable and does nothing out of season. For now, He is eager to establish this invisible spiritual rule in our hearts, changing us, saving us, and making us partakers of His nature (2 Pet. 1:4).

The second word is "**account**." The word *lógos* (translated "account" here) usually means simply "word," but it can take on the extended meaning of an accounting, a reason. Thus, Peter says, "But sanctify the Lord God in your hearts: and be ready always to give an answer [from *lógos*] to every man that asketh you a reason of the hope that is in you with meekness and fear" (1 Pet. 3:15). In modern Greek, an accountant is called a *logistḗs*.

[24] The accounting began:

And **when he began** [from *árchomai* {756}, to begin] **to reckon** [from *sunaírō* {4868}], one **was brought** [from *prosphérō* {4374} from *prós* {4314}, toward; and *phérō* {5342}, to carry or bring] unto him, **a debtor** [*opheilétēs* {3781}] of ten thousand talents. (a.t.)

The verb "brought" is chosen because the subject probably did not come willingly. The verb refers to bringing criminals to justice (Luke 12:11; 23:14) and animals for sacrifice (Mark 1:44; Luke 5:14; Heb. 5:1). The first debtor owed an incredibly large debt for an individual. A talent was the largest monetary unit in the Roman world. His debt equaled 240 pounds of silver and would have been worth about a thousand dollars in the first half of the twentieth century. Ten thousand talents, then, would have been worth about ten million dollars today. As A. T. Robertson points out, in New Testament times, the entire annual imperial tax debt for all five provinces of Palestine—Judea, Samaria, Galilee, Idumea, and Perea—was only eight hundred talents of silver. Ten thousand talents would be over twelve times this tax burden. Of course, this is typical of our failure to render the holiness that God has every right to expect from us.

An interesting difference occurs in the way Matthew and Luke present our petition in the Lord's Prayer. Luke 11:4 says, "And forgive us our **sins** (from *hamartía* [266])," while Matthew 6:12 says, "And forgive us our **debts** (from *opheílēma* [3783], that which is owed; related to *opheilétēs*, the word used here in Matt. 18:24 for **debtor**). Notice also that the word "debtor" is assigned to both the man who owed ten thousand talents and, as we will soon see, the man who owed one hundred denaria (v. 28).

[25] The king pronounced a severe penalty for defaulting on this loan:

> But because as he did not have [anything with which] **to pay back** [from *apodídōmi* {591} from *apó* {575}, from; and *dídōmi* {1325}, to give; "to give from one's own resources"], his lord commanded him **to be sold** [from *pipráskō* {4097}], and his wife and children and all that he had, and **to pay back** [from *apodídōmi*]. (a.t.)

Just as Adam's sin, guilt, and punishment passed on to his offspring (Rom. 5:18, 19), so the king imputed the servant's sin and guilt to his wife, children, and possessions. The king treated them as guilty of the debt because of their legal and natural association with the servant, and he punished them with the slavery necessary to pay off the bill.

[26] The servant plea bargained under the pressure of this terrible judgment:

> The servant, **having fallen down** [from *píptō* {4098}, to fall] **was worshiping** [*prosekúnei*, the imperfect of *proskunéō* {4352}; see below] him, saying, Lord, **have patience** [from *makrothuméō* {3114} from *makrós* {3117}, long; and *thumós* {2372}, wrath, anger; slow to anger towards persons as opposed to circumstances which is reflected in the verb *hupoménō* {5278}] with me, and I will pay you all. (a.t.)

The debtor panicked under the threat of being enslaved and requested extended time and individual accountability in the words, "I will pay." It was a desperate plea given the size of his debt but not desperate enough. He thought that with enough time he could repay the staggering debt and get back in the king's good graces. The servant neither comprehended the size of the debt nor his need for mercy that would cancel it altogether.

The verb *proskunéō* derives from *prós* (4314), towards; and *kunéō* (n.f.), to kiss. Lexically, it means "to throw a kiss towards [someone or something]"; however, syntactically the connotation was the humiliation attached to kissing the feet of a superior like a king.

The servant requested that his master be literally "**long-wrathed**" (*makrothuméō*), taking the same amount of time to get angry that the servant needed to pay off his debt. The second servant used the same request (and verb) (v. 29). "Long-wrathed" is more accurate than the archaic English adjective "long-suffering," since *makrós* (3117) means long, and *thumós* (2372) means wrath or anger, not suffering. The noun is associated with the verb *thumóō* (2373), to provoke to anger.

The related noun, *makrothumía* (3115), an intrinsic quality of deity according to Romans 2:4, is distinguishable from patience (*hupomonē* [5281]) in that the subjects responded to are persons rather than circumstances. The verb is used in 1 Corinthians 13:4: "Love is slow to anger" (a.t.), and this divine characteristic is one of the fruits of the Spirit (Gal. 5:22).

[27] The king knew the servant could never repay the debt and felt compassion for him.

> Then the lord of that servant **was moved with compassion** [*splagchnistheís*, the aorist passive deponent participle of *splagchnízomai* {4697}, to have compassion from the deepest level], and **loosed** [from *apolúo* {630}, to release, to free] him, and **forgave** [from *aphíemi* {863}, to send away from; the derivative noun *áphesis* {859} means forgiveness; Heb. 9:22] him the **debt** [*dáneion* {1156}, loan; see Sept. Deut. 24:11].

The verb here is clearly deponent and could be translated actively—"he compassionated." Moreover, the king revealed his compassion when he "released" the servant and "forgave" him the debt.

The verb *splagchnízomai*, to have compassion, is related to the noun *splágchnon* (4698), bowel, which became associated with deep feelings of empathy or sincere pity. The apostle John, for example, uses this metaphorical sense: "But whoso hath this world's good, and seeth his brother have need, and shutteth up his bowels of compassion [from *splágchnon*] from him, how dwelleth the love of God in him?" (1 John 3:17).

In spite of obvious parallels, the lord in this parable does not perfectly represent God. God never extends His forgiveness only to withdraw it if the forgiven does not forgive in return. And, of course, He would not hold the wife and children coresponsible for a man's sins, either. He who is not willing to forgive is not really repentant enough to receive forgiveness.

But to those who believe and accept Christ's grace, the Lord dismisses a debt that cannot be paid back with money or anything else. He Himself paid the debt with His blood, forever and completely. The debt is in the depths of the sea (Mic. 7:19), never to be found again. Sins are no longer willingly or habitually practiced (1 John 3:9).

"**Released**" (from *apolúo*) and "**forgave**" (from *aphíemi*) are synonymous, representing one gracious act of God. *Aphíemi*, to send away from, derives from *apó* (575), from; and *híemi* (n.f., to send). The prefix *apó* implies God distancing sins from a person. When He casts our sins into the depths of the sea, He removes them "from" us.

[28] The slave of sin was not changed by his master's grace since he did not show the same compassion that he was extended:

But the same servant went out, and found one of his **fellow servants** [from *súndoulos* {4889}], which owed him a hundred denaria: and **having seized** [from *kratéō* {2902}, to arrest] him, he took him by the throat, saying, **Pay** [from *apodídōmi* {591}] me what you owe. (a.t.)

The quantitative difference in debt was enormous. But the qualitative difference in attitudinal response was far greater. Accordingly, Jesus told this parable for one basic reason: to show the remarkable difference between God's merciful nature and the unbeliever's merciless nature. One person can be legally forgiven an unpayable debt by God and then subsequently refuse the payment terms of a small debt from another person. With this parable, Jesus showed that we not only must have our debts forgiven by God, but we must also have our hearts changed in order to have our self-centered natures changed into merciful ones. This evil servant did not turn toward God; in fact, there is no evidence that he even thanked God or his master for his release from debt.

Even if his family had been enslaved, the servant would not have changed his nature. We cannot change our sinful natures by human means but only through God's grace and power. His grace is free or gratis (Eph. 2:8–10). If we do not receive it, we will bring on ourselves God's judgment.

Instead of extending to his fellow servant the same compassion as that of the king, the evil servant demanded what was due him immediately, even though he was debt free and his fellow servant's debt was a small amount, representing only one hundred twelve-hour workdays.

[29] The demand for repayment was so strong that the fellow servant fell on his knees "at [*eis* {1519}] his feet [from *pous* {4228}], **begging** [from *parakaléō* {3870}, to beseech, to implore] him" (a.t.).

What was the request? "**Have patience** [from *makrothuméō* {3114}] with me, and I will pay the debt." Just as the first servant did not have the means to repay, this fellow servant asked for the mercy of time to repay the small loan.

[30] The first servant was unrepentant:

And he was not **willing** [from *thélō* {2309}, to determine] but went and cast him into prison **until** [*héōs* {2193}, see vv. 21, 22] he should pay the debt. (a.t.)

What this slave of sin did showed that he did not appreciate his master's kindness. The compassion was all one-sided. He did not even give the other man the courtesy of an answer, but immediately put his evil decision into practice.

[31] The evil servant's peers reacted to this maltreatment:

When his fellow servants **saw** [from *eídon*, the aorist of *horáō* {3708}, to see and perceive] the **things that occurred** [from *gínomai* {1096}, to take place],

they grieved [from *lupéō* {3076}] **exceedingly** [*sphódra* {4970}], and, having approached, **they reported** [from *diasaphéō* {1285} from *diá* {1223}, an intensive; and *saphéō* {n.f.}, to manifest, make clear] to their lord **all things** [from *pás* {3956}] that were done. (a.t.)

The man's fellow servants told their master "all things" that had transpired. They left nothing out of their report to the king.

Had the servant appropriated (accepted) his king's nature of forgiveness (2 Pet. 1:4), he would have forgiven the small debt his fellow servant owed him. Such hardness of heart happens when people do not accept God's offers of new natures through His forgiveness. When God's grace remains unappropriated, unaccepted, and unbelieved, a sinful person is unchanged. Like ripples on water, others are deeply affected. The evil servant's associates were disappointed, sorrowful, and "grieved exceedingly."

In the same way, Jesus became **very sorrowful** (*perílupos* [4037] from *perí* [4012], as an intensive; and *lupéō*, grief) when the rich young ruler turned down His command to sell his belongings, give the proceeds to the poor, and follow Him (Luke 18:24).

[32] The king reviewed his compassionate treatment of the evil, unforgiving servant:

> Then his lord, after that he had called him, said unto him, O thou **wicked** [from *ponērós* {4190}, malevolent] **servant** [from *doúlos*, slave {1401}], **I forgave** [from *aphíemi* {863} as in v. 27] thee **all** [from *pás* {3956}, the whole, the entirety, since "debt" is singular] that debt, because **thou desiredst** [from *parakaléō* {3870} from *pará* {3844}, alongside of; and *kaléō* {2564}, to call] me.

Jesus did not use such language often. In fact, only in Luke 19:22, with the parable of the pounds, is the expression "wicked servant" also found. It was addressed to a servant who buried his lord's talent.

The wicked servant here in Matthew 18 failed to appropriate the forgiveness offered him. God in Jesus Christ did His share in forgiving our sins, but in order for forgiveness to be effective, we have to receive it, believe it as real, and appropriate it, just as seed has to germinate to become fruitful.

[33] The king now impressed on the evil servant his moral obligation to have shown mercy:

> **Shouldest** [from *deí* {1163}, to be morally obligated] not thou also **have had compassion** [from *eleéō* {1653}, to pity] on thy fellowservant, even as **I had pity** [also from *eleéō*] on thee?

The incarnate God has offered mercy to His creation, but sinful people in their pride often refuse to accept it. God sent His Son into the world—not to judge it but to save it (John 3:17). If the sinful debtor would receive such mercy, he would be forgiven and become forgiving himself. Divine forgiveness possessed means divine forgiveness expressed.

Showing mercy (*eleéō*) is one quality any decent people can show. This does not mean they are saved, but it shows that they are civilized. (Study the author's volume entitled *The Beatitudes*, 355–414.) But refusing to show mercy is a clear indication that people have not been saved. True children of God share His nature.

[34] The master became angry and delivered this evil servant to "tormentors":

> And his lord **was angered** [from *orgízō* {3710}, to be angry] and **delivered** [from *paradídōmi* {3860}, to deliver from close by; from *pará* {3844}, close by; and *dídōmi* {1325}, to give] him to the tormentors **until** [*héōs*] **he should pay** [*apodṓ*, the aorist subjunctive of *apodídōmi* {591}] all **that was owed** [from *opheílō* {3784}] him. (a.t.)

Is the action taken by the king severe? Yes, the servant would never be able to repay such a huge debt.

We are told that hell (see Gehenna [1067]; Matt. 5:22, 30; 18:9; 25:41) is going to be a place of eternal fire. This is not a matter to be taken lightly. The verbs *basanízō* (928), to torment, or its corresponding noun *basanismós* (929), torment, occur in Matthew 8:29; Mark 5:7; Luke 8:28; Revelation 9:5; 14:10, 11; 18:7, 10, 15; and 20:10. Hell is not going to be a place where one enjoys being with those of his own kind, as some lightly say.

The statement of the king has an air of irrevocable finality. The verb *orgízō* is associated with the noun *orgḗ* (3709), anger. Just as Jesus Christ became angry at a crowd that objected to His healing a man's hand on the Sabbath (Mark 3:5), so the king in the parable became enraged by his servant's unwillingness to pass on a fraction of the compassion he had been shown.

In the same way, God, in His grace, has offered forgiveness of a debt that is impossible to repay. We can never earn forgiveness; we can only be forgiven and cleansed by grace through the blood of Jesus Christ (1 John 1:7, 9). If we accept His forgiveness, we also receive new natures, which encourage us to pass on this forgiveness.

[35] Now the Lord Jesus concluded this parable:

> **So likewise** [*hoútōs* {3779}, in the same manner] My heavenly Father **shall do** [from *poiéō* {4160}, to do] also unto you, if you from your hearts **forgive**

[from *aphíēmi* {863}, to release, to forgive] not every one his brother their **trespasses** [from *paráptōma* {3900}, a sideslip]. (a.t.)

Although God desires to do good (Matt. 19:17; Mark 10:18; Luke 18:19) and wills that all people be saved (1 Tim. 2:4; 2 Pet. 3:9), He will punish those who do not repent and believe in the atonement He has provided in His Son. Accordingly, Jesus concluded this parable by teaching that His Father will punish those who do not receive new, forgiving natures (2 Pet. 1:4) through faith.

Although the word for "trespasses" is not in some older manuscripts, it is found in most manuscripts. "Trespasses" (from *paráptōma*) are sins (see author's *The Complete Word Study Dictionary: New Testament*, words #'s 3895, 3900), but they refer to slips, unintended tripping aside that results in a recoverable fall that anyone is liable to experience. (For further study, see Heb. 6:6 where the verb *parapíptō* occurs; also the author's exegesis of Heb. 6:4–6 in his volume on James entitled *Faith, Love, and Hope,* 776–794).

CHAPTER

19

Marriage and Divorce
(19:1–12; Mark 10:1–12; Luke 16:18)

[1] Having concluded His ministry in Galilee, Jesus now "departed" (v. 1) toward the **coasts** (from *hórion* [3725], border region, coastal area) of Judea, particularly to Perea beyond the Jordan River. His ultimate destination was Jerusalem (Luke 9:51, 53; 13:22; 17:11; 18:31). Having proven time and time again who He was, the Father Himself testifying both at His baptism and transfiguration, and fully confident of His Person and destiny, Jesus approached the city to fulfill His planned death and resurrection (Matt. 16:21–23; 17:22–23; 20:17–19).

Jerusalem was the capital of Judea and the setting where Jesus' trial and crucifixion would soon take place. Knowing what lay ahead, He deliberately shifted His location to fulfill the plan of the Triune Godhead. His resolve was to be crucified, knowing that it was necessary to shed His blood for the remission of sins (Heb. 9:22). Nothing was going to cause Him to fail this purpose for His incarnation.

[2] Being followed by "**large** [from *polús* {4183}, much, many] **crowds** [from *óchlos* {3793}, unattached, unaffiliated individuals]," and taking time to heal them had become normal occurrences for Jesus by now. Mark 10:1 adds, "As He **had become accustomed** [from *éthō* {1486}], He **was teaching** [*edídasken*, the imperfect tense of *didáskō* {1321}] them again." (a.t.)

What was happening in the region beyond the Jordan River? For one thing, King Herod had removed John the Baptist from the castle of Machaerus (according to Jewish historian Josephus) and beheaded him (Matt. 14:1–12). Unafraid of Herod, Jesus proceeded in that direction, and the crowds "**followed** [from *akolouthéō* {190}] him." The verb *akolouthéō* derives from the alpha inclusive (or collective) *a* (1), together; and *kéleuthos* (n.f.), a road, path, way, meaning to accompany.

Certainly, part of the reason people were attracted to Jesus was that "**He tenderly healed** [from *therapeúō* {2323}, to tenderly attend to and heal physically] them" (a.t.). Crowds noticed this divine quality of Jesus Christ, but arrogant people like the Pharisees never did.

[3] Suddenly, the Pharisees interjected their own agenda, once again "**tempting** [from *peirázō* {3985}, to test] him," this time with the matter of divorce:

> Is it lawful for a man **to put away** [*apolúsai*, the aorist active infinitive of *apolúō* {630}, to dismiss; the aorist indicates once-for-all] his wife for every **cause** [from *aitía* {156}, reason]?

This type of temptation was effective, since there was hostile disagreement among the Jews. Two prevalent views on divorce existed at the time of Christ. The conservative view was attributed to Rabbi Shammai. His liberal rival, Hillel, believed that marriage could be dissolved for any excuse (*aitía*). The Pharisees, who were more conservative in ethics, and the Sadducees were violently divided on this particular subject. Consequently, the Pharisees could count on Jesus alienating at least one party whatever His answer, thereby dividing His following. Since some believed every cause for divorce was valid, and some who did not, the issue was controversial.

Here, the verb *peirázō* carries a contextual meaning of tempting with ill intent. This temptation was directed at Jesus' authority. Any inquiry related to the question of the "lawfulness" of some action immediately invoked divine authority. The Pharisees did not want to believe in Jesus Christ, but they hoped He would endorse their view that only a few reasons were valid for divorce. If He did, He would alienate the liberals and bring on Himself the condemnation of that whole group. But our omniscient Lord was too adroit to fall into that trap.

[4] Wisely appealing to the Torah—accepted by both parties, Jesus answered:

> Have you not **read** [*anégnōte*, the aorist tense of *anaginōskō* {314}, to read; the aorist means at any time, even once; from *aná* {303}, repetition; and *ginōskō* {1097}, to know by experience] that the One who [{TR, MT}, the One who created {UBS, Nestles}] from the **beginning** [from *arché* {746}] **made** [from *poiéō* {4160}, to do, to make] them **male** [from *ársēn* {730}] and **female** [from *thélus* {2338}]? (a.t.)

Here is an interesting variant describing God's action in the creation. The majority of Greek manuscripts, both ancient and later, have "the One who made" (the article with the aorist participle of *poiéō*), which agreed with the main verb, "made them male and female," emphasizing the result of creation. But a few manuscripts have "the One who created" (the article with the aorist participle of *ktízō* [2936], to create), emphasizing God's role as Creator.

But the Lord Jesus clearly accepted Genesis 1:27 and 5:2 as teaching that God originally created the genders of male and female and one member in each class. Since He spoke the truth, this puts an end to the theory of the evolution of humans from some other genus. The book of Genesis affirms the determination of independent species (Gen. 1:11, 12 [twice], 21 [twice], 24 [twice], 25 [three times]; 6:20 [three times]; 7:14 [four times]) by a class division separate from the genus of humankind (Gen. 2:18–23).

The phrase *ap' archḗs*, "from the beginning," rules out preexisting materials in the original creation of substances and relations.

[5] Jesus, as the One who made, also spoke:

> And He said, **Because of** [*héneken* {1752}] this, **a man** [*ánthrōpos* {444}; ordinarily generic but contextually the male is understood since the subject joins "his wife"] **shall leave** [from *kataleípō* {2641}, to forsake, to leave; from *katá* {2596}, according to; and *leípō* {3007}, to leave] father and mother and **shall be joined together** [*proskollēthḗsetai*, the future passive of *proskolláō* {4347} from *prós* {4314}, toward; and *kolláō* {2853}, to glue {*kólla* is glue}, to join] to his **wife** [from *gunḗ* {1135}, woman]; and the two **shall be** [from *eimí* {1510}, to be] one flesh. (a.t.)

Kataleípō is synonymous with *apotássomai* (657)—ordinarily translated "forsake"; however, both verbs preclude the idea of abandonment and convey rather the thought of arranging things properly prior to departure (Luke 9:61; 14:33). *Kataleípō* means to leave alone, to leave behind.

This is the scriptural protocol for marriage. Leaving parents, among other things, means economic independence. Marriage is permanent, two becoming "one flesh," just as "he that is joined unto the Lord is one spirit" (1 Cor. 6:17). When a child, regardless of age, becomes so "joined" to Christ, his spiritual responsibility becomes dual: to the Lord first, then to his family, one being a spiritual responsibility, the other a family responsibility. A bond always exists between father or mother and child, no matter what age, and that relationship only changes according to circumstances, not nature.

Although *gunḗ* means both "woman" and "wife," here and in Mark 10:7 the noun is restricted in meaning to "wife."

Proskollēthḗsetai is properly translated in the passive voice because verse 6 says that God has joined (see the aorist active verb *sunézeuxen* in the next verse) the two together. This does not mean the attachment is involuntary. Like salvation, marriage does not occur without personal consent, and it is interesting that the word implies that the two are "glued" together. There is no separating them now. Each one is "stuck" with the partner, whether for better or worse.

For persons entering marriage, the verb "leave" represents the proper attitude toward parents, the verb "cleave" represents the proper action toward one another, and the statement, "they shall be" represents the result—a Christian married couple, a new family.

[6] Jesus elaborated on the nature of marriage, concluding what He taught in verses 3–5:

> **Therefore** [*hṓste* {5620}], **they are** [from *eimí* {1510}, to be] **no more** [*oukéti* {3765} from *ouk* {3756}; and *éti* {2089}, yet, still] two but one flesh. **That which** [*hó*, the nominative singular neuter relative pronoun of *hós* {3739}, that which], therefore, **God** [*Theós* {2316}, i.e., the Father] **joined together** [from *suzeúgnumi* {4801}, yoked together; from *sún* {4862}, together; and *zeúgos* {2201}, yoke, pair], let not **man** [*ánthrōpos* {444}, generic man, either as a society decreeing or allowing a change in God's plan, or as the individual—husband or wife—choosing to defy God's plan] **separate** [from *chōrízō* {5563}, to divide, to separate]. (a.t.)

The experiential "they shall be" from the previous verse was now stated as a principle: "They are" an item, a fact created by the defining God. The couple will continue to experience what God has created in principle.

Godly marriage begins with God in the lives of two individuals indwelt by Him and led to join their lives together. Their union is not just a lateral union of two bodies but a triangle, with the sovereign Lord at the apex holding them together. God yokes together in actuality what He has willed in eternity.

Hó, "that which," a *neuter* singular pronoun, looks at marriage as one thing, namely the "one flesh" of this verse.

God does the yoking together, making marriage a binding institution, a contract between man and woman. People are not morally free to break this contract for any reason other than marital infidelity.

[7] The Pharisees, still tempting Jesus and rejecting His deity, now tried to position Jesus' view of marriage against that of Moses: "They say unto him, Why did Moses then **command** [from *entéllomai* {1781}] to give a writing of divorcement, and to put her away?"

Moses had a prophetic significance to Jesus. Moses announced the Messiah's coming (Luke 24:27, 44; John 1:45; 5:46; Acts 3:22 [cf. Deut. 18:15]); the resurrection of the dead (Luke 20:37 [cf. Ex. 3:15]); the preaching of the gospel to the Gentiles (Rom. 10:19 [cf. Deut. 32:21]); and the sovereignty of God's grace (Rom. 9:15 [cf. Ex. 33:19]). There's also a typological significance. As Moses was the mediator between God and Israel, so Christ was the mediator between God and all humanity (John 6:32; Heb. 3:1–6).

The writer of Hebrews spends some time comparing Moses and Jesus in his third chapter:

> For this One was counted worthy of more glory than Moses, inasmuch as He who has built the house has more honor than the house. For every house is built by someone; but He that built all things is God. And Moses, on the one hand, was faithful in all his house as a servant, for a testimony of those things that were to be spoken after; but Christ as a Son over His own house, whose house we are if we hold fast the confidence and the rejoicing of the hope firm unto the end. (Heb. 3:3–6; a.t.)

The writer informs us in this passage that Moses was a servant within a house, while Jesus actually built the house. Even the Law "through" (*diá* [1223]) Moses (John 1:17) first passed through the One "through" (*diá*) whom "all things" became (John 1:3). Accordingly, Jesus could speak with greater authority than Moses even in matters of the Law—thus, the very frequent, "But I say unto you."

Jesus had already said in Matthew 5:32 that the only legitimate reason for divorce was fornication (*porneía* [4202], marital infidelity). God had revealed His commandments to Moses, and they remained valid (Matt. 23:1–3; Acts 7:38), but Jesus intensified these imperatives by emphasizing internal violations (i.e., heart sins; Matt. 5:1–48; Mark 10:1–12) over against the external conformity of the Pharisees.

[8] Jesus further explained that God never commanded (from *entéllomai* [1781]) Moses to issue a regulation for divorce:

> Moses, because of the **hardness of your hearts** [from *sklērokardía* {4641} from *sklērós* {4642}, hard; and *kardía* {2588}, heart; inversely "cardiosclerosis" in English] **allowed** [from *epitrépō* {2010}, to permit; from *epí* {1909}, upon; and *trépō* {n.f.}, to turn around] you **to put away** [from *apolúō* {630}, to release from; from *apó* {575}, from; and *lúō* {3089}, to loose, the opposite of *déō* {1210}, to bind] your wives. **Nevertheless** [*dé* {1161}], **from the beginning** [*ap' archḗs* as in v. 4], it has **not been** [*ou* {3756}, absolutely not; *gégonen*, the perfect tense of *gínomai* {1096}] **this way** [*hoútōs* {3779}]. (a.t.)

This was Jesus' first correction of the Pharisees. What Moses permitted is not what God commanded. Permission is not commandment; permission is concession. A vast difference exists between permitting and ordering. God permits evil, although He designates the consequences of it. Divorce has terrible consequences, but this was not God's original plan when He created the world and people in particular.

Concerning God's attitude toward divorce, besides Malachi's often quoted, "He [God] hates divorce" (Mal. 2:16; a.t.), it is interesting to see the progression of thought in two tightly knit verses in Jeremiah. In Jeremiah 3:8 God says, "I gave faithless [i.e., adultery with foreign gods] Israel her certificate of divorce" (NIV), and yet a few breaths away, He adds, "Return, . . . for I am your husband" (3:14 NIV). Since God hates divorce, He hated His own divorce from Israel, which implies that He is going to do something about it. The implication becomes fact and prophecy in the book of Hosea. There, the Lord abrogated several of the Law's death penalties when He commanded Hosea to marry a whore and produce "children of whoredoms" (Hos. 1:2) to prove His undying love for the adulterous Israelites and His plan to "allure" (Hos. 2:14) them back from foreign gods (idol husbands) to Himself (Hos. 2:15 ff.; repeated in 3:1–5). In this narrative, we see that fine line between Law and grace, stoning and forgiveness, conditional and unconditional love. God divorced Israel for good cause; by His own Law, He could stone her to death, but He is still her husband, and He will win her back; in fact, He will remarry her (Hos. 2:19, 20), which, we saw above, was also forbidden once a woman had been defiled. When God divorces, then, it is temporary—a separation, but He transcends His own Law to be gracious. A good example for His covenant people!

God permitted divorce for the Jews because of "hard[ened] hearts" (a.t.; *sklērokardía*). This noun occurs here and in the parallel passage of Mark 10:5 regarding divorce. In Mark 16:14 where Jesus equated a hard heart to a heart of unbelief (*apistía* [570]), the reference was to the disciples' lack of trust. In Romans 2:5, Paul speaks of those who treasure up wrath for the day of wrath through their "hardness" (from *sklērótēs* [4643], the noun of the adjective *sklērós* [4642], hard) of heart.

Moses originally permitted divorce because of proof of some "uncleanness" (Deut. 24:1) that fell short of adultery, the penalty for which was death. Matthew 18:16 affirms the requisite of two or three witnesses that is found in Deuteronomy 19:15.

In conclusion, Jesus did not concede that Moses' permission was God's mistake. The full force of the perfect tense of *gínomai* is this: "The original intent of unconditional marriage has been from the beginning of human history until now." God never intended marriage to be annulled. Divorce is not the Law of God, nor was it anything other than the concession of Moses who did not absolutely forbid divorce.

[9] Jesus set Himself apart from and above Moses' concession immediately with the adversative, "But I say":

But [*dé* {1161}] I say unto you, that whoever **shall put away** [from *apolúo* {630}] his wife not **based upon** [*epí* {1909}] **fornication** [*porneía* {4202}, fornication, specifically adultery in this context] and **shall marry** [*gamése*, the aorist active subjunctive of *gaméō* {1060}, to marry] another woman **commits adultery** [from *moicháomai* {3429}]. (a.t.)

This is Jesus' second correction of the Pharisees. The man who puts away his wife for any reason other than fornication and marries another woman commits adultery.

Dé (but) is ordinarily used in an adversative sense in the expression, "But I say to you," as any student can see by examining the contexts where the clause is found (e.g., see Matt. 5:22, 28, 32, 34, 39; 12:6, 36; 17:12; 26:29; *plén* [4133], over and above, moreover, is used in Matt. 11:22, 24; *allá* [235], but, is found in Luke 6:27; and Luke 10:12, interestingly, has only "I say unto you . . ."). In most contexts, Jesus was not disagreeing with the Mosaic Law but intensifying it as, for example, "But I say unto you, That whosoever looketh on a woman to lust after her hath committed adultery with her already in his heart" (Matt. 5:28). Internal adultery per se was not recorded in the Mosaic Law, and most likely the Pharisees had conformed to much of the external code. Jesus reminded them that such physical congruity does not measure up to God's standard for internal holy living.

Here the flow of thought was clearly adversative: "Moses permitted, . . . but I say . . . from the beginning it was not so." In Matthew 5:32 Jesus said that *porneía* is a legitimate cause for divorce. Although *porneía* usually refers to premarital sexual relations, it can also refer to any illicit sexual activity, including adultery, homosexuality, or bestiality. Most Bible scholars assume it must refer only to adultery here and in Matthew 5:32, since Jesus made it clear that God gave Deuteronomy 24:1 only as a concession.

This means that even if—as many rabbis suggested—the uncleanness in Deuteronomy was premarital sex, divorce reflects only God's permission, never His preferred choice. Jesus did not say, for example, that when God spoke of uncleanness in Deuteronomy 24:1, He meant premarital sex and that God considers premarital sex a proper reason for dissolving the marriage relationship.

The only consistent way to take Jesus' saying here is that, in God's sight, marriage is a permanent relationship, broken only by infidelity after marriage (betrothal, or engagement, being considered as marriage). Notice, then, that while Old Testament Law prescribed death by stoning for adultery, Jesus permitted divorce for adultery here and in Matthew 5:32.

To illustrate, if, as Joseph assumed, Mary had been guilty of premarital sex, God would have permitted divorce, but that would not have been His preferred will. God intervened to prevent Joseph from making a mistake (Matt. 1:19–21).

Adultery is a destructive act. First, adultery is committed against God who forbids it. Second, adultery is a sin against one's own body as well as against one's spouse.

A few earlier Greek manuscripts, most Greek editions, and modern English versions omit the rest of verse 9 as it is in the King James Version regarding it as a copyist's assimilation of Matthew 5:32. However, since it is found in most Greek manuscripts, both ancient and later, we probably should include it here also:

> And whoever **marries** [from *gameō* {1060}, to marry] one **who has been put away** [from *apoluō* {630}] commits adultery. (a.t.)

This is the general principle, and the reader is directed to our extensive discussions of this topic in the author's books, *What About Divorce?* and *May I Divorce and Remarry?*

Theoretically, a married man has three opportunities to commit adultery: first, by committing fornication while married (including adulterous thoughts as in Matt. 5:28); second, by dismissing an innocent wife and marrying again; and thirdly, by marrying an adulterous woman divorced by her husband. Then, of course, the whole cycle can be repeated ad infinitum.

[10] Surprisingly, the disciples initially concluded that unless there were more "**cases**" or reasons for dissolving a marriage, the institution was not worth it:

> If the **case** [*aitía* {156}, reason, cause, matter] of the man be so with his wife, **to marry** [*gamēsai*, the aorist infinitive of *gameō* {1060}] is not **advantageous** [from *sumphérō* {4851}, to bring together]. (a.t.)

The literal Greek translation, "to marry does not bring together," highlights the disciples' fallacy. If marriage, like other contracts, did not carry the terms of its dissolution (many of them), then marriage did not unite in an advantageous way. It is incredible that the Twelve would hold to such loose morality, but this only shows how strongly they were steeped in the chauvinism of tradition prior to their walk with Christ.

From a practical standpoint, perhaps they also thought that no unmarried prophet or even Christ could be an authority on the subject.

[11] Jesus continued,

> But He said unto them, Not all men have room [*chōroúsi*, the present of *chōréō* {5562}, to receive, yield to, give way to. "Can" {KJV} is not in the Greek text; Jesus is discussing the reality, not the possibility.] for this **saying** [from

lógos {3056}, intelligent word], **but** [*all'* for *allá* {235}] they for whom it **has been given** [*dédotai*, the perfect passive of *dídōmi* {1325}] do accept it. (a.t.)

In response, Jesus neither affirmed that unconditional marriage was bad, nor denied that being single was good; nor did He promote one status over the other. What He did say was that God gave a subjective assent to the "saying" of celibacy to some, for "not all receive it." While both unconditional marriage and unconditional celibacy may be difficult, the disciples implied they believed celibacy to be the lighter load. As Paul would wisely say later, "Let every man be fully persuaded in his own mind" (Rom. 14:5), and as Jesus said here, this persuasion must come from God (cf. Gal. 5:8).

[12] Jesus now explained what He meant by God giving the "saying" only to some:

> For there are some eunuchs, which were so born from their mother's womb: and there are some eunuchs, which **were made eunuchs** [from *eunouchízō* {2134}, to eunuchize, to emasculate] **of** [*hupó* {5259}, by] men: and there be eunuchs, which **have made themselves eunuchs** [from *eunouchízō*; and *heautoús* {1438}, the reflexive pronoun "themselves"] **for** [*diá* {1223}, on the account of] the kingdom of heaven's sake.

The eunuch, by definition, is one who does not have testicles and therefore cannot have sexual arousal. According to Jesus, there are three categories of eunuchs: those born with the condition, others castrated by men for penalty or hire (e.g., to guard women), and some who made themselves eunuchs. There is no question concerning what Jesus meant by the first two categories, but the meaning of the last category poses some problems.

Some assume it must be interpreted literally, that one would castrate himself because of his love for the Lord Jesus. The most famous man to actually castrate himself was Origen (AD 185–254), the head of the Alexandrian school of theology and translator of the Hexapla, a six-column interlinear Bible (a tremendous one-man contribution to biblical study: one column for the Hebrew Bible, one column for the Greek transliteration of the Hebrew, and four columns for four different Greek versions of the Old Testament). Origen castrated himself in order to effectively teach a women's Bible study. He seems to have regretted his strong literalism later in life.

But what could the text mean if it does not refer to literal destruction of part of one's body? It must be a figure of speech for one voluntarily living a celibate life for the sake of Christ. We can see a parallel between this passage and the way Jesus responded to Nicodemus when the latter asked concerning the second birth, "Can a man [re]enter his mother's womb and be born again?" (John 3:4).

There is a new birth, but physical reentry into a womb is not what Jesus had in mind. Similarly, Paul refers to a spiritual gift of celibacy (1 Cor. 7:7).

Why would the Lord give a spiritual gift to a person to spiritually eunuchize himself for the kingdom of God? Persecution was one good reason, according to Paul:

> I suppose therefore that this is good for the present distress, I say, that it is good for a man so to be. . . . But this I say, brethren, the time is short: it remaineth, that both they that have wives be as though they had none; and they that weep, as though they wept not; and they that rejoice, as though they rejoiced not; and they that buy, as though they possessed not; and they that use this world, as not abusing it: for the fashion of this world passeth away. (1 Cor. 7:26, 29–31)

The "present distress" and the "fashion of this world passing away" may both refer to Nero's advancing persecution against the church. Under the threat of martyrdom, freedom from care would certainly be preferable to the attachments, encumbrances, and responsibilities of marriage.

Preempting Paul's words in 1 Corinthians 7:7, Jesus said,

> **He who is enabled** [from *dúnamai* {1410}] **to receive** [from *chōréō* {5562} from *chóros* {5566}, space; inferentially, "to make space for," "to fit" {i.e., in the heart}; see also v. 11] it, let him receive it. (a.t.)

"Not all men receive this saying" (v. 11) means that not everyone accepts celibacy. Jesus said the only ones who receive *it* (not in the Greek text but understood as His word) are those to whom the gift is given (v. 11). The saying is identified with the gift itself, since everyone can listen to [i.e., receive] words), as, for example, the apostle Paul (1 Cor. 7:7–9). Persons cannot snatch this gift out of heaven. They receive it because it is first given. Observe the verb tenses here: "does not receive [present active] . . . unless . . . has been given [perfect passive]." Since celibacy is a supernatural gift, God can control one's passions. The verb *dúnamai*, to be able, does not preclude the fact that God is the ultimate source of the ability; that is, He empowers some to be celibate.

Jesus Blesses Little Children
(19:13–15; Mark 10:13–16; Luke 18:15–17)

[13] Matthew (here) and Mark 10:13 record the bringing of **little children** (from *paidíon* [3813], the diminutive of *país* [3816], child), but Luke 18:15 describes them as babies (from *bréphos* [1025], infant).

The parents in this scenario wanted the Lord Jesus to "**pray**" (*proseúxētai*, the aorist middle deponent subjunctive of *proseúchomai* [4336], to pray) and "**touch**" (*hápsētai*, the aorist middle subjunctive of *háptōmai* [680], to touch; Mark 10:13; Luke 18:15) their young children and infants. They believed that even a single prayer (reflected in the aorist "pray") and the Lord's touch would influence their children.

According to Mark 10:16,

> **He took them in His arms** [from *enagkalízomai* {1723}, to take in arms; from *agkálē* {43}, arm] and, **having put** [from *títhēmi* {5087}, to place] His hands on them, **He was blessing** [from *eulogéō* {2127}, to speak well] them. (a.t.)

The disciples, however, "**rebuked** [*epetímēsan*, the aorist tense of *epitimáō* {2008}] them." They thought that Jesus' time could be used more beneficially than to be wasted with children. However, Jesus never wasted His time. If He valued children by spending time with them, so should we.

[14] While Matthew begins Jesus' response only with the adversative *dé* (1161), "**but**," Mark 10:14 fills in the fact that Jesus "**agonized**" (from *aganaktéō* [23], to agonize; from *ágan* [n.f.], very much; and *áchthos* [n.f.], pain, grief) over this rebuke. We, too, should agonize over false teaching, especially the lie that would attempt to block the Lord's touch on children.

Immediately countering their insensitivity, Jesus said,

> **Suffer** [from *aphíēmi* {863}, to permit, to release from oneself; from *apó* {575}, from; and *híēmi* {n.f.}, to let go] little children, and **forbid** [from *kōlúō* {2967}, to restrain] them not, **to come** [from *érchomai* {2064}] unto me: for of such is the kingdom of heaven.

Here Jesus emphasized the humility of little children as elsewhere in Scripture where we find a relative innocence assigned to them. For example, Jesus thanked His Father that He revealed truth to "babes" as opposed to the "wise and prudent" (Matt. 11:25; Luke 10:21). In a similar vein, Paul counsels the Corinthians: "In evil [from *kakía*], be children [*nēpiázete* from *nēpiázō* {3515}, from *nēpios* {3516}, infant]" (1 Cor. 14:20; a.t.).

Before going His way, Jesus mildly and patiently reminded His disciples that children are candidates for the kingdom of heaven. Mark 10:16 adds that Jesus "was blessing [*eulógei*, the imperfect tense of *eulogéō* {2127}, to speak well] them."

We find the general principle of this lesson in Luke 18:17:

> Verily I say unto you, Whosoever **shall** not **receive** [*déxētai*, the aorist middle deponent subjunctive of *déchomai* {1209}, to receive, the aorist tense

inferring once-for-all] the kingdom of God as a **little child** [*paidíon* {3813}] shall **in no wise** [the two negatives *ou* {3756} and *mē* {3361} combined as an intensive combination meaning absolutely not, never at any time] **enter** [*eisélthē*, the aorist active subjunctive of *eisérchomai* {1525}, to enter, the aorist meaning at any time] therein.

Indeed, this is an eternally inviolable rule that people can enter only once and for all into the kingdom.

Adults should never attempt to prevent the Lord from "touching" their children. This is no ordinary touch, but God's touch that fires up young lives like John the Baptist (Luke 1:14, 15). The sooner in life the Lord touches a young person, even in infancy, the better.

[15] Matthew now adds,

> And **having laid** [from *epitíthēmi* {2007}, to place] His hands on them, **He departed** [*eporeúthē*, the aorist passive deponent indicative of *poreúomai* {4198}, to go out] from there. (a.t.)

The Rich Young Ruler
(19:16–22; Mark 10:17–22; Luke 18:18–23)

[16] In all three gospels, the story of the rich young ruler follows Jesus' blessing of children. This is no coincidence; the events accord with the omniscient wisdom of the Lord Jesus Christ. Everything has its own proper season (1 Tim. 6:15), and this was one of them. The mature ruler contrasted with these young, relatively innocent children. He had experienced the corrupting influence of wealth and was unwilling to part with his possessions for the sake of the poor and his own eternal salvation.

Accordingly, Matthew begins this story with "**Behold**" (*idoú* [2400], the imperative of *eídon* [1492], the aorist of *horáō* [3708], to perceive, calling attention to the extraordinary [see Matt. 3:16]), to call attention to the fact that God can save little children before they plunge into the depths of sin.

In verse 20, Matthew calls the man "**young**" (*neanískos* [3495] from *néos* [3501), young, recent; and the diminutive suffix *-ískos*). He was probably in his twenties. We do not know if he had earned his wealth himself or had inherited either money or a lucrative business, but Luke 18:23 informs us that he was "**very** [*sphódra* {4970}] **rich** [*ploúsios* {4145}]." Luke 18:18 tells us he was a "ruler" (*árchōn* [758]), either a member of the Sanhedrin (cf. John 3:1 with 7:45–50) or a ruler in a local synagogue (cf. Matt. 9:18, 23; Mark 5:22; Luke 8:41).

Mark 10:17 says this young ruler "rushed forward [from the verb *prostrēchō* {4370}, to run forward; from *prós* {4314}, toward; and *trēchō* {5143}, to run] and kneeled [from *gonupetéō* {1120}] before Him" (a.t.) when Jesus "came out into the open" (a.t.; from *ekporeúomai* [1607] from *ek* [1537], out of; and *poreúomai* [4198], to march), probably a mad dash in response to something Jesus had done recently. Mark records the fact that the ruler knelt down (from *gonupetéō* [1120]). How this contrasts with the mock bow of the soldiers following His trial (Mark 15:19), and yet it does not touch the level of devotion of the woman who washed Jesus' feet with her tears and wiped them with her hair as she knelt at His feet (Luke 7:36–39). The ruler addressed Jesus,

> **Good** [from *agathós* {18}; TR, MT, not in UBS or Nestle's; see the discussion of v. 17] **Teacher** [from *didáskalos* {1320}], what **good thing** [*agathón*, the neuter singular of *agathós*] **shall I do** [from *poiéō* {4160}, to make, to do, perform], that I may have **eternal** [from *aiōnios* {166}] life? (a.t.)

The fact that the young man asked about eternal life tells us that he knew more about Jesus than the average Jew. Many Jews called Jesus "Teacher" at this point, but few connected Him with "eternal life." This is the first time the expression is recorded in Matthew. The only prior use of *aiōnios* in Matthew's Gospel is 18:8, where it is connected with "fire."

This successful young ruler had apparently witnessed enough of Jesus' compassion to call Him "Good Teacher." He knew that Jesus healed the sick out of a benevolent heart. In addition, Jesus' response to Jewish attacks was impressive. Peter says that "when He was reviled, He did not revile again [i.e., in turn or in kind]" (1 Pet. 2:23; a.t.). Something was different about the character of this Person, and the ruler had experienced some demonstrations of His character. But apart from accepting God's revelation, he could never know the truth of the Person of Christ.

Jesus came to save first—to bring salvation—and then to teach. Thus, Jesus directed the subject from achieving to receiving, from flattery to the critical issue of the man's relationship with the triune God. The Bible teaches that persons receive salvation as a free gift; eternal life is not earned by "doing some good thing."

In all fairness, the rich man knew something was missing from his life. For all his worldly advancement, he had not advanced spiritually.

[17] The rich young ruler had just called Jesus Christ "**good**" (*agathé*, the vocative singular masculine adjective of *agathós* [18], benevolent). Before answering the man's question, Jesus asked him a parenthetical question of His own:

Why **do you call** [from *légō* {3004}, to speak intelligently] Me **good** [from *agathós*]? There is **none** [*oudeís* {3762} from *ou* {3756}, "not"; the adversative *dé* {1161}, even; and *heís* {1520}, one] good **but** [*ei* {1487}, the suppositional "if"; *mḗ* {3361}, "not"; "except"] One, [the] God [i.e., the Father]. (a.t.)

A significant variant in a few older manuscripts in verses 16 and 17 is followed by most critical Greek editions and by most modern English versions of Matthew. Most Greek manuscripts, both earlier and later, agree with the King James Version in depicting the young ruler calling Jesus "Good Master," and Jesus as responding, "Why do you call me good? There is none good except one, God" (a.t.). Since all manuscripts of Mark present this conversation, we know that this is the way Mark's source understood the original conversation (in Aramaic). The Holy Spirit led Mark to record the conversation in this manner.

However, a few variant manuscripts picture Matthew as giving a completely different story. They leave out the word "good" in verse 16 (the ruler simply calls Him "Teacher"), and they present Jesus as responding, "Why do you say good? There is one good person." This person is not defined in most of the variant Greek manuscripts but is defined in the Latin manuscripts as God.

We feel that the variant versions represent Jesus' speech as confusing and hard to follow; the thoughts don't seem to be related. Since Mark records the conversation exactly like most Greek manuscripts of Matthew do, we will follow the King James Version account. It is easier to assume that some early copyists (who possibly did not speak Greek as their native language) made some careless mistakes rather than the Holy Spirit leading two Gospel writers to give such divergent accounts.

Notice that Jesus did not say, "Do not call Me good, because no one is good but the Father." Rather, His question can be read this way: Because of your assumptions that only the Father is benevolent, why then do you call Me benevolent? Are you admitting that I share this divine attribute with the Father?

While this ruler saw unique benevolence in the Son, he apparently did not realize the logical conclusion of calling someone other than the Father "benevolent."

[18, 19] Jesus did not wait for an answer to this question, which only broke the theme long enough for the ruler to consider the implication of what he had said. Jesus returned immediately to the subject at hand. The ruler's question was, "What good thing shall I do [to] have eternal life?" (v. 16; a.t.).

In response, Jesus suggested that if he wanted to gain eternal life because of something he did, he must keep the commandments. When asked which ones, Jesus listed some—not all—of the commandments as God, His Father, gave them. Matthew alone includes a definite article ("the") before the listing of the commandments. This is not apparent in English, but in Greek Jesus' answer is literally: "**The** [*tó*] do not murder. . . [etc.]". The equivalent English construction with the definite article would be "the following," and a list. The definite article implies all the authority associated with a verbatim quote.

> He saith unto him, Which? Jesus said, Thou shalt do no murder, Thou shalt not commit adultery, Thou shalt not steal, Thou shalt not bear false witness, Honour thy father and thy mother: and, Thou shalt love thy neighbor as thyself.

Without knowing the Father's gift to the world, the rich ruler did not understand the difference between "doing" and "inheriting." "Doing" is contrary to an inheritance; one does not "do" anything "to inherit" something. The young man was smart and advanced in life, but he did not understand grace. The Lord Jesus became man to die for us so that we might inherit eternal life. What remains for us to do is simply to acknowledge our need, confess our sin, and receive what He accomplished. Achievers think they have gotten where they are by their own efforts. They do not understand receiving something they cannot earn. God reduced Nebuchadnezzar's arrogant mind to that of an animal for seven years for priding himself on his achievements (Dan. 4:30–32).

The sixth to the tenth commandments direct action toward our fellow humans. Note that the positive command, "honor," is *tíma* (5091), the present imperative, inferring permanence. Whatever God does or commands is permanent and absolute.

The next command, to love our neighbor as ourselves, does not occur in the decalog; however, the identical command, including the verb *agapéseis*, occurs in the Septuagint version of Leviticus 19:18. Remember, the man did not ask, Which ones from the decalog? Jesus answered from the whole corpus of the Law—the Torah—and not just from Exodus 20.

The verb *agapáō* is infused with new content in the revelation of the Father's gift of His Son as the sacrifice for the sins of the world (John 3:16). This was the supreme demonstration of *agápē*. The apostle John uses the noun seven times and the verb thirty-seven times in his Gospel, and the noun twenty-one times and the verb thirty-one times in his three short epistles. He actually defines God as love in 1 John 4:8, 16.

[20] The young man's response showed confidence in his past obedience, yet an awareness that something was missing:

> All these things **I kept** [from *phulássō* {5442}, to guard] from my youth up: what **lack** [from *husteréō* {5302}] I **yet** [*éti* {2089}]? (a.t.)

Phulássō actually means more "to guard" than "to keep" (*tēréō* [5083]), but any difference between these words evaporated under the young man's plain meaning that he had conformed to the laws Jesus cited.

Yet he recognized something was lacking. Possibly he knew that his conformity to the Law did not touch his heart, that he did not love God with his "whole heart, soul, and might" (Deut. 6:5; a.t.). Beyond this, he had another reason for insecurity. The Mosaic Law did not promise eternal life. To move from the temporal to the eternal, then, must require something more. What could it be? Could Jesus reveal what more he must do to receive eternal life?

Since Jesus was dealing with legalism, He did not introduce the atonement nor expound on the verb "inherit" (*klēronoméō* [5692]), which He would introduce in verse 29. Rather, He addressed the man's blindness to his own shortcomings. Maybe he never murdered, committed adultery, stole, lied, dishonored his parents, but did he really love his neighbor as himself? Although he had so much wealth, was his neighbor getting his equal share?

This was the sore spot. The verb "**lack**" in Greek is *husteréō* (5302) from *hústeros* (5306), last. The full question, following the young man's claim to his obedience, might be rendered, What is the last thing I can do to ensure eternal life?

[21] Jesus answered him:

> If **you desire** [from *thélō* {2309}, to determine, want, wish] **to be** [from *eimí* {1510}] **perfect** [*téleios* {5046}, mature, complete], go and sell your **possessions** [*hupárchonta* {5224}; that which is at one's disposal, the present neuter plural participle of *hupárchō* {5225}, to subsist], and give to the poor, and you shall have treasure in heaven: and **come** [*deúro* {1204}, the singular adverb *hither* used as an imperative, *come hither* {see below}], **follow** [from *akoloutheō* {190}] Me. (a.t.)

Contextually, *téleios* is a relative perfection, not God's absolute perfection. Certainly, Jesus did not intend to say, "**If you desire to be God** [i.e., Perfect with a capital 'P']. . . ." The object or (better) goal (*télos*) Jesus had in mind was the *téleios* (perfect) *anér* ([435], man), the concept later developed by both Paul (Eph. 4:13) and James (James 3:2). The perfect God does not sell His possessions and give to the poor, but the perfect man does—the incarnate God who, "though he was rich, yet for your sakes he became poor, that ye through his poverty might be rich" (2 Cor. 8:9).

Jesus used the singular imperative adverb *deúro*, "**come**," and its plural *deúte* (1205), several times as an invitation to sinners to come to Him. For example, He used the plural, *deúte*, in Matthew 11:28 for all who are weary to come to Him for rest. And He used the singular, *deúro*, in John 11:43 to call forth Lazarus from the grave. Jesus says to sinners: "Come forth [from the graveyard of sin]." Coming to Christ changes us, converts us, reconciles us to God, justifies us, gives us God's nature, and will cause us to share the destiny of Jesus Christ—eternal life in heaven in the presence of the Father and His holy angels. We accomplish this not by our efforts but by receiving what Jesus Christ has done. We sinners are dead, but the Word of life "enlightens every man coming into the world" (John 1:9; a.t.), inviting us to receive spiritual life.

Notice that the command "to come" to Jesus is here followed by the command to "**follow** [from *akolouthéō* {190} from the collective *a* {1}, together; and *kéleuthos* {n.f.}, a way, meaning to attend, accompany, to follow a teacher; Matt. 4:20, 22, 25; 9:9, etc.] me." Jesus' command was like a magnet attracting iron. In Ephesians 2:1, 5, Paul tells us that people are dead (from *nekrós* [3498]) in their sins. The moment they hear Jesus Christ's words: "Come [*deúte*] unto Me, all ye that are laboring and are heavy laden, and I shall give you rest [from *anapaúō* {373}, to cause to rest, from *aná* {303}, again; and *anō* {507}, above; and *paúō* {3973}, to cease, refrain]" (Matt. 11:28; a.t.)—those who are tired and heavy laden are convicted of sin, believe, and follow Jesus. Those who resist are miserable. Believers are instantly transformed and become new creatures, recognizing others who have had the same experience and gathering with them into a fellowship of believers, the church.

[22] The rich ruler's original question was, "What shall I do that I may have eternal life?" (v. 16, a.t.). Jesus could have said, "Nothing! It's impossible! Nothing you do will merit eternal life." Instead, He said, "Sell that thou hast, and give to the poor, and thou shalt have treasure in heaven."

Jesus' intention was not to reintroduce salvation by the Mosaic Law but to show the man his need of the grace of experiencing what Lazarus experienced—a resurrection from the dead—a grace that would transform his character in such a way that he would freely part with his possessions. But the conversation never advanced this far.

Only in Mark 10:22 do we find the words, "And then, **having become saddened** [from *stugnázō* {4768}, to become gloomy, downcast] over this word, he went away grieving" (a.t.). All three narratives say, "He went away **grieving** [from *lupéō* {3076}, to grieve, here and in Mark 10:22; while Luke 18:23 has *perílupos* {4036} from *lúpē* {3077}, grief; and *perí* {4012}, all around, much]." *Perílupos* is used to describe Jesus' agony in the Garden of Gethsemane (Matt. 26:38; Mark 14:34) and also King Herod's grief that he had to live up to an oath and behead someone he liked—John the Baptist (Mark 6:26).

Although he clearly recognized that Jesus was telling the truth, this young man persisted in unbelief and went away sorrowing.

We never know how attached we are to possessions until the threat of losing them faces us squarely. This man did not even know himself until Jesus explained what regenerated humanity does. The young ruler had everything but the assurance of eternal life, and yet he was unwilling to give up his comfortable lifestyle and pleasures for peace of heart.

Possessions and the Kingdom of God
(19:23–30; Mark 10:23–31; Luke 18:24–30).

[23] After the rich young ruler left, Jesus generalized His teaching: "A rich man enters into the kingdom of heaven **with difficulty** [*duskólōs* {1423}]" (a.t.).

Verses 24 and 26 tell us just how difficult; "with men [it] is impossible" (v. 26). Since Jesus was not teaching that rich people can merit their way in "with difficulty," the certainty of salvation falls back on God.

[24] Jesus used an illustration to explain the bridge from "difficult" (*duskólōs*; v. 23) to "impossible" (from *adúnatos* [102], v. 26):

> And **again** [*pálin* {3825}; that is, "I am discussing the same subject"] I say unto you, It is **easier** [from *eukopóteros* {2123}, the comparative of *eúkopos* {n.f.} from *eú* {2095}, well, good; and *kópos* {2873}, toil, trouble; "better work or less work"] for a camel to go through **the eye** [from *trúpēma* {5169} from the verb *trupáō* {n.f.}, to perforate, bore a hole] of **a needle** [from *rhaphís* {4476} from *rháptō* {n.f.}, to sew], than for a rich man to enter into the kingdom of God.

From this picture, we hardly have to wait for Jesus' words that with people "it is impossible" (v. 26). God can pull a camel through the eye of a needle, and that's precisely the point. The things that are impossible for humans are possible for God. People cannot save themselves, and, generally speaking, rich persons can pull a camel through the eye of a needle sooner than they can change their tenacious grip on their money. Such hyperboles from Jesus were not intended to promote "real deals." It may be easier for a weightlifter to lift ten thousand pounds than twenty-five thousand pounds, yet no rational person will question the impossibility of his lifting the lighter weight.

[25, 26] The impossibility of a camel passing through the eye of a needle prompted the disciples to ask, "Who then can be saved?" to which Jesus responded,

With men this is **impossible** [from *adúnatos* {102}]; but with God **all things** [*pánta*, the neuter plural of *pás* {3956}] are **possible** [*dunatá*, the neuter plural of *dunatós* {1415}, possible; from the noun *dúnamis* {1411}, power].

It is impossible for us to save ourselves, to change our wills autonomously. Only the Spirit of God who "works in [us] to will" (Phil. 2:13; a.t.) can renew our natural wills, which are not neutral but anti-God (cf. Ps. 110:3; John 1:13; Rom. 9:16). The young ruler's will was bound to his possessions. Without regeneration, he remained in bondage to his riches, which is why he went away. His will was not free to do what Jesus commanded, namely sell his possessions and distribute the cash to the helpless. His natural mind, which Paul says is "enmity against God" (Rom. 8:7), was not free either. And even though he went away grieving, this was nothing more than the sorrow of the world that works death (2 Cor. 7:10). He grieved because he wanted all the benefits of eternal life without a change of heart and without losing his treasured possessions. Had the man asked Jesus for a new attitude toward his riches, He would freely have given it to him.

[27, 28] The salvation impossible for people is possible with God. Peter and the other disciples apparently did what the rich man could not do:

Behold [*idoú* {2400}, "perceive!"], **we left** [from *aphíemi* {863} from *apó* {575}, from; and *híemi* {n.f.}, to send; "to release"] all things and, we followed You. What, therefore, shall be for us? (a.t.; in modern colloquialism, What's in it for us?).

Jesus answered,

Verily [*amén* {281}, truly], I say unto you, that ye which have followed me, in the **regeneration** [from *paliggenesía* {3824}, from *pálin* {3825}, again; and *génesis* {1078}, generation; from the verb *gínomai* {1096}, to become] **when** [*hótan* {3752}] the Son of man shall sit in the throne of his glory, ye also shall sit upon twelve thrones, judging the twelve tribes of Israel.

Paul repeats this promise to the Corinthian church (1 Cor. 6:2, 3), and John gives it to all overcomers (Rev. 3:21).

[29] Jesus continued,

And every one that hath forsaken houses, or brethren, or sisters, or father, or mother, or wife, or children, or lands, for my name's sake, shall receive **an hundredfold** [from *hekatontaplasíon* {1542}, a hundred times], and shall inherit everlasting life.

Jesus stated here and in other places that the hundredfold return on what we sacrifice will be realized not only in our current world but in the new world to come. As Mark puts it:

> But he shall receive an hundredfold now in this time [from *kairós* {2540}], houses, and brethren, and sisters, and mothers, and children, and lands, with persecutions; and in the world to come eternal life. (Mark 10:30, cf. Luke 18:30)

[30] Jesus added a "but" to this teaching:

> But **many** [from *polús* {4183}] that are "**firsts**" [from *prŏtos* {4413}, "first ones"] shall be "**lasts**" [from *éschatos* {2078}, "last ones"]; and the "**lasts**" [*éschatoi*] shall be "**firsts**" [*prŏtoi*]. (a.t.)

The explanation of this statement follows in the parable of the workers in the vineyard of the next chapter. The first verse of the next chapter begins with "for" (*gár* {1063}), connecting the subjects, and verse 16 repeats the teaching of this verse.

CHAPTER

20

Two Categories of Workers
(20:1–16)

Jesus gave this parable to illustrate two categories of workers—those who contract for set wages and those who do not but trust in their manager's just discretion. The parable shows the need for laborers in the kingdom of God and the Lord's reward for those who serve Him.

[1–3] "The kingdom of the heavens" (a.t.) is "likened unto a householder" (a.t.), meaning an earthly king. The distinction is between the Lord God Almighty (Rev. 21:22, *Kúrios, ho Theós, ho Pantokrátōr* [3841]), the King of kings, and a man (*ánthrōpos* [444]), an earthly king. The manager "went out **early** [*háma* {260}] in the morning **to hire** [from *misthóō* {3409}, to hire; *misthós* {3408} is wages, payment for services rendered]."

The Greek word *háma* (260) is an adverb meaning "together" when it speaks of persons. The workers were hired to go together to the vineyard to work.

It is translated "early" in the KJV as an adjunct of the noun *prōí* (4404), morning. However, it is more an adjunct to *misthósasthai*, the aorist middle infinitive of *misthóō*, to hire, found only here and in verse 7 in the middle voice *misthóomai*, to hire for myself. Thus, Jesus, or God incarnate, told this parable of the workers as an illustration that believers should willingly serve Him without a pre-agreed salary.

The first group was hired at 6:00 a.m. and agreed to work for a specific amount of money.

The second group the manager hired went to work without an agreement for a predetermined wage. He had found them "**idle**" (from *argós* [692], inactive during work hours). The word *argós* comes from the negative particle *a* (1) and the noun *érgon* ([2041], work). *Argós* means not gainfully employed, therefore "idle." To this group of people belonged also those found at the third (9 a.m.), sixth (12 noon), ninth (3 p.m.), and eleventh (5 p.m.) hours, the twelve-hour workday beginning at 6 a.m. and ending at 6 p.m.

When those hired at the eleventh hour were questioned why they had not been working, they answered, "Because nobody **hired** [from *misthóō* {3409}] us."

Among other things, this parable teaches that the work of the kingdom requires many laborers and that the Lord will reward those who serve Him. The work in the vineyard—the church's work in the world—remains undone to a great extent because not enough people are willing to labor without first receiving guaranteed, immediate rewards. The work of the kingdom is partly done, but much more remains. It will be done if we who are redeemed understand the spiritual nature of the work involved, the rewards in the world to come, and our responsibilities to God.

The parable also illustrates Jesus' concern for His work, for He said, "The kingdom of heaven is like unto a **man** [from *ánthrōpos* {444}] that is **an householder** [from *oikodespótēs* {3617}, despot of a house or ruler]." "Like" stresses the similarity between a man's concern for the productivity of his vineyard and God's concern for His. The vineyard, which represents the kingdom of God, the church (Matt. 16:18) is His alone. When we are saved, we become partakers of the Master of this vineyard's nature (*phúsis* [5449]; 2 Pet. 1:4). As the Lord Jesus gave Himself sacrificially for the redemption of His church, so should we contribute to building its superstructure (1 Cor. 3:10; Col. 2:7).

[4–7] The first group hired accepted the wage of one dinar ("penny" in the KJV) for a twelve-hour day, but the manager promised the other groups only that he would "pay . . . whatever is **right** [from *díkaios* {1342}, right, just]" (NIV). The workers were to trust the recruiter for his sense of justice—which, in this case, turned out to be unmerited grace.

The twelfth hour was the end of the working day, and that meant the eleventh-hour laborers had only one hour to work. In spite of this, they seized the opportunity and were greatly rewarded for their diligence, as we will see.

[8] The time for payment came at the end of the day.

The master of the vineyard summoned his "**steward**" (from *epítropos* [2012], domestic manager, paymaster) and said to him, "Call the labourers, and give them their hire, beginning from the last unto the first." The last were paid first because the householder graciously rewarded them for their unconditional faith in His justice.

[9] Those who worked for one hour received a proportionately greater compensation rate (i.e., hourly; the compensation amount was the same) than the hired workers who had labored for twelve solid hours. They had been hired in the earliest part of the day and worked the longest and through the hottest hours. Now they complained that it was unfair for those who labored only one hour to receive equal pay.

The natural person hates sovereign grace, which gives more to some wholly apart from merit (Eph. 2:8, 9: "by grace . . . not of yourselves"). These people audaciously demanded equality when some were favored with higher pay for less work.

[10] When the first hired workers came in, Jesus said, "**They supposed** [from *nomízō* {3543}, to assume, presuppose] that they should have received more; and they likewise received every man a dinar" (a.t.). The master treated the workers in this group fairly and compensated them as he had promised.

[11–12] But these first workers become jealous when they were not compensated better than the last workers:

> And when they had received it, **they were murmuring** [*egógguzon*, the imperfect tense of *goggúzō* {1111}, to complain, grumble] against the **goodman of the house** [from *oikodespótēs* {3617}, the master of the house as in v. 1], saying, "These last ones have worked only one hour, and you have made them equal to us, who have borne the burden and burning heat of the day." (a.t.)

The parable deals not only with justifying grace but with work done by those already under grace. The first workers' incessant complaining (reflected in the imperfect tense) was well justified from a human standpoint, but the parable illustrates how far God's standards are above ours.

[13] The word translated "**friend**" in this verse is not from *phílos* (5384), a personal friend having the same interests but is from *hetaíros* (2083), a companion or business associate whose only interest is gain. In English he could be called a leech or a parasite.

The word is used three other times in the New Testament. It referred to the companions ("fellows") of the children playing in the market place (Matt. 11:16); to a guest who came to a wedding feast without the proper garment (Matt. 22:12); and to Judas Iscariot when he approached Jesus in the Garden of Gethsemane (Matt. 26:50).

Jesus called Judas *hetaíre* because he had joined the disciples for his own personal benefit. He was a selfish companion, a leech, a hanger-on who betrayed Jesus for only thirty pieces of silver.

In contrast, the Greek word for a real friend is *philos* (5384). Abraham, for instance, was "the friend [*philos*] of God" (James 2:23). The compound noun "philosophy" comes from *philos*, friend, and *sophós*, wise; thus, a philosopher is a friend of wisdom.

That the *hetaíros* in our parable under study is a worker for a salary is evident in his agreement to the terms of a proffered contract. Now he wanted a personal relationship without the security of a contract and the reward given to others—namely, to trust in the master's justice (see also our exegesis of Matt. 22:1–14).

The lesson concerns the proper response to the terms the master offered. Faith labor for the Lord for as little as one hour without a stipulated contract is well worth it. God's justice is always better than human justice, and His rewards are always superior to any people have to offer. Jesus confirmed this in Mark 10:30: "He shall receive an hundredfold now in this time . . . and in the world to come eternal life."

The emphasis here is not on specific rewards but on the Lord's character. Jesus did not give His disciples the promise of material blessings to motivate them to do more. His doctrine did not teach, "You do this for me, and I will do more for you!" There is nothing wrong with reward for work, but this should not be the primary motivation of our service for our Lord.

By saying, "Friend, **I do** thee no **wrong** [from *adikéō* {91}, to do injustice]," Jesus implied that this is what the murmuring servants thought. They had secured their compensation with a contract while the others depended on only a promise of justice. Surely, they were not in a good position to object.

The parable explains "justice." Jesus had earlier assured His followers that His judgments were both just (from *díkaios* [1342]; John 5:30) and true (from *alēthḗs* [227]; John 8:16). The first group agreed to work for a definite compensation; they did not have to hope in the master's justice. Such is the difference between natural and supernatural faith: The insecure worker secures a promise with a contract, but the hopeful one unconditionally trusts. When the day of rewards comes, the Lord will give the faith worker a hundredfold more than expected.

Note the question at the end of this verse: "Did you not agree with me for a penny?" (a.t.). We should not negotiate with God. What are we that we should bargain with our Creator? Considering what He has done for us, we should be willing to do anything for Him at any cost.

Because God in His grace bestows benefits beyond what we earn, how can anyone who contracts for less than grace complain of injustice? Such profit seekers (from *hetaíros*) are trapped by their own words. The master asked, "**Did** not **you agree** [from *sumphōnéō* {4856}; lit., sound together, from which the English word 'symphony' derives]?"

[14] The master added:

> Take what is yours, and **go** [from *hupágō* {5217}, to go quietly] your way; I will give unto this last even as I gave you. (a.t.)

The Greek text is a bit stronger, literally, "**I determine** [*thélō* {2309}; to wish, desire, associated with the noun *thélēma* {2307}, will, determination] **to give** [from *dídōmi* {1325}]." God calls the "counsel [from *boulé* {1012}] of His will [from *thélēma*]" (a.t.) (Eph. 1:11); a "mystery" (v. 9).

[15] The owner did not let the servant depart without demanding that he first consider another question: "**Or** [*ḗ* {2228}, a disjunctive] is it not **lawful** [from *éxesti* {1832}] for me to do what I will with mine own?" (a.t.).

Jesus called the human eye evil (*ponērós* [4190]) and, parabolically, Himself benevolent (*agathós* [18], good, full of grace). God exceeds even the good He promises (*epaggéllomai* [1861]), and the believer worker can abundantly rest on that.

[16] Jesus concluded the parable:

> **So** [*hoútōs* {3779}, thus, in this manner] the **lasts** [from *éschatos* {2078}] shall be **firsts** [from *prōtoi* {4413}] and the firsts lasts: for **many** [from *polús* {4183}, much, many] be called, but **few** [from *olígos* {3641}] **chosen** [from *eklektós* {1588}]. (a.t.)

The "lasts" are those who heard the call, responded, worked for the remaining hour, and were included among those who heard and went out. The "many" here stands for the workers who were called to service and agreed to a contract, while the "few" represent those who trusted in the justice of their master.

In the Greek, this expression, "for many be called, but few chosen," refers to the hiring of workers at different periods of the same day.

Only here and in Matthew 22:14 did Jesus make this statement, and both verses contain the same two but different Greek adjectives. One is *klētoi* (2822) from *kaléō* (2564), to call, to invite, and to give a name that reveals specifically what each individual will do in his or her life. The other adjective is *eklektoi* (1588) from *eklégomai*, the middle voice of *eklégō* (1586), to choose. God does the choosing, and He decides sovereignly how He will use every believer.

In giving this parable of believers as workers, Jesus wanted to show His disciples how appreciative He is when believers serve even the last hour of their working day without any prearranged committal of reward as the other workers received. But God in love provides salvation to all who accept His gift.

It was an unconscionable accusation of the 6 a.m. workers to accuse the master of injustice for paying the 5 p.m. workers the same amount for a single hour as they were paid for a full twelve hours of work. But God is not unjust for giving a preagreed amount to those who contracted for it.

In the Greek New Testament, God's promises are not called *huposchéseis* (n.f.), as commonly called in Modern Greek, but *epaggelía* (1860), a noun from the verb *epaggéllomai*, to publicly promise, a verb used only regarding God's promises. The result of *epaggéllomai* is *epággelma* (1862), in modern Greek meaning a trade or vocation, a job, but in New Testament Greek it means that which has a sure recompense. However, the surety is never equal to grace that is characterized by superabundance (*perisseúō* [4052]) or "abundant life" (John 10:10). God gives "grace for grace," grace superabundant. "The Word became flesh . . . **full** [*plérēs* {4134}] of grace and truth" (John 1:14; a.t.).

Jesus Again Predicts His Death and Resurrection
(20:17–19; Mark 10:32–34; Luke 18:31–34)

[17, 18] The Lord Jesus privately revealed to His disciples what would soon take place (see Matt. 16:21; 17:22, 23), events that would fulfill prophecies.

The first word in verse 18 is translated "**Behold**" (*idoú* [2400], the impersonal imperative of *eídon* [1492], the aorist of *horáō* [3708], to perceive, calling attention to the extraordinary [see Matt. 3:16]). Here it raised anticipation that a miracle was about to take place. This would not be the death of an ordinary man but rather the atoning death of the Son of man for the sins of the human race. Jesus Christ was God's unique (*monogenés* [3439]) Son who in reality was God (*Theós* [2316]; John 1:1), the Almighty (*Pantokrátōr* [3841]; Rev. 19:15; 21:22); and Lord (*Kúrios* [2962]; 2 Cor. 6:18; Rev. 1:8; 4:8; 11:17; 15:3; 16:7, 14; 19:6; 21:22). He had been prophetically revealed at the transfiguration to the inner circle of three disciples as Peter narrates in 2 Peter 1:16–21. "Behold" called the disciples to watch events unfold beyond human comprehension.

Although "we go up to Jerusalem" (a.t.) included the disciples, Jesus revealed what would happen to Him alone: "We shall all go up to Jerusalem, but the Son of man shall be betrayed." The Lord Jesus knew that what was going to happen to Him would not happen to His disciples at this time. The verb for "**betrayed**" is from *paradídōmi* (3860) from *pará* (3844), a preposition that indicates an extremely close proximity; and *dídōmi* (1325), to give.

The Son of man was giving Himself as a result of the divine will, but Judas was morally responsible for delivering the Lord Jesus to be crucified.

[19] Jesus now revealed something He did not disclose in earlier teachings about His death (Matt. 16:21; 17:22, 23), that is, how He would die: He would be delivered to the Gentiles who would "**crucify**" (from *stauróō* [4717]) Him.

Jesus knew every detail of how He would die before it happened. Through crucifixion, Jesus would fulfill the Father's eternal purpose of redeeming the world through the shedding of His Son's blood. The writer of Hebrews tells us that "without shedding of blood is no remission" (Heb. 9:22).

Jesus predicted He would be delivered into the hands of the "Gentiles" (from *éthnos* [1484], that is, the Romans) who would mock, scourge, and crucify Him, but He would rise again on the third day. Jesus also knew that Judas would betray Him to the Jews (see John 6:64) and that the Jewish Sanhedrin would condemn Him. Because the Jewish leaders could not execute Him according to Roman law, they would deliver Him to Pilate.

Following this, however, the Triune God would frustrate their purposes by raising Jesus from the dead.

Greatness Through Suffering and Service
(20:20–28; Mark 10:35–45)

[20, 21] Salome was the mother of James and John, the two sons of Zebedee (who was probably dead by now). They were two of the three who comprised the inner circle the Lord Jesus chose from among the Twelve (Peter was the third).

Three events portray the exclusive treatment accorded these disciples: Jesus allowed only these three to enter the room in which He raised Jairus' daughter from the dead (Mark 5:37); they alone observed the transfiguration (Matt. 17:1); and Jesus took just these three to be close to Him when He prayed in the Garden of Gethsemane (Matt. 26:37).

Two of these three events had already occurred at this point, prompting Salome to ask that Jesus would give her sons positions of honor and rulership in His kingdom. She and her sons had misunderstood His words concerning the invisible, spiritual kingdom to rule the hearts of believers (Luke 17:20, 21) long before the physical Second Coming. Since Salome had mistakenly thought that Jesus was about to establish His visible kingdom, her request was pertinent.

Matthew adds Salome's prostrating (from *proskunéō* [4352], to fall prostrate and kiss like a dog in absolute obeisance) herself before Jesus. Her submission to the Lord Jesus was absolute.

Jesus did not need to ask Salome what she wanted, but He wanted to hear her confession and that of her two sons (Mark 10:35, 36). In the expression, "What do you desire?" (a.t.), Jesus used the present tense of *thélō* (2309), generally to will. However, since Jesus determines a gift and the woman was merely asking for it, it is clear that *thélō* here is intentionally synonymous with *boúlomai* (1014), to desire. Jesus would hardly ask, What are you determining?

What she and her sons wanted (v. 21; Mark 10:37, respectively) was presumably something for nothing: "Grant that these my two sons may sit, the one on thy right hand, and the other on the left, in thy kingdom."

[22, 23] Note Jesus' reply:

> Ye **know** [to know intuitively; from *eídon*, the aorist of *horáō* {3708}, to see and perceive with emphasis on perception] not what **ye ask** [from *aitéō* {154}, to request from a superior]. **Are ye able** [from *dúnamai* {1410}, to be able by divine enablement in contrast to *ischúō* {2480}, to be able by human strength] **to drink** [*pínein*, the aorist active infinitive of *pínō* {4095}; the aorist indicates a single death, martyrdom, in thankfulness for His death] of the cup that **I shall** [*méllō* {3195}, "to be about to"] **drink** [*pínein*, the present active infinitive of *pínō*, to drink] of . . . ?

A few Greek manuscripts omit the last phrase concerning being baptized with the same baptism that Jesus would be baptized with. Most modern Greek editions and English versions omit it here also, assuming it is an assimilation from Mark 10:38. But since it is found in the overwhelming majority of both early and late Greek manuscripts of Matthew and since Mark records it as part of this conversation, we feel it belongs here, too.

In effect, Jesus was saying, You do not understand the situation, and this is the reason your request is such as it is. Consider what I will pass through from grace to glory. The cross stands before Me; I must first shed My blood, and you must be reminded of the "cross before the crown." Baptism will remind you of the passage from death to life in the Holy Spirit (John 1:33; Rom. 6:3; 1 Cor. 11:26; Eph. 4:5) and of the potential sufferings you face as you follow Me.

Jesus was willing and ready to endure this intense suffering to gain our salvation. Salome, James, and John also expressed a willingness, but they were unaware of future events. Indeed, James and John did ultimately become martyrs for Christ. God does not reveal all His truth at once. His revelation to us is progressive. We do not know when He is coming back as potentate (1 Tim. 6:15, 16), but we know for certain that He will return because He promised to do so (John 14:3).

Salome, James, and John needed patience, as we do today. Paul spoke about our need to serve sacrificially before glorification: "But in all things approving ourselves as the ministers [from *diákonos* {1249}, the same word used in vv. 26, 28 from *diakonéō* {1247}; 23:11] of God, in much patience, in afflictions, in necessities, in distresses, in stripes" (2 Cor. 6:4, 5; see also Rom. 8:17).

Jesus answered Salome and her sons politely while retaining the divine mystery of future exaltation. This answer was similar to the householder's when some complained he rewarded workers who had worked unequal hours with the same pay: "Is it not lawful for me to do what I will with mine own?" Similarly, now Jesus told this mother and her two sons to leave the seating in eternity to God.

Notice Jesus' comment in verse 23: "But to sit on my right hand, and on my left, is not mine to give, but it shall be given to them for whom it is prepared of my Father." Jesus disowned an autonomous, historic giving that was detached from the Father's eternal plan. In other words, it is not Mine alone (autonomy) to give now (historically) because this position "**has [already] been prepared** [from *hetoimázō* {2090}] by My Father" (i.e., in eternity; a.t.). And Jesus did not want to reveal what rewards would be distributed to whom. Can you imagine the arrogance that would well up in persons who knew the special places God had for them in His future kingdom?

The Father, the Word (John 1:1), and the Spirit are one God, one omniscience. Consequently, God, the Word who became flesh (John 1:1, 14) in the Person of Jesus Christ, prepared all seats in the kingdom of heaven. The same triune God prepared the eternal fire for the devil and his angels (Matt. 25:41).

[24] The spiritual imperfection of the disciples became clear:

> And when the ten heard it, they were **moved with indignation** [from *aganaktéō* {23} from *ágan* {n.f.}, very much; and *áchthos* {n.f.}, pain, grief; to be moved to emotional outburst, the first time this verb is used in the NT] against the two brethren.

Indignation is not necessarily sin, since it is sometimes a just response to injustice. The Lord Jesus Himself became indignant at times (Mark 10:14), and rightly so, but some of His disciples became indignant over actions that were not unjust, as when Mary poured expensive ointment over Jesus' head in Bethany (Mark 14:4).

Here, the cause of the indignation was no more than jealousy or covetousness. As the personification of divine kindness on earth, Jesus took advantage of this situation to instruct His disciples about indignation. Of course, we all can become irritated.

[25, 26] Note how the Lord Jesus handled the situation:

> **Ye know** [from *oídaleídō* {1492}, to intuitively know, from *eídon*, the aorist of *horáō* {3708} used as a present tense, to perceive] that the **princes** [from

árchōn {758}, ruler] of the **Gentiles** [from *éthnos* {1484}, any nation except Israel] **exercise dominion over** [from *katakurieúō* {2634}, to exercise lordship, to overpower] them, and they that are **great** [from *mégas* {3173}] **exercise authority** [from *katexousiázō* {2715} from *katá* {2596}, thoroughly, or *kátō* {2736}, down; and *exousiázō* {1850}, to control, to suppress] upon them.

The Lord Jesus now reassured the disciples who became jealous over Salome and her sons asking Him for superior positions in the kingdom of God. Rank, He said, will be established on a basis other than a request:

> But it shall not be **so** [*hoútōs* {3779}, so, thus] among you [disciples]: but whoever **will** [from *thélō* {2309}, to wish, desire] be great among you, let him become your **minister** [*diákonos* {1249}, deacon, servant; the verb *diakonéō* occurs twice in v. 28]. (a.t.)

[27] The Lord Jesus now further defined a "minister" as a "**servant**" (*doúlos* [1401], servant, slave):

> . . . and whosoever **will** [from *thélō* {2309}, to wish, desire] be **chief** [*prōtos* {4413}, first in rank] among you, let him be your **servant** [*doúlos* {1401}, servant, slave].

In other words, the path to exaltation is in direct opposition to that of the world. Exaltation is achieved by humility, not pride—by service, not rule. Distinction is earned by servicing the needs of others. Therefore, Jesus told Salome and her sons that the only way to ascend is to first descend as the Son of God did in His incarnation, "taking the form of a servant" (a.t.; Phil. 2:7).

[28] Thus, Jesus concluded:

> **Even as** [*hōsper* {5618} from *hōs* {5613}, in the manner of; and *per* {4007}, a particle indicating assurance and emphasis] the Son of man did not **come** [*élthe*, the aorist tense of *érchomai* {2064}, to come] **to be ministered unto** [from *diakonéō* {1247}, to serve, wait on] but **to minister** [also from *diakonéō*] and to give His life a **ransom** [*lútron* {3083}] for many. (a.t.)

The aorist tense refers to the incarnation of the Word, which was God (John 1:1) become flesh. The Word became sinless man (Heb. 4:15) to make atonement for sin and reconcile people to God. That purpose was shared by the Father and the Holy Spirit.

Jesus came not only to minister, but also to shed His blood to obtain remission (*áphesis* [859], forgiveness; Heb. 9:22), to put sins away as a cancellation (*athétēsis* [115] from *athetéō* [114], to put away, from the negative particle *a* [1] and *títhēmi* [5087] to put, place; Heb. 9:26) so people could acquire new natures. Jesus came humbly the first time in grace and truth (John 1:17), but one day He will return in physical power (see 1 Tim. 6:15, 16) and justice.

That will be a day of judgment, an accounting of all humanity—believers and unbelievers. Books will be opened—the Book of Life (Phil. 4:3; Rev. 3:5; 20:15) and a book of works (Rev. 20:12).

Delusioned about the future, Salome had asked Jesus to favor her children with the two highest possible ranks in His coming kingdom (v. 21). But Jesus responded that the subjects for these exalted positions had already been predetermined: "for whom it has been prepared by My Father" (v. 23; a.t.). The subjects may or may not be her sons, but no amount of special pleading on her or their part would alter the Father's planned connection between the "whom" and the "it." She and her sons, as all of us in the end, must acquiesce to God's wise but hidden plan. Jesus was not obligated to reveal whom He unconditionally (i.e., graciously) favored. This was a perfect rebuke to a presumptuous request based on presumed merit, a lesson for us all. He did, however, reveal a simple principle that we should heed: "Whosoever exalts himself will be humiliated" (Luke 14:11; a.t., cf. 18:14).

The works of both believers and unbelievers can be good and bad (2 Cor. 5:10). Judgment will be more tolerable (*anektóteron* [414]; Matt. 10:15; 11:22, 24; Luke 10:12, 14) for some unbelievers than for others. Some works are more heinous than others—for instance, the crimes of notorious criminals like Herod, Nero, and Hitler.

Another word to be noted in this verse is the word translated "**ransom**" (*lútron* [3083]; used only here and in Mark 10:45). The noun *lútron* derives from *lúō* (3089), to loose. It primarily denotes the release of captives from their chains. The spiritual analogy is release from the captivity (bondage) of sin (see Sept.: Ex. 30:12; Lev. 25:24, 51; Num. 35:31, 32). This is accomplished by the blood of Jesus Christ shed at Calvary as payment for the sins of all people, especially for the sins of believers (1 Tim. 4:10).

Two additional words to consider form the expression "**for** [*antí* {473}, in the place of] **many** [from *polús* {4183}, much many]." In 1 Timothy 2:6 the apostle Paul said, "Who [Jesus Christ] gave himself a ransom [*antílutron* {487}, ransom, from *antí* and *lútron*] for all." But not all who heard the gospel received (believed) it. Even among the Twelve Apostles, one, Judas, rejected the Lord and His message. Jesus called Judas "the son of perdition," as God foreknew he would be (John 17:12).

Thus it is with all who choose not to believe, in spite of the fact that "the living God . . . is the Savior of all men, especially [*málista* {3122}; very, particularly, chiefly, most of all] of believers [from *pistós* {4103}, faithful, the adjective associated with the verb *pisteúō* {4100}, to believe]" (1 Tim. 4:10; a.t.). The believer acquires forgiveness, remission (*áphesis* [859]; Heb. 9:22), and a new divine nature (2 Pet. 1:4) to defeat (Rom. 8:37) sin.

First John 2:2 confirms 1 Timothy 2:6 and 4:10 saying that Jesus Christ "is the propitiation [*hilasmós* {2434}, the atonement] for our sins: and not for ours only, but also for the sins of the whole world."

Jesus Heals Two Blind Men
(20:29–34; Mark 10:46–52; Luke 18:35–43)

Jesus performed His last recorded miracle as He traveled through Jericho for the last time in His earthly ministry as God incarnate.

[29] The word translated "departed" is from *ekporeúomai* (1607), a compound verb derived from *ek* (1537), out of; and *poreúomai* (4198), to march openly, which is in contrast to *hupágō* (5217) from *hupó* (5259), denoting stealth; and *ágō* (71), to lead, to drive with the intent of inducing. Jesus was not led stealthily and fearfully to Jerusalem for execution but rather, He marched publicly and courageously toward the fulfillment of the glorious, atoning death for which He came into the world.

We read here that "a great multitude **followed** [from *akolouthéō* {190}, to follow] him." (Read our exegesis of the verb *akolouthéō* in Matt. 4:25 to better understand the reason why this crowd followed Jesus.)

[30] Matthew records two blind men sitting by the roadside while Mark 10:46 (MT) and Luke 18:38 mention only one. This is not contradictory. Matthew says they both became aware that Jesus **was passing by,** and Mark and Luke inform us that one of them was continually begging (from *prosaitéō* [4319] from *prós* [4314], in addition to; and *aitéō* [154], to beg).

The Mark narration gives us the name of one of the beggars—Bartimaeus, the son of Timaeus. He cried out, saying, "Thou son of David, have mercy on me" (Mark 10:47). They apparently had heard that wherever Jesus went He showed compassion, as indeed He did on this occasion.

[31–34] The crowd was so annoyed by these noisy blind men that they told them to keep quiet. "But they cried the more, saying, Have mercy on us, O Lord, thou son of David." Jesus, however,

> **had compassion** [from *splagchnízomai* {4697}] on them, and touched [from *háptomai* {680}] their eyes: and **immediately** [*euthéos* {2112}, at once] their eyes **received sight** [from *anablépō* {308}, to see again], and they followed him.

The verb *anablépō* is also used in Mark 10:51 in Bartimaeus' answer when Jesus asked him, "What wilt thou that I should do unto thee?" Bartimaeus' answer implied that he previously had the ability to see. Obviously, he believed that Jesus had the miraculous power to restore his sight.

The miracle of giving sight to these two blind men was a demonstration of Christ's upcoming power to enable sinners who believe in God to regain what sin had caused them to lose. The Lord Jesus knew the purpose for which He became a sinless man and His innate power that He would soon use to save those who believed in Him (Col. 1:20; 1 Tim. 4:10; Heb. 9:14-20). Salvation was implicit in every one of His benevolent acts.

In Luke 4:18, the noun *anáblepsis* (309) is used (the only time in NT) to describe one aspect of the Lord's salvation of His people from their sins (see Isa. 61:1, 2). *Anáblepsis* is the noun associated with the verb *anablépo*, to see again. Just as these blind men had their eyesight restored, so the life of God that was lost in the Garden of Eden would be restored to believers.

"And **they followed** [from *akolouthéo* {190}, to follow] him." I believe "follow" here included the idea of believing as well as physically following (see our exegesis of the verb *akolouthéo* in Matt. 4:25). Jesus gave these two men spiritual sight in addition to restoring their physical eyesight.

This shows up clearly in Mark's and Luke's narrations (Mark 10:52; Luke 18:42, 43). Jesus said to the former blind man, Bartimaeus, "Go thy way; thy faith hath made thee whole" (Mark 10:52). His faith in Jesus' power caused his healing. The English translation, "made thee whole," is from the perfect tense of *sózo*, equivalent to "it [i.e., your faith] has saved you." The perfect tense means that the blind man believed in the Lord Jesus before his physical eyesight was restored.

The additional materials in Mark's and Luke's stories confirm that the salvation of the two blind men was first spiritual and then physical. The verb *sózo* is frequently associated with deliverance from disease or demon possession (Matt. 9:21, 22; Mark 3:4; 5:23, 28, 34; 6:56; 10:52; Luke 6:9; 8:36, 48, 50; 17:19; 18:42). In fifteen instances, the verb refers to physical life (Matt. 8:25; 14:30; 16:25; 27:40, 42, 49; Mark 8:35; 15:30, 31; Luke 9:24, 56; 23:35, 37, 39; John 12:27), and in the remaining twenty, to spiritual salvation (Matt. 1:21; 10:22; 19:25; 24:13, 22; Mark 8:35; 10:26; 13:20; 16:16; Luke 7:50; 8:12; 9:24; 13:23; 18:26; 19:10; John 3:17; 5:34; 10:9; 12:47). The blind men in Jericho were saved from both sin and blindness. In fact, the original sin of humankind causes all physical affliction (see the author's book, *Sickness Why, Healing How?*).

CHAPTER

21

Jesus Enters Jerusalem Triumphantly
(21:1–11; Mark 11:1–10; Luke 19:28–38; John 12:12–19)

This chapter and the two following relate events in Jesus' life during the week before His crucifixion, His last week on earth as the incarnate God. He had not come all the way to Jerusalem to be acclaimed king but to suffer rejection and die.

It was now nearing the Feast of the "**Passover**" (*páscha* [3957], the Greek transliteration of the Hebrew *pesaḥ* [6453, OT], lit. a leaping over), the great festival that commemorated the Jew's salvation during "the Lord's passover" (Ex. 12:11, cf. Lev. 23:5; Num. 9:2–6). Some historians estimate that two-and-a-half-million people with a quarter-of-a-million lambs—one to be sacrificed for every ten people—flocked into the city for this momentous occasion.

[1] After Jesus and His disciples had passed through the regions of Galilee and Samaria, the first village they came to was "**Bethphage**" (967). This compound name was derived from the Hebrew words for "house" (*bayith* [1004, OT]) and "unripe or green figs" (*pag* [6291, OT]), and so, "house of unripe figs." Bethphage was located near Bethany, about a mile and a half east of Jerusalem and the "**mount of Olives**" (Mark 11:1; Luke 19:29).

Jesus would accomplish many things in Bethany. He would raise Lazarus from the dead (John 11), visit the house of Simon (Matt. 26:6; Mark 14:3) whom He may have cured of leprosy, and would be anointed for burial. He was well known among the people there.

[2] Jesus sent two (unidentified) disciples ahead to prepare for His entrance into Jerusalem, telling them,

> Go into the village **before** [*apénanti* {561}, in front of] you, and **immediately** [*euthéos* {2112}, immediately, at once] **you will find** [*heurésete*, the future

tense of *heurískō* {2147}] an ass **tied** [from *déō* {1210}, to bind], and a colt with her; loose them and bring them to Me. (a.t.)

Note the emphatic "you will find," not "you may find." Had they failed to find a tied donkey, their faith in Jesus would have been greatly shaken. Jesus' directive was based neither on conjecture nor on prior arrangement but on supernatural foreknowledge. Although their faith in Christ's deity was intensified by this experience, the unmistakable sign (*sēmeíon* [4592] as given in Matt. 16:4), the resurrection, was yet to come.

Jesus further established His divine authority by commanding, "**Loose** [from *lúō* {3089}, to loose] them, and bring them unto me." From a human standpoint, this would be stealing. But Jesus declared His assurance that the owner would be glad to release the animals for His use, as we find in the next verse.

[3] Jesus anticipated some challenge:

> And if any man say ought unto you, ye shall say, The Lord hath **need** [from *chreía* {5532}] of them; and **straightway** [*euthéōs* {2112}, immediately] he will send them.

The "**need**" of course carried the idea of utility more than dependence. Jesus could easily have walked to Jerusalem, but God had sovereignly planned the use of these particular animals (Zech. 9:9).

In Luke 19:33 alone we read that the owners did in fact challenge the disciples: "Why loose ye the colt?" Once the disciples repeated what Jesus had told them to say, however, the owners immediately sent "them"—the donkey, the main subject (in the foreground) and her colt (in the background), thus the shift in object between "them" (i.e., the mother and colt; v. 3) and "him"; Luke 19:34, 35.

[4] This event was not prompted by impulse. Rather,

> All this **occurred** [*gégonen*, the perfect tense of *gínomai* {1096}, to become, take place] that [*hína* {2443}, in order that] **it might be fulfilled** [from *plēróō* {4137}] which **was spoken** [*rhēthén*, the aorist passive participle of *eréō* {2046}, to enunciate, speak specifically] **through** [*diá* {1223}, through the agency of] the prophet. (a.t.)

The perfect tense of "**occurred**" implies that the Father Himself was fulfilling the prophecy in accord with the general truth, "I have spoken it, I will also bring it to pass; I have purposed it, I will also do it" (Isa. 46:11; see also Gen. 41:32; 2 Kgs. 19:25; Isa. 37:26). God irresistibly brings to pass His prophecies: "For the LORD of hosts hath purposed, and who shall disannul it? and his hand is stretched out, and who shall turn it back?" (Isa. 14:27).

The "prophet" who "spoke" was Zechariah:

> Rejoice greatly, O daughter of Zion; shout, O daughter of Jerusalem: behold, thy King cometh unto thee: he is just, and having salvation; lowly, and riding upon an ass, and upon a colt the foal of an ass. (Zech. 9:9)

Isaiah also, with less detail, predicted this event (Isa. 62:11). The triune God ultimately spoke these prophecies, which accounts for the frequent "thus saith the Lord" in the Old Testament, but He spoke them "**through**" (*diá*) the human voices of His prophets.

[**5**] Matthew quotes only the pertinent sections of the Old Testament prophecies:

> **Tell ye** [*eípate*, the aorist imperative of *légō* {3004}, to intelligently declare] the **daughter** [from *thugátēr* {2364}] of Sion, **Behold** [*idoú* {2400}, the imperative of *eídon* {1492}, the aorist of *horáō* {3708}, to perceive, calling attention to the extraordinary; see Matt. 3:16], thy King **cometh** [from *érchomai* {2064}, to come] unto thee, **meek** [*praús* {4239}, humble, controlled, not given to premature anger; cf. Matt. 5:5 and the author's book, *The Beatitudes*], and **sitting upon** [*epibebēkós*, from *epibaínō* {1910}, to ride upon] an **ass** [from *ónos* {3688}, a donkey], and a **colt** [from *pólos* {4454}, a young ass] the **foal** [from *huiós* {5207}, son, offspring] of an **ass** [from *hupozúgion* {5268}, an adult ass, a domesticated animal placed under a yoke, cf. John 12:14–16; 2 Pet. 2:16].

The message the prophet Zechariah conveys in this verse is, first of all, that Jesus Christ is the coming King of Israel. Mount Zion is naturally associated with Jerusalem because it is the original site of Jerusalem. **Zion** (*ṣiyyôn* [OT 6726]), which derives from one of two roots— *ṣiyôn* (6724, OT) meaning desert, solitary place; or *ṣiyyûn* (6725, OT) meaning a guiding pillar—occurs 153 times in the Old Testament and the equivalent "Sion" seven times in the New, this being the first. In the Old Testament, Zion is identified as "the city of David" (2 Sam. 5:7; 1 Kgs. 8:1; 1 Chr. 11:5; 2 Chr. 5:2), "the city of the great King" (Ps. 48:2), "the city of the LORD" (Isa. 60:14; cf. Heb. 12:22, "the heavenly Jerusalem"), and the place where God does His "good pleasure" (Ps. 51:18). In the new Testament, the church, the bride of Christ, is identified as the New Jerusalem (Rev. 21:2).

The verb "**behold**" (*idoú*) is a dramatic call to pay attention to what God is about to do, here to highlight the personal coming of the Lord to the "daughter of Sion" (cf. Rev. 12:17: "the remnant of her seed, which keep the commandments of God, and have the testimony of Jesus Christ"), that is, Jewish and Gentile believers. The fulfillment of Zechariah's prophecy of some six hundred years before was about to unfold, but riding on the back of a donkey was not the messianic entrance the Jews expected. They were waiting for the conquering King of Zechariah's later prophecy to appear:

> Then shall the LORD go forth, and fight against those nations, as when he fought in the day of battle. And his feet shall stand in that day upon the mount of Olives, which is before Jerusalem on the east, and the mount of Olives shall cleave in the midst thereof toward the east and toward the west, and there shall be a very great valley; and half of the mountain shall remove toward the north, and half of it toward the south. (Zech. 14:3, 4)

Even though, on entering Jerusalem, people hailed Jesus as the king of Israel, this was only a prophetic entrance foreshadowing His coming in victory. Jesus Himself would predict that "when the Son of man **cometh** [from *érchomai* {2064}, to come] in His glory, . . . then He will sit upon the throne of His glory" (Matt. 25:31; a.t.). This entry into Jerusalem, by contrast, marked His humiliation, and the Pharisees, so far removed from humility, could not tolerate it. But this humble entry had been prophesied just as the triumphal entry still ahead.

The choice of a donkey was prophetically typological, anteceding and pointing to the cross. The donkey is a burden carrier. The verb that expresses the bearing of weakness and sickness in Greek is *bastázō* (941), used in Romans 15:1 and Galatians 5:10. We are commanded in Galatians 6:2 to bear one another's burdens (from *báros* [922]). Jesus Christ entered Jerusalem this time, specifically to carry the burden of sin so we might be made righteous in Him (2 Cor. 5:21). The donkey, then, was a symbol of the burdens Jesus carried to the cross. While Matthew 21:7 is ambiguous regarding who sat on what, Luke 19:30 adds the clear and significant detail that Jesus sat on the donkey "whereon yet never man [*oudeís* {3762}, 'not even one'] sat," a fitting choice for Jesus Christ, the "only One of His kind" (John 1:18; a.t.). The donkey had never been defiled by contact with a sinner; rather, like the "body You prepared Me" (Heb. 10:5; a.t.), God had created and retained this donkey as holy, separate, and set apart for this very purpose.

The Messiah is prophetically connected with the idea of "**lowly**" (*praús* [4239], a synonym of *práos* [4235], meek, gentle, mild), the King James' rendering of the Hebrew in Zechariah 9:9. Typically, a king rode on a horse or horse-drawn chariot to symbolize power and victory. However, at this significant juncture in history, Jesus the King came meekly, gently, with salvation, as Isaiah 62:11 prophesied nearly seven hundred years before: "Behold, thy salvation cometh; behold, his reward is with him, and his work before him." The "work before him" was the salvation accomplished through the shedding of His blood (Heb. 9:22).

When Christ returns, He will not be lowly but high and lifted up. As "Deliverer," He will appropriately sit on a white horse (*híppos* [2462]; Rev. 19:11), a symbol of victory, to conquer Zion's (Jerusalem's) enemies and save it from its own sin. Paul quotes Isaiah 59:20, 21: "And so all Israel shall be saved: as it is written, There shall come out of Zion the Deliverer, and He shall turn away ungodliness from Jacob" (Rom. 11:26; a.t.).

[6] In response to Jesus' instructions,

> The disciples, having gone, did **as** [*kathṓs* {2531} from *katá* {2596}, according to; and *hōs* {5613}, as, according as, i.e., following the instructions] Jesus commanded them. (a.t.)

[7] Thus, by divine arrangement,

> **They brought** [from *ágō* {71}, to lead] the donkey and the colt and put on them their **clothes** [from *himátion* {2440}, outer garment], and **they set** [from *epikathízō* {1940}, to set on; from *epí*, on; and *kathízō* {2523}, to cause to sit] [Jesus] on them [the clothes]. (a.t.)

[8] The crowd was not unanimous in welcoming Jesus into Jerusalem; however,

> . . . the **majority** [*pleístos* {4118}, the greatest number], on their way, spread their outer garments [from *himátion*]; **others** [from *állos* {243}, others of the same disposition, i.e., those favoring Jesus] **were cutting down** [*ékopton*, the imperfect tense of *kóptō* {2875}, to cut off or down; the imperfect stresses the duration] branches from the trees and **were spreading** [*estrṓnnuon*, the imperfect tense of *strṓnnumi* {4766}, to strew, spread] them in the way. (a.t.)

John tells us in John 12:13 that these were palm branches flat enough to prevent blocking the path.

[9] The procession into Jerusalem was led by crowds of parading people:

> And the multitudes that **went before** [from *proágō* {4254}, to go before], and **that followed** [from *akoloutheō* {190}, to follow, go after], **cried** [from *krázō* {2896}, to shout loudly], **saying** [from *légō* {3004}, to intelligently speak], Hosanna to the son of David.

"**Hosanna**" (*hōsanná* [5614]), a transliteration of the Hebrew term meaning *Save, we pray Thee!*, was a common acclamation (Ps. 118:25; John 12:13). It evidences the fact that the Jews expected their king to redeem them from Gentile dominion. In His own time (*kairós* [2540], season; see Luke 13:35; 21:24; Rom. 11:26), of course, Jesus will reenter Jerusalem as King.

These people applauded the royal lineage of their Messiah from king David: "son of David" (1055–1015 B.C.; see 1 Kgs. 8:25), a title often applied to Jesus in recognition that He was the Messiah of Israel (Matt. 1:1, 20; 9:27; 12:23; 15:22; 20:30, 31; 22:42; Mark 10:47, 48).

"**Blessed**" translates *eulogēménos*, the perfect passive participle of *eulogéō* (2127) meaning to speak well (to), bless; from *eú* (2095), well or good; and *légō*, to speak. The perfect tense covers Jesus' entire life: He was blessed from womb to tomb and beyond. The corresponding noun, *Eulogētós* (2128), "the blessed One," may be viewed as the One whom people bless or praise (predicated to the Father in Mark 14:61; Luke 1:68; Rom. 1:25; 2 Cor. 1:3; 11:31; Eph. 1:3; 1 Pet. 1:3, and to the Son of God in Rom. 9:5).

It is intriguing that the participle *eulogēménos* is, both here and elsewhere (see Matt. 23:39; Mark 11:9; Luke 19:38; John 12:13), followed by "**the coming One** [*ho erchómenos*, the present participle of *érchomai* {2064}, I am coming]." The present participle characterizes Christ's nature as "the coming One" across the whole of history. In Luke 19:38, He is designated "the coming One, the **King** [*basileús* {935}; a.t.]."

The expression, "in the **name** [from *ónoma* {3686}] of the Lord," could be read as a genitive of apposition, "in the name which is Yahweh." We read as early as Genesis 4:26 that the sons of Seth began to "call upon the name of Yahweh," the tetragrammaton (four Hebrew consonants). With respect to this "name," Jesus said, "I am come in my Father's name, and ye receive me not: if another shall come in his own name, him ye will receive" (John 5:43; see 12:28). One of the names of the holy Trinity is Yahweh or Jehovah.

"Hosanna in the **highests** [*hupsístois*, the dative *plural* of *húpsistos* {5310}]" (a.t.) is an interesting phrase. The adjective may reflect the plural majesty of God (*ᵉlōhíym* [430, OT], God; Deut. 6:4) or possibly the personified heavens or the highest archangels that are being called on to shout "Hosanna" to the Lord.

[10, 11] The commotion of this parade caught the attention of the citizens. As Jesus entered, the "whole city" was stirred, and the people asked, "Who is this?" The crowds that led the procession answered, "This is Jesus the prophet of Nazareth of Galilee."

Jerusalem was "**shaken**" (from *seíō* [4579], to shake), as if an earthquake had occurred. Later, when Jesus was crucified in Jerusalem, physical earthquakes actually did accompany His death (Matt. 27:54) and also His resurrection (Matt. 28:2).

As there was an earthquake at Jesus' crucifixion and resurrection, so there will be earthquakes when the Son of man returns in glory, for "the powers of the heavens shall be shaken" (Matt. 24:29; cf. Mark 13:25; Luke 21:11). This coming will be accompanied by cosmic disturbances described in Matthew

24:29–31; Revelation 6:12–14; 8:5; 11:13, 19; 16:18, and Hebrews 12:26: "Whose voice then shook the earth: but now he hath promised, saying, Yet once more I shake not the earth only, but also heaven."

Jesus Purifies the Temple
(21:12–17; Mark 11:15–17; Luke 19:45–48; John 2:13–25)

Although a few commentators identify this cleansing of the temple with the one in John 2:13–16, many others believe that the event in John occurred much earlier in Jesus' ministry. If so, this event, then, showed the Jews' apostate retreat to commercialism following Christ's first prophetic warning to remove trade from His Father's house of prayer. At two Passovers, that is, one at the beginning and one at the end of His ministry, Jesus sanctified the temple of God. How ironic that the Jews sank to such a low level even on the day of the feast that commemorated their salvation from Egypt. Trade in the temple marked their return to the slavery of sin, metaphorically to Egypt. Perhaps this is why John calls Jerusalem, "the great city, which spiritually is called Sodom and Egypt, where also our Lord was crucified" (Rev. 11:8).

[12] There are two words for "**temple**." One is *naós* (3485), the sanctuary, including both the Holy Place where the priests entered daily to minister at the table of showbread, the sacred lampstand, and the altar of incense. Here also was the Holy of Holies where the high priest met with God once a year on the Day of Atonement. Then the *hierón* (2411), the whole temple complex, included the outer courts where the people could gather.

Jesus entered the *hierón*: "Jesus **went** [from *eisérchomai* {1525}, to enter] into the **temple** [*hierón*] of **God** [from *Theós* {2316}]" (a.t.). Although at His ascension into heaven, Jesus, "with His own blood . . . entered once for all into the holy places [*hágia* the neuter plural of *hágion* {40}], having obtained eternal redemption for us" (Heb. 9:12; a.t.), the writer of Hebrews never used the term *naós*. This is probably because Jesus referred to His own body as the *naós* (John 2:19).

Jesus was now in the court of the Gentiles where business transactions, including currency exchange, were made. Here, we read,

> **He cast out** [from *ekbállō* {1544} from *ek* {1537}, out of; and *bállō* {906}, to throw or cast] all of them that sold and bought in the temple and **over-turned** [from *katastréphō* {2690} from *katá* {2596}, down; and *stréphō* {4762},

to turn] the tables of the **money changers** [from *kollubistḗs* {2855} from *kól-lubos* {n.f.}, a small coin] and the seats of those who sold **doves** [from *peristerá* {4058}; an offering of two young doves was made by the poor, according to Luke 2:24, cf. Lev. 5:7; 14:22]. (a.t.)

This is a small prophetic caption of the day when the Lord will much more violently "gather out of his kingdom all things that offend" (Matt. 13:41). Such things do not belong in God's presence: "Your eyes are too pure to approve evil, and You cannot look on wickedness with favor" (Hab. 1:13; a.t.).

In John's narrative of the first temple cleansing, Jesus drove sheep and oxen out of it but not doves and pigeons. He overturned only the seats of those selling these commodities. The sheep and oxen could be captured again, but had the birds been released, they would have flown away. We never read in the Scriptures that Jesus wasted anything; on the contrary, He was always careful that nothing was wasted (see John 6:12).

[13] As Jesus observed these commercial transactions occurring, His spirit was aroused, and He said,

> **It is written** [*gégraptai*, the perfect passive indicative third person singular of *gráphō* {1125}, to write; lit. "it has been written"; see Isa. 56:7], My **house** [*oíkos* {3624}] **shall be called** [from *kaléō* {2564}, to call] the house of prayer; but you have made it a **den** [*spḗlaion* {4693}, a cavern or cave, from which we get the English verb "spelunking"] for **open robbers** [from *lēstḗs* {3027}, one who steals openly]. (a.t.).

Mark's fuller text reads, "My house shall be called among all the nations the house of prayer" (Mark 11:17; a.t.). God chose the nation of Israel: "You only have I known among all the nations" (Amos 3:2; a.t.), but He also intended His people to preach His message to the world:

> It is a light thing that thou shouldest be my servant to raise up the tribes of Jacob, and to restore the preserved of Israel: I will also give thee for a light to the Gentiles, that thou mayest be my salvation unto the end of the earth. (Isa. 49:6)

This is why the offense of publicly making money in the temple of God was so great. Instead of using the temple to pray for the evangelization of both Jews and Gentiles, entrepreneurs had taken advantage of religious necessities for business opportunities. As far back as the days of Jeremiah, God's house was called "a **den** for open robbers" (a.t.; Jer. 7:11, where the same Greek words are found in the Septuagint). These people were indeed making God's house a covert place for those who robbed openly.

The merchants were unscrupulous in their dealings with worshipers. For example, if a worshiper brought an animal for sacrifice, the priests in charge did not usually approve it. Instead, they required him to buy a religiously approved animal from the merchants at an inflated price.

Similarly, holy (undefiled) currency needed to purchase these animals and pay temple taxes was equally inflated. As Passover approached, every Jew had to pay a temple tax of one-half shekel. Prior to this, the tax was collected at other places, but after a certain time, it could only be paid in the temple itself with coins of high-grade silver. This gave rise to an exchange market. The temple currency was available only from money changers at unreasonable exchange rates—a religious racket! To fulfill the Law of Moses, people were forced to submit to these exploitative practices.

[14] Handicapped people, such as the "blind and the lame" frequented the temple, especially the Court of the Gentiles (Acts 3:2). They hoped that worshipers would toss them small change left over from transactions. Many worshipers, however, were not compassionate and would not share with the needy.

When these blind and lame people noticed Jesus within the temple, they

> . . . **came** [from *prosérchomai* {4334}, to approach; from *prós* {4314}, in the direction of, toward; and *érchomai* {2064}, to come] to him in the temple; and **he healed** [from *therapeúō* {2323}, to tenderly heal and care for] them.

It was well known that those who came to Jesus received healing, and these people believed that they too would be healed (cf. Matt. 11:5; 15:30, 31). Although angry at the sin of the Pharisees, Jesus compassionately healed (*therapeúō* compares with *iáomai* [2390], to physically cure) the sick who came to Him. He not only restored physical health but showed interest and compassion for them.

[15] Such actions further aggravated the merciless traders as well as the chief priests and scribes.

> And when the chief priests and scribes **observed** [from *eídō* {1492}, to intuitively know, realize] the **wonderful things** [from *thaumásios* {2297} from *thaumázō* {2296}, to admire; in turn from *thaúma* {2295}, a marvel, wonder, admirable event; this is the only occurrence of *thaumásios* in the NT] He was doing, and the children shouting in the temple, saying, Hosanna to the Son of David, they were **sore displeased** [from *aganaktéō* {23} from *agán* {n.f.}, very much; and *áchthos* {n.f.}, pain; to become pained with indignance]. (a.t.)

They should have been exuberant at these "marvels," but they were not. They opposed Jesus Christ because He could do what they were unable to do and thereby turned the attention of the crowd away from them. They were simply jealous, and jealousy produces rage.

The chief priests included the official high priest and a group of ex-high priests who belonged to the party of the Sadducees, the Jewish aristocratic group. The Sadducees were satisfied with the present, giving little thought to the future. They rejected the ideas of resurrection and future life and denied the existence of angels and spirits.

Yet setting aside their doctrinal differences, they earlier joined with the Pharisees to ask Jesus for a sign from heaven (Matt. 16:1). Shortly afterwards, Jesus warned His disciples to beware of the leaven of both the Pharisees and Sadducees. These rulers resented Jesus' cleansing of the temple, and with the scribes and elders, they demanded proof of His authority to do so (Mark 11:27, 28). From then on, they tried to destroy Him (Mark 11:18). There is no record of any Sadducee accepting Christ which accords with their denial of the resurrection on which the church was founded.

The scribes (from *grammateús* [1122] from which comes our English "grammar") were learned Jews who devoted themselves to a diligent study of the Law. The name comes from their dealing closely with the letter (*grámma* [1121], from *gráphō* [1125], to write) of the Mosaic Law. Though inclined to sympathize with Jesus at first, they became disillusioned by His loose adherence to the letter of the Law and by His unauthorized actions.

Jesus did not perform miracles in the temple to draw admiration but to express loving compassion and to prove divine authority. But praise came nonetheless. Children were "**shouting** [from *krázō* {2896}, to cry out] in the temple, saying, Hosanna to the Son of David" (a.t.). These "**boys**" (from *país* [3816]) echoed the crowds' cries from the previous day (v. 9). The chief priests and scribes thought it was bad enough that adults had been duped into praising Christ, but now the younger generation was putting its trust in Him. The deception of children was intolerable.

[16] So they asked Jesus,

> Do you hear what **they are saying** [from *légō* {3004}, to intelligently speak]? And Jesus said to them, Yes, have you **never** [*oudépote* {3763}, not at any time; from *ou* {3756}, not; *dé* {1161}, even; and *poté* {4218}, any time] **read** [from *anaginōskō* {314}] that **out of** [*ek* {1537}] the mouth of **babes** [from *nēpios* {3516} from the prefix *nē*, not; and *épos* {2031}, word; thus "not a word," those who cannot speak, hence infants and therefore a miracle that they should "praise"] and **sucklings** [from *thēlázō* {2337}, to breast feed], **You ordained** [from *katartízō* {2675}, to set up, fit together, thoroughly prepare, constitute] **praise** [from *aínos* {136}]? (a.t.)

With an unambiguous example, Jesus argued that God prefers praise to the mature entrapments of worldly intellectualism, tradition, and self-righteousness.

Infants and sucklings are a step down from children, and Jesus intimated that the chief priests and scribes did not have this innocent, dependent faith. Moreover, since God dissolves His enemies with such praise, surely their callousness should melt in the presence of His care of totally helpless infants.

"**You ordained**" (*katartízō*) derives from *katá* (2596), in accordance with; and *artízō* (n.f.), to adjust, fit, finish, complete, related to the adjective *ártios* (739), fit, complete. In Matthew 4:21, it is used for the mending of fishing nets. God can as easily make infants praise Him as cause a donkey (Num. 22:28) or even stones (Luke 19:40) to speak. Each of these cases was a miracle. John the Baptist, for example, was "filled with the Spirit even from [*ek* {1537}, out of from within] his mother's womb" (Luke 1:15; a.t.). One evidence that John was filled with the Spirit prior to his birth is his leaping at the presence of the Son of God in Mary's womb (Luke 1:41, cf. 1:35).

[17] Not waiting for their response to this, Jesus,

> . . . **having left** [from *kataleípō* {2641}, to leave behind; from *katá* {2596}, an intensive meaning behind; and *leípō* {3007}, to leave] them [the chief priests and scribes], He went out of the city into Bethany [probably to the home of His friends, Lazarus, Mary, and Martha, about a mile and a half from the Mount of Olives], and **He lodged** [from *aulízomai* {835}, to lodge for the night, possibly outdoors in the *aulé* {833}, courtyard] there. (a.t.)

The only other occurrence of *aulízomai* is in Luke 21:37 which reads, "In the day time [Jesus] was teaching in the temple; and at night he went out, and abode [from *aulízomai*] in the mount that is called the mount of Olives."

Kataleípō is also used when Jesus left Nazareth for Capernaum (Matt. 4:13) and when He left the Pharisees and Sadducees who asked Him for a sign from heaven (Matt. 16:4). Similarly, in our ministry, the Lord may have us leave one city and move on to others where the gospel is welcomed.

The Barren Fig Tree
(21:18–22; Mark 11:12–14, 20–24)

[18] Jesus' true humanity was revealed in hunger, one of the specific pains through which the devil malevolently tempted Him in the wilderness (Luke 4:2, 3).

> Now in the morning **as he returned** [from *epanágō* {1877}, to lead back; from *epí* {1909}, upon, to; and *anágō* {321}, to bring back, to lead up] into the city, **he hungered** [from *peináō* {3983}, to hunger].

Mark 11:12 tells us that it was on "the next day [*epaúrion* {1887}], having gone out [from *exérchomai* {1831}, to go out] from Bethany, He was hungry" (a.t.). We do not know how early in the morning Jesus began His walk back to Jerusalem, but it seems He had not eaten.

[19] This hunger may have prompted Jesus to study "**a single** [*mían*, the accusative singular feminine numeral of *heís* {1520}, one] fig tree in the way" (a.t.), literally, "on the path." Since it had nothing but "**leaves**" (from *phúllon* [5444]), Jesus used this fig tree to symbolize the unfruitfulness of the Jewish nation that God had favored above the nations of the world. This action of Jesus immediately followed His cleansing the temple (Mark 11:12–14), further illustrating the spiritual barrenness of the Jewish religion.

Fig trees were usually cultivated, but sometimes, like this one, they grew wild in Palestine. The sprouting of fig trees was one of the earliest indications of summer (Song 2:13; Matt. 24:32; Luke 21:29, 30), and crop failure was a terrible calamity (Jer. 8:13; Joel 1:7, 12; Hab. 3:17, 18).

The fact that the fig tree had only leaves presents a clear analogy to the hypocrisy of the scribes and Pharisees, which the Lord had dealt with on the previous day. They displayed the outward trappings of devotion and religiosity but had no fruit. Theirs was only a pretense. "Every tree," John the Baptist preached to the Pharisees, "which bringeth not forth good fruit is hewn down, and cast into the fire" (Matt. 3:10).

Because the Jews were given the "advantage," as Paul calls it in Romans 3:1, of the Law and the prophets, they should have been the first to believe God's promises. Outwardly, they had leaves, "a form of godliness," but inwardly they denied "the power of God" (2 Tim. 3:5; a.t.). As Paul counsels, "from such turn away" (ibid.), so Jesus turned away from this fig tree, drying it up completely, right down to the "roots" (from *ríza* [4491]; Mark 11:20). This was prophetic of the Father's response to His Son's murder as set forth in a parable: "But when the king heard thereof, he was wroth: and he sent forth his armies, and destroyed those murderers, and burned up their city" (Matt. 22:7). This was accomplished in A.D. 70 when Titus destroyed Jerusalem and razed its temple. God took the kingdom away from the apostate nation of Israel and gave it to a nation that would produce fruit, in accord with Jesus' words in Matthew 21:43 (see Rom. 11:25).

Until this point, Jesus' miracles were beneficent. But He could not reveal only part of the truth. Those who persisted in disobedience would meet His justice (*ekdíkēsis* [1557], to bring out justice; from *ek* [1537], out, outward expression; and *díkē* [1349], justice; see Deut. 32:35; Rom. 12:19; Heb. 10:30) head-on. Jesus Christ gives eternal life to believers but destruction to the impenitent who choose for themselves the destruction prepared for the devil and his angels (Matt. 25:41).

The solitude of the fig tree reminds us that God will judge us as individuals. The certainty of this isolation in judgment cautions us to "not follow a multitude to do evil" (Ex. 23:2) but to "save [ourselves] from [a] crooked generation" (Acts 2:40; a.t.). No excuse here for peer pressure! Finally, the fig tree's inability to bear fruit symbolized Israel's rejection of its Messiah during His three-and-a-half years of testimony.

Jesus spoke directly to the fig tree:

> Let **no longer** [*mēkéti* {3371} from *mḗ*, not {3361}; and *éti* {2089}, more, longer, beyond] fruit be out of you **forever** [*eis* {1519}, unto; *tón* {3588}, the definite article; and *aiṓna* from *aiṓn* {165}, age]. **Presently** [*parachrēma* {3916}, immediately] the fig tree **withered away** [from *xēraínō* {3583}, to dry up]. (a.t.)

Once Jesus made this sovereign pronouncement, the tree died. Just as God's decree, "Let there be light," caused light—"and there was light" (Gen. 1:3), so this decree caused three things: no more opportunity to bear fruit, withering, and death. The "evil generation" (Luke 11:29) of Jews that Jesus had addressed was a "corrupt tree [that cannot] bring forth good fruit" (Matt. 7:18).

[20] Perhaps not understanding the full theological import and practical application of Jesus' action, the disciples "**marveled**" (from *thaumázō* [2296], to marvel) that even a tree would respond to His command. The One who imparted life to the fig tree in the first place now deprived that tree of life, as He can do to any individual or nation that persists in unbelief.

Distracted by the sensational and perhaps missing the meaning, the disciples stood amazed: "How **soon** [*parachrēma*; see above] the fig tree **dried up** [from *xēraínō* {3583}]!" (a.t.).

[21] Jesus' response to His disciples is worth noting:

> Verily **I say** [*légō* {3004}, to speak logically] to you, If you **have** [from *échō* {2192}, to have] **faith** [from *pístis* {4102}] and **doubt** [*diakrithête*, the aorist— and so, at any point—the passive subjunctive of *diakrínomai* {1252}, to hesitate, waver] not, you shall not only do what was done to the fig tree but also if you shall say unto this mountain [probably the Mount of Olives standing in front of Jesus], **Be thou removed** [from *aírō* {142}, to lift up], and **be thou cast** [from *bállō* {906}] into the sea, it shall be done. (a.t.)

Jesus gave a similar promise following His descent from the Mount of Transfiguration. In Matthew 17:20, He added, "and nothing [*oudén* {3762}, 'not even one thing'] shall be impossible unto you."

Faith is assent to truth, and in both Scriptures, the object was clearly God's omnipotence, His ability to do the things we ask. We believe God with the faith He implants in our hearts, reposing in revealed propositions, the first truth of which is His sovereignty over our lives. We should not doubt the Lord's sovereignty and never waver in our faith in His absolute power.

The specific power to curse a fig tree so that it no longer produces fruit may be an amplification of the corporate "binding" taught in Matthew 18:17–19 (see our exegesis of that section).

[22] The stress on adding prayer to faith discourages all forms of arrogance. While Jesus encouraged us to ask, we must never approach God demanding our way, for only He knows which way is best.

> And all things, whatever you shall ask in prayer, **believing** [*pisteúontes*, the present active participle of *pisteúō* {4100}, to believe, have faith in God; the present participle means continuous, uninterrupted], you shall receive. (a.t.)

As we saw in the parallel loosing and binding section of Matthew 18, this promise is properly limited to the will of God as revealed throughout Scripture: "Now we know that God heareth not sinners: but if any man be a worshipper of God, and doeth his will, him he heareth" (John 9:31).

An answer to prayer is assured, but the conditions are clearly delineated. We supplicants must have uninterrupted faith; we must ask for what agrees with the revealed will of God; we must come before omnipotent holiness and wisdom in utter humility, and we should be specific. To these conditions, we must concede our ignorance, knowing that some of the "will of God" is shrouded in mystery (Deut. 29:29; Eph. 1:9). In the final analysis, the best prayer is capped with, "Not my will, but thine, be done" (Luke 22:42).

Jesus' Authority Questioned
(21:23–27; Mark 11:27–33; Luke 20:1–8)

Jesus' teaching in the temple followed His healing the lame and the blind who had come to Him the previous day. After seeing this demonstration of power, people naturally wanted to learn more about Him. They could see a difference in His teaching "as one having authority [from *exousía* {1849}]" (Matt. 7:29).

As "the truth" (John 14:6), Jesus taught with an authority that disturbed His opponents. The chief priests and elders considered the temple their domain, and Jesus had presumptuously intruded. The elders (from *presbúteros* [4245]) were older men who sat with the chief priests as members of the highest Jewish court, the Sanhedrin, headquartered in the temple. These principals had to grant authorization to anyone who wished to teach there.

[23] Since they had not granted such authority to Jesus, the leaders questioned Him:

> By what **authority** [from *exousía* {1849}, physical and ethical power] doest thou these things? and **who** [*tís* {5101}, what individual] **gave thee** [from *didōmi* {1325}] this authority?

They queried Jesus' authority "to do," not "to teach." Teaching could always be questioned, even debated, but miracles were incontestable and evident to everyone. No one could do what Jesus did, and these miracles confirmed the authority of His teachings. One among them had miraculous power and authority, far more than they had, and they resented it. The miracles themselves should have been self-authorizing.

[24] Not only could Jesus outperform His adversaries, but He could easily outwit them with dilemmas:

> I also will ask you one **thing** [from *lógos* {3056}, rational sentence], which if ye tell me, I in like wise **will tell** [from *légō* {3004}, to intelligently speak] you by **what** [from *poíos* {4169}] authority I do these things.

The question was twofold, what and who, but Jesus answered the what, anticipating His own impersonal phrase "from heaven" (see next verse). The present tense, "I do," implied a certain regularity or frequency to His miracles. He could have added, "Not what I did, but those I am doing even now."

[25, 26] Many of Israel's rulers had evidently accepted John's baptism at the beginning of his ministry to escape God's wrath (see Matt. 3:7; Luke 3:7). Although Jesus spoke of him as being the greatest born of women, Israel's leaders had never publicly made a definite statement on John the Baptist's status.

Knowing that the people believed John's prophecy of the imminent coming of the Messiah (e.g., Matt. 3:11–12; John 1:26–30), Jesus wisely appealed to his baptism: "The baptism of John, whence was it? **From** [*ex* from *ek* {1537}, out of from within] heaven or **from** [*ek*] men?" (a.t.).

> And **they were reasoning** [*dielogízonto*, the imperfect middle deponent of *dialogízomai* {1260}, to rationalize] among themselves, **saying** [from *légō* {3004}], If **we say** [from *légō*] **from** [from *ek*] heaven, **He will say** [from *légō*] to us, Why **did you** not then **believe** [from *pisteúō* {4100}] him? But if we shall say of [from *ek*] men, we fear the people for all hold John as a prophet. (a.t.)

Because the general populace considered John a prophet on a par with those of the Old Testament, the chief priests and elders were now caught in a dilemma. After all, Jesus had already cited the testimony of John the Baptist as a witness to His deity (John 5:32–35). They had no good option favorable to their cause.

[27] All they could do was avoid answering. The dilemma posed by Jesus' question left them without argument. On the one hand, they could not acknowledge John as a prophet of God because he had predicted and later affirmed that Jesus was the Messiah of Israel. Nor could they, on the other hand, reject John because they feared the opinion of the general public. So they avoided the question altogether.

Hence, their answer was weak: "We **do** not **know** [from *oída*, the perfect of *eídō* [1492], to know intuitively] (a.t.)." They used the perfect *oída*, which is always used with a present-tense idea, emphasizing a present condition based on past results. So the effect of their statement was, "We cannot figure it out because we haven't seen sufficient evidence one way or the other."

Jesus' response was swift and firm: "**Neither** [*oudé* {3761} from the negative *ou* {3756}; and *dé* {1161}, even] tell **I** [*egō* {1473}, the emphatic 'I'] you by what **authority** [from *exousía* {1849}] I do these things."

The chief priests and elders had assumed the right to determine what happened in the temple. But Jesus is Lord of all and, therefore, His authority was not mediated through humans but given directly by the Father: "All authority [*exousía*] is given me in heaven and on earth" (Matt. 28:18; a.t.).

The Parable of the Two Sons
(21:28–32)

[28] Always appealing to reason, Jesus asked, "What do you think? A man had two **children** [from *téknon* {5043} from *tíktō* {5088}, to give birth; not *huiós* {5207}, a mature child]; and he came to the first, and said, **Child** [*téknon*], go work today in my vineyard" (a.t.). Jesus used "two children" the way Paul does in Galatians 4:24–31 where the two children of Abraham represent two nations.

The two in this parable are the basis for later Pauline theology that makes several contrasts: a Jew "outwardly" (Rom. 2:28) and a Jew "inwardly" (Rom. 2:29); "Israel" and "of Israel" (Rom. 9:6); "seed of Abraham" and "children [of Abraham]" (Rom. 9:7); "Israel" and "the election" (Rom. 11:7); and Mount Sinai (slavery) and Jerusalem against Mount Sion (freedom) and Jerusalem above (Gal. 4:24–31; cf. Heb. 12:18–24).

The two sons were both physical descendants of their father, just as the Jews were physical descendants of Abraham. But only the one who did the will of his father was born of the will (the spirit) of that father. Thus, Paul concludes, "They which are of faith [the spirit or faith of Abraham] are the sons [from *huiós*] of Abraham" (Gal. 3:7; a.t.).

The vineyard represents the father's line of work: sowing, reaping, and harvesting—all associated with the extension of the kingdom of God.

[29] Because all people are sinners by nature, their first choices concerning their father's will are impulsively negative. For this reason, the first son responds:

> I will [*thélō* {2309}, to determine, to wish] not: but **afterward** [*hústeron* {5305}, in the end, eventually], **having repented** [*metameletheís*, the aorist passive participle of *metamélomai* {3338} from *metá* {3326}, after, change; and *mélomai*, the middle of *mélō* {3199}, to be concerned about the future], he went out. (a.t.)

We have no idea how long this "afterward" lasted. The word is used in Matthew 4:2 to describe the Lord Jesus' hunger toward the end of His forty-day fast.

From the standpoint of strict justice, the father could have cut this first child out of his inheritance any time he wanted within this "afterward" period. God commanded Adam and Eve to leave the Garden of Eden and placed cherubim and a flaming sword to prevent their re-entry and partaking of the tree of life (Gen. 3:24). God's grace extends an afterward for repentance, as we read of Jezebel, "I gave her space to repent of her fornication; and she repented not" (Rev. 2:21). However, for Jezebel, "space" was only a temporary suspension of wrath since it did not result in repentance. God "grants repentance" (Acts 5:31; 11:18; 2 Tim. 2:25, 26) by creating new thoughts—the "mind of Christ" (1 Cor. 2:16)—within us, thoughts that are foolishness to the natural person (2:14).

A distinction in Greek exists between the verbs *metanoéō* (3340), to change one's mind, and *metamélomai*. The former is frequently associated with coming to faith in the gospel (Acts 11:18; 2 Tim. 2:25, 26), whereas the latter is a general anxiety about the future (*mélō*). Persons may repent (change their minds) for many other reasons besides concern for the future, and so the verb *metanoéō* is a broader genus of which *metamélomai* is a species. Here, on mature reflection, the first son finally realized that rebellion against his father would have bad long-term consequences. His concern for his future changed. This change of concern (*metamélomai*) produced a repentance of thought and action (*metanoéō*). Note the preceding action of the aorist participle to the main verb: "having changed concern, [then] he went out [repented]." According to Paul, "godly **sorrow** [*lúpē* {3077}] works repentance" (2 Cor. 7:10; a.t.).

Similarly, Peter, in a moment of weakness, denied his Lord. But afterward he became concerned about his future relationship with Christ and grieved for his sin, repenting bitterly. Judas also changed concern and even attempted to repent by trying to return the money he earned from betraying Christ. But his sin was of a different character than Peter's: he had not denied Christ, but he had betrayed Him. It was not a sin against identity with Christ but one of profiting from the death of an innocent Person. Peter's sin of denial would not cause Christ's death, whereas Judas' sin of betrayal immediately led to Christ's arrest. Moreover, unlike Peter, there is no evidence that Judas had ever put his faith in the Lord.

[30] The second child rebelled the more:

> And he came to the **other** [{MT} from *héteros* {2087}, another of a different kind {the difference is not specified}] and said **likewise** [*hōsaútōs* {5615}, here meaning "the same content"]. And he answered and said, **I** [*egō* {1473}, emphatic] go, sir: and **he went** [from *apérchomai* {565}, to depart] not. (a.t.)

The majority of the Greek texts have the adjective *hetérō*, another of a different kind, whereas the Textus Receptus and the Critical Texts (UBS; Nestle's) have *tō deutérō* (1208), "to the second"—which proved to be a qualitative difference in attitude and action.

Did this son intend to go and then afterwards change his mind, or did he just blatantly lie? We do not know. Both hypotheses read between the lines. Nor do we know whether he went to work at another job or was just lazy. The emphasis is plainly rebellion: "He did not go" where his father told him to go. Even if he had gone to work somewhere other than in his father's vineyard, he would have been rebelling. The father did not say, "Go find a job," but rather, "Go work [specifically] in my vineyard." This son expressed a willingness to work, but when it came time to actually do it, he did not. Either the willingness was temporary and died, or it was a pretense.

[31] Since both children could be condemned, the first because of an original unwillingness and the second because of a final unwillingness, Jesus raised the question, "Which of the two did the **will** [*thélēma* {2307}, the noun of the verb *thélō* {2309}, to determine, to wish, the suffix -*ma* associated with result] of his father?" (NASB). Note that the question is not which of the two willed but which of the two did?

The chief priests and elders answered, "The first." Jesus immediately affirmed their opinion with a direct application of the parable.

> Verily I say unto you, That the publicans [from *telṓnēs* {5057}, tax collector] and the harlots [from *pórnē* {4204}, prostitute] go [*proágō* {4254}, to go before], into the kingdom of God before you.

The first son's original and deliberate rebellion against parental authority corresponds to people's natural bent against God, which we also see in the publicans and harlots. Unless God has implanted new natures in humans (2 Pet. 1:4), they are naturally disobedient.

These sinners eventually, under the supernatural power of the Holy Spirit, recognize their sinfulness, confess it, seek the kingdom of God, and enter it (Matt. 19:23, 24). From a strictly legal standpoint, both sons could be condemned for unwillingness at one time or another. But the grace of God transcends the just punishment of the Law, transforming the old will into a new will (Ps. 110:3; Phil. 2:13) and repentance (Acts 11:18; 2 Tim. 2:25) as it did in the first child. That he ultimately did the right thing is even implied in the way Jesus structured His question, "Which of the two?" This phrasing would be incorrect if the right answer was neither. He would more aptly have asked, "Did either of these two do their father's will?" The fact that Jesus did not contend with the answer is corroborative evidence. Besides, the correct answer was a preplanned inducement to self-condemnation for the religious leaders.

Why did Jesus say that publicans and harlots would "**go before**" the chief priests and elders into the kingdom of God, implying that they too would make it? (*Proágō* [4254] actually carries the senses of leading and following.) Why didn't He say, "instead of" or something else which equates to "They go in and you don't?"

Let us note first that the verb is not necessarily a quantitative statement, that is, of chronology. A qualitative alternative is that He is referring to the relative difficulty of salvation reflected in Jesus' words, "It is easier for a camel to go through the eye of a needle, than for a rich man to enter into the kingdom of God" (Matt. 19:24). This text teaches that, while it is humanly impossible, it is easier for God to pull a camel through the eye of a needle than to pull the spirit of a rich man away from his wealth. (The poor man has no treasure from which to be pried away.) Similarly, it was easier for Jesus to draw (John 6:44) a guilt-ridden harlot to Himself than a self-righteous Pharisee. Some jobs produce greater obstinacy, and religious leadership is no doubt one of the greatest. "They go in before," then equates to, "They go in more easily" (as Peter says, even "the righteous scarcely be saved"; 1 Pet. 4:18). Self-righteous hypocrites are more offensive than prostitutes, which is why Jesus said that the self-righteous will "receive the greater damnation" (Matt. 23:14; cf. Luke 20:47; James 3:1). Thus, Jude counsels us to exert different pressures to save different types of sinners: "And of some have compassion, making a difference: and others save with fear, snatching them out of the fire; hating even the garment spotted by the flesh" (Jude 22, 23; a.t.).

If someone presses for the chronological meaning of *proágō*, to precede or go before, then we can appeal to Israel's partial blindness until the full number of Gentiles (the "fullness") is saved. The chief priests and elders represent that part of unrepentant Israel that remains blinded until Christ, the Deliverer, returns and turns sin away from Jacob.

> Blindness in part has occurred [*gégonen*, the perfect tense of *gínomai* {1096}, to become] to Israel, until the fulness of the Gentiles is come in. And so all Israel shall be saved: as it is written, There shall come out of Zion the Deliverer, and He shall turn away ungodliness from Jacob: for this is My covenant unto them, when I shall take away their sins. (Rom. 11:25–27; a.t.; cf. Zech. 12:7—13:2)

[32] While the analogy can be applied to God (or even Abraham, according to Gal. 4:22, 23) as the Father of the two children, one born according to the flesh (the Law) and the other according to the Spirit (the promise), Jesus now applied the parable to the ministry of John the Baptist whom He likened to the father of a disobedient child (represented by the chief priests and elders) and an obedient child (the harlots and prostitutes):

> **For** [meaning the analogy now interprets the "certain man who had two children" as John] John came unto you [all of you] in the **way** [from *hodós* {3598}, path] of **righteousness** [from *dikaiosúnē* {1343}, righteousness], and **you** [the disobedient child] **believed** [from *pisteúō* {4100}, to believe] him not, but the publicans and harlots [the obedient child] believed him; and you, **having seen** [from *eídō* {1492}, to perceive] it, **repented** [from *metamélomai* {3338}] not **afterward** [*hústeron* {5305}, at the end], **that you might believe** [*pisteúsai*, the aorist infinitive of *pisteúō*] him. (a.t.)

The message was clear. The publicans and harlots originally said no to John's message, but eventually (*hústeron*) they said yes (note: the aorist infinitive, *pisteúsai*, represents the once-for-all crisis of conversion) like the obedient child. In contrast, the chief priests and elders said *yes* with their lips and *no* with their hearts to John, as did the disobedient child. They rejected not only his message of a coming redeemer but the Redeemer Himself who said, "I have greater witness than that of John" (John 5:36).

Jesus gave both encouragement and warning in this parable. First, God can forgive vile sins like prostitution and self-righteousness. But Jesus warned that self-righteousness is the "greater sin" (John 19:11 uses this expression for the betrayal of Christ) because it is contrary to God's righteousness (Rom. 10:3). Judging our sins according to the Word of God is a vital part of our sanctification. We should guard our spirits against a lapse into self-justification.

The Parable of the Wicked Vine-growers
(21:33–46; Mark 12:1–9; Luke 20:9–19; cf. Isa. 5:1–7)

[33] Jesus continued His series: "**Hear** [*akoúsate*, the aorist imperative of *akoúō* {191}, to hear, the aorist inferring 'now'] **another** [from *állos* {243}, another of the same kind, one which illustrates the official Jewish rejection of their Messiah] parable." The term "official" refers to the chief priests and elders, the highest leaders of the Pharisaic and Sadducean parties.

This parable prophetically details how the religious leaders of Israel would treat the Son of God and what will happen to them as a result. Because of their broad exposure to scriptural prophecies, these leaders had a much greater opportunity to accept their Messiah than the laypeople. The parable thus warned all those who had some knowledge of Christ but *finally* (*husteron*) rejected Him.

Jesus likened the kingdom of God to

. . . a "**householder** [*oikodespótēs* {3617}, house master; from *oíkos* {3624}, house; and *despótēs* {1203}, despot, absolute ruler] **planted** [from *phuteúō* {5452}, to plant] a vineyard and **put around it** [from *peritíthēmi* {4060}, to place around] **a hedge** [*phragmón* {5418}, a thorny hedge; associated with the verb *phrásso* {5420}, to fence], and **dug** [from *orússo* {3736}, to dig] a winepress in it, and **built** [from *oikodoméō* {3618}, to construct, erect] a **watchtower** [from *púrgos* {4444}], and **let it out** [from *ekdídomi* {1554}, to hire] to **husbandmen** [from *geōrgós* {1092}, farmer], and **went into a far country** [from *apodēméō* {589}, to emigrate]. (a.t.)

The householder's care to grow a good crop of grapes and protect them was emphasized with several verbs. Unlike the verb *speírō* (4687), which carries the idea of scattering (seed), *phuteúō* implies the digging of individual holes and placing specific seeds or plants in properly prepared ground to ensure success (cf. Matt. 15:13; Mark 4:26–29, and the word *bállō* [906], to put, place). After this careful planting, the householder put a protective, thorny hedge around the vineyard to keep animals (i.e., intruders) out, built a watchtower to protect against thieves, and leased the vineyard to professional farmers.

The noun *oikodespótēs* is used in Matthew 10:25 for Satan, Beelzebub, who rules over the house of evil, which Jesus despoils whenever He robs Satan of one of his subjects. "How can one enter into a strong man's house, and spoil his goods, except he first bind the strong man? and then he will spoil his house" (Matt. 12:29). It's also used in Matthew 20:1 where Jesus said that "the kingdom of heaven is like unto a man that is an householder." It is not necessary for every detail in a parable to have an exact heavenly analogue.

This parable follows one in Isaiah where God (the Father) "hath a vineyard in a very fruitful hill" (Isa. 5:1) and does essentially the same things to it (5:2).

[34] Eventually, the owner sent servants to the tenant farmers to receive a full accounting of profits.

> And when the **time** [*kairós* {2540}, season, proper time] of the **fruit** [from *karpós* {2590}, fruit] drew near, he sent his **servants** [from *doúlos* {1401}, labors, slaves] to the **husbandmen** [farmers], that they might receive the fruits of it.

Scripture continually speaks of appointed seasons (from *kairós*). Here the singular *kairós* symbolizes the time for gathering the vineyard's fruit. This harvest does not illustrate the end of the church age, since the owner killed the husbandmen and leased the vineyard to new farmers. Jesus' explanation accords with the data—the transition of the kingdom from the Jews to the Gentiles: "The kingdom of God shall be taken from you, and given to a nation bringing forth the fruits thereof" (v. 43). The evil farmers were not able to prevent the master's harvest or to take over his vineyard, which they futilely attempted.

[35] The reaction to the owner's servants was inconceivably wicked:

> And the husbandmen, **having taken** [from *lambánō* {2983}, to take] his servants, on the one hand, **beat** [from *dérō* {1194}, to flay, take skin off, thrash] one, and **killed** [from *apokteínō* {615}] another, and **stoned** [from *lithoboléō* {3036} from *líthos* {3037}, stone; and *bállō*, throw] another. (a.t.)

Not a single servant, it seems, escaped unharmed. This abominable history of the apostate reaction to God's prophets stretches all the way back to the first death on the face of the earth:

> That upon you may come all the righteous blood shed upon the earth, from the blood of righteous Abel unto the blood of Zacharias son of Barachias, whom ye slew between the temple and the altar. (Matt. 23:35)

> And in her [Babylon] was found the blood of prophets, and of saints, and of all that were slain upon the earth. (Rev. 18:24)

[36] This treatment of the first round of servants (prophets) did not deter the owner of the farm from sending more slaves to the vineyard. "Again, he sent **other** [from *állos* {243}, another of the same kind] servants more than the first: and they did unto them likewise."

Like the first set, these servants were not warriors. They were innocent, peace-loving logistics managers sent to collect and transport what properly belonged to the owner. Again, the farmers mercilessly maimed and murdered every one of them, hoping to steal, the farm.

[37] The patience of the householder symbolizes God's patience with humankind (Rom. 2:4) in spite of their rejection of Him.

But **last of all** [*hústeron* {5305}, eventually, at the end; i.e., of those sent to gather fruit; see v. 32] he sent unto them his **son** [from *huiós* {5207}], saying, **They will reverence** [from *entrépo* {1788}, to reverence or make ashamed; from *en* {1722}, in; and *trépo* {n.f.}, to be ashamed of] my son.

The householder mistakenly assumed that they would respect his son more than they had his servants.

The human subject of a parable may make a mistake, but God the Father, analogously represented by the householder, is inerrant. Not every element of a parable has to be predicated to God (cf. e.g., *hō kritḗs tēs adikías* for the "unjust judge" in Luke 18:6; Christ's judgments are just [*dikaías kríses* in John 5:30]. Even though people killed His Son, they will fall down in respect before the Father either in this world on conversion (Zech. 12:10, cf. Rev. 1:7) or in the world to come before the judgment seat of Christ (Isa. 66:16; Luke 9:26; Phil. 2:10; 1 John 2:28).

The fact that the vineyard is "let out" again (v. 41) shows that this is not the final judgment scene.

[38, 39] The husbandmen jump at the new opportunity:

But the **husbandmen** [from *geōrgós* {1092}, farmer], **having seen** [from *horáo* {3708}, to perceive] the son, said among themselves, This is the **heir** [*klēronómos* {2818}]. Come, let us kill him, and **let us seize** [from *katécho* {2722} from *katá* {2596}, an intensive meaning down; and *écho* {2192}, to hold; thus, to hold down, suppress] his **inheritance** [from *klēronomía* {2817}]. And they caught him, **cast** [from *ekbállo* {1544}] him **out** [*éxo* {1854}, outside] of the vineyard, and **slew** [from *apokteíno* {615}, to kill, slay] him. (a.t.)

There is a minor variant in a few older manuscripts, followed by UBS and most modern versions, using the simple verb *écho* (2192), to hold or to have, rather than *katécho* (2722), to seize, but it doesn't really change the meaning of the farmers' proposal.

Katáschesis (2697) is an interesting modern Greek word, meaning a legal seizure of another's property. The phrase "out[side] of the vineyard" is equivalent to "without the camp" (Heb. 13:11, 13) and "without the gate" (i.e., of Jerusalem; Heb. 13:12) where Jesus was crucified. The vineyard itself was God's cultivated field entrusted to the Jews (Isa. 5:1–7).

These jealous and murderous farmers conspired together ("among themselves") to kill the heir in order to steal his inheritance. Their shortsighted stupidity made them think they would never have to contend with a Father who once said, "Vengeance is mine; I will repay, saith the Lord" (Rom. 12:19; cf. Deut. 32:35). Paul also tells us that "the unrighteous shall not inherit the kingdom of God" (1 Cor. 6:9). Not only will murderers not inherit, but also death will not prevent the Son of God from inheriting all things.

In the analogy, of course, Jesus Christ is the Father's heir: "[God] hath in these last days spoken unto us by his Son, whom he hath appointed heir [from *klēronómos*] of all things" (Heb. 1:2, cf. v. 4; Rom. 8:17; Gal. 4:7). Moreover, Paul tells us that the children of God are heirs with Christ according to God's promise (Gal. 3:29) through faith (Rom. 4:16) and even through suffering (Rom. 8:17, cf. 2 Cor. 1:5–7). Today more Christians are suffering and dying worldwide for the cause of Christ than ever before.

The murderous husbandmen thought they could obtain the inheritance by seizure. Earlier, Jesus had thus characterized all those who sought to be justified by the Mosaic Law once John the Baptist announced the kingdom:

> From the days of John the Baptist until now the kingdom of heaven is violated [from *biázō* {971}], and the violent [from *biastés* {973}] take it by force [from *harpázō* {726}, to snatch away by force, seize]. (Matt. 11:12; a.t.)

The unbelieving chief priests and elders thought they could both seize (*biázō*, *harpázō*) and forcibly retain (*katéchō*) the kingdom of God.

[40] The angry father returns, not as "householder," certainly not as "father"— he never had this relationship with the farmers—but as judge. This is not good news for the lessees.

"When the lord therefore of the vineyard **cometh** [from *érchomai* {2064}], what will he do unto those husbandmen?" By asking this question, Jesus prepared His opponents for self-condemnation. Also by saying "those," Jesus distanced Himself personally from the "wicked" men. Here we are reminded of those awful words, "I never knew you" (Matt. 7:23; see our exegesis).

[41] The parable overall reflected the same methodology Nathan used with David: Tell a parable about some malevolent person that angers your listener, then let him know, "Thou art the man!" (2 Sam. 12:7).

They say unto him, **He will miserably** [from *kakós* {2560}, badly] **destroy** [from *apóllumi* {622}, ruin] those **wicked** [from *kakós* {2556}; used in the same sense as earlier—they are wicked, so they will inherit wickedness] men, and **will let out** [from *ekdídomi* {1554}, to lease, the same verb used in v. 33] his vineyard unto **other** [from *állos* {243}, of the same profession, not character] **husbandmen** [farmers], which **shall render** [from *apodídomi* {591}, to give back, recompense] him the fruits in their **seasons** [from *kairós* {2540}].

The wicked will reap what they sow. The chief priests and elders understood what justice was, and the story was incredibly provocative, aimed, as it was, against them.

We cannot relate the events of the parable to the Second Coming of Christ because the householder leases to new tenant farmers. It is amazing that the chief priests and elders prophesy the end of their own Jewish dispensation and the reallocation of the kingdom to the church! They correctly deduced from the parable the justice associated with destroying the murderous farmers and giving the farm to others who would produce crops. God takes the kingdom away from apostates and gives it to believers. That this is a national judgment against apostate Israel will become evident in verse 43.

Fruitfulness in due season is the Lord's interest and demand. In the parables of the talents (Matt. 25:14–30) and the pounds (Luke 19:11–27), Jesus applauded investment returns of 500 and 1,000 percent while the one burying His talents was inexcusable. Here the owner turned the vineyard over to responsible men after removing it from the those who would seize the vineyard for themselves. The Jews had abused the many privileges they had been given (Rom. 3:1, 2).

[42] Since the chief priests and scribes were students of the Old Testament, the Lord Jesus quoted a relevant prophecy from Psalms 118:22, 23:

Did you **never** [*oudépote* {3763} from *ou* {3756}, not; *dé* {1161}, even; and *poté* {4218}, at some time; "not even at any time," ever] read in the Scriptures, The **stone** [from *líthos* {3037}] that the builders **rejected** [*apedokímasan*, the aorist tense of *apodokimázō* {593}, disapprove], this **became** [*egenéthē*, the aorist passive deponent of *gínomai* {1096}] the **head** [from *kephalé* {2776}] of the **corner** [from *gonía* {1137}]? This is the Lord's doing, and it is **marvelous** [from *thaumastós* {2298}, admirable] in our eyes. (a.t.)

The Davidic prophecy is general, a theme picked up later by Paul:

But God hath chosen the foolish things of the world to confound the wise; and God hath chosen the weak things of the world to confound the things which are mighty; and base things of the world, and things which are despised, hath God chosen, yea, and things which are not, to bring to nought things that are. (1 Cor. 1:27, 28)

Paul also asks the rhetorical question, "Who shall lay anything to the charge of God's elect? It is God that justifieth" (Rom. 8:33), that is, "Who will condemn what God justifies or reject what He has chosen?" David tells us some are depraved enough to do such things but only to their frustration. What people humiliate, God exalts. The rejected stone will become the cornerstone of the building. Such victories of God should excite us.

The historical aorist tenses, "rejected" and "became," summarize the premier instance of this—the Jews rejected Christ, and His Father accepted Him. As John says, "He came unto **His own** [*tá ídia*, the neuter accusative plural of *ídios* {2398}, one's own; i.e., 'his own things—country, land'], but **His own** [*hoi ídioi*, the masculine nominative plural of *ídios*; i.e., 'His own people'] received Him not" (John 1:11; a.t.). But God raised Him from the dead and exalted Him to His own right hand:

> The God of our fathers raised up Jesus, whom ye slew and hanged on a tree. Him hath God exalted with his right hand to be a Prince and a Saviour, for to give repentance to Israel, and forgiveness of sins. (Acts 5:30, 31)

Given unambiguous prophecy, the Israelites should have recognized and accepted their Messiah. Instead, they completed the sins of their fathers (Matt. 23:32) by killing another prophet, this time "**that** prophet" (John 1:21; cf. Deut. 18:18). But the Father "made that same Jesus . . . both Lord and Christ" (Acts 2:36). He is the "living [from *záō* {2198}, to live] stone [from *líthos* {3037}]" (1 Pet. 2:4), the "chief corner" (from *akrogōniaíos* [204] from *ákron* [206], extremity; and *gōnía* [1137], corner) stone on which the church is founded (1 Pet. 2:6, cf. Matt. 16:18; Eph. 2:20).

Those acquainted with construction would understand Jesus' words. Without a cornerstone, the walls of an edifice would not hold together. The marvel is how an obscure carpenter from a remote region could teach and minister for just three-and-a-half years of His thirty-three years of life, be crucified without cause, be despised and rejected by the majority, and have His resurrection classified as the pinnacle fraud of his followers. And yet He became the foundation of a multimillion-membered body that thrives to this day.

[43] The prophecy of the chief cornerstone came with a dire warning to the generation of Jews that rejected Jesus' messianic status:

> **On account** [*diá* {1223}, for] of **this** [*toúto* {5124}], I say unto you that the kingdom of God **shall be taken** [*arthḗsetai*, the future passive of *aírō* {142}, to take away] from you and **shall be given** [*dothḗsetai*, the future passive of

didōmi {1325}, to give] to a **nation** [from *éthnos* {1484}, Gentile nation or people] bringing forth the fruits **of it** [*autḗs* {846}, the genitive singular feminine personal pronoun, referring to the kingdom]. (a.t.)

This statement clearly depicted Israel's rejection of Christ and Christ's subsequent rejection of Israel from whom He would take (reflected in the passive voice of *arthḗsetai*) the kingdom away. There is no other way to read the words, "taken from you, and given to [another] nation." This is equivalent to His earlier words in verse 41, "He will destroy those wicked men and let out his vineyard to other farmers, who shall render him the fruits in their seasons" (a.t.). The general principle of deprivation (*airō*, to take away) is given in Matthew 13:12: "For whosoever hath, to him shall be given, and he shall have more abundance: but whosoever hath not, from him shall be taken away [*arthḗsetai* the future passive of *airō*] even that he hath."

The generation that murdered Christ, already oppressed by the Romans, was slaughtered in A.D. 70 when the Roman general, Titus, invaded and destroyed Jerusalem and leveled the temple. This was all in accord with Jesus' prophecy that the "house" of Jerusalem would be desolate until they say, "Blessed is he [Jesus] that cometh in the name of the Lord" (Luke 13:35, cf. Acts 3:21). According to Paul, Israel will remain partially hardened until the fulness of the Gentiles is in, implying that the new nation, which is the church, will be predominantly composed of Gentiles (Rom. 11:25). In terms of Israel's desolation, at a point beyond His turning away from the Jews and to the Gentiles, Paul summarizes:

> Ye also have suffered like things of your own countrymen, even as they have
> of the Jews, who both killed the Lord Jesus, and their own prophets, and have
> persecuted us; and they please not God, and are contrary to all men: forbidding us to speak to the Gentiles that they might be saved, to fill up their sins
> alway: for the [a definite article is present] wrath is come upon them to the
> uttermost. (1 Thess. 2:14–16)

All this will change when, as we noted earlier, the Deliverer returns and turns ungodliness from Jacob (Rom. 11:26). In the interim, the church, the universal body of Christ that incorporates believers from "every kindred, and tongue, and people, and nation" (Rev. 5:9), is itself called a holy nation (i.e., one that produces fruit): "But ye are a chosen generation, a royal priesthood, an holy nation [*éthnos* {1484}], a peculiar people; that ye should shew forth the praises of him who hath called you out of darkness into his marvellous light"(1 Pet. 2:9).

[44] Jesus elaborated on the roles of the chief cornerstone. When it is detached from the "house" of Jerusalem (Luke 13:35), that house will collapse. In addition, as a stand-alone, this huge rock judges both nations and individuals:

And **the one who falls** [from *píptō* {4098}, to fall] on this stone **shall be
shattered** [from *sunthláō* {4917} from *sún* {4862}, together; and *thláō* {n.f.},
to break, crush, dash in pieces; Luke 20:18; Sept.: Ps. 58:7; 110:5; Mic. 3:3]:
but on whomever it shall fall, **it will pulverize** [from *likmáō* {3039}] him. (a.t.)

He specified two judgments: the first will shatter those who take it lightly.
The second will pulverize those who willfully and continually reject Him.
These Jews militantly opposed Jesus. Many were Sadducees who denied the
vast majority of revelation from Joshua through Malachi—therefore the majority of the prophecies of a Messiah—and core truths like the existence of angels
and spirits and the resurrection from the dead.

This is the ultimate result of unbelief. The verb *likmáō* is associated with
the noun *líkmos* (n.f.), a winnowing fork used by ancient wheat farmers to
toss wheat in the air so that kernels would separate and fall to the ground
while the chaff would be blown away by the wind. This process of separating wheat from chaff was called *likmáō*, a type of judgment, the judging being
a separation.

[45] The parables were clearly aimed at the highest members of the Sanhedrin.
All three Synoptic writers, Matthew (v. 45), Mark (12:12), and Luke (20:19),
write that Jesus directed this parable "against" the chief priests and scribes:

When the chief priests and Pharisees **had heard** [from *akoúō* {191}, to hear]
His **parables** [from *parabolḗ* {3850}, that is, this one and the one about the
two sons {vv. 28–32}], **they knew** [from *ginṓskō* {1097}, to know by experi-
ence] that He spoke of them. (a.t.)

The accusation was terrible and the threat ominous. Jesus effectively called
them abusers, murderers (vv. 35–39), and "wicked" (from *kakós* [2556], v. 41).
He said that the kingdom of God would be taken from them and given to
others—their own judgment in verse 41—and, in the process, they would
either be broken in pieces or ground to powder as God judged that generation of their nation.

[46] Infuriated by jealousy and their humiliation before the crowds, the
Pharisees

. . . **were seeking** [*zētoúntes*, the present active participle of *zētéō* {2212}]
to arrest [*kratḗsai*, the aorist active infinitive of *kratéō* {2902}, to take by force,
the aorist implying once for all] Him, but **they became afraid** [*ephobḗthēsan*,
the aorist passive of *phobéō* {5399}, to frighten] of the multitude, because **they
were continuously having** [*eíchon*, the imperfect tense of *échō* {2192}] Him
for a **prophet** [from *prophḗtēs* {4396} from *pró* {4253}, before; and *phēmí*
{5346}, to speak; thus, one who predicts events]. (a.t.)

The chief priests' and scribes' resentment eclipsed all consideration of Jesus' miracles. Yet these leaders knew that the "**multitudes**" (from *óchlos* [3793], a disorganized crowd) accepted Jesus and followed Him. The organized authorities (v. 23) were always afraid of the multitudes, fearful perhaps that they could even turn the Romans against them.

These leaders were also cognizant of the disciples' faith and the favorable impression Jesus left on people. The crowds themselves had concluded that since John the Baptist, the forerunner of Christ, was a prophet (Matt. 14:5; 21:26), then Jesus of Nazareth was also a prophet (v. 11). The chief priests and the scribes (v. 15) thus ultimately feared Jesus' reputation. Unwilling to acknowledge His deity, they were forced to concede His exceptional popularity among the people He taught and healed.

22

cꝔᴏ

The Parable of the Marriage Supper
(22:1–14; Luke 14:15–24)

Jesus continued teaching in parables aimed at the leaders of the apostate Jewish nation. In general, parables teach a single point, and we must be careful not to build side inferences from minor points. Analogies are just that: they are like, not identical to.

[1, 2] This is the second parable (see Matt. 18:23) in which Jesus "**likened** [from *homoióō* {3666}] the kingdom of God to a certain **king** [from *basileús* {935}]" (a.t.). This time the king prepared royal "**wedding feasts**" (the plural of *gámos* [1062], not "weddings" but "wedding celebrations," parties, festivities, v. 3) for his son.

Homoióō derives from *hómoios* (3664), meaning like or similar. A correspondence or resemblance exists between the items being compared, not an identity or equality that would be expressed by the verb *eimí* (1510). Jesus made frequent use of similes, but He also used metaphors. For example, when He referred to Himself as the "door of the sheep" (John 10:7).

The most natural symbolism portrays the "**certain king**" as the Father and the "son" as the Son of God. Everyone else is either a slave or an invited guest. The Lord Jesus elsewhere is depicted as a bridegroom and His church as the bride (Matt. 9:15; 25:1; John 3:29; Eph. 5:25–32; Rev. 21:2, 9), and the marriage occurs in heaven. In the parable, the marriage is referred to as "the marriage" (*hó gámos;* see Rev. 19:7), while the preparation and the accompanying festivities of the marriage are given in the plural *gámous* throughout this chapter (vv. 2, 3, 4, 9). The event presupposes the prior rapture of the church, described by Paul in 1 Thessalonians 4:13–18.

The marriage is the final revelation of whom God saves, although this exact number—like the hairs on our heads (Matt. 10:30)—is infallibly foreknown by God in eternity past. Because God's foreknowledge is free from error, this number cannot be changed in history; it must be exactly what God foreknew, nothing more, nothing less (Eccl. 3:14). The Creator Himself is Lord of the history He foreknows: "I have spoken it, I will also bring it to pass; I have purposed it, I will also do it" (Isa. 46:11, cf. John 1:3). The bridegroom of Christ will encompass both Old and New Testament saints from all ages, including the final Tribulation period.

[3] In great detail, Jesus told about the original guests invited to the wedding festivities:

> And [the king] **sent forth** [from *apostéllō* {649}, to send forth on a mission] his **servants** [from *doúlos* {1401}, bond-slave] to call **them that were bidden** [*keklēménous*, the perfect passive participle of *kaléō* {2564}, to call, invite, bid] to the wedding.

The perfect tense implies that they had been invited at one time, and the invitation was still valid. Because everything was now prepared, the king now requested his servants to call those who had been invited earlier.

In the Gospels, the verb *kaléō* does not always reflect the effectual call to salvation that it does in the Epistles, especially those of Paul and Peter (Rom. 8:30; 9:11; 1 Cor. 1:9; 1 Pet. 2:9, 21; 5:10). Jesus gave a general call to all persons exhausted by their labors in Matthew 11:28—"Come unto me, all ye that labour and are heavy laden, and I will give you rest." But this was not Jesus' call of particular individuals to salvation such as He gave to Paul on his way to Damascus (Acts 9:3–9). God is not obligated to change the natural will of those who reject His standing invitation or general call.

However, on the day of judgment, no persons will be able to say they were not invited. In John 1:9, we read that the Word of God, which is God (John 1:1), was the "true Light which, coming into the world, enlightens [from *phōtízō* {5461}] every man" (NASB). Consequently, every person is responsible for his or her response.

Note the reaction of those invited: "And they would not come." The verb "**would**" is *éthelon*, "willed," the imperfect tense of *thélō* (2309), to will in a determinative sense—as compared with *boúlomai* (1014), to desire, to prefer—(literally, were not determining). It is followed by *eltheín*, the aorist infinitive of *érchomai* (2064), "**to come.**" This is not a physical handicap; the inability is obstinacy and rejection (reflected in the imperfect tense), the inflexible attitude of a will that is not neutral. The cannot is a will not. The aorist tense of *érchomai* indicates that these individuals did not make a single choice in favor of Christ. At the second invitation, this group made excuses for not coming.

Even though the call was indirect, that is, through the king's servants, the refusal to come constituted a personal affront to the king and his son. Perhaps, the subjects did not identify the servants with the king as much as they should have; they did not realize who ultimately was inviting them. God's specific call, by contrast, not only infallibly produces an effect but is direct (i.e., not mediated through servants) and is by name, as in the cases of the apostle Paul (Acts 9:4) and the sheep (John 10:27).

[4] At this point, the king clarified the incentives, implying that the invited guests had every reason to accept the offer:

> **Again** [*pálin* {3825}, once more], **he sent forth** [from *apostéllō* {649} as in v. 3] **other** [from *állos* {243}, others of the same kind] servants, saying, Tell **them that are bidden** [*keklēménois*, the perfect passive participle of *kaléō*, as in v. 3], **Behold** [*idoú* {2400}, the imperative of *eídon* {1492}, the aorist of *horáō* {3708}, to perceive, calling attention to the extraordinary {see Matt. 3:16}], **I have made ready** [from *hetoimázō* {2090}] my **dinner** [*áriston* {712}]. My **oxen** [from *taúros* {5022}, bull] and my **fatlings** [from *sitistós* {4619} from *sítos* {4621}, wheat; therefore, grain-fed cattle] **have been killed** [from *thúō* {2380}, to slaughter as for sacrifice], and all things are ready. Come unto the marriage. (a.t.)

"**Behold**" called attention to something wonderful that might otherwise be missed—here, that the food and "all things are **ready** [from *hétoimos* {2092}, prepared]." The first invitation did not include this information, so the level of accountability was now higher. Refusal at this point was absurd. "Behold" is intended to cause people to look beyond the human feast in the parable to the Divine One that celebrates not a marriage between humans but between the Messiah and His bride, the church.

"My **dinner** [*áriston*]" implied the best meal of the day (Luke 14:12)— here dinner, judging by the slaughter of oxen and cows, for which the king prepared the best possible food. Oxen and fatlings yielded the best meats.

The verb *hetoimázō* is related to the adjective used by Jesus when He advised His disciples to be ready at all times for His return: "Therefore, be the **ready** [from *hétoimos*] ones, for in such an hour as you do not think, the Son of man comes" (Matt. 24:44; a.t.). It is also used with respect to the preparation of the everlasting fire for the devil and his angels (Matt. 25:41).

In the analogy of the kingdom, preparation for this celebration is based on the king's determination that some will attend the feast, even if the first group invited turn it down (cf. note on Matt. 28:19). The verb *thúō*, "**killed**," is twice used in connection with the sacrifice of the Paschal Lamb, symbolic of the body of Jesus Christ (Mark 14:12; Luke 22:7) and in 1 Corinthians 5:7 for Christ's sacrifice.

"**Come!**" (*deúte* [1205], an interjection) is the concluding imperative. The king invited his subjects to respond because he had planned this wonderful feast.

[5] The poor response of those first invited is detailed in these next two verses.

> But **having made light** [*amelésantes*, the aorist active participle of *ameléō*
> {272}, to show no concern or care, to neglect; from the alpha privative *a* {1},
> without; and *mélei* {n.f.}, care or concern] of it, **they went their ways** [from
> *apérchomai* {565}, to go away], one to his **own** [from *ídios* {2398}, private]
> **farm** [from *agrós* {68}, a field], another to his **merchandise** [from *emporía*
> {1711}, business, commerce; from which we derive our English word "empo-
> rium"]. (a.t.)

In Hebrews 2:3, the same aorist participle of *ameléō* is translated by the stronger attitudinal verb "neglect": "How shall we escape, having neglected [*amelésantes*, the aorist participle assuming the prior truth of neglect to infer the conclusion of no escape] so great salvation?" (a.t.).

In general, the action of an aorist participle is most frequently prior to and causally related to a main verb. Thus, the attitude, "**having made light of**" something, not only comes first but determines the subsequent course of action—"**went away.**" Logically, attitudes precede actions, and actions result from predispositions.

The excuses offered are worldly. It is amazing how often the Gospels portray the "care [*mérimna* {3308}] of this age [from *aiōn* {165}] and the deceit [*apátē* {539}] of wealth [from *ploútos* {4149}]" (Matt. 13:22; a.t.) as powerfully dissuasive influences against following after the things of God.

Perhaps we can conclude from this that those specifically invited were financially secure, whereas those from the highways and byways were not so well off.

Those who refused could have accepted the invitation without neglecting their responsibilities. But they may have seen it as a threat. Perhaps they were hoarding wealth by defrauding laborers of proper wages or oppressing their best workers (see James 5:3–6)—vested sins for which they would have to repent if they followed Christ. In any case, they did not seek the kingdom of God as their first priority. In Matthew 19:29 Jesus had said that "every one who **has forsaken** [from *aphíēmi* {863}, to send away, to release, to forsake] houses, or brethren, or sisters, or father, or mother, or wife, or children, or lands, for My name's sake, shall receive a hundred times as much and shall inherit everlasting life" (a.t.).

The word translated "forsaken" here (*aphíēmi* [863]) indicates what our attitude ought to be when we forsake anybody or anything for Christ's sake. It comes from the preposition *apó* (575), away from, and the verb *híēmi* (n.f.), to send. We must send away, releasing our earthly cares as we dedicate ourselves to God.

But a synonym of *aphíēmi*, to forsake, indicates what our manner should be. In Luke 14:33 Jesus said: "So likewise, whosoever he be of you that forsaketh [from *apotássomai* {657}] not all that he hath, he cannot be my disciple." *Apotássomai* comes from the same preposition *apó* (575), away from, and the verb *tássō* (5021), to put in order, arrange. We should carefully arrange the disposal of our businesses or possessions (*apotássomai*) in consideration of those we must forsake in our priority of service to the King (*aphíēmi*). We should not neglect our families or possessions (Luke 14:33), but we should never value them in such a way that prevents our service to Him.

[6] Two groups of rejecters are portrayed in this parable: the first, in the previous verse, indifferent and callous, and now a second group that is much more violent:

> And the **remnant** [from *loipós* {3062}, the rest, the balance], **having taken hold of** [from *kratéō* {2902}, to seize, to violently take hold of] his servants, **treated them spitefully** [from *hubrízō* {5195}, to treat shamefully, act arrogantly and insolently in word and deed; from which we derive our English word "hubris"] and **killed** [from *apokteínō* {615}, to kill] them. (a.t.)

It is shocking to find sin so cruel in the face of kindness—this was an invitation to a wedding feast. They both insulted kindness and then killed it. The depravity shown in this parable weighs heavily against the idea of the natural goodness of humanity. The same treatment was given to the son of the householder in the parable of the wicked vinedressers (Matt. 21:39).

[7] When the king received word of the murders, he became enraged. The Greek word translated "**was wroth**" in the King James Version is *orgízo mai* (3710), to be angry.

This describes God's attitude toward those who insult and harm the servants who represent Him and His Son, the Lord Jesus Christ (Matt. 21:40). The noun from *orgízomai* is *orgé* (3709), wrath, anger. Paul tells us that God is not unjust when He brings wrath down upon evil: "Is God unrighteous [unjust] who taketh vengeance [from *orgé*, wrath]?" (Rom. 3:5). The answer of course is no!

Though aimed at the Jewish nation, this parable supports Paul's general contention that God intends His rich goodness (from *chrēstótēs* [5544], mellowness, gentleness), forbearance (from *anochḗ* [463], tolerance), and longsuffering (from *makrothumía* [3115], patience toward people) to lead people to repentance (Rom. 2:4). But natural persons, he notes, despise these qualities. Rather than repent, Paul observes in verse 5, "after your hardness and impenitent heart, you treasure up [from *thēsaurízō* {2343}] to yourself wrath [from *orgḗ*] against the day of wrath [from *orgḗ*] and revelation of the righteous judgment of God" (a.t.). God will not tolerate people's ongoing rejection of His gracious kindnesses forever. Wrath will meet wrath head-on, on the day of wrath.

Judgment is inevitable and, as the parable teaches, the king's anger is swift:

> And **having sent forth** [from *pémpō* {3992}, to send; contrasting with another verb, *apostéllō*, which means to send forth on a mission] his **armies** [from *stráteuma* {4753} from which we derive our English word "strategy", cf. Matt. 26:53; Rev. 19:14 where "the armies in heaven" follow the Word of God to battle at Armageddon; Rev. 19:19], **he destroyed** [from *apóllumi* {622}] those **murderers** [from *phoneús* {5406}] and **burned up** [from *empíprēmi* or *empréthō* {1714}, to set on fire, burn, blow a flame, kindle] their city. (a.t.)

Both individuals and their proud creations (cities) come under this judgment. The reference here is predictive of the overthrow of the people and the city of Jerusalem in A.D. 70 by armies of men and angels. (For God's warrior angels involved in earthly battles, see Deut. 7:20; Josh. 24:12; 2 Kgs. 6:15–18; Ps. 78:49; Dan. 10:13, 20; Acts 12:23; and Rev. 19:19.)

All this was anticipated by the Lord Jesus in His lamentation over Jerusalem, which was "left . . . desolate" after its final rejection—"ye **would** [from *thélō* {2309}, to determine, wish] not"—of His words (Matt. 23:37–39; Luke 13:34, 35). Israel's rejection of Christ was the apex of a long history of rebellion and murder of prophets:

> Not according to the covenant that I made with their fathers in the day when I took them by their hands to lead them out of the land of Egypt; because they continued not in My covenant, and I neglected [from *ameléō* {272}] them. (Heb. 8:9; a.t.)

If we consistently neglect the prophets God sends to us, He will inevitably punish us: "How shall we escape, having neglected [*amelḗsantes*, the aorist participle of *ameléō*] so great a salvation?" (Heb. 2:3; a.t.).

[8–10] Who finally came and ate the food the king prepared? Not those originally called but another group unrelated to this first one. Unhindered by rejection, the king redirected his servants:

> Then he said to his servants, On the one hand, the wedding is ready, but they that were bidden were not **worthy** [from *áxios* {514}]. Go therefore into

the **divisions** [from *diéxodos* {1327} from *diá* {1223}, through; and *éxodos* {1841} from *ek* {1537}, out of; and *hodós* {3598}, road, path; "intersecting"] of the roads, and as many as you shall find, **bid** [*kalésate*, the aorist imperative of *kaléō* {2564}] to the marriage. So those servants went out into the roads and **gathered together** [*sunégagon*, the aorist tense of *sunágō* {4863}] all whom they found, both **bad** [from *ponērós* {4190}, malevolent] and **good** [from *agathós* {18}, benevolent]: and the wedding was filled with guests. (a.t.)

Although the servants were to invite Jews and Gentiles alike—some "**bad**" and some "**good**"—as many as the servants could find. Those who originally rejected the invitation were not "worthy"—in the positive sense of reward—of the feast. They were, however, "worthy of death [from *thánatos*]" (Rom. 1:32).

This accords well with what Jesus had prophesied to the Jews earlier: "The kingdom of God shall be taken from you, and given to a nation bringing forth the fruits thereof" (Matt. 21:43). While individual Jews continued to respond to the gospel, God judged the nation represented by the Pharisees, other leaders, and the majority of ordinary people who demanded Christ's crucifixion. The Jews were scattered among Gentile nations following the destructive aftermath of A.D. 70.

The king commanded his servants in the parable to turn their attention from successful people to the common poor found in the "crossroads." They were not to make moral discriminations but were to invite "**both bad and good**" (see above). As in other parables, the kingdom in this present church age contains good and bad fish, wheat and tares, and here "good" and "evil" that symbolize the regenerate and unregenerate.

The single "**call**" (aorist) is effective, inasmuch as every person the servants find, they "**gather together**" (aorist). However, this is not God's call for salvation for two reasons: First, the call, once again (v. 4), is mediated by servants; second, one of the "bad" subjects is found within the feast but without a wedding garment and is immediately bound and cast into outer darkness (see below).

God alone "calls out" as Jesus said: "I have chosen you out [from *eklégomai* {1586}] of the world" (John 15:19, cf. Mark 13:20; Luke 6:13; John 6:70; 13:18; 15:16, 19; Acts 1:2, 24; 13:17; 15:7; 1 Cor. 1:27, 28; Eph. 1:4; James 2:5).

[11] The "bad" guest stood out from the rest, immediately catching the eye of the king:

And when the king came in **to see** [*theásasthai*, the aorist middle infinitive of *theáomai* {2300}, to see something; the infinitive carries the connotation of purpose, i.e., to inspect] the **guests** [from *anákeimai* {345}, to recline; "one reclining"], he saw there a man which had not on a **wedding garment** [from *énduma* {1742}, outer robe; and *gámos* {1062}, wedding].

A special wedding garment was required for entry and seating at these festive occasions. In oriental custom, this piece of clothing was presented to guests as a token of honor (cf. Judg. 14:12ff.). The guest without the wedding garment was obvious to the king.

The verb associated with the noun *énduma* (1742)—*endúō* (1746) from *en* (1722), in; and *dúō* or *dúnō* (1416), to go down—means to cover what the Greeks called the *chitōn* (5509), the undergarment worn next to the body. In the new covenant, the wedding garment is the "[array] in fine linen, clean and white: for the fine linen is the righteousness of saints" (Rev. 19:8). The "righteousness of saints" is given metaphorically as clothing to clarify that it is the objective righteousness of Christ, not the subjective righteousness of believers. Accordingly, God commands us to "put . . . on [from *endúō*; 'clothe yourself with'] the Lord Jesus Christ" (Rom. 13:14). Our righteousness can never match the pure and holy righteousness of Christ. This is why the lack of the wedding garment was so noticeable.

[12] His gaze fixed on the man, the king asked,

> **Friend** [from *hetaíros* {2083}, selfish comrade], **how** [*pōs* {4459}] **did you come** [from *eisérchomai* {1525}, to enter] in **here** [*hōde* {5602}] not **having** [from *échō* {2192}, to have] a wedding garment? And he was **speechless** [from *phimóō* {5392}, to muzzle]. (a.t.)

The word *hetaíros* is not the same as *héteros*, from which "heterogeneous," one of a different kind, comes. This is another good instance of the use of the word *hetaíros*, which strongly contrasts with *phílos* (5384) although it is commonly translated "friend" (mistakenly taken for *phílos*, as in Matt. 26:50); (cf. Matt. 11:16; 20:13). Jesus called Judas "friend" (from *hetaíros*) even at the point of betrayal, but He hardly considered him a friend. Judas was an associate, a fellow traveler, a comrade, but he had attached himself to Christ for selfish reasons. In modern Greek, *hetaireía* is used for a corporation, and the *hetaíroi* are members of the corporation who come together strictly for economic purposes and personal financial benefit. They rarely associate as "friends" when there is no profit in prospect.

Similarly, this man in the banquet hall did not qualify as a true friend of the king. He was not entitled to dine or attend the festivities, and the absence of the appropriate garment was conspicuous to everyone, especially to the king. As we mentioned, the garment represents the robe of the Christ's righteousness

(Isa. 61:10; Rom. 5:18, 19; Rev. 6:11; 7:9, 13, 14; 19:8, 14), which is acquired through faith (Eph. 2:8). Symbolized by clothing, it is apparent that such righteousness is external and objective—the righteousness of Christ.

The exposure among those fully clad with wedding garments was embarrassment enough, but we should not lose sight of the symbolism here. Since the man did not have a garment, he either ought to have had one or he ought not to have been at the feast. It is moral nakedness, guilt, which leaves one speechless, without any defense.

[13] Once again, the king acted promptly:

> Then the king told the **servants** [from *diákonos* {1249}, those serving at the tables], **Having bound** [from *déō* {1210}, to tie up] him, **hands** [from *cheír* {5495}, hand] and **feet** [from *poús* {4228}, foot], **take** him **away** [from *aírō* {142}, to lift up and remove] and **cast** [from *ekbállō* {1544} from *ek* {1537}, out of from within or among; and *bállō* {906}, to throw, place] him into outer darkness. (a.t.)

Both binding and taking away imply resistance. From Jesus' words that "men loved darkness rather than light" (John 3:19), at least one author has voiced the euphemistic opinion that "the gates of hell are locked on the inside" (C. S. Lewis in *The Great Divorce*). But these words, "binding" and "casting," work against this view. John's words cannot possibly mean that people prefer the fires of hell to the tranquility of heaven. The wicked neither bind themselves nor cast themselves into the furnace of fire, as though it were a preference. The gates of hell are locked on the outside, if at all.

The duty of binding and casting, here assigned to the "servants," reminds us of Jesus' commission: "Whatsoever surely [*eán* {1437}] you bind on earth has been bound in heaven" (Matt. 16:19; a.t.). But before we assume that these "servants" are saved persons in the church and that this is the church age, note that angels are also "servants" of God according to Hebrews 1:14: "Are they not all **ministering** [from *leitourgikós* {3010}, pertaining to liturgical service] spirits, sent forth unto **ministry** [from *diakonía* {1248}, the ministry of a *diákonos* {1249}, servant] for them who shall be heirs of salvation?" (a.t.). Angels also will bind and burn the tares at the end of the age, according to Matthew 13:30.

This is the second time in Matthew that we find the phrase "**outer darkness** [*exóteros* {1857}, the comparative of *éxō* {1854}, outside; and *skótos* {4655}, darkness]." The expression occurs only three times in the Greek New Testament, all three in the Gospel of Matthew concerning punishment for those who displease their Lord. In Matthew 8:12, it is for those who thought they were "children of the kingdom." Here in Matthew 22:13, it is for the guest who didn't care whether or not he was dressed appropriately for the wedding feast. And in Matthew 25:30, it is for the unprofitable servant who thought he would escape the master's wrath by hiding the "talent" that had been entrusted to him to use. In 1 John 1:5, we read that "God is Light, and in Him there is no darkness [*skotía* {4653}, obscurity] at all" (NASB).

In this verse, "outer darkness" is clarified as physically outside the illuminated banquet hall—evidenced by "cast outside." Moreover, the man without the proper garment did not ethically belong among the guests who are properly dressed. Morally bankrupt, he is physically banned from the hall. Having glimpsed and perhaps even having experienced some joy of the celebration, he was not allowed to remain and participate. This would cause extreme regret and frustration, expressed by the words: "There shall be **weeping** [*klauthmós* {2805}] and **gnashing** [*brugmós* {1030}, grating] of teeth."

Consider also the threat Jesus issued to the Jews in Luke 13:28:

> There shall be weeping and gnashing of teeth, when ye shall see Abraham, and Isaac, and Jacob, and all the prophets, in the kingdom of God, and you yourselves thrust out.

[14] Now the servants had "gathered" this man along with the rest, but he was evidently one of the "wicked" (from *ponērós* [4190], see v. 10), the result of the king's command to be indiscriminate among "as many as ye shall find." Jesus explained this in His summary: "For many are called, but few are chosen."

The word translated "called" is from the noun *klētós* (2822), derived from the verb *kaléō* (2564), to call, which is translated "bidden" in verses 4 and 8. The class of the called in the Gospels is broader than the class of the elect. This man was called but, extracting symbols from other parables, he lived as a tare alongside the wheat, a bad fish in the net with the good. So he was "called" into the field and into the fishnet, that is, into the church, but in the end he was a bad tare and a bad fish. He had no change of heart. This invitational meaning for "called" prevails in the Gospels, but the meaning changes in the Epistles to a call that actually changes the heart (Rom. 1:1, 6, 7; 8:28; 1 Cor. 1:1, 2, 24).

A statement in verse 8 has been left for consideration now, and that is: "But **they which were bidden** [from *kaléō*] were not **worthy** [from *áxios* {514}]." We know why they were not worthy, but what does this imply about the "good" persons gathered by the servants? Had they merited the banquet and marriage? As other Scriptures note, they were "worthy" (Luke 20:35; 21:36; 2 Thess. 1:5, 11; Rev. 3:4). But their worthiness is found in the wedding garment itself that they put on, the righteousness of the One who "is made unto us . . . righteousness" (1 Cor. 1:30; see also Rom 10:3; 2 Cor. 5:21; Phil. 3:9; Titus 3:5), meriting salvation for us in His perfect death and life. The "good," the personal righteousness of faith, holiness, and perseverance that we attain in this life, is inseparably linked to the objective justification in Christ represented by the external wedding garment. We "put on" the robe of justification, the wedding garment by faith.

Rendering to Caesar and to God
(22:15–22; Mark 12:13–17; Luke 20:20–26)

The parable of the wedding feast infuriated the Pharisees. They knew that Jesus accused them of rejecting the kingdom of God, of not possessing God's righteousness, and of having a futile righteousness of their own (Rom. 10:3). Beside all this, He had virtually predicted their personal deaths and the destruction of their city.

[15] Consequently, we read,

> Then went the Pharisees, and **took counsel** [*sumboúlion* {4824}, a body of advisers; from *sún* {4862}, together; and *boulé* {1012}, advice] how **they might entangle** [from *pagideúō* {3802}, to set a *pagís* {3803}, a trap] him in his **talk** [from *lógos* {3056}, logic, rational propositions].

They hoped to cause Jesus to say something they could interpret as an attack on Rome, a message the Herodians would carry swiftly to higher authorities. This would expedite His death. Imagine trying to trap the *Lógos* of God, God's personified Logic, with logic.

[16] "And **they sent out** [from *apostéllō* {649}, to send on a mission] unto him their disciples with the Herodians [from *hērōdianoí* {2265}]."

The Herodians were a Jewish political party loyal to the Romans, some of whom even considered Herod to be the Messiah. Because of the Pharisees' heavily compromised allegiance to Moses, they considered the Herodians their enemies. But the Pharisees willingly enlisted them as allies to entrap Jesus (cf. Mark 3:6). The expression "the leaven of Herod" in Mark 8:15 may be an allusion to the Herodians.

On approaching Jesus, the disciples of the Pharisees addressed Him with a long-winded, flattering barrage of lies:

> **Master** [from *didáskalos* {1320}], **we know** [from *oída*, the perfect of *horáō* {3708}, to see and perceive] that thou art **true** [*alēthés* {227}, genuine], and

teachest the **way** [from *hodós* {3598}] of God [meaning the Father as in John 1:1, 2] in **truth** [from *alḗtheia* {225}, truth], neither **carest** [from *mélō* {3199}, to care] thou for **any man** [from *oudeís* {3762}, not any one or anything]: for **thou regardest** [from *blépō* {991}, to see] not the **person** [*prósōpon* {4383}, face, appearance] **of men** [from *ánthrōpos* {444}, man].

What a preface! They believed none of these truths. Surely, they hoped the flattery would ensnare Jesus, please the crowd, or both. We know these were scheming and not honest appraisals.

[17] The attempt at entrapment began:

Tell us therefore, What **do You think** [*dokeí*, the third person singular of *dokéō* {1380}, to think; lit., "How does it seem {to you}"]? **Is it lawful** [*éxestin* {1832}, the third person singular impersonal of the verb *éxeimi* {n.f.}, to be lawful] **to give** [from *dídōmi* {1325}] **tribute** [from *kḗnsos* {2778}] to Caesar or not? (a.t.)

"Tribute" was a poll tax paid by each person recorded in the census, a polling of people and a property valuation. "Tribute" was the Latin word from which the Greek *kḗnsos* was transliterated (Matt. 17:25; Mark 12:14, 15 where it is called a "penny" or *dēnárion* [1220], the pay for one twelve-hour day of work [Matt. 20:2]) during the Roman occupation. Poll taxes collected from subjugated nations were called *phóros* ([5411]; Luke 20:22; 23:2; Rom. 13:6, 7).

Most Jews bitterly resented paying this tax imposed by Rome. So the question was filled with dangerous enticements. Any answer would necessarily enrage either the Jews (the Pharisees and their followers) or the Romans. If Christ's antagonists could get Him to say that it was unlawful, they could accuse Him to the Roman authorities and have Him apprehended. On the other hand, if they could get Jesus to say that it was lawful, the whole Jewish nation would be incited against Him and Rome. In either case, the Romans would retaliate against the instigator long before revolution or the threat of revolution broke out. The Pharisees knew either answer would cause Him a great deal of trouble.

[18] Jesus was cognizant of their evil intent:

But Jesus, **having perceived** [from *ginṓskō* {1097}, to know by experience] their **wickedness** [from *ponēría* {4189}, malice, evil intent], said, Why **do you tempt** [from *peirázō* {3985}, to tempt or test, here with the evil intention of causing trouble] Me, you **hypocrites** [from *hupokritḗs* {5273}, a stage-player, one who does not show his true self; cf. Mark 12:15]? (a.t.)

While Jesus had implied hypocrisy in the past (Matt. 6:2, 5, 16; 7:5; 15:7), this is the second time He explicitly called the Pharisees "hypocrites." He would do so many times later (Matt. 23:13–15). Mark 12:15 substitutes *eidōs*, the perfect participle of *oída* for *ginōskō*. But since *ginōskō* means experiential knowledge and *eidōs* derives from *horáō* (3708), to see and perceive—both of which are experiences—the two terms converge in meaning.

[19] Jesus was not intimidated by the request:

> **Shew** [from *epideíknumi* {1925}, to exhibit] me the tribute **money** [*nómisma* {3546}, the coin in use to pay the poll tax]. And they brought unto him a **penny** [*dēnárion* {1220}, a coin of very low value].

The "penny" or dinar is the most commonly mentioned coin in the Gospels (Matt. 18:28; 20:2, 9, 10, 13; 22:19; Mark 6:37; 12:15; 14:5; Luke 7:41; 10:35; 20:24; John 6:7; 12:5). The impression on it included the name, title, and image (effigy) of the reigning emperor or some member of the imperial family (Norman Fraser, *A Dictionary of Christ and the Gospels*, edited by James Hastings, pp. 199–200).

[20, 21] "And He saith unto them, Whose is this **image** [*eikōn* {1504}, likeness, profile] and **inscription** [*epigraphē* {1923}]? They say unto Him, Caesar's." (a.t., cf. Rom. 13:1, 5; 1 Pet. 2:13–17)

This was probably the image of the Roman emperor, Tiberius Caesar, who reigned in A.D. 14–37 (Luke 3:1).

> Then saith he unto them, **Render** [from *apodídōmi* {591}; from *apó* {575}, from; and *dídōmi* {1325}, to give; to give voluntarily something in fulfillment of an obligation or expectation, cf. Matt. 16:27; 21:41] therefore unto Caesar the things which are Caesar's; and unto God the things that are God's.

We cannot give to God as we would give to human rulers. God is almighty (*pantokrátōr* [3841] from *pás* [3956], all, the totality; and *krátōr* [n.f.], the one who holds, from the verb *krateō* [2902], to hold; see 2 Cor. 6:18), the absolute and universal Sovereign who needs nothing. He holds all things, maintains dominion, and therefore owns everything (John 16:15; 17:10; Col. 1:15, 16). We can only give back to God what He has given us, and we give indirectly to Him through His people (Matt. 25:35-45).

Paul commits seven verses of Romans 13 to the just payment of tribute (*phóros* [5411]; vv. 6, 7) to human governments as our civic duty. In most countries, taxes are allocated to defense, both externally (military) and internally (police and National Guard), to employment (governmental), and to social programs that benefit the retired and the poor. The "for" that connects Romans 13:5 to 13:6 implies that taxes finance the king's sword (from *máchaira* [3162]; v. 4], the "revenger [*ékdikos* {1558}, punisher] to execute wrath [from *orgē* {3709}] upon him that doeth evil" (Rom. 13:4).

Paul implies that an invisible theocracy is in place since "there is no power but of God: the powers that be are ordained of God" (Rom. 13:1). Therefore, a ruler is "the minister of God" (13:4), both of good to the good and of vengeance to the evildoer (v. 4).

[22] The leaders were impressed with Jesus' ability to avoid the trap:

> And having heard, **they marveled** [from *thaumázō* {2296}, to marvel, wonder, admire] and **having left** [from *aphíēmi* {863}, to leave alone] Him, they went their way. (a.t.)

Matthew records many times that people marveled at Jesus' words and actions: the disciples who witnessed the calming of the storm marveled (8:27); the crowd marveled when Jesus cast out a demon so that a dumb man could speak (9:33); the multitudes marveled when Jesus healed the dumb, the maimed, the lame, and the blind (15:31); Jesus' disciples marveled when He caused the fig tree to wither and die (21:20); and now the Pharisees and Herodians themselves marvel at Jesus' reconciling of civic and divine obligations.

Jesus was not trying to avoid death—that is why He came to Jerusalem in the first place—but He could never be tricked or arrested out of season. He planned to allow Himself to be betrayed (*paradídōmi* [3860]; cf. Matt. 17:22; 20:18, 19; 26:2, 24, 45) when the time was right.

As admirable as Jesus' response was, the Pharisees left. Repeatedly, the unrepentant hearts of people give lip service and toss a few peace offerings to God but inevitably returns to their vomit and mire (2 Pet. 2:22). As Jesus said, "If they hear not Moses and the prophets, neither will they be persuaded, though one rose from the dead" (Luke 16:31).

Jesus Answers the Sadducees about Life after Death
(22:23–33; Mark 12:18–27; Luke 20:27–40)

In the temple, Jesus dealt with the Pharisees, the scribes (from *grammateús* [1122]) who were students and teachers of the Jewish law, and the Herodians (*hērōdianoí* [2265]), a Jewish political sect favoring, as the name implies, the Roman occupation of Israel.

The chief priests were members of the Sanhedrin and mostly from the small sect of the Sadducees. They were wealthy, rationalistic, and more liberal than the Pharisees and Essenes (Matt. 3:7; 16:1, 6, 11, 12; 22:23, 34; Mark 12:18; Luke 20:27; Acts 4:1; 5:17; 23:6–8). Unlike the Pharisees, they restricted divine inspiration to the Pentateuch, the first five books of the Bible; they did not believe that the spirit survives death; and they rejected the ideas of bodily resurrection, final judgment, heaven, and hell. These last denials (cf. Acts 23:8) prompted the discussion that follows.

On Tuesday within the last week of His life, Jesus was in the temple. Many Sadducees no doubt had either heard of Lazarus' resurrection and/or seen him alive.

[23] On the same day that Jesus stumped the Pharisees and Herodians, the Sadducees came to Him with what they felt was a question He could not answer concerning the resurrection. The verb that Matthew uses implies that they did more than just ask a question; they demanded an answer. This verb is from *eperōtáō* (1905), from the intensive prefix *epí* (1909), upon; and the verb *erōtáō* (2065), to ask or inquire. The Sadducees tended to equate heaven with earth, like the Corinthians to whom Paul found it necessary to differentiate (1 Cor. 15:42–49) the earthly, natural (from *psuchikós* [5591]) body from the heavenly spiritual (from *pneumatikós* [4152] body; (see the author's works, *Conquering the Fear of Death: An Exegetical Commentary on First Corinthians 15*, and *Life After Death*, for a full treatment of objections to the resurrection).

[24–28] The story the Sadducees told Jesus may have been exaggerated fiction, but the expression "with us" (v. 25) argues for real history.

As it stands, there are seven brothers. The first marries a woman and then dies without offspring. Each successive brother performs his levirate duty (Gen. 38:8; Deut. 25:5) of marrying the widow to raise up seed to each prior, childless brother until all seven have married and died. Finally, the widow dies (vv. 25–27). The verb translated "**shall marry**" in verse 24 (from *epigambreúō* [1918]), derives from *epí* (1909), to or after; and *gambreúō* (n.f.), to marry after, which fits the context of remarriage.

It is not known whether this Mosaic law was kept during Christ's time, but the Pharisees and Sadducees, like contributing authors to the Talmud and Mishnah, often used exaggerated scenarios to engender controversy.

"**Issue**" in verse 25 translates the noun *spérma* (4690), sperm, seed, or offspring, the phrase meaning that no children had been born to any of the seven brothers.

"**Deceased**" (KJV) translates a Greek verb from *teleutáō* (5053), to end or finish (i.e., life in the body) in verse 25, which is followed by the synonymous verb died (from *apothnéskō* [599], to expire), referring to the death of the woman who had become the wife of all seven brothers (v. 27).

The question posed to Jesus was this:

In the **resurrection** [from *anástasis* {386}, a standing up from a prone position either "anew" or "again" {*aná* (303)}] whose wife shall she be of the seven? for they all had her. (v. 28)

[29] Without hesitation, Jesus answered,

You are deceived [*planásthe*, the present passive of *planáō* {4105}, to lead astray], not **having known** [from *oída* the perfect of *horáō* {3708}, to perceive] the Scriptures or the power of God. (a.t.)

Although Jesus would wisely extract His proof from the Pentateuch itself, it is possible here that by "**the Scriptures,**" He referred to the prophets whom the Sadducees rejected. Their "error" then would be not extending inspiration to such prophecies as Isaiah 26:19, "Thy dead men shall live, together with my dead body shall they arise," or Daniel 12:2, "And many of them that sleep in the dust of the earth shall awake, some to everlasting life, and some to shame and everlasting contempt."

Jesus went beyond this, however, to accuse the Sadducees of a limited application of a basic theistic premise—the omnipotence of God. In the matter of the resurrection, one must take into account what the Scriptures say specifically about the power of God. The Sadducees were not atheists. They did accept the five books of Moses as revelation.

Furthermore, they did not deny omnipotence. The Sadducees believed in the power of God to do all sorts of things, but they did not believe He would reclothe a spirit with a new body after death. There was nothing in their definition of omnipotence that required resurrection. An omnipotent God could choose to sustain spirits after death without bodily forms or to annihilate souls altogether. Because God can do anything He so desires, Jesus needed to show from the Torah that God does use His power to raise the dead, so He pointed them to Exodus 3:6.

While the Sadducees allowed for a power in man to "raise up" a full human body and soul out of "seed," they denied this power to God in the afterlife. Apparently, they did not think of the development of a body and soul from a seed as an impressive miracle. But if God cannot raise the dead, how did He create Adam out of dust in the first place? And the creation story is in the Torah!

[30] Jesus addressed the issue of marriage in the afterlife first by arguing that the resurrection body is spiritual in nature:

For in the **resurrection** [from *anástasis* {386}, i.e., in the life following the resurrection] they **neither** [*oúte* {3777}] **marry** [from *gaméō* {1060}, to marry, take a wife], **nor** [*oúte*] **are given in marriage** [from *ekgamízō* {1547}; an alternate of *ekgamískō* {1548}, to give in marriage as a father gives his daughter; see 1 Cor. 7:38], but are as the angels of God in heaven.

The groom marries (*gaméō*) the woman whose father gives her in marriage (*gamískō* [1061]). The purpose of God is that "they [the bride and the groom] twain [two] shall be one flesh" (Matt. 19:5).

While we are not taught a great deal about the resurrected body, we are told that it will be different from the one on earth. Paul says it will be a body that is primarily spiritual (from *pneumatikós* [4152]; see 1 Cor. 15:44) and glorious (from *éndoxos* [1741], gorgeous, honorable; see Eph. 5:27), manifesting the glory and power of God.

Jesus said we will be "**as** [*hōs* {5613}, like] angels [the definite article is not in the Greek text] of God in heaven." The small particle "as" (critical to the meaning) and the lack of a definite article (identity) preceding "angels" mean that we will not become angels when we are resurrected; rather, we will be "as" or "like" them—similar but not identical in basic nature. The additional qualification "in heaven" implies a predicate such as glory that would be absent from, say, the "angel of the abyss" (Rev. 9:11) or one of Satan's angels (Rev. 12:7). Tying this all together, believers will no longer pair off their angel-like bodies in marriage for the purpose of procreating the race. Procreation is obsolescent in immortality.

If we want to gain insight into our metaphysical state, we can study the resurrected body of Jesus Christ. His resurrected body was neither spaceless (omnipresent since it was seen in one place or another, although not two places simultaneously), nor timeless (an attribute of God, therefore also of Christ's divine nature) as He performed sequential actions like eating and walking. Yet He had transcendence over space so He could move from place to place quickly and even walk through walls. This latter ability should seem neither strange nor impossible to us, since, according to science, physical entities are mostly empty space, and the boundaries and charges that separate subatomic particles are God's creations. He is the cohesion that holds atoms together, and, as all nature, they are under His authority.

Jesus' resurrected body was apparently free from the necessities of food, water, and air. Since our bodies will be "spiritual" like Christ's (1 Cor. 15:44), they will not be enslaved to material things. However, we will enjoy both spiritual and material things as evidenced by Jesus' eating of a breakfast of bread and fish with His disciples (John 21:12, 13). This was a voluntary meal, enjoyed but not needed.

[31, 32] Jesus now confronted the Sadducees with their own Bible, the Pentateuch (Ex. 3:6):

Have ye not **read** [*anégnōte*, the aorist tense of *anaginōskō* {314}, to read, the aorist implying, "Didn't you ever read at any time"] **that which was spoken** [from *eréō* {2046}, to say precisely] unto you [i.e., for your own benefit even if you don't believe it now] **by** [*hupó* {5259}, by, which indicates direct cause] God, saying, I am the God of Abraham, and the God of Isaac, and the God of Jacob? God **is** [from *eimí* {1510}] not the God of the **dead** [from *nekrós* {3498}], but of the **living** [*zōntōn*, the present participle of *záō* {2198}, to live].

The Sadducees did not believe in the existence of human or angelic spirits (Acts 23:8), and they denied any resurrection—physical or spiritual. This did not mean, however, that, when Jesus spoke about the dead here, He agreed with their definition of "death" as nonexistence. Death is never juxtaposed to bare existence in Scripture, that is, as a state of nonexistence, which is a contradiction anyway (a state of nonexistence is a state of statelessness, which makes no logical sense). The true definition of "death" as "separation" (physical or ethical) implies the existence of two separated things.

Furthermore, the present participle, *zōntōn*, refers to those living now, not those who lived in the past, which would be expressed by the aorist participle. *Zōntōn* thus stands in opposition to *nekrōn*, "the dead," and since there is no definite article before the participle or the adjectival noun, Jesus spoke generically, that is, of comparative states rather than of persons.

Jesus did not reveal here any details of the kind of life human spirits experience behind the veil as He did elsewhere (Luke 16:19–31). In Luke's narrative, two men were assigned to two distinct locales following their deaths, one to a "place of torment" (v. 28), the other to a place of bliss. The areas were separated (see prior paragraph) by a great gulf (*chásma* [5490], chasm, impassable space) so that no one could pass from one place to the other. Their dwellings were fixed, they were both conscious, and they could sense their respective environments. These environments were customized to the way they reacted to God's offer of salvation.

If Abraham, Isaac, and Jacob were not raised from the dead before God spoke to Moses, how did the statement that "God is . . . the God of the . . . living" (note: Luke 20:38 adds "for all live unto him") impact Saducean beliefs?

It did so in two ways. First, even if Jesus had conceded to their definition of death as nonexistence, the Sadducees had to admit that God is not the God of nothing. God cannot say, "I am the God of Abraham," if Abraham does not exist. At best, then He should have said, I was the God of Abraham. If He says, "I am," then Abraham must exist at the time God spoke to Moses, which means either that he was bodily resurrected at death or that his spirit survived his body. Either way, Jesus overthrew one of the Sadducees' primary doctrines.

Second, if God is the God of the existing spirits of these men, then there is something to resurrect—something to reclothe with a body. On Sadducean premises, there might be a creation of another (new) person but not a resurrection, since this implies continuity, the restanding of something that formerly stood. That continuity, the real person, is the spirit that God attaches to a new body.

Jesus' point, then, was this: Since Abraham, Isaac, and Jacob exist, they (i.e., their spirits, their persons, not merely their bodies) can be resurrected—stand again inside new bodies. Resurrection is not a creation ex nihilo. By appealing to God's current sovereignty over these "dead" who "live unto him" (Luke 20:38), Jesus overthrew the primary Sadducean doctrine of annihilation, which in turn opened up the possibility for the resurrection of the body. If Abraham currently exists, then Abraham can be resurrected bodily.

[33] The people who heard this conversation of Jesus with the Sadducees were justifiably "**astonished**" (from *ekplēssō* [1605], to astonish; from *ek* [1537], out of from within or among; and *plēssō* [4141], to strike; thus to be hit from without by surprise).

Not only did Jesus silence the Sadducees on the doctrines of spirit and bodily resurrection, but He did so from within their own narrow set of inspired Scriptures, the Torah—an amazing feat!

The Two Great Commandments
(22:34–40; Mark 12:28–34)

[34] Even though the Pharisees agreed with Jesus on these two points—the immortality of the soul and the resurrection of the body—they seemed more threatened than overjoyed with Jesus' successful refutation of their nemeses:

> But when the Pharisees heard that **He silenced** [from *phimóō* {5392}, to muzzle, to cause to be silent] the Sadducees, **they were gathered together** [from *sunágō* {4863}, to lead, gather together] at the same place. (a.t.)

Apparently, the Pharisees did not gather to rejoice over their enemies; instead, they seemed to think He might disagree with them and lead people away from their authority as well. Consequently, they posed a question of their own.

The use of the verb *phimóō*, to muzzle, is interesting. The first time this verb is used in the New Testament is in this chapter: "Comrade [*hetaíre* {2083}], how did you enter here not having a wedding garment? And he was silenced [*ephimóthē*, the aorist passive indicative]" (v. 12; a.t.). The man was restrained by guilt and exposure. Here the Sadducees were trapped by the clarity of their own Scriptures.

We find this verb next in Mark 1:25 (see also Luke 4:35) when Jesus commanded an unclean spirit to come out of a demonized man in the Capernaum synagogue: "Be silent [from *phimóō* {5392}]!" (a.t.). The command was irresistible, and Jesus essentially stopped the unclean spirit from speaking.

A similar use of the verb is found in Mark 4:39 when Jesus addressed the raging sea, "Be silent [from *siōpáō* {4623}, to become silent] and be muzzled [from *phimóō*]" (a.t.).

In his first epistle, Peter says, "For so is the will of God, that with well doing ye may put to silence [from *phimóō*] the ignorance of foolish men" (1 Pet. 2:15). Good works, not always clever arguments, silence critics.

Notwithstanding their disagreement with the Sadducees, the Pharisees saw Jesus as a threat not to just Sadduceism, but to Judaism—their nation and their leadership—as a whole. Whenever they gathered together near Jesus, it was not for a good cause.

[35, 36] Matthew comments,

> Then one of them, which was a **lawyer** [*nomikós* {3544}, one skilled in the Mosaic Law], **asked** [from *eperōtáō* {1905} from *epí* {1909}, an intensive; and *erōtáō* {2065}, to ask as an equal] him a question, **tempting** [from *peirázō* {3985}, to tempt, to test] him, and saying, **Master** [from *didáskalos* {1320}, teacher], which is the **great** [from *mégas* {3173}] **commandment** [*entolé* {1785}] in the law?

This lawyer attempted to hide his evil intention by calling Jesus "Teacher." This title is used twenty-nine times in the New Testament to address Jesus directly. Twice Jesus referred to Himself as "Teacher," both times with the definite article, "the Teacher" (*ho didáskalos;* Matt. 26:18; John 13:14).

The question with which this lawyer hoped to entrap Jesus was this: "Which is the great commandment in the law?" (v. 36). The Pharisees' methodology had not changed. Just as they tried to force Jesus to choose one of two bad options with respect to paying taxes to Rome, so now they tried to make Him prioritize the 613 commandments of God. No matter what hierarchical order He imposed, someone would be offended, and their malevolent purpose would be accomplished.

[37] Jesus did not fall for this weakly disguised evil. He simply and wisely reduced the many commandments to two, the first of which is, "**Thou shalt love** [*agapéseis*, the future tense of *agapáō* {25}] the Lord thy God with all thy heart, and with all thy soul, and with all thy mind." This is an example of a future tense used as a categorical imperative—you will in the sense of you'd

better or you'd best do what I say. The lawyer had asked for the great command, not the great prophecy, and the verb form in the Septuagint version of Deuteronomy is the same (*agapéseis*).

The command to love God was not new, and the Jews would only accept Christ's teachings if they mirrored the contents of the Old Testament. This is why Jesus constantly referred to it. This particular command is found in Deuteronomy 6:5: "And **thou shalt love** [*agapéseis*] the LORD [Jehovah {3068, OT}; *kúrion* {2962, NT}, denoting supreme authority] thy God." The command is directed to all the faculties we have—our hearts, souls, and minds. This love must be total (from *hólos* [3650], complete, to the fullest extent; from which we get our English word "whole").

We should understand the quality of the sentiment that is involved in the word "love" (*agápē*). God's love must become ours, and the only way it can is if Christ becomes ours. We cannot love the way He does unless we acquire His nature (2 Pet. 1:4). In 1 Corinthians 13, the apostle Paul provides a checklist of behavior to see whether the love of God is the basic motivator of our thoughts and actions. (See the author's books, *To Live Is to Love* on 1 Cor. 13, and *The Epistles of John*.)

In coming into the world, the Lord Jesus demonstrated His love (*agápē*) when He sacrificed Himself on the cross for our sins (Isa. 53:10; 1 Pet. 2:24). This offering was accepted by the triune God (Heb. 10:10), and the acceptance of His sacrifice was the sealing (from *sphragízō* [4972]) of our redemption (from *apolútrōsis* [629]; Eph. 4:30).

God loved the world while the world had no respect for Him. In Romans 5:6 Paul expresses it this way: "For when we were yet without strength, in due time Christ died for the ungodly [from *asebés* {765}]," that is, those who have no respect for God. God's *agápē* "gave" sacrificially (John 3:16).

What did Jesus mean when He said that we should love Him with all our hearts, souls, minds, and strength? The "**heart**" (from *kardía* [2588]) is the faculty that thinks, chooses, and produces emotion. When the heart is made pure by God through Jesus Christ, then God befriends us. The "**soul**" (from *psuché* [5590]) is the living element within us, the immaterial part we hold in common with all living things. But the distinct faculty in us that sets us apart from animals is the cognitive element, called the "**mind**" (from *diánoia* [1271] from *diá* [1223], denoting separation; and *noéō* [3539], to contemplate). Finally, the "**strength**" (from *ischús* [2479]; Mark 12:30) is a general term applicable to the heart, soul, and mind.

The Holy Spirit within enables us to love with God's love, the way we ought to love: "Because the love of God is shed abroad in our hearts by the Holy Ghost which is given unto us" (Rom. 5:5).

[38] To make certain the lawyer understood that He was answering the question exactly as he asked it, Jesus used his own words:

This is the **first** [from *prōtos* {4413}, the superlative of *pró* {4253}, prior, foremost, chief, first not just in position or time but in rank or dignity] and **great** [from *mégas* {3173}, splendid, great in estimation, importance] commandment.

No matter what command of God we obey, if our obedience is not motivated or empowered by His love, it is nothing (1 Cor. 13:1–3). Each command is profitable only as it manifests God's love.

[39] Jesus continued, "And the second is like unto it, Thou shalt love thy neighbour as **thyself** [from *seautón* {4572}]."

It is interesting that this quotation from Leviticus 19:18 is expanded in Leviticus 19:34 to include the "stranger" (i.e., any foreigner) who lived in their land. Because sin naturally promotes the ego as the predominant object of love, we are commanded to love others as if they were ourselves (Matt. 19:19). Self-love, while not commanded, is presupposed. This is the rational limit God has placed on us. Had He commanded us to love our neighbors as He loves us, the command would be impossible to obey. Although "**neighbor**" (*plēsíon* [4139]) means the one near us, the parable of the Good Samaritan showed that Jesus intended to include the idea of the oppressed of the world in the term. Some next-door neighbors may reject us, while other people, far away but destitute, gladly receive our message and help.

[40] Finally, for the sake of the Sadducees who accepted only the Pentateuch as Scripture, Jesus added, "On these two commandments **hang** [from *kremánnumi* {2910}] all the law and the prophets." The Sadducees rejected the prophets, but the prophets pointed to Christ as the fulfillment of the Torah, the One who perfectly loved the Father and loved His neighbor as Himself.

Obviously, if something hangs, someone hangs it. Since the Law and the prophets are impersonal, they do not hang themselves on the two commandments to love; therefore, God must hang them.

David's Son and Lord
(22:41–46; Mark 12:35–37; Luke 20:41–44)

[41, 42] The Pharisees had had their day in court trying to entrap Jesus by His own words. It was now Jesus' turn to try them with a question of His own:

What **think ye** [from *dokéō* {1380}, to suppose] **of** [*perí* {4012}, about, concerning, regarding] **Christ** [from *Christós* {5547} from *chríō* {5548}, to anoint]?

whose [from the interrogative pronoun *tís* {5101}, who] son **is** [*estín*, the present tense of *eimí* {1510}, to be] he? They say unto him, The son of David.

"Christ" is preceded by a definite article, meaning "the Messiah," the anointed One of God anticipated in Old Testament prophecy.

By asking the question in the third person, Jesus directed attention away from Himself, perhaps to mitigate the effects of the ever-present, intimidating accolade, "Son of David," which throngs of people shouted out regularly. The definite article here points to a uniqueness that does not mimic the anointing on Old Testament kings like Saul (1 Sam. 10:1) and David (1 Sam. 16:13; see also 1 Sam. 26:11; 1 Kgs. 19:15; Ps. 2:2; Acts 4:26) or prophets like Elisha (1 Kgs. 19:16). In Psalm 105:15, the words "anointed" and "prophet" are used interchangeably. The "Servant of the Lord" said He was anointed to preach the gospel to the poor (Isa. 61:1), a prophecy Jesus applied to Himself (Luke 4:18).

The present tense of *eimí* (to be) has a timeless ring to it, perhaps because Jesus intended to discuss the subject in principle or because He wanted to imply that the Messiah was currently alive.

The expression, "son of David," means David's descendant. In Matthew 1:20 it is used for Joseph, Mary's husband-to-be, but it is frequently applied to Jesus as one of the messianic titles (Matt. 9:27; 12:23; 15:22; 20:30, 31; 21:9, 15; Mark 10:47, 48; 12:35; Luke 18:38, 39). A related messianic title predicated to Jesus Christ is the "root of David" (Isa. 11:1, 10; Rev. 5:5; 22:16; also the "seed of David" in Rom. 1:3). The kingdom of the Messiah is referred to as the "kingdom of David" (Mark 11:10), the "tabernacle of David" (Amos 9:11; Acts 15:16), and the "key of the house of David" (Isa. 22:22; cf. Rev. 3:7).

[43, 44] As soon as the Pharisees responded, Jesus asked,

Why then does David **in Spirit** [*pneúmati*, the dative singular of *pneúma* {4151}, spirit] call him Lord, saying, The **Lord** [*Kúrios* {2962}] said unto My **Lord** [also from *Kúrios*], **Sit** [*káthou*, the present middle reflexive deponent imperative of *káthēmai* {2521}, to seat oneself] on My right hand **until** [*héōs* {2193}] **I make** [from *títhēmi* {5087}, to place] Your **enemies** [from *echthrós* {2190}] a footstool for Your feet? (a.t.)

Although there is no definite article with "Spirit" here (lit.: "in spirit"), the definite article is usually implied in Greek prepositional phrases. Therefore, most English versions translate the phrase as reference to the Holy Spirit rather than to David's human spirit. (See Rev. 1:10; 4:2, which have the same phrase in Greek.)

The prophecy is Psalm 110:1, and Peter later quotes it in Acts 2:33–36 where he qualifies the "Spirit" in Matthew 22:43 as the "Holy Spirit" (cf. Mark 12:36). That the Jews understood Psalm 110 as messianic (110:4, 5) is incontestable, as did, later, the Apostles (see Eph. 1:20; Heb. 1:3; 5:6–7; 1 Pet. 3:22). The dative case means under the control of the Holy Spirit, the third Person of the Triune God (Matt. 28:19, cf. Rom. 9:1; 1 Cor. 12:3).

The one Greek word *Kúrios* does not translate the literal Hebrew which contains two distinct words for "Lord" (*Kúrios*): "Jehovah [3068, OT] said to my Adonai [113, OT]"; conceptually, however, Jehovah and Adonai are identical, meaning sovereign, and thus the one Greek word. Also, David calls Adonai "my Lord," not Jehovah, thus acknowledging the mediatorial role of the Adonai Messiah. Finally, David's Adonai is commanded to "sit" while Jehovah serves Him, a voluntary and temporal subordination of the Person of the Father to the Person of the Son.

On the other hand, the "right hand" is a position of functional equality, implying a fellow judge, one who shares equal authority and dignity (Matt. 20:21, 23; 26:64; Rom. 8:34; Eph. 1:20; Col. 3:1; Heb. 1:3, 13; 8:1; 10:12; 12:2; 1 Pet. 3:22).

This last statement tells us that the Messiah will have "enemies" throughout history "until" all enemies have been subjugated. Who are these enemies? All unbelievers, Gentiles (Luke 1:71, 74; specifically at the time, the Romans, Luke 19:43), apostate Jews (as we saw in the parable of the wedding feast), and so in general, any who do not want Christ to reign over them (Ps. 110:1; Mark 12:36; Luke 19:27; 20:43; Phil. 3:18; Heb. 1:13; 10:13), including Satan (Matt. 13:25, 39).

The apostle Paul describes the eschatological subjugation of all enemies to the Father's anointed One:

> Then cometh the end, when he shall have delivered up the kingdom to God, even the Father; when he shall have put down all rule and all authority and power. For he must reign, till he hath put all enemies under his feet. The last enemy that shall be destroyed is death. For he hath put all things under his feet. But when he saith all things are put under him, it is manifest that he is excepted, which did put all things under him. And when all things shall be subdued unto him, then shall the Son also himself be subject unto him that put all things under him, that God may be all in all. (1 Cor. 15:24–28; see author's volume on 1 Cor. 15 entitled *Conquering the Fear of Death*.)

[45] Jesus reiterated the question He asked in verse 43: "If David then calls him Lord, how is he his son?"

The question is framed in a way that implies that one of three possible statements is true. Either the Messiah is the human son of David, or He is the divine Lord over David, or as God and man He is both over and of David. Moreover, David's description does not seem to be just prophetic; rather, according to Peter, David was speaking about something that was true when he spoke it: "For David speaketh concerning him [Christ], I **foresaw** the Lord **always** before my face, for **he is** on my right hand, that I should not be moved" (Acts 2:25).

While the Pharisees could not answer Christ's question, Paul, a former Pharisee, later explains how both statements can be true in Romans 1:3, 4:

> Concerning his Son Jesus Christ our Lord, **which was made** [from *gínomai* {1096}, to become] of the seed of David **according to the flesh**; and **declared** [from *horízō* {3724}, to define, constitute, appoint] to be the Son of God with power, **according to the spirit of holiness**, by the resurrection from the dead.

Paul contrasted two verbs: "made" and "declared." Jesus, according to the flesh, was the descendant of David; hence, He is called the son of David. But according to the Spirit, He was Lord over David. Furthermore, the resurrection is a declaration of "God the Son" in that the Son of God raised up His own body from the dead (John 2:19; 10:17, 18).

The Pharisees had a theological problem with Jehovah addressing David's Adonai at His right hand, an exalted position reinforced by the unexpected inversion of Jehovah serving Adonai by subjugating His enemies (i.e., the Father working for the Son).

[46] Jesus' critics were again muzzled by their own Scriptures:

> And no one **was able** [from *dúnamai* {1410}] **to answer** [*apokrithênai*, the aorist passive deponent infinitive of *apokrínomai* {611}] Him a word, neither **dared** [from *tolmáō* {5111}, to dare] any one from that day forth **to question** [*eperōtêsai*, the aorist active infinitive of *eperōtáō* {1905}, to question intensely] Him **any more** [*oukéti* {3765} from *ou*, the absolute "not"; and *éti* {2089}, yet, hereafter]. (a.t.)

The Pharisees had no more questions for Jesus. The aorists *apokrithênai* and *eperōtêsai* mean that they could neither answer His questions nor ask Him questions that would trap Him. Their repeated attempts to trap Him *en lógō* ("with logic," v. 15) ended with their being entrapped by the *Lógos* (the Logic personified) who is God (John 1:1).

Thus, "the wicked [falls] by his own wickedness" (Prov. 11:5; a.t.), the arrogant by their own arrogance.

CHAPTER

23

The Pride of Pharisaism
(23:1–12; Mark 12:38–40; Luke 20:46, 47)

To prepare for this section, it is wise to review other narratives where Jesus called the Pharisees into account for substituting their traditions for God's commands (see Matt. 15:1–9; Mark 7:1–16).

As we saw in our discussion of Matthew 15:9, two words are translated "commandment" in the Greek New Testament. The first, *entolé* (1785), is the only one that defines God's authoritative, absolute rules including the Ten Commandments that He gave Moses. The second word is *éntalma* (1778) and always refers to man-made commandments, the religious precepts that the Pharisees mercilessly placed on the backs of people (see Matt. 15:9; Mark 7:7; Col. 2:22).

[1, 2] The Jews considered the decree or *éntalma* to be a prerogative that came with the "**seat**" (from *kathédra* [2515], seat of authority; from *kathézomai* [2516], to sit; we obtain the English word "cathedral" and the Latin expression "*ex cathedra*" from the noun) of Moses, as found in verse 2.

On this seat the scribes and Pharisees "**sat**" (*ekáthisan*, the aorist tense of *kathízō* [2523], to sit), the aorist summing up an extended history that began at some point in the intertestamental period. Even Jesus, in His use of the term, acknowledged that such a position—which was illegitimate—was considered to carry the same authority as that held by Moses. In other words, the precepts (from *éntalma*) were considered to be on a par with the imperatives (from *entolé*) in the Decalog and with other laws listed in the Torah. This, of course, was false. The concept of ex cathedra—"out of [or from] the chair"—is false because the *kathédra* (chair) was never established by Moses or any subsequent prophets.

[3] Interestingly, what follows is not so much a denunciation of the authority of the chair as a castigation of the hypocrisy of the chairpersons:

> All **therefore** [*oún* {3767}, in conclusion] **whatsoever** [from *hósos* {3745}, whatever] **they bid** [*eípōsin*, the aorist active subjunctive of *légō* {3004}, to intelligibly speak] you **to keep** [*tereín*, the present infinitive of *tēréō* {5083}, to guard], **keep** [*tēreíte*, the present imperative of *tēréō*] and **do** [*poieíte*, the present imperative of *poiéō* {4160}, to make, to do]. (a.t.)

The aorist verb *eípōsin* places the emphasis on instances of "saying," whereas the present infinitival verb *tēreín* means "**regularly** [habitually] **guard**." Similarly, "keep" and "do" are both present (habitual) imperatives.

By telling the multitudes and his disciples (v. 1) to both guard and do all the laws the scribes and Pharisees taught, Jesus acknowledged the authority of Moses' chair, but He rejected the hypocrisy of the chairpersons: "But **do** [*poieíte*, the present imperative of *poiéō*] not ye after their works: for they say, and do not."

[4] The Pharisees did more than speak but not perform God's commands (Matt. 22:36–40); they also did forbidden things. In fact, Jesus vividly described several evil things the Pharisees did (vv. 3, 5). The first was their imposition of the full load of the Law and its guilt on people, binding them without grace while not abiding by it themselves:

> For **they bind** [*desmeúousi*, the present tense of *desmeúō* {1195}, to tie up] **heavy** [from *barús* {926}, heavy] **burdens** [from *phortíon* {5413}, load, freight] and **difficult to carry** [from *dusbástaktos* {1419}, difficult to carry], and **lay** [*epitithéasin*, the present tense of *epitíthēmi* {2007}, to put on top; from *epí* {1909}, upon; and *títhēmi* {5087}, to place] them on men's shoulders; but **they** themselves **do not choose** [*thélousin*, the present tense of *thélō* {2309}, to determinately will] **to move** [from *kinéō* {2795}] them with one of their fingers. (a.t.)

Remember, Jesus had just said, "Whatever they tell you to observe, both observe and do!" (a.t.). Since He would not command such universal compliance to human precepts, the subject here must be the Mosaic Law. The problem, therefore, was not the Law per se but the scribes' and Pharisees' use of it. They did not use the Law to save souls because the Law could not do this anyway. As Paul says, "If there had been a law given which could have given life, verily righteousness should have been by the law" (Gal. 3:21). No such law had been given.

The scribes and Pharisees used the Law to imprison people in their sins—viewed metaphorically as placing heavy loads on their shoulders. They refused to extend grace, here analogous to physically lifting the loads off shoulders.

The aorist tense of *kinéō* means they would not make a single effort to remove an oppressive load. But why would they do something counterintentional? They placed the loads there in the first place. And they did it continuously; the verbs "bind," "lay," and "choose [not]" are all present tenses.

Paul explains the proper use of the Law: "The law was our schoolmaster to bring us unto Christ, that we might be justified by faith" (Gal. 3:24). Had the Pharisees recognized and accepted Christ's perfect obedience to the Law, they would rather have relieved the oppressive burdens by commanding people to place their faith in that perfection.

The problem here was that the scribes and Pharisees were not binding on themselves the heavy burdens they placed on other people's shoulders. They were inconsistent. What they demanded of others, they did not demand of themselves. This is why Jesus said in verse 3, "Whatsoever they bid you observe, that observe and do; but do not ye after their works: for they say, and do not."

[5] The second evil work of the scribes and Pharisees was ostentation:

> But all their works they do **for** [*prós* {4314}, toward the end purpose of] **to be seen** [from *theáomai* {2300}, to be displayed, theatricalized] of men.

Although Jesus earlier indicted the Pharisees' trumpeting their alms to be seen by others (the same verb, *theáomai*, is used in Matt. 6:1), here He extended hypocrisy to "all their works."

The inner motives of self-righteous persons are devious. They seem to have no consciousness that God is watching and that He can see motives as well as actions. Nor are self-righteous persons motivated to be seen by both God and others. Self-justification and pride overpower any good motives. They direct their ostentation toward people alone. Paul describes such persons as "boasters [from *alazōn* {213}, inventors [from *epheuretḗs* {2182} from *epí* {1909}, upon; and *heurískō* {2147}, to find] of evil things [from *kakós* {2556}, bad]" (Rom. 1:30). James tells us, "But now ye rejoice in your boastings [from *alazoneía* {212}]: all such rejoicing is evil" (James 4:16, cf. 2 Tim. 3:2).

The scribes and Pharisees paraded their arrogance in the culture of their day: "**They make broad** [from *platúnō* {4115}, widen, enlarge] their **phylacteries** [from *phulaktḗrion* {5440} from *phulássō* {5442}, to keep, preserve], and enlarge the borders of their garments [from *himátion* {2440}]," which made them more visible. Phylacteries were pouches or boxes in which the Jews stored scrolls of parchment on which they had written portions of the Law. Later, they would bind these to their foreheads and wrists (Matt. 23:5; see Ex. 13:8, 9, 11–16; Deut. 6:4–9; 11:13–21) as a display of their righteousness. Even certain groups of Jews today wear these small containers. In Jesus' day, the Jews superstitiously regarded them as amulets or charms that would preserve them from evil.

They also broadened the "**borders** [from *kráspedon* {2899}] of their garments" (Matt. 9:20; 14:36; Mark 6:56; Luke 8:44; see Num. 15:38; Deut. 22:12). Again, the purpose was to call attention to extraordinary piety and obedience to the Mosaic Law (Matt. 23:5). *Himátion* (2440) refers to the outer garments.

[6] The third evil work of the scribes and Pharisees was their love of prominence:

> [They] **love** [from *philéō* {5368}, to love conditionally] the **uppermost rooms** [from *prōtoklisía* {4411} from *prōtos* {4413}, first; and *klisía* {2828}, a chair or seat] at **feasts** [from *deípnon* {1173}], and the **chief seats** [from *prōtokathedría* {4410} from *prōtos*, first; and *kathédra* {2515}, chair, seat; see v. 2] in the synagogues.

Philéō is a fitting verb to describe the Pharisees, since the emphasis on conditionality shows that the scribes and Pharisees loved the topmost (*prōtos*) status for what they got out of it. Since *prōtos* has a qualitative element in it, the prefix "chief" is the preferable rendering to "numerically first" in both compound nouns above. What is numerically first is not necessarily first in rank. A person can be chronologically invited first to a wedding yet placed in the last row of the balcony. Chief (first in rank) seats at feasts and in synagogues were reserved for the rich and famous.

[7] Fourth, the conditional love continued, now for "**greetings** [from *aspasmós* {783} from *aspázomai* {782}, to salute; a salutation, an oral or written greeting] in the markets." Traditionally, the scribes and Pharisees expected formal greetings at three places: the evening meal (*deípnon* [1173]; see previous verse), the synagogue, and the markets.

They also loved being called "**Rabbi, Rabbi**" (*Hrabbí* [4461], Master). The noun "rabbi" is not found in the Old Testament, but the title emerged in the intertestamental period and continues to this day (Matt. 26:25, 49; Mark 9:5; 11:21; 14:45; John 1:38, 49; 3:2, 26; 4:31; 6:25; 9:2; 11:8).

Unable to see the forest because of his fixation on two or three trees, a fool either ignorantly loses a concept in a sound or deliberately destroys a concept with a sound. The sound here is "rabbi," but the concept is teaching authority. Today, the same love is attached to the title, "Doctor, Doctor"—a different sound but conceptually equivalent to *rabbi*. As with every title of teaching authority people bestow on themselves, this one especially applies to the Great Physician (v. 8).

[8] Accordingly, Jesus said bluntly:

> But **don't you be called** [*klēthēte*, the aorist passive subjunctive of *kaléō* {2564}, to call] Rabbi: for one is your **Master** [*Kathēgētēs* {2519} from *katá* {2596}, according to; and *hēgéomai* {2233}, to lead], even the Christ; and all of you are **brothers** [from *adelphós* {80}]. (a.t.)

Note how Jesus substituted "Master" (a "leading authority") for "Rabbi," identifying the two nouns in meaning.

The reasons assigned? First, Christ alone is your Master, and second, you are all equal. Plainly, there is no room for hierarchy below "the **anointed One** [*Christós* {5547} from the verb *chríō* {5548}, to anoint; note, the definite article is deliberately inserted to define uniqueness]," the Lord Jesus Christ. All believers are anointed with the Spirit of Christ according to 1 John 2:20: "But you have an anointing from the Holy One, and you all know" (NASB).

[9, 10] Jesus continued with His injunction:

> And call no one your father upon the earth: for One is your Father, who is in heaven. **Neither** [*mēdé* {3366} from *mē* {3361}, "not"; and the adversative *dé* {1161}, even] **be called** [*klēthēte*; see previous verse] **masters:** [from *kathēgētēs* {2519}] for One is your **Master** [*Kathēgētēs*], even the Christ. (a.t.)

"Father" is used in an absolute sense. This does not contradict Paul's relative use as, for example, when he says: "For though ye have ten thousand instructors in Christ, yet have ye not many fathers: for **in Christ** Jesus **I have begotten** you through the gospel" (1 Cor. 4:15). Even here, Paul's statement is carefully articulated: he is a "father in Christ"—having begotten "in Christ"—not a "father in himself" ("in" meaning "under the sovereignty of" [Christ]). Paul's sharp theological mind conveys the accurately sequenced thought that Christ fathered the Corinthians through Paul by the gospel (His Word). Moreover, Paul was not encouraging the incorrigible Corinthians to call him "father." He merely informed them of his right above other instructors to disciple them with the Word of Christ.

[11] An all-encompassing attitude characterizes greatness that is contrary to saying and not doing (v. 3), imposing law without extending grace (v. 4), performing to be seen by others (v. 5), and seeking status in public places (v. 6), including greetings and titles (vv. 7, 8): "But he that is **greatest** [from *mégas* {3173}, great, strong] among you shall be your **servant** [*diákonos* {1249}, a minister, one who waits on tables]." The true servant of Christ does not do the things the scribes and Pharisees did because he has a servant's heart.

This is the third time the word *diákonos* occurs in Matthew. In the first occurrence (Matt. 20:26), we find words similar to the ones in this verse addressed to Salome and her two sons, James and John: "Whosoever if he chooses [from *thélō* {2309}, to determine] to be great [*mégas*] among you, let him be your minister [*diákonos*]" (a.t.).

At the time, deacons were officers of banquets and synagogues or city officials. At banquets, they served or "ministered" (*diakonéō* [1247]) at tables (Acts 6:1–7). Deacons were not, however, designated as officers of the local church. Government was placed, rather, in the hands of elders (*presbúteroi* [4245]) who presided over a council (*presbutérion* [4244]; 1 Tim. 4:14). Elders were appointed to rule (Acts 14:23; 2 Cor. 8:19) while deacons served in the manner of the Lord Jesus who came "not to be served [from *diakonéō*] but to serve [also from *diakonéō*]" (Matt. 20:28; a.t.).

From Jesus' words above and from His own example, we conclude that every ruling elder in the church is a deacon (in the sense of being a servant [*diákonos*]) and the greatest elder (ruler) is the "servant [*deacon*] of all" (Mark 9:35).

[12] Now follows the general rule:

> Whosoever **shall exalt** [from *hupsóō* {5312}, to elevate] **himself** [from *heautoú* [1438], of himself] **shall be abased** [*tapeinōthḗsetai*, the future passive of *tapeinóō* {5013}, to humble, humiliate, be brought low]; and he that shall humble himself **shall be exalted** [*hupsōthḗsetai*, the future passive of *hupsóō*].

From the time of the fall of Adam, people seek status, glory, and positions of superior rank. But, for most, the highest rank they ever attain in this life is simply an appearance of superiority. According to James, God opposes (from *antitássomai* [498] from *antí* [473], against; and *tássomai*, the middle of *tássō* [5021], to set, place, arrange; "sets Himself against") such puffed-up persons (James 4:6; a.t.; cf. 1 Pet. 5:5).

In His opposition to the proud, God humiliates them. The passive voice of the verb *tapeinōthḗsetai* implies God's forced subjugation that Paul speaks of in 1 Corinthians 15:24, 25. Whenever the proud are humiliated from without, they resist, but not successfully; God's overpowering force prevails.

There is another side to this. Jesus added, "He that shall humble himself shall be exalted [*hupsōthḗsetai*]." This refers to the saved who believe by God's grace. Empowered by God's Spirit, we believers should voluntarily humble ourselves.

Hypocrisy, then, desires rank without change of character. The scribes and Pharisees needed to learn that God's eternal life is not superficial. Sin permeates the soul, and the soul itself needs saving, from its natural tendency to exalt itself over others. The first remedy for hypocrisy is the legal cancellation (*athétēsis* [115], annulling; Heb. 9:26) and removal (*áphesis* [859], remission; Heb. 9:22) of sin.

In verse 12, both verbs, "**abased**" (*tapeinōthḗsetai*) and "**exalted**" (*hupsōthḗse-tai*), are passive in voice with God the subject of the action. No matter how low or great we make ourselves, God has ways of exalting or humbling us.

The Eight Woes
(23:13–36; Mark 12:38–40; Luke 20:47)

[13] Jesus now pronounced a series of eight "**woe**"(s) (*ouaí* [3759], interjections of grief or indignation over an impending judgment) on the scribes and Pharisees. In the Majority Text of the New Testament, v. 14 precedes v. 13. Since most readers of this book will be using the King James translation of the New Testament, we shall follow its rendering. The first woe is directed against their legalistic theology:

> Woe unto you, scribes and Pharisees, hypocrites! **You shut up** [from *kleíō* {2808}, to shut, to lock] the kingdom of heaven against people: for you do not **enter** [from *eisérchomai* {1525}, to enter into] yourselves, **neither** [*oudé* {3761} from *ou* {3756}, "not"; and *dé* {1161}, even] **do you allow** [from *aphíēmi* {863}, to leave, i.e., alone] those **who are entering** [from *eisérchomai*] **to enter** [also from *eisérchomai*]. (a.t.)

What kind of power is this? How can hypocrites prevent others from entering the kingdom? Since when did the Pharisees possess the key to the kingdom? Could they actually "shut" (or "lock") this door?

It would seem that way in English, but let's look at the evidence in Greek. The key verb is *aphíēmi*. This is translated "suffer" in the older language of the King James Version. We don't use this word today, but we do have equivalent words, which are "permit" or "allow." However, the Greek word for "permit" is *eáō* ([1439]; Acts 14:16; 16:7). Ordinarily, nonpermission means stopping as, for example: "They determined to go into Bithynia: but the Spirit did not permit [from *eáō*] them" (Acts 16:7; a.t.), that is, the Spirit stopped them.

In the verse before us, *aphíēmi* does not carry this causal sense of stopping but rather, "[not] leaving alone." The Pharisees harassed—not stopped—those who were entering. While they attempted to block conversion, they did not and could not overpower the Spirit of God's regeneration of human hearts. It is safe to assume that "the ones entering" the kingdom did so by faith—the only way in.

Furthermore, the harassment was theological, political, and social—not physical. Pharisees even today try to lead the elect back onto the road of justification by works—legalism. Such Judaizers existed in the early church, and

Paul commits the entire book of Galatians to the refutation of the works-based salvation system. Stephen sums up the whole history of Pharisaism when he says, "Ye stiffnecked and uncircumcised in heart and ears, ye do always resist the Holy Ghost: as your fathers did, so do ye" (Acts 7:51).

But while they did "not leave alone those entering" (meaning they badgered or troubled them), the fact that they could not block entry to God's elect is found throughout Christ's teachings: "These things saith he that . . . openeth, and no man shutteth; and shutteth, and no man openeth. . . . I have set before thee an open door, and no man can shut it" (Rev. 3:7, 8). In agreement with this, Jesus said of His sheep, "A stranger will they not follow, but will flee from him: for they know not the voice of strangers" (John 10:5).

The Pharisees, then, shut up the kingdom of heaven against "men" only (not "sheep" who do not hear the voice of strangers)—in other words, against other Pharisees or converts of the Pharisees, all who attempted to be justified by works. "Ye neither go in yourselves" meant the Pharisees were included in the class of "men." They could only harass "them that are entering" by faith—thus, Luke's synoptic use of the verb form "to hinder":

> Woe unto you, lawyers! for ye have taken away the key of knowledge: ye entered not in yourselves, and them that were entering in ye hindered [from *kōlúō* {2967}, to hinder]. (Luke 11:52; note how "entered not" is contrasted with "hindered.")

The elect hear the voice of grace, not the Law. Disciples of Christ will do well to heed the apostle Paul's advice to "stand fast therefore in the liberty wherewith Christ hath made us free, and be not entangled again with the yoke of bondage" (Gal. 5:1).

[14] Jesus pronounced the second woe is pronounced on the sin of defrauding widows and then making long, pretentious prayers to cover up their wickedness.

> Woe unto you, scribes and Pharisees, hypocrites! For **you devour** [from *katesthíō* {2719} from the preposition *katá* {2596} or the adverb *kátō* {2736}, down; and *esthíō* {2068}, to eat; to devour] widows' **houses** [from *oikía* {3614}, home], and for a **pretense** [from *próphasis* {4392}, pretense, pretext] make long prayers. On account of this, you shall receive the greater damnation. (a.t.)

We are not told specifically what the practice was. Perhaps it was a scheme to claim that the house or estate of a deceased man belonged to the temple or to some charitable organization supervised by the particular scribe or Pharisee involved. Or, more likely, the scribe or Pharisee simply took advantage of a distraught widow by charging large fees for the burial of her husband. Whatever the practice was, the sin was so malevolent that Jesus threatened such practices with "greater condemnation." Apparently, there are degrees of judgment in hell (see the reference to "few" and "many" stripes in Luke 12:47, 48).

[15] The third woe qualified the first, explaining how Pharisees "shut up the kingdom . . . against men." Essentially, they did it by perverting Christian evangelism. We Christians proclaim good news when we evangelize (transliterated from *euaggelízō* [2097], to evangelize, from *eú* [2095], good or well, and *ággelos* [32], messenger or angel) and proclaim the truth of the gospel. The Pharisees, in contrast, proclaimed falsehood that became "bad news" when they roamed far and wide, making their disciples avid followers of their false teaching. We point people to heaven; they point them to hell. We should not be surprised, then, by the numeric success of false religions and cults. Against our message of grace, they preach legalism, the letter of the Law, which Paul says "kills" (2 Cor. 3:6) the soul. They consider themselves good enough to enter heaven and refuse to accept Christ's free gift of grace.

> Woe unto you, scribes and Pharisees, hypocrites! For **you compass** [from *periágō* {4013}, to encompass; from *perí* {4012}, around and about; and *ágō* {71}, to lead, carry, go] sea and land to make one **proselyte** [from *prosélutos* {4339} from *prós* {4314}, towards; and a form of the future of *érchomai* {2064}, to come], and **when he is made** [from *gínomai* {1096}], **you make** [from *poiéō* {4160}] him twofold more the **son** [from *huiós* {5207}, a mature son] **of Gehenna** [from *Géenna* {1067}] than yourselves. (a.t.)

This is a dire warning against leading others astray with the wrong message. One astonishing feature of Pharisees was their tireless zeal to produce a single convert. If unbelievers go out as missionaries of falsehood and people accept their message, Jesus made it clear that "the last state" of those persons "is worse than the first" (Matt. 12:45). Their converts sink to a lower level of depravity than that of the messengers. There is a degenerative aspect to hypocrisy; legalism begets an even greater hypocrite.

On the other hand, Christian missionaries locate people whose hearts have been prepared in advance by the Spirit of God to receive the gospel. In the book of Acts, such listeners are called either ones who "**reverence** [from *sébomai* {4576}, to be devout] God" (Acts 13:43, 50; 16:14; 17:4, 17; 18:7) or who "**fear**" (from *phobéomai* [5399]) God (Acts 10:2; 13:16, 26). They, in turn, desire to bring others into the kingdom of God through the good news of salvation in Christ.

Pharisees were known for extensive proselytism, and Jesus' mention of "sea" may have been a reference to their missionary work in Rome, which became proverbial. Luke records the presence at Pentecost of "Jews and proselytes" visiting from Rome (Acts 2:10). A number of Jewish proselytes were at Antioch in Syria (6:5). Jewish proselytes in Palestine at the time of Christ included the centurion, a Roman officer (Matt. 8:5–13; Luke 7:1–10); some Greeks (John 12:20); and possibly Pilate's wife (Matt. 27:19).

In Jesus' day, the Pharisees considered Gehenna to be the place where Gentiles and apostate Jews would be punished (Matt. 5:29, 30; 10:28; cf. James 3:6). The Greek word is a transliteration of the Hebrew *gā–Hinnom* (the Valley of Hinnom; Josh. 18:16; 2 Kgs. 23:10; 2 Chr. 28:3; 33:6; Jer. 7:31, 32; 19:2, 6), a valley where garbage was burned in perpetual fires. The word is found twelve times in the New Testament, eleven of which are in the Synoptic Gospels with Jesus speaking.

"Son of Gehenna" is an interesting metaphor, implying that Gehenna (hell) is the theological father of those who trust in justification by works. James uses a similar metaphor when he says that the tongue is "being set on fire [from *phlogízō* {5394}] by [the] Gehenna" (James 3:6; a.t.), a terrible picture of the fueling source of evil words.

[16] The fourth woe was a condemnation of materialism that valued sacred things for their worldly constituents—here the temple of God in terms of its gold content.

To understand Jesus' reasoning on this subject, we must assume that the temple current in His day was similar in construction to the first (Solomon's) temple. This first temple contained a great deal of gold:

> And the snuffers, and the basons, and the spoons, and the censers, of pure gold: and the entry of the house, the inner doors thereof for the most holy place, and the doors of the house of the temple, were of gold. (2 Chr. 4:22; cf. 1 Kgs. 7:50; 2 Kgs. 18:16; 24:13; 2 Chr. 4:7, 8; Ezra 5:14)

We can assume the presence of gold "in the temple" was in the form of tithes and offerings. But when Jesus said gold "of the temple" (the genitive case), He probably referred not only to removable articles like censers but also permanent gold inlays in parts of the temple like the doors.

Jesus aimed this woe, then, at the higher valuation the Pharisees gave to the gold content of the temple. To assume that gold was higher in spiritual value because it was higher in worldly value than other materials was false. Jesus did not break down the temple into material components that sanctified one another proportionately to their worldly values. Instead, He defined the true temple as the presence of God, which sanctifies every material. The Pharisees missed the point, blinded as they were by the relatively higher worldly value of gold.

Jesus called them by the depictive oxymoron, "**blind** [*tuphloí* {5185}] **leaders** [from *hodēgós* {3595}]." We don't expect the blind to follow, let alone lead, but as Jesus said elsewhere, "They are blind leaders of the blind. And if the blind lead the blind, both shall fall into the ditch" (Matt. 15:14; a.t.). This gives us further insight into the people whom the Pharisees "shut out of the kingdom"—the (equally) blind.

Jesus quoted the objectionable teaching:

> Whosoever **swears** [from *omnúō* {3660}] by the temple, it is nothing; but whosoever shall swear by the gold of the temple, **he is indebted** [from *opheílō* {3784}, to owe]. (a.t.)

[17] Jesus' accusation was strong:

> You **fools** [from *mōrós* {3474}, stupid and irresponsible person; the English word "moron" derives from this Greek noun] and **blind** [from *tuphlós* {5185}; the English medical term "typhlectomy" derives from this noun]: for which is greater, the gold, or the temple that sanctifies [from *hagiázō* {37}, to purify, make holy] the gold? (a.t.)

Jesus denied that the temple was definable by any of its materials. Gold, therefore, could not sanctify wood and stone, and the whole building could not sanctify any of its parts.

The temple ultimately was the earthly dwelling place of the living God, but He does not live in temples made by human hands (Acts 7:48; 17:24); He lives, rather, in the "souls [He has] made" (Isa. 57:16):

> For thus saith the high and lofty One that inhabiteth eternity, whose name is Holy; I dwell in the high and holy place, with him also that is of a contrite and humble spirit, to revive the spirit of the humble, and to revive the heart of the contrite ones. (Isa. 57:15)

Indeed, from the time the Shekinah glory departed from the temple under Babylonian rule (Ezek. 9), nothing was sanctified by the presence of God at all. The glory did not return to the temples built under Zerubbabel and Herod. Ironically, the Glory now stood unrecognized before the Pharisees in the "temple that was His body" (John 2:21; a.t.), pronouncing woes: "And we beheld his glory, the glory as of the only begotten of the Father, full of grace and truth" (John 1:14).

In the new covenant, the Spirit of God creates a new temple out of believing hearts: "Know ye not that ye are the temple of God, and that the Spirit of God dwelleth in you?" (1 Cor. 3:16, cf. 6:17). Hebrews 9:11 says, "But Christ, having come as a high priest of good things to come, by a greater and more perfect tabernacle, not made with hands, that is to say, not of this creation [from *ktísis* {2937}]" (a.t.).

[18, 19] Jesus continued to cite the offensive teaching:

> And, Whosoever shall swear by the **altar** [from *thusiastérion* {2379}, altar, sacrificial table], it is nothing; but whosoever sweareth by the gift that is upon it, he is guilty. Ye fools and blind: for whether is greater, the gift, or the altar that sanctifieth the gift?

The argument is the same. The Pharisees had inverted values, here substituting the physical materials of the altar in the temple for the true altar of God. Although the Hebrew word for "altar" meant, more broadly, "the place of slaughter or sacrifice," they were blinded to God's predestined place: Golgotha and the cross.

In the new covenant, the cross of Christ—the true altar—sanctifies gifts. Just as the true temple is His body, so the true altar is His cross.

Oaths were solemn statements used to validate promises, and they are found early in the Old Testament (Gen. 24:2, 3). Frequently, they included curses for noncompliance with contracted terms (Lev. 5:1; Judg. 17:2; 1 Sam. 14:24; 2 Sam. 3:35;). They were used to seal treaties (Gen. 26:28), even Israel's covenant to obey God (Deut. 27:11—28:68; 29:11–20). God sealed His promise to Abraham with an oath (Heb. 6:13–18).

Jesus' advice on swearing was clear:

> But I say unto you, Swear not at all; neither by heaven; for it is God's throne: nor by the earth; for it is his footstool: neither by Jerusalem; for it is the city of the great King. Neither shalt thou swear by thy head, because thou canst not make one hair white or black. But let your communication be, Yea, yea; Nay, nay: for whatsoever is more than these cometh of evil. (Matt. 5:34–37)

[20–22] That advice is reiterated in these verses:

> Whoso therefore **shall swear** [*omósas*, the aorist participle of *omnúō* {3660}] by the altar, sweareth by it, and by all things thereon. And whoso shall swear by the temple, sweareth by it, and by him that dwelleth therein. And he that shall swear by heaven, sweareth by the throne of God, and by him that sitteth thereon.

The aorist tense of "swear" (three times here) stresses the liability of single instances of this verbal action, supporting Christ's "swear not at all" ethics.

Jesus' point here was that by divine decree the altar (v. 20) was inseparately connected with God's plan of redemption (sacrifice), the temple (v. 21) with God's presence, and heaven (v. 22) with God's rule (throne). To swear by God's altar, His temple, or His throne as represented by heaven, was inevitably to swear by God Himself. The altar, the temple, and heaven were, in a valid sense, sacraments of the divine plan, presence, and rule.

[23, 24] The fifth woe condemned the external practice of Law without the internal qualities of justice, mercy, and grace:

> Woe to you, scribes and Pharisees, hypocrites! You tithe mint, anise, and cummin and have omitted the **weightier matters** [from *barús* {926}, weight; literally "weightier things"] of the Law: judgment, mercy, and faith. These you ought to have done and not to leave the others undone. You blind guides **strain out** [from *diulízo* {1368} from *diá* [1223], thorough; and *hulízo* {n.f.}, to strain, filter] a gnat and **swallow** [from *katapíno* {2666}] a camel. (a.t.)

While acknowledging that the scribes and Pharisees "ought to have" tithed these inexpensive spices as part of their general tithe, Jesus argued the futility of such external obedience at the expense of judgment, mercy, and faith.

In the Old Testament, the tithe was imposed on animals from herds and flocks (Lev. 27:32, 33) as well as grain, vegetables, and fruits (Lev. 27:30). Mint, anise, and cummin are not mentioned in the Torah, so this was an instance of how the Pharisaic tradition extended beyond the original Mosaic Law. Jesus commended this tradition—"ye ought to have"—since it was a logical deduction from the general tithe.

The heavier things of the Law include judgment, mercy, and faith as typified in the Torah: judgment (Deut. 28, 30), mercy (Ex. 34:6; Deut. 4:31), and faith in God's sacrifice (Ex. 4:5–9; 19:9; Lev. 17:11).

The "strain" refers to the ancient custom of filtering wine. The "gnat" exemplified the meticulous application of the tithe to small things such as spices (mint, anise, and cummin), even though Jesus conceded the correctness of the practice (see above). The "swallow a camel" hyperbole, on the other end of the extreme, corresponded to ignoring the weightier matters of the Law. The camel was selected not just because of its size but because it was an unclean animal. (Though it chews the cud, a camel does not "divide the hoof"; Lev. 11:4.) Obviously, a Jew who attempted to swallow a gargantuan unclean animal was not paying much attention to what he was doing. Justice, mercy, and faith apparently had no part in Pharisaic doctrine, ethics, and spiritual life.

[25, 26] Jesus pronounced the sixth woe on hypocrisy in general:

> **Woe** unto you, scribes and Pharisees, hypocrites! for ye make clean the **outside** [*éxothen* {1855}] of the cup and of the **platter** [from *paropsís* {3953}, a side dish consisting of delicacies like condiments or sauces; from the preposition *pará* {3844}, alongside; and *ópson* {n.f.}, bread], but within they are full

of **extortion** [from *harpagḗ* {724}, robbery, seizure] and **excess** [from *akrasía* {192}, intemperance, lack of restraint]. Thou blind Pharisee, **cleanse** [*kathárison*, the aorist imperative of *katharízō* {2511}, to make clean] first that which is within the cup and platter, **that** [*hína* {2443}, in order that] the outside of them **may be** [*génētai*, the aorist middle deponent subjunctive of *gínomai* {1096}, to become] clean **also** [*kaí* {2532}].

What a contrast! A good analogy would be a bathed robber or profligate. Jesus used these pictures to show the full contradiction between the outer and inner persons by nature. The Law cleaned up the outside like a coat of paint on rotted wood. Sooner or later, extortion and intemperance rise to the surface. Pharisees can fool people only for so long. But can they fool the Lord? Never!

Jesus explained that cleaning the outside had no impact on the inside, since God has decreed an inside-out change only. The *hína* clause—"in order that the outside of them may be clean also"—implied that veneers like paint are not cleaning agents. Only regenerated hearts produce both a clean inside and outside (the permanent effect is given in the aorist tense of *gínomai*).

Did Jesus command the Pharisees to regenerate themselves (the aorist tense of *katharízō* means "cleanse yourself once-for-all"; cf. "the washing [from *loutrón* {3067}] of regeneration" in Titus 3:5)? Regeneration is God's act alone; accordingly, those born "of God" are born "[not] of the will of the flesh" (John 1:13). However, the Lord does sometimes command the will of the flesh to do the impossible. His purpose, however, is to make us realize that in ourselves we cannot obey; we need the power of the Spirit of God. Thus, Paul notes, "The law [is] our schoolmaster to bring us unto Christ, that we might be justified by faith" (Gal. 3:24).

If the Pharisees tried to cleanse themselves once-for-all (*kathárison*) and failed, they might have conceded their impotence against the power of sin and put their faith in God's righteousness: "For they being ignorant of God's righteousness, and going about to establish their own righteousness, have not submitted themselves unto the righteousness of God" (Rom. 10:3).

[27, 28] The seventh woe was a repeat of the sixth with the added sense of decomposition:

Woe unto you, scribes and Pharisees, hypocrites! for **you are like** [from *paramoiázō* {3945} from *pará* {3844}, proximity; and *homoiázō* {3662}, to make like; "resemble"] **whited** [from *koniáō* {2867}, to whitewash with lime] sepulchres, which indeed appear beautiful outwardly but within are full of dead men's bones and of all uncleanness. Even so you also outwardly appear righteous to others, but within you are full of hypocrisy and iniquity. (a.t.)

The veneer of hypocrisy is whitewash. White might not have been the sole color the Pharisees painted their sepulchres; however, Jesus probably chose this color because of its symbolic connection to holiness and righteousness. The picture here is putrid. The closest analogy is the fictitious "zombie": a corpse painted with cosmetics (see *kosmeíte* in the next verse), animated, perhaps beautified on the outside but dead on the inside. Hypocrisy and iniquity are represented by "dead people's bones and . . . all uncleanness." The smell of decay is added to the picture. Among other things, sin, like dead men's bones, actually stinks, and Scripture implies that it is a stench in God's nostrils: "And I will make your cities waste, and bring your sanctuaries unto **desolation** [from *šāmam* {OT 8074}], and I will not smell the savour of your sweet odors" (Lev. 26:31, cf. Ps. 38:5; Amos 5:21).

These verses do not actually say that sin is a stench in God's nostrils, but the fact that He refuses to smell the "sweet odors" of incense implies some offsetting, corrupting stench.

[29] Jesus directed the eighth woe at the scribes' and Pharisees' hypocritical claim to be more faithful and reverent of God than their fathers were:

> Woe unto you, scribes and Pharisees, hypocrites! because you build the tombs of the prophets, and **cosmeticize** [from *kosméō* {2885}] the sepulchres of the righteous. (a.t.)

Some sepulchres that they had painted with whitewash and sanitized with cosmetics honored the prophets whom their own fathers had killed. Nothing had changed inside, however; the tombs were still filled with the repugnant bones of dead people.

[30] The woe continued:

> And you say, if we had been in the days of our fathers, we would not have been **partakers** [from *koinōnós* {2844}, sharer] with them in the blood of the prophets. (a.t.)

Children (especially teenagers) often think they are better than their parents. Here, the Pharisees attempted to detach themselves from their spiritual and natural lineages. But Jesus would not allow it because the Pharisees continued the murderous trends set by their natural fathers. They were persecuting Jesus, even planning His execution, just as their fathers had done to the prophets. Consequently, they inherited from their fathers not just their physical characteristics but their spiritual and moral ones as well.

[31] Jesus immediately addressed the self-incrimination:

> **Wherefore** [*hóste* {5620}, accordingly; i.e., a conclusion is coming] you are witnesses against yourselves that you **are** [note, the "**if**" of v. 30 is gone] the children of those who killed the prophets [i.e., not just the natural but the spiritual and moral children of murderers]. (a.t.)

To paraphrase verse 31, Jesus essentially said, "You just admitted that the people who killed the prophets are your fathers! Consequently, you are witnessing against yourself that you are their children!" Jesus called them hypocrites because, although they denied it, they were murderers just as their fathers were. They said, "If we had been there . . .," but Jesus refuted their "if" with their own testimony to the reality of their spiritual lineage.

[32] Jesus' language here was strong—an imperative:

> **Fill ye up** [*plērósate*, the aorist active imperative of *plēróō* {4137}, to fill up, complete] then the **measure** [*métron* {3358}, the part] of your fathers.

The aorist tense is proleptic, pointing to the event of the crucifixion. Jesus gave a similar injunction to Judas: "What you **do** [*poieîs*, the present indicative of *poiéō* {4160}] **do** [*poíēson*, the aorist active imperative of *poiéō*] quickly" (John 13:27; a.t.); that is, "What you are doing now, do it once for all (i.e., get it over with; by definition, imperatives command subsequent [i.e., to the imperative] behavior), and do it fast!"

The imperative was a reaction to their arrogance: "We would not have shared with them in the blood of the prophets" (v. 30; a.t.). But this boast contradicted their current attitude and behavior, and Jesus did not let them get away with it. They were personal—"our fathers"—sons of murderers on their own testimony, and their claim that they would not have shed innocent blood was a lie. By persecuting Christ and planning to murder Him, they proved that they were made of the same wicked stock.

[33] Jesus further described His opponents:

> *Ye* **serpents** [from *óphis* {3789}, a snake; here He defines His enemies with the same nature that belongs to "the serpent" from Gen. 3:1 through Rev. 20:2], ye **generation** [from *génnēma* {1081}, offspring, products; from the verb *gennáō* {1080}, to give birth to; and the suffix *–ma*, finished product] of **vipers** [from *échidna* {2191}, a poisonous snake].

Jesus selected the term "serpents" (*óphis*), the genus encompassing both poisonous and nonpoisonous species, to identify these persons with the one who "was more subtil [crafty] than any beast of the field" (Gen. 3:1). But Jesus also selected "vipers" (*échidna*) because this species poisons and kills people, further identifying with the one who "was a murderer from the beginning" (John 8:44; see "the serpent" above). *Génnēma* is picked to show that these murderers are true vipers from true vipers, "begotten, not made, of one being with their viper fathers." Vipers do not birth harmless snakes; they birth vipers. The offspring of a viper is a viper.

This is a terrible picture of natural depravity. The Pharisees were vipers by nature, and this nature determined their choices. They chose to bite, poison, and kill because they were biters, poisoners, and killers by nature. As Jesus addressed them in John 8:44: "You are out of your father the devil, and the lusts of your father you choose to do" (a.t.).

Given this nature, Jesus asked,

How [*pōs* {4459}] **might you escape** [*phúgēte*, the aorist subjunctive of *pheúgō* {5343}; i.e., "how is it possible for you to escape"] the [the definite article points to the final judgment] **judgment** [from *krísis* {2920}, judgment, separation] of **Gehenna** [from *géenna* {1067}]? (a.t.)

This rhetorical question was intended to make them realize that there was no "how" apart from God's mercy! The writer of Hebrews asks his readers the same question: "How shall we escape, if we neglect so great salvation[?]" (Heb. 2:3). Vipers cannot choose contrary to their natures. Even if they could choose to become something they are not—like sheep—the choice itself would not re-create them. This requires the Lord's power. He alone is the Creator, and He alone is the re-creator. "With men this is impossible; but with God all things are possible" (Matt. 19:26). When the Lord so re-creates, Saul the viper who was persecuting and killing off the church like his fathers, became Paul the sheep.

The final eschatological punishment is mentioned here—"Gehenna": the Valley of Hinnom, the final place of "destruction from the presence of the Lord" (2 Thess. 1:9).

[34, 35] Jesus reviewed God's supply of prophets to Israel throughout its long history of disobedience:

Wherefore [*diá* {1223}, on account of; *toúto* {5124}, the neuter of the pronoun *hoútos* {3778}, this, i.e., reason forthcoming], **behold** [*idoú* {2400}, the imperative of *eídon* {1492}, the aorist of *horáō* {3708}, to perceive, calling attention to the extraordinary {see Matt. 3:16}], I send unto you prophets, and wise men, and scribes: and some of them ye shall kill and crucify; and some of them shall ye scourge in your synagogues, and persecute them from city to city: **that** [*hópōs* {3704}, so that] upon you may come all the righteous blood shed upon the earth, from the blood of righteous Abel unto the blood of Zacharias son of Barachias, whom ye slew between the temple and the altar.

"Upon you" is equivalent to the "upon this generation" of the next verse. However, since Cain and other murderers down the line were guilty of the blood they shed in their respective generations, it was a simple deduction to include them in "you" (here) and "this generation" (v. 36), generic classes encompassing the entire line of vipers ("generation of vipers," v. 33) from Cain forward. Some commentators restrict "this generation" to the specific people contemporary with Christ. Yet Cain was the beginning of the "generation of vipers" and therefore was properly included in the classes of "you" and "this generation." The latter expression, therefore, is equivalent to Paul's "present [from *enístēmi* {1764}] evil age [from *aión* {165}]" (Gal. 1:4; a.t.), which has stood from the time of Cain.

"Some of them" should not be construed to mean that some prophets escaped. They were all persecuted but not in the same manner. This was implied in Stephen's rhetorical question just before he was martyred: "Which of the prophets have your fathers not persecuted? And they have slain them that showed before the coming of the Just One, of whom now you have been the betrayers and murderers" (Acts 7:52; a.t.).

[36] Jesus continued the theme:

> Verily I say unto you, All these things **shall come** [from *hēkō* {2240}, to come, frequently in a hostile sense: Matt. 24:50; Luke 19:43; 2 Pet. 3:10; Rev. 3:3; 18:8] upon this generation.

"All these things" will come on the whole line of prophet persecutors and murderers, that is, God's judgment and wrath including, from the context, Gehenna (v. 33). On the day of judgment, the whole judgment will descend on the whole "generation of vipers"—the line of prophet abusers starting with Cain.

Jesus Laments over Jerusalem
(23:37–39; Luke 13:34, 35)

[37] Jesus now mourned over the current desolation of Jerusalem, evident in the present tense of *aphíetai* (v. 38) and the fact that the Pharisees were persecuting Him just as their fathers had done to the prophets God sent from the time of Abel.

> O Jerusalem, Jerusalem, the **one killing** [from *apokteinō* {615}] the prophets and **stoning** [from *lithoboléo* {3036}] **those who are sent** [from *apostéllō* {649}] to **her** [from *autē*, the feminine of *autós* {846}, him]! **How often** [*posákis*

{4212}] **I would** [from *thélō* {2309}, to will] **gather together** [from *episunágō* {1996} from *epí* {1909}, upon; *sún* {4862}, together; and *ágō* {71}, to lead] your **children** [from *téknon* {5043}, a younger child; from *tíktō* {5088}, to give birth], even as a hen gathers her chickens under her wings, and **you determined** [also from *thélō*] not! (a.t.)

The two *thélō(s)* are in diametric opposition to one another: I would gather . . . you determined to resist. Although the Pharisees attempted to shut out people from the kingdom of God, their theological, social, and political leverages did not prevent God from saving His people.

Here are three subjects: Jesus; the opposing Jerusalem (represented by the Pharisees, the generation of vipers from the context); and a believing Jerusalem, the "children" or the "men" (v. 13) who accepted Christ in spite of Pharisaic opposition.

The "many times" (*posákis* [4212]) is not necessarily limited to the period of the historic incarnation. It may well stretch back to Cain's legalistic oppression of Abel, since Jesus was interested enough in the universal history of persecution to cite this first instance. From Hebrews we learn that long before His incarnation, the *Lógos* (word of logic) of God spoke "at sundry times [*polumerōs* {4181}, many sided] and in diverse manners [*polutrópōs* {4187}, in many ways, in a variety of ways]" (Heb. 1:1). None of this persecution and murder was strange to the preincarnate Word (John 1:1), who witnessed the first murder of Abel by his brother Cain (John 1:1, 2, 14, 18). Indeed, Jesus had seen the whole line of vipers beginning with Cain.

Jesus does indeed gather together His little children, because "the gates of hell [do] not prevail against [His church]" (Matt. 16:18; a.t.).

[38] The next word, **"Behold"** (*idoú* [2400], the imperative of *eídon* [1492], the aorist of *horáō* [3708], to perceive, calling attention to the extraordinary, [see Matt. 3:16]), calls attention to something important. Jesus expected Jerusalem to see its own desolation that issued from two thousand plus years of abusing prophets.

> Your house **is left** [*aphíetai*, the present passive indicative of *aphíemi* {863}, to leave alone, to let be] unto you **desolate** [*érēmos* {2048}, deserted, a desert or wilderness; see Matt. 11:7; 24:26; Luke 5:16; 7:24; 8:29; Rev. 12:6, 14; 17:3].

The "house" spoken of here in verse 38 is not the whole of the "Jerusalem" as in verse 37. We may think of Jerusalem as consisting of two parts: in verse 37, "your children" (the good part of Jerusalem that would indeed be gathered together), and in verse 38 "your house" (the bad part of Jerusalem that would be left desolate), which perpetually attempted to shut people out of the kingdom. This house would be judged, and it already had been since *aphíe-tai* is a present tense. The spirit had been saved, but "Israel according to the flesh" was under judgment.

[39] This judgment will remain for a period of time:

> I say unto you, you shall **not** [*ou* {3756}, "not"; and *mḗ* {3361}, "not"; an intensive combination meaning not ever, not at any instant, no never] **see** [from *eídon*, the aorist of *horáō* {3708}, to perceive] Me **from** [from *apó* {575}, from] **now on** [*árti* {737}, now, from which *ártios* {739}, complete, is derived] **until** [*héōs* {2193}, a temporal preposition] you shall say, Blessed is He that **comes** [from *érchomai* {2064}, to come] in the name of the Lord. (a.t.)

The end of this period of time is what Paul calls "the fulness of the Gentiles" (see below). Although individual Jews will be saved in the ages to come, Jerusalem's "house" will remain a "desert" until the Jews en masse repent and confess Jesus Christ as Lord. Even here the reference is eschatological, a point in the future when together they call Him blessed and acknowledge His coming. Paul develops this theme in his Epistle to the Romans:

> For I would not, brethren, that ye should be ignorant of this mystery, lest ye should be wise in your own conceits; that blindness in part is happened to Israel, until the fulness of the Gentiles be come in. And so **all Israel** shall be saved: as it is written, There shall come out of Sion the Deliverer, and shall turn away ungodliness **from Jacob.** (Rom. 11:25, 26)

The verb "blessed" (Matt. 23:39) is better translated "having been blessed" (*eulogēménos*, the perfect passive participle of *eulogéō* [2127], to speak well of or to; from *eú* [2095], good, well; and *légō* [3004], to speak). Since this participle is used with reference to other people, the subject is no doubt the human nature of Christ; that is, His Father blesses Him. Interestingly, the full adjective *eulogētós* (2128) is attributed only to the deity of the Father (Mark 14:61; Luke 1:68; Rom. 1:25; 2 Cor. 1:3; 11:31; Eph. 1:3; 1 Pet. 1:3) and of the Son (Rom. 9:5). Christ is "God over all," the "One who is blessed [spoken well of] forever," or "the One who shall be blessed forever."

24

⚘

Jesus Predicts His Return in Glory
(24:1–8; Mark 13:1–8; Luke 21:5–10)

The twenty-third chapter of Matthew closes with Christ's final denunciation of Jerusalem, the capital of Judaism (vv. 34–39), following eight woes He pronounced on the scribes and the Pharisees (vv. 13–16, 23, 25, 27, 29).

[1] Most Bible scholars assume that the questioning of Christ's authority in chapter 22 and His denunciation of the Pharisees in chapter 23 take place on Tuesday of the Passion Week and that the Olivet discourse of chapters 24 and 25 takes place later on the same day. Thus, while leaving the complex of the "**temple**" (*hierón* [2411]) on Tuesday and before crossing the Kidron Valley to the Mount of Olives in view of the temple structure still under construction, we read,

> His disciples **came to** [from *prosérchomai* {4334}, to come near] him for **to shew** [from *epideíknumi* {1925}, to exhibit, display, show off] him the **buildings** [from *oikodomé* {3619}, buildings under construction] of the temple.

The stones used in the construction of this temple were huge, some measuring 40 by 12 by 20 feet each and weighing up to one hundred tons. The disciples were evidently impressed by the immense size and apparent indestructibility of these building blocks. The arches of the temple were 24 feet long. The porches (Solomon's and the Royal) were upheld by pillars of pure marble. First Kings 6 describes the remarkable opulence of this temple. It was covered within and without—the walls, doors, floors, altar, and many other things—with pure gold. Historians recorded that these huge stones were thrown down in A.D. 70 and the gold recycled.

Why would the disciples show off the temple to Jesus? They were impressed, and they may have thought Jesus was less familiar with the architecture than they. *Epideíknumi*, "**to exhibit**," derives from *epí* (1909), upon; and *deíknumi* (1166), to show. But how could Jesus possibly be impressed when He had just left the glories of heaven?

[2] Jesus made full use of their awe at human construction. He used an intensive negative to predict the certain destruction of this admittedly glorious edifice, a prophecy fulfilled by Roman armies under Titus in A.D. 70:

> And Jesus said unto them, See ye not all these things? **verily** [*amēn* {281}, truly] I say unto you, There shall **not** [the two negatives *ou* {3756} and *mē* {3361} combined as an intensive combination meaning absolutely not, never, at any time] be left here one stone upon another, that **shall** not **be thrown** [from *kataluō* {2647}, to throw down] down.

Kataluō derives from the preposition *katá* (2596) or the adverb *kátō* (2736), down; and *lúō* (3089), to loose. Paul uses it to describe the dissolution of our physical bodies that house our spirits like tents (from *skēnos* [4636]). These present bodies, he says, will be dissolved (from *kataluō*) and replaced with a new building from God in heaven (2 Cor. 5:1).

From this ominous prediction and another teaching (John 2:19), the Jewish opposition concluded that Jesus personally was going to destroy the temple. At His trial, they claimed, "We heard him say, I will destroy [*katalúsō*, the future tense of *kataluō*] this temple that is made with hands, and within three days I will build another made without hands" (Mark 14:58). But their conclusions were incorrect. Here Jesus predicted the destruction without any reference to Himself. The record in John 2:21 includes John's comment that "He was speaking of the temple of His body" (NASB). In plain language, the opponents deliberately misconstrued Jesus' words or did not listen carefully and got it wrong! Since they rejected Jesus' deity, it was absurd for them to suppose that a mere man could destroy such a massive edifice and reconstruct it in three days!

Since the Greek manuscripts do not contain question marks, Jesus' question could be taken in the indicative mood: "You do not see all [that is related to] these things." This would be a fitting introduction to the prophecy that began with the strong adverb, "**truly**" (a.t.; *amēn*). To paraphrase Christ's words, "There is more in respect to this magnificent building," Christ was intimating, "and you do not see the whole picture. When the panorama is extended to A.D. 70, the stones are no longer standing one upon the other."

Apocalyptic vision is unique. Whenever we are awestruck by the edifices of the world, we are blinded to higher realities. The cure is prophecy—the ability to foresee God's judgments on human pride.

Eventually, the material structures of this world are destined to destruction and replacement by spiritual structures: "And this word, Yet once more, signifieth the removing of those things that are shaken, as of things that are made, that those things which cannot be shaken may remain" (Heb. 12:27). As Jesus said, absolutely not (*ou mḗ*) a single stone would remain on another!

[3] Before expounding on the dramatic events leading to the overthrow of the temple, Jesus sat on the Mount of Olives and further taught His disciples.

And **as he sat** [from *káthēmai* {2521}] upon the mount of Olives, the disciples came unto him **privately** [*kat'* from *katá* {2596}, according to; *ídian* {2398}, private, own, personal], saying, Tell us, **when** [*póte* {4219}, an interrogative adverb meaning at what time] shall these things be? and **what** [*tí*, the **singular** neuter pronoun of *tís* {5101}, "what one thing," meaning, from the context, "what one sign"] shall be the sign of thy **coming** [from *parousía* {3952}, presence, appearance], and of the **end** [from *suntéleia* {4930}, the noun associated with the verb *suntéleō* {4931}, to bring together to completion, as e.g., in Heb. 12:2 where Jesus is called the *teleiōtḗs* {5051}, the finisher of our faith] of the **world** [from *aiṓn* {165}, age]?

Just as the Pharisees spoke authoritatively from the chair (*ex cathedra*; Matt. 23:2) of Moses and as a king would from his throne, now Jesus sat to describe the sweep of history to the end of the age, including dire predictions for the city and temple of Jerusalem. Actually, Jesus spoke in this manner from two mountains—the Mount of Beatitudes in Galilee (see Matt. 5:1 and author's, *The Beatitudes*) where He taught His disciples how to pray (see Matt. 6:9–13 and the author's book entitled, *The Lord's Prayer*) and the Mount of Olives in Jerusalem. Here at the close of His earthly ministry, His disciples asked Him about His Second Coming (*parousía*) and the consummation of the age.

The Second Coming of the Lord Jesus will begin with the snatching away of believers to be with Him in glory. The word *parousía* derives from *pará* (3844), which denotes close proximity; and the feminine participle of *eimí* (1510), to be (spiritual and/or material). It is used frequently with respect to the Second Coming of Christ (see vv. 27, 37, 39; 1 Cor. 15:23; 1 Thess. 2:19; 3:13; 4:15; 5:23; 2 Thess. 2:1, 8). *Parousía* describes single events as well as processes of several events. There is no doubt that Jesus will return physically to earth in His glorified body. Revelation 1:7 says, "Every eye [*ophthalmós* {3788}] shall see [from *optánomai* {3700}, to see physically] him" (cf. Acts 1:11).

The *parousía* includes the Day of Christ (the rapture) followed by the Tribulation and then the Day of the Lord (Isa. 2:12; 13:6, 9; Ezek. 13:5; 30:3; Joel 1:15; 2:1, 11, 31; 3:14; Amos 5:18, 20; Obad. 15; Zeph. 1:7, 14;

Zech. 14:1; Mal. 4:5; Acts 2:20; 1 Cor. 5:5; 2 Cor. 1:14; Phil. 1:6, 10; 2:16; 1 Thess. 5:2; 2 Thess. 2:2; 2 Pet. 3:10). The phrases "that day," "the day," or "the great day" together occur more than seventy-five times in the Old Testament. Zechariah 14:1–4 speaks of the Day of the Lord as an event of the Second Coming in the program of God. Second Peter 3:10 appears to include the entire millennial age within this period. During this "day," Jesus will personally come to raise dead believers (1 Cor. 15:23), transform living believers, and take them to be with Him forever (1 Cor. 15:50–54; 1 Thess. 4:13–17).

This "coming" is also described by the Greek words *apokálupsis* (602), revelation (Rom. 2:5; 8:19; 1 Cor. 1:7; 1 Pet. 1:7, 13; 4:13), and *epipháneia* (2015), manifestation (2 Thess. 2:8; 1 Tim. 6:14; 2 Tim. 1:10; 4:1, 8; Titus 2:13).

Thus, the coming of Jesus and His *parousía* is a series of events and comings, not just one single event. The disciples had no doubt that the events Jesus predicted were going to take place, but they wanted to know "**when**" (*póte*) and what one sign would confirm or verify His presence and the consummation of the age. When the scribes asked for signs, Jesus answered that no sign would be given but the sign of the resurrection, typified by Jonah's incarceration in the belly of the great fish (Matt. 12:39–41; 16:4; Luke 11:29–32). Accordingly, the resurrection would be the basic assurance that events predicted in this "Olivet Discourse," as it is called, would occur. At least five hundred people witnessed Christ's resurrection, over half of them alive at the time Paul wrote his first epistle to the Corinthians (1 Cor. 15:6; see author's, *Conquering the Fear of Death*).

Notice that, in the Greek, the disciples did not ask concerning "the end [KJV, as if from *télos* {5056}] of the world [KJV, as if from *kósmos* {2889}]" but rather concerning "the **completion** [a.t.; *suntéleia* {4930}] of the **age** [a.t.; *aiṓn* {165}]." "Completion" adds conceptually to the term *aiṓn*, age, the qualitative idea that events within the age will all contribute to the completion like bricks to a building (e.g., we speak of a building's completion, not its end). The Second Coming will be a process, a consummation of foreknown events rather than a disjointed series of crises. All the events will tie together, contributing to a culmination, a climax in which the old order will be superseded by the new.

An *aiṓn*, age, itself is not a *chrónos* (5550), mere measured time like a delay or interval but rather a dispensation—time with a divinely appointed content. Although the disciples requested a single sign (*tí*), they also inquired about "**these things**" (*taúta* [5023])—a number of observable events that will complete the age (*aiōn*). This age has *kairoí* (2540), seasons, opportunities that God extends to people to repent. Jesus also taught, however, that "blasphemy against the Holy Spirit would not be forgiven him [man] . . . in this age nor in the one to come" (Matt. 12:31, 32 a.t.).

In Mark 13:33, Jesus told His disciples to "Take heed, watch and pray; for you do not know when [*póte* {4219}] the time [*kairós*, season] is" (NKJV). *Póte*, then, refers not to an instant of time but to a season, a period. Similarly, in Luke 21:8, the "time [*kairós*] [that] **has drawn near** [from *eggízō* {1448}]" (a.t.) includes a series of events: earthquakes, wars, portentous signs in the sky, persecutions, etc.

[4, 5] Because this age will be characterized by unique deception, Jesus issued the warning: "Take heed that no one **deceives** [*planḗsē*, the aorist subjunctive of *plandō* {4105}, to lead away from the proper course; the aorist tense means even once] you" (NKJV).

"**Take heed**" translates the Greek verb *blépete*, the present imperative of *blépō* (991), to see, heed. The present tense means that believers should constantly watch for signals in the prophetic future. Jesus did not directly answer the disciples' question "when?" because the emphasis lies not on when but on what to look for.

When false prophets fix the date of Christ's return, they deceive believers. They cause them to lose their commitment to the Savior in exchange for escape from the very tribulations intended to glorify Christ's power. "Thou hast left thy first love" (Rev. 2:4), the church of Ephesus was told. New believers are consumed with love and enthusiasm when they first come to know Jesus as their personal Lord and Savior. When anything leads them away from this first love, even the study of eschatology (events in the last times), then they should beware (1 Pet. 1:5, cf. John 6:39, 40, 44; 11:24; 12:48; Acts 2:17; 2 Tim. 3:1; Heb. 1:2; James 5:3; 2 Pet. 3:3; Jude 18).

[6] Adam and Eve's rejection of God brought suffering and death into the world. We cannot escape this sorrow and trouble (John 16:33), but God has promised to give us victory.

Christ's message to believers is, "See to it that you do not **become panicked** [from *throéō* {2360}, to disturb, trouble, terrify]" (a.t.). The verb *throéō* is found in the two recordings of the Olivet Discourse (Matt. 24:6; Mark 13:7) and in Paul's counsel to the Thessalonians that they should not panic in the face of events attending the Day of the Lord (2 Thess. 2:2). Panic, the syndrome that now fills whole shelves of large bookstores, involves a subordination of logical thinking to highly vacillating emotions. Since Jesus commanded

His disciples to neither panic (above) nor be afraid (*phobéō* [5399], fear; see Matt. 14:27; 17:7; 28:5, 10), panic is a response contrary to faith. Of course, we all need the Lord's grace to overcome fear.

Jesus told the disciples that all these things "**must**" (*deí* [1163], it is bound to be, or necessary) occur. God, therefore, will work out His purposes through these events; they should neither take us by surprise nor plunge us into despair. Wars, and there will be many, must not cause us to lose hope because "the end is **not yet** [*oúpō* {3768}; derived from the negative *ou*; and –*pō* {4452}, yet]." In John 16:33, Jesus said, "These things I have spoken unto you, that in me ye might have peace. In the world ye shall have tribulation [from *thlípsis* {2347}, pressure, squeezing]." The Lord will allow us to be pressured by individuals, nations, and events during this age (*aiōn*) in order to strengthen our faith and commitment to Him.

[7] Natural disasters such as "**famines**" (from *limós* [3042]; Mark 13:8; Luke 21:11), plagues or "**pestilences**" (from *loimós* [3061]; Luke 21:11), and "**earthquakes**" (from *seismós* [4578], shaking as, of the earth or even the heavens; Mark 13:8; Luke 21:11; Rev. 6:12; 11:13, 19; 16:18) all operate within the power and wisdom of our God.

[8] As terrible as they are, these tribulational pressures should not cause us to panic. Jesus said they are the beginning of "**sorrows**" (from *ōdín* [5604], birth pangs), comparable to the labor pains a woman forgets when her child is finally born (John 16:21). By analogy, we can expect sudden and painful stress, but we should not be overwhelmed because the Lord will deliver us from these evils as surely as He delivers a mother from her labor pains.

The Threats of Betrayal and Martyrdom
(24:9–14; Mark 13:5–13; Luke 21:8–19)

[9] The false notion that believers are exempt from affliction (*thlípsis* [2347], squeezing, suffering) is being spread today. In this section, Jesus said this is not true. Here *tóte* (5119), "then," covers the whole period from Christ's first coming to His triumphant return in glory to reign on earth after the tribulation (Matt. 25:31).

Given the nature of the persecution that follows and the reference to endurance to the end (v. 13), the "then's" in verses 9 and 10 extend through the time of the "Great Tribulation" specified in verse 21. But the emphasis of *thlípsis* without the definite article (as in v. 21) is on the quality of persecution as opposed to its identity or duration. It is then that "**they** [an undefined subject but presumably agents of the Antichrist] **will deliver** [from *paradídōmi* {3860}, to deliver]" (a.t.) believers into affliction by superior but temporary physical force. As the devil focuses on earth, having been cast out of heaven, he "knows that he has only a short time" (Rev. 12:12; a.t.). Panic sets in, and he will rage against the victorious "saints" (Rev. 13:7).

His agents will "**kill**" (from *apokteínō* [615]; in this context, murder) many believers unjustly during this time. As all nations hated the Jews, so the world will "**hate**" (from *miséō* [3404]) Christians during this season (Matt. 10:22; John 15:18, 19). Believers do not need to do anything to incite hatred. Resentment is aroused simply by bearing and declaring the name of Christ before unbelievers.

During this time of intense persecution, believers will rise to the call of the hour to be on a polite but an assertive offensive.

The last persons saved in the Tribulation period are the fruit of assertive believers that includes two special "witnesses" from heaven (Rev. 11:2, 3). The beast rises out of the abyss to war against these two witnesses and kills them (Rev. 11:7). During this time, the devil furiously attacks believers (Rev. 12:17). Hatred and persecution will be intense against the physical church, which will be sifted to separate true believers from false (Matt. 13:24–30, 36–43). All offenses (from *skándalon* [4625]) will be uniquely dealt with by divine intervention (Matt. 13:41).

[10] Hypocrites will be "**offended**" (from *skandalízō* [4624], to trip up, to scandalize) as their secret unbelief is exposed when they desert Jesus Christ.

Persecution brings out publicly those who "have no root in themselves, but are temporary [from *próskairos* {4340} from *prós* {4314}, toward, pertaining to; and *kairós* {2540}, a season]" (Mark 4:17; a.t.). These will be "**offended**" (see above), quickly falling away under trial. By contrast, true believers are snatched away by (1 Thess. 4:17) but never from (John 10:28) the omnipotent hand of Christ.

[11] From within the ranks of the deceived multitudes, false leaders will arise. Here they are called "**false prophets**" (*pseudoprophētai* [5578]) who "**shall deceive**" (*planēsousi* [4105]) many of their own kind. They will be blind guides of the blind.

[12] Jesus warned His disciples that lawlessness will be "**multiplied**" (from *plēthúnō* [4129], to increase, to make full).

Anarchy, the casting off of legal and moral restraints, is the most detrimental attack on society. The increase of sin will correlate with an objective relaxation of the law. We see this in our society today. Our laws condone both homosexuality and abortion (see Rom. 1:26, 27). More and more people will follow such "death styles" where "**iniquity** [*anomía* {458}, lawlessness] shall abound."

Can you imagine what human behavior will be like when no enforceable laws will govern conduct? The result will be chaos and anarchy, a great milieu for a campaigning Antichrist's promises of peace, stability, and prosperity. When people become a law unto themselves, they will clamor for a universal dictator. Even satanic order is preferable to the evil apex of anarchy, and from Jesus' words that imply that Satan is not against Satan, we can infer that Satan himself would prefer evil rule to an evil anarchy that would pit every demon against every other demon.

"The **love** [*agápē* {26}] of many [i.e., the majority]" probably refers to the unbelieving majority. We should not be distracted by the term *agápē*, which Jesus (using the verb form *agapáō* [25]) said exists between "sinners" (Luke 6:32) in the Pharisees' love for the "chief seats" of the synagogue (Luke 11:43), and between a person and an evil master like money (Luke 16:13). Accordingly, "**shall wax cold**," translating a verb form of *psúchō* (5594), to render cool, to chill, akin to *pnéō* (4154), to breathe or blow on in order to cool, refers to the degeneration of what little love exists between unbelievers. Possibly their love moves from cold to colder; certainly nothing implies that it was "hot" (Rev. 3:15, 16) in the first place. Moreover, with lawlessness and sin abounding, even some believers' first love for Christ will cool (Rev. 2:4).

[13] However, a minority will exist whose first love for Christ does not cool off. This group is introduced by the adversative particle "**but**" (*dé* [1161]), followed by the expression "**he that shall endure** [*hupomeínas*, the aorist participle of *hupoménō* {5278}, to persevere against adverse circumstances]."

The adversity of this time is highlighted in verses 9–14. Believers will be "hated of all nations" (v. 9). At that time, many will be offended (v. 10). Many false prophets (religious leaders) shall arise to deceive many (v. 11). Iniquity shall abound, and the love of many shall wax cold (v. 12). In the midst of this, however, a minority endures: "But the one who endures. . ." (NASB). God saves individuals even out of wicked generations (Acts 2:40). John 1:12 says, "As many as [from *hósos* {3745}, as many individuals] received him, to them gave he power to become the sons [children, from *téknon* {5043}] of God, even to them that believe on his name." Personal admission to the kingdom of God is secured by personal faith. "Every one" (*hékastos* [1538]) stands alone before the Lord in judgment (2 Cor. 5:10; Rev. 20:13).

To emphasize personal victory in the end of the age, the demonstrative pronoun "**this one**" (*hoútos* [3778], the masculine demonstrative pronoun), translated "the same" in the King James Version, is used, followed by the future verb "**shall be saved**" (from *sṓzō* [4982]). The verb does not refer to salvation from sin but, specifically, salvation from the persecution of the end times (Matt. 10:22; 24:22; Mark 13:20).

God's rescue is accomplished even if believers are killed (v. 9). In 2 Timothy 4:17, 18, Paul uses both verbs, *rhúomai* (4506), to deliver, and *sōzō*. They have the same meaning, which is to deliver from some objective danger. Paul, for example, "was delivered [from *rhúomai*] out of the mouth of the lion" (2 Tim. 4:17). He says also that the Lord will deliver (also from *rhúomai*) him "from every evil work . . . unto his heavenly kingdom" (v.18). This will be the ultimate victory for Christians who are rescued from the oppression of wickedness and spiritual death (2 Cor. 1:10).

The word "**end**" (*télos* [5056]) in the phrase "unto the end" certainly means the end of this life. This seems to be the case when we compare Revelation 2:10, "Be thou faithful unto death," with verse 2:26, "He who overcomes and keeps My works to the end" (a.t.). It is a simple inference that "unto death" is equivalent to "until the end." If "the end" meant when Christ returns, then the Lord would expect a first-century believer to be faithful not just "unto [his] death" but milleniums beyond it.

[14] The gospel will be "**proclaimed** [from *kērússō* {2784}] in all the **inhabited earth** [*oikouménē* {3625}]" (a.t.). In Revelation, John gives us a glimpse of the impact of this preaching in the scene of an innumerable crowd from all nations victoriously coming out of the Great Tribulation (Rev. 7:9, 14).

The Greek word for "**witness**" here is the neuter noun *martúrion* (3142) and probably refers to positively witnessing for Christ, but it could refer to a negative witnessing against the nations, pointing out their sins. Nations may reject the gospel, but an innumerable crowd of individuals out of every nation will exit the Tribulation in victory (see previous paragraph).

In the day of condemnation, all nonbelievers will be faced with the testimony (*martúrion*) that they had an opportunity to receive Christ but rejected it. Since "the gospel of the kingdom" will reach the entire inhabited earth, no one will be able to claim ignorance.

"And then **shall come** [from *hēkō* {2240}] the **end** [*télos* {5056}]" (a.t.), that is, the consummation (*suntéleia*) of the age. After these successive events, the end will occur at a specific time (*tóte*, then; see v. 9).

The Abomination of Desolation
(24:15–22; Mark 13:14–22; Luke 21:20–24)

[15] The word "therefore" (*oún* [3767]) connects "the end [*télos* {5056}, terminal point]" in verse 14 with the event being introduced here.

"**When**," the Greek conjunction *hótan* (3752), focuses on a specific event within the nation of Israel, which will be miraculously preserved. The appearance of the abomination of desolation is connected with the worldwide preaching of the gospel of the kingdom at "the end." This is the closest Jesus gets to answering the disciple's question of when in verse 3. However, the "when" is eclipsed by a "what", that is, some physical object called an "abomination of desolation" is given in place of a date. There will be a day and hour when this profane, sacrilegious idol will be erected, but the disciples were to deduce the time from the sign, not the sign from the times.

Once in this discourse, *hótan* is qualified only by anticipatory waiting (*prosdokáō* [4328]; v. 50). In three other instances, the expectation of "then" is connected with signs that are empirically observed (here the abomination of desolation, in v. 32 the branch putting forth leaves as summer approaches, and in v. 33 "all these things").

In looking at the magnificent temple, Jesus had said (v. 2) that one stone would not be left on another, but the entire structure would be "thrown down" or destroyed (from *katalúō* [2647]).

Jesus now spoke of "the abomination of desolation." **Abomination** is the Greek noun *bdélugma* (946) from the verb *bdelússō* (948), to emit a foul odor or to turn away through loathing or disgust. The abomination, then, whatever it is, will cause desolation. The verb translated "**shall see**" is *ídēte*, the aorist active subjunctive of *eídon* from *horáō* (3708), to see and perceive with emphasis on perception. Believers will see or perceive this disgusting thing at the completion of the age (*suntéleia toú aiōnos*; v. 3). Furthermore, they will need to "mind" what was written in the book of Daniel to perceive accurately how this event fits into the general scheme.

In 1 John 2:18 we read,

> Little children, it is the last hour: and as you have heard that **antichrist** [*antíchristos* {500} from *antí* {473}, against; and *christós* {5547}, anointed one] **comes** [from *érchomai* {2064}, to come], even now there are many antichrists; so we know it is the last hour. (a.t.)

An antichrist is one who opposes Christ. "Anti" also means in place of, so this last Antichrist will be a supplanter; he will try to replace the true Messiah. The "little horn" on the fourth beast of Daniel 7:8 and "the beast" (*thēríon* [2342]) of Revelation 11:7; 13:1–8 are then both Antichrist. Three-and-a-half years into Daniel's seventieth week, this beast will attempt to replace Christ (Dan. 9:27; 2 Thess. 2:3-10; Rev. 13:5). This ultimate Antichrist surpasses the attempts of former antichrists to replace God as the object of worship (Rev. 13:12). Satan will energize him (Rev. 13:2, 3) and aid his cause by performing miracles through him and deceiving the world into worshiping him through "another beast" (Rev. 13:11, 12). Elsewhere the Antichrist is called "that lawless [*ánomos* {459}] one" (2 Thess. 2:8 NASB), the "man of sin," and the "son of perdition" (2 Thess. 2:1–12). He will be destroyed on and by the "Day of Christ" (2 Thess. 2:2). This final Antichrist may be the "angel of the abyss," the "king" of Hades (Rev. 9:11), whose name in Hebrew is "Abaddon" (*abaddṓn* [3]) and in Greek "Apollyon" (*apollúōn* [623]), both names signifying "the destroyer."

This final Antichrist is so obnoxious (*bdelússō* or *bdéō* [n.f.], to stink) that Jerusalem and the temple will be desolated as prophesied by Christ (Matt. 23:38; Luke 21:20) and earlier by Jeremiah (Jer. 22:5). This is not so much a military conquest as moral abandonment, far worse than defeat. The amazing thing is that all this was predicted so long ago in Daniel 8:13 and 9:27. Daniel 11:31 says, "And they shall pollute the sanctuary of strength, and shall take away the daily sacrifice, and they shall place the abomination that maketh desolate."

The activities of this supreme world leader are given in historical narrative in Daniel, chapters 7–12. Satan himself empowers him according to Revelation 13:2, warring against the people of God (13:7). The conflict that ensues is unimaginable. At the end, the Messiah stops the transgression and the "wicked one" (2 Thess. 2:8; a.t.). All this centers in Jerusalem (Dan. 9:26).

According to Daniel 11:36 (cf. 2 Thess. 2:4), this Antichrist magnifies himself above every god, including the almighty God, arousing His indignation. While two words in Greek (*orgḗ* [3709], wrath; Matt. 3:7; Luke 3:7; John 3:36; Rom. 1:18; 2:5; 3:5; 9:22; Eph. 2:3; 5:6; Col. 3:6; 1 Thess. 1:10; 2:16; 5:9; Rev. 6:16, 17; 11:18; and *thlípsis* [2347], tribulation; Matt. 24:21, 29; Mark 13:19, 24; 2 Thess. 1:6; Rev. 2:22; 7:14) are both characteristics of this time, Paul makes it clear that believers are not appointed to the wrath (from *orgḗ*; 1 Thess. 5:9) of God. The Lord, rather, "rescues us from the coming wrath" (1 Thess. 1:10 NIV).

Jesus now said parenthetically that understanding this prophecy is essential and should occupy our careful attention:

> Whoso **readeth** [from *anaginṓskō* {314} from *aná* {303}, **again**; and *ginṓskō* {1097}, to know by experience], **let him understand** [*noeítō* from *noéō* {3539}, to comprehend, understand].

Each individual should read these Scriptures over and over again until he or she understands what is meant. Of course, this will take place in the middle of the Tribulation period. We who are alive today probably will have already been raptured. But many will seek the truth in that day. These people must learn what Christ would have them do when the abomination of desolation approaches. This is impossible apart from a careful study of Daniel chapters 7–12 and other related portions of Scripture (2 Thess. 2:1–12; 1 John 2:18; Rev. 13).

As disciples, we all ought to read the biblical lessons given by God's inspired prophets like Daniel. Eschatology is a set of templates (patterns) that fit over the whole of history, revealing how God works and what He does. Accordingly, we should not read prophecy casually, but carefully interpret it and apply it to our own experiences.

[16] When believers recognize the identity of the Antichrist, Jesus continued, they should take certain measures.

The adverb **"then"** (*tóte* [5119]) here agrees with the "then's" of verses 9 and 10, referring to the second half of the seven-year, seventieth week of Daniel. Conditions in Jerusalem will be so bad that Jesus forewarned His disciples to leave the region of Judea and escape to the mountains. The verb **"let them flee"** is *pheugétōsan*, the present imperative of *pheúgō* (5343), to flee (cf. Mark 13:14; Luke 21:21).

[17, 18] Other specific instructions are worth noting. If any one is on the roof of his house, Jesus warned,

> **Let him** . . . **not come down** [from *katabaínō* {2597}, to go down] **to take** [from *aírō* {142}, to take away] anything out of his house. Nor let him who is in the field **return** [from *epistréphō* {1994}] **back** [*opísō* {3694}] **to take** [also from *aírō*] his clothes. (a.t.)

No material possession is worth a human life. As Judea will be surrounded by armies (Luke 21:20), panic and anarchy will set in. People will no longer find safety in status or possessions. Jesus' clear advice here is to flee from the land.

[19] A specific exhortation is given to expectant and nursing mothers:

> And woe unto them that are with child, and **them that nurse** [from *thēlázō* {2337}, to breast feed a baby] in those days. (a.t.)

"Those days" may extend to the full forty-two months or 1,260 days noted in other places (Dan. 7:25; 9:27; 12:10–12; Rev. 11:2, 3; 13:5; see below for further discussion). (Note that the "Great Tribulation" comes after the appearance of the abomination of desolation [vv. 15, 21], which, according to Dan. 9:27, occurs in the middle of the seventieth week.)

[20] Within this period, apparently, there will be favorable times to escape:

> But **pray ye** [from *proseúchomai* {4336}, to pray to God] that your **flight** [*phugē* {5437}] **be** [from *gínomai* {1096}, to become] not in the winter, neither on the Sabbath day.

As Paul tells us generally, we should "pray without ceasing" (1 Thess. 5:17), but this prayer has a specific content. A desperate flight out of Judea would violate the command to rest on the Sabbath, and winter is generally a time of food scarcity, even apart from the threat of an invasion. But God will be tolerant throughout the Tribulation, His grace reaching down to save souls from "all nations" from the evil one. Among these will be great numbers of Israelites.

[21] The reason for praying that the escape out of Judea is not in the winter or on a Sabbath day follows:

> For then shall be **great** [from *mégas* {3173}] **tribulation** [*thlípsis* {2347}], such as **was** [from *gínomai* {1096}, "to be"] not **since** [*ap'* from *apó* {575}, from] the **beginning** [from *archḗ* {746}, commencement] of the **world** [*kósmos* {2889}] to this time, no, nor ever shall be.

The words "great" and "tribulation," occurring without definite articles, should be taken generically, introducing us to a special kind of tribulation. "**Such**" translates a form of the relative pronoun *hoíos* (3634), such a one. The contrast that follows is between this and every other tribulation. This will be the severest.

"**To this time**" translates *héōs* (2193), until this time. The last phrase, "**no, nor ever shall be**," begins with the negative *oudé* (3761), "but not." This is a contrasting compound conjunction of the two negatives *ou* (3756) and *mḗ* (3361) combined as an intensive combination, meaning absolutely not, never at any time. The intensive negative means that this tribulation will be absolutely unprecedented.

Though dreadful and unique, the Tribulation will be under God's full control. Satan and his demons are sometimes called world rulers (from *kosmokrátōr* [2888]; see Eph. 6:12), but God is the ruler of all, the *pantokrátōr* (3841), the almighty, the ruler of all heaven and earth, the universe (2 Cor. 6:18; Rev. 1:8; 4:8; 11:17; 15:3; 16:7, 14; 19:6, 15; 21:22). Because Satan's time will be short, he will no doubt command his malevolent ranks to carry out their evil plans efficiently. But Revelation 17:14 assures us who will be victorious: "These [the forces of evil including the Antichrist] shall make war with the Lamb [*arníon* {721} a living lamb], and the Lamb shall overcome them" (see also Rev. 5:6, 8, 12, 13; 6:1, 16; 7:9, 10, 14, 17; 12:11; 13:8; 14:1, 4, 10; 15:3; 17:14; 19:7, 9; 21:9, 14, 22, 23, 27; 22:1, 3).

[22] The King James Version here translates the Greek conjunction *ei* (1487) *mḗ* (3361), "**if not**," as a clause of exception:

> And **except** [*ei mḗ*] those days be shortened, **no** [literally, **none** {from *ou* (3756)} of **any** {from *pás* (3956), all, any}] flesh [*sárx* {4561}, the emphasis is

on physical preservation, not spiritual salvation] would [*án* {302}, "then" as a potential] be **saved** [from *sōzō* {4982}, to save]. (a.t.)

The contextual referent of "those days" is the Great Tribulation, the period when Gentile armies invade Jerusalem to quell the religious anarchy created by positioning the abomination of desolation in the holy place (Dan. 9:27). Such furious oppression will take place in those days that unless the time is shortened, everyone will die physically.

Will God shorten the days? Here, it would be better to think of the Greek verb translated in the King James Version as "**should be shortened** [from *koloböō* {2856}]" as "to be cut short." Or, to put it another way, God has already determined shortened days. If He had not, the text says, the destruction would be total. Another way to translate the first part of the verse is:

> **If** [*ei*, on the supposition that] those days **were not shortened** [*ekolobóthēsan*, the **aorist** indicative of *koloböō* {2856}; the indicative—in place of the subjunctive—implies that God already shortened], **then surely** [*an* {302}] no one will escape alive. (a.t.)

Since God's foreknowledge is absolutely accurate, it already includes shortened days, but to what extent? No doubt the original three-and-a-half years prophesied in Daniel and marked out as a unique period of oppression also in Revelation (see Dan. 7:25; Rev. 11: 2, 3, 7; 12:7, 11, 14; 13:5) have already been shortened from a longer period that would have been (see, e.g., Matt. 11:21, 23 for events that "would have been" had God determined otherwise). It is not necessary for us to know what the reduction in time is in order to know that it is.

The balance of the verse tells us for whose sake God cut the days short: "For the elect's sake those days shall be shortened" (which means the shortening is included in God's eternal decree. There's no "if" about this here; they "shall be" shortened).

The "**elect**" (from *eklektós* [1588], chosen one) are those saved from all nations during the Tribulation (Rev. 7:1–17; 12:17; 13:7; 15:2, 3). The persecution by the Antichrist will stimulate believers of this period to pray fervently: "The effectual fervent prayer [*déesis* {1162}, prayer for what is needed] of a righteous man availeth much" (James 5:16). Many will be saved through these prayers.

This does not indicate a change of God's plan and mind but the exact execution of His will as planned. The time of the severe persecution by the Antichrist will be no longer than the length of time to which God has shortened it. The time would be longer if God were not merciful, but since He is, He will shorten the period in which the Antichrist expends his fury.

False Christs and Prophets
(24:23–26; Mark 13:21–23)

[23] The terror caused by the Antichrist during the second half of Daniel's seventieth week will be so great that the only hope will be Christ's direct intervention. The word "then" here, as we find in Matthew 24:9, 10, 16, 21, does not refer to an instant of time but to a period. Here the antecedent is "those days" (v. 22) which in turn points back to "great tribulation" (v. 21).

Then **if** [*eán* {1437}] **anyone** [*tís*, the masculine or feminine enclitic indefinite pronoun {5100}, anyone—false prophet of either sex] **say** [from *eípon*, the aorist of *légō* {3004}, to say meaningfully] to you, **Lo** [*idoú* {2400}, behold, see, the imperative of *eídon* {1492}, the aorist of *horáō* {3708}, to perceive, calling attention to the extraordinary, {see Matt. 3:16}], **here** [*hṓde* {5602}] is the Christ, or there, **believe** [*pisteúsēte*, the aorist active imperative of *pisteúō* {4100}] it not. (a.t.)

This will be an unprecedented time of messianic claims—a proliferation of false christs and false prophets. The entire paragraph warns believers against single events of deception: first, by the use of the indefinite pronoun *tis*, anyone, and secondly by the presence of three verbs in the aorist tense: "say . . . behold . . . believe."

[24] For there shall arise false Christs, and false prophets.

At this time, those who claim to be anointed will be "**false Christs**" (from *pseudóchristos* [5580] from *pseudḗs* [5571], false, pretentious). The true Christ is "the **truth**" (John 14:6; *alḗtheia* [225]—the opposite of false, *pseúdos* [5579]). Since there is only one Truth, there is only one Christ.

False prophets promise but cannot deliver. The word "**prophet**" (*prophḗtēs* [4396] from the preposition *pró* [4253], before or ahead of time, or possibly a truncated *prós* [4314], toward; and *phēmí* [5346], to speak, to affirm) designates one who accurately foretells the future. According to Deuteronomy 13:1–3, a true prophet must have the added stipulation of acknowledging previously revealed truth. When Christ said He was going to rise from the dead, He did so. Having fulfilled His own prophetic word, He established His veracity.

The purpose, "**insomuch that**" (*hṓste* [5620], consequently), of false christs and prophets is "**to deceive**" (from *planáō* [4105], to deceive) the multitudes. To deceive, they shall show "great **signs** [from *sēmeíon* {4592}, a sign post] and **wonders** [from *téras* {5059}, an extraordinary event which causes astonishment and/or terror]." Wonders (*téras*) also accompanied Moses (Acts 7:36; Sept.: Ex. 7:3; Deut. 6:22; 7:19; Jer. 32:20); Christ (John 4:48); and the apostles and teachers (Acts 2:43; 4:30; 5:12; 6:8; 14:3; 15:12; Rom. 15:19; 2 Cor. 12:12; Heb. 2:4).

Signs and wonders are not easily differentiated, but wonders (*téras*) are associated with the verb *tēréō* (5083), to keep or watch, adding the ideas of startling, imposing, amazing, and memorable to observation. As empirical events, "wonders" are not intrinsically predictive, and so they can as easily point to falsity as to truth. However, since the same can be said for "signs," their difference may be no more than the degree.

The persuasive power of the signs and wonders of these false prophets and christs will be so great that "if it were **possible** [from *dunatós* {1415}], they shall deceive the very elect." The "**if**" (*ei* [1487]) is an "if" of supposition, not of reality. The effort and purpose will be to deceive, if it were possible, "**also** [*kaí* {2532}, in the ascensive sense of 'even'] the elect," meaning true believers in the Tribulation period. Physical signs and wonders can deceive the elect in the same manner in which they can be fooled by a magician but never by false propositions. As Jesus said of His sheep, "They will not follow a stranger because they have not known the voice [not the sounds but the false propositions] of strangers" (John 10:5; a.t.).

The "**elect**" (from *eklektós* [1588] from *eklégomai* [1586], to select, choose) are those chosen for salvation. Many are called (from *klētós* [2822] associated with the verb *kaléō* [2564], to call), but not all respond to God's call. Those who do respond to His call are His elect, the ones He chooses. These include believers saved during the Tribulation period who are mentioned in verse 31 (cf. Mark 13:27).

[25] "**Behold**" (from *eídōn*, the aorist of *horáō* [3708], to see and perceive) means to see in the sense of understanding. Jesus told His disciples they should not be surprised when these things happen because He "**foretold** [from *proeréō* {4280}, to predict, from *pró* {4253}, before; and *eréō* {2046}, to speak precisely] them" (a.t.). Forewarned is forearmed; we believers must prepare theologically and ethically for these false prophets and false christs.

[26] A qualification followed:

Wherefore if **they shall say** [*eipōsin*, the aorist active subjunctive of *légō* {3004}, to meaningfully say] unto you, Behold, he is in the desert; **go** [*exélthēte*, the aorist active imperative of *exérchomai* {1831}, to depart] not forth: behold, he is in the **secret chambers** [from *tameíon* {5009}, special rooms where the owner kept things secretly; in modern Greek, a place where treasures are kept]; **believe** [*pisteúsēte*, the aorist active imperative of *pisteúō* {4100}, to believe] it not.

Wild reports of the appearance of Christ in esoteric places like deserts and secret chambers will surface, all of which contrast with Christ's coming public appearance which will be like lightning.

We are to wholly reject these false claims of Christ's return in our actions ("do not go out") and in our attitudinal faith ("do not believe"). The punctiliar nature of the aorist stresses the importance of not going out or believing a single instance of these false claims. If we should reject the formal claim of anointing, then we should reject the accompanying content—the predictions, ethics, and theology, as well.

The Return of the Son of Man
(24:27–41; Mark 13:24–33; Luke 17:24–36; 21:34–36)

[27] "**For as**" introduces the reason why the local appearances of prophets, so-called christs, signs, and wonders do not constitute valid testimony of the appearance (*parousía* [3952]) of "the Son of man . . . in his glory" (Matt. 25:31). Christ's return will not be secretive at all but "like [*hósper* {5618} from *hós* {5613}, as; and the emphatic enclitic particle *per* {4007}, wholly, very much; 'exactly like'] the **lightning** [*astrapé* {796}] coming out of the east and shining even to the west" (a.t.).

This verse stresses the dramatic universal display of Christ's coming against the localizations picked up by news reporters that happen to be in the area.

"**Coming**" is actually *parousía*, presence. Jesus' visible presence is also referred to as an *epipháneia* (2015), a manifestation, a visible revelation (*apokálupsis* [602], an uncovering). It is associated with the verb used here of the lightning that "**shineth**" (from *phaínō* [5316]), especially in Paul's epistles (2 Thess. 2:8; 1 Tim. 6:14).

Everyone who is living will see this event that ushers in the eternal reign of Jesus Christ with believers of all ages (Rev. 1:7).

[28] Jesus will return in judgment:

> For wheresoever the **carcase** [*ptóma* {4430}, corpse; Luke's Synoptic text uses *sóma* {4983}, body] is, there the **eagles** [from *aetós* {105}, an eagle or vulture, a species of rapacious birds that prey on dead bodies] **will be gathered together** [*sunachthésontai*, the future passive tense of *sunágō* {4863}, to lead together]. (a.t.)

The picture is clearly one of judgment, a scenario of predatory birds perched on a dead body (*sóma*), intent on feeding. (Note: "the body [*sóma*] without the spirit [from *pneúma* {4151}] is dead [from *nekrós* {3498}]," meaning a corpse [*ptôma*] according to James 2:26—thus our reference to a dead body.) What eagles or vultures feed on is worthless apart from its value as fodder. A similar picture is painted in the book of Revelation:

> And I saw an angel standing in the sun; and he cried with a loud voice, saying to all the fowls that fly in the midst of heaven, Come and gather yourselves together unto the supper of the great God; that ye may eat the flesh of kings, and the flesh of captains, and the flesh of mighty men, and the flesh of horses, and of them that sit on them, and the flesh of all men, both free and bond, both small and great. (Rev. 19:17, 18)

The context in Revelation is Armageddon, thus the reference to the flesh of captains, mighty men, and horses (Rev. 19:18, 21).

Jesus never answered His disciples' question concerning the when of His coming; it is a divine secret (Matt. 24:36; Mark 13:32; Acts 1:7). But Revelation 22:20, 21 reveal that the series of events leading up to the physical return of Jesus Christ will take place in rapid succession (*tachú* [5035], quickly and suddenly; used as an adverb, it means speedily; Rev. 2:16; 3:11; 11:14; 22:7, 12, 20). Living believers will be transformed "in an instant [from *átomos* {823}, an indivisible unit of time], in the twinkling of an eye" (1 Cor. 15:52; a.t.).

Divine chronology does not always fit human speculations (2 Pet. 3:7–15). In general, the events will catch unbelievers by surprise, like a "thief in the night" (1 Thess. 5:2; see Matt. 24:43; Luke 12:39; 2 Pet. 3:10; Rev. 3:3; 16:15).

[29] The events described in this verse occur "**immediately** [*euthéōs* {2112}] **after** [*metá* {3326}, succession, sequence] the tribulation of those days." This refers to the troubles described in verse 21 (without the definite article as here), the Great Tribulation, in the last three-and-a-half years of the seventieth week. This is the period of the worst activity of the Antichrist who wages war against "the saints" (Dan. 7:25; Rev. 13:5–8).

The events of "those days" are similar to those on the day the Lord Jesus was crucified, especially during the last three hours He hung on the cross. We read in Matthew 27:45, "Now from the sixth hour there was darkness over all the land [*gê* {1093}, earth] unto the ninth hour," a time when the sun should have been the brightest. Yet darkness (*skótos* [4655], a word symbolic of spiritual darkness, i.e., sin) prevailed over the whole earth where people, separated from God because of sin, were doing their worst. Jesus' tribulation on the cross was a prophetic type of the Great Tribulation.

Jesus added, "The sun **shall be darkened** [from *skotízō* {4654}, a verb associated with the noun *skótos* {4655}, darkness], and the moon shall not give her **light** [*phéggos* {5338}]" (a.t.). *Phéggos* refers to the light (*phós* [5457]) of the sun reflected by the moon, which is analogous to the church's reflection of the glory of Christ.

This culminating darkness will end when He who is the "bright and morning star" dispels it once and for all (Rev. 22:16).

[30] In verse 3, the disciples asked, "When will all these things be, and what is the [single] sign of your coming [*parousía* {3952}] and the consummation of the age?" (a.t.). Jesus now spoke of the sign.

> And then **shall appear** [from *phaínō* {5316}, to shine, to give light; from *phós* {5457}, light] the sign of the Son of man in **heaven** [from *ouranós* {3772}, heaven, sky]: and then shall all the tribes of the earth mourn, and they shall see the Son of man coming in the clouds of heaven with power and great glory.

The disciples asked about a variety of events that are designated by "these things" to which they expected Jesus to give a specific time. Jesus, however, described different events that will not take place simultaneously but at different times connected with the total process. We must, therefore, study these events from God's revelation in the totality of Scripture.

Jesus told His disciples that He was going to heaven to prepare a place for them (John 14:3, 4). Just after His ascension into heaven, angels told His followers that He would descend from heaven at some future date to take them to Himself (Acts 1:11). He has not yet fulfilled that promise, which the apostle Paul also gives in 1 Thessalonians 4:13–18. We must, therefore, understand this event as the resurrection of dead believers and the transformation of living believers (1 Cor. 15:51–53), called "the rapture of the church," the next event to take place. The Scriptures delineate the role of angels as ministering spirits in heaven at the service of Christ in all His appearances, beginning with the incarnation (Matt. 1:20, 21; Luke 1:28–33) and ending with the final establishment of His kingdom (Matt. 25:31).

This "sign" of the "Son of man in heaven," however, is at the end of the Tribulation period, when Christ comes back to earth to defeat His enemies and set up His kingdom for a thousand years (see Rev. 19:11—20:4). The appearance of the visible "sign" implies that the heavenly perturbations referred to in verse 29 will be temporary. Neither the sun nor the moon will stop shining permanently, although these disturbances will impact everyone on earth.

The sign appears "in heaven," in this case, visible to all humanity. The Jesus has already used the verb *phaínō* (5316) in the immediate context (v. 27) to liken His return to wild streaking (from *phaínō*) of lightning towards the west, vividly contrasted to the claims of false prophets that He is "in" their tamed, esoteric environments, the "desert" and the "secret chambers" (v. 26).

It is most natural, then, to take the genitival expression, "of the Son of man in heaven," appositionally—"of" meaning "which is," that is, the sign which is the physical appearance of Christ in the sky. Corroborative evidence for this is that Jesus cited Zechariah's prophecy, "They shall look upon me whom they have pierced, and they shall mourn for him" (Zech. 12:10), a clear prediction of the conversion of Jews who personally witness Christ's physical return. "Behold, he cometh with clouds; and every eye shall see him, and they also which pierced him: and all kindreds of the earth shall wail because of him" (Rev. 1:7; cf. Rom. 11:26).

This sign is similar to the sign Jesus gave during His first coming to that "generation" (Mark 8:12). When the Pharisees demanded proof of His authority, Jesus characterized their generation—and every generation that seeks signs—as wicked and adulterous, adding that no sign would be given other than His resurrection typified by Jonah's supernatural rescue from the body of the great fish (from *kḗtos* [2785]; Matt. 12:39, 40; see Jon. 1:17) after three days.

Christ's resurrection became the basis for all future resurrections, according to the apostle Paul:

> But now is Christ risen from the dead, and become the **firstfruits** [*aparchḗ* {536}] of them that slept. For since by man came death, by man came also the resurrection of the dead. For as in Adam all die, even so in Christ shall all be made alive. But every man in his own order: Christ the firstfruits; afterward they that are Christ's at his coming. Then cometh the end, when he shall have delivered up the kingdom to God, even the Father; when he shall have put down all rule and all authority and power. (1 Cor. 15:20–24)

As the firstfruits, Christ secured the resurrection of all those who believe. As Paul says in verse 23, "every man in his own order." Christ was clearly the firstfruits. After the temple veil was rent in two parts during the crucifixion, "the graves were opened; and many bodies of the saints which slept arose, and came out of the graves after his resurrection, and went into the holy city, and appeared unto many" (Matt. 27:52–53). If this represents their permanent resurrection and not a temporary resurrection similar to what Lazarus experienced in John 11, these saints would be the first order. The resurrection accompanying the rapture will be the next order (1 Thess. 4:13–18). We are not told of any resurrection taking place during the Tribulation period, but we assume that all the Tribulation-period saints will be resurrected before the millennium begins. We gather this from Revelation 20:4, 5 that says that the Tribulation-period saints have already been resurrected and will live and reign with Christ for a thousand years during the millennium. We also assume that no believers will die during the millennium and that only those unbelievers who deliberately rebel will die (see Isa. 65:20) as well as those who follow the released dragon into the Battle of Armageddon after the millennium (Rev. 20:8). These will be resurrected with unbelievers of all ages in the second resurrection, as implied in Revelation 20:5, 6, to face the great white throne judgment of Revelation 20:11–15.

At the sign of the Son of man in heaven, the "**tribes** [from *phulē* {5443}, tribe, nation; Rev. 1:7] of the **earth** [*gē* {1093}, the earth or land] **shall mourn** [*kópsontai*, the future middle of *kóptō* {2875}, to cut down to size, cf. Zech. 12:10–14]." The Lord works in two arenas: heaven, the dwelling place of God, angels, and departed saints; and earth (Matt. 5:18, 35; 6:10, 19; Luke 2:14; Acts 2:19; 7:49). What takes place in heaven affects those living on earth.

Those on earth "**will see** [from *horáō* {3708}, to see and perceive; or *óptomai* {3700}, to see, from which the English word 'optometrist' derives] the Son of man coming." *Horáō* contrasts with *blépō* (991), to see physically, gaze, look at. The fact that they will see and understand the significance of what is happening will cause many to lament.

Note that *erchómenon*, "**coming**," is the present participle of *érchomai*, I come, or I am coming. If a single coming had been intended, another tense would have been selected, like *eleusómenon*, the **future** participle. The present participle of érchomai is used frequently to describe Jesus' return to earth (cf. Mark 11:9; 13:26; Luke 21:27; John 1:15, 27; 3:31; 6:14; 11:27; 12:13). The whole future is a series of comings of the Lord Jesus in salvation and judgment.

Two Greek words are translated "cloud." One is *néphos* (3509), a cloudy, shapeless mass covering the sky, used metaphorically for a crowd or throng (Heb. 12:1). The other is *nephélē* (3507), a feminine diminutive, meaning a small, formed cloud, such as the pillar that guided the Israelites in the desert during the day (1 Cor. 10:1, 2). This latter word is used in connection with the transfiguration of Christ (Matt. 17:5; Luke 9:34, 35); His ascension (Acts 1:9); and His coming again (Matt. 24:30; 26:64; Mark 13:26; 14:62; Luke 21:27; 1 Thess. 4:17; Rev. 1:7; 14:14–16).

Jesus will come in a final sense (*élthē*, the aorist subjunctive of *érchomai*, I come) in clouds of glory as in Matthew 25:31: "When the Son of man shall come [*élthē*] in his glory, and all the holy angels with him, then shall he sit upon the throne of his glory." At this time, the Lord, the victorious Lamb, will defeat the Antichrist and come to earth not only with angels, but with the called, chosen, and faithful (Rev. 17:14). The defeat of Antichrist will manifest Christ's "**power**" (from *dúnamis* [1411], accomplishing power) and "**glory**" (from *dóxa* [1391], glory, derived from the verb *dokéō* [1380], to think or recognize, therefore His recognition). This power and glory is qualified as "**great**" (from *polús* [4183], much), issuing from the victorious "Lion of the tribe of Judah" (Rev. 5:5). Christ will be properly recognized as the One who was eternally with the Father (John 1:1, 2; 17:5; 1 John 1:1, 2) and became flesh (John 1:14), without sin (Heb. 4:15), so that He might be the sacrificial lamb (*amnós* [286]; John 1:29, 36; Acts 8:32; 1 Pet. 1:19, in contrast to *arníon* [721], a living lamb).

[**31**] There are three places where we find the phrase "**shall send** [from *apostéllō* {649} from *apó* {575}, from; and *stéllō* {4724}, to send; 'to send off from'] his angels": Matthew 13:41; 24:31, and Mark 13:27. These all refer to the final separation of the righteous from the wicked who are cast into eternal fire at the consummation of the age (Matt. 13:39–42). Both here and in Mark 13:27 we read that the "elect" are gathered from "the four winds," probably the four points of the compass—"the four corners of the earth."

"His angels [from ággelos {32}]" are all ministering (from leitourgikós [3010]) spirits who serve the needs of the "heirs of salvation" (Heb. 1:14). They are closely associated with Christ's incarnation and subsequent comings. An angel brought "tidings of great joy" (Luke 2:10) at the birth of Jesus our Savior. Each occasion of a sinner's repentance heralds a message of great joy to the messengers in heaven (Luke 15:10), implying that angels carry the good news of salvation in both directions. Their numbers are very great (Matt. 26:53; Heb. 12:22; Rev. 5:11).

Jesus Christ will send angels to earth at the consummation of the age (Matt. 13:39–42) to gather believers and unbelievers for judgment at the end of the Tribulation. But this coming (*parousía* [3952]) is subsequent to the rapture of believers (1 Thess. 4:16, 17). This event will truly be the arrival (*parousía*) of the Lord Jesus to the earth, His coming to sit on His glorious throne (Matt. 25:31). (To study the word *parousía* in reference to Christ's various comings, see Matt. 24:3, 27, 37, 39; 1 Cor. 15:23; 1 Thess. 2:19; 3:13; 4:15; 5:23; 2 Thess. 2:1, 8; James 5:7, 8; 2 Pet. 1:16; 3:4, 12, and 1 John 2:28.)

The final ingathering of unbelievers and believers at "the consummation of the age" is mentioned in Matthew 24:3 and in the parable of the wheat and the tares (Matt. 13:24–30). The wheat represents the seed of the gospel that grows and bears fruit, and the tares represent the work of the devil (vv. 38,

39). These two, the wheat and the tares, will coexist on earth until the Lord sends His angels to make a final separation at the time of harvest. In reality, the wheat will be gathered in two stages. First, believers of the church age will be gathered at the rapture. Only unbelievers will remain on the earth after the rapture, but the Holy Spirit will immediately begin sowing seed, which produces believers again. Then will come the complete gathering of both, but this time, the wheat will be left alive for the millennium after the judgments described in Matthew 25. The tares will be placed in hell until the second resurrection and the great white throne judgment of Revelation 20:11–15. These events constitute the consummation of the age.

The gathering of believers of the Tribulation will be worldwide. "With a great trumpet," Jesus will send out His angels to "**gather together** [from *episunágō* {1996} from *epí* {1909}, upon; and *sunágō* {4863}, to lead; to bring together, to group] His elect" (a.t.). In 2 Thessalonians 2:1, a form of the related noun *episunagōgḗ* (1997) is used in conjunction with the "coming" (*parousía*) of the Lord and "our gathering together unto him."

[32] "Now **learn** [*máthete*, the aorist active imperative of *manthánō* {3129}, to learn]," Jesus continued, "a parable of the fig tree." The aorist tense means "learn once and for all!"

"Disciples" (v. 3) are *mathētaí* (from *mathētḗs* [3101]), learners. In the matter of prophecy, Jesus gave neither a simple chronology nor a series of exact dates regarding His return. Matthew 24 and 25 together constitute the longest reply Jesus ever gave to such a short question. Because the events that point to His return are not easily discernible, people will begin to mock the prophecies (2 Pet. 3:3–5). But Peter said "that one day is with the Lord as a thousand years, and a thousand years as one day" (2 Pet. 3:8).

The signs mentioned in Matthew 24:4–14 can be misconstrued because they are general in character. But the signs given in verses 15–28 are specific and discernible. Then in verse 29 the sun, the moon, and the stars will be involved, signs that immediately follow the seven-year period of the Great Tribulation. These signs point clearly to Christ's appearance on earth. In the same way, the fig tree, when "its twigs get tender and its leaves come out" (NIV), points to summer's approach.

[33] Jesus said that if we are alert when we "shall see all these things" take place, we will then "**know**" (from *ginōskō* [1097], to experientially know) that the coming of the Lord is "**near**" (*eggús* [1451]), at the very doors. The adjective *eggús* is relative and should be contrasted to *hḗkō* (2240), to be here, to arrive (2 Pet. 3:10). "These things" refers to the sensational heavenly disturbances

referred to in verse 29. Through these visible events, the Lord will knock at the doors of people's hearts.

[34, 35] Jesus concluded His teaching with these words, "Verily I say unto you, This generation shall not pass, till all these things be fulfilled." When the sun and moon are darkened and stars fall from the skies, Jesus advised us to realize that the end is near. These events will take place in rapid succession.

The word "**generation**" (*geneá* [1074]) means the average duration of a human life. In the age of the patriarchs, a generation spanned about one hundred years (cf. Gen. 15:13, 16 with Ex. 12:40, 41). However, as the ravages of sin slowly deteriorated the average span to three score and ten or seventy years (Ps. 90:10), we find the term "generation" narrowing down to approximately forty years. Thus, the generation that grieved the Lord in the desert died out in forty years (Ps. 95:10). The period from the beginning of the Babylonian Captivity (586 B.C.) to Christ, specified in Matthew 1:17 as fourteen "generations," yields five hundred and eighty-six fourteenths or about forty-two years per generation. Ancient Greeks counted three generations in each one hundred years, or about thirty-three and one-third years each.

In general, Jesus taught that the generation that "see[s] all these things" (v. 33) will not pass away without witnessing the completion of all the events prophesied. "All these things" were typically fulfilled in the forty years from A.D. 30 to 70 when Jerusalem was destroyed. Jerusalem's destruction was a sign for believers to prepare for the rapture of His church and *parousía*. Typical fulfillment of prophecy enhances imminence—the nearness of the Lord's return.

Imminence in these verses refers to Christ's coming in judgment after the Tribulation period and is aimed squarely at unbelievers; as Paul says, "Ye, brethren, are not in darkness, that that day should overtake you as a thief" (1 Thess. 5:4). The parable of the fig tree helps us realize how rapidly the events predicted will take place. Lack of preparation is not excused: the evil servant who in verse 48 says, "My lord delayeth [from *chronízō* {5549} from *chrónos* {5550}, a space of time; see also Matt. 25:5; Luke 12:45; Heb. 10:37] his coming," is assigned a place with the hypocrites. Christ will come as a welcome (from *apekdéchomai* [553]; Rom. 8:19, 23, 25; 1 Cor. 1:7; Gal. 5:5; Phil. 3:20; Heb. 9:28) liberator to the elect in the end times but as a plundering thief in the night (Matt. 24:43; Luke 12:39; 1 Thess. 5:2, 4; 2 Pet. 3:10; Rev. 3:3; 16:15) to unbelievers.

[36] Jesus continued,

> But of that day and hour **knoweth** [from *eídō* {1492}, the aorist of *horáō* {3708}, to see and perceive with emphasis on perception] **no man** [*oudeís*

{3762} from *ou* {3756} "not"; *dé* {1161}, even; and *heís* {1520}, one; "not even a single man"], no, not the angels of heaven, **but** [*ei* {1487}, "if"; and *mē̂* {3361}, "not"; i.e., "if not"] my Father **only** [*mónos* {3441}].

Mark 13:32 adds a significant detail: "But of that day or hour [*ē̂* {2228}, or *hōras* {5610}, exact hour] no man knows, nor [*oudé* {3761}] the angels that are in heaven, neither [*oudé*] the Son, but the Father" (a.t. [MJ]). In the fourth century A.D., Arians used Mark's text to try to disprove Christ's deity by arguing His ignorance regarding the timing of His return. The argument is quite simple: if the Son of God does not know a particular proposition—the time of His return, He cannot be omniscient by definition, that is, knowing all propositions.

The verse is difficult to exegete. Without exhausting all the logical possibilities, Jesus no doubt clearly taught that "the Father only" knows the time of His return, *ei mē̂* best interpreted as in all the English versions either as "but" or "except."

As God, Jesus Christ is omniscient and knows all things innately. The Father does not reveal things to the Son of God as He would to an angel or a human. Since the Son of God is omniscient by definition, revelation to Him is meaningless. Innate omniscience cannot "receive" revelation. (Note: While *oíden*, derived from *horáō* [3708], normally means knowledge gained through the five senses, here it means innate knowledge. God does not have physical senses, and He does not obtain knowledge by perceiving creation.)

If we take the unqualified "Son" here as the Son of man—not the Son of God—then we can offer the rational interpretation that the triune God, the Father, the Word, and Holy Spirit, did not reveal to the human nature of Christ (the "Son of man" who "increased in wisdom" [Luke 2:52]) the time of His return of which the *Lógos* or Infinite Wisdom had no need of revelation. In His humanity, He may have laid aside this particular detail as He did His glory.

This is logically scriptural, and it was the mainstay argument of the most famous Greek trinitarian in Christian history, Athanasius. It was used successfully against the Arians in the fourth century, the Nestorians in the fifth, and against every cult that has denied the Trinity since.

The fact that Jesus said "Son" in the third person implied that the Word (*Lógos*; see John 1:1, 14), the divine Person, was speaking. In other words, the *Lógos* did not say, "I do not know" but rather, "neither the Son [i.e., 'Son of man,' the third person; see Mark 13:32]." Though the end product is complex, no contradiction results from the Word incarnating in flesh. The Chalcedonian Christology accurately summarized this complexity: Jesus Christ is true God and true man, without mixture and without confusion.

When Jesus spake of the day and hour (both singular), we should recall Peter's words that "one day is with the Lord as a thousand years, and a thousand years as one day" (2 Pet. 3:8). He did not say one day with the Lord is one thousand of our years. He used "**as**" (*hós* [5613]) to guard his readers from creating useless equations. The simile is anthropomorphic. Because God is timeless and immutable, He does not experience time at all. For example, He doesn't wait for things to happen, watch a clock, or get bored and impatient. Some events within the Day of the Lord, like the transformation of believers' bodies to conform to Christ's glorified body, will take place in an "instant" (from *átomos* [823] from *a* [1]; and *tomé* [n.f.], cut, from *témnō* [n.f.], to cut, divide; 'indivisible time'), the "**twinkling** [*rhipē* {4493}; from *rhíptō* {4496}, to cast, throw] of an eye," that is, the time it takes to change the direction of a glance (1 Cor. 15:52). By definition as divisionless, an instant is timeless since time is always divisible.

[37, 38] Jesus again substituted signs of the times for the times themselves:

> **But** [*dé* {1161}] **as** [*hósper* {5618}] the days of Noe were, so shall also the coming of the Son of man be. For as in the days that were before the flood they were **eating** [from *trōgō* {5176} from *trúo* {n.f.}, to injure, wear away, e.g., the teeth when chewing nuts, tough meats, etc., but here as in the NT generally for eating, therefore practically equivalent to *esthíō* {2068}] and **drinking** [from *pínō* {4095}], **marrying** [from *gaméō* {1060}, to marry] and **giving in marriage** [from *ekgamízō* {1547}, to give away in marriage], until the day that Noe entered into the ark.

We have translated *dé* as the adversative "but," which is corroborated by the use of the conjunction *hósper* from *hós* (5613), as; and *per* (4007), indeed, much; "just indeed" in verses 27, 37, 38. As suddenly as lightning strikes, so indeed Christ's Second Coming will come without warning. The condition of the world will be dreadfully similar to its condition in the days of Noah.

What were the conditions just before the flood? They were characterized by excessive evil and the distractions of everyday events: "And God saw that the wickedness of man was great in the earth, and that every imagination of the thoughts of his heart was only evil continually" (Gen. 6:5). Similarly, Paul describes the "perilous times" of the "last days" (2 Tim. 3:1):

> For men shall be lovers of their own selves, covetous, boasters, proud, blasphemers, disobedient to parents, unthankful, unholy, without natural affection, trucebreakers, false accusers, incontinent, fierce, despisers of those that are good, traitors, heady, highminded, lovers of pleasures more than lovers of God; having a form of godliness, but denying the power thereof: from such turn away. (2 Tim. 3:2–5)

Again, the days of Noah included "eating and drinking, marrying and giving in marriage"—all morally neutral if not accompanied by excess, such as gluttony, drunkenness, or multiple marriages. The Synoptic narrative in Luke 17:28 adds buying, selling, planting, and building. As we approach the end of the age, the world will ignore God, distracted by excess pleasure and greed. While created things are good in moderation and as a means to glorify God as the provider, they are evil as ends in themselves. People committed to these gods ignore the true God and the pleasures that come from knowing Him. Distracted, they are not prepared for the sudden advent of His Son.

This should strike caution in our hearts. Both excess consumption and the distraction of this world's goods work against preparing for Christ's imminent return when we are taken away from such things.

Ekgamízō means to give away a woman in marriage as a father today "gives away" his daughter, a moral obligation virtually ignored by couples who decide to live together. Jesus did not focus on sinful relationships such as fornication or adultery but rather on the distractions of ordinary marriage and routine work to the exclusion of spiritual life, as the preflood conditions that brought judgment. (See the author's studies, *What About Divorce?* and *May I Divorce and Remarry?*)

This reinforces the proverb, "The plowing of the wicked, is sin" (Prov. 21:4). Even routine obedience to legitimate institutions of God should be subordinated to the motive of seeking first the kingdom of God and His righteousness. But from Paul's prophecy to Timothy (cited above), we know that debauchery and sinful practices will increase in the last days (2 Tim. 3:1–7).

Judgment is based on the immutable character of God, specifically His unchanging intolerance of sin. Jesus Christ, "the same yesterday, and today, and forever" (Heb. 13:8), continuously hates and overthrows sin with grace and judgment. While God's goodness (from *chrēstótēs* [5544], kindness) causes repentance and belief (Rom. 2:4), the wicked must not construe this as a license to sin. If they continue to do so, judgment is ahead for them as surely as it was for the people in Noah's day.

Before such events, God never leaves Himself "without witness" or people without an ark to enter. As only those who entered through the door of Noah's ark were saved, today we enter through the door, which is Christ (John 10:9) based on the remission of sins accomplished once for all time. But we must enter this door through faith before physical death, after which there is "judgment" (Heb. 9:27).

[39] Entrance into the ark preceded the flood, which took unbelievers by total surprise: "And [they] knew not until the flood came, and took them all away."

The phrase "**knew not**" combines *égnōsan*, the aorist tense of *ginōskō*, to experientially know, and the absolute negative *ouk*, "not." Unbelievers had no experiences to confirm the coming judgment; all they had was Noah's proclamation (2 Pet. 2:5), which they rejected. No doubt they mocked Noah's hard labor to design and construct an ark. The flood came roaring in, drowning all but those God had called into the ark.

The adverb "**until**" (*áchri* [891], duration up to a limit in v. 38), marks out the temporal limit God places on sin. Sin abides "until" judgment, at which time God stops it.

The flood destroyed those who did not believe, not sparing any. The verb "**took them all away**" is from *aírō* (142), to lift and remove; and *hápas* (537), all. The destruction was absolute.

[40, 41] When Christ returns, the wicked will be separated from the righteous:

> Then shall two be in the field; the **one** [*heís* {1520}] **shall be taken** [*paralambánetai*, the present passive of *paralambánō* {3880}, to receive to oneself, from the preposition *pará* {3844}, alongside, expressing close proximity; and *lambánō* {2983}, to take or receive], and the **other** [*heís*, "one" again] **left** [from *aphíēmi* {863}, to be left behind]. Two women shall be grinding at the mill; the one shall be taken, and the other left.

The passive voice of the root verb *lambánō* and the prefix *pará*, meaning "alongside of," both express the gentleness with which angels will gather believers and bring them before the Lord. According to Luke 17:34, "the one" left behind is called "other" (*héteros* [2087], another of a different kind, a tare [*zizánia* {2215}] contrasted with wheat). While God will not send a physical ark as in the days of Noah, He will command His powerful angels to gather His people together before He storms in wrath against wicked unbelievers.

Aphíēmi is used for abandonment as, for example, when Jerusalem, on rejecting Christ, was "left . . . desolate" (Matt. 23:38). The days before the Second Coming will be like those of the preflood days of Noah—"life as usual." No advance warning will be given beyond Jesus' prophetic words. What happens will happen suddenly and unexpectedly. Believers expect Christ's return; unbelievers do not. Believers watch for it; unbelievers do not (1 Thess. 5:3, 4).

Watching for Christ's Return
(24:42–44; Mark 13:33–38; Luke 17:30–36)

[42] From the example of the days of Noah, Jesus instructed believers to

watch [*grēgoreíte*, the present imperative of *grēgoréō* {1127}, to watch, stay alert, a verb deriving from *egeírō* {1453}, to stay awake, to not succumb to anxiety and fear, to maintain watchfulness] therefore: for ye **know** [from *oída* {1492} from *horáō* {3708}, to see and perceive with emphasis on understanding] not what hour your Lord **doth come** [*érchetai*, the present middle deponent of *érchomai* {2064}, to come].

The believers have absolutely no perception or revelation of the precise hour Christ will come. The timing is hidden from us. In the parallel passage in Mark 13:33, the word used is *kairós* (2540), season, a bit broader than "hour," showing the fluidity of eschatological time references in Scripture (see also Acts 1:7; 1 John 2:18: "it is the last hour" [a.t.; *hōra* {5510}]). Consequently, the return of Christ is always imminent. In Revelation 3:3, the Lord warned the church of Sardis, "You will absolutely not [the two negatives *ou* {3756} and *mē* {3361} combined as an intensive combination meaning 'absolutely not,' never, at any time] know what sort [from *poíos* {4169}] of hour I will come upon you" (a.t.)—referring to a local judgment.

The present (as opposed to the aorist) imperative of *grēgoréō* stresses the need for a constant vigil since Christ's return is soon. This is the first time Jesus said to maintain an attitude of alertness based on (*oún* [3767], "**therefore**") our having absolutely no experiential knowledge of the hour of His return.

We watch with expectation not only for Christ's return but also for the events associated with that return as described by Paul (1 Thess. 4:13–18). For us, His return means resurrection to a qualitatively new life (John 5:29) and reunion with believers of past ages, some of whom may be close relatives. The expectation of redemption that offsets our groaning to be released from our present dying bodies (Rom. 8:10, 11, 19) is described with the verb *apekdéchomai* (553), to sincerely and eagerly await, expect (Rom. 8:23; see 1 Cor. 1:7; Gal. 5:5; Phil. 3:20; Heb. 9:28). Christ's return also means our appearance before His judgment seat (*bēma* [968]) to receive rewards for benevolent (*agathós* [18]) works done "through the body" (2 Cor. 5:10; a.t.), that is throughout the course of our physical lives. One phrase that captures the full meaning of the Lord's return to and for believers is the "**blessed** [from *makários* {3107}] **hope** [from *elpís* {1680}]" (Tit. 2:13).

The writer of Hebrews says unbelievers have "a **fearful** [from *phoberós* {5398}] **expectation** [*ekdochē* {1561}] of judgment and a zealous fire coming to devour the adversaries" (Heb. 10:27; a.t.). To them, Christ's coming is the same threat to worldly values, goals, and living that it was to those in the days of Noah (Matt. 24:37). Their expectation, cued by consciences stamped with the guilt of vile things done throughout their lives (2 Cor. 5:10), is terror.

Guilt is a negative premonition that produces cowering and running for cover (Rev. 6:16: "Hide us from . . . the wrath of the Lamb!"). But there will be no cover. The hypocrite even "say[s] in his heart, My lord delays his coming" (Matt. 24:48; a.t.), as if an omniscient Lord would not notice.

In modern Greek, *grégora* means quickly, implying a need to hurry because of danger. Something is about to take place that is not within one's control. An unpredictable, uncontrollable, and undesirable storm is brewing. The Noahic flood was such a storm. Anyone who has survived a major flood understands how quickly life-sustaining water turns into life-threatening power. The need is not philosophical conjecture but escape. Jesus did not say when the storm is coming, only that it is coming. He cautioned us to prepare and wait for His ark. There is always an ark for He is "the true Light, which lighteth every man that cometh into the world" (John 1:9).

But we are told in 1 Timothy 6:16 that the true Light, like our natural sun, is unapproachable (from *aprósitos* [676], a compound from the alpha privative *a* [1], without; *prós* [4314], toward; and *eimí* [1510], to be). We cannot live without the sun, but we do not try to colonize it. We receive from it, but we cannot control or regulate it; it is not within the scope of scientific manipulation. Unlike the sun, the Son of Righteousness is fast approaching. He will return in "yet a little while" (Heb. 10:37), so we must "watch" in a hurried (i.e., urgent) manner.

There are several imminent events. The rapture of the church is imminent, but death is always close. People's spirits are either peaceably "carried by the angels" (Luke 16:22) or violently snatched out of their bodies. We never know when our physical lives will be taken from us. Hebrews 9:27 says, "It is appointed unto men once to die, but after this the judgment." While the fact of death is appointed, the time is not an intuition or even a private revelation. Consequently, we must live our lives with ongoing watchfulness and expectation, treating death as an imminent coming of the Lord to take us to Himself.

What can we do?

[43, 44] An interesting shift of emphasis occurs in the text by the use of the two verbs for "**know**" in verses 42, 43. Verse 42 uses the verb for intuitive knowledge (*eídō* [1492]), knowledge independent of reasoning. Ultimately, only God has perfect intrinsic knowledge that is timeless and underived from external sources. God does not get His knowledge from someone (e.g., a higher god) or something (creation). Neither does God derive knowledge over time by reasoning through syllogisms. He is omniscient, so all His knowledge is immediate and therefore timeless. While all three Persons of the Trinity are defined by omniscience, no creature has such knowledge. Whatever truths we possess are revelations from God. One proposition the triune God has chosen not to reveal is the hour of His Son's return (v. 36; Mark 13:32).

But here in verse 43, we read, "**Know this**" (*ginṓskete*, the present imperative of *ginṓskō* [1097], to know by experience or by learning, a verb that contrasts with the root verb *eídō* in v. 42). Jesus did not command us to determine by experience what is knowable only by revelation. He revealed that godly experience is a continuous state, not an occasional event.

> If the master of the house had known in what **watch** [from *phulakḗ* {5438}, a three-hour period of the night] the thief would come, he would have **watched** [*egrēgórēsen*, the aorist tense of *grēgoréō* {1127}], and would not have suffered his house to be broken up. (a.t.)

This illustrates ungodly concern or assuming the risks of watching intermittently or not at all for the Master's return and behaving accordingly. Although we believers do not know the time of Christ's return, we should expect Him at all times and obey consistently. When a man assumes he will live to the age of 103, he plans his life accordingly. But when he knows that death is beyond his control and always imminent, he plans differently. The Lord, however, does not want us to focus on death, the appointed enemy (1 Cor. 15:26). Instead, we should focus on Him who appoints eternal life beyond.

One Greek word behind the phrase "**master of the house**" is *oikodespótēs* (3617) literally "housemaster." How the adjective "good" in "goodman" ever got into the English text is a mystery, for this compound term is a polite, euphemistic translation of a Greek word accurately rendered "despot" (*despótēs* [1203], absolute master), the emphasis on power, not moral character.

The thief does not announce his coming to rob. Rather than assume he is imminent, the householder counts on a "delay," as the evil servant does. The enemy here is "the **thief** [*kléptēs* {2812} from which we get our English word 'kleptomaniac,' one who robs in secret, in contrast with *lēstḗs* {3027}, one who robs openly]."

The doctrine of imminence, then, points to unbelievers throughout Scripture (Luke 12:39; 1 Thess. 5:2, 4; 2 Pet. 3:10; Rev. 3:3; 16:15). The Lord will pounce on them like a thief. Of course, He owns all things and so, technically, He cannot steal, although He can take things from anyone "like a thief," that is, unexpectedly.

What does He take? God can take those things the master of the house thinks he owns—his wealth, his physical life, his opportunity to believe, and possibly even a believing spouse or child. All of these may be lost in an instant, since they belong ultimately to the Lord who merely lends for a season.

By contrast, God tells believers:

> But ye, brethren, are not in darkness, that that day should overtake you as a thief. Ye are all the children of the light, and the children of the day: we are not of the night, nor of darkness. Therefore let us not sleep, as do others; but let us watch and be sober. (1 Thess. 5:4–6)

Our attitude should be that which Paul described in Titus 2:13: "**Looking for** [from *prosdéchomai* {4327}, to wait with confidence and endurance] that blessed hope, and the glorious appearing [from *epipháneia* {2015}, epiphany] of the great God and our Savior Jesus Christ" (see also Jude 21).

Another aspect of our waiting is found in the word *apechdéchomai* (553), to expect with eagerness, as in Philippians 3:20: "For our **conversation** [*políteuma* {4175}, place of citizenship] is in heaven; from whence also we look for [*apechdéchomai*] the Savior, the Lord Jesus Christ" (see also Rom. 8:19, 23, 25; 1 Cor. 1:7; Gal. 5:5; Heb. 9:28).

Another word used to describe our attitude is *prosdokáō* (4328), to anticipate, to look and hope for, found in Matthew 24:50 where it describes the unfaithful servant who is not expecting (from *prosdokáō*) his master (cf. Luke 12:46). According to 2 Peter 3:12, believers are "looking for [from *prosdokáō*; ongoingly looking for] and hasting [from *speúdō* {4692}, continually speeding up] unto the coming [*parousía* {3952}] of the day of God" (cf. 2 Pet. 3:13).

A third synonym, *anaménō* (362), to wait with anticipation, occurs in 1 Thessalonians 1:10: "And to wait for his Son from heaven, whom he raised from the dead, even Jesus, which delivered us from the wrath to come."

We should follow the admonition of Jesus Christ: "For this reason, become ready; for in such an hour as you think not the Son of man comes" (a.t.). "**Become**" (from *gínomai* [1096]) tells us that this should be a permanent state of mind for the true believer.

The Faithful and Unfaithful Servants (24:45–51)

[45] This parable follows naturally from the previous teaching. Christ's Second Coming will be like God's coming in judgment in the days of Noah. A catastrophic separation will occur between the righteous and the wicked. It will come suddenly; no one knows the day or the hour, and therefore the appropriate response is to watch constantly. The "evil servant" who expects his lord to delay his return (v. 48) and does not watch for him is cut off when the master

returns, just as unbelievers will be cut off when Christ returns as a thief in the night to gather His own. The "faithful and wise servant," on the other hand, waits for his master with eager anticipation (vv. 45, 46).

The first point of interest for us here and in the Synoptic section of Luke 12:41–48 is the meaning of the word translated "**servant**." The Greek word *doúlos* (1401) has the distinct meaning of slave. It is associated with the verb *doulóō* (1402), which means to bring into bondage. By definition, slaves are subjugated and forced into a state of slavery. In the spiritual realm, the human will is enslaved or addicted to sin. In the New Testament, unbelievers are called slaves or servants of sin (Rom. 6:16, 17, 20). When Christ saves us, he liberates us from sin (John 8:33–36). Paul explains this great truth:

> But now you, having been freed [*eleutherōthéntes*, the aorist passive participle of *eleutheróō* {1659}; i.e., by God] from sin, and having been enslaved [*doulōthéntes*, the aorist passive participle of *doulóō* {1402}, i.e., by God] to God. . . . (Rom. 6:22; a.t.; Paul calls believers slaves of righteousness in 6:18.)

The aorist passive of the two verbs ("enslave" and "free") means that God does the actions, enslaving us to His righteousness and taking away our addiction *to* sin by making us "free from sin."

Paul considered himself a slave of Jesus Christ (Rom. 1:1; Titus 1:1, etc.) and remarked that "yielding" does not cause slavery but is rather defined by slavery: Do you not know that to whom you yield yourselves slaves to obey, his slaves you are [i.e., not 'have become'] to whom you obey; whether of sin unto death or of obedience unto righteousness?" (Rom. 6:16; a.t.). We don't yield ourselves to be or to become slaves. We yield ourselves as slaves because we are slaves, and we are the slaves of someone or something, not ourselves. If a master enslaves us, we are not free from that master. We can be nothing else but his slaves. The idea of being our own slaves is contradictory. A willing slave is a rational coupling of terms; a free slave is a contradiction.

Before slavery was eliminated in the United States, people yielded themselves as slaves, but they did not yield themselves to be or to become slaves. They did not yield themselves to enter the institution of slavery nor were they free to leave it once sold into it. The slave master, not the slaves, determined both the quantity and the quality of slavery. However much slaves desired to flee the farm, they made themselves get up in the morning and work, but this can hardly be called free will.

Sin enslaves people because it is addictive: "For God imprisoned [from *sugkleíō* {4788}] all unto [*eis* {1519}, unto, i.e., the end of] disobedience that He might have mercy upon all" (Rom. 11:32; a.t.). When in mercy Jesus Christ saves sinners, He does two things: He lifts the burden of sin—guilt and its paralysis, and He frees people, the sinners, from the power of sin. The two elements are parts of salvation. The first is called *áphesis* ([859]; Heb. 9:22), remission, pardon; and the second is called *athétēsis* (115), as the King James Version translators render it in Hebrews 9:26, the power "to put away" sin. Both are the result of the power of Christ's blood shed on Calvary's cross.

We can learn much from the "author and finisher of our faith" (Heb. 12:2) who willingly took the "form [from *morphē̂* {3444}] of a slave [from *doúlos*]" (Phil. 2:7; a.t.). While the incarnation, ministry, and cross were all foreordained (Luke 22:22; Acts 2:23; 4:28; 1 Pet. 1:20; Rev. 13:8), Christ voluntarily entered this slavery of obedience to death (Phil. 2:8). "For I came down from heaven [i.e., voluntarily], not to do mine own will [therefore, His human doing and willing were not free of but according to the plan of the triune God], but the [determinate] will of him that sent me" (John 6:38, cf. Luke 22:42; John 5:19; 1 Pet. 1:20; Rev. 13:8). The language could not be stronger: Jesus' human willing and doing were not "[His] own"; they were determined to be the same as the good willing and doing of His Father. Thus, He could say, "I do always [*pántote* {3842}] those things that please him" (John 8:29). There was never a time when Jesus' human will or actions were free from or contradictory to the Father's plan.

Jesus contrasted the "**faithful**" (*pistós* [4103]) and "**prudent**" (*phrónimos* [5429]) slave here with the "**bad**" (*kakós* [2556]) one in verse 48. The faithful (*pistós*) servant has the faith (*pístis* [4102]) to believe that Jesus told the truth about God and about His own Person and work. One of the fullest definitions of this mental content of faith is found in Hebrews 11:1 where faith is called the

> . . . substance [*hupóstasis* {5287} from *hupó* {5259}, under; and *hístēmi* {2476}, to stand; "that which stands below," i.e., the foundation] of things hoped for [from *elpízō* {1679}, to hope], the evidence [*élegchos* {1650}, proof] of things not seen [from *blépō* {991}, to see physically].

Notice that the evidence is not seen physically. "Faithful" is not just a quality of mental cognition; it is also a quality of volition, namely, unreserved loyalty and trustworthiness. In Matthew 25:23, when the lord of the parable commended his servant at the judgment, among other things he said, "Thou hast been faithful [*pistós*] over a few things, I will make thee ruler over many things." Here, *pistós* with "over" is not commitment to doctrine but rather loyal rule over the talents and other physical and spiritual possessions given by the master.

The prudent (*phrónimos*) servant applies moral brakes (*phrēn* in modern Greek) when things get out of control or head toward some dangerous situation—in this case, sin, which is always downhill. He uses the wisdom God gave him to think with the "mind [coherent thoughts] of Christ" (1 Cor. 2:16) rather than with the "wisdom of this world" (1 Cor. 1:20), the natural person (1 Cor. 1:26), and the devil (James 3:15)—all of which God Himself "made foolish" (from *mōraínō* [3471]; 1 Cor. 1:20). God grants true wisdom to people because, as both Paul and Jude say, our God is "the **only** [from *mónos* {3441}, alone, singly] **wise** [from *sophós* {4680}] God" (see Jude 1:25; Rom. 16:27).

We are told that the master delegated rule to this servant. He is

. . . **given charge** [from *kathístēmi* {2525} from *katá* {2596}, according to; and *hístēmi* {2476}, to stand, establish] **over** [*epí* {1909}, upon] his household to the **care** [*therapeías*, the genitive of *therapeía* {2322}, compassionate care] of them by **giving** [from *dídōmi* {1325}, to give] them food at the **right time** [from *kairós* {2540}, proper season]. (v. 45; a.t.)

Instead of "**care**" (from *therapeía*), the United Bible Society's and Nestle's texts read "**domestic affairs**" (from *oiketeía* [3610]—a type of care appropriately qualified by the context). The faithful and prudent servant carefully attends to the domestic affairs of his household and thus is ready for the coming of his lord at any time. He not only meets schedules but, according to Luke 12:42, he gives proper portions of food (*sitométrion* [4620] from *sítos* [4621], wheat; and *métron* [3358], measure). This is not restricted to food alone but no doubt extends to all physical and spiritual needs of the household.

[46] A further simile of the faithful and prudent servant of Jesus Christ is given in the term *makários* (3107), blessed—the beatitude word that means to be indwelt by God and thereby fully satisfied (Rom. 8:9; see the author's study of *makários* in his book, *The Beatitudes*). "Blessed is that servant, whom his lord when he cometh [*elthōn*, the aorist participle of *érchomai* {2064}; cf. Luke 12:43] shall find so doing." The aorist tense here underscores Christ's appearance at any instant.

We believers who are truly blessed should serve the Lord with faith and prudence every waking moment of our lives so that when Christ does appear suddenly, we will be "caught" "**doing**" (from *poiéō* [4160], "continually doing") the right thing.

[47] The master rewards the faithful and prudent servant with extensive sovereignty over his kingdom:

Verily [*amēn* {281}, truly] I say unto you, that **over** [*epí* {1909}, upon] all things of his **possessions** [*hupárchousin*, the neuter plural dative present active participle of *hupárchō* {5225}, to be, belong to], **he will establish** [from *kathístēmi* {2525}] him. (a.t.)

The master will entrust those who prove worthy in small things with greater authority (Luke 16:10; 19:17) as well as His possessions.

[48, 49] The adversative "**but**" (*dé* [1161]) introduces another servant who contrasts vividly with "the faithful and prudent one":

> But if that **evil** [*kakós* {2556}] servant shall say in his heart, My lord **delays** [*chronízei*, the present tense of *chronízō* {5549} associated with the noun *chrónos* {5550}, a space of time] his **coming** [*elthein* {TR, MT}, the aorist infinitive of *érchomai* {2064}; in the analogy, the aorist refers to the crisis of the Second Coming of the Lord] and shall begin **to beat** [*túptein*, the present infinitive of *túptō* {5180}, to strike or beat] his **fellow servants** [*sundoúlous* {4889} from *sún* {4862}, with, together; and *doúlos* {1401}, slave] and **to eat** [from *esthíō* {2068}] and **to drink** [from *pínō* {4095}] with the **drunken** [from *methúō* {3184}, to drink to excess]. . . . (a.t.)

The evil of the servant is twofold. The first is internal—a belief with a bad attitude: My lord is taking his time—procrastinating! This, of course, is false, and it brings to light this servant's faithlessness against the faithfulness of the other servant. The second is external—two actions that issue from this bad attitude and belief: He beats his fellow servants and gets drunk with other drunkards, his new associates. The evil servant's "unwise" mind contrasts with the "prudent" (*phrónimos*) mind of the other servant.

True believers in Christ do not have these beliefs, attitudes, or actions. They believe their Lord's coming is imminent because that is what He taught, and He always spoke the truth. Interestingly, Jesus connected a denial of the imminence of His Second Coming with bad attitudes and actions. The evil servant's use of *chronízei* carries a sarcastic tone. It's not a neutral but an attitudinal statement that implies his lord's procrastination and an excuse to behave irresponsibly.

Logic does not follow. Even if the lord does delay, it does not mean his servants are not accountable. What makes the man think that he will not be held accountable for beating his fellows (peers)? The irrational postulate is this: "If I am not punished right away, then I won't be punished. Or, to put it another away," "If my lord delays his return, then he doesn't care what I do." Both assumptions are absurd, yet most people act as if God will overlook the evil details of their lives.

A minor textual variant occurs here, but the thought is the same. Some manuscripts (followed by the KJV) have present participles for "to eat" and "to drink," following the present participle for "to smite": "He shall begin to be smiting his fellow servants and to be eating and drinking with the drunken."

Other manuscripts have the present subjunctive for "to eat" and "to drink": "He shall begin to be smiting his fellow servants, and he shall be eating and drinking with the drunken." Notice that in both readings, a pattern of excess—gluttony and drunkenness—emerges after the servant abuses his fellow servants. (For a thorough study on the impact of beliefs on habitual attitudes and actions, see the author's *Faith, Love, and Hope*, an exegetical commentary on the Epistle of James.)

[50] The master of the evil servant returns suddenly without warning:

> The lord of that servant **shall come** [from *hḗkō* {2240}, to appear, arrive, become present] in a day when **he does not look** [from *prosdokáō* {4328}, to expect] for him, and in an hour that he does not **know** [from *ginṓskō* {1097}, to experientially know]. (a.t.)

It is evident that the hypocrite, described here as an example of those who confess Christ with their mouths but accuse Him of delay in their hearts, are unbelievers and behave accordingly. They do not really expect (*prosdokáō*) Christ's Second Coming at any time. The text does not say that such evil servants do not look at all for the master's return; in fact, the wording, "in a day when [they] look not for him," implies that they were looking on other days. It was a good start with slow deterioration. At first they look every day; but then as time passes, they look intermittently, then finally not at all. The day they give up is the day they begin to beat their fellow servants.

Christ will pounce as a thief in the night on those who live in darkness like this (vv. 43, 44, 50, 51; 1 Thess. 5:2, 4; 2 Pet. 3:10; Rev. 3:3; 16:15). We should take warning to persevere in faith and holiness while remembering Paul's encouraging words: "Ye, brethren, are not in darkness, that that day should overtake you as a thief" (1 Thess. 5:4). The Lord will not come as a thief on those who continually watch for Him.

Much to the contrary, we believers should "eagerly look forward to" (*prosdéchomai* [4327]) the blessed hope (Titus 2:13; a.t.) and "wait with anticipation for" (*anaménō* [362]) the return of Christ (1 Thess. 1:10; a.t.).

[51] The master will punish the evil servant at this unexpected return:

> And **shall cut him asunder** [from *dichotoméō* {1371}, to cut in two or in half, from *dícha* {n.f.}, separately; and *tomḗ* {n.f.}, a cut] and appoint his **part** [*méros* {3313}] with the hypocrites: there shall be **weeping** [*klauthmós* {2805}, lamentation] and **gnashing** [*brugmós* {1030}, grinding] of teeth. (a.t.)

Only here and in Luke 12:46 do we find this interesting verb, *dichotoméō*, from which comes our English word "dichotomy." Evil servants who claim to be Christians and perhaps even think they are Christians will be cut in pieces and assigned to hell with other unbelievers, the destiny of all hypocrites. The parallel passage in Luke has additional material (Luke 12:47, 48) that indicates that those who profess Christ without possessing Christ will receive greater punishment than those who know nothing about God's will for their lives:

> And that servant, which **knew** [from *ginōskō* {1097}, to know by experience] his lord's **will** [*thélēma* {2307}, determinative will, the –*ma* suffix viewing it as a product], and **prepared** [from *hetoimázō* {2090}, to prepare] not himself, **neither** [*mēdé* {3366} from *mē* {3361}; and *dé* {1161}] **did** [from *poiéō* {4160}] **according to** [*prós* {4314}, toward, in the direction of] his will, **shall be beaten** [from *dérō* {1194}] with many stripes. But he that knew not, and did commit things **worthy** [from *áxios* {514}] of **stripes** [from *plēgé* {4127}, stripe], shall be beaten with few stripes. For unto whomsoever much is given, of him shall be much required: and to whom men have committed much, of him they will ask the more.

Degrees of punishment correlate with degrees of experiential knowledge. Those who know their Lord's will and do not do it will be punished more severely than those who do not know His will and do not do it. The more light given to us, the more accountable we are.

25

The Parable of the Ten Virgins
(25:1–13)

The Tribulation period as described in chapter 24 ends with the return of our Lord Jesus Christ to earth to set up His millennial kingdom. When the millennium starts, no unsaved people will be on earth. Those who follow the Antichrist into the Battle of Armageddon will have been cast into the lake of fire (Rev. 19:19–21). But what about other people born during the millenium who have not given their hearts to the Lord by the end of that period? In the second part of the Olivet discourse, Jesus addressed the separation of these unbelievers from believers in three parables that illustrate what will take place at that time.

Although there will probably be only one judgment (John 5:29), these parables show three aspects of what separates believers from unbelievers. They indicate who goes into the millennial kingdom and who does not.

The first parable concerns watchfulness and discusses the difference between **prudent** (*phrónimos* [5429]) and **foolish** (*mōrós* [3474]) people on earth when Christ returns. The primary focus here is on those who claim to be God's people, either as the nation of Israel or as members (both possessing and professing) of His church.

While many aspects in this parable parallel the rapture, the context describes the end of the Tribulation period. The rapture at the beginning of the Tribulation period is when Christ will come for His bride. The virgins in this parable were not expecting to become the bride. The bridegroom had not proposed to ten women and then married only five of them because the other five weren't ready. Nobody who heard Jesus give this parable would think that for a moment because the Jews in Christ's day were totally monogamous. Instead, these virgins were waiting for the wedding reception. The bridegroom had taken the bride from her house to his house to consummate the marriage and celebrate the wedding, paralleling the rapture of the church and our ascent to heaven to be with Christ forever. These virgins were coming to a pre-arranged place to meet the newlyweds. They would place the lamps they carried in little niches on the wall to provide illumination for the festivities (differentiate between *gámos* [1062], wedding in the singular [Matt. 22:8–10, 12; John 13:4; Rev. 19:7, 9] and *gámous*, celebrations in the plural [Matt. 22:2–4, 9; 25:10; Luke 14:8]).

[1, 2] The parable begins with the adverb "**then**" (*tóte* [5119]), referring to a specific time in the future, in this case, the return of Christ with His Bride to earth at the end of the Tribulation period.

Jesus compared those who are alive when He comes back to the ten virgins, five of whom are **wise** (from *phrónimos* [5429]) and five of whom are **foolish** (from *mōrós* [3474]).

Because these two words are antithetical in character, we can consider *mōrós* to be the opposite of *phrónimos* and, therefore, synonymous with *áphrōn* (878), which means lacking *phrēn* (5424), moral understanding and self-control. For example, the rich farmer who built larger barns (Luke 12:16–21) is called a "fool" in the English text (v. 20), but the Greek term is *áphrōn*, lacking wisdom. Similarly, Jesus called the Pharisees "fools" (also from *áphrōn*; Luke 11:40) because they believed that outer cleanliness proved inner purity. The "fool"—not the occasionally foolish believer but the completely immoral and godless person—is not born from above (John 3:3, 7) and is thereby not restrained by the power of the Holy Spirit. The one who lives for himself only is not indwelt by God (Luke 16:19–31).

Phrēn, the noun from which *phrónimos* comes, is prudence, the quality of applying God-given moral wisdom correctly. We use the English word "diaphragm," a device that curbs. In Modern Greek, *phréna* (the plural of *phréno*) are the brakes on a car. Figuratively, we can think of prudence as the moral brakes we apply before we collide with immorality.

In Koine Greek, *phrēn* means "mind" (equivalent to *noús* [3563]). *Áphrōn*, therefore, indicates "mindlessness." The ability to exercise prudence, as exhibited by the wise virgins, is part of God's wisdom given to His people through His Word.

People do not have the innate wisdom God has. We all have a measure of wisdom because we were created in the image of God (Gen. 1:27; Luke 16:8; James 3:9), much of which was lost in Adam's fall. But all true wisdom comes from redemptive revelation, that is, the gospel: "But we speak the wisdom of God in a mystery, even the hidden wisdom, which God ordained before the world unto our glory" (1 Cor. 2:7). God's wisdom (*sophía* [4678]) is distinctly differentiated (Mark 6:2; Luke 11:49; 1 Cor. 1:21, 24, 30; 2:7; Eph. 3:10; James 3:15, 17; Rev. 5:12) from human wisdom which is always qualified by limiting adjectives like "of the world," "of this age," or "earthly, sensual, devilish" (James 3:15, cf. Matt. 12:42; Luke 11:31; Acts 7:22; 1 Cor. 1:19, 20, 22; 2:5, 6, 13; 3:19; 2 Cor. 1:12).

The apostle Paul contrasts *mōrós* and *phrónimos* in 1 Corinthians 4:10: "We are fools [from *mōrós*] for Christ's sake, but ye are wise [from *phrónimos*] in Christ." In the context, Paul was looking at an apostle's office from a worldly perspective. Apostles were appointed to martyrdom (v. 9), humiliation (v. 9), weakness (v. 10), hunger, thirst, and poverty (v. 11), nakedness, blows, and homelessness (v. 11), persecution (v. 12), defamation and degradation (v. 12, 13). Such a life is for fools, and the comfortable are the wise, from a worldly perspective. Paul clearly was making use of sardonic irony. The Corinthians, no doubt, understood his point. They should follow his foolish (from a worldly perspective) but wise (from God's perspective) path.

The ten virgins equally conformed to one law of God—chastity, but they were not moral equals in other areas. Today's church contains diligent students, who accept the Word of God and adapt to it, and sloths who have never completely adapted to the Word of God. Five virgins did not believe that the Bridegroom's return was imminent so they did not prepare for it.

[3] The five foolish virgins took their lamps (v. 1) but no additional oil when they went to meet the bridegroom. Essentially, they were morally unprepared like the "**evil** [*kakós* {2556}, bad] servant" of Matthew 24:48 who counted on a delay (from *chronízō* [5549], to take time) in his lord's return.

To understand this parable, we can refer back to the contrast between the two servants given in Matthew 24:45–51. One is faithful (*pistós* [4103]; v. 45), wise (*phrónimos* [5429]; v. 45), and blessed (*makários* [3107]; v. 46), while the other is evil (*kakós*; v. 48), hypocritical (from *hupokritḗs* [5273]; v. 51), and beats his fellow servants (v. 49).

In Matthew 25:3, five virgins are called "foolish" (from *mōrós* [3474]), but this should not be understood as the innocent ignorance of infants. It is the accountable, conscious foolishness of adult women. The fact that they remembered their lamps evidences conscious thinking about oil from the beginning; after all, lamps require oil. But they "took no oil." They chose not to take oil for the same reason the lazy servant buried his talent in the subsequent parable of the talents (vv. 14–30). They were too foolish and lazy to buy the oil needed for the extended journey. The critical point is that the text says they "took no oil", not that they forgot oil. Had they used their God-given intelligence and properly responded to His call, they would have been prepared.

[4, 5] The wise virgins, on the other hand, prepared themselves:

> But the wise took oil in their vessels with their lamps. While the bridegroom **tarried** [from *chronízō* {5549}, to take time, linger, delay, defer], they all **became** drowsy [from *nustázō* {3573}, to become sleepy] and **were sleeping** [from *katheúdō* {2518}, to sleep]. (a.t.)

During the bridegroom's absence, all ten virgins became drowsy and fell asleep. No blame is attached to this; rather, accountability began when they first "took their lamps . . . to meet the bridegroom," some with and some without extra oil, long before they fell asleep (v. 1).

[6] At midnight, an hour when most people do not expect visitors, a "**cry**" (*kraugḗ* [2906]), presumably from an advancing messenger, announced that the "**bridegroom**" (*numphíos* [3566]) was coming. The sudden and swift appearance of the bridegroom is likened to the explosive rush of the Noahic flood in other Scriptures (Matt. 24:37–39; Luke 17:26, 27; Heb. 11:7; 1 Pet. 3:20; 2 Pet. 2:5).

The cry goes forth, "**Behold** [*idoú* {2400}, the imperative of *eídon* {1492}, the aorist of *horáō* {3708}, to perceive, calling attention to the extraordinary; see Matt. 3:16], the bridegroom **cometh** [from *érchomai* {2064}]." When the bridegroom came in that culture, he brought the bride with him. We sing, "Here comes the bride"; they cried out, "The bridegroom cometh." The "**behold**" was intended to awaken the virgins. All ten are then commanded to "go . . . out to meet him."

[7] Then all those virgins arose, and **trimmed** [from *kosméō* {2885}, to put in proper order] their lamps.

All ten virgins got ready to meet the bridegroom, but five lacked oil, the source of the flame that represents the inner spiritual life. Five virgins neglected this oil, which may represent the Holy Spirit, the fiery source of all Christian graces (Gal. 5:22, 23). Although they maintained their lamps in good order, they could not function without oil, just as Christians cannot function without the Spirit of God.

The five prudent virgins attended to the right thing. They not only kept their lamps in good order, but they were filled with the oil of God's presence. Accordingly, they "adorn[ed] [also from *kosméō* from which comes the English 'cosmetics'] the doctrine of God our Saviour in all things" (Titus 2:10). The wick of a lamp may be carefully trimmed, but if the lamp contains no oil, no light can shine forth.

The good servant in Matthew 24:45, who corresponds to the five prudent virgins, was called "faithful" (*pistós* [4103], believing and loyal). He believed his master would return soon, he watched for him expectantly, and he behaved accordingly. The evil servant, who corresponds to the five foolish virgins, on the other hand, was faithless and morally disloyal. He believed his master was procrastinating, and he took advantage of the time to beat his fellows.

[8] The five foolish virgins said to the wise virgins:

> Give us some of your oil; for our lamps are being extinguished. (a.t.)

This was a presumptuous request since they already had the opportunity to bring their own oil. True believers, conscious of the imminent return of the Bridegroom and dependent on the oil of the Holy Spirit, work and sacrifice, always alert and ready. They know that no other believers—pastors, doctors, psychologists, or friends—can give them what they need when the Bridegroom returns. When He comes, He will come for His own, not strangers. We believers should prepare by purchasing things of eternal value and forgoing the excessive consumption of the transient goods and services of a perishing world (2 Cor. 4:18). Rewards in heaven will not be transferable; they are earned individually and uniquely. True believers do not borrow oil. A relationship with Christ cannot be begged, borrowed, or stolen from someone else. We must have our own oil, and we must have it now. The time to solidify our relationships with the Master is not at the moment of His return: "Today if ye will hear his voice, harden not your hearts, as in the provocation" (Heb. 3:15). "Behold, now is the accepted time; behold, now is the day of salvation" (2 Cor. 6:2).

[9] The response of the prudent virgins may appear to run contrary to the spirit of Christ's generosity, but, in fact, it was the only real advice they could give:

> Not so; lest there be not enough for us and you: but go ye rather to **them that sell** [from *pōléō* {4453}], and **buy** [from *agorázō* {59}] for yourselves.

The "sellers" could illustrate the Father, Son, and Holy Spirit. The ascended Lord so addressed the church in Laodicea:

> I counsel thee to buy [also from *agorázō*] of me gold tried in the fire, that thou mayest be rich; and white raiment, that thou mayest be clothed, and that the shame of thy nakedness do not appear; and anoint thine eyes with eyesalve, that thou mayest see. (Rev. 3:18)

According to the Lord's counsel, the purchase is not mediated through the church's ministers. It is a direct transaction between the believer and the Lord. Simon the sorcerer tried to buy the power of the Holy Spirit, and Peter severely rebuked him:

> And when Simon saw that through laying on of the apostles' hands the Holy Ghost was given, he offered them money, saying, Give me also this

power, that on whomsoever I lay hands, he may receive the Holy Ghost. But Peter said unto him, Thy money perish with thee, because thou hast thought that the gift of God [i.e., not the Holy Spirit but the power to bestow the Holy Spirit; v. 19] may be purchased with money. (Acts 8:18–20)

Some things cannot be shared, and the fact that the ascended Lord told the church of Laodicea to "buy of me" means that the goods—"gold tried in the fire" and "white raiment"—are not transferable, just as the Holy Spirit is not transferable. We cannot make others believe, and we cannot sell or give them either God's Holy Spirit or our own personal faith. They must purchase their own "oil of gladness" (Ps. 45:7), their own "gold tried in the fire," directly from God through the Lord Jesus Christ. The cost is personal repentance and faith: "I will not offer burnt offerings unto the Lord my God from that which has cost me nothing" (2 Sam. 24:24; a.t.). A morally pure and religiously obedient life will not merit salvation. This comes through Christ alone.

[10] The shut door closed down the opportunity to participate in the wedding festivities of the bridegroom:

> And while they went **to buy** [from *agorázō* {59}–the same verb as in Rev. 3:18; see previous verse], the bridegroom came; and the **readied** [from the adjective *hétoimos* {2092}, prepared] went in with him to the marriage: and the door was shut. (a.t.)

Was the advice of the five prudent virgins heartless? Did they know the bridegroom was coming so soon after the messenger's first "cry" (v. 6)? No, they did not. They gave sound counsel to their foolish counterparts. We should counsel people to turn directly to the Lord, whether His coming is near at hand or far off, for none of us knows the precise time of His return (Mark 13:32). John the Baptist was "continually crying [a present participle] in the wilderness, prepare ye the way of the Lord" (Matt. 3:3; a.t.). He warned the Pharisees of "wrath to come" (3:7), although the wrath did not come until A.D. 70 when Jerusalem and its temple were destroyed.

The five prudent virgins could not know the time of the groom's return since he did not reveal it (Matt. 24:36; Mark 13:32). So it was not their fault that the bridegroom came so quickly after the "cry" of the messenger. Neither was it the bridegroom's lack of wisdom. Many people will expect some delay between the cries of the Lord's prophets and His return. But then one day, "The Lord . . . shall suddenly come to his temple" (Mal. 3:1). Toward the end of this age, ministers of the gospel will issue stern warnings to repent, and many will consider it. But then, unexpectedly, the Lord will come, whether people are prepared or not.

Notice how true believers are called "the readied" or "the prepared"—a full adjective used substantivally as the subject. When we do things from time to time, they can be described by verbs, and when we do them habitually, by participles; but when those things are part of our natures, then only an adjectival noun does justice to the reality. Believers are "the prepared," conforming to the image of Christ (Rom. 8:29).

[11–13] The foolish virgins cry out desperately when the door was shut. The spiritual implication of the answer is terrifying:

> Afterward came also the other virgins, saying, Lord, Lord, open to us. But he answered and said, Verily I say unto you, **I know** [*oída*, the perfect tense of *eído* {1492}, the aorist of *horáo* {3708}, to perceive; here used to know innately, i.e., "I have known"] you not. Watch therefore, for ye know neither the day nor the hour wherein the Son of man cometh.

Like the evil subjects of prior parables, the five foolish virgins were neither alert—because they rejected the bridegroom's imminence—nor prepared, because their works corresponded with the falsity of a delay.

The figure of a door being shut is strong, naturally suggesting that the five are closed out of whatever the prepared five received on the other side of the door (v. 10). If we add to this the metaphor of Christ being the "door of the sheep" (John 10:7), it is obvious that salvation issues are at stake. To those who claimed to have prophesied and have done mighty works in His name, Jesus will say, "**I never** [from *oudépote* {3763}] **knew** [from *ginósko* {1097}, to know by experience] you: depart from me, ye that work iniquity" (Matt. 7:22–23). This would seem to have the same impact as the bridegroom's statement here, "I know you not" (*ouk oíde* contrasted with *oudépote égnon humás*, "I never knew you" of Matt. 7:23). No salvation takes place at or following "the marriage supper of the Lamb (Rev. 19:9).

Jesus used the term "virgins" to describe the five foolish persons. In the Old Testament, Babylon and Egypt in their worst states were called "virgin" (Isa. 47:1; Jer. 46:11) as was apostate Israel under God's judgment (Jer. 18:13; Lam. 1:15; 2:13; Amos 5:2). It is neither scriptural nor logical to deduce absolute moral purity from virginity. A virgin can be a liar, a thief, and a murderer but still a virgin. As James says, "Whosoever shall keep the whole law, and yet offend in one point, he is guilty of all" (James 2:10). We also learn from this parable that "clean" lives of good works (they were virgins and had trimmed their lamps) are not enough. God's Holy Spirit must indwell us and make us grow (*auxáno* [837]; 1 Cor. 3:7). Ultimately, those who do not believe the Lord is "near" and do not prepare themselves accordingly for His sudden appearance are not true believers. Their grievous sin has led to irreversible consequences.

The parable, then, conforms to others in which persons profess faith but ultimately distance themselves from the Lord of truth (John 6:66). In this case, the lack of oil was a rejection of the Lord and His teaching, the imminence of His return, and the importance of watching and waiting. Those who disbelieve this teaching do not watch and behave foolishly. In the prior parable, Jesus called the unprepared servant (*kakós* [2556], evil or bad) who assumed a delay in his lord's return and beat his fellow servants (Matt. 24:48).

It is unlikely that Jesus was shifting from the dichotomies of belief and unbelief, good and evil, and integrity and hypocrisy to two types of believers. Surely, it is unlikely He would call believers by the same "fools and blind" He called the Pharisees (Matt. 23:19) or that He would shut the door on them with the words, "I do not know you." If this latter statement reflected a timeless innate knowledge (*eídō*), then He never knew these five (cf. Matt. 7:23). Congruently, Jesus did not say, I have not known your faith (i.e., some aspect of you) but rather, I have not known you (*ouk oída humás* your whole person). This is strong language indeed, but it cannot equal the *oudépote égnōn humás*, "I never knew you" of Matthew 7:23.

Belief in the imminent return of Christ, watching for that return, and living a holy life in accord with this belief, therefore, are not options for us as believers. Both faith (Rom. 16:26) and actions that correspond to the faith (James 2:26) represent obedient love.

The Parable of the Talents
(25:14–30)

Jesus gave this parable and the related parable of the minas (pounds) in Luke 19:11–27 during His last trip to Jerusalem and the last week of His earthly life. They both teach another aspect of God's servants: faithfulness. Those who love God will do what God tells them to do.

[14] As the King James Version notes in italics, the phrase, "*the kingdom of heaven is*," is not in the Greek text. The phrase is, however, found in verse 1, and this parable offers another instance of similarity to the kingdom of God:

For the kingdom of heaven is as [*hōsper* {5618} from *hōs* {5613}, as; and *per* {4007}, surely] a man **travelling into a far country** [from *apodēméō* {589}, to travel abroad], who called **his own** [from *ídios* {2398}, own, personal] **servants** [from *doúlos* {1401}, bond-slave], and **delivered** [from *paradídōmi* {3860} from *pará* {3844}, close proximity; and *dídōmi* {1325}, to give voluntarily] unto them his **goods** [*hupárchonta* {5224}, possessions, the participle of *hupárchō* {5225}, to be at one's disposal].

As with the parable of the ten virgins, we in this present church age can learn many lessons from this parable as we face the rapture and the judgment seat of Christ. However, the primary context is at the end of the Tribulation period. Christ has given a charge to us as His people to supervise His "goods." The "goods" are the gospel, the gifts of the Holy Spirit, and the talents He has given us to work with and produce while He is away.

[15] The talent was the largest monetary value used in the Greek world, equivalent to 240 pounds of silver, worth about one thousand dollars in the first half of the twentieth century (see Matt. 18:24). The Lord imparts these to His servants individually:

> And unto one he gave five **talents** [from *tálanton* {5007}], to another two, and to another one; to every man according to his own [from *ídios* {2398}, personal] **ability** [from *dúnamis* {1411}, strength]; and straightway took his journey. (a.t)

When He made us, God gave each of us a special ability (from *dúnamis*). He augments those abilities with various quantities of talents. In modern Greek, the word *tálanton* retains the general meaning of aptitude or money. In Koine Greek, the language of the New Testament, the word "talent" meant a certain weight. In Greek mythology, the chief god, Zeus, placed "talants" on scales to weigh the copper, gold, and silver used to make coins.

In the parallel parable of the pounds, the Lord called ten servants and gave each of them one pound saying, "Occupy [from *pragmateúomai* {4231}, to trade, to put into *prágma* {4229}, practice, from which we get our English words 'pragmatic' and 'practical'] till I come" (Luke 19:13).

[16, 17] The one who received five talents did not waste any time.

> Then he that had received the five talents **went** [from *poreúomai* {4198}, to go out publicly in contrast to *hupágō* {5217}, to depart stealthily] and **traded** [from *ergázomai* {2038}, to work] with the same, and **made** [{MT, TR} *epoíēsen*, the aorist indicative of *poiéō* {4160}, to make; {NES, UBS} *ekérdēsen*, the aorist indicative of *kerdaínō* {2770}, to gain] them other five talents. And likewise he that had received two, he also **gained** [*ekérdēsen*] other two.

The work here is clearly investment, *ergázomai* defined in the context as *kerdaínō*, to gain. Profit is indicated in *kerdaínō*, a verb used for the first time in Matthew 16:26 where Jesus said, "For what is a man profited, if he shall gain [from *kerdaínō*] the whole world, and lose his own soul?"

The successful servants in this parable gained the world to come by putting the Lord's talents to use in ways that extended His kingdom. The aorist tense of *kerdaínō* sums up a lifetime of ministry. Here in verses 16 and 17, each servant produced 100 percent return on his lord's investment.

[18] The third servant produced nothing:

> But he that had received one went and digged in the earth, and hid his lord's money.

He was both lazy and indifferent. As noted above, successful investment (*kerdaínō*) is work (*ergázomai*). Unlike the other two servants, this servant did not want to work at all and had no excuse for not working.

[19] Inevitably, their lord returned to account for the talents he gave his servants:

> After a **long** [from *polús* {4183}, much] **time** [from *chrónos* {5550}, space of time, interval], the lord of those servants **comes** [from *érchomai* {2064}, to come], and **settles** [from *sunaírō* {4868} from *sún* {4862}, together; and *aírō* {142}, to lift up and take away, to resolve] **accounts** [from *lógos* {3056}] with them. (a.t.)

Although the interval in which the servants were expected to invest seemed long, the lord did return within their lifetimes. In our own period, the rapture for us is just as imminent. But should the Lord tarry in His physical return to earth, a temporary and limited judgment will take place immediately at death (see Luke 16:22, 23).

The accounting that follows was rather simple. The master wanted to know what his investors did with the initial capital he gave them.

[20–23] The accounting scenario unfolds:

> And so he that had received five talents came and brought other five talents, saying, Lord, you gave me five talents: **behold** [*íde*, the imperative of *eídon*, the aorist of *horáō* {3708}, to see and perceive with emphasis on perception, the personalization of the impersonal *idoú*; see Matt. 1:20, 23; 2:1, 9, 13], I have gained **beside** [*ep'* from *epí* {1909}, upon] them five talents more. (a.t.)
>
> His lord said unto him, Well done, thou **good** [from *agathós* {18}, benevolent] and **faithful** [from *pistós* {4103}, trustworthy] servant: thou hast been faithful over a **few things** [from *olígos* {3641}], **I will make** thee **ruler** [from *kathistēmi* {2525} from *katá* {2596}, down; and *hístēmi* {2476}, to set or place, to constitute, appoint] **over** [*epí* {1909}, upon] **many things** [from *polús*

{4183}, much]: **enter thou** [*eiselthe*, the aorist imperative of *eisérchomai* {1525}, to come into] into the **joy** [from *chará* {5479}] of thy lord.

He also that had received two talents came and said, Lord, thou deliveredst unto me two talents: behold, I have gained two other talents beside them. His lord said unto him, Well done, good and faithful servant; thou hast been faithful over a few things, I will make thee ruler over many things: enter thou into the joy of thy lord.

An interesting switch—servants telling their lord to "behold!" Normally, God, speaking through His prophets, commanded His people to take notice of some upcoming miracle. "Behold" here dramatizes the servants' enthusiasm over what they did. They know that by God's grace they were successful, and so they were excited to display the results to the one they deemed their human lord (Matt. 12:8; John 16:30; 21:17). They wanted to hear his "well done"— the "praise of God" (John 12:43; 1 Cor. 4:5). (See the author's exegetical commentary on 1 Cor. 4, *Seeking the Praise of God*.) And rightly so, since the returns on the lord's investments were 100 percent.

(Note in addition to the verb *kerdaínō*, to gain, the TR and MT use of *epí*, upon, meaning "on top of" in vv. 20, 22.) Yet since grace is never outperformed, the rewards far outweighed the work: "many things" for "few things" (see our exegesis on Matt. 13:23.) Also, in this parable the lord delegates rulership in the spiritual kingdom: "To him that overcometh will I grant to sit with me in my throne, even as I also overcame, and am set down with my Father in his throne" (Rev. 3:21; cf. John 16:33).

The lord commended these servants with the adjectives "**good**" (from *agathós* [18], benevolent), and **faithful** (from *pistós* [4103], trustworthy, which includes the meanings of keeping the faith [Col. 4:9; 1 Pet. 5:12; Rev. 2:10] and dependability [1 Cor. 1:9]). Since "there is none good but one, . . . God" (Matt. 19:17), any benevolence in a believer is part of God's new creation (2 Cor. 5:17; Gal. 6:15; Eph. 2:10) and is, therefore, the work of the benevolent God. The greatest benevolence, of course, was God's sacrifice of His Son for the sins of the world (John 3:16; 1 John 4:9).

There is an objective joy to "enter," which shows that heaven has its own space and time. Space is implicit in the imperative "enter." Time is implicit not only in the aorist—once-for-all—tense of the verb "enter" but also in the subsequent, ongoing action implied in "**rul[ing]** over many things." But heaven is not just space, time, and work; it is "the joy of [our] [L]ord," and therefore joyful space, time, and work with no more "thorns and thistles" and "sweat of [the] brow" (Gen. 3:18, 19 NIV). For such joy set before Him, the Lord Jesus endured the cross and despised its shame (Heb. 12:2).

[24, 25] The third servant presented a different case:

> Then he which received the one talent came and said, Lord, **I knew** [from *ginōskō* {1097}, to know experientially] that you are a **hard** [*sklērós* {4642}, callous, harsh, inconsiderate] man, **reaping** [from *therízō* {2325}, to harvest] where you have not **sown** [from *speírō* {4687}, to sow] and **gathering** [from *sunágō* {4863}, to assemble, bring together] **where** [*hóthen* {3606}, from whence] you have not **strawed** [from *diaskorpízō* {1287}, to scatter]. And **I was afraid** [from *phobéō* {5399}, to frighten] and went and hid your talent in the earth: lo, there you have what is yours. (a.t.)

What exactly was the complaint, and what was the excuse? The servant complained that the lord was "callous" or inconsiderate (*sklērós*) because he reaped where he did not sow; that is, he expected others to do all his work. The servant resented the thought that his master would profit from his work, and he resented the master for it. But he completely ignored the fact that the capital by which he could gain anything came from his master. He also had a duty as a slave to do what his owner asked him to do. His master simply told him in effect, "I can't be around to oversee the investment of my money; I want you to invest it for me while I am away." Once again a person claims to be God's servant but does not really know Him at all. He thinks he knows God from experience (from *ginōskō*), but he has no real understanding of God or His character.

In the parable, this servant was prejudged already by the success of the first two servants. Also, he was guilty of blaming his lord, as if a master answers to a servant. But he had no excuse for hiding the money when a bank was available.

In the parable of the pounds, one servant amassed a 1,000 percent gain: "Then came the first, saying, Lord, thy pound hath gained ten pounds" (Luke 19:16). A second servant produced a gain of 500 percent (19:18). Given these results, the third servant had no valid basis for fear or excuse for nonperformance. Obviously, he was strong enough to work since he dug a hole and buried the talent.

[26, 27] The lord's response was wise and just:

> His lord answered and said unto him, **Wicked** [from *ponērós* {4190}] and **slothful** [from *oknērós* {3636}, lazy] servant, you knew that I reap where I did not sow, and gather where I have not scattered. **It was morally necessary** [from *deí* {1163}, it must be], **therefore** [*oún* {3767}], **to place** [from *bállō* {906}, to cast or place; the aorist indicates a one time placement] my **money** [from *argúrion* {694}, silver coin, talent, money, investment] with the exchangers, and then at my coming I would have received my principle with **interest** [*tókos* {5110}]. (a.t.)

The master called him a wicked and lazy servant because he did not act properly according to his own words. The master's words, "You knew that I reap where I did not sow and gather where I have not scattered," with the following statement could be paraphrased: "If you really believed that I was a harsh master, you should have been afraid to deliberately disobey me." The master then pointed out that the servant could have invested the money in a bank if he were really afraid of losing it in a business venture. Burying or hiding the money was inexcusable. Even if he did not want to purchase and work at a business, he could have made a simple deposit in an interest-bearing account that involved no subsequent work. Of course, in human investing, there is always the slim possibility that a bank may go bankrupt and the investment be lost. But Christians who really know their Lord and have faith in Him should never have such a fear: God will never allow any effort we make for Him go unrewarded.

Notice that the lord calls it "my money," as does the servant—"your talent" (v. 25). The *argúrion*, silver, was understandably on loan, and it properly belonged in a bank if not exchanged for capital goods that could be increased. This is why the servant's claim was an utterly indefensible excuse. Who buries money?

There is an implicit approval of bank commerce here. In fact, the legal charging of business interest originated with the Torah (Deut. 23:20), though God told His people not to place this burden on the poor (Ex. 22:25; Lev. 25:36, 37; Deut. 23:19).

The master did not bother refuting the accusation that he was a "hard man, reaping where [he] hast not sown." In fact, he assumed the truth of the premise:

> You knew that I reap where I have not sown, and gather where I have not scattered seed. So you ought to have deposited my money with the bankers, and at my coming I would have received back my own with interest (NKJV).

By appealing to the bank sector, the lord refuted the servant with his own premise. There was an institution where the servant could have leveraged his lord's creative power in his favor without any effort on his part—a bank! The money just sits there and earns interest; no effort is involved following the initial deposit. To not perform this minimal act is sheer laziness.

[28–30] While it was not too late to learn the lesson, it was too late to apply it. Judgment followed:

> **Take** [from *aírō* {142}, to pick up and take away], therefore, the talent from him, and give it to him that has ten talents. For to the one who has, all things

shall be given [from *dídōmi* {1325}, to give voluntarily], and **he shall be made abundant** [from *perisseúō* {4052}, to abound, gain]: but from him that has not **shall also be taken away** [from *aírō*] even that which he has [here, the original talent]. (a.t.)

This last verse is an explanatory parenthesis between two imperatives. The original Scriptures had no punctuation marks. Verse 30 now reverts to the command of the lord:

> And **cast ye** [from *ekbállō* {1544}, to cast out, from *ek* {1537}, out of from within or among; and *bállō* {906}, to cast, put] the **unprofitable** [from *achreíos* {888} from *a* {1}, without; and *chreía* {5532}, utility, usefulness; thus, useless] servant into outer darkness: there shall be weeping and gnashing of teeth.

Notice the analogy with the parable of the profitable and unprofitable servants in Matthew 24:45–51. As the lord in that parable promised the faithful servant he would be ruler over all his goods, so in this parable the master promised the faithful servants that they would rule over many things. And as the lord in that parable commanded that the wicked servant who beat his fellow servants should be cut asunder and placed with the hypocrites where there was weeping and gnashing of teeth, in this parable the wicked and slothful servant also was cast into outer darkness where there was weeping and gnashing of teeth. The only appropriate place for a wicked, lazy, valueless servant is outer darkness. Some of the frustration expressed in "weeping and gnashing of teeth" may be due to the comparative success of the two other servants and the consequent reallocation of the one talent, the same frustration the isolated rich man experienced in Hades while watching Lazarus and Abraham together across a vast chasm (Luke 16:19–31).

All three occurrences of the expression "outer darkness" are in Matthew (here and 8:12; 22:13), who, more than any other Gospel writer, highlights Jewish apostasy and the subsequent allocation of the kingdom to Gentiles:

> And I say unto you, That many shall come from the east and west, and shall sit down with Abraham, and Isaac, and Jacob, in the kingdom of heaven. But the children of the kingdom shall be cast out into outer darkness [*skótos* {4655}]: there shall be weeping and gnashing of teeth. (Matt. 8:11, 12)

> The kingdom of God [much more than a talent] shall be taken from you, and given to a nation bringing forth the fruits thereof. (Matt. 21:43)

In Matthew 22:13, we find a similar command concerning the one who attempted to enter the wedding feast without the proper garment: "Bind him hand and foot, and take him away, and cast him into outer darkness [*skótos* {4655}]; there shall be weeping and gnashing of teeth." *Skótos* means spiritual darkness and eternal misery (Matt. 4:16; 8:12; Luke 1:79; Acts 26:18; 1 Thess. 5:4; 1 Pet. 2:9; 2 Pet. 2:17; Jude 13).

The Son of Man Returns in Glory to Judge the Nations (25:31–46)

[31] The last parable in chapter 25, the parable of the sheep and the goats, brings out a third aspect of judgment in determining who goes into the millennial kingdom: actions in befriending and protecting God's people, which in this context indicates salvation. We now see a judgment scenario that follows the defeat of the beast and the false prophet, as recorded in Revelation 19:11—20:1–15.

When the Son of man **comes** [*élthē*, the aorist active subjunctive of *érchomai* {2064}, to come; the aorist tense denotes a crisis in human, redemptive history] in **His** [from *autós* {846}, His own] **glory** [from *dóxē* {1391} from *dokéō* {1380}, to appraise] and all the **holy** [from *hágios* {40}, internally righteous] angels with Him, then He shall sit on the throne of His glory. (a.t.)

There are several glories of the Son: There is the pristine or original glory of the pre-incarnate Word: "And now, O Father, glorify thou me with thine own self with the glory which I had with thee before the world was" (John 17:5). This glory was the praise of angels long before creation (Job 1:6; 38:7; Prov. 8:22–26). Then there is the glory of the incarnate Word: "And we beheld his glory, the glory as of the only begotten [from *monogenḗs* {3439}] of the Father, full of grace and truth" (John 1:14). This glory attaches to the uniqueness (*monogenḗs*, only begotten, one of a kind, sole member of a class) of the incarnate Word.

Finally, there is a glory that attaches to judgment; thus, the verse ends with the captivating phrase, "throne of his glory." It is a glorious throne, a throne characterized by the glory of the One sitting on it; therefore, a glorious judgment is about to unfold. In the Gospel of John we read, "For the Father judgeth no man, but hath committed all judgment unto the Son. . . . and hath given him authority to execute judgment also, because he is the Son of man" (John 5:22, 27). The Son judges both as God and man, by deity through sinless humanity, the standard being that omniscient wisdom that redeemed people have through the perfect human life—Jesus Christ, the benchmark of all judgment.

Christ promises to share His throne, as we saw in Matthew 19:23 (cf. Luke 22:30) and also in Revelation 3:21. According to the apostle Paul, believers will "judge angels" (1 Cor. 6:3). Thus, when He returns, He comes "to be glorified in his saints" (2 Thess. 1:10), that is, His elect people.

[32, 33] Holy angels will not only accompany Christ at His return but also will gather all people before Him to be judged:

> And before him **shall be gathered** [from *sunágō* {4863}, to lead together] all **nations** [from *éthnos* {1484}]; and **he shall separate** [from *aphorízō* {873}, to separate] them one from another, as a shepherd divideth his **sheep** [from *próbaton* {4263}] from the **goats** [from *ériphos* {2056}]: and he shall set the sheep on his right hand, but the goats on the left.

Though gathered as nations, people are judged as individuals; accordingly, the nations will be divided into believers (sheep) and unbelievers (goats). Judgment will be a separation, and the task is assigned to angels: "The Son of man shall send forth his angels, and they shall gather out of his kingdom all things that offend, and them which do iniquity" (Matt. 13:41). That is, even the gathering will include a differentiating factor, as the angels sort the wheat and the tares (Matt. 13:30; 25:31).

In God's foreknowledge, the separation is already done: "He who believes on Him is not judged [*krínetai*, the present passive tense of *krínō* {2919}], but he who believes not already [*ēdē* {2235}] has been judged [*kékritai*, the perfect passive tense of *krínō*]" (John 3:18; a.t.). The judgment was completed when Christ died on the cross, a historical event with a timeless impact on humans and angels. His death imputed judgment to all unbelievers (note in this last verse that the judgment, a perfect tense, is prior to unbelief, a present tense). Thus, Christ's words: "For judgment I am come into this world, that . . . they which see might be made blind" (John 9:39). Similarly, "Ye believe not, because ye are not of my sheep" (John 10:26). Sheep wander without shepherds (see, e.g., Ezek. 34:6), but goats are the more wild of the two.

Note also the contrast between "his right hand" and "the left." The "right hand of God" is the position of privilege.

[34] Jesus addressed His people:

> Then shall the King say unto them on His right hand, Come, you **who have been blessed** [*eulogēménoi*, the perfect passive participle of *eulogéō* {2127}, to speak well, to decree good] of my Father, inherit the **kingdom** [from *basileía* {932}] **that has been prepared** [*hētoimasménēn*, the perfect passive participle of *hetoimázō* {2090}] for you from the foundation of the world. (a.t.)

The participle and other constructions of *eulogéō*, blessed, are frequently used of the saints, but God is the only one who is innately *eulogētós* (the descriptive adjective predicate). This adjective is used only of God the Father (2 Cor. 1:3; Eph. 1:3; 1 Pet. 1:3) and God the Son (Rom. 9:5).

In the immediate context, *eulogeménoi*, "**you who have been blessed**," contrasts with the parallel perfect participle *katēraménoi* (v. 41), "**you who have been cursed**." Just as Christ's "right hand [position of privilege]" is contrasted with "the left" (previous verse), so "you who have been blessed of My Father" is contrasted with the unqualified "you who have been cursed." The curse rests on those God does not know personally: "I never knew you" (Matt. 7:23, cf. Amos 3:2; see v. 41 for further discussion).

The contrast between the sheep and the goats continues in the commands given to the two. The King will invite the sheep with the personal "**come**" (*deúte* [1205]), the same personal invitation given in Matthew 11:28 to the "burdened and heavy laden." But He will command the goats to "**depart**" (*poreúesthe*, the present imperative of *poreúomai* [4198], to march publicly; v. 41). This command is a decree; it cannot be disobeyed. The goats will be cast into the lake of fire. The Lord doesn't ask them to remove themselves; He commands them to leave.

The participial phrase that describes the kingdom as having been "prepared for you from the foundation of the world" is paralleled by Paul's statement in Ephesians 1:4 that we were chosen in Christ "before the foundation of the world, that we should be holy and without blame before him in love." In other words, God prepared from the foundation of the world both a kingdom and a people to rule in it. To predetermine a specific kingdom is to predetermine particular rulers—the believers—since, by definition, there is no kingdom without rulers.

[35, 36] The invitation to come and inherit is based on (*gár* [1063], because) the ministry of sheep to other sheep, proof of their faith in the Shepherd:

> **For** [*gár*] I was hungry, and you gave Me meat: I was thirsty, and you gave Me drink: I was a stranger, and you took Me in: naked, and you clothed Me: I was sick, and you visited Me: I was in prison, and you came unto Me. (a.t.)

Jesus identifies with His sheep. When they are hungry, thirsty, naked, sick, and imprisoned, then He is (vicariously) also. The Scripture says that even now He is able "to sympathize [from *sumpathéō* {4834} from *sún* {4862}, together; and *páschō* {3958}, to suffer; 'to suffer together with'] with our weaknesses" (Heb. 4:15; a.t.), since He Himself was crucified because of the physical weakness He assumed in His incarnation (2 Cor. 13:4).

In general, the New Testament teaches that Jesus "suffered" (1 Pet. 2:21, 23); He "suffered in the flesh" (1 Pet. 4:1); He "suffered being tempted" (Heb. 2:18); He suffered a sorrow unto death in the Garden of Gethsemane (Matt.

26:38), and spiritual and physical pain on the cross (Luke 24:26; Heb. 13:12; 1 Pet. 3:18). Jesus personally experienced hunger (Matt. 4:2) and thirst (John 19:28). He was also a "stranger" (*xénos* [3581]) since He had no place to lay His head (Matt. 8:20) and was "despised and rejected of men" (Isa. 53:3), as well as being rejected by "His own" (John 1:11). The Roman guards stripped Him (Matt. 27:28), so He was at least partially and temporarily naked on one occasion. He was imprisoned according to Matthew 27:2, 15. Scripture is silent concerning Christ personally suffering from illness, but the judgments that He bore in His humanity were due to the sins of others, not His own—"who knew no sin" (2 Cor. 5:21).

The remarkable identity between the Shepherd and His sheep is given elsewhere in Scripture. For example, when someone told Jesus that His mother and brothers were waiting outside, He responded, "Who is my mother? and who are my brethren?" (Matt. 12:48). Immediately after, pointing to believers, He said, "Behold my mother and my brethren!" (12:49).

The indwelling Christ initiates and empowers ministry among believers. Paul tells us that coming to faith and subsequent good works are all part of the creative, saving work of God:

> For we are His **products** [*poíema* {4161}, the *–ma* suffix treats the "work" as a resultant product], **created** [from *ktízō* {2936}, to create] in Christ Jesus for good works, which God ordained in order that [*hina* {2443}] we should walk [from *peripatéō* {4043}] in them. (Eph. 2:10; a.t.; cf. 3 John 11)

[37–39] The sheep are profoundly bewildered by these words. In true humility consistent with that displayed throughout their lives, they do not seem to be aware of the impact of their ministry:

> Then shall the **righteous** [from *díkaios* {1342}, justified] answer him, saying, Lord, when saw we thee an hungred, and fed thee? or thirsty, and gave thee drink? When saw we thee a stranger, and took thee in? or naked, and clothed thee? Or when saw we thee sick, or in prison, and came unto thee?

How different this is from hypocrites who perpetually advertise and applaud their own works and demean others. The wicked, the Scripture says, will promote their products and services even before God (Matt. 7:22), only to have them condemned as void of any compassion for the Lord's people (1 Cor. 13:1–3).

The "righteous" are those who are justified by the meritorious life and death of Jesus Christ:

> Therefore as by the offence of one judgment came upon all men to condemnation; even so by the righteousness of one the free gift came upon all men

unto justification of life. For as by one man's disobedience many were constituted sinners, so by the obedience of one shall many be constituted righteous.
(Rom. 5:18, 19; a.t.)

God's wrath is propitiated through "faith in [Christ's] blood" (Rom. 3:25),
so believers are "justified by faith" (Rom. 5:1).

[40] Jesus enlightened the sheep: "And the King shall answer and say unto
them, Verily I say unto you, Inasmuch as ye have done it unto one of the **least**
[from *eláchistos* {1646}] of these my brethren, ye have done it unto me."

Who are the brethren who are befriended here? One clue may be found in
the word **nations** (from *éthnos* [1484]) in verse 32. When used in the plural with
no other modifier, the Greek word *éthnos* usually means every nation but one's
own, in this case, every nation but the Jews. Indeed, the plural of *éthnos* is frequently translated as "Gentiles" in the King James Version (e.g., Matt. 6:32;
12:21; 20:25; Acts 4:27; 9:15; 11:18; 14:2, 5; 18:6; etc.). If this is true here,
then this is primarily a picture of the judgment of the Gentiles. One thing on
which they will be judged is how they treated Christ's brethren, the Jews. This
is especially crucial during the Tribulation period when the Antichrist and his
followers mount their attack against the Jews. Only born-again Christians will
dare risk their lives to protect these persecuted new believers (Rom. 11:26). Here
we see actions that indicate whether persons are redeemed or not.

[41] The goats are forced to hear a terrifying command:

> Then shall He say also unto them on the left, **Depart** [*poreúesthe*, the pres-
> ent imperative of *poreúomai* {4198}, to march] from Me, **you who are cursed**
> [from *kataráomai* {2672}], into **everlasting** [from *aiónios* {166}, eternal, forever]
> **fire** [*púr* {4442}] **which has been prepared** [*hētoimasménon*, the perfect passive
> participle of *hetoimázō* {2090}] for the devil and his **angels** [*aggélois* {32}]. (a.t.)

A "**curse**" in the Bible does not carry the connotations that the word has
in today's English. Throughout Scripture curses are identified with God's righteous judgments on the wicked (Gen. 3:14, 17; 4:11; 5:29; Num. 23:8; and
the entire chapters of Deut. 28—30, e.g., 30:7: "God will put all these curses
[i.e., judgments of sickness and death] on your enemies" [a.t.; cf. Gen. 12:3;
Deut. 29:27; Josh. 6:26; 2 Kgs. 2:24; 2 Chr. 34:24; Jer. 17:5; Mal. 2:2; 3:9]).
A curse is a decree of judgment, a just punishment, the final decision of the
judge. The perfect tense of *kataráomai* defines those who have already reached
the mature state of liability for judgment, those who have filled up their sins
(Gen. 15:16; Matt. 23:32), having given themselves over to ruin.

The ultimate destiny of unbelievers will be in an everlasting fire that God
has prepared for the devil and his angels.

The finality of this judgment is also supported by Revelation 20:14, which says that death (*thánatos* [2288]) and Hades (*hádēs* [86]) will be cast into the lake of fire, here defined as the "second death." Note that unlike the kingdom, the everlasting fire is not described as "prepared . . . from before the foundation of the world" (Matt. 25:34).

[42–45] Jesus now gave the reason for the destiny of everlasting fire:

> For I was hungry, and you gave Me nothing to eat; I was thirsty, and you gave Me no drink; I was a stranger, and you did not take Me in; naked, and you did not clothe Me; sick and in prison, and you did not visit Me. Then shall they also answer Him, saying, Lord, when did we see You hungry, or thirsty, or a stranger, or naked, or sick, or in prison, and not minister to You? Then shall He answer them, saying, Verily I say unto you, Inasmuch as you did not do it to one of the least of these, you did not do it to Me. (a.t.)

This is the other side of the coin. Interestingly, the goats did not perform a single act of compassionate ministry. Sacrificial love (*agápē* [26]), which God is (1 John 4:8, 16), was entirely missing. Since these goats did not respond properly to the love of God, they did not receive the love of God into their hearts. Their actions were concordant with their natures.

[46] The finality of the destinies is repeated here:

> And these **shall go away** [from *apérchomai* {565} from *apó* {575}, from; and *érchomai* {2064}, to come or go, to depart] into everlasting **punishment** [from *kólasis* {2851}] but the righteous into everlasting **life** [from *zōē* {2222}]. (a.t.)

In the context, everlasting punishment is contrasted with everlasting life, which means that it cannot be life. The sheeps' sanctification will be complete in heaven. They glory in "eternal life," that mature state of perfect love for God.

The double use of the preposition "into," especially in conjunction with the local verb *apérchomai*, to depart, implies that "life" and "punishment" are places. Of course, this is given elsewhere in Scripture when, for example, hell is likened to a valley (Isa. 30:33; Jer. 7:31); a furnace (Matt. 13:42, 50; Rev. 9:2); a lake (Rev. 19:20; 20:10); or simply "this **place** [*tópos* {5117}] of torment" (Luke 16:28). Similarly, heaven is spoken of as a house with many "mansions" that Christ has prepared for His own (John 14:2, 3).

CHAPTER

26

❧

The Plot to Kill Jesus
(26:1–5; Mark 14:1, 2; Luke 22:1, 2; John 11:45–53)

[1, 2] The When Jesus finished this extended teaching on future events, He told the disciples about His impending death.

And it came about as Jesus finished all these sayings, He said to His disciples, "You know [*oídate*, from *eídō* {1492}, to know intuitively {see v. 24}] that after two days the Passover is celebrated, and the Son of man will be delivered to be crucified." (a.t.)

It was now almost the "**Passover**" (*páscha* [3957]), an important festival that commemorated God's sparing the Jews through atonement when He destroyed the firstborn of the Egyptians. This was celebrated yearly on the fourteenth day of the month of Nisan (April). At the festival, the Jews sacrificed paschal lambs to God to atone for sin, usually one lamb for every ten people (cf. Ex. 12; Lev. 23:5; Num. 9:2–5). According to the historian Josephus, 256,500 lambs were sacrificed in Jerusalem between the ninth and eleventh hour (3 to 5 p.m. our time) on the day of celebration.

Jesus here predicted that He would be crucified. When the Lamb (*amnós* [286], a sacrificial lamb not *arníon* [721], a living lamb) of God would take away the sin of the world (John 1:29, 36) through His own sacrifice on the cross, thousands of innocent lambs would no longer have to be sacrificed. The shed blood of the perfect Lamb of God is sufficient to take away the sins of those who confess them and ask for mercy and deliverance (1 John 1:7).

Jesus now informed His disciples about what was going to take place soon when He would be **betrayed** (from *paradídōmi* [3860], to deliver over; from the preposition *pará* [3844], denoting proximity; and *dídōmi* [1325], to give). Judas Iscariot betrayed Him to the Jewish leaders, and they delivered Him to the Roman authorities. Only the Romans had the authority to put anyone to death, which, in the Roman judicial system, was by crucifixion.

Although Judas planned the betrayal for evil, God used it for good by delivering the Son of man into the hands of sinners to be crucified for our sins. Christ said in Matthew 26:53 that He could have called twelve legions of angels to His rescue. Instead, He willingly died in our place for our sins. Satan used Judas as his instrument.

The purpose for Jesus' delivery into the hands of godless men is given in the preposition *eis* (1519), **into** (or unto), and the aorist passive infinitive of *stauróō* (4717), **to crucify**; thus, He was delivered "**to be crucified**" (Matt. 26:2).

The manner of death was divinely predetermined. Ultimately, Jesus' enemies did not determine how He would die; but the triune God did make the decision. From a strictly human viewpoint, Jesus might have been put to death in another manner. But through crucifixion He shed His blood without which "[there] is no remission" of sins (Heb. 9:22). Little did these evil people realize that they were acting out God's foreordination (see Acts 2:23; 4:27, 28).

[3–5] **Then assembled together the chief priests, and the scribes, and the elders of the people, unto the palace of the high priest, who was called Caiaphas, and consulted that they might take Jesus by subtilty, and kill him. But they said, Not on the feast day, lest there be an uproar among the people.**

Those who "assembled together" sought to apprehend Jesus that morning, but they were afraid of the teeming mobs (from *óchlos* [3793], an unorganized crowd) that had poured into Jerusalem for the Passover.

Many people considered Jesus to be a prophet (Matt. 21:46). Previously, the Sanhedrin had sent officers to arrest Him, but the officers were so impressed by His teaching that they decided to do nothing (John 7:32, 45–49). Verse 4 tells us that the Sanhedrin had previously met unofficially to plan some subtle (from *dólos* [1388], deceit and trickery) way to have Jesus taken into custody. For them, their plan used craft and deceit; for Jesus, the Father's plan was predetermined. Prophets had been predicted God's plan many times and for many years.

Jesus Is Anointed Prior to His Burial
(26:6–13; Mark 14:3–9; John 12:1–8)

Jesus traveled approximately two miles from the temple to Bethany—a familiar town where Lazarus, Mary, and Martha had extended hospitality to Him.

[6] Now when Jesus was in Bethany, in the house of Simon the leper . . . (a.t.).

Matthew uses the participle "**having come**" (*genoménou*, the aorist middle deponent participle of *gínomai* [1096], to begin to be) to emphasize Jesus' arrival. Mark 14:3, on the other hand, uses "being" (*óntos*, the present participle of *eimí* [1510], to be), starting his narrative after Jesus had been in Bethany for a while.

Jesus probably stayed in the home of Lazarus, Mary, and Martha during this time, even though He visited the house of Simon the leper. We can speculate from these visits that Jesus sought comfort in the presence of these godly friends, knowing that His terrible suffering and death were imminent.

Comparing and studying the three passages concerning Jesus' anointing and the time He was in Bethany, we can assume that He stayed in Bethany six full days, with frequent visits to the temple in Jerusalem. We cannot be sure on which day the anointing took place since no text gives us this information. John 12:1, 2 tells us that while Jesus was there, "they made him a supper." The meal was served in the house of Simon the leper. This may have been a large dinner party to which local residents were invited. Lazarus and his sisters were there, and Martha helped with the serving (John 12:2).

Simon is a common name in the New Testament (Matt. 4:18; 10:4; 13:55; 27:32; Luke 6:15; 7:40, 43, 44; John 6:71; Acts 8:9, 13, 18, 24; 9:43). The only distinction given to this Simon is that he was a leper, and probably Jesus had healed him. In a small community like Bethany, a miraculous cure of an otherwise incurable disease would not be easily forgotten. Possibly this Simon was the leper Jesus healed in Galilee. He may have moved to Judea where Jesus visited him from time to time. We can only surmise the fellowship the Cleanser would have with the cleansed on these occasions. The former leper would be accepted in the community of the small town of Bethany.

[7] Suddenly, a woman appeared:

> There came unto him a woman having an **alabaster box** [*alábastron* {211}, a small vessel carved from alabaster stone, a valuable marble] of **very precious** [from *barútimos* {927}, highly valuable; from *barús* {926}, heavy, weighty; and *timé* {5092}, honor, attributed value] ointment [from *múron* {3464}].

The word *timé* denotes high cost but sentimental value as well. The ointment was nard ([3487]; Mark 14:3; John 12:3), a special oil derived from a plant grown in India.

Matthew does not identify the woman, but John records "Mary" (John 12:3), undoubtedly the sister of Lazarus and Martha. Matthew and Mark inform us that the woman anointed Jesus' head, whereas John mentions the feet. The body parts don't contradict, however. Mary obviously anointed both, perhaps pouring oil on Jesus' head and rubbing some on His feet with her hands. Washing another person's feet was a common courtesy shown to guests since most traveling was done on foot. The parts of the body selected agree with the theological purpose of the Gospel writers. Matthew emphasizes Christ as King (the head), whereas John emphasizes Christ as the divine servant (the feet, cf. John 1:14; Phil. 2:6, 7).

[8, 9] The disciples are outraged at what seemed to be a total waste of money:

> But when his disciples **saw** [from *horáō* {3708}, to perceive] it, they had indignation, saying, To what purpose is this **waste** [*apóleia* {684}, loss, both physical and spiritual]? For this **ointment** [*múron* {3464}, myrrh] **might have been sold** [from *pipráskō* {4097}, to sell] for much, and given to the poor.

Although all the disciples became indignant, John 12:4 tells that Judas spoke up for the group. Ironically, Judas had been designated to hold the money for the group (John 12:6) and perhaps stirred up the grumbling among the rest.

[10, 11] Jesus immediately rebuked the disciples:

> When Jesus **knew** [*gnoús*, the aorist participle of *ginóskō* {1097}, to experientially know; "having known"] it, He said unto them, Why do you give **troubles** [*kópous*, the accusative plural of *kópos* {2873}, toil, labor, trouble] to this woman, for she has wrought a good work on Me. For you have the poor always with you, but Me you have not always. (a.t.)

The poor would continue throughout the present age, while opportunities to show love to Jesus "in the days of his flesh" (Heb. 5:7) would soon be over.

[12, 13] Jesus explained further:

> For in that **she hath poured** [from *bállō* {906}, to cast or place] this ointment on my body, she did it for my **burial** [from *entaphiázō* {1779}, to entomb]. **Verily** [*amén* {281}, truly] **I say** [*légō* {3004}, to speak intelligently] unto you, **Wheresoever** [*hópou* {3699}, where; and *eán* {1437}, if] this gospel **shall be preached** [from *kērússō* {2784}, to proclaim] in the whole world, there shall also this, that this woman hath done, be told **for** [*eis* {1519}, unto, for] a **memorial** [*mnēmósunon* {3422}, a reminder] of her.

This woman is still remembered for her single act of humble devotion. Jesus rewarded her by placing the event in Scripture. Some actions, seemingly nominal, done only once, and criticized by the majority, live forever. This anointing for burial tells us that Jesus' death was approaching.

Judas Volunteers to Betray Jesus
(26:14–16; Mark 14:10, 11; Luke 22:3–6)

Although Judas was numbered with the Twelve (John 6:70), he was never really one of them (John 13:18, cf. 1 John 2:19). In His intercessory prayer, Jesus said, "While I was with them in the world, I kept them in Your name: those that You gave Me I have kept, and not even one [*oudeis* {3762}] of them is lost but the son of perdition in order that the Scripture might be fulfilled" (John 17:12; a.t.).

Judas was never a true disciple of Jesus. He guarded and probably managed the disciples' funds (John 12:6; 13:29), a great temptation to any stranger to the grace of God. The fact that money was a problem for Judas was evident in his decision to profit from the chief priests' hatred and jealousy of Christ.

[14] Judas "went unto the chief priests," and Luke adds that Satan entered him (Luke 22:3). Later, Paul said that Satan energizes all the "sons of disobedience" (Eph. 2:2; a.t.).

Jesus knew that Judas was dishonest but tolerated him to the very end. Yet John explains that "Jesus knew from the beginning who they were that believed not, and who should betray him" (John 6:64).

[15] The verb translated "**will deliver**" is the future of *paradídōmi* (3860), to deliver over, the same verb translated "**betrayed**" in verse 2.

Implied in the meaning of betrayal is a victim who is close to the betrayer. Acquaintances betray, not strangers; familiarity is not only presupposed but desirable for efficiency. Judas had lived close to Jesus for over three years, yet he had never truly repented, choosing instead to identify with the "mystery of lawlessness" (2 Thess. 2:7; a.t.).

And **they covenanted** [from *hístēmi* {2476}, to establish, agree] with him for thirty pieces of **silver** [from *argúrion*, a silver coin].

[16] From the time Judas approached the Jewish leaders to negotiate his wage,

he sought **opportunity** [from *eukairía* {2120}, favorable occasion, proper time] to **betray** [*paradṓ*, the aorist active subjunctive of *paradídomi* [3860], to deliver over] him.

The conspicuous aorist tense of "to betray" emphasizes Judas' attempt to betray once for all, that is, to get the job done.

The Last Supper (26:17–30; Mark 14:12–26; Luke 22:7–23; John 13:21–30; 1 Cor. 11:23–25)

[17] Passover was a weeklong celebration that started on Thursday in A.D. 30 with the feast of "**unleavened bread**" called *ázuma*, the neuter plural of *ázumos* (106), unleavened. The verb *zumóō* (2220) means to cause fermentation.

Both feasts, commemorating the Hebrews' liberation from slavery in Egypt, were celebrated in Jerusalem. The Passover began on Thursday after six in the evening when ceremonially the new day began with each Jewish home searching for leaven (used to make dough rise) in their houses and removing it. It takes much less time to make unleavened dough than leavened. The shortened preparation and baking period was to remind the Jews of their hasty departure from Egypt (Ex. 12:33, 34).

Because of its permeating effect, leaven became a symbol of the spread of evil (Matt. 16:6, 11, 12) and also of the kingdom of heaven (Matt. 13:33) throughout the world.

The word "**passover**" (see v. 2) comes from the Hebrew *pesaḥ* (6453, OT), derived from the Hebrew verb *pāsaḥ* (6452, OT), to leap over. When the angel of death saw the blood of the slain lamb sprinkled on the lintel and doorposts of a house, he would "pass over" that house, sparing its firstborn children (Ex. 12:27, 28).

The disciples asked Jesus, "Where do You want us to prepare for You to eat the Passover?" (a.t.); similarly, Mark 14:12: "that You may eat the Passover?" (a.t.). They knew Jesus wanted to share the Passover meal with them, but they were not expecting Him to lay down His life as the Passover Lamb in a few short hours.

[18] Jesus told them to "go into the city." Jerusalem was crowded during this time, but the Passover had to be celebrated inside the city.

Jesus sent them "**to** [*prós* {4314}, toward] **such** [*deína* {1170}, an indefinite pronoun used when a person does not wish to disclose a name] a man [not in the original]." Though from a human perspective Jesus had probably not made prior arrangements, the triune God foreknew the person and the meeting. Luke 22:8–12 tells us that Peter and John went into the city to meet and follow a man bearing a pitcher of water into a house. Jesus told them to tell this person that the Master was going to eat the Passover meal with His disciples at his house:

The **Master** [*didáskalos* {1320}, teacher, the title by which Jesus was acknowledged] saith, My **time** [*kairós* {2540}, season, appointed time] is **at hand** [*eggús* {1451}, near, ready]; I will keep the passover at thy house with my disciples.

[19] The disciples then

. . . did as Jesus **appointed** [from *suntássō* {4929}, arranged together; from *sún* {4862}, together; and *tássō* {5021}, to order, arrange] them; and **they made ready** [from *hetoimázō* {2090}, to prepare, to make ready] the passover. (a.t.)

[20, 21] In the **evening** (*opsías* [3798], the close of the day just before darkness), Jesus ate supper with His disciples within the city limits. While eating, He addressed the disciples:

Verily [*amēn* {281}] **I say** [*légō* {3004}, I say intelligently and firmly] unto you, that one **of** [from *ek* {1537}, out of from within, i.e., the circle of disciples] you **shall betray** [from *paradídōmi* {3860}, to betray or deliver] me.

In the strongest manner, Jesus asserted that one of those nearest to Him would betray Him.

[22] Only Matthew records the fact that the disciples became "**exceedingly** [*sphódra* {4970}] **sorrowful** [from *lupéō* {3076}, to make someone sorrowful or grieved]" twice during the latter part of Christ's ministry (here and in 17:23). In 17:23, they became sorrowful because of Jesus' predicted death. The fact that Jesus promised that He would be raised from the dead should have comforted the true disciples, but they did not understand this.

Now the true disciples became sorrowful because Jesus told them that one of them would betray Him. "**Every one**" (*hékastos* [1538], each) individually asked whether he himself were the one. They all use the negative *mē*, which in Koine Greek, is used in a direct question to indicate an expected answer of no. "It is not I, is it?" They all felt certain they could never stoop so low.

[23] Jesus did not answer them directly but said,

He that dips [*embápsas*, the aorist participle of *embáptō* {1686}, to dip in; from *en* {1722}, into; and *báptō* {911}, to dip; thus, proleptically, "the one having dipped" or "the one who dips {once}"] his hand with Me in the **dish** [from *trúblion* {5165}, a bowl or dish], the same **shall betray** [from *paradídōmi* {3860}, to deliver] me. (a.t.)

John tells us that Jesus originally spoke these words only to John himself as he leaned back onto Jesus' breast as they reclined at the table (John 13:22–26).

[24] Here in Matthew, Christ explained that the "the Son of Man goeth" to conform to Scripture "as it has been written [*gégraptai*, the perfect passive of *gráphō* {1125} a.t.]." But in Luke 22:22 Christ gave a more specific reason why "the Son of Man goeth," using *hōrisménon* (the perfect passive participle of *horízō* [3724], to define or specify), "as it is specified" or "defined [by the Father]" (a.t.).

Not every detail was prophesied, however, as for example, Judas' name. Psalm 41:9 says rather generally, "Yes, My own familiar friend whom I trusted, who ate My bread, has lifted up his heel against Me" (a.t.). Does this mean that Jesus on this occasion became aware that Judas was going to betray Him? No, the Scripture says, "**Jesus knew** [from *oída* {1492}] **from the beginning** . . . who would betray Him" (John 6:64; a.t.).

Oída, the perfect (used as a present) of *eídō* (1492), to know innately, is also the verb used in John 13:18: "I know whom I have chosen." This innate knowledge contrasts with *ginōskō* (1097), a knowledge acquired by experience. Jesus knew when He chose His disciples who among them were genuine and who were not.

In John 13:18, Jesus stressed a personal knowledge based on prior choice:

> I speak not of all of you. **I know** [*oída*, from *eídō* {1492}, to know innately; there is no indication here that there was ever a time that the Lord did not know] whom **I selected** [from *eklégomai* {1586}, to select for myself]. (a.t.)

There is no verb *eklégō* in the active voice. All the references in the New Testament are from *eklégomai* (Mark 3:20; Luke 6:13; 9:35; 10:42; 14:7; John 6:70; 13:18; 15:16, 19; Acts 1:2, 24; 6:5; 13:17; 15:7, 22, 25; 1 Cor. 1:27, 28; Eph. 1:4; James 2:5). In John 13:18, Jesus spoke of the true disciples, not of Judas. Thus, Jesus' personal knowledge of His disciples was not based on any historic experience but on innate divine foreknowledge. Nevertheless, He pronounced a "**woe**" (*ouaí* [3759]) on the one who would betray Him, the same threat spoken repeatedly to the scribes and Pharisees in Matthew 23:13–16, 23. The two Greek verbs "**goeth**" (from *hupágo* [5217]) and "**is betrayed**" (from *paradídōmi* [3860]) indicate deliberate actions. What Jesus did ("goeth") and Judas did ("betrayed"), they both did willingly.

Jesus concluded the sad story of Judas by saying, "It would have been **good** [from *kalós* {2570}] for that man if he had not **been born** [*egennéthē*, the aorist passive of *gennáō* {1080}, to give birth]" (a.t.).

"Good" referred to Judas' [that man's] good; in other words, it would have been better for Judas if he had never been born. Judas' actions were disastrous to his own destiny. Had he died in the womb, his destiny would have been far better than his living to betray the innocent Son of God.

[25] Judas repeated the disciples' question but with one conspicuous difference. They addressed him as "Lord" (v. 22), whereas Judas addressed Jesus as "Master" or "Rabbi." To him, Jesus was just a teacher, not a personal lord and certainly not the Lord.

Jesus answered, "Thou hast said," confirming the fact but not making an accusation. We are not told that after this exposure, Judas left Jesus and the disciples immediately (John 13:30).

Some believe Jesus distributed the bread and wine after Judas left. But how then could Judas have dipped the bread in the dish with Jesus? Jesus said, "The hand of him that betrayeth me is with me on the table" after He distributed bread and wine according to Luke 22:19–22.

Local churches are called to observe the Lord's Supper in remembrance (from *anámnēsis* [364], recollection, memorial) of what He did to take away the sins of believers (Luke 22:19). Furthermore, Paul states that no one should participate in this event unworthily (1 Cor. 11:29). Those who partake of the Lord's Supper valuelessly or worthlessly repeat Judas' spite toward God's redemption. Paul says we should approve ourselves before partaking of the elements (1 Cor. 11:28) to avoid judgment (11:31).

If Jesus did not exclude Judas from participation in this meal, no minister should limit the Lord's Supper to those he thinks are worthy of it. In a pure sense, no one is worthy of what Jesus did, but faith in the Lord's shed blood is a reverence that values Christ's sacrifice. Nevertheless, every minister of Christ should warn people to examine themselves so they participate worthily as eleven of the Twelve Apostles did (1 Cor. 11:28).

[26] Jesus took in His hand a "**loaf of bread**" (from *ártos* [740], bread, a loaf) and blessed it. To commemorate Passover, this was a flat disk of bread made without yeast.

The Textus Receptus and the United Bible Society version have "**blessed**" (from *eulogéō* [2127], to bless or speak well [to]; from *eu* [2095], good, well; and *légō* [3004], to speak), while the Majority Text has "**thanked**" (from *eucharistéō* [2168], to thank). The two verbs are related, both rooted in the preposition *eu*, good, with gracing (*charístō*) simply being the content of the speaking (*légō*). "To speak well [or good]" and "to bless" are the same action.

Jesus then "broke" (from *kláō* [2806], to break into small pieces) the bread and "gave" (from *dídōmi* [1325], to give) it to the disciples, and said, "Take, eat; this is my body." The broken bread symbolized His body that was about to be sacrificed on the cross.

[27] Jesus then blessed the cup of wine. During the Passover feast, four cups of wine represented four promises given to the Jews prior to their exodus:

[1] I will bring you out from under the burdens of the Egyptians, and I will rid you out of their bondage, and I will redeem you with a stretched out arm, and with great judgments: [2] And I will take you to me for a people, and I will be to you a God: and ye shall know that I am the LORD your God, which bringeth you out from under the burdens of the Egyptians. [3] And I will bring you in unto the land, concerning the which I did swear to give it to Abraham, to Isaac, and to Jacob; and [4] I will give it you for an heritage: I am the LORD. (Ex. 6:6–8)

[28] Jesus then said,

For this is my blood of the new testament, which **is shed** [*ekchunómenon*, the present passive participle of *ekchúnō* {1632}, to pour out, "which is being poured out," spoken proleptically] for many **for** [*eis* {1519}, in order that, for the purpose of] the **remission** [from the noun *áphesis* {859}, removal, forgiveness, putting away; from the verb *aphíēmi* {863}, to send away, forgive] of sins.

The blood of Jesus still coursed through His veins when He spoke these words, but it was soon poured out on the cross. It would atone for all sins, no matter what kind. Jesus did not mean that the symbol, the wine itself, would be shed to forgive sins, only the reality behind the symbol—His physical blood, for "without shedding of blood [there] is no remission [*áphesis*]" (Heb. 9:22).

In John 6:54 Jesus said, "Whoever eats My flesh and drinks My blood has eternal life" (a.t.). But this should be taken in light of the immediate context: "It is the Spirit that gives life; the flesh profits nothing: the words that I speak to you are spirit and are life" (v. 63; a.t.). Accordingly, "Man does not live on bread alone but on every word that proceeds from the mouth of God" (Matt. 4:4; Luke 4:4; a.t.). The Word of God is food to us, and we should treat it as such.

Metaphors based on eating foods and drinking fluids are common in the Bible. Unbelievers are said to have "drunk of the wine of the wrath of [the whore of Babylon's] fornication" (Rev. 18:3); to have "blood to drink" (Rev. 16:6); and they would drink of "the wine of the wrath of God" (Rev. 14:10). In 1 Corinthians 10:2–4, Paul tells us that those baptized into Moses at the crossing of the Red Sea drank from the spiritual rock that was Christ. No one would question the metaphorical nature of these statements and, in light of their extensive use throughout the Bible, it is foolish to press for relative literalism here. We say relative, because even here an absolute literalism would require Christ's physical body and blood—not so-called "converted" bread and wine.

Nothing we do materially can result in our regeneration. Faith, specifically "in his blood" (Rom. 3:25), secures eternal life. Paul says, "For by grace you are saved through faith; and that not of yourselves: it is the gift [*dōron* {1435}] of God" (Eph. 2:8; a.t.). Physical bread and wine cannot propitiate the wrath of God. Only faith in Jesus' atoning death produces the legal remission of sins and sanctification. Jesus qualified this as the blood of

> ... the **new** [from *kainós* {2537}, qualitatively new, i.e., of a different kind, no longer the blood of lambs and bulls that could not take away sin; Heb. 10:4] **testament** [from *diathḗkē* {1242}; a person's will to his heirs upon his or her death; see author's *Complete Word Study Dictionary: New Testament*, 424–428].

The United Bible Society and most modern English versions, following a few older manuscripts, do not have the adjective "new" (from *kainós*) but only "the blood of the testament [or covenant]." But in Luke 22:20, Christ clearly said, "This cup is the new testament in my blood, which is shed for you." The Father wills to His heirs eternal life—His own life—on the death of His Son. Believers become "joint-heirs with Christ" (Rom. 8:17, cf. v. 29; Heb. 2:11). The life of God in humans was lost when Adam sinned at the beginning of history. In the Old Testament, it was regained by faith in the promises of God.

That is what Abraham did (John 8:56). He looked forward to what Christ came to do as we look back to what He did. A new chronology would have given us a *néa* (from *néos* [3501]) subsequent but not qualitatively distinct) testament, but we have a *kainḗ* (from *kainós*, qualitatively new) testament (Luke 22:20). What is new is based on the death of the Testator, Jesus Christ.

Why does Matthew 26:28 say "for many" (1 Tim. 2:6; 4:10; cf. 2 Cor. 5:17)? Did Jesus Christ in becoming flesh (John 1:14) die only for many or for all? He died for all by giving all an opportunity to believe, and among the "all," we find those who did believe, those who do believe, those who will believe, and those who did not or will not believe. But this latter group refuses to accept His free gift of salvation and thus do not obtain it. That is why Paul, in 1 Timothy 4:10, calls Him "the Saviour of all men, specially of those that believe."

The present participle, "**being shed**"—reflecting once again Jesus' fluctuation between the timeless plans of the Father and the temporal realizations—does not contradict the once-for-all (*hápax* [530]; Heb. 9:28; 1 Pet. 3:18) nature of the atonement. Jesus does not die again (Rom. 6:9, 10; Heb. 6:4–6).

[29] The single "**not**" in English translates the two Greek words *ou* (3756) and *mḗ* (3361). The two combined gives the strongest negative possible in Greek: never at any time, never in any way, absolutely not.

The aorist tense of the verb "**drink**" (*píō*, the aorist subjunctive of *pínō* [4095], to drink) implies "at any one time." "Until that day" brings us to the return of Christ. Jesus did not tell us just how this new (from *kainós*, qualitatively new) commemoration will be celebrated.

In 1 Corinthians 11:26, the apostle Paul tells us that whenever (*hosákis* [3740]) we celebrate the Lord's Supper, it shows forth His death till (*áchris* [891], continually) He comes. This celebration will extend through the age of grace, until Christ returns in glory (Matt. 25:31) to create His new (from *kainós*) heaven and a new (from *kainós*) earth (Rev. 21:1, 4). A new order will supplant even death.

[30] When Jesus and His disciples finished their last meal together, they "**sang a hymn**" (from *humnéō* [5214], to praise with a hymn), possibly from Psalms 113—118, which the Jews called their *Hallel*, from the Hebrew verb "to praise" (2 Chr. 7:6; Ezra 3:11). Psalm 114 especially celebrated Israel's exodus from Egypt.

The Prophecy of Peter's Denial
(26:31–35; Mark 14:27–31;Luke 22:31–34; John 13:36–38)

Jesus now gave His disciples more detailed prophecies concerning coming events. Only God could predict precisely such a vast number of events and make no mistakes.

[31] The word "**all**" (from *pás* [3956]) emphasizes the totality of the believing disciples, the sum of every individual. "**Shall be offended**" is translated from *skandalisthḗsesthe*, the future passive of *skandalízō* (4624), to offend or scandalize.

The disciples were going to be offended with Christ because they neither understood nor believed the gospel enough to commit to the point of death. And for Jews in general, death could never be harmonized with the Messiah's predicted rule over Israel's enemies. Peter was so appalled at the idea of a dead Messiah that he rebuked Christ (Matt. 16:21–23).

Jesus then assured them that His coming arrest and death were within His Father's sovereign purpose by quoting the prophet Zechariah: "I will **smite** [from *patássō* {3960}, to strike] the shepherd" (cf. Zech. 13:7). It was the Trinity's plan that Jesus be smitten. Here for the first time in the New Testament, the strong word *patássō*, to strike, is used (see also Mark 14:27).

Jesus called Himself the "good [*kalós* {2570}, intrinsically good] shepherd" (John 10:11, 14), and Peter later refers to Him as the "chief Shepherd" (from *archipoimḗn* [750]) in 1 Peter 5:4. The Lamb of God who sits on God's throne will shepherd believers by guiding them to fountains of living waters and wiping away their tears (Rev. 7:17).

[32] The scattering of the sheep was only temporary as seen in the immediate disjunctive clause, "But after I am **risen** [from *egeírō* {1453}, to raise] again, I will go ahead of you into Galilee" (a.t.). This is the only time a living person made an appointment to meet others after death and kept it.

[33] Peter understood scattering to mean disowning Christ. Although this is exactly what happened when the threat of death came and Jesus' followers ran away (see v. 56), Peter was confident that he would never desert His Lord. Peter remained nearby but disowned Christ publicly.

At this point, Peter arrogantly set himself apart from the other disciples:

> **Though** [*ei* {1487}, the subjective "if"] all men **shall be offended** [from *skandalízō* {4624}] **because of** [*en* {1722}, in] thee, yet will **I** [*egṓ* {1473}, an emphatic pronoun] **never** [*oudépote* {3763}, never, not even once, derived from *oudé* {3761}, "not"; and *poté* {4218}, at any time] be offended.

[34] Jesus' response to this indicated that He knew every one of His disciples, particularly Peter, more intimately than they knew themselves. Peter was a bit of a braggart, and Jesus did not want him to think he was superior to the other disciples. Besides, he had missed the point. Zechariah had prophesied that not only would the Shepherd be smitten but the sheep would "be scattered." In other words, Peter certainly would scatter along with the rest of the disciples. This in fact was what happened, as we read in Mark 14:50: "And they all forsook him, and fled."

Jesus needed to deflate Peter's ego, knowing his natural tendency to preserve his physical life: "Truly I say to you that in this night, before the cock crows, you will deny Me three times" (a.t.). The verb "**deny**" is the Greek *aparnḗsē*, the future middle of *aparnéomai* (533), to deny, from the preposition *apó* (575), from; and *arnéomai* (720), to disavow, abnegate, contradict. The middle voice shows reflexive action—denial is done for the sake of the one denying; there is some benefit to be gained. This compound verb is the same word Jesus used in Matthew 16:24: "If any man will come after me, let him deny [*aparnēsásthō*, the aorist imperative of *aparnéomai*] himself, and take up his cross, and follow me." To avow Christ, we must disavow ourselves—a straight exchange. The verb *aparnéomai* presupposes a previous attachment to Christ.

This compound verb was used here in verse 34 and again in verses 35 and 75: "Before the cock crow, thou shalt deny [from *aparnéomai*] me thrice."

Interestingly, in verses 70 and 72, the simple verb *arnéomai* is used: "But he denied [from *arnéomai*] before them all, saying, I know not what thou sayest. . . . And again he denied [also from *arnéomai*] with an oath, I do not know [*oída*, from *eídō* {1492}, to know, recognize] the man." These words advance far beyond the affirmation of a severed relationship with Christ, such as, I no longer know the man. Peter acted as if he had never heard of Jesus, denying even an acquaintance, let alone familiarity—an amazing state to end up in after boasting that he would never be offended under any circumstances.

[35] Peter carried his boast to the point of death:

> And if **it is necessary** [from *deí* {1163}] for me to die with you, yet will I **not** [the two negatives *ou* {3756} and *mé* {3361} combined as an intensive combination meaning "absolutely not," never, at any time] deny thee. (a.t.)

Peter used strong language here to portray his courage under attack. How little he knew himself, and how little did the rest: "**Likewise** [*homoíōs* {3668}, in a similar manner] also said all the disciples."

Jesus in Gethsemane
(26:36–56; Mark 14:32–52; Luke 22:39–53; John 18:1–12)

[36, 37] Jesus and the eleven remaining disciples walked from the temple area to a "**place**" (*chōríon* [5564], an enclosed area, a plot of ground, a field less than an acre in size) called **Gethsemane** (*Gethsēmanē* [1068], oil press) at the foot of the Mount of Olives. It was between midnight and morning. At the entrance, Jesus said to His disciples,

> Sit here while I go and pray there. And having taken with Him Peter and the two sons of Zebedee, He **began to be sorrowful** [from *lupéō* {3076}, to grieve] and **very heavy** [from *adēmonéō* {85}; cf. Mark 14:33; Phil. 2:26]. (a.t.)

We do not know the exact derivation of the verb *adēmonéō*, but it is always used with verbs that express grief or sorrow. Here it is used with *lupéomai*, to sorrow, and in Mark 14:33 it is used with the verb *ekthambéomai* (1568), to be distressed, astonished, or greatly amazed. Paul writes to the Philippians about how Epaphroditus had nearly died while he was with him in Rome (Phil. 2:26–30; 4:18), adding, "He **longed** [from *epipothéō* {1971}, to desire earnestly] after you all, and was **full of heaviness** [from *adēmonéō*], because that ye had heard that he had been sick" (Phil. 2:26).

John records some additional words of Jesus as He contemplated His approaching death: "Now my soul has been troubled [*tetáraktai*, the perfect passive of *tarássō* {5015}, to be agitated]; and what shall I say? Father, save Me from this hour? But for this reason came I unto this hour" (John 12:27; a.t.).

[38] Jesus had selected three disciples—Peter, James, and John—to share His deepest sorrow. It was important for them to learn about suffering for the sake of the kingdom of God:

> My soul is **exceeding sorrowful** [*perílupos* {4036} from *perí* {4012}, all around; and *lúpē* {3077}, sorrow, grief; therefore, encompassed with and hemmed in by grief; cf. Mark 14:34], even unto death: **tarry ye** [from *ménō* {3306}, to remain, stay] here, and **watch** [from *grēgoréō* {1127} from *egeírō* {1453}, to arise, arouse, to watch, refrain from sleep] with me.

This was no ordinary sorrow because Jesus was not facing an ordinary death. Now as He began to bear unimaginable suffering, Jesus wanted these three disciples to remain and watch with Him as He entered the terrible sorrow and agony of bearing the sins of the world (cf. Mark 14:34, 37, 38).

[39] It was inevitable, however, that the "Man of Sorrows" face this alone, so eventually "he went a little farther." Jesus then "fell on his face, and **prayed** [from *proseúchomai* {4336}, to pray], saying, O my Father." God was Father to Jesus in a unique way. Even though the Lord Jesus taught His disciples to pray, "Our Father," as the Son of God, He stood in a completely different relationship to the Father.

"If it is possible, let this cup pass from Me: **nevertheless** [*plēn* {4133}] not as **I will** [*thélō* {2309}, to intend, to purpose] but as You will" (a.t.). Though He would not hesitate to accomplish the purpose for which He was sent, Jesus was not looking forward to the suffering associated with the death that lay before Him. From a human perspective, He had no prior experience of being "forsaken" (Matt. 27:46) by a Father whom He knew "was able to save him from death" (Heb. 5:7). Bearing the sins of the world was not going to be an easy event, to say the least.

[40] When Jesus returned to the three disciples, He found them "**sleeping**" (from *katheúdō* [2518], to fall asleep; used here as elsewhere as an antonym of *grēgoréō* [1127], to watch, stay awake, be alert).

Though He spoke to Peter directly, indirectly He addressed all three with the plural "ye": "What, **could ye** [from *ischúō* {2480}, to be able naturally] not **watch** [from *grēgoréō*] with me one hour?"

[41] Jesus had called the three disciples to watch for a short time. His question now implied that this was a reasonable request. Perhaps if they had

comprehended Jesus' mission of redemption, they would have mustered the energy to stay awake. Jesus appropriately reminded them that special tasks that require fighting against natural inclinations of the body such as fatigue require prayer for supernatural power: "**Watch** [from *grēgoréō*] and **pray** [from *proseúchomai*, to pray]"—that is, for yourselves. Jesus never asked other people to pray for Him.

The need was specific: "that **ye enter** [*eisélthēte*, the aorist subjunctive of *eisérchomai* {1525}] not into temptation." Temptation is always present, especially when we are tired. This explains the use of the aorist tense—to highlight those particular times when we are weak.

What "**temptation**" (from *peirasmós* [3986]) did Jesus warn His disciples about? They would be tempted to avoid suffering, the escape route Satan offered Jesus in the wilderness. Jesus clarified this in the words that follow:

> The spirit **indeed** [*mén* {3303}, on the one hand, forming a contrast with *dé* {1161}, "but" which follows] **is willing** [*próthumon* {4289} from *pró*, forward; and *thumós* {2372}, mind, temperament, passion, predisposition; cf. Mark 14:38], **but** [*dé*] the **flesh** [*sárx* {4561}] is **weak** [*asthenḗs* {772}, strengthless].

Here we observe the fundamental struggle between the nature that resists God (flesh) and the nature that responds to Him (spirit), as Paul graphically describes in the entire chapter of Romans 7. Our spirits may be willing to obey the Lord, but the flesh that God desires to kill (from *thanatóō*, to put to death; Rom. 8:13) hinders holy living. Human nature interrupts the mechanism between willing and doing; as Paul confesses, "In me (that is, in my flesh,) dwelleth no good thing: for to will is present with me; but how to perform that which is good I find not" (Rom. 7:18).

Jesus shared our human weakness: "For though he was crucified through [*ek* [{1537}, out of, from within] weakness [from *asthéneia* {769}], yet he liveth by the power of God. For we also are weak in him, but we shall live with him by the power of God toward you" (2 Cor 13:4).

[42] In His second prayer, Jesus requested,

> O my Father, if this cup may not **pass away** [from *parérchomai* {3928}, to pass near, by, or over; from *pará* {3844}, near, denoting the closest possible proximity; and *érchomai*, to come, go] from me, except I drink it, thy will be done.

Jesus knew He had to die, because this constituted the Triune God's plan of redemption. It was the very purpose for which the Word became flesh (John 1:1, 14).

Accordingly, as Jesus continued His prayer, we see a "willing spirit," a holy resolution operating against a natural repulsion to suffering: "Thy **will** [*thélēma* {2307}, accomplished will or desire] **be done** [from *gínomai* {1096}, to come to be realized].” The human nature of Christ was in full accord with the sovereign determination of the Triune God to accomplish salvation. The —*ma* suffix views its root as a completed product; thus, *thélēma* means completed or finished will.

This was not progessive thinking in Christ’s mind, an evolution from weakness to power, from doubt to faith, from sin to recovery. From His first prayer in verse 39—“not as I will [as man], but as thou wilt”—to the last concession in verse 42—“thy will be done”—Jesus determined to submit to the eternal will of the Trinity. His disciples, however, were not capable of understanding this tension within Jesus’ human will.

[43] When Jesus returned to His disciples, He found them “**sleeping**” (from *katheúdō* as in v. 40).

Since it was beyond midnight, the time they ordinarily slept, they were naturally tired. “Their eyes **were** [*ésan*, the imperfect tense of *eimí* {1510}, to be] **heavy** [from *baréō* {916} used with the imperfect indicative of *eimí* as a periphrastic tense: lit., ‘their eyes had become very heavy’].” As their eyes became heavier, it became more difficult for them to stay awake.

[44] Jesus did not wake the three disciples but left them to return to pray to His Father.

[45] When He returned this time,

He said to them, Do you **sleep** [*katheúdete*, the present active indicative or imperative] and **rest** [*anapaúesthe*, the present middle indicative or imperative of *anapaúō* {373}, to rest]? (a.t.)

There are several ways to interpret this statement. For example, since the original Greek had no punctuation marks, the indicative mood can be taken as either a declarative statement, “[I see that] you are still sleeping and resting” or as an interrogative question, “Are you still resting and sleeping?” And since the forms are the same in the present tense for the second person plural in both the indicative and imperative moods, this could also be understood as a command. “Go on sleeping and resting.” We could also combine the first and third possibilities, “You are sleeping. Go on resting now because the hour of betrayal has already arrived.”

No English versions understand these statements to be simply declarative statements. A few English versions understand both statements as commands like the King James Version. But most Greek editions and most English versions understand both statements to be questions, as we do. Why do we interpret both as questions? There are several reasons. First, Luke quotes Jesus as saying “Why [*tí* {5101}] sleep ye?” (Luke 22:46). Second, a command to sleep under conditions that had not changed—namely, temptation to sin under the threat of arrest—would contradict Jesus' prior command to remain awake and pray. His response is not a concession to sin—and falling asleep was a sin since He commanded, "Watch and pray" (v. 41)—as if He had given up. Jesus never concedes to sin in general, and here, specifically, He did not relax His imperatives to watch and pray under the pressure of persecution. Third, a command to sleep does not easily attach to what immediately follows: "Behold, the hour is at hand [for Christ to be betrayed] . . . . Rise, let us be going" (vv. 45, 46). It is unlikely Jesus wanted them to sleep for the microsecond before His command to get up.

Behold [*idoú* {2400}, the imperative of *eídon* {1492}, the aorist of *horáō* {3708}, to perceive, calling attention to the extraordinary {see Matt. 3:16}], the hour **is at hand** [from *eggízō* {1448}, to approach or has approached], and the Son of man **is betrayed** [from *paradídōmi* {3860}, to betray, deliver; "is now actually delivered"; cf. the word "smite" in v. 31 and "betrayed" {from *paradídōmi*} spoken of Judas as the human instrument] into the hands of sinners.

God the Father struck the Son for the redemption of humankind but used the evil motive and act of Judas to accomplish it. And Jesus fixed His mind on the joy (from *chará* [5479]) that lay beyond the cross (Heb. 12:2).

Jesus fully realized that sinners (from *hamartōlós* [268]) were going to crucify Him. The betrayer delivered Him into the hands of the jealous (the Jewish leaders) who in turn delivered Him over to the paranoid (the Gentile rulers threatened by His kingdom). The full gamut of sinful motives was included: personal, religious, and political.

[46] Addressing the three disciples, Jesus said,

Rise [from *egeírō*, to raise, rise, get up], **let us be going** [from *ágō* {71}, to lead, go]: **behold** [*idoú* as in v. 45], he is **at hand** [from *eggízō*, indicating that Judas had already arrived] **that doth betray** [from *paradídōmi*, to betray or deliver] me.

[47] Matthew comments that while Jesus was still speaking to His disciples,

Behold [*idoú* {1492}, as in vv. 45, 46], Judas came and with him a great **multitude** [*óchlos* {3793}, a mob, an unorganized multitude as in our English word "ochlocracy" which means mob rule] with **swords** [from *máchaira* {3162}, a slaughter knife; from which the Spanish word "machéte" is probably derived] and **staves** [from *xúlon* {3586}, a wooden club]. (a.t.)

The chief priests and elders from the Sanhedrin (vv. 14–16) sent this contingent; apparently, they prearranged everything.

[48] Judas, here infamously titled "he that **betrayed** [from *paradídōmi*] him," conspired to betray Christ with a kiss—the fatal, intimate nearness (*pará* [3844]) of betrayal (*paradídomi*).

[49] What a treacherous greeting follows:

> **Hail** [from *chaírō* {5463}, to rejoice], **Master** [*rhabbí* {4461}, master, teacher, a title of honor in the Jewish schools]; and **he kept kissing** [from *kataphiléō* {2705} from *katá* {2596}, an intensive; and *philéō* {5368}, to kiss] Him. (a.t.)

A kiss and a virtual stab in the back—perfect hypocrisy and a perfect cover-up had he not been dealing with the One who "knew from the beginning . . . who would betray Him" (John 6:64; a.t.).

[50] Jesus never called Judas "**friend**" as the King James Version translates here. The Greek word is not from *phílos* (5384), friend (from *philéō*, to befriend or love) but from *hetaíros* (2083), meaning selfish comrade (Matt. 11:16; 20:13; 22:12). (For a full comparison of these two words, see author's *The Complete Word Study Dictionary: New Testament*.)

> Why **are you come** [*párei*, the present tense of *páreimi* {3918}, to be present; from *pará*, denoting the closest possible proximity; and *eimí* {1510}, to be]? (a.t.)

We can paraphrase this question as, "What is the purpose of your coming?" Jesus, of course, who knew the answer to this question, intended only to expose Judas's hidden motives.

> Then came they, and **laid** [from *epibállō* {1911} from *epí*, upon; and *bállō* {906}, to lay, put] hands on Jesus, and **took** [from *kratéō* {2902}, to take hold, arrest] him.

[51] And, behold, one of them which were with Jesus stretched out his hand, and **drew** [from *apospáō* {645}, to draw; from *apó*, from; and *spáō* {4685}, to pull] his sword, and **struck** [from *patássō* {3960}, to smite, see v. 31] a servant of the high priest's, and **smote off** [from *aphairéō* {851}, to take off] his ear.

While three synopticists say only "one of them" (cf. Mark 14:47; Luke 22:50), John 18:10 records that Peter protectively overreacted: "Then Simon Peter having a sword drew it."

[52] Jesus disapproved of this action and said,

> **Put up again** [*apóstrepson*, the aorist tense of *apostréphō* {654}, to turn away; from *apó*, from or back again; and *stréphō* {4762}, to turn] your sword into its place: for all they that **take** [from *lambánō* {2983}] the sword shall die by the sword. (a.t.)

Jesus meant this as a general principle that those who resort to a sword to resolve problems generally end up dying in battle. He obviously does not mean that every person who draws a sword will be killed with a sword. Only hours earlier, He had reversed His earlier instruction to go out into evangelism without staves or other normal provisions (Luke 9:3). From now on, He said, each disciple, if necessary, should sell his cloak to purchase a sword for protection (Luke 22:35, 36). Not all who resort to violence die a violent death. Consider Moses, for example (Ex. 2:11, 12; Deut. 32:49, 50).

This may be a reference to capital execution by the Roman government for anyone who would raise a sword against its representatives. Those who used a sword in Israel while Rome was dominant, especially against Rome, could expect to be executed by Rome.

[53] To correct the mistaken notion that God can save only through people, Jesus asked Peter,

> Or do you think that I am not able now **to pray** [from *parakaleō* {3870}, to call upon] to my Father, and He shall presently **give** [from *parístēmi* {3936}, to place beside, to present] Me more than twelve **legions** [from *legeōn* {3003}; assuming the Lord's use of a culturally conditioned term, the average legion of Roman soldiers was between 3,000 and 6,600 soldiers. A reasonable total would be 12 × 4,800 = 57,600 of angels? (a.t.)

Nothing in Jesus' question (as we will note in our comments in the next verse) implied that "yes" was a bad or incorrect answer. Apart from a predetermined plan to redeem, the Father could have sent enough angels to rescue His Son from arrest and death. Revelation 5:11 says that the number of angels around the throne of God is "ten thousand times ten thousand [a hundred million], and thousands of thousands [millions more]." Hebrews 12:22 speaks of an "innumerable company of angels."

But the Father had planned to redeem humankind through the sacrifice of His only Son, so why should His disciples attempt to hinder that plan by rescuing their Master?

[54] The Triune Godhead predetermined Christ's death, which is why Jesus immediately added,

> How then will the Scripture be fulfilled, that thus **it is necessary** [*deí* {1163}] **to be** [from *gínomai* {1096}, to become]? (a.t.).

The atonement was necessary for the human race to be redeemed (Heb. 9:22). Judas, the high priests, and the Sanhedrin may have thought they were creating history, but in reality they were enacting the Father's plan.

Jesus wanted His disciples to understand why such a prayer was impossible for Him. His purpose in asking the question was not to imply the possibility of His praying to be rescued and being rescued but just the opposite—to prove why the prayer and the answer were impossible for Him to even consider. They were impossible because the Triune Godhead had decreed otherwise in eternity; thus, the immediate connection, "But how then? . . . [and] **it is necessary** [*deî*] to be"; that is, it must be this way because it has so been predestined from eternity past.

If the Lord Jesus had prayed to be rescued from the cross and His Father ignored Him because the plan was immutable, then Jesus would have sinned against the plan and been dragged unwillingly to the cross—not an inspiring sacrifice. This option was logically and morally impossible. Additionally, if the Father had changed His mind about atoning for sin just to comply with a cowardly request, then the immutable God would have changed. Neither alternative was scripturally or logically valid. Not only was it impossible for Jesus to pray this prayer, but it was equally impossible for the Father to change His mind about redeeming the world. A perfect plan can only be exchanged for an imperfect one. God does not make mistakes.

[55] Jesus now turned to the militant crowd who had come to the garden with Judas and said,

> Have you come out against a **thief** [from *lēstḗs* {3027}, a confrontational robber as opposed to a *kléptēs* {2812}, a stealthy thief] with swords and staves **to take** [from *sullambánō* {4815}, to grasp together, to capture by force; from *sún* {4862}, together with; and *lambánō*, to take] me? (a.t.)

The question was unanswerable. They had no excuse for their weapons because Jesus' gentle, didactic character had been publicly displayed for more than three years.

Jesus appealed to this very thing:

> **I was sitting** [*ekathezómēn*, the imperfect middle of *kathézomai* {2516}, to sit down; from *katá*, down; and *ézomai* {n.f.}, to sit] daily with you **teaching** [*didáskōn* {1321}, the present active participle] in the temple, and you did not lay hold on me. (a.t.)

The imperfect and participial verb forms add the sense of customarily, a regularity to His actions over the course of His ministry (cf. the aorist form, *etélesen*, finished, v. 1). To come at Him with such violence made little sense.

[56] "But," we read for the second time (see v. 54), God's sovereign plan stands in contrast to people's plans. The Jewish leaders might have arrested

Jesus on many occasions during the regular course of His ministry, but God's plan overruled since "his hour was not yet come" (John 7:30).

All [from *hólos* {3650}, the whole] this **was done** [*gégonen*, the perfect tense of *gínomai* [1096], to take place, become; "has taken place"], **that** [*hína* {2443}, for the purpose of, in order that] the **scriptures** [from *graphḗ* {1124}, Scripture, writing] of the prophets might be fulfilled.

What Scriptures? Certainly, Zechariah 13:7: "Awake, O sword, against my shepherd, and against the man that is my fellow, saith the LORD of hosts: smite the shepherd, and the sheep shall be scattered [cf. Matt. 26:31]: and I will turn mine hand upon the little ones."

Then the prophet Isaiah predicted, "He is despised and rejected" (53:3), and "He made his grave with the wicked . . . because he had done no violence" (53:9). Many messianic Psalms speak of the violent abuse of the anointed One. Isaiah even says, "It pleased the LORD to bruise him" (Isa. 53:10), but the entire Triune God and the human nature of Jesus were all "pleased" to accomplish redemption. What the Son of God did, He did willingly "for the joy that was set before him" (Heb. 12:2). The "joy" or "pleasure" was the redemption provided for humankind.

Matthew's point is simply that the innocent Teacher did not deserve such treatment, "but" the Triune God had so predicted that the Messiah would be hated "without a cause" (*dōreán* [1432], literally, "as a gratuitous gift," freely; from *dōréa* [1431], gift; John 15:25).

Then all the disciples **forsook** [from *aphíemi* {863}, to leave where one is and depart] him, and **fled** [from *pheúgō* {5343}, to flee, depart, go away].

It was not that the disciples did not care about what happened to Jesus; they just put their own protection first in fulfillment of Zechariah's prophecy cited above, and they, "scattered." This scattering of the disciples, abandoning Jesus and fleeing for safety, was only temporary. Jesus had told Peter, "I have prayed that your faith not fail, and when you **have turned back** [from *epistréphō* {1894}, from *epí* {1909}, to; and *stréphō* {4762}, to turn; to turn toward], strengthen your brothers" (Luke 22:32; a.t.).

From a strictly legal standpoint, Jesus could have condemned Peter for denying Him before men—that was Jesus' warning (Matt. 10:33). Moreover, He had taught the disciples much about persevering while undergoing severe trial: "Whosoever will save his life shall lose it" (Matt. 16:25), and "He that endureth to the end shall be saved" (Matt. 10:22). He had warned the disciples adequately about apostasy.

Jesus' prayer for Peter's faith to be rekindled after such an episode was pure grace. Thank God, He perpetually intercedes in prayer for His chosen people (Heb. 7:25) so that our faith does not lapse permanently.

Jesus Is Tried Before the Sanhedrin
(26:57–68; Mark 14:53–65; Luke 22:54, 55, 63–71; John 18:12–14, 19–24)

[57] Having arrested Jesus, the band from the guards of the temple (John 18:3, 12) led Him to Caiaphas the high priest where the scribes and elders were assembled in a meeting of the Sanhedrin. Caiaphas was the son-in-law of Annas, a former high priest. The members of the family were Sadducees who did not believe in the resurrection.

[58] We do not know where the disciples fled to from the garden, but we read that one of them, Peter, "**followed** [*ēkoloúthei*, the imperfect tense of *akolouthéō* {190}, was following] him **from** [*apó* {575}] **afar off** [*makróthen* {3113}, from a distance]."

Though removed from Jesus to protect himself, Peter could see that they led Him to the high priest's "**palace**" (*aulḗ* [833], an open courtyard around an edifice such as a palace). Apparently, Peter and John were the only ones brave enough to follow and enter the palace area. Peter was sitting with the servants "**to see** [from *eídō* {1492} the aorist of *horáō* {3708}, to see and perceive] the **end** [*télos* {5056}]," that is, what would become of Jesus. His courage was short-lived, however, for when he was queried, Peter denied that He knew Jesus.

[59] This was not a just court session. A court is supposed to seek truth, but this one, on the defensive from the beginning, needed and therefore "sought **false witnesses** [from *pseudomarturía* {5577}, literally, false testimony] against Jesus, **to** [*hópōs* {3704}, in order to] put him to death."

[60, 61] Unfortunately for the Jewish leaders, they "found none: yea, though many false witnesses came, yet found they none [repeated for emphasis]." Near the end of the trial, they found the incriminating testimony they wanted: "**At the last** [*hústeron* {5305}, eventually, at the very end] came two false witnesses" that agreed with one another.

These rogues quoted Jesus as saying, "**I am able** [*dúnamai* {1410}] **to destroy** [from *katalúō* {2647}, to throw down] the **temple** [from *naós* {3485}, temple sanctuary] of God and build it up in three days" (a.t.).

Ironically, by misinterpreting the "temple" Jesus had referred to, the Jews originally wrote off such ability as insane, since the temple had taken forty-six years to build (John 2:20). The testimony of these witnesses was not entirely consistent with each other, perhaps differing on when or where Jesus allegedly made this statement (Mark 14:59).

However, their testimony was similar to something Jesus actually said but not in complete agreement. In John 2:19 Jesus did say, "Destroy [*lúsate*, the second plural aorist active imperative of *lúō* {3089}, to loose, with the actual significance of, 'if you destroy,' or 'when you destroy,' but He did not say, 'I will destroy'] this temple [from *naós*], and in three days I will raise it up."

When they misinterpreted the "temple" Jesus referred to, they considered it an insane boast, since the temple was immense and had taken years to build. But Jesus spoke of the "temple of his body" (John 2:21). He used the word *naós*, which always referred to the temple sanctuary, rather than the more normal word *hierón* (2411), which usually referred to the whole temple complex. *Naós* was used several times in the Epistles to speak of the human body as a temple sanctuary of God (1 Cor. 3:16, 17; 6:19; 2 Cor. 6:16; Eph. 2:21).

Although the leaders took *naós* as referring to the temple complex and therefore accused Jesus of blasphemy, they actually understood that He used it as a figure of speech to refer to His own body. When they approached Pilate to ask for a guard for Jesus' tomb, they told him: "Sir, we remember that that deceiver [Jesus] said, while he was yet alive, After three days I will rise again" (Matt. 27:63).

These false accusations were irrationally evil. They not only distorted or ignored facts, but they were rooted in covetousness and political fear.

[62] The high priest (usually the chairman of the Sanhedrin) listened to the proceedings for a while. Then he rose and asked Jesus, "Do You answer nothing? What is it that these are testifying against You?" (a.t.). Because the high priest recognized how inconclusive the inconsistent testimony of the false witnesses actually was, he tried to goad Jesus into a more damaging statement.

[63] Consistent with His teachings, Jesus did not "cast [His] pearls before swine" (Matt. 7:6). No matter what reply He gave, they would turn it against Him. Once you have determined that your opponent has an evil character, it is senseless to continue to argue. Silence is the best answer in such situations. "But Jesus was **silent** [*esiópa*, the imperfect tense of *siōpáō* {4623}, to keep silence; 'was keeping silent']." (a.t.)

Jesus was not disturbed by these proceedings. But the peace in His heart and responses upset the high priest; in fact, it infuriated him. He demanded an answer:

I adjure [*exorkízō* {1844}, to exact an oath; the only time this verb is used in the NT] thee **by** [*katá* {2596}, the preposition with the genitive that replaces the accusative noun with oaths representing the one who is to oversee an oath and guarantee its veracity: "before, or in the presence of"] the living God [as if God were in court listening to the testimony], that thou tell us whether thou be the Christ, the Son of God.

The definite article before "Christ" implies one Messiah, so the high priest demanded that Jesus openly admit if He considered Himself to be that One.

It is intriguing that any Jew of that period, especially a high priest, would identify the Messiah as "the **Son** [*huiós* {5207}] of God." This was not common among Pharisees or Sadducees for a good reason. The Hebrew Old Testament did not contain the singular expression, "the Son." There is no definite article accompanying the singular "son" in the Aramaic phrase "son [from *bar* {1247, OT}] of God [from *ʾᵉlāh* {426, OT}]" in the original text of Daniel 3:25 (Dan. 2:4—7:28 in the original Hebrew OT was written in Aramaic). The Septuagint, the Greek translation of the original Hebrew and Aramaic Old Testament, interprets the Aramaic as *ággelos* (32), "angel of God." Also, there are no definite articles with the plural "sons" in the Hebrew texts of Genesis 6:2, 4; Job 1:6; 2:1; 38:7. God calls the collective nation of Israel in Exodus 4:22 "my son" and the anointed individual King in Psalm 2:7 "my Son" (identically in Hebrew, *bᵉniy*, and in Greek, *huios . . . mou*) but neither with definite articles. Even Isaiah 9:6 has simply *bēn* (child) in the Hebrew and *paidíon* (child) in the Septuagint (Isa. 9:5), neither, again, with preceding articles.

Thus, for a chief priest to qualify the Messiah as "the [presumably unique] Son" reflects a messianic expectation of the times that advances beyond the precise wording of the Old Testament.

[64] Jesus finally spoke, masterfully. First He said, "**Thou hast said** [*eípas*, the aorist tense of *légō* {3004}, to intelligently speak]." The aorist indicates that the high priest had already made the assertion (literally, "You said it!"), not that he believed it. Jesus just acknowledged that he spoke the truth.

But Jesus did not stop there:

Nevertheless [*plḗn* {4133}, an adverb contracted from *pléon* or *pleíon* {4119}, more, besides, meaning He has more to say], I say to you, **Hereafter** [*ap' árti*, from now; from *apó* {575}, from; and *árti* {737}, now] you shall see the Son of man sitting on the right hand of power and coming on the clouds of heaven. (a.t.)

The prepositional phrase *ap' árti* occurs in two other places in Matthew, and all three are eschatological references. In Matthew 23:39 it occurs at the end of Jesus' lament over Jerusalem: "For I say unto you, Ye shall not see me henceforth, till ye shall say, Blessed is he that cometh in the name of the Lord." We also find the expression in Matthew 26:29 where Jesus said He will not drink *ap' árti* the fruit of the vine until His kingdom is established.

From here forward, Jesus said, they will see the Son of man exalted and coming in clouds of glory. The phrase "Son of man" occurs eighty times in the Gospels, including thirty times in Matthew. In humiliation, the Son of God vacated His proper position at the right hand of the Father. In His ascension, He reassumed that position. This prediction is actually a fulfillment of Hebrew prophecies with which the high priest would be familiar (e.g., Ps. 2:1–12; 110:1–7; Dan. 7:13, 14; Zech. 14:3, 4).

Psalm 110:1 (cf. Acts 2:35; Heb. 1:13) teaches that the Father works on behalf of the Son, who remains seated "at [His] right hand," a position of exaltation. The Jewish leaders were inexcusable for treating Jesus as they did in light of their thorough familiarity with these oracles entrusted to them (Rom. 3:1, 2). Christ predicted that He would personally occupy the throne of David promised to the Messiah (Matt. 19:27, 28; 25:31; see also Luke 1:32; Rom. 8:34; 2 Cor. 5:10; Eph. 1:20–23, cf. Isa. 16:5; Col. 3:1; Heb. 1:3, 13; 8:1; 10:12; Rev. 3:21).

The verb "**you shall see**" is from *horáō* (3708), to see and perceive. The same Son of man incarnated, humiliated, and killed would be exalted to the right hand of the Father, "**sitting** [*kathḗmenon*, the present participle of *káthēmai* {2521}, to sit] on the right hand of power." "Sitting" and "coming" are both present participles, arguing not only that sitting and coming are not contradictory but that the coming of Christ is a process of salvation and judgment that would start at the ascension (note: *ap' árti* is proleptic, pointing forward—"you shall see"—to the time when Jesus would actually sit at the right hand of the Father) and carries forward to the end of the age.

"Sitting" infers that the work of redemption, the remission of sins (*áphesis* [859]), was accomplished (v. 28). What remains is the regeneration (*paliggenesía* [3824]; see 19:28), justification, sanctification, and bodily redemption of believers (Rom. 8:23; 1 Cor. 15:51–57; 1 Thess. 4:11, 13–18).

God is presented as the God of real "**power**" (*dúnamis* [1411]), a dynamic power that always energizes all things (Rom. 11:36; Eph. 1:11)—not potential power—**strength** (*ischús* [2479]; see Matt. 12:29). Christ's ongoing "sitting" is not antithetical to His ongoing "coming." Though the Father is subduing His enemies, Christ Himself subdues all things (Phil. 3:21) as He promised the disciples when they pray in His name, "Because I go to my Father, I will do it" (John 14:12, 14; a.t.). So He is not "sitting down on the job," as the expression goes, but is always interceding for His own (Rom. 8:34; Heb. 4:16; 7:25; 10:19–25; 1 John 2:1) and judging the rest (Matt. 19:28; 25:31; Mark 14:62; 2 Cor. 5:10).

The Lord Jesus is coming in the "**clouds** [from *nephélē* {3507}, the diminutive of *néphos* {3509}, cloud; therefore, a small cloud] of heaven" (see also Matt. 24:30; Mark 13:26; 14:62; Luke 21:27). These clouds showed up first at Jesus' transfiguration (Matt. 17:5; Mark 9:7; Luke 9:34) and later at His ascension (Acts 1:9). *Néphos*, a normal-sized cloud, is used metaphorically in Hebrews 12:1 to picture crowds of heavenly spectators watching the saints on earth.

[65] Upon hearing Jesus' claim to be the messianic Son of God, "The high priest **rent** [from *diarrésso* or *diarrégnumi* {1284}, to tear, break, rip; from the preposition *diá* {1223}, denoting separation; and *rhéssō/rhégnumi* {4486}, to tear, rip] his clothes [outer garments; see below]."

This was strictly forbidden for a high priest (Lev. 21:10). It is amazing that at Jesus' confirmation of the truth, even the high priest sinned against the very Law he was committed to uphold. The distinctive clothes he wore (Ex. 28, 39) symbolized his religious authority. The noun translated "**clothes**" (from *himátion* [2440]) in the King James Version, refers to any garments but particularly the outer ones distinctive of the high priestly office.

Following this action, the high priest accused Jesus: "**He has blasphemed**" (a.t.). The Greek word used here is *eblasphémēse*, the aorist tense of *blasphēméō* ([987], to speak irreverently concerning God or holy things; derived from *bláx* [n.f.], sluggish, slow, stupid; and *phēmí* [5346], to say, speak, affirm). In no context, however, does the root noun *bláx* conjure up any pity as if a handicapped person were being addressed. Blasphemy was not a pitiful stupidity but rather a rational, ungodly offense against God and persons and was punishable by death (Lev. 24:15, 16).

The high priest continued, "What **further** [*éti* {2089}, yet, beyond, additional] need have we of witnesses?" Previously, they had only the false witnesses, but now they had the actual testimony of Jesus, which they considered blasphemy. It was on this basis that the high priest requested the Sanhedrin to condemn Jesus.

[66] So he asked, "What **think** [*dokeí*, the present tense of *dokéō* {1380}, to suppose, assume; lit., 'how does it seem' to you] ye?" What a rhetorical question! He had rent his garments, pronounced that Christ spoke blasphemy, asked what further need they had for witnesses, and then noted that the audience had heard the blasphemy. Who would dare defy all this? Every angry word and mannerism showed he was not interested in objectivity, having signaled loud and clear exactly how he wanted them to vote. Who defies a high priest that breaks the Mosaic Law to make his point?

The response, without the deliberation of fair jurisprudence, came from all the other members of the Sanhedrin present. No doubt, Nicodemus and Joseph of Arimathea were deliberately omitted from the list of members receiving an invitation to attend the trial because their honesty or loyalty to Christ was well-known (see Matt. 27:57; Mark 15:43; Luke 23:50–51; John 7:50–52): "He is **guilty** [*énochos* {1777} from *enéchō* {1758}, to have an involvement in] of death."

[67] Perhaps to visibly support their chief's garment-rending, "They spit in his [Jesus'] face, and **buffeted** [from *kolaphízō* {2852}, to slap with the palms of the hands] him." What utter humiliation of the One who "laid Himself down" (from *tapeinóō* [5013], to bring low, to humiliate; from *tápēs* [n.f.], a carpet; a.t.), taking the form of a man and becoming "obedient unto death, even the death of the cross" (Phil. 2:8).

[68] The command, "Prophesy unto us, thou Christ," was derisive. After covering His face (Mark 14:65), they punched and slapped Him, saying, "Who is he that smote thee?"

Jesus knew who struck Him, but He was under no obligation to answer these wicked people. The question showed that even unbelievers expect supernatural knowledge from a prophet. Although the action was complete: "Who hit you?"—and, therefore, the predictive role of the prophet was not being called into question—as, for example, in the question, Who will hit you?—it takes supernatural vision to see beyond a blindfold.

Peter's Denials
(26:69–75; Mark 14:66–72; Luke 22:54–62; John 18:15–18, 25–27)

[69] Peter's denial of Jesus at the palace of the high priest started here where he sat "**without**" (*éxō* [1854], outside) the palace but within the courtyard (*aulē* [833]).

When he arrived, Peter entered, sat down (v. 58), arose, then went out, and sat down again (v. 69). A "**damsel**" (*paidískē* [3814], a young girl, maiden) approached him with the accusation, "And you also were with Jesus of Galilee" (a.t.). The "also" implies that someone else had been recently accused—most likely John (John 18:15–18), who was with Peter at the court of the palace.

[70–72] Peter responded simply but adamantly out of fear:

[70] But **he denied** [from *arnéomai* {720}, to deny] before them all [the other servants who were there], saying, **I know** [*oída* {1492}, to perceive, understand] not what thou sayest. [71] And when he was gone out into the **porch** [from *pulón* {4440}, the vestibule, further away than the courtyard], **another** [*állē*, the feminine of *állos* {243}, meaning another damsel] maid saw him, and said unto them that were there, This fellow was also with Jesus of Nazareth. [72] And again he denied with an oath, I do not **know** [*oída*] the man.

It seems Peter moved to another place to hide from recognition. "I do not know the man!" What a fall from his original confession, "Thou art the Christ, the Son of the living God" (Matt. 16:16). However, Peter may have denied knowing Jesus to distract his accusers.

[73] An hour later (Luke 22:59), a man came forward with, "Surely you also are one of them; for your **speech** [*laliá* {2981}, idiom; implying dialect or pronunciation] **betrayeth** [from *poiéō* {4160}, to make; and *dḗlos* {1212}, clear, evident] you." (a.t.) Galileans had a distinct accent.

[74] At this point, Peter's adamancy became hostile:

Then began he **to curse** [*katanathematízein*, the present active infinitive of *katanathematízō* {2653}, to call down a curse upon oneself, from *katá* {2596}, either as an intensive or with the directional idea "down"; and *anathematízō* {332}, to bind with an oath; from *aná* {303}, upwards, up; and *títhēmi* {5087}, to place] and to swear [*omnúein*, the present active infinitive of *omnúō* {3660}, to vow with an oath], saying, I know not the man.

Most Greek manuscripts have a variant verb for "to curse," *katathematízō* (n.f.), which would have the same meaning. To emphasize that he was telling the truth, Peter did two things: He cursed (calling down judgment on himself if he was not telling the truth), and he swore (invoking God or a sacred object as a witness and judge if he was not telling the truth). In that day, neither cursing nor swearing involved the profanity that these words conjure today with the curser calling down judgment on another person. The present infinitives used with "began," indicate repetitive cursing and swearing. He began doing both continuously.

There is a proper way to swear with an oath, *omnúō*, because we are told in Hebrews 6:16, 17, that God took such an oath (see also Luke 1:73; Acts 2:30). The verb *ommúō* could have any number of objects invoked as witness.

For example, one could swear by his own head (Matt. 5:36); the heavens (Matt. 5:34; Rev. 10:6); the earth; or Jerusalem (Matt. 5:35). In His pronouncement of "woes" upon the Pharisees, Jesus condemned those who swore by certain objects as more valid or sacred then others, pronouncing that both the temple and its gold, the altar and the gifts upon the altar, the throne of God and God seated on His throne are all valid objects of such an oath (Matt. 23:16, 20, 22).

On Peter's third denial, "**Immediately** [*euthéos* {2112}] the cock **crew** [from *phōnéō* {5455}, to cry out]." This fulfilled Jesus' prophecy (v. 34) of the events and their sequencing ("immediately after," "deny me three times," etc.), proving that the Lord directs not just the animal kingdom but time itself—"all things [including events] through Him became" (John 1:3; Heb. 1:2; a.t.).

[75] Matthew continues,

> And Peter **remembered** [from *mnēmoneúō* {3421}, to remember] the **word** [from *rhéma* {4487}, a statement spoken] of Jesus, which said unto him, Before the cock crow, **thou shalt deny** [from *aparnéomai* {533}, to deny personal acquaintance] me thrice. And he went out, and **wept** [from *klaíō* {2799}, to cry] bitterly.

This was true repentance (*metánoia* [3341]) flowing out of godly sorrow (2 Cor. 7:9, 10). We must repent after falling into sin, as Peter did. David says godly persons will make this a habit:

> I acknowledged my sin unto thee, and mine iniquity have I not hid. I said, I will confess my transgressions unto the LORD; and thou forgavest the iniquity of my sin. Selah. For this shall every one that is godly pray unto thee in a time when thou mayest be found: surely in the floods of great waters they shall not come nigh unto him. (Ps. 32:5, 6)

Each time true believers sin, they experience bitter remorse (Matt. 11:21; Luke 10:13; 17:4). Judas, on the other hand, never really repented and believed. Although the verb *metamélomai* (3338), to regret, described his change of emotion, it was not a godly sorrow producing repentance but a worldly one that drove him to suicide (Matt. 27:3, 5).

Jesus' Condemnation and Judas' Suicide
(27:1–10; Mark 15:1; Luke 23:1; John 18:28–32; Acts 1:18, 19)

The meeting of the Sanhedrin, which continued throughout the night, was illegal because it dealt with a crime punishable by death. The *Mishnah*, a book of traditions and oral doctrine of the Jews, specified that meetings of the Sanhedrin to try criminal cases had to be held during the daytime. A decision to acquit could be made the same day. On the other hand, a death sentence had to be postponed until the next day, so the decision to put Jesus to death was taken up the next morning with the high priests present. We are not told exactly how many were there.

Sunédrion (4892), Sanhedrin, derives from the noun *súnedros* (n.f.), which means "counselor" from the roots *sún* (4862), together; and *hédra* (n.f.), a firm seat. From this last term, we obtain our English word, "cathedral." The Sanhedrin was composed of a high priest and seventy counselors from the ranks of previous high priests and elders (*presbúteroi* [4245]). A chairman presided, but other counselors (*súnedroi*) were consulted in decision making.

[1] "When the morning was come," the Sanhedrin convened again in Caiaphas' palace and "**took counsel**" (*sumboúlion* [4824], counsel, consultation; from *sún*, together; and *boulé* [1012], advice or a council of advisers; from *bouleúomai* [1011], to advise or counsel). In Greece today, the parliament is called *boulé*. The elders and former high priests deliberated under the current high priest (*archiereús* [749]).

It seems that the counsel determined Jesus' guilt during the night. This is evident from the fact that they now took counsel "**against** [*katá* {2596}] Jesus to [*hóste* {5620}, in order to, so that] put him to death." The Greek preposition *hóste* shows that their intention was to obtain a result—His death.

[2] They again became physically abusive:

And when **they had bound** [*désantes*, the aorist participle of *déō* {1210}, to bind] him, **they led him away** [*apégagon*, the aorist indicative of *apágō* {520}, to lead away; from *apó* {575}, from; and *ágō* {71}, to carry, lead, implying an abduction], and **delivered** [*parédōkan*, the aorist indicative of *paradídōmi* {3860}] him to Pontius Pilate the **governor** [*hēgemóni*, the dative of *hēgemōn* {2232}, the Roman prefect or procurator of Judea; see 27:11, 14, 15, 21, 23, 27; 28:14; Luke 20:20].

Pilate's authority level was fairly high, but he was accountable to the Roman senate.

[3] The judgment against Jesus had an impact on Judas:

Then Judas, the **betrayer** [*paradidoús*, the present participle of *paradídōmi* {3860}, used as a predicate and not as a time reference; like Satan, Judas was "a murderer from the beginning," John 8:44] of Him, having seen that He was condemned, **having changed concern** [*metamelētheís*, the aorist middle participle of *metamélomai* {3338}]. . . . (a.t.)

Unlike *metanoéō* (3340), which means to change one's mind, *metamélomai* means to change one's concern. The verbs *mélō* (n.f.), **to care**, and *méllō* (3195), to be imminent, about to happen, are clearly related. Imminent events frequently cause alarm, nervous expectations, and care. But Judas was not repentant. In spite of his confession of betraying innocent blood (next verse), Judas became fearful that he would either be identified with Jesus and arrested himself or suffer divine punishment (or both).

So Judas "**brought again** [*apéstrepse*, the aorist tense of *apostréphō* {654} from *apó* {575}; and *stréphō* {4762}, to turn back or away; thus, to return, i.e., back to where he received them] the thirty pieces of silver to the chief priests and elders,"

[4] Saying, **I sinned** [*hēmarton*, the aorist tense of *hamartánō* {264}, to sin], **having betrayed** [*paradoús*, the aorist participle of *paradídōmi*] innocent blood. (a.t.)

Judas accepted the sole responsibility of betraying the Lord Jesus although he realized that Christ's blood was innocent (*athôon* [121], free from guilt). To be innocent means to be free from sin and therefore free from the necessary punishment for sin. Judas knew that Jesus had not sinned over the three plus years of His public life. Hebrews 4:15 says that He was entirely "without sin." The sins Jesus died for were not His own but those of the world (2 Cor. 5:21). Because He was innocent, His blood was an acceptable sacrifice for our sins.

The members of the Sanhedrin did not wish to share Judas' guilt, though they had agreed with him for thirty pieces of silver in the first place (Matt. 26:15). They even dared to say, "What is that to us? see thou to that." The verb translated "**see thou**" (*ópsē* [3700]) is actually not an imperative but a future middle, which can be translated, "You shall see [i.e., the consequences] for yourself!" In other words, You'll be responsible yourself! This sounds brave, but it is pompous, making them as "innocent" as Pilate when he washed his hands (see v. 24).

[5] Judas literally burst from guilt. Here we read that

> . . . **having thrown down** [*rhípsas*, the aorist participle of *rhíptō* {4496}, to cast or throw] the pieces of silver in the temple, having departed and having gone away [both aorist participles], **he hanged himself** [*apégxato*, the aorist middle indicative of *apágchomai* {519}, to strangle; from *apó*, used as an intensive; and *ágchomai* {n.f.}, to strangle]. (a.t.).

Judas was responsible for his own sin. Although Christ "save[s] his people from their sins" (Matt. 1:21), those who refuse to be "His" cannot blame Him for not being saved. Responsibility begins and ends with the individual. Judas may have believed that hanging would be an appropriate penalty for betraying the Son of God. How wrong he was (see Heb. 10:28–30). Even after his suicide, the branch on which he had hung himself broke so he fell headlong (*prēnḗs* [4248], bending forward, prostrate), and his bowels or intestines burst open (*elákēse*, the aorist tense of *láskō* [2997], to burst; Acts 1:18), a providential, grim reminder of his punishment after death, having gone, "to his own place" (Acts 1:25).

[6] After the chief priests of the Sanhedrin took the thirty pieces of silver, they said,

> It is **not** [*ouk* {3756}, the absolute "not"] **lawful** [*éxesti*, the present tense of *éxeimi* {1826}, permitted by custom or law] for **to put** [*baleín*, the aorist infinitive of *bállō* {906}, to place] them into the **treasury** [*korbanán*, the accusative of *korbanás* {2878}, a place for depositing the *korbán* {7133, OT}, vow money considered sacred; Mark 7:9–13, cf. Lev. 2:1, 4, 12, 13], because it is the **price** [*timḗ* {5092}, attributed value, not true value, which is *axía* {n.f.} from which the adjective *áxios* {514}, worthy, is derived] of blood.

Thirty pieces of silver was the price (*timḗ*) Judas attributed to the blood of Jesus, whereas its true value in accomplishing atonement was incalculable. Peter speaks of the blood of Jesus Christ in 1 Peter 1:19 as precious (*timíō*, the dative of *tímios* [5093], dear, honorable, most precious). It was as precious to

Peter as it is to all true believers. Because Jesus was innocent, the payment for betrayal was defiled. Accordingly, it was unacceptable for admission into the treasury of the temple.

[7–9] What alternate use could there be for this money? Once again, the Sanhedrin "**took counsel** [*sumboúlion*; see v. 1] and bought with them [the thirty pieces of silver] the potter's field, to bury **strangers** [*xénois*, the dative plural of *xénos* {3581}, a foreigner] in." Judas, of course, was from out of town, namely Galilee.

> **Wherefore** [*dió* {1352}, for this reason] that **field** [*agrós* {68}, an area of cultivated ground, cf. Matt. 13:24, 27, 44] was called, The [the definite article "the" is not in the Greek] field of blood, **unto** [*héōs* {2193}, until] this day [i.e., when Matthew was writing, possibly as late as A.D. 50–70].

Perhaps the potter's field was renamed once Judas "the betrayer" was buried there.

> Then **was fulfilled** [*eplērōthē*, the aorist passive indicative of *plēróō* {4137}, to fulfill] **that which** [*tó*, the definite article] **was spoken** [*rhēthén*, the aorist passive participle of *erhéō* {2046}, to say specifically] by Jeremy the prophet.

It was God who spoke, as Matthew 1:22 tells us, "That it might be fulfilled which was spoken of [*hupó* {5259}, 'by' as the immediate source] the Lord by [*diá* {1223}, 'through' as the agent or intermediary] the prophet, saying. . . ." The prophets were simply God's mouthpieces.

These words are not found in Jeremiah but Zechariah 11:12, 13. Several explanations have been offered. Perhaps the least satisfactory is the "abridged-names" theory that suggests that a Hellenistic copyist mistook the Greek abridgment *Zriou* for *Iriou*, the difference of only a single letter. Others have argued that the book of Jeremiah headed up the "Book of the Prophets." In this case, Matthew was referring to the set of prophets under the name of the first book, which was Jeremiah. The best solution may be that Zechariah, who lived roughly one hundred years after Jeremiah, simply quoted a detailed prophecy that was not incorporated in Jeremiah's book.

> And they took the thirty pieces of silver, the price of him that was **valued** [*tetimēménou*, the perfect passive participle of *timáō* {5091}, to attribute value], whom [Jesus Christ] they [the religious leaders and Judas] of the children of Israel **did value** [*etimēsanto*, the aorist middle indicative of *timáō*, to value according to their own estimate of Jesus]; and gave them for the potter's field.

Thirty pieces of silver was considered the common price to buy a slave. For example, it was the price paid when an ox gored a male or female servant, presumably to death (Ex. 21:32).

[10] This contemptuous amount of money now reappeared in history. The first time was when Zechariah asked the people of Israel to determine a wage for his pastoral work. The thirty pieces, a rate paid for a slave, showed contempt for him and his messages of judgment.

Jesus Goes Before Pilate
(27:11–26; Mark 15:2–15; Luke 23:2, 3, 13–25; John 18:29–40)

Although Jesus was condemned by the highest Jewish court, the religious leaders did not have the authority to put Him to death. The Romans retained the right of capital execution, and they determined the criteria.

[11] When Jesus was led to the judgment hall, Pilate asked Him, "Art thou the King of the Jews?" Matthew presents the ensuing trial much more compactly than does John (18:20–24, 28–37) who goes into great detail.

John 18:37 has a word that does not appear here: "Are thou a king **then** [*oukoún* {3766}, a combination of the Greek *ouk*, the absolute 'not'; and *oún* {3767}, therefore, certainly]?" It can be translated, "Is it not therefore that You are a king?" This gives an implied meaning of "certainly." And the question necessitates a positive answer, "Therefore You are a king."

The accusation in Luke 23:2 was not only that Jesus declared that He was Christ, the King of the Jews, but that He perverted (*diastréphonta*, the present participle of *diastréphō* [1294], to seduce, corrupt; from *diá* [1223] denoting separation; and *stréphō* [4762], to turn) the nation. The Jews told the Roman governor that this Man who had been preaching for over three years was attempting to turn the loyalty of the Jewish people away from the Romans, as though it were God's will for them to be governed by Rome and they were satisfied with it. No wonder Jesus condemned them repeatedly for hypocrisy (Matt. 23:13–15, 23, 25, 27, 29).

Among the cited examples of political dissent, the Jewish religious leaders stated that Jesus forbade payment of taxes to Caesar. This was more effective than the threat of Jesus becoming King of the Jews—a role He seemed far too pacifistic to fit. Possibly Pilate was not aware of the tax issue the Jews contrived to prove Christ's insurgency (see Matt. 22:17–21).

Jesus explained to Pilate that His kingdom was not a worldly kingdom (John 18:36), but He accepted the accusation that He was a "King," though different from an earthly king. In Matthew, however, Christ accepted the accusation by saying to Pilate, "Thou sayest," the response He gave in all four Gospels.

Pilate was reluctant to condemn Jesus. John records that he said, "Take ye him, and judge him according to your law" (John 18:31), since from the perspective of Roman law, He was not a criminal (John 18:38). Pilate seriously doubted He was the malefactor (*kakopoiós* [2555], a doer of evil; John 18:30) He was accused of being. Even his wife warned him not to execute Jesus (Matt 27:19), but Pilate finally succumbed to the pressure from the religious leaders. He did not condemn Jesus out of personal conviction but from fear that the Jews would riot if he did not. At heart, Pilate was a coward who chose to let an innocent man be killed rather than to stand on his convictions against public pressure.

Most ancient traditions teach that Pilate committed suicide, but "where" has been the subject of debate. One tradition says Germany, since Mount Pilatus in that country was named in his commemoration. Another is Switzerland. Eusebius claimed that he was exiled to Vienne in Gaul (France). Probably like Judas, he bitterly regretted (*metaméleia* [n.f.], see v. 3) what he did, though without repentance.

[12] Jesus' silence in the face of His accusers is particularly noteworthy, a good example for us. Once we find out that certain people have made up their minds to believe lies and reject truth, we ought, like the Master, to be silent.

[13] The silence was too much for Pilate:

> Hearest thou not how many things they **witness against** [*katamarturoúsi* {2649} from *katá* {2596}, against; and *marturéō* {3140}, to bear witness] thee?

These Jewish leaders were not interested in establishing the truth about Jesus Christ; all they said was distorted and opposed to Him (Matt. 26:59–62). Pilate later recognized that their opposition grew from envy (see v. 18).

[14] And he answered him to **never** [*oudé* {3761} from *ou*, the absolute "not"; and the adversative *dé* {1161}, but not even] a [*hén* {1520}, one, single] **word** [*rhéma* {4487}].

The emphasis here is that Jesus did not utter a single word or statement in His own defense, even when He had the opportunity to respond to a more favorable audience—Pilate, standing for Rome.

The result of His silence, expressed with the Greek conjunction *hóste* (5620), "**so that**" or "therefore," produced admiration: ". . . so that the governor **marveled** [*thaumázein*, the present infinitive of *thaumázō* {2296}, to admire] greatly" (a.t.). The present tense indicates Pilate's continuing admiration of

Jesus Christ. Indeed, Jesus had lived His entire life the way Peter describes Him in his epistle: "Who, when he was reviled, reviled not again" (1 Pet. 2:23). Jesus' actions and silence resulted in curiosity in people like Pilate who had some interest in the truth.

The Jewish leaders had arrested Jesus on fallacious charges (v. 1) and continued their maligning until they achieved their purpose of having Him condemned to death by the Roman authorities, which they themselves legally could not do (John 18:31). Pilate, afraid to displease them although he did not like them, decided it was expedient to bow to their wishes and reluctantly accepted their word that Jesus was a criminal.

[15] Matthew now informs us that sometime during the Jewish feast of Passover,

> the governor **had been accustomed** [*eiōthei*, the pluperfect tense of *éthō* {1486}, to have a custom; translated "was wont" in the KJV] to release unto the people a prisoner, whom they would. (a.t.)

While the verb *éthō* is now obsolete, the noun *éthos* (1485), custom (from which comes our English word "ethnic"), is used in modern Greek to refer to an accepted custom, especially the plural *éthē*. This was not some law Rome had imposed on itself. It was merely an instance of what they believed to be ethical behavior toward the Jewish people, hoping perhaps to quell rebellion with these occasional crumbs from their table. Since some prisoners had been jailed as would-be messiahs and for other strictly political crimes, the Jews were happy to receive these men and women back into their fold instead of Jesus.

[16] One such "**notable**" or **notorious** (*epísēmon* [1978] from *epí* [1909], upon; and *sēma* [n.f.], sign; from *sēmaínō* [n.f.], to point out) person was Barabbas, with whom they classified Jesus as equally criminal.

[17] When the Jews gathered together to observe this custom, the governor asked,

> Whom will ye that I release unto you? Barabbas, or Jesus **which is called** [*legómenon*, the present passive participle of *légō*, to call, e.g., who is called by some] Christ?

The governor apparently had been told that a significant number of people persistently (the present participle) considered Jesus to be their Messiah.

Mark's Gospel supplies more details (15:6–15). The chief priests urged Pilate to choose Barabbas even though he was a known murderer. Pilate then mockingly identified Jesus as the King of the Jews.

[18] Both Matthew and Mark say that Pilate could perceive their real motive for delivering Jesus:

> For **he had known** [*édei*, the pluperfect tense of *oída/eídō*, to perceive] that **for** [*diá* {1223}, with the accusative meaning "on account of"] **envy** [*phthónon* {5355}] **they had delivered** [*parédōkan*, the aorist tense of *paradídōmi* {3860}, to deliver] him. (a.t.)

On somewhat of a play on Greek words, one was imprisoned for *phónos* (5408), murder (Mark 15:7), the other for *phthónos* (5355), envy.

[19] Only Matthew relates this incident about Pilate's wife's concern over Jesus' innocence. She perhaps had had some experience with Jesus, since He was well known in the region. Calling Him, literally "**that** [*ekeínō* {1565}] **Just One** [*dikaíō* {1342}]" (a.t.) shows prior superlative reflection with respect to His character. Moreover, God apparently troubled her with a nightmare that her husband did not take seriously—though he should have. How intriguing that God can temporarily turn even a heathen wife into an inspired prophet!

[20, 21] Finally, the chief priests and elders persuaded the crowds "**to plead**" (*aitḗsōntai*, the aorist middle subjunctive of *aitéō* [154], to request, plead) for Barabbas and "**to destroy**" (*apolésōsin*, the aorist active subjunctive of *apóllumi* [622], to do away with) Jesus.

At this point, Pilate repeated his question: "Which of the two do you want me to release to you?" (a.t.).

[22, 23] Jesus had predicted that He would die by crucifixion. In His third prophecy (Matt. 16:21–23; 17:22, 23; 20:17–19), He added the details of being delivered to the Gentiles, then mocked, scourged, and crucified (Matt. 20:19).

The chief priests, elders, and the crowd, therefore, did not realize that when they shouted, "Let him be crucified" (vv. 22, 23), they were executing God's plan of salvation as prophesied by their own prophets. Pilate insisted that Jesus had done nothing wrong, and his wife confirmed that Jesus was a just man. Judas confessed that Jesus was innocent (v. 4) and he had sinned in delivering Him. But now, even the crowd, intimidated by the question—"Why, what evil hath he done?"—could only respond irrationally, repeating the imperative to crucify Him.

[24] Realizing that he could "**gain** [*ōpheleí* {5623}, to be profitable or advantageous] **nothing** [*oudén* {3762}, not a single thing]" but that "**confusion**" (*thórubos* [2351], noise, clamor, uproar) was beginning to reign, Pilate decided to borrow the prescribed Old Testament ablution of Deuteronomy 21:6–9 (cf.

Ps. 26:6) to declare his innocence before the crowd. The inference here is that if Pilate could have benefited from releasing Jesus, he would not have ordered the execution.

Accordingly, he "**washed**" (*apenípsato*, the aorist middle indicative of *aponíptō* [633], to wash off; from the preposition *apó* [575], from; and *níptō* [3538], to wash; found only here) his hands in front of the crowd, saying, "I am innocent of the blood of this Just One" (TR)—finally conceding His wife's opinion and mimicking her words.

Then Pilate added, "**See ye** [*ópsesthe*, the future middle deponent indicative of *horáō* {3708}, to see and perceive] to it." Of course, both Pilate and the Jews knew that the crowds were not permitted to crucify anyone.

[25] Then the people did a senseless thing as a last resort. They called a curse down on themselves and their children. In other words, they were willing to risk their physical lives, their progeny, their nation, perhaps even eternity in this decision. It's worth it, they said, to lose our own souls and the souls of our children for the sake of being right. Though they could not cite a single crime at Pilate's request, they were totally unwilling to accept Jesus' claim to be the Messiah.

Jesus had clearly prophesied that within "this generation," as Josephus recorded, Galilee was turned into a sea of blood, Jerusalem was destroyed, and the temple was razed. God gave the people precisely what they asked for—the penalty for killing the innocent Messenger from God. Jesus had predicted, "He will miserably destroy those wicked men, and will let out his vineyard unto other husbandmen, which shall render him the fruits in their seasons" (Matt. 21:41).

In their refusal to recognize Jesus Christ as the incarnate God, the Jewish people willfully imputed guilt to their children (*tékna* [5043]). Parents' choices can have serious consequences for their children. God said, "For I the LORD thy God am a jealous God" (Ex. 20:5). Keeping mercy for thousands, forgiving iniquity and transgression and sin, and that will by no means clear the guilty; visiting the iniquity of the fathers upon the children, and upon the children's children, unto the third and to the fourth generation" (Ex. 34:7). How odd that they should actually ask for this! They knew their own Scriptures.

[26] Under this pressure, Pilate released Barabbas, then "**scourged**" (*phragellōsas*, the aorist participle of *phragellóō* [5417], to whip, akin to the noun *phragéllion* [5416], a whip—a Roman punishment) Jesus and sent Him off to be crucified. John uses the synonymous verb *emastígōse*, the aorist tense of *mastigóō* (3146), to whip (John 19:1).

"He delivered him **to be** [*hína* {2443}, in order that or for the purpose of being; Mark 15:15; John 19:6] crucified." Luke 23:25 adds, "He delivered Jesus **to their will** [*thelḗmati*, the dative singular of *thélēma* {2307}, their predetermined will or desire]."

Jesus Ridiculed and Mistreated
(27:27–31; Mark 15:16–23; Luke 23:26–32; John 19:16, 17)

[27] Pilate's band of soldiers (*speíra* [4686], a cohort of between four hundred and six hundred Roman foot soldiers), then took Jesus into the large hall in the Praetorium.

[28] This was the third time Jesus was mocked, the first being before the Sanhedrin as described in Mark 14:65 and Matthew 26:67, 68 and the second being before Herod as described in Luke 23:11. This third time took place in the palace of Pilate as described also in John 19:2, 3.

And **they stripped** [*ekdúsantes*, the aorist participle of *ekdúō* {1562} from *ek* {1537}, out of; and *dúnō* {1416}, to go down, to sink, as contrasted to *endúō* {1746}, to dress; from *en* {1722}, in; and *dúnō*; v. 28] him.

To the Greeks, dressing was conceived as dipping into something, and undressing was emerging out of it. Thus, "dress" (*énduma* [1742]; Matt. 3:4; 6:25, 28; 7:15; 22:11, 12; 28:3; Luke 12:23) was usually plural because of the various items of clothes one wears.

The Roman soldiers clothed Jesus with a "**robe**" (*chlamús* [5511], an outer garment of dignity) to mock His alleged kingship. "**Scarlet**" (*porphúra* [4209]) was a dye derived from a reddish/purple shellfish found in the Mediterranean. It was of great value in biblical times (Mark 15:17). In this verse, the robe was designated simply as scarlet or **red** (*kokkínēn* [2847]).

[29] The soldiers also braided a "**crown**" (*stéphanos* [4735], a wreath) from thorn bushes, a further sign of mockery and humiliation (Mark 15:17; John 19:2, 5). A common bush in Israel today grows sharp thorns over an inch long, which could have been the type used. The soldiers conveyed a message of scorn to the Jews that this Man could not possibly be their hope of freedom from Roman domination.

There Jesus stood, seemingly helpless, wearing a crown of thorns. Peter comments, "**being reviled** [*loidoroúmenos*, the present passive participle of *loidoréō*

{3058}, to revile, reproach, make fun of], **He reviled** [*anteloidórei*, the imperfect tense of *antiloidoréō* {486}, to revile against] **not** [*ouk*, the absolute 'not'] again" (1 Pet. 2:23; a.t.). The imperfect tense means it was not His custom to treat others as they were treating Him. Jesus did not react to their ridicule and torment.

The soldiers also put a "**bamboo reed** [*kálamos* {2563}] in His right hand" (a.t.). They may have wanted to tempt Him into striking them, though the attempt would have been futile because the instrument was innocuous.

To complete the royal mock-up, the soldiers "**having kneeled**" (*gonupetḗsantes*, the aorist active participle of *gonupetéō* [1120], to fall down on the knees; from *gónu* [1119], knee; and *píptō* [4098], to fall) to feign worship, they "**mocked**" (*enépaizon*, the imperfect tense of *empaízō* [1702], to deride, ridicule, scoff; from *en* [1722], in; and *paízō* [3815], to play, make fun of) Him. The imperfect tense implies that this went on for some time. While doing this, they repeated, "**Hail** [*chaíre*, the present tense of *chaírō* {5463}, to rejoice, be glad, cf. Luke 1:28], King of the Jews!"

[30, 31] The soldiers then "**spit**" (*emptúsantes*, the aorist participle of *emptúō* [1716]) on Jesus.

Spitting was a common mark of derision and contempt, as it still is in the Middle East. The word "spitting" occurs only in the Gospels and always in connection with Christ. Jesus even prophesied that He was going to be spat on as the Messiah (Mark 10:34; Luke 18:32). During His passion, He was spat on by both Jews (Matt. 26:67; Mark 14:65) and Roman soldiers (v. 30; Mark 15:19). Old Testament references to the insult associated with spitting are Numbers 12:14, Deuteronomy 25:9, and Isaiah 50:6.

After taking the reed from Jesus' hand, the soldiers "**were striking**" (*étupton*, the imperfect tense of *túptō* [5180], to smite) Jesus on the head, the imperfect tense indicating a repetitive beating. Following all this abject humiliation, the soldiers put His original clothing back on Him and led Him to the place of crucifixion.

The Crucifixion and Final Mockery of Jesus
(27:32–44; Mark 15:22–32; Luke 23:33–43; John 19:17–24)

[32] After mocking Jesus inside Pilate's majestic hall, the Roman soldiers then led Him outside where the Jews were waiting. There they compelled a man named Simon to carry Christ's cross.

Simon may have been a black man since he was from Cyrene, a Greek settlement on the north coast of Africa. Today Cyrene is called Benghazi or Barca. In 96 B.C., this region became a Roman senatorial province and in 27 B.C. united with the island of Crete. It was progressive in commerce and philosophy, producing men like philosophers Aristippus and Carmeades, the poet Cellimachus, and the Christian orator and bishop Synesius. As Roman provinces, Cyrene and Palestine were economically linked. Mark 15:21 introduces Simon as the father of two sons, Alexander and Rufus. Possibly Paul refers to the latter son when he says, "Salute Rufus chosen in the Lord, and his mother and mine" (Rom. 16:13). If this is the same Rufus and Paul sent greetings to his mother, we can infer that the family came to faith in Christ. She must have been loving and caring because Paul speaks of her as his own mother.

We read that "**they compelled**" (*ēggáreusan*, the aorist tense of *aggareúō* [29], to press into service, draft) Simon to carry the cross. In an interesting combination of determinism and freedom, Jesus commanded His followers to freely volunteer the second mile after being compelled (*aggareúsei*) to go the first (Matt. 5:41).

Up to this point in Scripture, the noun "cross" (*staurós* [4716]) and the verb "crucify" (*stauróō* [4717]) have been used symbolically to mean the burdens of life and bearing those burdens. The root derives from the verb *hístēmi* (2476), to stand.

The burdens we carry in life are of two kinds. Those we carry to survive are called "loads" (*phortía* [5413]), similar to the weighted cargo a boat carries. Each boat is sized to carry a certain load without sinking. There is a correlation between the weight of the load and the amount of water displaced when afloat. Disobedience to this law results in catastrophe.

A second noun is called a "burden" (*báros* [922], weight). One chooses to shoulder this weight for others. And persons have their own (*ídion* [2398]) loads to bear, according to their created capacity and training.

The Greek verb for "bear" is *bastázō* (941), to carry or bear something and remain standing. The Greek verb for the action of taking up and transferring a burden to oneself that others cannot bear is *aírō* (142), to take or lift up, to raise. This is the verb used here: "Him they compelled to **bear** [*árē*, the aorist subjunctive of *aírō*] his cross" (cf. John 15:2). Before this occasion, the Lord Jesus used the verb *aírō*, to take up one's cross symbolically, meaning the load that is his or hers to lift up and carry. Now the theology was being enacted in the physical event.

The word "cross" does not occur in the Septuagint. In the Greek classics, a cross (*staurós*) was like a stake (*skólops* [4647]), used to enable something to stand (*histēmi* [2476], a derivation of *staurós*). According to A. T. Robertson, Plutarch, a famous Greek biographer and philosopher, wrote that each malefactor carried his own cross (A. T. Robertson, *A Dictionary of Christ and the Gospels*, 395).

If Simon of Cyrene carried Christ's cross, why then does John report, "And [Jesus] bearing [*bastázōn*, the present participle of *bastázō*] his own cross [TR, MT] went forth into a place called the place of a skull . . . ." (John 19:17)? Luke 23:26 says that as the soldiers led Christ out, they took hold of Simon and placed the cross on him to carry behind Jesus. Apparently, after the scourging and torment, the cross was placed on Jesus, and He began to carry it. But then perhaps He fainted or was too weak to continue. On seeing a man passing by (*parágonta*, the present active participle of *parágō* [3855], to go along or near in Mark 15:21), the soldiers compelled him to lift up (*árē*) the cross from (off) Jesus. This implies that Jesus was about to collapse—if He had not already—under the weight of the cross.

[33] Golgotha was called the place of the "**skull**" (*kraníon* [2898] from which we get our English word "cranium"). Here, outside the walls of Jerusalem (John 19:16, 17; Heb. 13:12), yet near the city proper (John 19:20), criminals were commonly executed (Mark 15:22; John 19:17).

Golgotha was a conspicuous place (Mark 15:22; John 19:17) located near a well-traveled road. Also nearby was the garden containing Joseph of Arimathaea's new tomb (Matt. 27:57, 60; Mark 15:43, 46; Luke 23:53; John 19:41).

[34] Before crucifixion, the soldiers "gave him **vinegar** [*óxos* {3690}, sour wine] to drink mixed with **gall** [*cholē* {5521}, bile]" in fulfillment of Psalms 69:21.

After tasting it, Jesus "was **not** [*ouk* {3756}, the absolute 'not'] **electing** [*éthele*, the imperfect tense of *thélō* [2309], to determine, choose] to drink it" (a.t.), not because the mixture was bitter or because He was not thirsty. Later, however, He said, "I thirst" (*dipsō* [1372]; see John 19:28). The most reasonable hypothesis is that Jesus did not want to mitigate the pain associated with redemption.

[35] After the crucifixion, four soldiers cast "**lots**" (*klēros* [2819], a term used for an inheritance, which, of course, is "free"; more specifically called *klēronomía* [2817]; see Acts 26:18; Gal. 3:18; Eph. 1:14). They cast lots twice, first to allocate His four garments, then to decide who would take his robe since it was seamless and they did not want to rip it (John 19:24).

Little did these soldiers realize that they were fulfilling the prophecy given in Psalm 22:18, "They part my garments among them, and cast lots upon my vesture."

The soldiers might have sacrificed the inheritance of garments for the inheritance of eternal life. The Scriptures frequently spoke of inheriting (*klēronoméō* [2816]) eternal life (Matt. 19:29); the kingdom of God (Matt. 25:34; 1 Cor. 6:9, 10; 15:50; Gal. 5:21); salvation (Heb. 1:14); and the blessings of God (Heb. 6:12; 12:17; 1 Pet. 3:9; Rev. 21:7). These estates, however, are only granted to the children of God (John 1:12) who are born from above (John 3:3, 7; Rom. 8:17).

[36] After the soldiers divided Jesus' garments among themselves,

> **sitting down** [*kathēmenoi*, the present middle of *káthēmai* {2521}], **they were guarding** [*etéroun*, the imperfect tense of *tēréō* {5083}, to keep, guard] Him there. (a.t.)

These low-ranking bandits probably considered themselves quite the conquerors. But they did not know with whom they were dealing.

[37] Here we see that the heathen ended up acknowledging the very kingship of the Messiah they denied, in fulfillment of Psalm 2:2–4.

Totally contrary to the Jews who requested the wording, "He said He was King of the Jews," the Romans defiantly displayed the words: "THIS IS JESUS THE KING OF THE JEWS." The double-edged offense was that this was both a lie and an insult to the Jews who frantically demanded that the unpaid-for advertisement be changed (see John 19:19–22). From God's vantage point, this was the objective truth. And so David's messianic prophecy came to pass: "He that sitteth in the heavens shall laugh: the Lord shall have them in derision" (Ps. 2:4) when they gather against the Lord and His Christ (2:2), thinking they can tear away God's sovereign "cords" (2:3).

[38] Isaiah prophesied that the innocent Lamb led to the slaughter would be "numbered with the transgressors" (Isa. 53:12). As it turned out, "two **thieves** [*lēstaí* {3027}, violent thieves]" were crucified with Jesus.

[39, 40] Apparently, regular "**passersby**" (*paraporeuómenoi*, the present middle deponent participle of *paraporeúomai* [3899], to pass near by) shook their heads negatively. They believed that Jesus' condition did not match His boast of destroying the temple and rebuilding it in three days. So they mocked Jesus, saying,

> Thou that destroyest the temple, and buildest it in three days, save thyself. **If** [*ei* {1487}, supposing, assuming] thou be the Son of God, **come down** [*katábēthi*, the aorist imperative of *katabaínō* {2597}, to descend] from the cross.

To unbelievers, those who either were ignorant of or who consciously rejected Isaiah's clear prophecies, it made no sense for the Creator to be destroyed, for the providential One to be manipulated, for the holy and righteous One to suffer a penalty. If the Trinity had not planned otherwise, Jesus could have come down. But He would not because He would not contradict the timeless mind and will of the Trinity. To do otherwise would be schizophrenia. God's mind and will are one timeless entity: "He is of one mind; who can turn Him?" (Job 23:13; a.t.).

[41, 42] The passersby were joined by the chief priests, scribes, and elders, and they

> **were saying** [*élegon*, the imperfect of *légō* {3004}], He saved others; He cannot [*ou* {3756}, the absolute "not"] save Himself. **If** [*ei* {1487}, the subjective assumption] He be the King of Israel, let Him **now** [*nún* {3568}, at this present time] come down from the cross, and we will believe on Him. (a.t.)

Amazing how often people not only think that God should do this or that, but He should do it "now!" If you want peace in your life, never forget this study on "His hour." "Wait for the LORD" (Ps. 130:5), and never ask, "Why should I wait for the LORD any longer?" (2 Kgs. 6:33; a.t.).

[43] Continuing their criticism, growing out of the assumption that "sons of God don't die," they said,

> **He trusted** [*pépoithen*, the perfect tense of *peíthō* {3982}, to persuade, put one's confidence in] upon God; **let Him deliver** [*rhusásthō*, the aorist middle deponent imperative of *rhúomai* {4506}, to deliver] Him **now**, if **He desires** [*thélei* {2309}, to choose or select] Him: for He said, I am the Son of God. (a.t.)

It is interesting how they shifted the subject from Christ's deity—"himself he cannot save" (v. 42), to His humanity—"Let him [God the Father] deliver him!" Their connection between the Father's deliverance and His selective will (*thélei*) was far removed from Isaiah's prophecy: "It pleased the LORD to bruise him" (Isa. 53:10).

Jesus Christ would, of course, save Himself, and the Father would deliver him as He willed, not now, but in the three days Christ prophesied on three occasions (Matt. 16:21; 17:22, 23; 20:19). Peter tried to persuade Jesus to avoid the cross (Matt. 16:21–23), but Jesus knew He was going to rise from the dead. This would provide the greatest proof to believers that He was what He claimed to be.

People are in no position to limit how and when God acts. To attempt to do so is blasphemy. If God took orders from humans, He would cease to be God; in fact, they would become God-prime, that is, a higher god.

The Lord delivers in many ways; and we attain the meaning from the preposition associated with the verb *rhúomai*. Sometimes He delivers positionally as, for example, "**from** [*apó* {575}, a position outside its object] evil" (Matt. 6:13);

at other times, transitionally as, for example "**out of** [*ek* {1537}, out of from within] them [i.e., persecutions] all" (2 Tim. 3:11, cf. 2 Tim. 4:17). From these examples, we gather that the Lord delivers either through physical repositioning (*apó*) or through victorious emergence (*ek*).

Specifically with respect to Christ, the writer of Hebrews says, "Who in the days of his flesh, when he had offered up prayers and supplications with strong crying and tears unto him that was able to save him from [*ek*] death, and was heard in that he feared" (Heb. 5:7). Here, the preposition *ek* shows that Christ entered into the sphere of death, and the Father saved Him out of—from within—it. This occurred at the resurrection, when Christ was raised "out of [*ek*, from among] the dead ones" (Acts 4:10; a.t; see Rom. 7:4; 1 Thess. 1:10; 2 Tim. 2:8). Similarly, innumerable (Rev. 7:9) believers will be "coming [a present participle] out [*ek*] of the great tribulation" (Rev. 7:14; a.t.), emerging victoriously over the beast (Rev. 15:2).

[44] Both robbers originally "reproached Him" (a.t.) as well. Luke 23:32 calls them "malefactors" (*kakoúrgoi* [2557], criminals). *Kakoúrgoi* not only openly steal property, but they may kill to do so. In modern Greek, a *kakoúrgēma* is a felony—one of the worst crimes.

The King James Version has the interesting phrase, "[They] cast the same in his teeth." All of this translates a single Greek verb, *ōneídizon*, the imperfect tense of *oneidízō* (3679), to reproach, revile, assail with abusive words. The imperfect indicates that the thieves displayed this disdain much of the time they were alive on the cross. They were abusing while "**being crucified together**" (a.t.; *sustaurōthéntes*, the aorist passive participle of *sustauróō* [4957] from *sún*, together [see v. 38]; and *stauróō* [4717], to crucify). Jesus had lived as the personification of virtue and benevolence but died like a common criminal, surrounded by enemies.

One of the thieves ridiculed Jesus to the end of His life; the other, perhaps on hearing Jesus pray to the Father to forgive His enemies, repented and was forgiven (Luke 23:34–43).

Jesus' Death
(27:45–54; Mark 15:33–41; Luke 23:44–49; John 19:30–37)

From Mark 15:25 we learn that Jesus was placed on the cross at 9 a.m. Although the sun is brightest at noon, a strange phenomenon occurred. Mark 15:33 tells us "darkness was over the whole land" and lasted until 3 p.m.

[45] Darkness "**became**" (*egéneto*, the aorist middle of *gínomai* [1096], to occur, take place) on all the "**earth**" (*gēn*, the accusative of *gē* [1093], earth) for three hours.

Gē sometimes includes the earth, but more frequently it means the land. Most translations render it "the land" here, meaning the land of Palestine (see v. 51 where the earthquake was most likely restricted to Jerusalem and its environs). Metaphorically, the cross was darkness to the entire universe—the culmination of evil.

[46] By mid-afternoon, Jesus cried out to His Father:

> **About** [*perí* {4012}, around] the ninth hour [3 p.m.], Jesus **cried** [*aneboēsen*, the aorist tense of *anaboáō* {310} from *aná* {303}, an emphatic, or *ánō* {507}, up or upward, suggesting the direction of His cry toward His Father; and *boáō* {994}, to cry] with a loud voice, saying, Eli, Eli [Hebrew: "My God, My God"], **why** [*lāmāh* {4100, OT}, for what reason?] **hast thou forsaken me** [*sabachthaní* {7662, OT}]?

As Matthew moves us from Hebrew/Aramaic to the Greek translation, we have,

> My God, my God, **why** [*hinatí* {2444} from *hína* {2443}, for what purpose; and *tí* {5101}, to what end specifically] **hast thou forsaken** [*egkatélipes*, the aorist tense of *egkataleípō* {1459}, to forsake; from *en* {1722}, in; and *kataleípō* {2641}, to desert] me?

This last verb literally means to leave behind, abandon or forsake from *katá* (2596), an intensive, or *kátō* (2736), down; and *leípō* (3007), to leave.

What happened here? Let us start with what did not happen. The Trinity did not fragment; that is, there was no ontological disjunction between the Father and the Son who "are one" (John 10:30). The Trinity cannot decompose because it is not a composition as, for instance, chemicals. The writer of Hebrews tells us that the Son of God took human nature on Himself in order to die (Heb. 2:9, 14). When He was forsaken, however, it was not for His own sin, which He did not have (Heb. 4:15) but for the sins of humanity (2 Cor. 5:21).

On the cross, Jesus said to one of the thieves, "Today you will be with Me in paradise" (Luke 23:43; a.t.). At His death, according to 1 Peter 3:18, 19, He emptied Hades of its believing inhabitants and brought them to Paradise (*parádeison* [3857]; Acts 2:27).

From Jesus' why? we can take heart. The first thing we say when things go wrong or we must suffer is, "Why, Lord?" But note how quickly Jesus' why? turned to "It is finished!" Let us not condemn ourselves too severely when we question God's temporal actions in our lives, but let us eagerly wait for His eternal purposes.

We should also keep in mind that the very question, "Why hast thou forsaken me?" was addressed to "My God, my God." At no time was Jesus' faith in or His personal relationship with His Father interrupted. Jesus confirmed that in spite of the ordeal He was enduring, He was conscious of the eternal, unbroken relationship He always had with the Father (John 17:5).

[47] When some who stood there heard Jesus cry out, they thought He was calling for the prophet Elijah to save Him. They might have inferred as much from Malachi 4:5, which says, "Behold, I will send you Elijah the prophet before the coming of the great and dreadful day of the LORD." Perhaps Elijah's physical translation into heaven, added to this prophecy, raised their expectations for some glorious reappearance in history.

[48] The thought that Jesus was calling for help aroused sympathy among some hearers. One ran, took a sponge, filled it with vinegar, put it on a reed, and gave Jesus a drink. "Having put it on a reed," the text continues, "**he was giving [Him] something to drink** [*epótizen*, the imperfect tense of *potízō* {4222}]" (a.t.). We get the impression that the man was caring for Jesus over a period of time, although his actions could have been another form of ridicule.

"**Vinegar**" (*óxos* [3690], a sharp wine that tasted like vinegar; the noun *óxos* is related to the adjective *oxús* [3691], sharp) was a cheap, poor wine mixed with water, a common drink among the poorer classes (Sept: Num. 6:3; Ruth 2:14). This time the vinegar did not contain the bitter substances that the first offer had, which Christ refused (v. 34). Possibly a guard gave Him a drink from his own vessel (John 19:29, 30) after hearing Jesus pray for the forgiveness of His enemies.

[49] We can see how easily the two names, Eli and Elias, might be confused, especially when articulated from a dry, thirsty throat (see John 19:28). The callous individuals who thought Jesus called for Elias actually rebuked the man who mercifully gave Him a drink, urging him instead to see if Elias would come in response to Jesus' call.

[50] In spite of the abusive mockery and physical pain Jesus endured for six hours, He still had the strength to muster a final, loud cry just before His death. However, this time He was unable to enunciate any words but simply "**cried out** [*kráxas*, the aorist participle of *krázō* {2896}, to cry; a verb related to the onomatopoeia *krá*, the raucous sound of a crow, roughly corresponding to our English 'caw'] again with a loud voice and yielded up the **ghost** [*pneúma* {4151}, spirit]" (a.t.).

The verb "**yielded up**" is *aphḗke*, the aorist tense of *aphíēmi* (863), to let go; from *apó* (575), from; and *híēmi* (n.f.), to send. In other places, the verb *exépneusen* (*ekpnéō* [1606], to breathe out) is used to describe the departure of the spirit (*pneúma*) from the body (see also Mark 15:37; Luke 23:46). At a specified time, Jesus committed His human spirit into the hands of His Father, separating from His living body (*sṓma* [4983]), which then became a corpse (*ptṓma* [4430], a dead body). A good example of this is found in Luke 8:55 where Jairus' daughter's spirit "came again" (*epéstrepse*, the aorist tense of *epistréphō* [1994], to turn back) to her body at Jesus' command. Her person returned to her body.

In Luke 23:46, Jesus added, "Father, into thy hands I commend [*parathḗsomai*, the future middle deponent of *paratíthēmi* {3908} from *pará* {3844}, near, a preposition denoting close proximity; and *títhēmi* {5087}, to put, place] my spirit." As a deponent verb, the voice is active, that is, "I place My spirit by My own initiative and power into Your hands." Similarly, John 19:30 says that He "gave up [*parédōke*, the aorist tense of *paradídōmi* {3860} from *pará*, near; and *dídōmi* {1325}, to give] the spirit" (a.t.).

[51] Some supernatural events attended the crucifixion of the Lord Jesus. The three-hour darkness that affected the whole land or earth was one of them (v. 45). A similar darkness will occur when Christ comes to earth again, according to Matthew 24:29.

Jesus' death had a severe impact on the Jewish temple, particularly the sanctuary (*naós* [3485]). The "**veil**," a heavy curtain (*katapétasma* [2665]) that divided the Holy Place from the Holy of Holies, was torn from top to bottom, a sign that God Himself was terminating the Levitical priestly office and system. Mark 15:38 and Luke 23:45 are the only other references to the veil of the temple in the New Testament. In Psalm 28:2, the Holy of Holies is referred to as the "holy oracle" (1687, OT), a sanctuary or inner room, the former Holy of Holies of the tabernacle in the wilderness.

The veil in the temple Herod had built was about one cubit (*pḗchus* [4083]) or twenty-one inches thick. The splitting of such a thick curtain was an act of God, especially "from the top [hardly accessible to a human] to the bottom," as the text reads. Moreover, the common person was not permitted into the Holy of Holies. Only the high priest could enter once a year to offer a blood sacrifice for sins. Thus, the splitting of the veil symbolized the access Jew and Gentile together now have to come into the presence of God Himself, claiming the blood of Jesus Christ as their own personal, sacrificial offering. The access is obtained from above—God revealing Himself to humans—not from below, that is, people raising themselves to God's level (cf. the verbs *anakalúptō*

[344], 2 Cor. 3:14, 18; *apokalúptō* [601], and the noun *apokálupois* [602], revelation, 1 Cor. 1:7; 2 Cor. 12:1; Gal. 1:12; Eph. 1:17; 3:3; 2 Thess. 1:7; 1 Pet. 1:7, 13; 4:13; Rev. 1:1).

The reference to the "second veil" in Hebrews 9:3 is likely this veil that was torn from top to bottom. Assuming the temple Herod built was patterned after the original design given to Moses, the inner and outer veils are described in Exodus 26:31–37. The "first" or outer veil (a deduction from Heb. 9:3), serving as a "hanging for the door of the tent" (26:36), was composed of three colors of cloth and fine twined linen and was suspended on five pillars of shittim wood covered with gold. The second inner veil, separating the Holy Place from the Most Holy Place, was made of similar materials, was suspended on four pillars, was more elegantly embroidered.

Not only was the veil torn, but "**the land**" (*hḗ gḗ*, as in v. 45 above) also "**was shaken**" (*eseísthē*, the aorist passive of *seíō* [4579], to shake), an event mentioned only here. Later, an earthquake occurred at Jesus' resurrection (Matt. 28:2), and earthquakes will prevail before His return (Matt. 24:7).

The same verb used for the tearing of the veil is used with respect to the **splitting** (*schízō* [4977]) of the **rocks** (*pétrai* [4073]) as well. Matthew's use of the definite article implies that he had some particular rocks in mind. Unfortunately, he leaves us without qualification. Possibly "the tombs" in the immediate context were made from these "[the] rocks."

[52] Now we read about a strange phenomenon, which Matthew alone has recorded. He says, "The tombs **were opened** [*aneṓchthēsan*, the aorist passive of *anoígō* {455}, to open]" (a.t.), obviously by God.

The Greek word for "tomb" is *mnēmeíon* (3419) from *mnáomai* (3415), to remember. The tomb, therefore, is a memorial or monument in contrast to *mnḗma* (3418), which is a grave (*táphos* [5028], sepulchre or grave). The Jews artistically hewed tombs out of rocks or in the sides of hills in various forms and sizes, sometimes with several compartments. Many had doors and entrances that were whitewashed and decorated with ornaments.

Matthew continues his unique report,

> And **many** [*pollá*, the neuter plural of *polús* {4183}, much] **bodies** [*sṓmata*, the accusative plural of *sṓma* {4983}, body] of the **saints** [*hagíōn* {40}] **which have been put to sleep** [*kekoimēménōn*, the perfect passive participle of *koimáomai* {2837}, to lie outstretched] **arose** [*ēgérthē*, the aorist passive of *egeírō* {1453}, to raise]. (a.t.)

Two Greek verbs refer to natural sleep: *koimáomai* (2837) and *katheúdō* (2518) from *katá* (2596), down; and *heúdō* (n.f.), to sleep. The expression "had been put to sleep" might refer to martyrs who died for their testimony, and God honored them in this special way.

In Matthew 28:13, *koimáomai* is used of soldiers who were "sleeping" when they should have been guarding Jesus' tomb. While both *katheúdō* and *koimáomai* are most frequently used this way, both are also used metaphorically to describe the transient nature of death prior to the final judgment (see, e.g., Sept.; Dan. 12:2: "Many of those sleeping [*katheudóntōn*] in the dust shall awake, some to everlasting life, and some to shame and everlasting contempt" [a.t.; cf. Matt. 9:24; Mark 5:39; Luke 8:52; 1 Thess. 5:6; for *koimáomai*, see also Acts 7:60; 13:36; 1 Cor. 7:39; 11:30; 15:6, 18, 20, 51; 1 Thess. 4:13–15; 2 Pet. 3:4]). This state includes unbelievers (Dan. 12:2) since their bodily slumber, too, is temporary, pending the "resurrection of the . . . unjust" (Acts 24:15, cf. John 5:29).

As here, John 11:11 uses the perfect passive of both *koimáomai* (*koímēsetai*; "has been put to sleep") and in John 11:12 *sṓzō* (*sōthḗsetai*, "shall be saved" meaning "awakened") to describe God's particular sovereignty respectively over Lazarus' physical death and resurrection. The middle voice is unlikely: Lazarus has not put himself to sleep [killed himself, which is the lexical meaning of the verb in the context and the requirement of the perfect tense—as opposed to the present active "he is sleeping"] any more than he awakens (meaning resurrects) himself. "I am the Lord; I kill and I make alive" (Deut. 32:39; a.t.; cf. Rev. 2:23).

In the New Testament, the state of wakefulness is often metaphorically compared with sleep (*húpnos* [5258]) as the moral to the immoral (Rom. 13:11–13; 1 Cor. 15:34; Eph. 5:14). Sometimes authors equivocate meanings in a single discourse. For example, it is highly questionable whether Paul uses the verb *katheúdō* (the present active subjunctive) in the same ethical sense between 1 Thessalonians 5:7 and 5:10, which (the latter) reads, "Whether we wake or sleep, we should live together with [Christ]." The context of 5:2–9 clearly identifies those who sleep in darkness during the night as unbelievers— not dead believers. Accordingly, for Paul to conclude with "whether we obey [wake] or sin [sleep], we should live together with him" contradicts the context's meaning, the child of light behaving one way, the child of darkness quite another. Paul likely is stylistically equivocating *katheúdō*, returning to the death/life, sleep/wake conditions of believers he introduces in the prior chapter (4:13–16).

Concerning the identity of the subjects of this newsworthy report of resurrection in Matthew, we know nothing. Most commentators in the early church connected this event to Christ's preaching "to the spirits in prison"

(1 Pet. 3:18, 19) and "to . . . the dead" (1 Pet. 4:5, 6). But Matthew spends no time explaining (interpreting) the event, his apologetical purpose different than Peter's. Peter's event is placed in an extended, complex argument of suffering for Christ's sake, while Matthew is content with simply reporting. He may be typifying the power of God to raise all people with the resurrection of the "firstfruits" (1 Cor. 15:20, 23), the "firstborn from the dead" (Col. 1:18; note: believers, also, are referred to as "firstfruits" [James 1:18; Rev. 14:4]). Jesus Christ was the firstfruits (*aparchē* [536]) of the resurrection in which each person will be raised in preordained order (*tágmati*, the dative of *tágma* [5001], arrangement) at the *parousía* (3952), Christ's Second Coming. At that time, all saints who have been "put to bed" (*kekoimēménoi*), so to speak, in Jesus will be raised, and He will bring them with Himself (1 Thess. 4:14).

> And, **having come out** [*exelthóntes*, the aorist participle of *exérchomai* {1831} from *ex* {1537}, out of; and *érchomai* {2064}, to come] **after** [*metá* {3326} with a subsequent accusative is "after"] His resurrection, **they entered into** [*eisēlthon*, the aorist indicative of *eisérchomai* {1525}] the holy city, and **they were made apparent** [*enephanísthēsan*, the aorist *passive* tense of *emphanízōmai* {1718}, to appear; the verb may be passive—in the sense that Jesus made them appear just as He made Moses and Elijah appear in glory at the transfiguration {Luke 9:31}—or deponent: "they appeared"] to many. (a.t.)

[53] Notwithstanding the simultaneity of Christ's dying (v. 50), the earthquake with the tearing of the temple veil, the splitting of the rocks (v. 51), and the opening of the graves (v. 52), the actual resurrection of these saints seems to have been subsequent to (*metá*) Jesus' resurrection (v. 53) three days later (v. 63).

The passive voice of *emphanízō* may mean that the Lord Himself made these saints appear in the holy city (note: the voice is passive, not middle; see above reference; i.e., made them apparent, as in English today: "The judge made me appear in court"; the middle reflexive has no meaning anyway, as in "they appeared themselves"). Moreover, this appearance was not universal but "unto many," that is, many believers.

As the memorials were opened and sleeping believers literally exited their tombs, so it will be when Christ returns in due time, an event fully described in 1 Thessalonians 4:13–18 and referred to in 1 Corinthians 15:23.

[54] A "**centurion**" (*hekatóntarchos* [1543]) was a Roman officer who was responsible for the command of one hundred soldiers.

This is the second centurion mentioned with regard to Jesus. The first in Capernaum (Matt. 8:5–13) was so impressed by Jesus' healing power that he asked Him to heal his servant. Jesus marveled at the centurion's faith and commended him for a faith He did not see among the Jews, the "children [*huioí* {5207}, mature sons as contrasted with *tékna* {5043}, children] of the kingdom" (Matt. 8:12; 13:38).

This second centurion and his soldiers were astonished as they observed Jesus' crucifixion and the supernatural events accompanying it: "Truly this was the Son [*huiós*] of God," they concluded.

The guards experienced the earthquake and "**those things that were done** [*tá genómena*, the aorist middle deponent participle of *gínomai* {1096}, to become, thus events that had already transpired]." The verb "**saw**" (*idóntes*, the aorist active participle of *eídon/eídō* from *horáō* [3708]) implies a perception beyond physical sight, an understanding of the miracles.

The whole scenario produced terror, for "**they feared**" (*ephobéthēsan*, the aorist passive of *phobéomai* [5399], to frighten; and from which we derive our English word "phobia"). For the second time, this verb is qualified with the adverb "**greatly**" (*sphódra* [4970]). The fear was not ordinary, and soldiers don't frighten easily.

Yet this godly fear produced faith: "Truly," they said, "this was the Son of God." "**Truly**" (*alēthōs* [230], indeed, surely) derives from the noun *alētheia* (225), truth, reality, something that is objective as contrasted to products of the imagination.

The imperfect *ēn*, "**was**," here may evidence the eternity of the Word of God who was with the Father and was God (John 1:1, 2), even if the centurion had not advanced to this level of understanding.

Jesus' Burial
(27:55–66; Mark 15:42–47; Luke 23:50–56; John 19:38–42)

[55] Several women had been with Jesus Christ from the beginning of His earthly public ministry in Galilee, "**helping**" (*diakonoúsai*, the present participle of *diakonéō* [1247], to serve) to meet His physical needs. Matthew does not give details of how many women were present to suffer through the sight of the crucifixion.

In this verse we are told only that the women followed Jesus all the way from Galilee, ministering to Him (Luke 8:2, 3). This terrible, excruciating scene they "**from** [*apó* {575}, from] **afar off** [*makróthen* {3113}] **were . . . beholding** [*theōroúsai*, the present participle of *theōréō* {2334}, to look with awe]" (a.t.).

We deliberately inserted the word order from the Greek text because it is possible that *makróthen* does not modify "beholding." The phrase, in the order of the Greek text, reads, "There were there women many **from afar off** beholding." As you can see, it is possible that "from afar off" attaches to "were there" instead of "beholding" from a distance. Most commentators prefer "beholding from afar"; however, we have to reconcile Mary Magdalene and other women being *makróthen*, from afar off, according to Matthew (v. 56) with their being *pará* ([3844], near, proximate) the cross according to John (John 19:25). The completed picture is that Mary Magdalene and some of the other women originally came "from afar off" (Matthew) but now were near the cross and beside John at the death of Jesus.

[56] We cannot identify all of the women. However, Matthew informs us that "among them were Mary Magdalene, and Mary the mother of James" (a.t.). Mark 15:40 adds, "James the less and of Joses, and Salome." Because Joanna, the wife of Chuza, Herod's servant, and Susanna "ministered unto him of their substance" (Luke 8:3), and Mark records that the group, "among whom" were the two Marys and Salome (Mark 15:40), consisted of those who "used to . . . minister to Him" (Mark 15:41 NASB), some have conjectured that Joanna and Susanna also were present.

Possibly "among them" also were the widow of Nain whose son Jesus raised from the dead (Luke 7:11–17), the sinful woman who anointed Jesus' feet (Luke 7:36–50), and Mary and Martha of Bethany, the sisters of Lazarus (John 11:1). This event would certainly draw them out. Although they no doubt were fearful, they also desired to support their Master in any way they could.

John 19:25 mentions "his [Jesus'] mother, and his mother's sister, Mary the wife of Cleophas, and Mary Magdalene." It is possible that both Joseph's wife and sister-in-law had the name "Mary," but the Greek has a slight variation in the name of Jesus' mother, sometimes referring to her as Miriam or Mariam (Matt. 1:20).

[57] Joseph of Arimathaea, Matthew stresses, "also **himself** [*autós* {846}, the personal pronoun inserted for emphasis] was Jesus' disciple." The verb is *emathēteusen*, the aorist tense of *mathēteúō* (3100), to disciple. This active voice given by the Textus Receptus means the initiative was personal and voluntary— Joseph "discipled" or "learned" under Jesus. We wonder how this member of the Sanhedrin found it possible to personally disciple under Jesus. Both his wealth and activities in the Sanhedrin could take a great deal of time. Moreover, the Sanhedrin was clearly opposed to Jesus' teachings. Joseph had the courage to learn from Jesus in spite of this group's protest.

The critical texts (UBS and Nestle's Text) defer to manuscripts that have the passive voice *ematheteuthe*, "**he was discipled**," meaning he was discipled by Jesus. John 19:38 informs us that Joseph was "a disciple of Jesus, but secretly for fear of the Jews." Like Nicodemus who also appeared at the cross (John 19:39), he eventually confessed the Lord openly.

[58] According to the Law, if someone were "hung on a tree" for a crime, the body was not to remain there overnight (Deut. 21:22, 23).

Accordingly, Joseph went to Pilate to ask for the body of Jesus at the very time the Jews thought they had achieved their greatest victory—Jesus' death. God used Joseph to fulfill prophecy because he believed Jesus' prophecy that He would rise from the dead in three days. So he volunteered his newly carved tomb for the Lord's burial. Disciples who are the genuine product of the Holy Spirit are generous and do not count the cost. They deem any sacrifice worthwhile for Him who gave His life for them.

[59] Joseph wrapped Jesus' body in a clean linen cloth out of respect. Nothing dirty or defiled touched even the dead body of our dear Lord.

Here, an interesting question arises. Where would Jesus have been buried had Joseph not given Him his own tomb? Jesus was not from Jerusalem. At that time, dead bodies could not be transported back home because the Law required immediate interment. But Jesus had no personal assets for local burial expenses. We have to conclude that the Father Himself planned the burial of His Son, raising up a rich believer for this purpose.

Joseph found companionship in Nicodemus who helped take down the body (John 19:39–42). Where were Christ's eleven disciples? How strange that this honorable task was performed by those outside of Christ's "little flock" (Luke 12:32). The disciples did not attend to the body of Jesus after His burial except Joseph and Nicodemus. And the women brought sweet spices early in the morning to anoint His body on the day of resurrection. Where were the disciples then?

Perhaps they were still cowering in fear or were in deep depression over the turn of events. The Holy Spirit sometimes raises up others to temporarily replace weakened brethren in order to complete the work of ministry.

[60] These events fulfilled many prophecies recorded in Isaiah 53. Now a further prophecy was fulfilled when the Lord "made his grave with the wicked [the two robbers], and with the rich in his death [Joseph of Arimathaea]; because he had done no violence, neither was any deceit in his mouth" (Isa. 53:9).

Something must be said about the burial customs of Jews. In the words of George Milligan (*A Dictionary of Christ and the Gospels*, 241, 242):

Immediately after death the body was washed (Acts 9:37) and wrapped in linen clothes in the folds of which spices and ointments were placed (John 19:39, 40). The face was bound about with a napkin, and the hands and feet with grave bands (John 11:44; 20:7). Meanwhile the house of the deceased had been given over to the hired mourners (Matt. 9:23; cf. 2 Chr. 35:25; Jer. 9:17) who lamented for the dead in some strains as are preserved in Jeremiah 22:18, and skillfully improvised verses in praise of his virtues. The actual interment took place as quickly as possible, mainly on sanitary grounds; very frequently, indeed, on the same day as the death (Acts 5:6, 10; 8:2), though it might be delayed for special reasons (Acts 9:37f.).

The place of burial in New Testament times was always outside the city (Luke 7:12; John 11:30; Matt. 27:52, 53), and frequently consisted of a natural cave, or an opening made in imitation of one. These rock-sepulchres were often of considerable size, and sometimes permitted the interment of as many as thirteen bodies. Eight, however, was the usual number, three on each side of the entrance and two opposite. The doorway to the tomb was an aperture about 2 feet broad and 4 feet high, and was closed by a door, or by a great stone that was rolled against it (Matt. 27:60; Mark 15:46; John 11:38, 39).

In the same reference, Milligan adds that in addition to family sepulchres (Gen. 23:20; Judg. 8:32; 2 Sam. 2:32), there were private tombs such as the tomb of Joseph of Arimathaea (Matt. 27:60).

According to Herkless, special provisions were made for the interment of strangers (Matt. 27:7, 8; cf. Jer. 26:23):

Jewish law required that the body of a person who had been executed should not remain all night upon the tree, but should "in any wise" be buried (Deut. 21:22, 23). This law would not bind the Roman authorities, and the custom in the empire was to leave the body to decay upon the cross. But at the crucifixion of Jesus and of the two malefactors, the Jews, anxious that the bodies should not remain upon the cross during the Sabbath, besought Pilate that the legs of the crucified might be broken and death hastened, and that then the bodies might be taken away (John 19:31). According to Roman law, the relatives could claim the body of a person executed. But which of the relatives of Jesus had a sepulchre in Jerusalem where His body might be placed? Joseph, wishing Jesus' burial to be according to the most pious custom of his race, went to Pilate and asked for the body. The petition required boldness (Mark 15:43), since Joseph, with no kinship in the flesh with Jesus, would be forced to make a confession of discipleship which the Jews would note. Pilate, too, neither loved nor was loved by Israel, and his anger might be kindled at the coming of a Jew, and the member of the Sanhedrin to be assailed with insults. Pilate, however, making sure that Jesus was dead, gave the body. Joseph, taking down the body of Jesus from the cross (and other hands must have aided his), wrapped it in linen which he himself had bought (Mark 15:46 [see John 19:39–42]). (J. Herkless, *A Dictionary of Christ and the Gospels*, 901, 902)

After Joseph buried the body of Jesus, he departed, having done his best for His Lord.

[61, 62] The two Marys remained near, "sitting **opposite** [*apénanti* {561}] the sepulchre" (a.t.). The Jews referred to Friday as *paraskeué* (3904), preparation, the day on which to prepare for the Sabbath. Mark 15:42 literally calls Friday "the pre-Sabbath" (*prosábbaton* [4315], fore-Sabbath).

Only Matthew reports that the chief priests and Pharisees requested Pilate to post a guard at Jesus' tomb. Their fear lay not so much in the belief that Jesus would rise from the dead but that the disciples would steal the body and say that He had risen. Such a report would mean nothing to the Sadducees, since they rejected the theory of bodily resurrection, but it might deceive Pharisees like Nicodemus and laypeople sympathetic with Pharisaic doctrine. Because they had no jurisdiction beyond the temple or outside the city where Jesus was buried, the priests and Pharisees had to ask Pilate, the only one who could order armed soldiers for that area.

[63] So they said to Pilate,

Sir, we remember that that **deceiver** [*plános* {4108}, impostor] said, while he was yet alive, After three days **I will rise** [*egeíromai*, the present middle of *egeírō* {1453}, to raise] again.

The middle voice again stresses Jesus' initiative and ability to raise Himself from the dead. The present tense accentuates the certainty of it, as if it were a principle: "I raise Myself."

[64] They anticipated a conspiracy. To negate the possibility, they requested Pilate to

command therefore that the sepulchre **be made sure** [*asphalisthénai*, the aorist passive infinitive of *asphalízō* {805}, to secure] until the third day.

Since Jesus' prophecy was so specific, it did not matter what happened after the third day.

Joseph had rolled the stone against the door, but the chief priests and Pharisees were not satisfied. They wanted a seal and a guard against the threat that the disciples would steal the body Friday or Saturday evening and then on Sunday proclaim that Jesus rose from the dead.

[65] If Pilate had not considered the threat reasonable, he would not have responded as he did:

> **Ye have** [*échete* {2192}, either an imperative or an indicative—the same morphologically, i.e., "have at your disposal"] **a watch** [*koustōdían* {2892}]: **Go** [*hupágete*, the present imperative of *hupágō* {5217}, to go; derived from *hupó* {5259}, under, a preposition that denotes stealth] your way, **make it as sure** [*asphalísasthe*, the aorist middle deponent imperative of *asphalízō* {805}, to secure oneself against enemies, cf. Acts 16:24] as ye can [humanly speaking].

The middle voice of *asphalízomai* implies, "Secure it yourselves." Make it as safe as you think necessary; in other words, given your evident familiarity with conspiracy, do whatever you have to do. One wonders here what Pilate thought of this paranoid messianism. But, in deference to Jews, others, like Theudas (Acts 5:36), had jeopardized the leadership role of the chief priests and Pharisees as well as the little security the oppressed nation of Israel had.

[66] So they went, and made the sepulchre **sure** [*ēsphalísanto*, the aorist middle deponent indicative of *asphalízō*].

The middle voice emphasizes their personal objectives—"for themselves"— over and against any concern they might have for Pilate's motives. In all probability, he did not take the threat seriously. After all, Jesus was not a typical general or king.

After all this preparation, neither soldiers nor cement could match the power of angels.

28

⤮

Jesus' Resurrection
(28:1–10; Mark 16:1–14; Luke 24:1–35; John 20:1–8)

Matthew informs us of the day that Jesus came forth from the grave but did not specify the exact time. The Jews measured time by blocks of time (*chrónos* [5550]) and seasons (*kairós* [2540]). Unlike a measured period of time (*chrónos*), a season (*kairós*) was significant not because of minutes and hours but because of important events that transpired within it. For instance, we divide our year (a measured block of time) by seasons (summer and winter, spring and fall). Most of our memory relates to events, not necessarily the day, month, or year. We remember, for example, where we were when some significant event took place because of the event itself, not because it was Thursday and 3:00 p.m. If we remember the time, it is because of the event, not vice versa.

Jesus predicted several times that He would rise on the third day (e.g., Matt. 16:21; 17:23; 20:19). In Matthew 12:40, He also predicted that He would be in the grave for three days and three nights. This has caused some Bible scholars to assume that Jesus must have been crucified on Wednesday to allow a full seventy-two hours in the grave. The traditional view is that He would be in the grave for portions of three day/night periods or, more properly, three "night/day" periods.

When we in the Western world think of a twenty-four hour period, we usually consider a day starting at midnight and extending to the next midnight. But we may also think of a day starting at dawn and extending through the night to the next dawn. The Jewish view of this twenty-four hour period begins at sunset and extends through the night and daylight hours to sunset the next day (see, Gen. 1:5, 8, 13, 19, 23, 31). Paul expresses this idea in 2 Corinthians 11:25 when he uses a single word—*nuchthēmeron* (3574), literally, "night/day," to describe his being adrift in the open sea for a night and a day.

I believe that the term "three days and three nights" in Matthew 12:40, understood in its own cultural setting, simply means three portions of consecutive "night/day" periods. Assuming that the crucifixion took place on a Friday, darkness was over the land from the sixth hour to the ninth hour (i.e., from noon until 3:00 in the afternoon) (Matt. 27:45). Jesus must have died around that time, because He was already dead when the soldiers came to break the bones of those being crucified as requested by the Jewish authorities. This hastened death so that no dead bodies would be on the cross during the Sabbath day (John 19:31; see also Deut. 21:22, 23). Joseph of Arimathea buried Him soon afterwards (Matt. 27:57, 59; Mark 15:43, 45). If Christ was crucified on Friday, as traditionally held, then He was in the grave for a portion of Friday, all of Saturday, and part of Sunday. Any part of a twenty-four hour period was considered a day. From the Jewish point of view, this would satisfy the term "three days and three nights."

[1] The word translated as "end" in the King James Version (*opsé* [3796]) means "late in the day" when used by itself as an adverb referring to the last hours before sunset (see Mark 11:19; 13:35). But most recent lexicographers agree that, when used as a preposition with a noun, it simply means "after."

> And after the Sabbath, **as it dawned** [from *epiphṓskō* {2020} from *epi* {1909}, upon, toward; and *phṓskō* {n.f.}, to shine; see Luke 23:54] toward the first day of the week came Mary Magdalene and the other Mary to see the sepulchre. (a.t.)

Sometime before 6 a.m. on Sunday morning when the third day was dawning, Jesus rose from the dead. Mark 16:2 says the women arrived "very early in the morning . . . at the rising [from *anatéllō* {393}, when the sun had already risen] of the sun." Luke 24:1 says "**very early** [from *bathús* {901}, deep, meaning very early] in the **morning** [from *órthros* {3722}, at the daybreak or dawning of the day]." John 20:1 says "when it was yet dark."

Matthew mentions two women, Mary Magdalene and another Mary, coming to the tomb. They were among many who had followed Jesus from Galilee (Matt. 27:55, 56), had probably observed Joseph burying the body, and had watched the sealing of the tomb and the posting of the guard (Matt. 27:61). They did not expect a resurrection but had come to the tomb to anoint Jesus' body (Mark 16:1; Luke 24:1). According to John's account, Mary Magdalene arrived first and, on seeing the stone removed from the tomb, ran to tell the disciples that Jesus' enemies had stolen His body (John 20:2).

[2] "**Behold**" (*idoú*, the imperative of *eídō* [1492], to perceive; from *horáō* [3708], to see and perceive; see Matt. 1:20, 23, et al) calls our attention to something supernatural, in this instance an "**earthquake**" (*seismós* [4578], a shaking).

Earthquakes accompanied both Jesus' death and resurrection. This one is described as "**great**" (*mégas* [3173]) because an (the Greek text has no definite article before "angel")

> angel of the Lord **descended** [from *katabaínō* {2597}, to descend] **from** [*ek* {1537}, out of from within] heaven, came and **rolled back** [from *apokulíō* {617} from *apó* {575}, from; and *kulíō* (2947), to roll away] the stone from the door, and **was sitting** [from *káthēmai* {2521}] on it. (a.t.)

[3] The angel's "**countenance**" (*idéa* [2397] TR; or *eidéa* UBS) was his external appearance, which, Matthew says, was like lightning, while his clothing glistened like snow. This reminds us of Jesus' brilliant appearance at the transfiguration (Matt. 17:2). However, this is the only place that this word occurs in the New Testament.

[4] Until now, the soldiers had faithfully guarded the tomb, but as soon as they witnessed the earthquake and the angel, they became paralyzed with "**fear**" (from *phóbos* [5401], associated with the verb *phobéō* [5399], to fear).

Fear will also grip people when Jesus returns to earth accompanied by heavenly signs and disturbances (Luke 21:25–27). Scripture says that

> men's hearts [will be] failing [from *apopsúchō* {674}, expiring as if the soul {*psuchē*} were departing "from" {*apó*} the body, literally being scared almost to death] them for fear [from *phóbos*], and for looking after those things which are coming on the earth: for the powers of heaven shall be shaken. (Luke 21:26)

What Paul calls "that blessed hope" of believers in Titus 2:13 will be "the cursed despair" of unbelievers. Fear either causes persons to flee in terror from God or to fall prostrate in worship before Him.

The terror the soldiers experienced was due to their ignorance of the gospel:

> And for fear [terror] of him [the angel of God], **the keepers** [from *tēréō* {5083}, to guard] **were shaken** [from *seíō* {4579}, to shake or agitate], and became **as** [*hōseí* {5616}, an adverb from *hōs* {5613}, as; and *ei* {1487}, "if"] dead. (a.t.)

As they sensed the shaking and saw the brilliant angel, all their strength left them. They evidently collapsed out of sheer terror and became paralyzed with fear.

[5] The angel ignored the terrified soldiers but spoke to the women who had already entered the sepulchre (Mark 16:5).

Luke 24:4 and John 20:12 inform us that two angels were in the tomb. Evidently, a number of angels were present at Christ's resurrection; however, only one spoke that we have record of. Meanwhile, Mary Magdalene returned to the tomb with several women, according to Luke 24:10, which says "and other women that were with them." They had come to anoint the dead body of Jesus, but He was not in the tomb.

The angel who spoke said, "Fear you not: for I know that you seek Jesus, who was crucified" (a.t.). We do not know to which of the several women present the angel spoke. John 20:1 names only Mary Magdalene as coming to the sepulchre, but apparently she was accompanied by "another Mary" (Matt. 28:1; a.t.). She did not say, "I do not know where they have laid Him" but rather "we" (John 20:2). Mary Magdalene and the other Mary may have started out together, but Mary Magdalene took the lead, seeing the stone from a distance. Then, returning from the tomb, they met the other party of women who were on their way to the sepulchre and told them what they had seen. They also told the eleven disciples (Luke 24:9).

The angel identified the risen Lord as "Jesus, the **crucified One** [a.t., *estauroménon*, the perfect passive participle of *stauróō* [4717], lit., the One who has been crucified]." Since they thought He was dead, the women carried spices to anoint His body (Luke 24:1).

[6] Because of this and thus confirming Christ's veracity, the angel immediately told them,

He is not **here** [*hóde* {5602}, in this place]: for **he is risen** [*egérthē*, the aorist passive of *egeírō* {1453}, lit., he was raised] as he said. (Cf. Matt. 16:21; 17:23; 20:17–19; John 2:19).

Had Jesus not risen from the dead "as he said," everything else He had said would have been questionable.

The angel challenged them to an on-site inspection:

Come, **see** [*ídete*, the aorist—"see once for all"—the imperative of *eídon/horáō* {1492}, to see and perceive] the place where the Lord lay.

[7] Then the angel commanded the women,

Go quickly, and tell His disciples that He is risen from the dead; and behold, He goes before you into Galilee. There you shall see Him (a.t.; see Matt. 26:32).

Just seeing "the place where the Lord lay" was not conclusive; it was still possible that someone had stolen the body. So the angel pointed the women in the direction of His physical presence: "Behold [i.e., *Pay attention!*], **He**

goes before [from *proágō* {4254}] you into Galilee" (a.t.). As Jesus said about the Good Shepherd, "When he putteth forth his own sheep, he goeth before them" (John 10:4).

Why did the angel say, "Go **quickly** [*tachú* {5035}]"? He implied that there was no time to waste. We, too, should waste none of the precious time the Lord has given us on worldly priorities. We cannot get the gospel out fast enough! Twice in his epistles, Paul tells us to redeem "the time" (Eph. 5:16; Col. 4:5).

The women could certainly testify that Jesus had risen "**from**" (*apó* [575]) the dead because He had put space between Himself and the dead. Additionally, He was now physically removed from the tomb. More frequently, the preposition *ek* (1537), out of from within or among, is coupled with "the dead" to describe the resurrection (John 2:22; 21:14; Acts 3:15; 4:10; 13:30; Rom. 4:24; 6:4, 9; 7:4; 8:11; 10:9; 1 Cor. 15:20; Gal. 1:1; Eph. 1:20; Col. 2:12; 1 Thess. 1:10; 2 Tim. 2:8; Heb. 11:19; 1 Pet. 1:21).

The verb "**you shall see**" (*ópsesthe* [3708], the future of *optánomai* [3700], to physically see, and *horáō*, to perceive) includes physical sight. Through a physical sighting, especially of Jesus' wounds from the crucifixion, the women would be able to perceive that it was the same Person.

[8] And they departed quickly from the sepulchre with **fear** [from *phóbos* {5401}].

This kind of anxiety was more of a healthy expectation than a terror, but perhaps the women were, notwithstanding the message from the angel, uncertain about what had transpired. Nevertheless, their fear was mixed with great joy (*chará* [5479] from *cháris* [5484], grace)—a wonderful blend of anxious expectation for the best.

Notice that the women ran "**to tell**" (from *apaggéllō* [518], announce) the disciples what had happened. When we have good news to announce, we must not delay but move quickly.

[9] While the women were on their way to tell the eleven disciples the news of Christ's resurrection, Jesus appeared to them personally.

As **they went** [from *poreúomai* {4198}, to go, proceed] to tell his disciples, **behold** [*idoú* {2400}, the imperative of *eídon* {1492}, the aorist of *horáō* {3708}, to perceive, calling attention to the extraordinary {see Matt. 3:17}], Jesus **met** [from *apantáō* {528}, to meet, possibly coming from the opposite direction] them, saying, All **hail** [*chaírete*, rejoice, the present imperative of *chaírō* {5463}, to rejoice, not a common greeting].

"*Chaíre*" in Luke 1:28 was the angel Gabriel's special greeting to the virgin Mary, followed by "*kecharitōménē*, from the verb *charitóō* (5487), from *cháris*

(5485), the grace of which Jesus Christ was full. John 1:16 says "of his fulness have all we received, and grace for grace." The verb *charitóō* is a transitive verb ending in *óō* equivalent to the middle voice *charízomai* [5483] Luke 7:21, 42, 43; Acts 3:14; 25:11, 16; 27:24; Rom. 8:32; 1 Cor. 2:12; 2 Cor. 2:7, 10; 12:13; Gal. 3:18; Eph. 4:32; Phil. 1:29; 2:9; Col. 2:13; 3:13; Philem. 22). The verb *charitóō*, however, occurs only in Luke 1:28 in the case of the virgin Mary whom the angel Gabriel greeted with the verb *chaíre* followed by the participle *kecharitōménē* meaning "that has been highly favored or graced." This means that the omniscient God has foreseen (*proégnō*, from *proginōskō* [4267], to fore-know, which is part of God's wisdom [Rom. 16:27]). As Rom. 8:29 says, "For whom he did foreknow (*proégnō*), he also did predestinate (*proórise*) to be con-formed to the image of His Son, that he might be the firstborn among many brethren." Here the distinction must be emphasized between the adjective *monogenḗs* (3439) from *mónos* (3439), only one, and *génos* (1085), stock and *prōtótokos* (4416), referring to rank and honor, "the preeminent" (Luke 2:7), which birth was brought about by the Holy Spirit. Colossians 1:15 calls Jesus Christ "the image of the invisible God," the preeminent (*prōtótokos*) of every creature who gave birth to everything that was made. John 1:3 states that "all things were made by him: and without him was not any thing made [*oudé* {3761} a compound word from *ou* {3756}, the absolute 'not' and *dé* {1161}]."

zOnly Matthew records the event of verse 9. The women had left the tomb with "fear and great joy" (see v. 8), in spite of the angel's command to "fear not." Now Jesus commanded them to fully "**rejoice!**" (see translation for "hail"). When they recognized Him, they

> . . . **approached** [from *prosérchomai* {4334}, to come close to; from *prós* {4314}, toward, close to; and *érchomai* {2064}, to come] and **held** [from *kratéō* {2902}, to take hold of] His feet, and **worshiped** [from *proskunéō* {4352} from *prós* {4314}, to; and *kunéō* {n.f.}, meaning to kiss, worship, reverence by show-ing respect and devotion] Him. (a.t.)

Holding someone by the feet was not merely an act of humiliation but a worshipful desire that the person being held would not walk away, as when Jacob said, "I will not let thee go, except thou bless me" (Gen. 32:26). A cer-tain detainment is implied in the word that stands out in John's account of Jesus' appearance to Mary Magdalene:

> Jesus saith unto her, Touch [from *hápto* {681}, to hold on to] me not; for I am not yet ascended to my Father: but go to my brethren, and say unto them, I ascend unto my Father, and your Father; and to my God, and your God. (John 20:17)

Proskunéō, to worship, is sometimes used in the Greek translation of the Old Testament in the general sense of doing homage or reverence toward a dignitary like a king (Sept.: Gen. 19:1; 48:12). In the New Testament, however, it is almost exclusively used for the worship of God. In two instances, men were rebuked for falling prostrate to someone other than God: Cornelius who "prostrated" before Peter (Acts 10:25, 26), and the apostle John who was about to "prostrate" before an angel (Rev. 19:10), perhaps thinking that he was a theophany. In Revelation 13:12; 14:11, those not written in the Book of Life "prostrate" before the beast.

The worship accorded to Jesus, however, is divine. As the writer of Hebrews quotes the Septuagint: "When He bringeth in the first begotten into the world, He says, And let all the angels of God worship [from *proskunésō*] Him" (Heb. 1:6; a.t.; annotating the Sept. of Deut. 32:43). Since "all," not some, angels are included, the writer excludes Jesus from angels, which he sets out to prove in the first chapter of Hebrews. Worship of the Son of God (Heb. 1:2), he insists, is not worship of an angel but designates Jesus as "the Son" (*en huiō*, in and through "the Son") by "his Son" (KJV). The King James Version translates correctly *en Huiō*. When we humans become related to God, we are called children (*tékna* [5043]) of God. We become first babies, then children, then *huioí* (5207), mature people. So when God became sinless Man incarnate, He was born a babe (cf. Luke 1:41, 44; 2:12, 16). When He became mature at the age of thirty, He manifested His deity for three calendar years till God permitted His enemies to crucify Him. His shed blood redeems those who believe on Him, and cleanses from sin(cf. *katharízō* [2511], 1 John 1:7). However, when God allowed the death of His incarnate Son, it was meant for all those who would believe at any time of history. As God is the creator of time (*chrónos* [5550]), He also ordained that the birth, crucifixion, and death of His incarnate Son took place for the purpose of saving "his people from their sins" (Matt. 1:21). Observe that the verb *sōsei* is the future active indicative of *sōzō* [4982]). This salvation (*sōtēría* [4991]) is immediately effective and continue to the end of human life. Jesus is the author (*archēgós* [747]), the initiator and finisher (*teleiōtēs* [5054]), and the perfector (NIV) of our faith (Heb. 12:2).

Hebrews 1:2 says God has spoken and is still speaking (*laléō* [2980], to speak) by His Son (*en Huiō*). The Son of God (John 1:1) became incarnate but when crucified and risen again, He proved to be forever God (*aídios* [126], from *aeí* [104] and *ídios* [2398]).

[10] Jesus reinforced the command the angel gave the women at the tomb in verse 5, "Be not **afraid** [from *phobéomai* {5399}]." This was not a time for fear

but for joy. Jesus had risen as He promised (v. 6). They had seen both the empty tomb and the living Christ.

Jesus commanded the disciples to meet Him in Galilee. Whom did He have in mind when He said, "Tell my brethren?" Were these physical or spiritual brothers? We can only guess. His physical brothers were apparently unbelievers according to John 7:5: "For neither did his brethren [from *adelphós* {80}] believe [from *pisteúō* {4100}, to believe] in him," the imperfect tense covering some indefinite period in which they had not yet believed. But Acts 1:14 shows that they came to faith: "These all continued with one accord in prayer and supplication, with the women, and Mary the mother of Jesus, and with his brethren." Their unbelief may be the reason Jesus assigned the care of His mother to John, the beloved disciple (John 19:25–27). But the resurrection was most likely the miracle that penetrated his brothers' hearts of unbelief.

The Conspiracy
(28:11–15)

The Roman soldiers had been assigned to guard the tomb so that the disciples would not be able to steal the body of Jesus. Pilate was satisfied that he had secured Rome against such a conspiracy.

[11] But then the report came in that the body was missing. Some of the guards went to the chief priests. They seem to have reported the facts without bias as "**occurrences**" (*tá genómena*, the aorist middle participle of *gínomai* [1096], to become) and reported "**all**" (from *hápas* [537], each and all) the pertinent news (note the specific *hápanta* from *hápas*).

[12] What did these chief priests and elders do now?

> And when they were assembled together with the elders and had taken **counsel** [*sumboúlion* {4824}, a discussion], they gave **large** [*hikaná* {2425}, sufficient, that is bribe] money unto the soldiers. (a.t.)

This was not the first time the Pharisees marshaled against Jesus. They had tried to trap Him with words (Matt. 22:15–17) and to deceive the people concerning His character (Mark 3:22; John 9:24); they had plotted His death (John 11:53); had bribed Judas to betray Him (Matt. 26:14, 15); had perverted and misrepresented His teaching at the trial (Matt. 26:59–62; Luke 23:1, 2); and had influenced Pilate to crucify Him (John 19:12). And now, following the glorious, irrefutable resurrection, they attempted to hide the truth. They did not hesitate to endanger the lives of the soldiers that might be condemned to death by Pilate, who only reluctantly gave permission to crucify Jesus.

[13] The lie was self-incriminating, which meant that the money had to be high enough to compensate for the risk of falling asleep on duty—a capital offense. The Romans had no allegiances to the Jews, but the soldiers were trapped because the body was missing. It had disappeared on their watch, and they desperately needed an excuse.

[14, 15] Along with the payment, the chief priests and elders also offered these soldiers further aid if Pilate heard what happened.

> **We will persuade** [from *peíthō* {3982}, to convince] him and **make** [from *poiéō* {4160}, to do or make] you **secure** [from *amérimnos* {275} from the privative *a* {1}, without; and the noun *mérimna* {3308}, worry]. (a.t.)

In other words, for confirming the lie, they would make the soldiers free from anxiety by eliminating the danger.

> So they took the **money** [from *argúrion* {694}, silver], and did as they were **taught** [from *didáskō* {1321}].

They were "taught" not "told," as the King James faithfully translates the original. It was rational instruction and didactic skill, not orders or a bullying negotiation. The priests and elders convinced the soldiers that this was the best and perhaps the only strategy. Persuasion like this is typical of the cults who use propaganda and the suppression of truth to retain their members.

The aftermath of all this? "And this saying **is commonly reported** [from *diaphēmízō* {1310}, to advertise] among the Jews until this day." The body was gone! What else could they do but lie? This "conspiracy theory" has continued into the twentieth century, republished in the work of Jewish author Hugh Schonfield (*The Passover Plot*, New York: Bernard Geis Assoc., 1965).

The Great Commission (28:16–20; Mark 16:15–18;Luke 24:36–49; John 20:19–23; Acts 1:6–8)

Today the Jewish nation as a whole still rejects Jesus' resurrection, His atonement for sin, and His deity. But all this will change when He returns: "So all Israel shall be saved: as it is written, There shall come out of Sion the Deliverer, and shall turn away ungodliness from Jacob" (Rom. 11:26). At that time, Jews will repent collectively.

[16] In obedience to Jesus' command (vv. 9, 10), the eleven disciples departed for Galilee to encounter the risen Christ. They

> **marched on** [from *poreúomai* {4198}, to proceed] to Galilee, to a mountain that Jesus **had appointed** [from *tássō* {5021}, to arrange, appoint] to them. (a.t.)

So certain was Jesus of His resurrection that He even told His disciples on which mountain to meet Him afterward. Possibly this was the mountain (*óros* [3735]) near the Sea of Galilee where Jesus retired to pray during His ministry (Matt. 14:23). No other person has ever made an appointment to meet someone following his or her death and kept it. In Matthew 26:32 Jesus had prophesied, "But after I am risen again, I will go before you into Galilee."

[17] Again, Jesus was worshiped, this time by the eleven disciples:

> And **when they saw** [from *eídon*, the aorist of *horáō* {3708}, to see and perceive] Him, **they worshiped** [from *proskunéō*] Him, but some **doubted** [from *distázō* {1365}, to doubt or to hesitate]. (a.t.)

An alternate translation of the verb *distázō* is "to **hesitate**." The Greek has two verbs for doubt. The one is *amphibállō* (n.f.) and the other *distázō* (1365). Only *distázō* is used in the New Testament. Matthew 14:31 says, "O thou of little faith, wherefore didst thou doubt?" In our present verse, it is translated "but some doubted" (28:17). This concerned the eleven true disciples of Jesus Christ who had already marched into Galilee to see the risen Jesus at the mountain where Jesus said He was going to meet them. Now they had no reason to doubt the resurrection of Jesus. He was not in the grave. That was a fact. Even the guards could not explain it.

The verb *edístasan* refers to the true disciples, who were persuaded about the risen Christ, but they hesitated about the evangelization of the world. The verb *distázo* in Matthew 14:31 is used in conjunction with the adjective, calling Peter "a man of little faith" (*oligópiste* [3640]) for hesitating to go to Jesus Christ who walked on the water (Matt. 14:22–33; Mark 6:45–52; John 6:15–21). The same Jesus also told the disciples to disciple all nations, baptizing them in the name of the Father, the Son, and the Holy Spirit.

Jesus' appearance was changed (*hē idéa*, from *eídon*, aorist of *horáō* meaning to perceive). The noun "idea" in English derives from *idéa*. It is the recognition a person has of a past acquaintance. Mary Magdalene recognized Jesus after He spoke her name at the tomb. Having been freed from demons who had possessed her, she became a follower of Jesus (Luke 8:2, 3). She proved faithful to Him and His cause to the very end. She was at His crucifixion (Matt. 27:56; John 19:25) and burial (Matt. 27:61; Mark 15:40, 47); she helped prepare the materials to embalm Him (Mark 16:1); and she was the first to go to the sepulchre after the resurrection (Matt. 28:1; Luke 24:10).

At Christ's Second Coming, those who died in Christ will be raised first, then those believers who are still alive will be caught up together with them to meet Christ (*háma* [260]) (Matt. 13:29; 24:26–27; 1 Thess. 4:13–18; 5:10). The verb used in 1 Thessalonians 4:17 referring to what will happen to believers is expressed by the Greek verb *harpagēsómetha*, translated "we . . . shall be caught up" from *harpázō* (726) to catch up, to pluck, to snatch away, especially used for the rapture (Acts 8:39; 2 Cor. 12:4; Rev. 12:5). Second Corinthians 12:2 says that Paul was caught up into paradise, the third heaven (*trítou ouranoú*), where he heard unspeakable words—*arrēta* (731), inexpressible, *rhēmata* (4487) specific words having divine significance. The rapture refers to the saved people who make up the church (*ekklēsía* [1577]). The believers resurrected and those living when Jesus Christ comes again have a dual relationship with Christ. His Spirit took possession of the believers' spirits and made them one spiritual family. In Matthew 18:20, Jesus said, "For where two or three are gathered together in my name, there am I in the midst of them."

This is why Matthew 28:17 states, "but they hesitated" because they were believers of little faith (*oligópistoi* [3640]). Today believers' little faith is the culprit for not accomplishing great things for God. The great things are *megaleía* (3167), and the verb is *megalúnō* (3170), which Mary, the mother of Jesus, used in her Magnificat (Luke 1:46–56), translated "magnify" which seeks to manifest God's greatness (*megaleiótēs* [3168], Luke 9:43; 2 Pet. 1:16). In Luke 1:47, Mary acknowledged her unborn Son as the Lord her God and Savior. The same verb *echarítōsen*, an intransitive verb in the case of Mary, was used in the angel Gabriel's greeting in Luke 1:28. The same word is used in Ephesians 1:6 for believers as a result of their active faith in Christ (*toís pisteúousin* [John 1:12]). Their faith in Christ makes it possible for Him to give them His grace (*charízomai*, which is equivalent to *charitóō*).

Jesus' promise that He would precede His disciples into Galilee implied some ministry to be done there. Perhaps now, even after the resurrection, they still were hesitant to take a stand for His name.

The disciples had difficulty accepting the bodily resurrection of Jesus Christ at first. Mark 16:11 says they did not believe Mary Magdalene even after she had seen Christ risen from the dead. And Mark 16:12, 13 says they did not believe two other disciples (probably Cleopas and his companion, as recorded in Luke 24:13–31) to whom Jesus appeared in another form while they were walking into the country. But when they heard later testimony from Peter,

John, and the women that Jesus rose and the tomb was empty (John 20:2–18), some believed. Thomas doubted, but when he physically "handled" the risen Christ, he believed (John 20:26–29).

[18] Once the resurrection was verified, Jesus dispelled the disciples' hesitation and assured them of the promise He gave in John 14:12–14 that believers would perform greater works when the Holy Spirit personally came on them (John 16:7). Oddly, even the ascension bewildered the disciples. The angels asked, "Why stand ye gazing up into heaven?" (Acts 1:11).

Before His actual ascension, Jesus explained its full theological import: "All **authority** [*exousía* {1849}, moral right and physical power] **is given** [from *dídōmi* {1325}, to give] to Me in heaven and in earth" (a.t.).

[19] The giving of all authority in heaven and earth to the Son is the foundation for world evangelism (Mark 16:15). In Matthew's presentation of the Great Commission, Jesus gave only one imperative command: **make disciples** (*mathēteúsate*, the aorist active imperative of *mathēteúō* [3100], to disciple or teach a student). The first verbal phrase in the verse is translated by almost all English versions into idiomatic English as an imperative itself, "Go ye . . . ." But, in Greek, it is an aorist passive participle (*poreuthéntes* from *poreúomai* [4198], to proceed), designed to indicate a circumstantial action that accompanies the main verb. When used with an imperative command, as here, the participle of attendant circumstance presents an activity to accompany the fulfilling of the imperative. It takes on the character of an imperative command itself, which explains why most English versions translate it as "go and make disciples."

The verb *poreúou*, second person singular present middle/passive deponent imperative of *poreúomai* (4198), as *poreuthéntes* of Matthew 28:19 is followed by the imperative "make disciples" (*mathēteúsate*, from *mathēteúō* [3100]) of all nations. The expression *poreuthéntes mathēteúsate*, having marched on to make disciples, would be futile if the parable of the true vine did not teach that every believer should produce as much fruit as humanly possible with God's divine enablement (John 15).

We fulfill the Great Commission only when we go to reach others and make disciples of them. The proper translation is "having gone [or 'as you go'], **make disciples. . . .**"

This is the same thing that Mark describes in his version of the Great Commission as given in Mark 16:15:

> **Having gone** [*poreuthéntes*, the same participle of attendant circumstance as used in Matt. 28:19] into all the world, **preach** [*kērúxate*, the aorist active

imperative of *kērússō* {2784}, to proclaim, preach] the **gospel** [from *euaggélion* {2098}] to every **created being** [from *ktísis* {2937}]. (a.t)

We make disciples through preaching or proclaiming the gospel to people. The gospel of the death and resurrection of Jesus Christ must be preached "first" (1 Cor. 15:12). The Great Commission should always be connected with the Lord's resurrection and the authority He has in heaven and on earth.

The Lord Jesus Christ is unique. Because "all authority" (v.18) presupposes a divine nature, He does not pass all this power to created individuals or institutions. Accordingly, when the Lord commanded the Eleven to make disciples of all nations, He did not mean they were to force nations to acknowledge Christ, as some attempted in the Crusades.

In addition to the participle of attendant circumstance, "having gone," two adverbial participles of manner describe how to make disciples, that is, what is involved in fulfilling the command to make disciples. Both participles are in the present tense, indicating that they are to be performed over and over again as often as the need arises. The first present participle of manner is "**baptizing** [from *baptízō* {907}] them." The pronoun in the phrase, "baptizing them," removes the idea that whole nations are in view. *Autoús* is masculine, whereas *éthnē* is neuter (*tá éthnē*). Thus, "them" refers to persons within the nations rather than the nations themselves. We are commanded to disciple individuals from all nations. Those who respond in faith (presupposed here) must be baptized.

These believers are to be baptized "in the [one] name of the Father, and of the Son, and of the Holy Spirit," that is, the Triune God. The single name embraces Father, Son, and Holy Spirit in one distinct Deity; otherwise, Matthew would have said "names." "**Baptizing**" (from *baptízō* [907]) means primarily an identity that signifies burial with Christ and resurrection with Him into newness of life (Rom. 6:4).

[20] Beyond baptizing, Jesus commanded the disciples to be

... **teaching** [from *didáskō* {1321}] them **to observe** [from *tēréō* {5083}, to hold fast, keep faithfully] all things as many as **I commanded** [from *entéllomai* {1781}, to command] you. (a.t.)

Jesus taught, "On these two commandments hang all the law and the prophets" (Matt. 22:40), and the greatest is "love" (*agápē* [26], v. 38) toward God and toward our fellow humans (vv. 34–40). And John forever links our love for the Lord with our obedience to Him. Jesus said, "Ye are my friends, if ye do whatsoever I command you" (John 15:14).

After the Lord's final commands came the promise of His special presence:

And **lo** [*idoú* {2400}, "behold" something special, the imperative of *eídon/eidō* {1492} from *horáō* {3708}, to see and perceive], I am with you all the **days** [*hēméras* {2250}] **until** [*héōs* {2193}, unto] the **end** [from *suntéleia* {4930}, completion, consummation; from *sún* {4862}, together with; and *télos* {5056}, end, completion, goal] of the **age** [from *aiōn* {165}]. Amen. (a.t.)

The definite article before "days" marks out a specific age that will terminate at the end of people's opportunity to repent and accept God's free gift of forgiveness—the church age. "**Until**" (*héōs*) does not mean that the Lord will abandon us after this period. It simply means that during this particular time that may be characterized by persecution, He will manifest His special presence to us. *Suntéleia*, the end or consummation, also occurs in Matthew 13:39, 40, 49; 24:3 and Hebrews 9:26 (where it appears with the plural "ages") and defines the purposeful goals God determines and executes.

"World" is a mistranslation in the King James Version of *aiōn*. The word means "age" and, similarly to the way "hour" is used in the New Testament, this period or age is filled with redemptive content flowing out of the eternal plan of God. *Kósmos* (2889) is better translated "world." Technically the term *kósmos* (from which we get the English "cosmetics") includes outer adornment and structure; it does not mean empty space. Structure includes a philosophy of life. Since the fall, human philosophy has been predominantly anti-God. Therefore, the term "philosophy" is a misnomer, since no one can hate God and love (true) wisdom, which is what true philosophy is. "For the wisdom of this world is foolishness with God. For it is written, He takes the wise by their own craftiness" (1 Cor. 3:19; a.t.).

The risen Christ promises to be "**with**" (*metá* [3326]) His disciples, as well as being "in" (*en* [1722]) them in the Person of the Holy Spirit (John 14:17; Col. 1:27). No wonder the Lord tells us to "Behold!" His presence should excite and motivate us to endure under the worst of trials and to persevere against the worst of persecutions.